o—o—o—o—o—o o—o—o—o—o—o—o—o—o—o—o—o

Resources for Teaching

WAYS OF READING

An Anthology for Writers

Sixth Edition

o—o—o—o—o—o—o—o—o—o—o—o—o—o—o—o—o

o–o–o–o–o–o–o–o–o–o–o–o–o–o–o–o–o–o–o–o

Resources for Teaching

WAYS OF READING

An Anthology for Writers

Sixth Edition

o–o–o–o–o–o–o–o–o–o–o–o–o–o–o–o–o–o–o–o

Prepared by

David Bartholomae

UNIVERSITY OF PITTSBURGH

Anthony Petrosky

UNIVERSITY OF PITTSBURGH

BEDFORD/ST. MARTIN'S
Boston • New York

For information, write: Bedford/St. Martin's,
75 Arlington Street, Boston, MA 02116 (617-399-4000)

ISBN: 0–312–39382–2

Instructors who have adopted *Ways of Reading: An Anthology for Writers,* Sixth Edition, as a textbook for a course are authorized to duplicate portions of this manual for their students.

Acknowledgment

Stephen R. Graubard, "Preface to *Myth, Symbol, and Culture.*" Reprinted by permission of *Daedalus,* Journal of the American Academy of Arts and Sciences, from the issue titled, "Myth, Symbol, and Culture," Winter 1972, Volume 101, Number 1.

o—o—o—o—o—o—o—o—o—o—o—o—o—o—o—o—o—o

Preface

Ways of Reading is designed for a course where students are given the opportunity to work on what they read, and to work on it by writing. This manual is a guidebook to such a course. We cannot begin to imagine all the possible ways that the selections might (or should) be taught. The best we can do is to speak from our own experience in such courses. If we seem at times to be dogmatic (to be single-minded in saying what should be done or how it should be done), it is because we are drawing on our own practices as teachers and they are grounded, finally, in our beliefs about what it means to read, write, and teach. We don't mean to imply that we have a corner on effective teaching or that there is no other way to help young adults take charge of what they do with texts.

In Part I of this manual, you will find a brief introduction to the textbook and the opportunities it offers a teacher. A second section addresses the questions instructors often ask us about teaching with *Ways of Reading*, and a third details how the book is used in the training program for Teaching Assistants and Teaching Fellows at the University of Pittsburgh. Part II of the manual is composed of individual discussions of the selections and the three sets of questions that follow each selection, "Questions for a Second Reading," "Assignments for Writing," and "Making Connections." The third part provides a similar discussion of the "Assignment Sequences." We have also included four additional "Assignment Sequences" to give you even more options in the classroom. In Part IV, we have reprinted fourteen papers by instructors who have taught with *Ways of Reading*. Most were written by graduate students or former graduate students in our department who developed their work in a seminar on the teaching of composition. Also included is an essay by one of our former colleagues, Bill Hendricks. Bill taught with us for several years. He is a fine teacher, but more than that he has the rare talent of being able to write well about teaching. There is no more difficult genre than the pedagogical essay.) Bill talks about the shape and the conduct of a course in reading and writing, and he looks at some sample student papers. Part V features an interview with a colleague of ours who has taught a version of the ninth sequence, "History and Ethnography: Reading the Lives of Others." She talks about the logistics of preparing both students and local librarians for an archival project.

Contents

Contents

Part III: Working with the Assignment Sequences   125

These writing assignments provide an opportunity for students to test the arguments in the individual essays by weighing them against scenes and episodes from their own schooling.

SEQUENCE TWO   *The Arts of the Contact Zone*

This sequence asks students to work closely with the argument of Mary Louise Pratt's "Arts of the Contact Zone," not so much through summary (repeating the argument) as through extension (working under its influence, applying its terms and protocols).

Assignments

SEQUENCE THREE   *Autobiographical Explorations*

What is suggested by the title of this sequence is a use of writing (and the example of one's experience, including intellectual experience) to investigate, question, explore, inquire.

Assignments

SEQUENCE FOUR   *Autobiographical Explorations (II)*

This sequence provides an alternative set of readings for sequence three. All of these assignments can be used to represent personal narrative as a writing problem, as something to work on carefully, not as something simple or easy or to be taken for granted.

Assignments

SEQUENCE FIVE   *Close Reading/Close Writing*   142

Eash assignment in this sequence provides (or asks students to select) a sample sentence or paragraph from the text, one that is characteristic or exemplary of the author's style. It asks them to imitate that sentence or paragraph (that is, to write in parallel). And it asks them to describe sentences, not through textbook terms (subject, predicate, direct object), but in terms of what the sentence *does*.

Assignments

SEQUENCE SIX   *The Documentary Tradition*   146

This sequence is designed to both introduce students to a key text in the history of documentary work, James Agee and Walker Evans's *Let Us Now Praise Famous Men,* and to raise questions about the past and present of the documentary tradition.

Assignments

SEQUENCE SEVEN   *Experimental Readings and Writings*   150

Each of the writers in this sequence is experimenting, pushing against or stepping outside of conventional ways of writing and thinking. This is an opportunity to learn about these experimental ways of writing from the inside, as a practitioner, as someone who learns from doing the very thing that he or she is studying.

Assignments

SEQUENCE EIGHT   *Experts and Expertise*   154

These assignments give students the chance to consider familiar settings or experiences through the work of writers who have had a significant effect on contemporary culture. In each case, students will be given the opportunity to work alongside these thinkers as an apprentice, carrying out work these writers have begun.

Assignments

SEQUENCE NINE   *History and Ethnography: Reading the Lives of Others*   157

This sequence is designed to give students a chance to write a history or an ethnography and to think about and revise that work through the work of critics and theorists.

Assignments

SEQUENCE TEN   *On Difficulty*   162

The six assignments in this sequence invite students to consider the nature of difficult texts and how the problems they pose might be said to belong simultaneously to language, to readers, and to writers.

Assignments

SEQUENCE ELEVEN   *Reading Culture*   **166**

In this sequence, students will be reading and writing about culture — the images, words, and sounds that pervade our lives and organize and represent our common experience.

Assignments

1. *Looking at Pictures* [BERGER]   **166**
2. *The Ideology of Hunger* [BORDO]   **167**
3. *Ideology and Agency* [BORDO, BERGER]   **168**
4. *On Agency* [FOUCAULT]   **168**
5. *Reading Images* [MITCHELL]   **168**
6. *Visual Culture* [BERGER, BORDO, FOUCAULT, MITCHELL]   **169**

SEQUENCE TWELVE   *Reading Culture (II)*   **169**

This sequence provides and alternate set of readings for sequence eleven.

Assignments

1. *The Work of Art in the Age of Mechanical Reproduction* [BENJAMIN]   **170**
2. *Thinking about Cases* [BENJAMIN]   **170**
3. *Ways of Seeing* [BERGER, BENJAMIN]   **171**
4. *Ways of Listening* [FRITH]   **171**
5. *Back to Benjamin* [FRITH, BENJAMIN]   **171**
6. *Conclusions* [BENJAMIN, BERGER, FRITH]   **172**

SEQUENCE THIRTEEN   *The Uses of Reading*   **173**

This sequence focuses attention on authors as readers, on the use of sources, and on the art of reading as a writer. It combines technical lessons with lessons on the practice and rhetoric of citation.

Assignments

1. *The Scholarship Boy* [RODRIGUEZ, HOGGART]   **174**
2. *Sources* [BENJAMIN]   **174**
3. *Contrary Instincts* [WALKER]   **175**
4. *Ways of Reading* [BARTHOLOMAE AND PETROSKY]   **175**

SEQUENCE FOURTEEN   *Ways of Seeing*   **175**

This sequence works closely with John Berger's "Ways of Seeing" and his argument concerning the relationship between a spectator (one who sees and "reads" a painting) and knowledge, in concerning this case a knowledge of history.

Assignments

1. *Ways of Seeing* [BERGER]   **176**
2. *A Painting in Writing* [BERGER]   **176**
3. *Berger Writing* [BERGER]   **177**
4. *Picture Theory* [BERGER, MITCHELL]   **177**
5. *Revision* [MITCHELL, BERGER]   **178**

SEQUENCE FIFTEEN   *Working with the Past*   **178**

These assignments examine instances in which authors directly or indirectly work under the influence of others.

Assignments

SEQUENCE SIXTEEN   *Working with the Past (II)*   **181**

This sequence provides a variation on sequence fifteen. It provides similar assignments but with different readings.

Assignments

SEQUENCE SEVENTEEN   *Writing History*   **184**

This short sequence has two goals: to present two views of the "problem of history" and to use these accounts as an introduction to academic life.

Assignments

SEQUENCE EIGHTEEN   *Writing Projects*   **187**

The purpose of this sequence is to invite students to work closely with pieces of writing that call attention to themselves as writers, that make visible writing as a problem, a fundamental problem of representation and understanding.

Assignments

ADDITIONAL ASSIGNMENT SEQUENCES   *191*

Reading Walker Percy   *191*

This sequence is designed to provide students with a way of reading Walker Percy's essay "The Loss of the Creature." There are six assignments in this sequence, all of which offer a way of rereading (or revising a reading of) Percy's essay; and, in doing so, they provide one example of what it means to be an expert or a critical reader.

Assignments

A Way of Composing   *196*

This sequence is designed to offer a lesson in writing. The assignments stage students' work (or the process they will follow in composing a single essay) in a pattern common to most writers: drafting, revising, and editing.

Assignments

Ways of Seeing   *201*

This sequence calls for an examination of the claims that John Berger makes about our ways of seeing art.

Assignments

Working with Foucault   *204*

This sequence asks students to work their way through "Panopticism" by summarizing Foucault's argument, by interrogating the summary (as it does and doesn't "capture" Foucault), and by putting Foucault to work in a Foucauldian analysis of primary materials.

Assignments

Contents

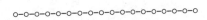

Resources for Teaching

WAYS OF
READING

An Anthology for Writers

Sixth Edition

Part I: Teaching with *Ways of Reading*

o–o–o–o–o–o–o–o–o–o–o–o–o–o–o–o–o–o

Introduction

Several years ago we were asked by the dean of our college to put together a course that combined instruction in reading and writing. The goal was to make students proficient users of the varieties of texts they would encounter in undergraduate education. When we began working on this course, we realized that the problems our students had when asked to write or talk about what they read were not "reading problems," at least not as these are strictly defined. Our students knew how to move from one page to the next. They could read sentences. They had obviously been able to carry out many of the versions of reading required for their education — skimming textbooks, cramming for tests, stripmining books for term papers.

Our students, however, felt powerless in the face of serious writing, in the face of long and complicated texts — the kinds of texts we thought they should find interesting and challenging. We thought (as many teachers have thought) that if we just, finally, gave them something good to read — something rich and meaty — they would change forever their ways of thinking about English. It didn't work, of course. The issue is not only *what* students read, but what they can learn to *do* with what they read. We have learned that the problems our students had lay not in the reading material (it was too hard) or in the students (they were poorly prepared) but in the classroom — in the ways we and they imagined what it meant to work on an essay.

In the preface and introduction to *Ways of Reading*, we provide an extended glimpse into that classroom. The preface is addressed to teachers; it speaks of the design of the book and the assumptions about reading, writing, and teaching that have informed our work. The introduction is addressed to students. It is also, however, a demonstration of how we have learned to talk to our students about reading and writing, about their work and ours. If you haven't read the preface and introduction, we suggest that you begin there before working with this manual. Many instructors assign the introduction as one of the "readings" for the course. Some have asked students to reread the introduction later in the semester — perhaps after reading the essays by Wideman or Rich — and to write a response to it, to provide a student's introduction to *Ways of Reading*. This is a way for students to reflect on the work they have been doing and to articulate a sense of the course in terms that can stand alongside or outside of the terms that dominate the book. It is a way for students to have a conversation with Bartholomae and Petrosky, to imagine us as writers or as characters, to represent the book as having a point of view.

What follows is a brief additional list of tips and afterthoughts — the sorts of things we find ourselves saying to each other over coffee or in the staff room.

Be Patient. We remind ourselves of this more often than anything else. The argument of this text is that students should be given the very types of essays that are often denied them — those that demand time and attention. The purpose of the course, then, is to teach

1

students how to work on those essays and, in particular, how to work on them by writing. There is work for a reader to do. It is important work and part of the process of a liberal arts education. And yet, because the essays cannot be quickly handled, students' first efforts with them are often halting. You cannot expect to walk into class and have a dazzling discussion of Geertz's "Deep Play," or to pick up a set of papers and see commanding readings of that essay. At least not all at once. You have to teach students to do this. As we have taught such courses, the rhythm goes something like this: Students write papers on "Deep Play" that are beginning attempts, footholds on a difficult essay. It is only through further discussion and revision that students will begin to shape these early drafts into more confident and impressive performances. With time, students will learn to take great pleasure in their accomplishments. They will see that they are beginning to be able to enter into conversations, to do things with texts, that they never imagined they could do. If you move too quickly from one work to the next, however, students will experience more frustration than anything else. They will sense what they might have been able to do, without getting a chance to show their best work.

Write First or Write Later? When students are working regularly from essays, much depends on whether they write before or after those essays are discussed in class. The issues are these: If you talk through an essay in class, there is a way in which the students' papers are prewritten. If a teacher takes a strong line and speaks convincingly about how he or she reads Geertz's references to *King Lear,* it is a rare student who will do anything but say back what the teacher has already said. This student has not been in a position to author, or take responsibility for, a reading. The enabling moment for a reader is the moment of silence, when the student sits down before a text — a text that must remain silent — and must begin to write and to see what can be made of that writing. Even if a teacher is skilled at being slippery in front of class, even if a teacher avoids taking a stand and serves primarily to encourage and orchestrate the various comments of the students, there is still a way in which the pressure to write is taken from a writer by discussion. One student may sit down to write about Geertz and find that whatever she says sounds just like what she heard others say in class. Another student may sit down with the intention of doing no more than trying to piece together what went on in class. In many cases, it is best to let students write first. And then, after a discussion of their papers and perhaps a discussion of the selection, let them go back to those papers to work on them again.

This is not cut and dried, however. While all this makes sense, we have often felt that we would have given students a real head start by anticipating problems in students' readings of the essays before they wrote, and so we often hold discussions before they begin. The discussion to have *before* students write is the discussion that will enable students to be better readers of the essays — a discussion preparing students to deal with Foucault's language or to anticipate the temptation to ignore the difficult sections and stick to the familiar in "The Loss of the Creature." We will often speak directly to these special requirements in the discussions of each selection in the first part of the manual.

Be Patient. This is worth repeating. Students will learn to take charge of the work they do as readers and writers when they are given a chance to go back to the work — when they are given opportunities to reread and revise. If they have a chance to go back to a paper on "Deep Play," they can see themselves as readers in what they have written; they will be able to work on the reading by working on the essay. The act of revision we are thinking of, then, is not just a matter of tightening or correcting a paper; it is a matter of going back to the primary text and reworking what one might say about it. Students will not learn the same lesson by jumping ahead to a new assignment. Getting started on an essay on "Deep Play" is not, in itself, preparation for an essay on Percy. Students will learn more if they can spend time working again and again on a single essay than they will if they start a paper on one subject and then jump forward to something new. If you think of your course as a course in reading and writing, there is no pressure to cover material. There is pressure to read and write, but it makes no difference whether you cover three selections in the textbook or eleven.

On Revision. Revision has been a standard part of the courses we teach — and by that we mean that revision is part of the weekly schedule of work. It is not an afterthought or something students might do on the side. It is part of the assigned work from class to class. Our students, in other words, know that they can expect to work their way toward a final draft. And they can expect to receive help from us through written comments or conferences, and from their colleagues through class discussions of sample mimeographed papers and through group conferences. Since revision is a group process in our classes, we find that we have to make a point of ensuring that revision is not (at least necessarily) a drive toward consensus. When students write first drafts on, for example, "The Loss of the Creature," we will get quite a variety of responses. When we discuss these papers in class, we call attention to the variety of responses — particularly the strongest ones — in order to demonstrate that there are ways of reading "The Loss of the Creature," not just one way, and that these ways of reading are driven by different strategies and serve different ends. We want students, in other words, to see their papers as evidence of choices they made in talking about the text. And we want them to see those choices in the context of choices made by other writers. The purpose of revision, then, is to enable students to take their approach to a text and to make the most of it. We do not want students to revise in order to say what we would say, or what the group has said about "The Loss of the Creature." Our goal as teachers has always been to try to bring forward the paper that seems to be struggling to be written. That's the paper we want the student to work on in revision. These revisions should show again the variety of the first drafts. We do not want students to rework their papers so that they all say the same thing. We want students to work on readings of an essay; we do not insist that they come to a common point of view.

Background Information. There are classes where it is a teacher's job to know all that he or she can about the backgrounds to the texts under discussion. These are not necessarily composition classes, however. We would be paralyzed if we felt we had to be specialists on Freire, Geertz, and Rich before we could walk into our classes. It would keep us from teaching what we want to teach. So what do we want to teach? We want to teach students how to make what they can out of essays that don't lend themselves to quick summary. We want to show students, or lead them to show each other, how to work with what they have. We want to teach them how to draw on their own resources. As a consequence, we have avoided *Norton Anthology*–like footnotes (the footnotes you find are in the original texts), and we have avoided headnotes that cast the essays in the context of the history of ideas. Readers read outside of their areas of professional expertise. And they take pleasure and instruction from reading unfamiliar material. We don't want students to get the notion that, because they lack specialized knowledge, they are unable to read essays like "Deep Play." The essay may be difficult, but we don't want students to imagine the difficulty in those terms. If they do, then there is nothing to do but give up. The argument of the textbook, then, is that readers and writers make use of what they have. No reader catches all the allusions or understands all the words or translates all the foreign phrases — yet readers can make texts meaningful by what they do with them when they act as though they had the ability to make a text meaningful. Your students will learn most as they discover how to deal with complex or unfamiliar material. They will be learning about learning.

So What Is This Course About? It is about composing — reading and writing. You are not teaching Limerick or Geertz, history or anthropology. You are teaching reading and writing. You stand for a method, a way of working with texts, and not for a set of canonical interpretations, a series of approved statements used to represent an understanding of those texts. Your authority as a teacher in this course comes from your ability to do things with texts, not from your experience with all the fields of inquiry represented by these essays. The best way to prepare for your teaching is to imagine the varieties of ways these texts might be read. Then you will not be surprised by what your students want to do when they read, and you will be better able to encourage them to work out the potential of their own approaches to the essays. The worst thing to do is to come to class ready to expound or defend a single reading, one that all your students are expected to speak back to you by the end of the day. Then students will sit back and wait to be told what the essays say; they won't feel empowered to forge a reading on their own. You need to be able to monitor and assist your students as they work on these essays. To do that you will have to be able to enter into their ways of reading. You must do more, that is, than tell them whether they are wrong or right.

Who's the Boss? You are, of course. But this means that you are responsible for evaluating the performance of your students. You may ask the class an open question, one reasonable people can disagree on. This is not, however, the same thing as saying that everyone has a right to his or her own opinion. Some opinions are phrased powerfully, some work closely with material from the text, some acknowledge and represent counteropinions, some push against easy commonplaces and clichéd thinking. Whether they are writing or speaking, students are composing ways of talking about these essays, and the job of a teacher is to encourage, monitor, and evaluate those performances. There is nothing worse than a class where discussion is an end in itself — where a lively fifty minutes is its own justification. Whether students are discussing Geertz's essay or an essay of their own, the point of the conversation should be to bring forward a textual problem and to demonstrate how, with care, attention, rigor, and precision, a person might work on it.

Reading against the Grain. We have tried to write a book that leaves plenty of room for a student to move around in, one that is strongly voiced, or as strongly voiced as the conventions of textbook publishing will allow. In the introduction and headnotes, in the questions and assignments, we wanted students to get a sense of two characters speaking. We did not want them to hear the disembodied voice of Truth or Reason. We wanted, in other words, to encourage students to read the text *as* a text, to see it as representing a point of view, to argue with it, to take it as a prompting to respond in a voice of their own. Students can read with or against the text — with it by participating in its form of instruction, against it by seeing its bias or limitations. Students are asked to read not only with but against the grain of the authors represented in *Ways of Reading*. While it is important for students to pay generous attention to what they read — to give in, to think through someone else's words — it is also important that students feel what it is like to step outside a text, in order to ask questions about where it might lead, what it leaves out, and whose interests it serves and why. We wanted students to imagine that they could read in the name of a collective set of interests. Students need to feel their power to step outside a text, and they need to learn how and why it is OK to ask difficult questions or resist the forces of tradition, power, and authority.

Using This Book. And we have tried to write a book that leaves plenty of room for a teacher. You'll notice that the teaching materials are placed both after the selections and at the end of the book. There are second-reading questions and writing assignments after each piece and assignment sequences at the end. This is not to insist that a teacher use either one set of materials or the other. All the assignments in the sequences, for example, assume that students will reread the selections, and the second-reading questions are designed to help students imagine where to begin and how to proceed — so that they are not just reading the words one more time. We hope that students will work back and forth between the questions at the end of an essay or a story and the writing assignments in the sequences. Many instructors have found the assignment sequences a powerful way of representing writing as a tool for learning and inquiry, particularly inquiry as it involves the close and critical reading of texts. The assignment sequences are meant to suggest possible courses of instruction, but they are not meant to be limiting. We have used the book for twelve years at the University of Pittsburgh, teaching different sequences each year. We always revise the sequences at the end of the book by leaving out some readings and adding others, using the "Assignments for Writing" in place of the writing assignments in the sequence. We have also known several instructors who put together semester-long sequences out of a combination of questions in "Assignments for Writing" and "Making Connections."

4

Reader's Journal. A reader's journal can serve as a useful adjunct to the more formal writing students do. We think of a reader's journal as both a commonplace book and a double–entry notebook. We encourage students, in other words, to copy out and reflect on passages that grab them in what they read. There are powerful lines and phrases in these essays, and this is one way of acknowledging to students that readers grab on to the minute specifics as much as they do the general argument in what they read. The journal can also serve as a way for students to record the process of reading. They can, for example, make two columns in the journal, using one to note puzzles or problems or reactions after a first reading and the other to comment on those entries after a second reading.

And, Finally. Assume that students will need to read each selection at least twice before they do any of the assignments. First readings should give a sense of the selection and its language; subsequent readings should be focused by the questions or directions in the assignment.

Tell students there are no quick-and-easy ways to read these selections. They will need to reread and pay attention to the passages and moments in each selection that allow them to address the questions in the assignments.

Ask students to take notes and mark passages on their second and third readings of the selections.

Use class discussions of the "Questions for a Second Reading" to help students prepare for the writing assignments.

Ask students to come to class prepared to discuss the "Questions for a Second Reading." They should have notes and numerous references to the selection for each question.

Discuss writing with students before they do any of the writing assignments. Use examples of past students' papers to demonstrate such things as notetaking, drafting, revising, and editing.

Duplicate students' papers for class discussions. Use complete papers and parts of papers to demonstrate students' work on such matters as interpretation, critical commentary, text references, paraphrase, and risk-taking.

Encourage students to take notes from the texts and to record their thoughts, other students' comments, class discussions, and their responses to your comments on their papers.

Encourage students to reread their drafts, paying attention to what they say and how they use the selection, and to redraft whole drafts or parts of drafts before they hand in their papers.

Accept students' drafts as drafts. Allow them the opportunity to use drafts and revisions to think through the problems posed by the assignments.

Encourage or require revisions for the assignments that warrant them, especially if a student is particularly involved in an assignment.

Respond to students' writing in stages. Respond first to their completion of the task, then to what they have to say and how they use (or don't use) the text, then to editorial matters.

Write comments and raise questions on students' papers. Press them back into the texts and push against their generalizations and quick summaries.

Limit the number of comments you write on students' papers. Pick two or three things to focus on and avoid mixing comments for revision with editorial suggestions.

Teach students to edit their papers. Show them how to use a ruler and a red pencil and to read line by line through their final revisions.

Teach students to work in peer editing groups. Ask them to read each other's papers and to explain to each other the errors that they find.

Try to avoid grading individual papers. Ask students to be responsible for keeping all their papers, including all their drafts, in a pocket folder or portfolio, and grade the portfolio of work at mid-semester and at semester's end.

Hold two or three twenty- to thirty-minute conferences with each student during the semester. Go over papers and note what you would like each student to work on during that semester. Keep a record of these conferences for your files, and use your notes to help with grading.

o–o–o–o–o–o–o–o–o–o–o–o–o–o–o–o–o–o–o

Questions We Are Often Asked

The writing assignments are often long and difficult, even confusing. Why is this? How do you prepare students to read and work with the assignments in *Ways of Reading*?

Let's take the last question first: "How do you prepare students to read and work with the writing assignments?" It's true that the assignments are long. In comparison to what students are used to (test questions, for example, or writing assignments that look like test questions), they take time to read. This is part of the design of the assignments. Even in their format, we want them to challenge or call into question the assumption that the project before students, their writing, is simple or simply a matter of following instructions.

Our goal, rather, is to set a context, to define the outlines or possibilities of a project (we say to our students) within which students can find interesting work to do. Our students say, "Just tell us what you want." And we say, "We want you to do something interesting, something you care about." But, as teachers, we also want to help our students imagine unimaginable projects, work they couldn't do without our help.

From our point of view, the worst way to read the assignments is to find one sentence or one question and to say, "Aha, *here* is what this assignment is *really* about," as though the rest of the words were simply distraction, a smoke screen. This is a version of the standard technology of mastery, similar to reading an essay for its main idea. You find one passage you can control and you let it stand for the whole essay. You find one question you can answer quickly and you let it stand for the whole assignment. We want our assignments to open up a process of questioning for students, not to present a single question or to signal a routine school task.

The other problem we have observed, and again we can link this to the history of American education, is that students are tempted to take the questions in the assignments and answer them one by one, thus using them to structure their essays. One reason there are several questions in each assignment is to suggest that there are several ways in, several ways to begin to think about a response. They are not meant to serve as a checklist for a writer to follow, item by item. A question, for many students, becomes a straitjacket, an order, a command, a test. We want our questions to be an exercise in questioning.

Most of the questions are designed to turn against what we have taken as the flow of the assignment, to open it up and to suggest a new direction. As we just said, we don't want students to think of writing as following a series of orders. In any case, the questions (at their best) don't function that way. They *aren't* a series but a set of interruptions. They are designed to frustrate the very patterns the assignment has set into play.

The writing assignments, then, are meant to suggest a project. This project usually asks students to do two things: to go back to reread the essay, this time with a specific problem in mind; and to write an essay as a way of thinking through an answer to that problem. Our goal is to set some specific limits on students' work — the assignment might

7

direct students to perform a close reading of passages or to apply the terms of one essay to examples of their own choosing or to read one essay as it is framed by another. At the same time we want to provide room for students to move around; we want to make the assignments "readable" in the sense that there is room for interpretation. We want students to be able to find *their* work in *our* assignments. Now, we're realists. Sometimes they do and sometimes they don't. We realize that. If we have done our work well, students will often find ways of making the work their own. In our own classes, we certainly never set ourselves up as assignment police. We expect our students to read the assignments carefully. We expect them to be able to explain how they read the assignments and how their work constitutes a response. But we do not have a specific answer in mind to our questions and we do not have a particular essay in mind as a response to our assignments. When students ask us, "What do you want?" we answer, "What do *you* want to do?" In a class of twenty-two students, our goal is to get as many different kinds of responses as we can. We use the assignments as starting points. They suggest an approach to the readings ("Look at the poems in 'When We Dead Awaken' and think about how they might represent a series") and they suggest a project ("Write an essay describing what you consider to be the most significant pattern of change in Rich's poems. When you are done, compare your account with Rich's account"). Because as teachers we can begin with what our students imagine to be the most profitable (or possible) directions to take with this (their sense of what the assignment might mean for them as they prepare to write), our discussions about the work they might do have a focus and a motive they would not have if students were left to determine projects on their own. We think that our assignments intervene in productive ways and enable students to want to do things they would never have imagined doing on their own.

Perhaps it might help to look closely at a couple of assignments. Because we have begun using Rich as an example, we have chosen another assignment from "When We Dead Awaken" and, for the sake of comparison, one of the assignments that followed Virginia Woolf's "A Room of One's Own" in the fifth edition of *Ways of Reading*. The discussion will treat them paragraph by paragraph (or section by section).

In the opening of her essay, Woolf says that the "I" of her text "is only a convenient term for somebody who has no real being." And at the beginning of the last chapter (in reference to a new novel by "Mr. A"), she says,

> But after reading a chapter or two a shadow seemed to lie across the page. It was a straight dark bar, a shadow shaped something like the letter "I." One began dodging this way and that to catch a glimpse of the landscape behind it. Whether that was indeed a tree or a woman walking I was not quite sure. Back one was always hailed to the letter "I." One began to be tired of "I." (p. 766)

It's hard to know what to make of this, as an argument about either the position of women or writing. Read back through Woolf's essay, noting sections you could use to investigate the ways an "I" is or is not present in this text and to investigate the argument that text makes about a writer's (or speaker's) presence. (See the third "Question for a Second Reading.")

Write an essay in which you examine the ways Woolf, a writer, is and is not present in this piece of writing. Where and how does she hide? And why? Whom do you find in her place? How might this difficulty over the presence of the writer be said to be a part of Woolf's argument about women and writing? And what might this have to do with you and the writing you are doing, either in this class or in school generally?

The first paragraph was written to prompt a close reading and to resituate a student in relation to the text of "A Room of One's Own." We focus on a passage, making it a key passage. When students reread, they will be reading for the definition of both the authorial I (the writer) and the presentation of the character who speaks in the first person throughout the essay. And, following the passage, we do what we often do. We take something that we suspect students might feel to be straightforward and announce that it is strange, mysterious or problematic ("It is hard to know what to make of this"). In a sense, the writing assignment sets students the task of making something out of the ways in which Woolf, both in what she says and in what she does as a writer, challenges the standard notions governing the status and presence of a "Person" in writing.

The first paragraph, then, defines the project as a directed rereading of "A Room of One's Own." The last paragraph turns specifically to the essays students are to write. The first few questions are there for students who can't quite figure out where to begin ("Think about how and why Woolf might hide. Think about where she is present"). The remaining questions are there to complicate this project: first, by asking students to think about the connections between the argument in "A Room of One's Own" and the argument represented in its style or method; second, by asking students to think about how this essay might be written for them, as writers, how it might have a bearing on the work they are doing in a composition course. In most of our assignments, we try to find a way of saying to students, "Hey, this isn't just academic, it is speaking directly to you about the way you think and write, about how you live your life."

There is a similar pattern in the Rich assignment:

Rich says, "We need to know the writing of the past, and know it differently than we have ever known it; not to pass on a tradition but to break its hold over us." That "us" includes you too. Look back over your own writing (perhaps the drafts and revisions you have written for this course), and think back over comments teachers have made, textbooks you've seen; think about what student writers do and what they are told to do, about the secrets students keep and the secrets teachers keep. You can assume, as Rich does, that there are ways of speaking about writing that are part of the culture of schooling and that they are designed to preserve certain ways of writing and thinking and to discourage others.

One might argue, in other words, that there are traditions here. As you look at the evidence of the "past" in your work, what are its significant features? What might you name this tradition (or these traditions)? How would you illustrate its hold on your work or the work of students generally? What might you have to do to begin to "know it differently," "to break its hold," or to revise? And, finally, why would someone want (or not want) to break its hold?

This assignment defines a different kind of project from the Woolf assignment. The Woolf assignment asked for a close reading of the text. This one asks students to use a text (its terms, its interpretive frame, its motives) to "read" their own experience, including the material record of that experience.

The opening paragraph sets the terms for this project. The "we" of Rich's essay, it says, is also "you." It suggests where students might go to begin to gather material to write about (not just memory but also old textbooks, old papers). And the end of the paragraph returns to frame their work in Rich's terms, terms that would remain hidden or lost or invisible in the text if we did not bring them forward and make them key terms. We want students to think not just about *"my"* school or *"my"* teacher, but about the past, about tradition, about patriarchy (a word we wish we had featured more prominently in the assignment), and about culture.

The final paragraph restates the goal of the project and then tries to question or complicate students' (or any readers') desire to say — "Oh, I get it, what they want is simply this." We want to forestall the desire to see it "simply." We do this by pointing, again, to the larger social, historical, and cultural context of the examples students will be writing about, a context we know from experience will be lost without our prompting. We do this by turning, again, to the words of the text. Our goal is to make this essay also a reading of

"When We Dead Awaken." We are hoping that students will refer to Rich and use some of her terms in their discussion ("Nothing in this textbook even suggests, as Rich does, that I might not only need to write a topic sentence but 'know it differently,' even 'break its hold' on my writing"). And, finally, we want students to imagine that the essay speaks to them directly as students in a writing course — that in a sense, "When We Dead Awaken" can be read as a lesson in writing.

How do you construct assignment sequences?

We always begin with the readings. Our teaching is driven, in other words, by what we want to teach — that is, what we want students to read. The process of selection is described in both the preface and the introduction, but we begin by locating challenging readings, readings with some currency in the academy. We look for work in writing that we think can provide important examples to young writers, that can provide interesting work for a required course, and with authors, ideas, terms, and subjects that can be useful in the education of young scholars. Each selection, then, must be something students can profitably write from and about; it must also, itself, be a lesson in writing.

Once we have decided on the readings, the key question becomes one of how to engage writers with the material over an extended piece of time. How might these readings define a project and not simply serve as independent units to be processed and then left behind? It is important to us that the semester be defined by a project, an evolving body of work that asks students to think of one text in terms of another, usually with some general subject or question in mind, and, by thinking about them, to revise, extend, and rework earlier essays and earlier positions. The assignments, then, are written to broker that engagement, to call attention to certain problems in the text that students might otherwise overlook, and then to move from that piece of reading to the next, to both focus attention on its ways of thinking and writing and to invite students to see it in relation to what they have read before. They move into one piece and then back to the general project in a pattern that will include revision as well as addition. Because we know how easy it is for students to be overwhelmed by the readings, the sequences are generally punctuated by assignments that ask students to stop, take stock, and find a place to enter, as writers, into the discussions begun by others, by the authors they have read.

How many readings do you teach in a semester?

This is an easier question to answer than the first. Usually four. Sometimes three, sometimes five, but never more than that. We could imagine assigning more essays and using them for discussion, in groups or in class, but only if students' writing was limited to three, four, or five essays.

Our semester has fourteen weeks. We spend at least two weeks on every essay and generally leave time for what we call "retrospective" essays. These essays, which we assign at mid-term and at the end of the term are designed to give students time to reflect on the work of the course (and to give us a sense of what students are thinking).

We give students at least two weeks to work on the readings they write about. There is a simple and standard pattern here. Students write a draft in the first week and revise it in the second. The readings are difficult enough to warrant giving students the extra time, particularly the time to reread and revise, tasks we have come to think of as almost identical. We also want students to feel their achievement as readers and writers. If we were moving quickly from one essay to the next each week, we would worry that students would feel only frustration at their failure to understand. Each first draft would give them a sense of what they might be able to do with an essay, but they would never be able to complete that work — or at least take it to its next stage.

What are your courses like? What is the daily routine?

We have taught from *Ways of Reading* every year. In fact, the first edition began with a collection of the materials we had been teaching over the past several years. The first thing to say is that even at the University of Pittsburgh, where a large staff has been teaching this or similar material for a long time, there is a surprising range of differences in the shape of the courses and in the daily routine. Teachers need to teach from their strengths. They need to believe in their courses. Most teachers who work with us make regular revisions in the sequences or in individual assignments, both before the semester begins (to create a different emphasis, for example) and once it is under way (to respond to issues that have come up in class).

There are some generalizations to make, however. We regularly reproduce student essays and use them (often in pairs) as the center of class discussion. Instead of having a general discussion of "When We Dead Awaken," for example, we would focus on two specific readings by two different students. Rather than talk about revision generally, we would use those same two papers to discuss how and where and why they might usefully be revised. As we have already stated, revision is a central part of the course. Students revise as part of their weekly schedule of assignments, not on their own or for extra credit; they do one of the writing assignments one week, receive our comments, then revise it the next week. Revision in this case is represented as something other than "fixing" an essay. We ask students to put in the same amount of time as they did on the first draft. Their goal is to rethink the essay they have begun and to take it on its next step.

Perhaps the best way to illustrate one of our classes is to present an example of a course description and a syllabus. The following course description comes from one of Bartholomae's courses taught from an earlier edition. (You should feel free, by the way, to take any of this and use it in your courses. Good teachers borrow from each other all the time.)

Sample Course Description
David Bartholomae

COURSE DESCRIPTION

Introduction. The subject of this course is writing. Writing, as I think of it, is an action, an event, a performance. It is a way of asserting one's presence but, paradoxically, in a language that makes the writer disappear. No matter what you write, the writing is not yours; it's part of a larger text, one with many authors, begun long ago. And its end is outside your control. In spite of what you think you are saying, your text will become what others make of it, what they say you said.

One of my goals in this course is to arrange your work to highlight your relationship (as a writer) to the past and to the words of others (to history and culture). This is the reason for the assigned readings, and this is the primary role reading will play in this writing course. You will be asked to read a series of assigned texts and to write in response what you have read. I want to foreground the ways in which your writing takes place in relation to the writing of others. My goal, as your teacher, will be to make that relationship interesting, surprising, and productive. These meetings between the past and the present, writing and a writer, those places in your essays where you work with someone else's words and ideas to my mind represent the basic scene of instruction; they are the workplaces, the laboratories, the arenas of what is often called a "liberal" education. It is there, on the page, that the key work of a student is done and not in some private, internal mental space. This is why a writing course is fundamental to undergraduate education.

The Course. I have asked you to think of a writing course as the representative workplace of a liberal arts education. You might also think of our course as a studio course, like a course in painting or sculpture or composition. You will be practicing your art by working on specific projects. I will be looking over your shoulder, monitoring your progress, and, at various points in the semester, assessing the work you gather together in a portfolio.

In this sense, the course is one where you practice writing. You can expect to write regularly, at least one draft or essay each week. You will need to develop the habits and the discipline of a writer. You will need a regular schedule, a regular place and time for writing. There is nothing fancy about this. You need to learn to organize your time so that there is time for writing, so that it becomes part of a routine.

You'll need to learn to work quickly but also to keep your attention inside sentences for hours at a time. This requires discipline, a kind of physical training I can best describe as athletic. Writers need to be able to sit in one place and to think inside of sentences for long periods of time. You'll have to set your own goals. I would suggest four hours a week in two two-hour sessions. These are writing times, when you will be sitting in one place and working closely with words, yours and others'. You should do nothing else during these sessions. You should work in the same place at the same time every week.

I can insist on this kind of care and attention, but I can't teach it. I can, however, teach you ways of working on your writing. I have come to believe that the most important skill I can teach in a writing course is reading — the ability to read closely and critically. In this sense a writing course is like any other course in an English department. There is one difference, however. In a writing course we are interested in how you can apply criticism to production, to the production of your own writing, your texts. In a course on Shakespeare, you may write about Shakespeare, you may be said to "produce" Shakespeare's plays by interpreting them and writing about what you have read. But there is a fundamental difference in what you produce, in your writing, and how your writing is valued. In a writing class it is *your* work that is the center of critical attention, not Shakespeare's. The pressing question is what your writing might say about our culture, about language and imagination, not what his might say. Writing requires the skills of endurance and attention. In revision, it requires critical reading, a form of practical criticism, a protocol that will allow you to read your own writing in order to go back to work.

I have learned that the essential work of any writing course is revision. There is more to writing than first thoughts, first drafts, and first pages. A writer learns most by returning to his or her work to see what it does and doesn't do, by taking time with a project and seeing where it might lead. This class is a place where you will practice writing, but it is also a place where the writing is expected to change. You will be writing regularly, but I will also be asking you revise — to step outside your writing, to see what it might represent (not just what it says), and to make changes. I will teach you how to read your own writing, how to pay close and critical attention to what you have written, and I will teach you how to make this critical attention part of the cycle of production, part of your work as a writer.

The course will be organized so that you will work a single essay through several drafts; each essay will be a part of a larger project. When I assess your writing I will be looking primarily at the progress from draft to draft.

Schedule and Routines. I have planned for fourteen weeks and divided the semester into three units, each with a particular focus.

You should plan to read each assigned reading *twice* before I begin to discuss it in class. The first time through you should read quickly, to get a general sense of what the writer is doing, what the piece is about. Then you should read through a second time, this time working more closely and deliberately with the text, focusing on those sections that seem difficult or puzzling or mysterious. You should read with a pen or pencil, marking

he text in a way that will help you when you go back to it (particularly when you go back
o it as a writer). If you can't bring yourself to write in your book, you should begin to
levelop a system using note cards or Post-it notes.

Each week you will write one essay and/or revise one essay, both as stages in a larger
project. Each week you should make two additional copies of everything you have writ-
en, one for me and one for a peer reader. My graded copy of *everything* you write for this
course must be gathered together in your portfolio. Keep back-up copies in a separate
folder. In order to monitor your progress, I will review your portfolios at three points in
the term — around the fifth week, the tenth, and at the end of the term. Your final grade
will be based on my final reading of your portfolio. It will be an assessment of your work
in the course over the term. I will be particularly interested in the development I see in
revision and across the portfolio. I will be looking for evidence of your involvement with
the course and of your willingness and your success in working on your writing. I will *not*
add together and average the grades from the earlier reviews.

I will also read individual essays carefully each week and write comments on them. I
spend a lot of time on these comments and I will expect you to take time to read what I
have written. If you find that I have written much on your paper, you should take this as a
sign of love, not of desperation. It means I was interested, engaged.

The best way to read my comments is to start at the beginning of your essay, reread
what you have written, and stop to read my comments along the way. This is how I write
the marginal comments, while I am reading. They show my reactions and suggestions at
that moment. The final comment is where I will make a summary statement about your
essay. Be warned: I tend to be blunt and to the point. If I sound angry, I probably am not. I
want to get your attention, I want to be honest, and I see no reason to beat around the bush.

If your work seems thoughtless or quickly done, I will notice. I have taught writing
for many years and I know when writers are working hard and when they are fooling
around. I will tell you if I think you are fooling around.

I will not put grades on individual essays. I will grade your performance over fourteen weeks, but I see no reason to grade each and every piece you write. In many cases, I
will be asking you to extend yourself and to do what you cannot do easily or with grace. It
would make no sense for me to grade everything you do. (Please see the separate handout
on "Error and Plagiarism." I will expect you to consistently and successfully proofread all
papers, including first drafts.) I will be available to answer questions or to look at an essay
immediately before and after class. I know that my handwriting can be a problem. I will
not be embarrassed if you ask me to decipher what I have written. I will, however, be
heartbroken if you simply skip over what is hard to read.

Class Participation. I will regularly reproduce your papers (with names removed)
and use them for class discussion. Most of our class time will be spent discussing copies of
your essays. This is as important to your education as the time you spend alone working
on your writing. I expect you to attend all classes. If you are absent, you are not taking the
course and I will ask you to drop or give you a failing grade. Similarly, all written work
must be completed on schedule. Because you will be writing every week, and because one
week's work will lead to the next assignment, you cannot afford to fall behind. I will not
accept work that is late. If you are not doing the writing, you are not taking the course and
I will ask you to drop or give you a failing grade.

Writing Groups. I will divide the class into groups of three. Few writers work alone;
they rely on friends and colleagues to listen to ideas, to read drafts, and to help with
copyediting. You will be responsible for commenting on one group member's essay or
draft each week. When you do, you are to sign your name to your comments. (See the
handout on "Working as a Reader and Editor.")

Workshop. Throughout the semester you can receive free tutorial help at the Writing Workshop, CL 501. It is open Monday through Friday, with evening hours Tuesday through Thursday. I will also set aside three or four class sessions as tutorial workshops. I will meet with you individually and ask you to work together in your writing groups.

End of Term. I will not put comments on the work in the final folders. You will have heard plenty from me throughout the semester and I don't want to waste time writing comments that won't be read. This does not mean, however, that I am not interested in talking with you about your work. If you would like to review the folder or individual essays, come see me first thing at the beginning of the next semester. There is no final exam.

Materials. You will need:

A handbook (I have ordered one for the course)

A dictionary (there are copies of *The American Heritage Dictionary* at the Bookcenter)

Ways of Reading, Fourth Edition, Bartholomae and Petrosky

Photocopied handouts

You will need a sturdy folder with pockets to hold your work and everything I hand out in class. This will become your portfolio.

A Word to the Wise. All your work for this course *must be typed.* If you have not yet begun to use a word processor, now is the time to begin. In a course like this, where you are expected to revise and to revise regularly, you will make your life a lot easier if you can do your revisions on a computer screen. Typing papers over and over again is tiresome and inefficient. If you need help getting started with a computer or a program, see me immediately.

COURSE SCHEDULE Readings: Pratt, Anzaldúa, Jacobs, Greenblatt (Sequence Two: The Arts of the Contact Zone)

Writing and Revising: "Long, intense absorption," "logic and imagination," "practical criticism"

Sept. 3	Introductions
Sept. 8, 10	Read Pratt, "Arts of the Contact Zone"
Sept. 15, 17	Assignment 1 due: The Literate Arts of the Contact Zone [Pratt]
Sept. 22, 24	Revise Assignment l; Read Anzaldúa, "Entering into the Serpent" and "How to Tame a Wild Tongue"
Sept. 29, Oct. 1	Assignment 2 due: Borderlands [Pratt, Anzaldúa]; Portfolios due, 9/29

Working with Texts: "Historical awareness"

Oct. 6, 8	Revise Assignment 2; Read Jacobs, "Incidents in the Life of a Slave Girl"
Oct. 13, 15	Midterm retrospective writing assignment
Oct. 20, 22	Assignment 3 due: Autoethnography [Pratt, Jacobs]; Read Greenblatt, "Marvelous Possessions"[1]
Oct. 27, 29	Revise Assignment 3
Nov. 3, 5	Assignment 4 due: Writing America [Greenblatt]; Portfolios due, 11/3

[1]This essay appeared in the fourth edition of *Ways of Reading.*

Fine-Tuning: "Linguistic precision"

Nov. 10, 12	Assignment 5 due: Writing the Other [Greenblatt]
Nov. 17, 19	Revise Assignment 5
Nov. 24	Assignment 6: On Culture [Pratt, Anzaldúa, Jacobs, Greenblatt]
Dec. 1, 3	Revise Assignment 6
Dec. 8, 10	Final retrospective essay
Finals week	**Final Portfolios Due** Friday, December 18th, 4:00 P.M.

Aren't these readings too hard? What do you do with students who claim that they can't read them or that the work is boring? What do you do with students who become angry or who give up?

We get this question all the time. Or people say, "Maybe you can teach this stuff at Pitt, but it would never work on our campus."

The course represented by *Ways of Reading* began several years ago, prompted by our sense that students were being cheated. Textbooks and courses were founded on the assumption that students would be bored or frustrated or angry with the intellectual materials that we ourselves found most interesting, fascinating, compelling, or important. And so, ostensibly to protect students, composition courses gave them simple things to work with. ("Don't worry your pretty little heads," the profession said. "Work on simple essays for simple minds.")

We designed our course, as we say in the preface, to teach students *how* to work with difficult materials. We wanted to bring them into the conversation, to give students a way to begin to work the materials that mattered to us, that we valued.

We don't hide the fact that these essays are difficult and frustrating. They were for us when we read them the first time. Our goal is to give students a course to show them how and why they might negotiate the difficulty. This is why rereading is such an important feature of our courses. This is why the writing assignments are designed to help students work with the readings.

Nevertheless, the questions about the difficulty of the texts are valid, and we don't ignore them. Even if you make difficulty one of the acknowledged features of the course, how do you keep students interested? How do you allow them to believe that they can do the work? One way is to show your enthusiasm and pleasure in the work they are doing. It is important, we've said, for teachers to be patient. If students are going to work on these essays, that work will take time. There will be halting steps along the way. Even at the end, a student's account of Rich's "When We Dead Awaken" will most likely not reproduce the level or intensity of the lecture on American feminism that you or a colleague might be able to give. The point of a course like this is to give students a chance to work on the materials and concerns important to the academy. They will not, however, all attain the eloquence or the conclusions of their professors. So patience is more than a matter of waiting. It requires a willingness to value and show enthusiasm for work that is partial, unfinished, the work of novices, work that we have been prepared to call "error."

The book also offers a protocol for dealing with difficulty. It says indirectly (and we say directly in our classes), "Read through quickly as though it all made sense, get the big picture, get a feel for what the piece is about. Then go back to read more closely, taking time to work on passages that seem difficult or mysterious. Assume that these passages are hard for you because they are indeed difficult and would be hard for any reader, not because you are stupid." We offer questions to help direct this rereading. Students should also think of this stage as pencil work, writing in the margins, connecting sections of the text, working out provisional responses and definitions. We've also found that it is important to help students know when and where to use a dictionary.

The other approach we often take is to use class time to model ways of working on difficult passages. We will begin a discussion by asking students to identify passages that they would like us to work on together, as a group. Then we will use the discussion to work out possible readings and to chart, on the blackboard, the strategies that have enabled them. We will also do this in our discussion of students' essays, asking students to notice how a writer has made sense of a difficult section or (often early in the semester) where a writer has carefully avoided dealing with the parts of text that resisted his or her reading.

Your course seems to put so much emphasis on reading. Where is there time for writing instruction? How is your course a writing course?

We have never thought of our course as anything *but* a writing course. As we interpret reading (working on a text, working out a response), it becomes almost synonymous with writing. Reading, too, is a way of working with meaning and language. We also feel that writing students can learn some of the most important lessons only by writing from readings. By doing so students learn that their ideas aren't simply their own. They learn about convention and context. They learn that they don't invent a subject. They learn what it means to work in the context of a history of writing that comes into play when they sit down to write. This is how we make sense of the metaphor of the "conversation of humankind." There are other speakers already speaking. You enter this moment not alone but in the company of others.

But we are avoiding the crux of the question: Where and how do we give the kinds of instruction traditionally associated with the writing course? There are two answers to this question. The first is simple. The work that surrounds the production and revision of students' essays each week, in class, in groups, in conference, and in our comments on their papers represents our most immediate intervention with the students' writing. In this sense our writing courses follow the standard pattern of "workshop" courses. The one major difference is the degree to which revising here also requires rereading. As we have said elsewhere in *Resources,* the one surprising feature of our classes is the small amount of time we spend, as teachers, talking about the readings. Almost all of our discussion of the readings takes place *through* the discussion of student essays, which we reproduce and use to represent specific acts of reading and writing. Most of the questions we address to the assigned texts, in other words, are delivered through questions we ask about writing. Rather than talk generally about introductions, for example, we would talk about the ways a writer has introduced a project or a text or a quotation. Rather than talk about examples in the abstract, we would discuss the use of examples in a student essay — what examples were chosen from the assigned reading; what examples were ignored; what use was made of the examples; what counterexamples there might be; where and how the writer might bring in examples *not* prefigured in the assigned text.

The second "writing lesson" is represented in the readings themselves. Because we have chosen readings that are about writing, they offer lessons to writers, some directly ("When We Dead Awaken: Writing as Re-Vision") and some indirectly ("Our Time"). And the assignments ask students to consider the readings as having immediate import on their work as writers. "Our Time," the assignment says, can help them to write a similarly multivocal text; "When We Dead Awaken" can help students to imagine why writing and a writing course might matter, how it can be about something other than fulfilling college requirements.

The sequences — how do you write them? How do you use them? Why put so much emphasis on the broad sweep of a course?

These are questions we have tried to address in the introductions to the textbooks and to the sequences. The brief section of the textbook just before the sequences begin ("Working with Assignment Sequences," pp. 795–798) explains the idea of a sequence to students. You might want to ask your students to read this before they begin their work, perhaps at the same time as you ask them to read the Introduction. Many teachers have found both these introductions to be useful.

Why do we put so much emphasis on the broad sweep of a course? Writers work differently if they are working on single, discrete weekly exercises than if they are working on longer, academic projects. We think of our course as a project course; and we want our students, as writers, to see and pace their work for the long haul. This requirement is not just a matter of endurance, although endurance counts. Students need to learn that *the subjects that matter aren't quickly exhausted,* that the best ideas come when you think there is nothing else to say, that it is important to turn from the security of newfound conclusions to consider alternative points of view. Students also learn to imagine drafts and revisions differently when they are in service of a longer project. In particular, they learn to imagine revision as a way of opening up an issue rather than finishing it, closing it down, and getting it out of the way. We want to teach our students to imagine intellectual life differently than they have imagined it before (with the pieces they read and the pieces they write standing alone, as single exercises), and we want them to imagine reading and writing as they serve in the long term and not just the short.

The best way to work with the sequences is to imagine that they suggest the possibilities for a project students can begin to believe in and imagine as their own. This approach requires flexibility. We have never taught a sequence, whether in the textbook or not, without making changes along the way. We go into a course with a sense of how to put together some interesting readings, readings that speak back and forth to each other in productive ways, readings that we feel we can use to enable students to think about reading and writing. Once we are into that course, however, and get a chance to watch how our students are reading and working with our assignments, we begin to make revisions. Sometimes, when students are not doing what we want, we revise to get better control of the class; sometimes, when students are doing productive work we hadn't imagined them doing, we revise to respond to directions they have taken.

You need to be flexible, to adjust assignments and readings so that they make sense to you and your students as the semester goes along. In this sense, you and your students are readers. The sequences won't automatically make sense. There is no guaranteed payoff if you only follow from step to step. They represent a plan and, in almost every case, a course we have taught. But during the course of the semester or quarter, you will need to feel that you and your students have begun to take the sequence over, so that it begins to make your kind of sense.

As mentioned earlier, we also have found it useful to ask students at mid-term and at the end of the term to write a "retrospective" assignment. This short essay, in which students stop to reflect on the course and its materials, has a double benefit. It allows us to hear our students' versions of the course they are taking. More important, however, it formalizes our concern that students take an active role in making sense out of the course. We don't want the course to just happen to them; we want them to see it as something they can use to frame and enable their work in school.

The question of how we put the sequences together is a bit harder to answer. This process has changed, actually, since we began to work on *Ways of Reading.* Initially, we would get together with our friends and colleagues to design a course we would teach in the upcoming year. Often we would begin with a single book or essay that had knocked us out over the summer. We would start to gather readings to surround this core text, provide interesting ways of going back to it. In most cases, we would look for readings that would profitably counter the piece we began with.

We continue to use these same principles when we design the sequences for *Ways of Reading*. We collect pieces we would like to teach; we then find other pieces suggested by those we have collected. And then we think about teachable combinations. The biggest difference now is that we will have three or four courses going in a semester, Tony teaching one, Dave another, some of our students teaching the third and fourth.

So we gather materials that we think can be profitably read together. A good example is the "Arts of the Contact Zone" sequence. We loved the Pratt essay, and Pratt's work generally, and found pieces that could be used to put her argument to the test. In a sense we looked for essays that could stand as alternatives to the Guaman Poma example Pratt employs. When we wrote the assignments, we wanted them to represent a stage to various uses of Pratt's texts; we wanted students to work closely with Pratt's text, to apply the metaphor of the "contact zone" to local scenes, and to use her interpretive scheme to look at alternative examples of writing that could be said to be produced by the contact zone.

The general pattern in most of the sequences takes students into one of the readings (asking them to work closely with the text and to produce a "close reading"). Then students are asked to apply and test a set of terms (and, sometimes, an argument) by turning to alternative examples. Finally, students are asked to step back from what they have done to take a position of their own, adding their voice to the conversation among authors, making space in their essays where they speak and speak at length.

We like to think of the sequences as projects and not as arguments. We would be disappointed, for example, if people saw the sequence "The Aims of Education" as an argument we are making about American education. It would be wrong, to our minds, to work through the sequence asking what point it makes or what the correct final position might be. We would hate students to be trying to guess *our* version of the "right" answer to the implied question, "What are the appropriate aims of education?" The sequence is offered not as an argument but as a way of raising questions about education. Now these selections are not neutral or value-free, of course, but we have tried to offer a variety of positions. The questions have their own thrust and direction. But we have written many questions; and we try to turn the issues back to students and to their understanding (in the case of their sequence) of their own participation in the history and culture of schooling. The argument of the textbook is that readers can read both generously and critically and that such reading does not happen naturally but reading requires work, labor. The argument extends to the sequences. To our minds they would be misread if used as a series of fixed steps or seen as representing an argument students are bound to reproduce.

How do you know your class is going well? What are the signs that a class is working?

It sounds corny to say it, but we can feel it when a particular class works well, or when class meetings have gone well. When they do, it almost always means that students feel comfortable — they talk about the examples of writing before them, and they get involved responding to each other and commenting on each other's remarks. We invariably conduct our classes around two or three examples of students' writing, and we always work from examples that demonstrate students' successes or admirable struggles with particular "moves" in their writing. We tend to focus on what we call "moves" that occur in students' writing; they depend, of course, on the particular assignment and the student work, but generally we look at papers to see how closely students are reading, speculating about, or interpreting sentences and passages from their readings. We also look at how students use others' sentences and language in their writings, and we pay attention to how students create and use such things as summary statements and paraphrases. And, of course, we look for the "moves" that students make when they revise passages in their papers or whole papers. Such examples of typical "moves" in student writing, represent the kinds of student work that we would bring into class for discussion, given, of course, our particular agenda for the class and for the assignment at hand. Our classes generally run for ninety minutes twice a week, and this allows us enough time to work with two or three student papers or excerpts from papers during each meeting. We focus the discussions with our own questions, even though we invite students to respond and ask questions, because we don't want students' comments to be haphazard. We want them to discuss the work in front of them for the reasons that we've brought it into class. We might, for example, bring into class excerpts from two students' papers that show the students interpreting particular passages from a text. We might ask the class then to discuss these excerpts by first restating what each student seems to be saying that the text says. How, in other words, does each student author read his or her passage? We might then, after that initial discussion, ask the class to comment on these readings. At this point, the class would be working well if the students were involved, if they were talking and speculating and commenting and drawing conclusions about the excerpts from the students' papers in front of them. And the discussion would seem truly accomplished if students were speaking substantively about particular sentences in the work before them rather than talking in general, abstract, terms ("I think she makes her point well," "He has a lot of evidence to back up his point") about why a student's paragraph seems good or strong. These discussions are going well, of course, when students are involved, participating, but it takes more than enthusiasm for a class to work well. Students have to be doing the detailed work of writers, and that means that they have to be commenting on sentences and chunks of prose in the examples of writing before them, whether those examples be from students' papers or from the essays or stories they are reading and writing about. This is the "local," important work of talking about writing, and when students do it in class discussions, we feel good.

What do you do about sentence errors?

We approach sentence errors in a number of ways. First, we make distinctions between "accidental errors" that students can and do catch and fix when they proofread carefully and "error patterns" that students regularly make and don't notice, or notice, but don't know how to fix. We have a routine for dealing with both kinds of errors that involves individual work with students' papers and whole-class instruction. The key, at least for us, to working on sentence errors has to do with the atmosphere and rhythm of the class. We want to encourage students to experiment with sentences, and we want them to proofread. Both of these tasks can be accomplished without heavy-handed attention, as a part of the regular routine of the class. Five or fifteen minutes here and there throughout the semester seems much more effective than large blocks of time or whole days of instruction given over to sentences and errors.

Before we describe what we do in class, we would like to make a few comments about how we encourage our students to experiment with complex sentences. Generally, we do this in two ways. First, we like to bring interesting sentences to students' attention. Sometimes this exercise is as casual as reading sentences aloud in class and commenting on why they are interesting or compelling, and other times we might put sentences on the chalkboard and study them more closely for the work that's taking place in them. We use examples from the readings and from students' writing for this kind of casual attention drawing. Occasionally, we might conduct a whole class lesson on a particular kind of sentence (e.g., those that use conjunctions to show causal relationships) or sentence construction (e.g., complex, related sentences joined by a semicolon). Here again, we work from examples in the readings and from students' writing. Tony, for instance, regularly asks his students to use embeddings and appositives to qualify and specify subjects and nouns in sentences. He sees this kind of instruction as a way of helping students understand how qualifications that modify nouns and subjects can help wring vagueness and generality out of sentences. When we do this kind of instruction and attention drawing, we feel it's important for students to realize that they'll make errors as they try kinds of sentences they aren't yet familiar with. Such experimentation can give writers another dimension or plane to work on, but they need to feel there's room for it, and this feeling depends a great deal on how we establish the work of the class when it comes to editing and errors.

From the start of the semester, we ask students to buy and use a writer's handbook. They must proofread their papers, including their drafts. We want them to get into the habit of using a handbook and of proofreading as a regular part of writing. Sometimes we ask them to proofread using red pencils so that we can see which errors they catch and which they don't, in other words, those that are accidental and those that might indicate regular error patterns. If students are proofreading, catching what we call accidental errors, but still having problems identifying or correcting recurring errors, then we step in and help. Usually, for students struggling with errors that repeat from one paper to the next, we'll place a check mark in the margin next to the lines where errors occur. We explain to students that when they get their papers back with these check marks, they should find and fix the errors by turning to their handbooks, getting help from friends, and by going to the English Department's Writing Workshop for help. As part of this work, we ask the students who have persistent errors in their sentences individually to keep logs or error journals where they record their errors, explanations of why they made them, and then the corrected sentences. We seldom ask whole classes to do this kind of error journal, but we have. It's important to conduct this kind of error work individually, as a part of the rhythm of the class, and not to make a big deal of it. If students are proofreading and working to correct their errors, we feel that we can show them how to help themselves.

At times, when it seems appropriate, we conduct whole-class lessons, using students' sentences and paragraphs as examples, on the conventions of punctuation and the more common usage errors we see in our students' writing (e.g., noun-verb agreements, noun-pronoun agreements). We don't belabor this kind of instruction, which we do on the chalkboard as graphically as possible, using circles around phrases and clauses and boxes around the punctuation as part of a visual demonstration of how commas, for example, or semicolons or colons work in sentences. Of course, students can always turn to their handbooks for additional help, but we don't assign exercises. When we conduct whole-class instruction like this, we always center it on discussions and demonstrations involving students' work. We work toward establishing an atmosphere in which students get a feel for sentences as plastic and malleable, as language that can be shaped and formed with the help of a few conventions and procedures.

What about the research paper?

Our students regularly write assignments and work on projects that ask them to read various kinds of texts closely, to study texts for particular purposes, and to work across texts. These ways of reading and studying prepare them for the intellectual work of academic research and writing, which historians, scientists, anthropologists, engineers, and market researchers, among others, must be able to do. As part of their work on these assignments and projects, they learn to use quotations and paraphrases; they learn, that is, to use the writings of others in their research. A number of the instructors who use our book ask their students to cite references and document sources in their papers in one of the commonly used styles (that is, MLA, APA) as yet another way of preparing them for academic research.

We don't, however, teach what might be called the traditional research paper in which students compile research on a subject or issue, although many of our assignments ask students to conduct library research (see, for instance, the assignments for Patricia Limerick's selection), observations, and interviews. Assignments, for example, for Mary Louise Pratt's selection offer students opportunities to do both observations and interviews as part of their work on individual texts and larger projects involving multiple texts.

Ways of Reading as Part of a TA/TF Training Program

TA/TF Training and Ways of Reading

The readings and assignments (and assignment sequences) in *Ways of Reading* have served for many years as the central documents in the TA/TF training program at the University of Pittsburgh. Perhaps it would be useful to begin by briefly describing that program and its history. (See also the essay by our colleagues, Paul Kameen and Mariolina Salvatori, "The Teaching of Teaching: Theoretical Reflections," in *Reader,* Spring/Fall 1995, pp. 103–25.)

At Pittsburgh, all new Teaching Assistants (TA) and Teaching Fellows (TF) teach a common set of materials in the first year. It is called the "staff course." The faculty design a new course each year, a sequence of assignments engaging students with a long-term writing project organized through a set of readings. We write a new course each year not only to finesse the plagiarism problem but also as a way of paying attention and remaining closely involved with this area of the curriculum.

The new TA/TFs, as is the case with any large program, bring a wide variety of preparation and professional goals to their first year of teaching at Pitt. They are M.A., M.F.A., and Ph.D. students; some are teaching for the first time; some bring with them considerable experience. Some plan for careers in colleges and universities, and so see their teaching as essential to their professional preparation; but this is not the case with all, particularly with the M.F.A. students, many of whom go on to work outside the academy. All new TA/TFs are sent materials over the summer (including the readings and assignment sequence); there is a brief orientation before classes begin in August. This is largely a welcome session, an introduction to the faculty, the office staff and the facilities in support of instruction. It serves also as an introduction to policies and procedures and, particularly for the new teachers, it provides a way of imagining the first week or two of classes. We often have previous years' TA/TFs lead sessions and give papers. (Some of these are collected in *Resources for Teaching Ways of Reading.*)

During the first semester, the work of the first-year staff is supported by a Teaching Seminar (more on this later) and by a committee charged to run staff meetings, to provide one-on-one support, and to organize classroom observations (called CEAT, or the Committee on the Evaluation and Advancement of Teaching). The committee is made up of advanced graduate students and faculty. Ideally, there is close communication between the faculty running the Teaching Seminar and CEAT.

The Teaching Seminar began in 1974 and has been a regular part of the program ever since. Most members of the composition faculty have taught it; it is often team taught, sometimes with a member of the literature or writing faculty. CEAT was developed in the eighties in order to increase the opportunities for making teaching visible and for providing occasions for the staff to talk together about their work.

Perhaps the most distinctive feature of this program is the insistence that all new TA/TFs teach a common, core set of materials, no matter their prior training. After the first year, graduate students have much more freedom to develop their own courses (and to teach courses in other programs: film, literature, creative writing); it is often the case that they will make some revisions to the core course in preparation for the second semester of the first year (revising the core either individually or as a group). In the first year, however, we have two concerns: that our graduate students work with a course that represents our common practice and history as a faculty, and that all students in the first year have a common point of reference as they work to develop ways to talk about (and to think about) teaching.

We feel that there is something distinctive about composition at the University of Pittsburgh. While the course changes from year to year, and changes as it is designed by different members of the faculty, there are features and concerns that represent both a tradition of teaching and our determination to work together as a collective: the assignment sequences, the sets of readings, an emphasis on revision, a desire to represent students as intellectuals, a respect for difficulty. The core course also provides a common point of reference for the Teaching Seminar and the staff meetings (and the informal conversations in the hallways and offices) throughout the year.

We have learned that there is much to be gained with discussions of teaching that are grounded in reference to common (and therefore specific) readings, assignments, materials, and practices. The discussions, then, are not about general topics ("teaching revision") but about what specific, representative students are doing in the first papers they are writing on John Edgar Wideman's "Our Time," about what they have written, and how and why they might reread and revise. Because all are working with the same assignments, the staff can trade student papers, looking for examples that can help to open up discussion and focus attention on a particular problem. TA/TFs and faculty can (and will) argue and take different positions on these papers and what they represent, leading to different next steps, and the results of those next steps too can be presented and shared. The approaches to particular pedagogical problems will differ, as they must, but everyone's teaching is shaped by their participation in a common project and in relation to the rest of the staff. A common set of materials enables teachers, as Bill Coles used to say, to put their cards on the table. It is a way of making teaching visible. And it is a way of enabling individual teachers to define themselves in relation to a faculty and a program, its ideas and history.

The Teaching Seminar

The Teaching Seminar is a regular, full, 3-credit graduate seminar. It meets during the fall semester. It is one of the distinctive features of our graduate program and has a long and colorful history.

From the beginning, the seminar was designed to place the freshman course and its materials (materials in *Ways of Reading*, for example) in relation to the problems central to English studies as represented in the work graduate students would be doing in other graduate courses. The Teaching Seminar has never, then, served as an "Introduction to Composition Studies." It does not survey approaches to the freshman course, theories of composition, or major books and figures in the field. There are other courses to do that work and to do it for graduate students who elect advanced work in composition.

The teaching seminar, rather, is organized around three sets of texts: the readings in the freshman course (selections in *Ways of Reading*, for example), student papers, and a selection of books and articles from the professional literature designed to focus theoretical attention on fundamental problems of language, writing, reading, and reception. It is to our advantage to choose readings likely to be present and important to the graduate students as they prepare for conferences and for other courses. This part of the reading list, hen, looks similar to what you would expect in an "Introduction to Graduate Studies" or any introduction to theory and method. The seminar gives the graduate students a chance to work through these materials slowly and in relation (often surprising relation) to the "everyday" concerns of the first year writing class.

In a year that we are teaching the selections by Wideman, Pratt, Griffin, and Foucault for example), the teaching seminar would organize the students work in the following ways.

1. The seminar would be the place to work on these as primary texts (and for some of he students, this will be the first time). As in any graduate seminar, this is a matter of discussion, writing, research, and group presentation. The seminar, however, asks students always to think about these texts as they might serve writers and writing courses. What do you need to know to prepare writers to make the best use of these texts? What does it mean to read these texts as a writer? What writing lessons do they contain? As a result, the work on Foucault or Wideman is very different than it would be for another graduate seminar.

2. There is work on the texts as texts. There is also work on the texts as they are read and understood by our students. Student papers, then, are some of the central materials for the Teaching Seminar. How might we understand the ways of reading Wideman, Pratt, Griffin, or Foucault as reading is represented in sample student papers drawn from the course, the course everyone is teaching (including the faculty member teaching the Teaching Seminar)? And, from those student papers, how might we best understand revision — the next step, whether that next step be a class discussion of one or two sample papers, or directions for re-reading and revision? We have long felt that the central skill for a writing teacher is knowing how to read student writing. Student writing is not a genre we are prepared to read or to value. Learning to read student writing has immediate and practical consequences, providing a context for evaluation or for marginal, editorial commentary, for example; but it is also crucial for understanding the first-year writing course as a course. First-year writing not only names a spot in the curriculum; it names a genre, a subject position, a way of reading and writing. You can't teach student writing unless you have an informed and determined sense of what student writing is and what it is good for. And, of course, Wideman, Pratt, Griffin, and Foucault provide powerful tools to think about the writing produced by the students in the course. The readings can be turned to, used as tools to examine the work of students as writers. Wideman provides a powerful way for thinking about "beginnings" or for thinking about who speaks in an essay and how and why. Wideman writes wonderful sentences, sentences that provide a way of talking about sentences. Pratt provides terms for analysis, terms like the "rhetoric of sincerity," and for imagining the position and practice of the student writer. Griffin provides a powerful counterexample for the classroom pieties about unity, order, and coherence. Foucault we have used often to think about the paragraph and about examples.

3. And, finally, there are the "outside" readings, critical and theoretical texts drawn from the standard reading lists in graduate education in English. They are brought into the mix in order to demonstrate that the work on language, literature, literacy, and culture is also always about writing and schooling, about the work of students in any given term in a first year writing class as they try to represent themselves and others, to represent knowledge, tradition, and authority. We have taught, for example, Gates, Spivak, Said, Foucault, Butler, Bove, Williams (Patricia and Raymond), Fish, Clifford and Marcus, Spillers, Gallop, and Tompkins. Their work (and others) becomes surprisingly appropriate to the course. The specific selections are suggested by the readings from *Ways of Reading* and by whatever is pressing and in the air at a given moment.

In this sense, the seminar is an argument that writing is writing and that student writing can be read into the theoretical literature; it is also an argument that pedagogy is a theoretical concern and can be well served by books and projects that don't specifically name the classroom as their topic. We always also bring in a work from the field of composition. Again, the seminar is not an "Introduction to Composition Studies"; composition however, has much to offer our discussions. We want to make that clear, while also making clear that composition doesn't have to stand alone. And we have been concerned to bring in material from creative writing and its representations of writing, the problems of writing, and the process of learning to write.

Ways of Reading

Ways of Reading argues for the connection between students' work and some of the most interesting writing of our time. This is, finally, how it serves a TA/TF training program; it argues that the first-year writing course is connected to the general concerns of English studies and its graduate students. The textbook provides the occasion for graduate students to think about teaching and about student writing in relation to some of the key figures and arguments in their field. For some of our students, the textbook has been a safe space to think for the first time about Foucault and/or the death of the author and what these arguments might say to a young scholar trying to find a way of thinking about writing, teaching, and a career. For others it has been the surprising occasion to think from theory into practice, not only the practice of teaching but writing practice as well, including their own.

When we hear from graduate students, we tend to hear that they appreciate the book for providing a course that they can take seriously (and that will allow them to take their students seriously). We also hear, however, that it has made a difference to their own writing. It seems an odd thing to say, but advanced students in English, including M.A. and Ph.D. students, have a very limited sense of what they can and can't do as writers. The "experimental" assignments in *Ways of Reading* have provided the invitation to write like Griffin or Wideman or Anzaldúa — not just about them. And the M.F.A. students are given a sense of the power and range of the essay (and of academic writing) beyond what they had learned to expect, including within the domain of "creative nonfiction."

Part II: Working with the Readings

o–o–o–o–o–o–o–o–o–o–o–o–o–o–o–o–o–o–o

GLORIA ANZALDÚA

Entering into the Serpent (p. 23)
How to Tame a Wild Tongue (p. 36)

Anzaldúa's book, *Borderlands/La Frontera,* is a compelling example of postmodern, fragmented writing that can introduce students to the plasticity of writing, to its possibilities beyond the tired, rationally argued essay that they (and everyone else) have been forced to write for all their academic years. These two chapters from Anzaldúa's book capture the spirit, style, and argument of the book and demonstrate that it is possible, feasible, and perhaps desirable to compose in "montage," presenting complex subjects like identity, sexuality, religion in understandable, passionate, and compelling writing while at the same time allowing for the inherent contradictions and paradoxes of such subjects and such writing. We loved teaching Anzaldúa, and for our students this kind of text was both new and challenging (and fun, once they allowed themselves to work with it rather than trying to "get it"). It's a genuine "assemblage" or "montage" a "crazy dance," as Anzaldúa calls it, made up of sections written in a variety of styles (prose poems, endnotes, stories, anecdotes) and languages. Its argument is unconventionally cast. Rather than logically presenting a case for her mixed identity and languages as a *mestiza,* Anzaldúa juxtaposes passionate statements on her heritages, identities, sexualities, religions, and cultures with stories, poems, and anecdotes. The effect is jarring, powerful, but students will need to spend time sorting out the text's mixed style and arguments.

Immediately questions will arise about the Spanish interspersed in the text. Students will want to know if they need to read Spanish to understand Anzaldúa's arguments. It might be difficult for them to understand, at first, that they don't, that the text reveals its use of the Spanish sections as a part of its style and argument, that they'll be able to work through it as they come to see the text as a representation of Anzaldúa's mixed identity. The best advice for students, then, is to read as if the Spanish passages will defy any attempts at a complete understanding but, at the same time, will offer up sentences, phrases, and larger stylistic patterns that they'll be able to make sense of and connect to the rest of her writing.

QUESTIONS FOR A SECOND READING (p. 45)

1. This is an important discussion question to pose for students, especially since this kind of text will be new and challenging (and fun) for most of them. The central question (So how do you read this text if you don't read Spanish?) is a natural one for breaking the ice before any other discussion or writing assignments. It allows students to relate how they read the selection, how they worked with it, and it serves beautifully as an opening to other questions about Anzaldúa's style and arguments.

2. The idea of an author inventing a reader as she writes gives students a way of understanding a text's creation aside from (or alongside) notions of arguments and "points" being put forward. If students begin their work with this text through the first ques-

25

tion in this section on how they read the three chapters, then they are ready to consider how Anzaldúa invents a reader or a way of reading and what her expectations or demands might be. A number of sections, like the one quoted in this question, obliquely reveal Anzaldúa's expectations, and students shouldn't have trouble finding and working from them. They should be encouraged, especially, to work from their own experiences reading the chapters. What kinds of readers were they? How would they describe the ways in which they read?

3. This question prompts students to discuss Anzaldúa's arguments but its primary emphasis is on asking students to explain the arguments' connections across the chapters. Anzaldúa's key terms involve issues of identity, sexuality, religious experience, and consciousness, especially what she refers to as *la facultad,* the ability to see deeper realities in surface phenomena. It's fair to say that there is no specific number of correct terms that students must identify and explain; but some terms and arguments and examples do carry across the chapters, and students would do well to look to these for their discussions of Anzaldúa's arguments and how they're connected across the chapters. It's critical to place the emphasis on *arguments,* as opposed to *argument,* because Anzaldúa makes numerous arguments, some of which contradict others — this is not a unified text, nor a unified, seamless argument.

ASSIGNMENTS FOR WRITING (p. 46)

1. This is a wonderful writing assignment that allows students to experience the creation of a mixed style from their various positions, voices, and backgrounds. Of course, as the assignment points out, students have not been prepared to write this kind of text, but Anzaldúa's example is strong enough to enable them to do so. The key moment in the assignment is the one that asks students to consider the different positions they occupy. What does this mean? Resist the temptation to tell them. Let them come to see that they are students, sons and daughters, friends, authorities, novices, swimmers, skateboarders, lovers, bikers, enemies, ballplayers, music listeners, concertgoers, inheritors of particular cultures and traits, and so on. Let them realize that these various selves have voices, often contradictory that students can bring forward in writing, as Anzaldúa does, when they set out to explain who they are, how they understand their experiences and, in particular, what their key or significant experiences are and in what form or style they might be presented.

2. Like the first question in "Questions for a Second Reading," this writing assignment asks students to tell the story of their reading of these two chapters, but the assignment goes beyond the simple recounting of a reading. It asks students in addition to consider themselves as readers, who feel at home in the text and then lost in it, who occupy a position in relation to the text and, especially, who read or don't read as Anzaldúa expects. Some passages in the text, like the one quoted in the assignment, voice Anzaldúa's expectations about her readers, and they ask to be answered. Students may align themselves with Anzaldúa's expectations or be put off or angered by them; or they might have different responses at different times in their reading. The goal for this assignment is to let students speak back to Anzaldúa's expectations of them as readers and to use their experiences reading these chapters in that essay.

3. This assignment would work well with the first writing assignment, which asks students to write a mixed text like Anzaldúa's. Students might write this assignment first. It's straightforward in its request to students to locate and define Anzaldúa's woman's voice, her sexual voice, and her poet's voice, to work from specific passages to do this locating and defining, and to speculate how these voices differ from each other and from what Anzaldúa imagines a "standard" voice to be. Although the assignment is straightforward, the task is challenging. It opens up the discussion of what constitutes a voice, where voices come from (the self? language?), and how they're defined. It's not unusual for students to see these voices mixing into each other or to

26

begin naming the voices by the emotional reactions they elicit. The goal of this assignment is to open up the conversation for students to the idea of voice, not to have them find rock-solid examples of one kind of voice or dictionary or literary definitions of voice. The text offers students plenty to work with, and they should puzzle these voices out from it and from their own reactions to the various shifts in style and tone.

4. This assignment is a slightly different version of the first writing assignment. Like that first assignment, it asks students to write in different voices that are a part of them or a part of an argument they want to make. Unlike the first assignment, this one focuses specifically on students creating an argument (rather than expressing their own selves or their understandings of their situations). For this assignment to work well, students will need to write an argument about which they feel passionate, yet one on which they can see themselves taking various positions, given the different roles (students, sons and daughters, friends, skateboarders, lovers, bikers, swimmers, enemies, and so on) they hold in relation to the argument. In other words, students need to make an argument in which they allow their various voices to speak, as Anzaldúa does; they shouldn't expect to have a logical, unified, seamless case.

The second part of this assignment, the two-page assignment on why a student's argument is worth a reader's attention, serves as a way for students to consider the importance of their arguments. It's a way of asking students to think of their readers and their writing in order to present arguments worth a reader's attention, which will teach, challenge, or show readers something rather than simply reiterating commonplace clichés or generalities. In short, the two-page coda is a way of forcing the issue of asking for writing that is worth a reader's time and attention. If this assignment is to work, students will have to invest the time and energy to create arguments that they care about, that they feel confused or uncertain about, as Anzaldúa does (even though she comes across at times as certain), that they can actually explain in terms of being worth a reader's attention. If the explanation turns to clichés or generalizations, then the argument is most likely not worth a reader's attention. The two-page coda can be used, then, as a way to begin the discussion of the arguments that students produce. The first question might be, "Is this argument worth our attention? Why or why not?"

MAKING CONNECTIONS (p. 48)

1. Students will need to have read both the Pratt essay and the Anzaldúa chapters before working on this assignment. It would be worthwhile for students to work with at least one other assignment (either a second-reading or writing assignment) for each selection before they turn to this one. The key terms and notions for this assignment reside in Pratt's use of autoethnographic or transcultural texts as writing in which the writer engages in some way the representations others have made of him or her. Anzaldúa continually refers to and critiques various representations of her identity, sexuality, religion, and culture, and students will need to locate those two or three representations that they would like to work from. But the task they face is larger than simply presenting Anzaldúa's text as autoethnographic or transcultural, because they are also being asked to present Pratt's argument for autoethnographic texts and Anzaldúa's text to readers who haven't read either. In other words, they are being asked to re-present both texts and to use Anzaldúa's as a further example for Pratt's discussion of autoethnographic or transcultural texts. Students, of course, will have to produce some sort of summary or paraphrase of both texts in order to complete the assignment, but that summary or paraphrase is only the frame. They must then go on to present Anzaldúa's writing as part and parcel of Pratt's argument. The summary or paraphrase of these texts serves the purpose of orienting readers unfamiliar with either Pratt's essay or Anzaldúa's text, and this assignment offers a good opportunity for students to test their drafts against readers outside their class.

2.   The heart of this assignment resides in students identifying the differences in Anzaldúa's and Rich's arguments about writing, identity, politics, and history and then in attributing them to the positions each writer occupies. Students will need to resist the tendency to attribute differences in the authors' arguments to personal differences, to the fact, that is, that different people hold different opinions, and to examine carefully the positions each author holds as a writer. How, for instance, they might be asked, does Anzaldúa create her identity in writing? How does Rich? How does each locate herself in her culture? What positions do the two hold in relation to their respective histories? What key examples and terms do they put forward? And how do these terms and examples reflect the different positions that they hold as writers? as people working out identities in writing?

JAMES BALDWIN
"Notes of a Native Son" (p. 52)

We are of the generation who read Baldwin, and particularly *The Fire Next Time*, (1963) while neighborhoods were burning in our home cities: Akron, Ohio, and Buffalo, New York. He was one of the figures we turned to with the hope that he could explain and understand what we could not, and that he could explain it with a force and eloquence that would make a difference, particularly to our fathers.

"Notes of a Native Son" is a remarkable piece of writing — to us it is one of the key documents in the history of writing in the United States. In the headnote and in the assignments, we try to situate it in between *Native Son* (which we suspect students will not yet have read) and rap and hip-hop, each as attempts to give voice to anger and desire in an urban, African American setting. As our students read "Notes of a Native Son," we want them of course to pay attention to the family story at its center, a frank and powerful story of men of two generations, one that allows identification across race. We have always wanted to insist, however, that "Notes" must be read with regard to the specific location of its narrator — a young, African American man in Harlem in the early 1940s. Determined context is one of the great achievements of this essay. The story of Baldwin and his father is to be read in relation to slavery, to the black migration to northern cities, to World War II and the ways the experience of black soldiers changed race relations in the United States and, finally, to the riots in Detroit and in New York. The father and son, who they are, their love, hatred and despair, are part of this history, produced by it. This is not the story students are prepared to read — a story about individuals, self-determined, defined primarily in relation to narratives of love, marriage, and professional ambition. To teach this essay, we've found, we need to ask students to re-read in order to pay attention to background and context, to all (and it is most of the essay) that is not just the "universal" story of father and son.

We've also learned that students need help placing the "voice" of the narrator. Our students are products of a moment when "black voices" are represented by (thought to be equivalent to) a standard "black" urban vernacular common to contemporary music, film, and advertising. Baldwin doesn't sound "black" and this is often said by students to be problematic. (The voices of John and Robbie in John Wideman's "Our Time" can help to frame this problem — or to bring it to the next generation. Martin Luther King is another common point of reference.)

It is important, then, to help students to place the voice in "Notes of a Native Son." We usually begin with the scene of the funeral in section 3, where the narrator slips easily into the language of the preacher and of eulogy:

Only the Lord saw the midnight tears, only He was present when one of His children, moaning and writing hands, paced up and down the room. When one slapped one's child in anger the recoil in the heart reverberated through heaven and became part of the pain of the universe. And when the children were hungry and sullen and distrustful and one watched them, daily, growing wilder, and further away, and running headlong into danger, it was the Lord who knew what the charged heart endured as the strap was laid to the backside; the Lord alone who knew what one *would* have said if one had had, like the Lord, the gift of the living word.

It is such a remarkable passage and from it students can begin to hear biblical cadences throughout the text and see the degree to which a mode of analysis which might be said to be (loosely) "sociological" is accompanied by a language of explanation that relies on references to pride, hatred, rage ("a pounding in the skull and fire in the bowels") and the deep truths of the heart. The body represented here is not the body of pop psychology (where there are issues to be resolved) but of the old and new testament, where souls are won and lost and where sacrifice can be redemptive. We can also ask students to examine the way of thinking through narrative that places family stories in relation to the story of the nation; and the way of thinking represented by the other language of argument, perhaps best represented in the penultimate paragraph, where Baldwin (the writer) sets the narrative voice in relation to the language and rhetoric of the sermon — "All my father's texts and songs, which I had decided were meaningless, were arranged before me at his death like empty bottles, waiting to hold the meaning which life would give them for me." The concluding paragraph is quite remarkable for the way it moves from argument to sermon to narrative:

> It began to seem that one would have to hold in the mind forever two ideas, which seemed to be in opposition. The first idea was acceptance, the acceptance, totally without rancor, of life as it is, and men as they are: in the light of this idea, it goes without saying that injustice is a commonplace. But this did not mean that one could be complacent, for the second idea was of equal power: that one must never, in one's own life, accept these injustices as commonplace but must fight them with all one's strength. This fight begins, however, in the heart and it now had been laid to my charge to keep my own heart free of hatred and despair. This intimation made my heart heavy and, now that my father was irrecoverable, I wished that he had been beside me so that I could have searched his face for the answers which only the future would give me now.

Moving from "two ideas" carefully held in counterpoise to a battle in the heart and a new covenant — "and it now had been laid in my charge to keep my own heart free of hatred and despair" — Baldwin returns in the final sentence to his father, earlier referred to as "an old man dead." "Why," we ask our students, "does he wish to search his face for answers? Why doesn't he wish for words, for what his father could say?" With all the talk of the heart, this is not a sentimental narrative. It is not *that* language of the heart that drives this essay.

"Notes of a Native Son" is an extraordinarily rich text. It is distant enough from contemporary culture to be an important history lesson, including a lesson in the history of writing. That is the challenge it brings to the classroom, the challenge of teaching students to read it as strange rather than as familiar. If they can, it teaches as well a lesson in how autobiography can be a rich genre, serving more than trivial celebrations of the local and the personal.

QUESTIONS FOR A SECOND READING (p. 68)

1–2. These questions ask students to reread in order to think about the writing as writing, to think about form and style. Question 1 asks about form or arrangement and phrases the question in terms of the way prose organizes a reader's time and attention. Why are there two sections? What is gained by this arrangement — what are the two parts and how might they serve a reader? Within each section, how might you chart the development of ideas and/or story? What are the key transitions? Are there moments of climax or conclusion (or provisional conclusion)? The order of this essay is nothing like the textbook definition of an essay's order (the march from thesis to conclusion). It is important for students to be able to carry away a visual or verbal representation of the order of "Notes" — so that this essay can serve as a formal model and not simply as evidence of Baldwin's "genius" or "inspiration."

The second question refers to style, defined here as "voice." We spoke at length about how we direct students attention to voice in the introduction. The key part of the exercise is for students to choose characteristic passages and to be prepared to report on them. We prompt the question of whether and how "voice" can or should be racialized only because we know from experience that this is an issue students will bring to the classroom (and yet fear that it is out of place). Does it make sense, does it matter, whether we can define Baldwin's voice as a "black" voice? He is certainly quick to speak for the black experience: "There is not a Negro alive who does not have this rage in his blood — one has the choice, merely, of living with it consciously or surrendering to it." As we say above, the voice in "Notes" is significantly (and importantly) different from the standard urban black voice as it is produced for and reproduced by popular music, film, and advertising.

3.   We have wanted more and more to focus students' attention on sentences. Baldwin is a remarkable writer of sentences. One of the characteristic sentence patterns is represented in the example:

> He was not a young man when we were growing up and he had already suffered many kinds of ruin; in his outrageously demanding and protective way he loved his children, who were black like him and menaced, like him; and all these things sometimes showed in his face when he tried, never to my knowledge with any success, to establish contact with any of us. When he took one of his children on his knee to play, the child always became fretful and began to cry; when he tried to help one of us with our homework the absolutely unabating tension which emanated from him caused our minds and our tongues to become paralyzed, so that he, scarcely knowing why, flew into a rage and the child, not knowing why, was punished.

For discussion, we like to ask "What do these sentences do?" We are not looking for a formal description (or a formal description alone). We want students to note the length of the sentences and the use of commas and semicolons in relation to an expressive project — as a necessary or determined way of doing something with words. Baldwin is not, for example, being dismissive even though he is being critical. This is not the rhetoric of simple statement: "He was outrageous and demanding with his children. He never established contact. He caused his children to become paralyzed with a fear of his rage." Thus the long elaborated sentences. The semicolons insist on the link and proximity of utterances: the father's experience as a child and adult; the form of his love; his failure to establish contact. And the forward movement of the sentences, their inevitability, are regularly interrupted with qualifications and secondary statements. It is not "he flew into a rage and the child was punished." It is, rather, "he, scarcely knowing why, flew into a rage and the child, not knowing why, was punished." Rather than simply resting agency in the father, both the father and the child are products of moment (a family moment, a national moment) that neither can understand or control.

4.   We have been increasingly careful to remind students that research is part of reading and writing. While learning to work *with* the text is crucial and important, it is not the only kind of work a scholar performs. Or, while a reader has the responsibility to read

closely and carefully, there are other responsibilities to the text. Here we are asking students not only to have more information about the riots in Detroit and Harlem in 1943, but also to look for newspaper accounts. This is another way for students to understand that there were different ways of thinking about and talking publicly about race in the 1940s. This is a way of situating Baldwin's essay (written in 1955) in a history of racial discourse.

ASSIGNMENTS FOR WRITING (p. 69)

1. The assignment begins with an extended passage from Richard Wright's *Native Son*. It is unlikely that first year students will have read the novel; we wanted to give some sense of Bigger Thomas and how he is represented. The assignment says, "The speaker in 'Notes of a Native Son,' like the 'Thoreau' in *Walden*, is one of the exemplary characters of American letters." And it asks students to write an essay on the character of the speaker, or narrator, in "Notes of a Native Son." It is important to help students to distinguish between the character the narrator (represented by a way of speaking) and the character, James Baldwin, that is part of the narrative. The essay is not asking students to summarize a series of actions and events but to write about a way of thinking about and representing family, nation, and race. The assignment may not put enough emphasis on the question, "How does he think and speak?" You might need to call attention to it as you prepare students to write. And the assignment asks students to think about "a comparable voice today, in the twenty-first century." Comparable does not have to mean similar. We are looking for students to turn to an example of a contemporary text (our students tended to write about Spike Lee movies or sitcoms). These are not likely to be similar. In fact, it might be useful to prompt students to think about differences.

2. In many ways, this assignment is a reworking of the first. This point of this assignment is a comparison with a contemporary text; and it makes the question of the style and method of "Notes of a Native Son" a secondary concern. The success of this assignment will depend upon the time and care students' give to presenting and developing examples. It is not easy to write about music or a music video or a film or a television show. Students should not underestimate the task. In fact, if you are working with draft and revision, it will most likely be the case that the work of revision will be to further develop the examples and to further articulate the comparison with Baldwin.

3. This assignment asks students to write about "Notes" as a representative essay, an example of style and method that can serve as a model (or whose usefulness can be questioned for contemporary purposes). Irving Howe referred to Baldwin as a writer whose essays represented an art form, "a form with possibilities for discursive reflection and concrete drama." And, he said, "The style of these essays is a remarkable instance of the way in which a grave and sustained eloquence . . . can be employed in an age deeply suspicious of rhetorical prowess."

Our age is not deeply suspicious of rhetorical prowess. It is either blind to it or drawn by it. Because our age is preoccupied with autobiography, testimonial, and life stories, we do, however, have much to learn about the possibilities for "discursive reflection and concrete drama." Students do not, however, need to feel bound by the terms of Howe's appreciation. The crucial thing is that they find ways of describing and naming the key features of "Notes" as an example of the genre of the essay. It is useful, we have found, if they think of this essay in relation to what they have heard or learned about the essay (usually something about importance of thesis and "logical" order). And it is important for students to take the final set of questions seriously. The temptation will be to say that Baldwin is a great writer and thus everyone should be allowed a similar freedom of expression — or something like that. Students should feel the pressure (or students will benefit, we've found, from the pressure) to think seriously about what an essay like this can and can't do, the purposes and occasions it can and cannot serve.

4. We have had great success with assignments like these. This one asks students to consider the style and method of "Notes of a Native Son" and then to write an essay that is in direct imitation or to write as an act of homage. The first step, of course, is crucial. Students need to develop a sense of what Baldwin does and how he works before they can try to write from inside his example. The key here, we've found, is for students to think primarily about method rather than subject. They don't have to write about fathers, in other words. They should think about a family story that can be written against the story of nation, state, city, or community.

    And you should take time to think with your students about voice and style. We would recommend some short, in-class exercises in writing Baldwin-like paragraphs as starting points. You need to have the Bible deeply in your history to write old testament narrative or to work within a sermonic style. It is perhaps a more useful instruction to ask students to work from within the discursive world of the central secondary character in their narrative (the figure occupying the father slot) and to move into and out of that discursive frame.

5. This assignment was prompted by our students' frequently phrased concern for the appropriateness (or the ethic) of Baldwin's treatment of his father. It is an appropriate question, rooted more (we think) in what students are used to reading than in a different experience or sense of obligation, child to parent. The text provides the frame for this question — Baldwin invites it, that is, in the way he presents the funeral and in the extended discussion of eulogy. We direct students' attention to this section, although we don't suggest (in the wording of the assignment) that their response should be based on a reading of this section. A reading of this section, however, might be useful as a form of preparation. You could read from this section aloud in class (or invite readings). It is brilliantly readable. And then you could ask students to discuss what Baldwin is saying about eulogies in the black church. And then you could ask how he might be using this section to address a reader and to answer questions a reader might harbor.

    The students' essays, though, should ideally reach beyond this section to address "Notes" more generally. The essay begins, "I had inclined to be contemptuous of my father for the conditions of his life, for the conditions of our lives." The essay does not idealize the father; it struggles against simple sentimental narratives (or simple dismissal); it is not, however, contemptuous. That is a position marked in the past tense: "I had inclined to be." In fact, *inclination* is an important word here, since it begs the question of who or what had put the speaker in a position to take this attitude. In our teaching, we have found it important to ask students to think of the essay in its completion — from beginning to end — at some point in their papers.

MAKING CONNECTIONS (p. 72)

1. The first of these assignments points to the obvious connections with other selections written by African American writers that, in one way or another — and in relation to a particular period and audience — have tried to think through what Baldwin refers to as "the American Negro problem."

    The writers identified in the assignment are Harriet Jacobs, Alice Walker, and John Edgar Wideman. The Wideman connection is perhaps the most potentially interesting and promising, particularly as an example of another generation of writers considering a common project, since it too places a family narrative against the larger questions of race in America. As always, the success of this assignment will depend on students taking time to present and to develop examples from the texts. Certainly summary and paraphrase will be required strategically to prepare the comparison. You can help students feel the pressure, however, to turn to block quotation and to specific and extended points of comparison.

2.   This assignment asks students to think about "Notes of a Native Son" in relation to other essays that use autobiography and family history to think about large questions — race, patriarchy, nation, war. The assignment identifies Susan Griffin's "Our Secret" and Adrienne Rich's "When We Dead Awaken." Students could also write about Anzaldúa, Rodriguez, Walker, or Wideman. In Howe's terms, all their work combines discursive reflection and concrete drama.

As we said before: The success of the writing to this assignment will depend on students taking time to present and to develop examples from the texts. Certainly summary and paraphrase will be required strategically to prepare the comparison. You can help students to feel the pressure, however, to turn to block quotation and to specific and extended points of comparison.

And, again: It is important for students to take the final set of questions seriously. The temptation will be to say that these are great writers and of course everyone should be allowed a similar freedom of expression — or something like that. Students should feel the pressure (or students will benefit, we've found, from the pressure) to think seriously about what an essay like this can and can't do, the purposes and occasions it can and cannot serve.

WALTER BENJAMIN

The Work of Art in the Age of Mechanical Reproduction (p. 75)

This challenging selection offers students interesting historical and critical work to do. To begin, you will want to be certain that everyone reads the headnote. It contains key information about Benjamin, sets the historical context for the piece, and sketches out two of the key terms — *superstructure* and *substructure* — that students will need to understand to begin the reading. These are standard Marxist terms. Superstructure refers to a culture's way of enacting and regulating itself through such things as education, culture, art, law, philosophy, religion, and politics. Substructure, in the context that Benjamin uses it, refers to economic forces, the work people engage in to produce the necessities of life — food, clothing, shelter, and so on. It's possible to be more precise and technical about these terms with more research on them, but these definitions are certainly enough to get students into the reading, especially the preface where Benjamin uses them to frame his essay.

You will want also to be certain that students read the footnotes as they read the selection. Footnotes are critically important for reading Benjamin. He collected notes — often clipping them from sources then pasting them into collages — so we treat them as integral to the whole text here, and if students read them as they read the essay, they'll get a sense of how Benjamin's mind works — moving from one thing to another in an associative way — and they'll understand that the notes aren't just further examples (although some are) but that they extend his thinking in key passages.

If you are inclined to set students to do research while they read this selection, we'd recommend bypassing the Marxist terminology in favor of work on the historical contexts for Benjamin's essay. He references Marxist notions to frame his essay, to set its ground, but the critical understandings of this piece will come from students' work on the essay itself and from their research into the politics, art, work conditions, and history of the

1930s. He wrote this piece in 1936, so students would benefit from being able to paint a picture for themselves of Benjamin's world at that time. As we mention in the headnote, he seems fascinated with the ways photography and motion pictures affect art, culture, and human perception. There were "loud" debates at the time about whether photography could be considered art (he briefly mentions these in the selection), but rather than engaging in these, Benjamin's focus takes the revolutionary possibilities of these art forms for people and cultures as his subjects. Still, students might find them interesting, especially given our new technologies and multimedia that have become, of course, new art forms very much in the spirit of Benjamin's understandings of photography and motion pictures.

Students could benefit enormously from research on Benjamin's historical time in Europe. He refers to photography in contrast to Dadaist arts, and it's our experience that not many students know about Dadaist art, so it's a good research project — to find examples of it and present it to the class in light of Benjamin's comments. And, of course, the 1930s present students with opportunities for research on everything that influences Benjamin — historical events in Europe (particularly the rise of the Fascists and their ideas of culture, art, work, and so on), the range of photography and motion pictures that might have caught Benjamin's attention, and the place of Marxist thinking in global culture. Students could also delve into work — into what it meant to work, the kinds of work people did, and the labor movements that politicized work.

QUESTIONS FOR A SECOND READING (p. 99)

1. This question is designed to enable students to bring forward Benjamin's argument about the changes in the superstructure (the society's engagement with such things as education, art, politics, and so on) by locating the sentences in his writings about paintings, movies, music, and photography that refer back to his remarks in the preface. It seems fair to assume that students will be engaged with his comments on the various arts but the underlying arguments about revolutionary change to the superstructure will be elusive. To bring those underlying arguments forward, students might work, then, with specific sentences or groups of sentences that refer to the "larger" Marxist political arguments Benjamin makes. They could do this individually or in groups of two or three students, perhaps with each group taking a particular section of the piece, then the groups (or individuals) might report to the class before the class begins a discussion of Benjamin's political argument and the ways it evolves through his references to changes in art forms.

2. Although this appears to be a straightforward question, pointing students to the notion that art is "constructed" with and from the elements of culture — rather than pulled mysteriously from personal creativity or genius — and historically situated, it will challenge most students' notions about art. They will want to argue for personal creativity and genius and the eternal value for good art, and possibly gloss over or erase Benjamin's countervailing notions, so it's critically important that students stay close to the text for this discussion — moving from specific passages that point to Benjamin's notions of the creation of art and how it might be valued.

3. For this question, students might work in groups of two or three to identify one or two footnotes, and in their work together, they could connect those to the text in whatever ways they imagine. The idea is to see how the footnotes work with the text, so they might find examples in the footnotes that elaborate on the text, serve as examples to it, pose additional problems, or situate the text in some way. This is a good assignment to teach students about footnotes, and they get to work with a master footnoter whose primary works, according to Hannah Arendt, were his notebooks filled with notes, clippings, and footnotes.

4. The epilogue will seem to be tacked on to the essay to many students unless they have the opportunity to relate it back to the essay, so we begin this question with that task by asking students to find those moments in the essay that prepare readers for the epilogue. This is another question that lends itself to small group work (with groups of two to three students — although we prefer to work with groups of two). Students will need to have read the essay and, perhaps, to have begun a discussion of it — either through the second reading questions or through a writing assignment — before they begin this work. Once they have found ways to relate the epilogue back to the essay, they can formulate the notions of war Benjamin discusses, their requisite politics, and Benjamin's stance in the epilogue. It will be curious for most students to encounter Marinetti's manifesto on the Ethiopian colonial war, and they'll need to find a way to read it in the context of the epilogue. And what, finally, is Benjamin's position? Why is he so concerned about the introduction of aesthetics into politics? What does he imagine as the antidote to this?

ASSIGNMENTS FOR WRITING (p. 100)

1. Extending Benjamin's work, as this assignments invites students to do, involves the creation of arguments about art forms (such as film and video, or painting, music, and so on) and about the interrelation of these forms to the superstructure of the society. Students will need to begin by, in some way of their own, representing Benjamin's arguments about both the evolution of art forms and their connections to the culture's superstructure. How, they might then ask themselves, after they have represented Benjamin's work, have the forms they are writing about now evolved since Benjamin's time? How has the superstructure of the culture evolved? What marks these evolutions? What visible signs, that is, would they point to to say "this is what Benjamin sees" and this is what we see now (while keeping Benjamin's underlying notions of the superstructure)?

Once students set the ground for their work by providing that careful account of Benjamin's arguments (for art forms and their relation to the superstructure), they can go on and extend his work by writing about a single area of art they know well enough to focus on. They might write a fairly traditional piece in which they say "this is what Benjamin thinks and this is how my example fits into it," or they might take a more challenging tack and write in conversation with Benjamin's piece by picking up his notions, weaving in their own with examples, using footnotes as he does, and taking their examples to some conclusion about the culture, as he does with the final epilogue on war. Benjamin's piece itself can serve as an example of how one might write in conversation with others' ideas. Students could study the ways he uses his sources before they begin this so that they might have a sense of writing that speaks to other writing before they begin.

2. The third question for a second reading offers students a way to begin studying Benjamin's use of footnotes, and this writing assignment asks them to take that work into their writing by finding a way to tell others — readers not familiar with Benjamin's essays or his use of footnotes — how he uses footnotes. The key for student's work is to stay close to the text, to work with particular footnotes as examples of their arguments for the ways Benjamin's writing is a style that involves footnotes. When we ask students to offer this essay "not only as an interesting spectacle but as evidence of a style of writing or a theory of writing," we are inviting students to imagine a way of writing that could not be itself without the footnotes as Benjamin uses them. What might they call this style? How does it work? What can they as beginning writers (at least as they might compare themselves to Benjamin) learn from this style? And how does this way of writing affect the reader? How, that is, does it affect them?

Students might extend this project in class by studying the ways in which other authors in *Ways of Reading* use footnotes. To do this , they'll need to read the selections by those others (we might suggest Susan Bordo's selection or Clifford Geertz's) and study their use of footnotes in contrast to Benjamin's use of them. Such an extension would work well *after* students complete this assignment and before they move on to the Making Connections questions.

3. One could argue that a key to Benjamin's argument about the change in art (and in the superstructure of the culture because of the change) resides in his relegation of "authenticity" and "aura," in connection to art, to a tradition that is forever changed by the possibilities of mechanical reproduction of art. Traditional notions of art as authentic, or as art having an aura about it, no longer have bearing in a world where art can be reproduced massively for the masses. There are major passages in the text where Benjamin makes these arguments, and, of course, he uses fairly extended examples involving painting and drama and photography and film.

    When students work on this assignment, they'll want to be certain that they first follow Benjamin's arguments about the traditional notions of authenticity and aura through to the end of the essay, because Benjamin continues to build and modify them, especially when he writes about photography and film towards the end of his essay. The assignment also asks students to work with examples of their own that they might place alongside his in order to extend his argument with twenty-first century examples.

4. Benjamin asks how changes in art forms, which change the superstructure of cultures, change human perceptions — the ways in which we see and imagine. Film is his most powerful example. He says in the footnotes (number 21, for instance) that mass movements are difficult to perceive without the aid of mechanical reproductions, so that films of mass movements of people or things change the ways we perceive and imagine such images. The change in what we can imagine, then, changes our perceptions for good. This assignment invites students to consider Benjamin's notions of how perceptions are changed by mechanical reproductions of film and then to comment on his thinking given their experiences with film — with their experiences growing up on film, for example, as Benjamin as his readers did not.

    To complete the assignment, students will need to first follow through Benjamin's argument on the ways in which film changes our perceptions. It might be useful for students to imagine the ways film changed the perceptions of those who were not born to it but experienced it, as Benjamin did, as a new art form in juxtaposition to such art forms as painting and drama. What, then, does film change? What does it allow us to see or imagine that we couldn't see or imagine without it? How do these ways of seeing and imagining evolve through them, the students, as a generation saturated with film and multimedia? What do they see that Benjamin didn't or couldn't?

5. This assignment extends the fourth question for a second reading into a writing project by asking students to explain the epilogue as a conclusion. Students also are invited to write for readers who have not read Benjamin and who do not have the text at hand, so they will need to re-present Benjamin's essay and his epilogue to those readers. This itself is a substantial piece of writing, one that students will have difficulties with because Benjamin's essay is complex and they'll want to reduce it to a string of generalizations about art. They'll need to be reminded in revisions that they also have to present his arguments about the superstructure, changing human perceptions, and changed notions of art (the loss of the authentic, for instance). As students work on re-presenting Benjamin to these readers, they'll need to find ways to explain to them the ways in which his essay prepares readers in general for the epilogue on war while, at the same time, coming to a conclusion about Benjamin's two accounts of war and his position on war, art, and aesthetics.

This is to be sure a demanding piece of work and students might complete it in stages of a week's worth of writing. You might help them stage it by building it into class discussions over a week's worth of time, so that they can see examples of how their colleagues have handled the tasks. A writing workshop environment might offer everyone the flexibility to do both individual and group work over that week before they set about producing final versions.

MAKING CONNECTIONS (p. 102)

1. This is a lovely assignment for students to study the influences of one author on another. Berger, as the assignment points out, acknowledges his debt to Benjamin by including a picture of Benjamin at the end of his essay, but the influence is much more particular than this gesture. He appropriates and transforms much of Benjamin's arguments, and his terms, so there is much for students to learn and do with these two pieces.

    First, of course, students will need to read both essays. They can begin with Benjamin and then move on to Berger with an eye towards locating those ideas and terms that he takes from Benjamin's work. This is an extended project, one that can easily involve discussions and writings about Benjamin and Berger before turning to these connections. Students benefit from having been close to both of these texts before beginning this connections project, so if you're imagining the amount of time this assignment might take, it would be helpful to imagine it as a concluding project, perhaps after extended work with both essays.

    Once students are ready to begin this connections project, they might work in small groups to identify those ideas and terms in Benjamin that Berger appropriates before they begin writing individually. At times students help themselves if they can work together and see what others identify and the connections they make to Berger. This could easily evolve into a whole class project, with students doing all of the work, so that you don't inadvertently value a particular set of connections and end up reading about them in everyone's essays. After the class work, the individual writing might begin. With this, students will need to experiment with ways to present these connections so that every essay does not read like "Benjamin says this and Berger says this." Class discussions of students' work in their first drafts could focus on the connections students make and the ways they write those connections, so that the class could see multiple examples of different ways of working and, then, imagine other methods as well.

2. For Walker Percy, the loss of the "authentic" is the loss of the creature. In response to this loss, he studies the ways in which we present experiences to ourselves and others. Benjamin does not lament, like Percy, the loss of the authentic or the aura of works of art. He notices them instead as artifacts of a different technology of art, one that was not involved in mass production but relied on individual perceptions for individuals to view.

    Students, of course, will need to have read and worked with both of these essays before beginning this connections assignment. The assignment suggests that they write a general introduction first, one in which they orient readers to the comparisons they are about to make. They might work closely, for instance, with each author's use of "authentic" by setting the context for each essay. They might say what it means for Percy and what it means for Benjamin, then go on to locate each author's position toward the loss of the authentic. Or they might begin with how the authentic varies for both while holding each to some common ground. We can imagine many ways to begin within the call for a general introduction. However, once students are ready to work on the comparisons — with emphasis on the differences across each author's use of notion — they would benefit from working closely with parallel passages from

Percy and Benjamin, so this becomes, then, a close reading assignment. They read a passage from Benjamin on the "authentic" next to one from Percy, beginning with the assumption that each passage might represent a significant position by each author. Students are also asked to write in response, for themselves, after they have completed the comparison.

3. This is an enormously challenging (and rewarding) piece of work for students. Foucault's notions of power reside in arrangements of mechanisms — those here in this essay concerned with overseeing and the power of panopticism to regulate and control — in which individuals are caught. Benjamin's notions of power reside in the uses of art by cultures and politics. His most compelling example is film and the ways in which it has the power to change human perceptions and politics.

    For students to complete this assignment, they will need to spend considerable time with Foucault's selection. The question for them has to do with how Foucault imagines power and the ways in which that power is situated in a society. Students will want to read his notions of power as something individuals hold, by being people of influence or wealth, for instance, but that is not Foucault's notion, and it often takes considerable work for students to see past their preconceived notions of power because they are so commonly held in our culture. If you would like to engage students in this connections project, we would suggest that you spend about a week's worth of work on the Foucault essay, beginning with a discussion about power and then, perhaps, with a writing assignment in which students are asked to formulate Foucault's notion of power with a close reading of passages from his essay.

    Once students have worked on Foucault (and after they have worked on the Benjamin selection), they're ready to begin this project. You might ask students to work closely from a passage or two from each essay so that they avoid sweeping generalizations and work, instead, from their close readings of passages that they feel they can use to represent each author's notions of power.

JOHN BERGER

Ways of Seeing (p. 105)
On Rembrandt's Woman in Bed *(p. 129)*
On Caravaggio's The Calling of St. Matthew *(p. 131)*

As the headnote says, this selection is the first chapter of a book, *Ways of Seeing*, drawn from John Berger's television series with the BBC. The book actually has five authors — or, as the page opposite the title page says, it is "a book made by" John Berger, Sven Blomberg, Chris Fox, Michael Dibb, and Richard Hollis. Both the spine and the title page, however, carry Berger's name only. For convenience, we refer to the essay as his. Possession and ownership, as Berger argues in the essay, are difficult and problematic concepts.

Berger creates books that are hard to classify, and this one is certainly no exception. There are chapters in *Ways of Seeing* that have no words, only pictures. In the chapter we've included, there are pictures that are clearly part of the text (the argument instructs the reader to look at them), but there are other pictures included as well, and they have a less official status. Some could be said to be illustrations of points in the text. Others have to be worked into the chapter.

We were attracted to this piece by the way it allowed us to extend the concept of reading beyond written texts (to the way one "reads" paintings or images, to the way one "reads" one's culture), and for the act of reading it requires. There is a strong argument in the essay, to be sure, particularly in the discussion of the paintings by Frans Hals, and students can reproduce it without great trouble. But there is still much work left for the reader. There are paintings and pictures that go without discussion. There are moments when common words like "history" are wrenched out of common usage. Berger wants to take common terms and make them problematic, just as he wants to take familiar images and give us a new way of seeing them, yet he is not pushy about definitions; terms remain open to discussion. The structure of the essay also presents a challenge to its readers. While students can begin through discussion to work out the argument of various sections in the essay (his reading of the Hals paintings, the example of mystification, his argument about reproduction, the section on the use of museums), there is no single answer to how these various parts should fit together in a single discussion.

This, then, is one way to teach this essay. Students can begin by focusing on individual sections in order to figure out what Berger is saying and what, as a group, they feel it means. (How do you make sense out of the "yet" in "Yet, although every image embodies a way of seeing, our perception or appreciation of an image depends also upon our own way of seeing" [text p. 107]?) As teachers, we are willing to be a resource at this point: to say what we see in the painting by Magritte or the figures on museum attendance, or to help students see the lines of demarcation that underlie their various points of view on, for instance, what it means to say that the prose on text page 112 is mystification. We are unwilling to tell our students everything we know about Magritte or Benjamin — at least not until very late in the discussion, when this section of the course is over. We don't want the textual problems in an essay to seem like problems of information. The question is not what students can be told about Magritte but what they can make out of that painting, placed as it is in the text. The issue is not how much they know about Walter Benjamin, but that they know that Berger felt the need to bring forward Benjamin's name and one of his books.

The fun of the discussion comes when students find they have gained a foothold on various sections of the essay and you ask, "How does it fit together? How do you put together the section on the *Virgin of the Rocks* with the section on Van Gogh and Hals? What does this have to do with what you've learned to say about history or about the relationship between a person, an image, and ways of seeing?" These are questions that don't have any quick answer. The uncertainty they create can only in a limited sense be resolved by returning to the text. Berger, in other words, loses his capacity as the authority here. Students might test what they have to say by talking about the charts on text page 119 or the painting on text page 117, but they won't find answers. These are answers that they must create, present, and defend both for themselves and for their colleagues, and in discussion as a prelude to work they might do as writers.

Some Additional Notes

The man pictured on text page 127 is Walter Benjamin and not, as it appears, John Berger. The reproductions in Berger's book are of about the same quality as those in the textbook. They too, are in black and white. Many of the frames are dark. The physical relationship of image to text is as close to that of the original as we could make it, so the images you see are similar to those a reader confronts in the original text. There is no reason, of course, why a teacher should not seek out slides or better, full-color reproductions, nor should a teacher apologize for black and white. The images your students will be studying are those in Berger's book, and since part of Berger's argument concerns the use and reproduction of images, there is reason to pay attention to — rather than try to overcome — problems with his use and reproduction of images.

QUESTIONS FOR A SECOND READING (p. 133)

1. These questions are designed to take one of the key terms of this essay, "history," and to make its possible meanings the central textual problem for students as they read back through the text. For Berger, who is both an art historian and a Marxist, history is something of a technical term, and he uses it to frame his argument. He puts pressure on the term and forces it to mean more than it does when it is used loosely in conversation. The job for students is to see how they might make sense of these sentences — what, for a reader of Berger, might it mean to be "situated" in history, or to be "deprived" of history?

    Students are directed to pay attention to Berger's use of this term. Once they begin to develop a way of accounting for that use, the remaining questions ask them to put their sense of this term, "history" to the test by using it in sentences that discuss the Hals paintings. Students are asked to develop a specialized use for a common term and then to use that term to enable a discussion of an example they share with their colleagues in class (and with Berger, their author). They are asked, that is, to produce a Berger-like discussion, or a discussion that demonstrates their way of reading Berger.

2. This question is intended to allow students to imagine a position outside of Berger's, one from which they can critique Berger's argument. On the one hand, Berger argues that mystification hides that which is "really" there. The assumption, at least at a first reading, seems to be that there are some people who can see with that kind of clarity. On the other hand, Berger argues that we see what we have learned to see. Students are asked, then, to work out Berger's position on the relationship between seeing and understanding, between the individual and the culture, and to turn the terms of that discussion back on Berger himself. Could you say that he sees the truth in the Hals paintings? Is his perception "shaped" or pure? If you find that you can say that Berger too sees what he has learned to see, does that discredit his argument?

ASSIGNMENTS FOR WRITING (p. 133)

1. This first assignment is an opportunity for students to closely study Berger's essay to resay his arguments about what gets in the way when we look at paintings and what we might do to overcome the barriers. Berger claims, in a broad sense, that culture gets in the way of our readings of paintings and history, but his examples are examples of culture as it appears in different enacted forms — in the machinery of "mystification," for example, and in the social positioning of experts or critics. So students will need to work closely from Berger's examples of things and people getting in the way and to use these examples as the grounds for making their claims for his argument. With this assignment, students also are asked to imagine that they are writing to an audience unfamiliar with Berger's essay.

2. Accepting the implied invitation of the essays, this assignment asks the reader to see what he or she can make of one of the paintings that is given a prominent position in the text. While Berger has something to say about *Woman Pouring Milk*, he does not give it a full discussion. The problem posed is "What can you make of this painting, if you work on it in Berger's spirit?" One way of framing a discussion of these papers or of preparing students for revision is to turn to Berger's own words: "What we make of that painted moment when it is before our eyes depends upon what we expect of art, and that in turn depends today upon how we have already experienced the meaning of paintings through reproductions" (text p. 125). Students might begin by considering what the authors of the papers under consideration expect of art, how they might have experienced the meaning of paintings through reproductions. What, in those papers, might be attributed to the authors' work with Berger? What might be attrib-

uted to our general culture? What might be taken as a sign of some individual or idiosyncratic vision?

In our experience, the key features for students who have worked on this painting have been the identity of the box and pot on the floor behind the woman, the woman's relationship to this room — is it hers, for example? — and the nature of the task she is performing. One question for a teacher here is the degree to which this project could, or should, involve research. It would be a good idea to decide beforehand whether to provide additional information about Vermeer; to provide art historians' readings of the painting; to suggest that students make use of the library; or students work without any secondary sources.

3. We've had a good deal of success with this assignment. Ideally, students should have ready access to a museum. Berger talks about the ways we have come to experience paintings in museums, and a trip to a museum to look at a painting will give students a way of adding to or reflecting on Berger's argument. But he also talks about reproductions, so we felt justified in adding the option of using art books. If you can reasonably expect your students to get to a museum, however, we think the trip will hold some interesting surprises for you. We usually schedule a class meeting at the museum — just to get the students walking around to think about which painting might be "theirs." Warn students against docents and taped tours — for your purposes, prepared readings of paintings will be a real barrier to writing.

The students who have had the most success with this assignment have been fairly literal in their sense of what it means to have a "conversation" with a painting. Their essays do not read like museum-guide interpretations, rather like more open-ended and speculative pieces, sometimes cast as a narrative with dialogue, sometimes as pure dialogue. The key is to invite students to talk to the painting, to ask questions, and to imagine rich and ambiguous responses. You want to avoid papers in which students begin with an idea of what a picture is about and simply impose that reading on the material. The paintings need to be imagined to talk back, to counter or open up a student's desire to master and control.

For revision: In some cases we've found we needed to send students back to the painting and the original assignment, usually because they were more concerned to push through a single reading than to have a conversation with their material. In most cases, however, we used the revision as the occasion to send students back to the Berger essay. As they became involved with the museum assignment, students forgot about Berger, so we used the revision to send them back to see what use they could make of his way of talking about paintings or the museum. "How, for example, could you use the example of your essay to explain what Berger might mean when he talks about 'history'?" The idea is to engage students in a conversation with Berger, where they can draw on their expertise to enter his argument.

4. Berger offers interesting and compelling readings of Rembrandt's *Woman in Bed* and Caravaggio's *The Calling of St. Matthew* as ways to talk with his lover. Students will see a slightly different Berger in these two pieces than in "Ways of Seeing," and this assignment offers them both the opportunity to use these readings to clarify and elaborate on Berger's claims that he makes in "Ways of Seeing" for what it means to "read" paintings and as the opportunity to see readings of paintings created in meditative space as a part of a long love letter. How, they might be asked, does this kind of reading differ from the readings in his essay? What would account for those differences? What, in other words, are these readings able to accomplish that the readings in the essay do not or can not?

MAKING CONNECTIONS (p. 135)

1. The assignment points to the common starting point in Percy's and Berger's essays. Both work with the assumption that people see what they have learned to see — we don't "naturally" or "truly" receive scenes in nature or pictures in a museum. Both argue that, if this is the case, one ought to think about ways of seeing, worry about one's habitual understanding of the world, and plan strategies or approaches to improve one's vision. With this Percy/Berger sense of the problem, students are asked to put themselves (and the essays) to the test by imagining approaches to a painting in a museum (although there is no reason why a teacher should insist on a museum — it would be possible to use slides or handouts or the images in the text). Students must step back from what they have done and use what they have written in their essays to compare and evaluate the two essays.

    The only real difficulty in this assignment is the number of steps: grasp the argument of the essays, write a series of approaches, and evaluate what you have done. There is no reason why these steps can't be separate stages as students work on this essay. Each might be written individually and discussed in class or in groups. All three might then be put together into a single essay in a final revision.

2. Before writing this assignment, students will undoubtedly need to do some preliminary work with the Foucault selection and would certainly be helped by preliminary work with the Berger piece. The second-reading questions for class discussions of both the Foucault and the Berger selections will help students orient themselves to these challenging texts.

    Neither Berger nor Foucault directly defines what he means by power. However, Berger is more direct in his attribution of power to the ruling class and invites us to imagine how power relations might change if people were to understand history in art, whereas Foucault presents power as a force of production in culture that, in a sense, has a life of its own. If students approach this assignment as a single project to explain theories of power, rather than to make a critical judgment about either theory, they'll have a clearer sense of purpose as they reread the texts and mark passages that they can use to represent each author's notions of power. Students will find it more challenging to write about Foucault's arguments about power, which he invests not in people or classes of people but rather in culture as a force that those knowledgeable enough about power can use to channel and manipulate people. But it is difficult to say from either Foucault's or Berger's arguments how power works and how you might know it when you see it. Students will be frustrated if they think that they can get either author's arguments about power down pat, and they will need to write this assignment in an atmosphere of experimentation so that they can acknowledge and write about the sections of both texts that they have trouble understanding. It helps our students to know that anyone reading these texts will have a challenging time of trying to come to grips with the discussions of power, and that this difficulty is an opportunity to speculate and venture explanations that are tentative and uncertain.

3. The best way to approach Geertz's essay might be through this one-sentence representation of his method: The cockfights are a story the Balinese tell themselves about themselves. American teenagers walk around shopping malls doing peculiar but characteristic things. College students decorate dorm rooms in peculiar but characteristic ways. To begin to carry out a Geertzian project, we might say that in each case these are stories people are telling themselves about themselves. What are these stories? What are the key features? How might an outsider interpret them? *What*, then, are they telling themselves about themselves?

    This is the basic pattern — from it, and by returning to Geertz's essay, a class can begin to account for the special expertise of an anthropologist and the special concerns Geertz shows for the limits and potential of such a method of analysis.

42

Students are asked to speak, with Berger's help, about the peculiar but characteristic ways we make use of images from the past (for Berger, of course, this includes the use of those images outside of museum walls). And the assignment asks students to speculate on what stories we are telling ourselves about ourselves.

A note on the final caveat: Berger's argument about the ruling class will quickly consume the speculative ardor of most students. He says it in a nutshell, they will argue, so there is nothing else to say. We've found that it makes sense to insist that students ought to work toward some other account; then, if they and you choose, they can go back to consider Berger's.

SUSAN BORDO

Hunger as Ideology (p. 139)

Bordo's work is compelling. Few students will read this essay and remain silent. It's the kind of work that prompts students to speak back, although not necessarily in agreement. Bordo reads what seems so obvious to most of us — advertisements having to do with bodies, food, hunger, and caring — and she sees more at play in these advertisements than capitalistic desires to make money. She sees representational conventions of gender differences that have changed little since the nineteenth century. She demonstrates close readings of sophisticated advertisements that often put women in double-binds by inviting them to indulge in forbidden foods rich in calories while, at the same time, asking them to withhold or control their desires so that they can be the reproduction of male images of women. It's OK to indulge but don't get fat. Men are treated differently, according to Bordo's readings, and unlike women, they are seldom portrayed as caretakers who enact that caretaking in food preparation, or as people who do not have carefree and easy relationships with food.

Students have interesting reactions to Bordo's readings. Many students take sympathetic positions, but others argue something along the lines that these are only ads, and we know they want to sell us food by playing on our desires for control and sexuality, so what's the big deal. In the extreme, a few male students always seem to be ready to take the devil's advocate position to argue that woman are caretakers, and they should indulge themselves once in awhile and what's wrong with being tall and lean and sexy anyway. Whatever students read into this essay, it's important to keep them close to Bordo's argument and examples. She reads the ads closely, always looking for the ways in which they represent gender and the assumptions that they make about women and men. As such, her examples can be models for students to work with when they read her essay and when they read other ads. They can ask questions, for example, about her essay that play with the same strategies she uses when she reads ads. They can ask about her assumptions about gender and about how she represents women and men and herself. And, of course, students can read other ads with her strategies.

QUESTIONS FOR A SECOND READING (p. 172)

1. Students are being asked to identify cultural pressures that Bordo sees at play in specific advertisements, so they'll need to work closely with her examples as they reread. This is an occasion for students to take notes or to make marginal comments as they reread. It's also a good opportunity for students to demonstrate in class how they read these cultural pressures in Bordo's critiques. After they have discussed their readings in terms of these cultural pressures, students can be asked to put them together, so that they form larger pictures. If one of the pressures has to do, for example, with

women being asked to indulge themselves, how might this be connected to the pressure to be caretakers through food preparation? It's important to remember that these pressures operate both individually and as systems. Individually they might be clear and coherent, but as a system they might be incoherent and schizophrenic. And, finally, once students have done this kind of discussion, they can turn to questions of who these cultural pressures being brought to bear (mostly on women) benefit. This identification is an integral part of the critical work posed by this question, but so are the students' explanations of how those benefits accrue.

2. This question challenges students to investigate Bordo's critical terms. It's pretty straightforward. Students can identify passages where Bordo uses terms outside of students common language to explain how the terms work and what they allow her to say and do in her readings of the ads. The same is true of the figures, such as John Berger, she refers to. The figures, like the terms, allow her to say things, to see the ads (and their assumptions or motives) in particular ways, and students can be asked to explain how the examples they've marked during their rereadings allow her to do this kind of work. They can also be asked to speak to the limitations of her terms and references. Just as metaphors allow us to say things and see things in particular ways while masking other ways to speak and see, so do terms and references allow ways of seeing and speaking while masking others.

3. Students will need to reread Bordo with an eye towards identifying those passages where she contrasts ads designed to appeal to women and those designed to appeal to men. How do they differ? How, that is, do they appeal to men differently? And what assumptions do they make about men that are different from the assumptions that they make about women? Students can also speak to the question of how these ads represent men and women differently. They appeal to images and psychological states of being and they portray those images and states of being, according to Bordo, quite differently. Once students have worked their way through her examples, they might, as the question suggests, try their hands with ads they find that seem powerful and attractive to them. They can literally put the ads they find against her examples and read them using her strategies.

ASSIGNMENTS FOR WRITING (p. 172)

1. Students will be challenged by this assignment. It invites them to write out their understandings of Bordo's central arguments and to use her central examples to do this, but it also asks them to establish a point of view of their own in the name of the group that they imagine they represent. Keeping students focused on both aspects of this assignment will be a major piece of any instructor's work with their revisions. Students will want to quickly do one aspect of the assignment, and they'll be tempted to overgeneralize Bordo's argument and move rapidly to their points of view. When this happens, we have asked students to step back into Bordo's essay to closely read her central examples and to write from these examples what they take to be the attendant arguments. Bordo's essay can be read from a number of perspectives, and identifying central arguments is always dicey because readers will see and weigh Bordo's various arguments differently, so the challenge here for students is not that they get the arguments nailed down in some right hierarchy or map, but that they make the case from Bordo's examples for what they think her central arguments are. As they write their own perspectives into their essays, students will also need to work from their own examples. If they want to develop a point of view on Bordo's arguments that is different from hers, then they need to work, as she does, from compelling examples, so students will want to read ads as well. Much of this work will have to be done in revisions, so it's helpful if you take the tack that the first drafts of this assignment will be beginning "think" pieces as students work their way into multiple revisions.

2. Here you'll want to turn students to the section of Bordo's essay towards the end where she discusses her students' work with counterexamples to what she takes to be the traditional gender dualities at play in ads having to do with body images, eating, and nurturing. For students, the assignment asks that they work with a way to present her arguments for the gender dualities, so that they can then offer examples that don't seem to play by the rules. Bordo will tell them in her essay that although the examples do not seem to play by the gender duality rules, even the best of them will have traces of those dualities because they are so sedimented and unquestioned in our culture and particularly in the culture of advertising that propels capitalism, through desires for things, including desires for images and states of being.

   Bordo uses the terms *stabilize* and *destabilize* to label the images and representations in ads that either confirm (stabilize) or challenge (destabilize) conventional gender dualities. Nurturing men, for example, in ads might destabilize conventional gender dualities while women trimming down to please men would stabilize those dualities. Students can work with these terms in their own readings of the ads they select to work with to test Bordo's use of the terms. They might think about whether it's always this or that. Do images or representations operate in clear-cut ways to either stabilize or destabilize gender dualities in all of these ads? How might they explain contradictory examples or ones in which both things seem to be happening?

3. This is a straightforward request to students to study two examples from Bordo's essay so that they can write about her methods. They will want to reread the essay to identify the examples they wish to work with, then they can interrogate her readings of the examples for how she selects the ads, the questions she asks about them, the strategies she uses in her criticism that they think defines her particular expertise. What, in other words, does she do that's characteristically Bordo? How does she do it? She's particularly good at drawing out the assumptions about gender that inform specific images and particular rhetoric, and she makes some wonderful moves where she relates these assumptions to issues of agency and power. Who is in control? she asks. Who benefits if things are as the ad would have them be? She reads in layers and stages. She reads the ad for its positioning of a product in relation to women and men. She reads the positioning of women and men in the images and rhetoric. She reads the positioning as a representation of an ideology that gives and takes power to and from women and men, that gives and takes agency and specific roles (such as nurturance, independence, rebellion, conformity, and so on) as well.

   What Bordo doesn't see is much more difficult for students to write about. They can work with the same examples, of course, but they'll have to read them outside of or adjacent to Bordo's critical mechanisms, so that they can ask themselves what she misses or doesn't see in these examples. They might begin by thinking about Bordo's assumptions about the relationships of people — women and men — to food. What does she think food is for? or about? What does eating represent to her? What doesn't it represent? What, that is, doesn't she talk about in relation to people eating?

MAKING CONNECTIONS (p. 174)

1. The Berger and Bordo essays are substantial pieces of work, and they have much to say to each other, but this assignment asks students to reconsider Berger's essay in light of Bordo's. Here students will need to think about what it might mean to reconsider Berger's critical work on art, reproductions, and the ways we are taught, according to Berger, to read paintings. He makes a lot of the mystification of art from the past by art critics, and he asks us to read paintings particularly as representations of artists' positions towards their subjects and what their subjects might represent to them by taking into consideration the situations of the artists and the situations of their times. How do Bordo's arguments about the manipulations of ads directed towards women

and men allow for a reconsideration of Berger's examples? of his arguments? Working with one or two of Berger's examples, students might begin by studying his arguments about them. Do his arguments for the ways in which paintings are read by art critics, for example, seem like Bordo's arguments that are critical of ways ads portray gender differences? Students can study the arguments and the critical readings of examples to see how these two theorists cross and differ in their agendas and in their methods.

Students might also begin with Berger's terms. Do ads, as Bordo sees them, mystify our relationships to body images, food, hunger, and nurturance? Here is an opportunity for students to consider how it might (or might not) be possible to use one of Berger's central notions to say that ads mystify these relationships. What terms might Bordo use to describe the ways art critics have mystified the art of the past, according to Berger? Students can be asked to study these questions along gender lines too. Are there examples in Berger where gender dualities can be said to be at play?

With this assignment, as with others that ask students to find ways into critical work, the important thing is the work students do. Much of this will be done through revisions and class discussions of those revisions. There are no cut-and-dried ways to put Berger's and Bordo's arguments and examples together, even though they seem to be related and even though Bordo references Berger. It's the work that students will do that matters, and it's the critical perspectives they take on each others drafts of their readings of Berger and Bordo that matters. No one, in other words, gets this assignment right — there are many ways into it, and students should be encouraged to follow leads, test assumptions, and argue from examples as Berger and Bordo do.

2.   The comparison of concerns and methods that this assignment asks students to make with the Bordo and Coles essays is pretty straightforward, yet the issues are complex in both essays, so students will need to think about how they might represent each essay's concerns as they relate to their uses and critiques of images. Coles works with documentary projects, and he's careful to avoid harsh distinctions between fiction and nonfiction with these projects, yet he also draws our attention to the ways documentary projects represent their composers' visions or interpretations of their subjects. These visions, in Coles's view, are social commentaries; they locate their subjects in their composers' social views and beliefs while, at the same time, they reveal the social situations of the subjects. Documentary work is not, according to Coles, naive representation of "actual" or "true" or "natural" reality. It's composed work, work that bears its makers' influences and interpretations. Bordo challenges notions of true or natural representations of bodies and gender roles that emanate from Madison Avenue's campaigns to sell us food and states of being and images. These ads desire to convince us that the images, states of being, and relationships to food they portray are in fact "natural" and representative of "real" states of affairs. Within this broad overlap of concerns, there is a good deal of work that students can do with the ways both authors see the construction of images by their makers and the readings of those images by their readers.

There is also a good deal of work for students to do here with each author's terminology and orientation towards images. Bordo critiques ads to reveal their ideology concerning gender dualities. Coles studies images as artifacts of social situations and the concerns of their makers. Their perspectives differ in substantial ways, yet they both question notions of "true" and "natural" realities. Here again, though, students will help themselves by staying close to the authors' work with images by taking examples from each essay to ground their comparisons. One or two examples from each would give them all that they need to comment on the concerns, terminology, and methods of each author. Anything more than that would be unmanageable for most students, even with multiple revisions of their writings, and it would tend to pull them into overgeneralizations without the specific grounding of the examples.

ROBERT COLES

The Tradition: Fact and Fiction (p. 176)

This is a wonderful essay to use to immerse students in the complexities of fact and fiction through documentary works. It adds another dimension to this subject — a familiar one that has been raised in *Ways of Reading* by John Edgar Wideman ("Our Time") and Susan Griffin ("Our Secret") — with Coles's attention to both photographic and written projects. He comments extensively on the photographic essays of Dorothea Lange and Walker Evans —which are readily available from most college libraries in various editions — his own writings about children in crisis in the South during desegregation, and on two lengthy anecdotes about William Carlos Williams and Erik Erikson.

Coles takes a reverential posture towards his subjects in this work, but it doesn't conceal the fundamental questions that he's interested in raising about our common notions about factual and fictional work. And these are questions that he has raised with students, so we benefit from his thinking on paper about their responses to these distinctions. Coles argues compellingly for the complex mix of fact and fiction in documentary projects. He says that documentary work is shaped by its maker's visions and beliefs, so it is then always an act of interpretation. He dances a bit on the edges of this argument, because it inevitably leads into questions of how anything made by a person, including such commonly objectivized things as photographs and interviews, can be anything but this mixture, always under the influence of human vision and interpretation.

Students can have good fun with this essay, and they can test its claims by rereading the projects of Coles's subjects and by creating their own documentary work and, then, by studying that work and how it might be said to be this mixture of fact and fiction, shaped by their own interpretations. We have been taken with the idea of asking a number of students to create documentary projects on the same subjects and to work independent of each other, so that the similarities and differences in their projects could be subjects of further study. The other reading selections in *Ways of Reading* that take up this subject are, too, additional points of entry into study that students can take advantage of with their own self-reflective essays on documentary projects (whether they are their own or others).

QUESTIONS FOR A SECOND READING (p. 218)

1. With this question students have the opportunity to study the way Coles has structured his essay (and his argument) into five sections. After each section, students stop to note what he seems to be saying about documentary work. It's a good idea to also ask students to note Coles's major examples for each section and to write briefly in their notes on how they think he uses the examples to produce his arguments. In this way, they'll have a sense of his train of thought, the way he proceeds with different kinds of examples, and a sense of how a complicated, lengthy argument can be structured in sections around powerful examples.

2. This assignment can lead students in an interesting discussion of the choices photographers make when they crop pictures to orient them in particular ways. Coles discusses three examples, and he presents his father's alternative response to one of them. In doing so, he opens up the subject for all students to comment on the cropped photographs and the discarded images. He also opens up the subject of what it means for a photographer to orient a photograph by cropping. At times it can mean a radical

change in the original document — as it does for the photograph of the couple in the car — and at other times it seems to be more a matter of focus. At the heart of this issue is the question, then, of what it means to create documentary work when it is possible to significantly alter photographs to reorient them along the lines of a photographer's desires or vision. This is, of course, the beauty of this essay — it raises and reraises these questions with different works and with different consequences.

3. Coles thinks through the problems he raises concerning the influences of artists on their documentary work. He creates two categories of influences — social/cultural/ historical and individual/idiosyncratic — then he uses these categories to discuss the influences on the work of his subjects. Students can be asked to use these categories also to reexamine Coles's claims, and they can use them to study their own influences on their own documentary projects, but they can also question the categories. How is it possible, after all, to separate the cultural from the individual? or the historical from the individual? What, students can be asked, do the categories allow Coles to envision of these works, and what do they mask? And how might it be said that these categories inform Coles's overall argument about the distinctions between fact and fiction in documentary work? They are fundamental categories to his thinking, and it is possible to argue that they are the hinges to his argument. How might his argument change if someone thought, for instance, that these forces — cultural and individual — could not be separated as Coles does? Where might that lead?

4. It seems like a genuine missed opportunity to not ask students to research the work of Lange, Evans, and Agee when they work with this essay. These projects are readily available at most libraries, and most libraries hold multiple editions and copies of these works because they are so popular. It would be interesting to ask students to study these works before reading the Coles essay, and to then work with the essay and the photographic essays after they have done the initial work. Students might also study the Lange, Evans, and Agee work after they have read Coles to refigure their readings, to see how immersion in the complete works can alter their responses and readings. It would be interesting also for students to read reviews and comments on this work, particularly those that deal directly with the issues of artistic influences on the projects. These too can be researched at the library or on the Internet.

ASSIGNMENTS FOR WRITING (p. 219)

1. This assignment to chart out and summarize Coles's issues works nicely with the first of the "Questions for a Second Reading." Students could first reread, taking notes on their rereadings with attention to Coles's arguments and examples in each of the five sections of the essay, and then write first drafts of this writing assignment. The heart of the issue here is their discussions of how Coles thinks about these issues of fact and fiction in documentary work and how he uses his examples to generate that thinking. The first of the "Questions for a Second Reading" gives them the opportunity to study each section in detail while taking notes and rereading before they write. Students, of course, can also rewrite to shift their attention once they have produced a draft.

2. This is an assignment that can be a lot of fun and enormously instructive. The key to students creating their own documentary projects is in their beginning it as a written documentary, a documentary, that is, in which they rely on writing to do the work with additional support from whatever else is available to them — photographs, interviews, observations, research, and so on. This is not, in other words, an invitation to create a photographic essay. It is an invitation to create an essay that makes use of other materials, including photographs. Students will also need to think of this as an extended project. Many will want to put it together once and think its finished. They would help themselves if they begin with the understanding that they'll revise the documentary, perhaps a number of times, and perhaps with the comments and evalu-

ations of their colleagues and instructor. During revision, other students can raise hard questions about how the work represents others — what does it say about them? What does it leave out? What seems sensitive to their situations? What seems insensitive?

The second part of the assignment asks students to study the ways in which they might say (or the ways in which others might say) they are filters for their documentaries. They can use Coles's language and categories (social/cultural/historical versus individual/idiosyncratic) or they can find other ways to write about how their visions and beliefs influenced their work. They need to have guidance here because they'll want to generalize about this filtering. The guidance might best help them by asking them to work from examples in their work — from sentences or paragraphs or from photographs and the text they wrote that accompanies them or from interviews and the questions they asked and the ways they relayed the responses and interpreted them in their projects. Students might be given the opportunity to revise their projects after they have completed this second part of the assignment and shared it with others.

3. Here's another writing assignment that follows well from the "Questions for a Second Reading" assignment. The second question asks students to study the three examples of cropped photographs that Coles uses. This assignment picks up that invitation by asking students to represent the photographs, their history, and the points that Coles seems to be making about them for readers who are not completely familiar with the essay. Then the assignment invites students to find a way to enter into the discussion of those cropped photographs. Do they think the decisions to crop them as they are cropped were good decisions? What, then, constitutes a good decision about documentary work? How would they argue for or against those original decisions? What is at stake here when they are cropped? if they were not cropped?

·The important part of this assignment is the invitation for students to enter the discussion with their thinking about the photographs and the issues that they raise having to do with the ways they were cropped and the fact that they were cropped. Students' first drafts will want to hover around the representations of the photographs and Coles's arguments about them; the work of revision will be to get students to enter the discussion, to see their thinking carrying weight in the essay along with their representations of Coles's thinking.

4. This is an excellent opportunity for students to test Coles's notions about the ways in which the real is filtered through an individuals imagination and point of view. There is a range of books and films in the list that they might study, and they can find more in Coles's book. This is a substantial project, and students should be prepared to take the time necessary to complete it. They will need to read and reread the books (or see and resee the films) that they choose to study, and they'll need to work from specific moments in the works. They will want their examples to speak to Coles's notion that individual imagination is a filter for documentary work and that filter can be said to be social/cultural/historical or individual/idiosyncratic. They need to understand that these influences are things they must see in a work. It is their readings that will determine what is a cultural influence and what might be called an individual or idiosyncratic influence. How, they will need to ask, can a cultural or historical influence be determined or argued? What would they expect of the examples at hand in these contexts? And, similarly, what would determine or argue for individual influences?

MAKING CONNECTIONS (p. 221)

1. The comparison of concerns and methods that this assignment asks students to make with the Bordo and Coles essays is pretty straightforward, yet the issues are complex in both essays, so students will need to think about how they might represent each essay's concerns as they relate to their uses and critiques of images. Coles works with

documentary projects, and he's careful to avoid harsh distinctions between fiction and nonfiction with these projects, yet he also draws our attention to the ways documentary projects represent their composers' visions or interpretations of their subjects. These visions, in Coles's view, are social commentaries; they locate their subjects in their composers' social views and beliefs while, at the same time, they reveal the social situations of the subjects. Documentary work is not, according to Coles, naive representation of "actual" or "true" or "natural" reality. It's composed work, work that bears its makers' influences and interpretations. Bordo challenges notions of "true" or "natural" representations of bodies and gender roles that emanate from Madison Avenue's campaigns to sell us food and states of being and images. These ads desire to convince us that the images, states of being, and relationships to food they portray are in fact "natural" and representative of "real" states of affairs. Within this broad overlap of concerns, there is a good deal of work that students can do with the ways both authors see the construction of images by their makers and the readings of those images by their readers.

There is also a good deal of work for students to do here with each author's terminology and orientation towards images. Bordo critiques ads to reveal their ideology concerning gender dualities. Coles studies images as artifacts of social situations and the concerns of their makers. Their perspectives differ in substantial ways, yet they both question notions of "true" and "natural" realities. Here again, though, students will help themselves by staying close to the authors' work with images by taking examples from each essay to ground their comparisons. One or two examples from each would give them all that they need to comment on the concerns, terminology, and methods of each author. Anything more than that would be unmanageable for most students, even with multiple revisions of their writings, and it would tend to pull them into overgeneralizations without the specific grounding of the examples.

2. While this assignment asks students to compare the issues and problems of representing the past raised by both Limerick and Coles, it is also, and more significantly, an opportunity for students to extend both of these writers' projects into one that represents the problems and difficulties of doing documentary work from two quite different perspectives. Students will need to focus on the issues that each author raises, but they'll also need to work closely with the examples and sources of each author's project. Limerick uses quite different sources than Coles, and she has different training from Coles. She's a historian, and she wants to read (or reread) historical materials. Coles could approach the photographic essays he works with this way, but he doesn't. He's more interested in forming an argument about the work of documentaries, so Limerick's historical orientation is not his, although he does at times consider the photographic essays as historical documentation, and he does write about the influences on them from a quasi-historical perspective.

MICHEL FOUCAULT
Panopticism (p. 225)

We've taught Foucault over several semesters and, as surprising as it may seem, he always emerges as one of the most revisited figures in the course. When students are given the option of going back to an essay, they often go back to their Foucault essays. When asked which selection we should be sure to retain in the course, they often choose Foucault.

The reading is difficult and frustrating, to be sure, but students take great pleasure in working with this text and, for reasons that should not be so surprising, they are eager to have an analytical tool (and a fancy vocabulary) they can use to think about power, about the "disciplinary mechanism" at play in the academy and in their lives. We have heard this story over and over again: students and teachers who approached Foucault with hesitation end by finding the work with Foucault is among the most memorable ever. Most recently the story came from a group of instructors teaching extension courses in Oregon, who talked with great pleasure about the work of students in a technical curriculum who love to quote Foucault to each other in the shop or the hallway.

Foucault offers students surprising examples and dramatic new ways of thinking about and talking about power, knowledge, and life in the midst of institutions, ominous institutions quick to define themselves as benign and benevolent. There is something very seductive, too, about Foucault's willingness to write prose that always attempts to be all-inclusive. His essays, and his sentences, are thick, qualified, and, it seems, always moving to the edge of abstraction.

Some of the ways our students have found "Panopticism" difficult or daunting are predictable. You will find that students will want to begin with (rather than work toward) definitions, including a definition of the title word. The key with Foucault is to allow students to work within their own limits and uncertainty. We find we have to school students to write sentences that are tentative — that say, for example, something like, "While I don't completely understand what Foucault means by a 'disciplinary mechanism,' it seems to me that . . ." In writing and in discussion, students need to acknowledge what they don't understand. And they need to feel the invitation to try to translate the difficult phrases or to work toward examples of their own. We have found it useful to get a class to come up with a list of what they take to be the key phrases in "Panopticism," then to type the list for use as a kind of tool kit during the weeks they are working on, and with, the essay.

In this selection, length functions as more of a barrier than, say, in Susan Griffin's "Our Secret," where it at least makes some remote sense to say that the length extends our fascination with the piece. With Foucault, since his prose does not follow structures of elaboration familiar to American students, readers have to simply make their way from beginning to end. The apparatus we provide can help with this, but it is worth making the point that work on this essay requires fortitude and endurance. We've asked students to chart, and to account for, the structure of the piece as an alternative to the structures they have learned to take for granted. This motivates them to think about Foucault's argument or about the way he imagines the work of the historian.

Finally, in our teaching (and in the assignments in *Ways of Reading*), we have tried to invite students to make connections between the technologies of power revealed by Foucault and those common to the classroom and its practices, turning attention, for example, to the *controlling* idea of the standard classroom rhetoric or to the ways in which writing is normalized by American instruction. The summary assignments, for example, ask students to think of "mastery" as both an achievement and a problem, and to connect writing techniques with other techniques of political control.

Foucault makes these connections in *Discipline and Punish*. Among the illustrations in the book are pictures from students' penmanship guides. We found it an extremely useful exercise, in fact, to ask students to think both inside and outside English as a system designed to discipline language and language use — that is, to think both generously and critically about English as a scene of discipline and control. This provided a parallel to the prison as an organizing term. The technology of control in English was readily available in ways that the technology of control in the law was not. It was easy for students to play the role of the professor and to speak for English. In fact, there was some subversive pleasure in this act of ventriloquism — where students could "correct" a piece of writing and then think about how and where they had made it worse — more predictable, less interesting, less "personal," and so on. These discussions gave students a sense of the basic oppositional move in Foucault; and it gave them a sense of how he ignores traditional historical or disciplinary boundaries (connecting schools and prisons, the seventeenth century and the twentieth).

These were our goals in teaching Foucault. We did not use the word "poststructuralism"; we did not make any attempts to connect this chapter to the body of Foucault's work or to the larger critical project he has inspired. That, to our minds, would be the work of a different kind of course. We wanted students to work with the peculiar difficulties of Foucault's text and to put into lay terms what they could imagine to be his critical project. We did not bring in terms from his earlier or later work. For our classes, Foucault was only the figure represented in "Panopticism."

QUESTIONS FOR A SECOND READING (p. 254)

1. Like the questions that follow, this one is designed to give students a way of working back through the essay to make connections, to see it as an evolving project rather than as an assortment of interesting or arresting moments. Here the question is designed to have students make an inventory of the various instances of the "dream" of order and to think about how Foucault accounts for the differences between present and past. It might make sense to invite students to extend their inventory to even more contemporary instances — items they might add to Foucault's list.

2. We have found it useful for students to try to imagine the kind of work Foucault is doing in relation to their sense of academic traditions. Like Susan Griffin, Foucault can be thought of as a historian who is unwilling to write the usual kind of narrative history. If he doesn't do what he is supposed to do, what *does* he do and how might one generously account for what he does?

3. The numbered sections can be imagined as parodic — Foucault is calling attention to the poverty and the inevitability of the desire for ordered "sense," for a 1, 2, 3 — but they can also be seen as straightforward summary gestures, places where the text alludes to other forms of order or to the more conventional needs of readers. This question uses those sections as reference points and asks students to chart the chapter as an argument.

ASSIGNMENTS FOR WRITING (p. 254)

1. Although this assignment presents itself as an opportunity for students to write an essay that summarizes "Panopticism," it is important that students take the position of presenting Foucault's arguments and key terms to other readers, perhaps to members of their class who are also trying to figure out what Foucault is saying. It is equally important that they understand this as work in progress on a text that will refuse to be mastered or re-presented in a summary. Most likely students will attend to the discussion of Bentham and the prison and shy away from everything else — from the difficult terms and connections that define what Foucault *does* with Bentham and his design for a prison. In other words, Foucault will likely be left *out* of the summaries or perhaps made to stand as the same figure as Jeremy Bentham. You can, in advance, direct students to draw on three different sections of the text in their account of the text, or you can ask them to account for the unfolding of the text (for where it begins and where it ends and for the key steps along the way). And (or) you can make this the work of revision, where students go back to think about what they have left out or ignored, about what the consequences are of their desire to master the text.

2–3. These are fairly standard *Ways of Reading* assignments. Whereas the first assignment asks students to work closely with the text, its terms and examples, these two ask students to extend the argument to examples of their own selection.

MAKING CONNECTIONS (p. 250)

1. Students will need to reread both assignments, taking notes toward this essay. In their notes, students will need to identify passages that represent how each author thinks about (talks about) power — where it comes from, how it works, and so on. Berger thinks power comes from privileged positions, from individuals with the wealth and heritage to mystify art and to turn it into a commodity. Basically, he allows members of the ruling classes to hold power as a form of control over others and their perceptions, but he also makes it possible for ordinary people, those without wealth and privilege, to have power when they learn to demystify the art of the past and thereby come to "see" that art is situated, opinionated, not in any way "objective," and always, then, a commentary on the relationship of its subjects and its creators. Foucault, working from examples of how punishment changes (rather than progresses), thinks of power in terms of social relations, but where there is no single, identifiable agent (like the "ruling class"). For Foucault, people like jailers, priests, and psychiatrists use and direct power by virtue of their control over others. It is harder to think with Foucault, since he does not think in terms of the usual narratives of domination and revolt.

    Of the two authors, students will find Foucault's notion of power new and compelling, but they'll have to work to unpack abstract sentences where he describes power in terms of its technologies and filiations. It is important, we have learned, to push for differences, since the easiest tack is to collapse both into a familiar accounting of anti-establishment thinking.

2. The goal of this assignment is to bring to light what would otherwise remain invisible — the difficulty of the pose in these two texts. We want students to think about difficulty and to consider it as strategic, as an achievement, and not simply as a mistake or a sign of arrogance or proof of the fact that writers are smart and students are dumb. We want students to think about how and why these texts represent work (and demand work) and we want them to think about how this work relates to the usual ways of doing things in school. It will be crucial for your students to work from examples — not only passages from the text but also closely realized examples of their own work, as readers, with these passages.

3. This is an enormously challenging (and rewarding) assignment for students to work on. Foucault's notions of power reside in arrangements of mechanisms — those here in this essay concerned with overseeing and the power of panopticism to regulate and control — in which individuals are caught. Benjamin's notions of power reside in the uses of art by cultures and politics. His most compelling example is film and the ways in which it has the power to change human perceptions and politics.

    For students to complete this assignment, they will need to spend considerable time with Foucault's selection. The question for them has to do with how Foucault imagines power and the ways in which that power is situated in a society. Students will want to read his notions of power as something individuals hold, by being people of influence or wealth, for instance, but that is not Foucault's notion, and it often takes considerable work for students to see past their preconceived notions of power because they are so commonly held in our culture. If you would like to engage students in this connections project, we would suggest that you spend about a week's worth of work on the Foucault essay, beginning with a discussion about power and then, perhaps, with a writing assignment in which students are asked to formulate Foucault's notion of power with a close reading of passages from his essay.

    Once students have worked on Foucault (and after they have worked on the Benjamin selection), they're ready to begin this project. You might ask students to work closely from a passage or two from each essay so that they avoid sweeping generalizations and work, instead, from their close readings of passages that they feel they can use to represent each author's notions of power.

PAULO FREIRE

The "Banking" Concept of Education (p. 259)

This essay provokes students. They either feel strongly sympathetic to Freire's condemnation of "banking" education, where students are turned into "containers" to be "filled" by their teachers, or they feel strongly that "banking" education is the very education they need to be competitive and successful.

Assume that your students will need to reread this selection a number of times as it poses challenging conceptual problems, and Freire's terms, like "problem-posing" and "creative transformation," are usually part and parcel of the conceptual problem. The essay has momentum, though, and once students begin to follow his argument — that education that only transmits information, that is conducted through teacher narratives and student silences, stands opposed to "problem-solving" education, which is conducted by teachers and students working together in a dialogue to solve genuine problems — they'll react to it, largely because their personal experiences serve as quick validations of Freire's central concepts.

QUESTIONS FOR A SECOND READING (p. 270)

1. This discussion assignment is designed to allow students to "problem-pose" Freire's concepts by testing them against their own experiences and by imagining them in classes and subjects with which they are familiar. You will want to move slowly, perhaps allowing two or three class sessions to work your way through the assignment's questions. Students will need to be constantly moving between the essay and examples they come up with. When they discuss problem-posing in English, for instance, they'll need to turn to Freire to put his concept in their own language. Then they'll need to imagine an English class where reading, writing, and discussion are used by the teacher and students to "work" a problem that has some significance to them — for example, growth and change in adolescence. When they turn to Freire's examples, as the second half of this assignment asks them to, they'll need to pay particular attention to what he means when he discusses students as spectators and students as re-creators. You can make connections between their examples and his by asking them to include a discussion of students as spectators and students as re-creators in their examples of problem-posing classes in the various subjects.

2. This assignment focuses students on two important concepts that Freire borrows from Marxist thought, and it serves as a good follow-up discussion to the first assignment. Because of its narrow focus, it's not good as an opening assignment, although a discussion of praxis and alienation could certainly be broadened to include Freire's concepts of banking education and problem-posing education.

   Students will need to stay close to the text to discuss these terms, and you'll want to ask them to reread to find those passages and moments that present Freire's use of the terms. Once they've located and noted those, they're ready to put them into their own words and create what I. A. Richards calls a "radical paraphrase."

3. There is a way in which Freire's voice and his explanations invite response. Readers often mention their inclination to talk back as they read and reread Freire. Although some of this can be explained by his accessible subjects (education and teachers and students) and his accessible metaphors (banking and working together in problem-

posing), he takes a stance that both gives information and invites response by posing education as a problem for readers to work on. Although he frames the question with descriptions, explanations, and a few examples, he doesn't offer any definitive solutions. Instead, he insists through his posture and commitment that readers begin to examine their experiences from this problem-posing perspective. Still, he does offer information and it is quite strong stuff, raising the question of whether banking and problem-posing are as clear-cut as Freire would have us believe. Students will need to speak from his text, so they'll need to reread to find those moments when Freire can be said to be both depositing information and allowing for a dialogue. You might turn your students' attention to his voice by asking them to characterize the kinds of voices that speak in banking education and the kinds that speak in problem-posing. Ask them to recall those times when they experienced each. Where, you might ask, would Freire's voice put him — in banking or problem-posing? What passages or moments in the text lead them to make this appraisal?

ASSIGNMENTS FOR WRITING (p. 271)

1. This challenging writing assignment offers students the opportunity to see a significant learning experience of their own through Freire's eyes. You might consider turning to this assignment after some extended discussion of the essay, perhaps after spending two or three class sessions working with the questions for the first of the "Questions for a Second Reading." Students will then be familiar with the essay and with framing their own experiences in its terms.

You might consider asking students to identify a rich and illustrative incident in which they learned something from their own experience, without paying much attention to whether it fits or doesn't fit in Freire's view of education. Once they have identified the incident — and it should be one that they can write quite a bit about — they can begin the work of seeing it through Freire's terms. They'll need to reconstruct the incident with as much detail as they can, and they'll need to pay attention to conversations and what specific people did during or as a result of the incident. If the incident involved school experience, they'll want to write about what they worked with (textbooks, assignments, etc.) and how they worked (what they did, what other students did, what teachers did). Once they've reconstructed the incident, you'll want to turn their attention to a Freirian reading of it. They might consider whether it could be said to be a banking experience or a problem-posing one. What about the experience allows them to talk about it as one or the other? Was it an experience that would allow them to write about an "emersion" of consciousness? or perhaps a submersion?

For revision: In their first drafts for this essay, students often tell lively stories of an individual's experience in school or provide a tightly organized demonstration that their experiences show that Freire was right. The goal of revision, we feel, should be to open these accounts up, to call them into question.

Perhaps because they are young adults, and perhaps because they are, by and large, Americans, students translate Freire's account of social, political, and historical forces into a story of individuals — a mean teacher and an innocent student. One way to pose problems for revision, then, would be to send students back to Freire's essay to see how he accounts for "agency" — who is doing what to whom in Freire's account of education. Once students have reread the essay with this in mind, they can go back to their own pieces, making this story of individuals a story of *representative* individuals. Here, teacher and student play predetermined roles in the larger drama of American education and are figures through which the culture works out questions of independence and authority, production and reproduction of knowledge, and the relationship of the citizen to society.

The first drafts often make quick work of Freire. We asked one of our students how he was able to sum up in three tidy pages everything Freire said. He replied, "It was easy. I left out everything I didn't understand and worked with what I did." This is a familiar strategy, one that is reinforced by teachers who have students read for "gist." Another strategy for revision is to have students go back to the sections of Freire's essay that they *didn't* understand, or couldn't easily control, and to see how they might work those sections into what they have written. This is an opportunity for a dialogue with Freire — not a debate, but a chance to put his words on the page and to say, in effect, "Here is what I think you are saying." This revision will put pressure on students' resources for including quotations and representing and working on text. It makes a big difference, for example, whether a student uses Freire to conclude a point or uses Freire's language as material to work on. These different approaches to Freire provide handy illustrations for a discussion of problem-posing education.

2. This writing assignment would follow nicely from two or three class sessions devoted to a discussion of the first of the "Questions for a Second Reading." You might also consider using the third question as part of prewriting discussions.

Students will have to imagine themselves as teachers determined to adapt Freire's practices to a class working with his essay. They'll have to enact problem-solving through a writing assignment or a set of discussion questions, guidelines, or instructions for this essay. You might consider asking them to examine the questions and assignments in the book to see which, if any, they think fit Freire's notions of problem-solving tasks. They'll need to engage in some discussion of the questions and assignments to say why the tasks do or do not reflect Freire's thinking about problem-solving, and this could help them begin to conceptualize criteria for translating his theory into learning tasks. Once they've participated in these discussions, they'll be ready to write their problem-solving tasks. Then they'll have to complete their own assignments. You might consider a follow-up discussion on what students thought their tasks were asking of them. From there, they could go on to revise their tasks.

MAKING CONNECTIONS (p. 272)

1. Students need to use one of the essays in the book as a starting point for posing a Freirian problem. Then they need to begin working on that problem, responding to it in writing. It's difficult to say ahead of time which essays or stories will trigger students' thinking about a genuine problem that interests and involves them. You might go through the text table of contents and comment on the essays and stories with an eye toward presenting their subjects or issues so students can pinpoint essays to consider. The introductions to each selection will give you a sense of what each one touches on.

Once students have decided on an essay or story to use as a starting point, they'll need to pose a problem or question. It will probably be one that is raised by the selection, but they should understand that the problem can extend far beyond the selection itself. For example, if students were working on Rich's essay "When We Dead Awaken: Writing as Re-Vision," they might raise questions about what a famous poet's account of her position within a patriarchal culture might have to do with their position as students in a writing class or as participants in the general culture. In what ways might they be said to be "drenched in assumptions" they cannot easily understand? What does this have to do with revision or the writing of the past, both familiar concepts, neither appearing to have anything to do with sexual politics nor, in Rich's terms, survival? It is possible to read Rich's essay as though it were not addressed to students, as though it could not make contact with their lives. To pose the essay as a problem means finding, even mechanically at first, such possible connections. "How might I use this phrase in a sentence or paragraph about myself, a sentence, or a paragraph I believed in?"

These become difficult questions, to be sure, but they can lead students to imagine genuine problems. They can bring to consciousness strong, often unspoken experiences. They can make the usual, familiar language seem suddenly fraught with danger or previously unthought-of implications. They can lead writers to be smarter about themselves and the language they use to represent their world.

When students have posed their problems, you might consider conducting two or three class discussions to examine those problems so students can revise them before they write. They'll have to present their problems, including brief summaries of the selections they have worked from, and they'll need to explain why, in Freire's terms, their problems are Freirian. Consider using questions about how this writing differs from what they are accustomed to doing. Another assignment might ask them to look back on the essays they wrote in response to their own problems or questions.

2. Students will have to have read Rodriguez's essay and to have spent some time discussing it, perhaps in response to the "Questions for a Second Reading," before they can write this imagined dialogue between Freire and Rodriguez. You might suggest that they begin by imagining questions Freire and Rodriguez might ask each other. They could also reread the Rodriguez selection and note passages or moments that they think Freire would comment on, and they can do the same for the Freire selection by rereading from Rodriguez's point of view. It's important for the dialogue that students avoid turning this into a debate where someone challenges someone. The stance should be conversational — two people from different backgrounds and different sets of beliefs talking with each other about education. They ask questions and comment on things each has said in the essays, and try their best to answer and further explain their comments.

SIMON FRITH

The Voice (p. 276)

We have followed Simon Frith's work for many years and we have often considered his essays and chapters for *Ways of Reading*. He brings to contemporary music, rock in particular, an unusual combination of scholarship and theory, enthusiasm and passion. As we say in the headnote, Frith is a serious scholar; he is also a serious fan. And he is not only a fan, he is a regular reviewer and an occasional concert promoter. It seems like he listens to everything and remembers everything he hears.

He is among the most important cultural critics working today. We met him almost fifteen years ago at a remarkable conference that brought a number of British scholars and writers to our campus, including Frith, Stephen Heath, and Salman Rushdie. We were eager, then, to read *Performing Rites* when it was published in 1996. One difficulty with cultural criticism (or, one difficulty bringing it into a textbook) is that it deals with particular cultural materials (artists, songs, performances) that are quickly dated. And the theoretical discussions are often incredibly dense. *Performing Rites* is extremely readable; it situates contemporary performance in a history of music, musical performance, and reception; and it is organized by topic (rather than artist, period, or genre). It might be interesting to have a general sense of the book. It is organized in three sections. The first, "Music Talk," is about value and the language (and necessity) of criticism. The second, "On Music Itself," is organized by topics: Sounds, Rhythm, Songs as Texts, Voice, Performance, and Technology. The final section, "Why Music Matters," returns to an argument for the function of criticism at the present time and lays out the terms of a "popular aesthetic," a way of valuing popular music (and popular culture).

The chapter we have chosen, "The Voice," is a wonderful demonstration of critical scholarship, to our minds an ideal introduction for students to how and why popular culture can become the subject of serious work, how writing about pop music might be something an interesting adult could do for a living. In the best tradition of criticism, Frith takes something that seems simple and obvious, the presence of "voice" in song, and renders it complex and problematic, not so simple at all. And the language of analysis is drawn from the traditions of rhetorical analysis — that is, the discussion of "voice" (and style and rhetoric) in popular music can serve discussions of voice, style, and rhetoric in writing. Frith begins, for example, by making a careful distinction between voice as "gesture" and voice as "utterance" — the standard distinction in a writing class where students are asked to consider not only what the language says but what it does. Later, in talking about voice as "person" and as "character," he is making another distinction fundamental to the writing class, the distinction between the writer and the "I" on the page.

The chapter announces its organization at the very beginning. Frith says, "What makes the voice so interesting is that it makes meaning in these two ways simultaneously [as gesture and utterance]." And he says, "We have, therefore, to approach the voice under four headings: *as a musical instrument; as a body; as a person; and as a character.*" The organizing principles become subtle as the chapter unfolds. It is not written in textbook style, in other words, since the categories merge and become problematic; they are not simple or fixed terms. It is useful, we've found, in teaching this essay to help students to see how it is organized, or to return to these four headings and to see what he attempts to do under each.

The other thing both significant and odd about the chapter is that it talks at length about a subject that is always absent — voices. This will be troubling to students, partly because it makes the essay seem abstract, partly because Frith will allude to some voices that are unfamiliar, and partly because music television has prepared them to expect to hear the text under consideration. In response to this concern (or in advance of it), it is important for students to understand the kind of work Frith is doing. While he is definitely interested in (a fan of) specific artists, like Sinead O'Connor or Billie Holiday, he is not trying to give us direct access to their voices; he is not promoting them, he is thinking analytically about the category of voice in the act of listening; he is promoting critical inquiry and a careful discussion of terms. This is not MTV-on-the-page, in other words. The argument he makes, in fact, is that we can never have direct access to these voices, voice is always something that we produce as listeners, a production based on experience, habit, and knowledge; and he argues that the more we understand about the role we play the better we can become as listeners and the better we can become at articulating the sources and terms of our pleasure — better to argue not only in the hallways but in the classroom.

Still, it can help to hear the voices. Frith assumes a reader with a better musical memory and a wider range of listening experiences than is usual, normal, or (perhaps) even possible. The chapter defines, then, its own necessary course of study. (Like much good writing, this is a chapter one has to live up to and not just receive.) Accordingly, we have set assignments that ask students to collect recordings carefully noted in the "works cited" page and to bring in recordings that they can add to Frith's collection. It can be useful as an opening gesture for you to bring to class songs recorded by Bing Crosby, Frank Sinatra, Bob Dylan, Billie Holiday, and Barbra Streisand. These singers figure prominently in the opening discussion and it is likely that students may not be familiar with all of them.

QUESTIONS FOR A SECOND READING (p. 298)

1. This question invites students to chart Frith's argument as it is counterintuitive. He starts (and we hope students can see this as playful), by defining the obvious position as "stupid." A move like this both names us as readers and allows us to want to occupy a different space, one whose terms and understandings he will help to provide.

The essay is long enough and dense enough that it can be useful for students to pre-pare some kind of outline or chart or organized set of notes that traces the primary line of argument. As we said earlier, this can be organized under the four headings provided at the beginning of the essay. Voice as *"a musical instrument; as a body; as a person;* and *as a character."*

2. This question points to the key distinction Frith draws between classical and pop music. The classical performer disappears behind the work; the pop performer "draws atten-tion to performance itself, to the *relationship* between the performer and the work." It is the relationship that interests Frith. Our goal here is to make this distinction a key to the chapter and to invite students to read back over the text to see where and how this distinction is articulated throughout the discussion.

3. As we said in the introduction above, the absence of recordings as examples is both inevitable and characteristic in the work Frith does. It is important for students to understand this (that it is not just a failure of print technology that makes the page silent). Still, Frith assumes that his readers will have heard and remembered at least some of the examples he cites (citations carefully indicated in the endnotes). This ques-tion asks students (perhaps most profitably in groups) to track down his sources, to bring recorded examples to class, and to be prepared to present them as a way of using and deploying Frith's key terms and as a way of experimenting with Frith's method and style of presentation. You will find that these provide lively and useful exercises in class.

4. We wanted to provide some sense of Frith's conclusion. "The Voice" chapter moves toward a conclusion but it does not articulate one. (It is a chapter, after all, and in service of the larger structure of the book.) The question asks students to read the paragraph (and it might be useful to have some discussion in class) and then to re-read, thinking about where and how the discussion of voice is leading to these conclu-sions (which seem importantly utopian to us, and which will most likely seem odd to students):

> It follows that an identity is always already an ideal, what we would like to be, not what we are. In taking pleasure from black or gay or female music I don't thus identify as black or gay or female (I don't actually experience these sounds as "black music" or "gay music" or "women's voices") but, rather, participate in imagined forms of democracy and desire, imagined forms of the social and the sexual. And what makes music special in this familiar cultural process is that musical identity is both fantastic — idealizing not just oneself but also the social world one inhabits — and real: it is enacted in activity. Music making and music listening, that is to say, are bodily matters; they involve what one might call *social movements*. In this respect, musical pleasure is not derived from fantasy–it is not mediated by daydreams — but is experience directly: music gives us a real experience of what the ideal could be.

The question also invites students to engage with this argument. We focused on two elements: the statement that "music gives us a real experience of what the ideal could be," and a view of the ideal as imagined forms of democracy and desire (the social and the sexual).

ASSIGNMENTS FOR WRITING (p. 300)

1. The first writing assignment begins with an exercise. It invites students to take the models presented in the opening pages of the chapter and to write their own descrip-tions of voice in performance, working with an example that is close to them, that they know well and care about. The task is to put onto the page something that is not

writing. (In this sense, the problem falls into the range of W. J. T. Mitchell's concerns in "The Photographic Essay: Four Case Studies.")

We suggest that the assignment involve draft and revision. If this is possible, the first draft (or drafts) would be the production of the exercises — descriptions of voice in the manner of Sandow, Day, Gould, and Frith. The revision would be to bring these examples to a discussion of Frith's project in "The Voice." This would involve summary and paraphrase and then (or also) a move from Frith to a consideration of the student's examples and how they extend, engage, or modify his argument.

2–3. Both assignments begin with the four "headings" Frith uses to organize his approach to voice: *as a musical instrument*; as *a body*; as *a person*; and as *a character*. The assignment assumes that students have a sense of how these terms work for Frith. If you use this assignment, it would be useful to work in advance of the writing along the lines suggested in the first of the "Questions for a Second Reading." Assignment 2 asks students to use Frith's terms to examine an example of their own, one that is close to them and that they care about. And they are asked to return from this discussion to Frith's argument, to see how their work extends, engages, or modifies what Frith has to say. Assignment 3 takes this frame for analysis and applies it to writing rather than to musical performance. The one immediate formal difference will be the need to use block quotation. In writing about writing (in presenting a close reading), writers have the advantage of being able to work the primary text into their own texts. The project, however, remains the same in both. Apply Frith's method to a new set of examples, using that project to authorize the student as expert so that he or she can speak back to or alongside of "The Voice."

4. This is more specifically a summary assignment. Students are asked to occupy the position that is *not* naive (that is, the position beyond "stupid") and to write from that position for a naive audience, an audience who knows something about music but hasn't read Frith. As in the case above, students are asked to bring their own examples and positions to the discussion. The summary, paraphrase, and quotation from "The Voice" are meant to be strategic, to get Frith out on the table so that another writer can have something to say as well. Here, that something is imagined as extension, dialogue, qualification, homage, or rebuttal. This list certainly does not exhaust the range of responses.

5. This assignment takes one of the more striking and conceptually difficult ideas in the essay, the idea of embodying voice, and asks students to work with it. It would certainly be useful to bring the final "Question for a Second Reading" into play with this "Assignment for Writing", since the "conclusion" presented there turns again to the question of the body and, in a surprising turn, from "bodily matters" to "social movements." The assignment situates students first as a generous reader, trying to represent Frith's sense of this — of voice embodied and what is at stake; it then asks them how and why and if this makes sense to them. Students most likely will try to make experiential sense ("I don't do that when I talk on the phone"). They should be invited to think of this conceptually and, following Frith, in terms of fantasy. The issue is not "Do you do this?" but "Can you imagine this and can you imagine its consequences?"

MAKING CONNECTIONS (p. 302)

1. This connection is a natural. Frith's work is shaped by the traditions of British cultural study, which were shaped by the Frankfurt school. Students do not need to have the history or to know the theory in order to work on this assignment. Good work can be done trying to think through the differences between Benjamin and Frith and to think them through in detail (thinking about the differences in time and place, thinking about the differences in film and music, thinking about the different positions the two writers take on popular culture and its audiences).

Adorno is the representative Frankfurt figure for Frith. Here are some sections of a 1991 article in *Diacritics* (Winter 1991, 102–15) where Frith thinks through his objections for the Frankfurt representation of the consumer. The first begins with a discussion reproduced in "The Voice":

> In universities, then, just as in high schools, there is still a split between what Frank Kogan describes as the discourse of the classroom (with its focus on a subject matter) and the discourse of the hallway (with its focus on one's feelings about a subject matter). In this respect (and despite first impressions) academic approaches to popular culture still derive from the mass cultural critiques of the 1930s and 1940s, particularly from the Marxist critique of contemporary popular culture in terms of the production and circulation of commodities. For the Frankfurt School, analyzing the organization of mass production on the one hand, and the psychology of mass consumption on the other, the value issue was, in a sense straightforward — if it's popular it must be bad! — and Adorno and his colleagues developed a number of concepts (such as standardization) to show why this must be so.

He continues,

> In the cultural studies tradition with which I'm most familiar, British subcultural theory, this reworking [to look for the redeeming features of commodity culture in the act of consumption] took on the particular form of identifying certain social groups with what we might call "positive mass consumption" (which became — and remains — the pithiest academic definition of "popular" culture). The value of cultural goods could therefore be equated with the value of the groups consuming them — youth, the working class, women, and so forth.

And finally,

> It is hard to avoid the conclusion that the more celebratory the populist study, the more patronizing its tone, an effect, I think, of the explicit populist determination to deny (or reverse) the usual high/low cultural hierarchy. If one strand of the mass cultural critique was an indictment of low culture from the perspective of high art (as was obviously the case for Adorno, for example), then to assert the value of the popular is also, certainly, to query the superiority of high culture. Most populist writers, though, draw the wrong conclusion; what needs challenging is not the notion of the superior, but the claim that it is the exclusive property of the "high."

In the end, Frith wants to maintain the distinction between high and low but to deny that it is distributed along lines of class or defined by the traditions of high culture. Popular music, he argues, *can* contain serious pleasure; distinctions of value belong not just to the bourgeoisie but to all consumers; and the goal of academic criticism should be to improve the ways we (all of us) talk about and think about the cultural materials we value.

2. The second "Making Connections" question is a version of the third "Assignment for Writing" (see above), although it specifies Wideman or Anzaldúa as the authors whose texts can provide a case study of "voice" in writing. What we said earlier still holds. Students can organize the discussion under the four headings provided in the text — voice as instrument, as body, as person, and as character. They will need to work out equivalences for "instrument" and "body." And they will need to work closely with examples, most often from extended block quotations. In writing about writing (in presenting a close reading), writers have the advantage of being able to work the primary text into their texts. The project is to apply Frith's method to a new set of ex-

amples, using that project to authorize the student as expert so that he or she can speak back to or alongside of "The Voice."

3. This is probably the most difficult of the three "Connections" assignments. This one asks students to use W. J. T. Mitchell and his discussion of the relationship between text and image in the traditions of the photographic essay ("The Photographic Essay: Four Case Studies") in order to think about the practical and theoretical problems of writing about music and performance.

    In this assignment (which can usefully be linked to the first "Assignment for Writing,") students are asked to write about voice following the models provided in Frith's chapter: Sandow, Day, Gould, and Frith. They are asked to use the models presented in the opening pages of the chapter and to write their own descriptions of voice in performance, working with an example that is close to them, that they know well and care about. The task is to put onto the page something that is not writing (hence the connection with Mitchell). The exercise of writing about voice can give students a sense of the problem in practice (of what it looks like on the page and feels like at the ends of one's fingers) that they can take to their reading of Mitchell.

CLIFFORD GEERTZ

Deep Play: Notes on the Balinese Cockfight (p. 305)

"Deep Play" is a brilliant performance and a rare example of the potential for wit and playfulness in academic writing. Geertz speaks in different voices and runs through a range of styles as he demonstrates the methods by which an anthropologist tries to represent and understand his subject.

While it will be hard for students to get a fix on Geertz and what he is doing, it is not a difficult essay to read until the final two sections (beginning with "Feathers, Blood, Crowds, and Money"). Part of the difficulty here is that Geertz suddenly begins talking about literature and literary criticism, and he does so as if he hasn't changed subjects at all. The last two sections are truly difficult — conceptually difficult. We have read them many, many times and, while we have found ways of speaking about what we have read, we wouldn't say for a minute that we are confident that we have "got it" or exhausted those pages. Students need to know that reading presents difficulties that one can only respect or work on, difficulties that one can't resolve. These difficulties are no reason for shame or silence.

The best way to teach the essay might be to lead up to, even dramatize, the turn in the final two sections. We have taught classes where we conscientiously avoided the last two sections until late in the lesson. And our interest in the opening sections, beyond the opening questions that try to chart out the argument — what does Geertz see? what does he say about what he sees? — is directed toward the stylistic differences in the various sections. We are interested in having students consider how a way of writing could be said to represent a method, a way of seeing and understanding. The narrative in "The Raid," the punning and wordplay in "Of Cocks and Men," the careful exposition in "Odds and Even Money," the numbered list in "Playing with Fire" — all represent different ways of approaching or shaping information. All say something about Geertz's skill and method as an observer. All give us a different view of the cockfight. We want our students to sense the various textures in the essay, and to speculate on why Geertz would have made use of them. It is only after we have had such discussions, or after students have written about these problems, that we are willing to invite students to make what they can of the final two sections.

The essay is drawn from a special issue of *Daedalus* (vol. 101, 1972). In the preface, the editor speaks about the origins of the essay and includes a letter from Geertz and Paul de Man inviting scholars to a conference on the "Systematic Study of Meaningful Forms." "Deep Play" accompanied the letter. The full text of the preface follows.

Stephen R. Graubard
Preface to the Issue "Myth, Symbol and Culture"

As many readers of *Daedalus* are aware, almost all issues of the journal depend on a series of closed conferences where authors discuss their draft essays with interested critics. Such conferences generally follow smaller meetings where the issue is planned. On occasion, the deliberations of the planning group persuade the Editors and planners that the time is not propitious for a particular subject to be treated in *Daedalus*, and that there is some advantage in not proceeding. More frequently, the planning committee's decision is to go ahead and to ask for papers from authors who have an obvious interest in the subject.

This issue of *Daedalus* has a history that is worth telling. It began with the suggestion from Clifford Geertz, now at the Institute for Advanced Study at Princeton, and Paul de Man, now of Yale University, that we consider inviting scholars from many disciplines, but principally from anthropology and literature, to discuss the possibility of a *Daedalus* issue on what they called the "Systematic Study of Meaningful Forms." Invitations went out to twelve scholars, both in this country and abroad, for a conference that was to meet in Paris. The planning sessions persuaded all of us that the problems of interdisciplinary discourse are even more substantial than is generally admitted. Disciplines have languages that are specific to themselves, it is not always easy for a scholar in one discipline to appreciate the significance of the intervention of a scholar who comes from a quite different field. More than that, the relations between the particular disciplines are not always apparent, even after days of intensive discussion.

In this instance, the subject itself was so intrinsically difficult that a decision to abandon our original intention, and not go forward with plans for a *Daedalus* issue, would have been entirely understandable. We were dissuaded from that course by three considerations. first, the letter of invitation to participants in the planning meeting seemed to many of us a document of major import; second, though the conference itself had not seen any single theme emerge, individual interventions at the meeting had aroused very substantial interest; finally, one of the conveners, Clifford Geertz, had been moved by the meeting to write more fully on a theme he had treated in one of his lengthy conference interventions.

The Editors were persuaded that there were good reasons for going forward. Clifford Geertz's paper, "Deep Play: Notes on the Balinese Cockfight," together with an invitation to write, went to scholars in widely separated disciplines. They were invited to write on texts or themes that had significance for them. The results of their efforts are apparent in this issue.

We believe that there may be some purpose in reproducing the original letter of invitation that went to members of the planning group. Professors Geertz and de Man wrote as follows:

> We write to tell you about a conference that the American Academy of Arts and Sciences, through its journal *Daedalus*, proposes to hold in Paris on October 29, 30, and 31, 1970. We hope very much that your schedule will permit you to attend this meeting. Its purpose is to plan an issue of *Daedalus* on a theme whose importance is increasingly recognized. The idea for the conference and the *Daedalus* issue arose out of a shared feeling that the question of the relationship between the social sciences and the humanities is often approached in the wrong way.

General efforts to connect the work of scholars we take to be occupied with "The Humanities" with those we take to be occupied with "The Social Sciences" tend to adopt a "two cultures" sort of formulation. The "relations" between humanistic and social scientific methods, outlooks, concerns, ambitions, and achievements are described in a rather external fashion, as though two wary sovereign powers were drawing up a treaty of mutual coexistence in order to allow a certain level of carefully regulated commerce between them while guaranteeing their mutual autonomy and right to live their separate lives. Thus one gets discussions, whether or not they are actually called such, of "The Implications (Impact, Convergence, Irrelevance...) of Structuralism (Evolutionism, Gestalt Psychology, Generative Grammar, Psychoanalysis...) for History (Literary Criticism, Musicology, Law, Philosophy...)" and so on. (The Sciences being masculine and the Humanities feminine, the causal arrow is only rarely pointed in the other direction.) Some of these discussions have their uses, if only as statements of a larger faith — or, in some cases, lack of it; but they tend not to contribute much, or at least as much as the grandness of their conception would seem to promise, to the specific development of the fields of study thus "related." They are, a few exceptions aside, part only of parascholarship, public declarations for public occasions which, like Auden's "poetry," make nothing happen.

Yet, in the face of all of this, the conviction continues to grow among leading figures in the Humanities and the Social Sciences that, as the cliché goes, "they have something to offer one another." The problem is how to effect the offering, reasonably unburnt.

It is our assumption that this will best be done not by general, programmatic considerations of how the humanities, or some corner of them, and the social sciences, or some corner of them, are "related" to one another, or even of what overall presuppositions they share in common, nor again of their supposedly complementary or contradictory roles in the functioning of modern culture. Rather, it will be done, if it is done at all, when some of the more creative people in specific disciplines discover that they are in fact working, from their contrasting methods, on quite similar problems or ranges of problems.

It is when two (or more) scholars realize that, for all the differences between them, they are attacking highly similar issues, trying to solve closely related puzzles, that communication between them begins to look like a practical policy rather than an academic piety. Specific commonalities of intellectual interest make scholarly interchange possible and useful; and the creation of such interchange demands, and indeed consists in, the discovery and exploitation of such commonalities. It is the coincident perception by historians concerned with the authorship of the Federalist papers and by statisticians concerned with Bayesian interpretations of probability theory that they are confronted with the same kind of problem — how to evaluate "subjective" judgments — which causes them to become genuinely interested in one another. Academic ideologies celebrating the unity of knowledge, decrying the evils of specialization, or dissolving substantive differences into rhetorical agreements do not achieve the same objectives.

Clearly, such commonalities of concern among otherwise discrete disciplines cannot be formulated without prior inquiry. Looking both at the work of our own fields, literary criticism and cultural anthropology, and at that of fields more or less adjacent to them, it seems to us that one such commonality is what might be called — or, when we actually come to look into it, might not — "the systematic study of meaningful forms."

There are a lot of elastic and ill-used words crowded into this little formula — only the article and the preposition seem straightforward — but that it points, in its awkward and preliminary way, to a general area in which "humanists" and "social scientists" (even, in a few cases, some we call natural scientists) are simultaneously engaged in study is beyond much doubt. In the social sciences, structuralist anthropology, sociolinguistics, cognitive psychology, and phenomenological sociology, merely to list a few labels, all represent a sharp turn toward a concern with the analysis of meaningful forms, whether they be South American Indian myths, urban speech styles, children's categorical systems, or the taken-for-granted assumptions of everyday life. In the humanities, where the study of meaningful structures has been a traditional concern, recent developments in the philosophy of language and in the analysis of artistic and literary forms all show a markedly heightened awareness of the need for devising ways of coping more effectively with such structures.

What, dimly perceived, these assorted enterprises seem to have in common is a conviction that meaningful forms, whether they be African passage rites, nineteenth-century novels, revolutionary ideologies, grammatical paradigms, scientific theories, English landscape paintings, or the ways in which moral judgments are phrased, have as good a claim to public existence as horses, stones, and trees, and are therefore as susceptible to objective investigation and systematic analysis as these apparently harder realities.

Everything from modern logic, computer technology, and cybernetics at one extreme to phenomenological criticism, psychohistory, and ordinary language philosophy at the other has conspired to undermine the notion that meaning is so radically "in the head," so deeply subjective, that it is incapable of being firmly grasped, much less analyzed. It may be supremely difficult to deal with such structures of meaning but they are neither a miracle nor a mirage. Indeed, constructing concepts and methods to deal with them and to produce generalizations about them is the primary intellectual task now facing those humanists and social scientists not content merely to exercise habitual skills. The surge of interest in "myth," "fiction," "archetype," "semantics," "systems of relevance," "language games," and so on is but the symptom that this transformation in viewpoint has in fact taken place, and — from the very multiplicity of the terms — that it has taken place in intellectual contexts much more isolated from one another than the commonality of their concerns would warrant.

Considerations such as these have led us, in collaboration with Professor Stephen Graubard, editor of *Daedalus*, to summon a small group to Paris in late October. Our hope is that some of the commonality of concern that undoubtedly exists may be concretely expressed and that this may have, as one of its effects, a reduction of the mutual isolation that is so frequently noted.

The focus of this conference will not be on a general discussion of the study of meaning, nor on the virtues of interdisciplinary communication, but on specific examples of such study, so cast that their arguments and conclusions, and particularly the conceptual foundations upon which they rest, may be accessible to others working toward similar ends in different ways. The conference will include a variety of scholars from various of the social sciences and humanistic disciplines (and possibly some from the natural sciences as well), actively working, in one way or another, on the systematic analysis of meaningful forms, and especially on the theoretical bases for such analysis. As we do not envisage a generalized discussion of "the meaning of meaning," so also we do not envisage a set of particular empirical studies presented crystalline for admiration, but rather the exemplification and explication of a range of theoretical approaches to our topic on the part of people not ordinarily in one another's company. In such a way, not only should the subject of the conference be advanced, but the usefulness of the work of humanists and social scientists for one another be demonstrated rather than merely debated or proclaimed.

This issue of *Daedalus* is, at best, a first tentative step toward realizing certain of the objectives outlined in this letter. Our gratitude to Professors Clifford Geertz and Paul de Man is very real. They have done much to make this issue possible. We wish also to express our deep appreciation to the Ford Foundation for the grant it has made to the Academy to support interdisciplinary study.

QUESTIONS FOR A SECOND READING (p. 339)

1. The first of these questions directs students to think about Geertz's stated objective as they reread the essay. It is possible to assume that all of the exposition is devoted to a demonstration of what the cockfight says, its commentary upon Balinese life. If that is the case, then one can reread to get a fuller sense of that story, including a fuller sense of the key details and episodes. When Geertz says that the cockfights don't reinforce the patterns of Balinese life but comment on them, he is also arguing with his colleagues. Students don't need to know all the details of that argument (we don't), but they can feel the force of the distinction he is making and his insistence that observed behavior be treated as text.

2. This question directs students to the stylistic differences in the various subsections. We spoke earlier about why these have been important in our teaching. It is important not only to invite students to notice the differences but to give them a way of talking about what the differences represent, particularly in a project of observation, interpretation, and report.

3. This question is an invitation to students to read against the grain of Geertz's essay. Each of the sections in "Deep Play" could be said to reveal its own ideological apparatus. In the first section, for example, both Geertz's wife and the Balinese are turned quickly into cartoon figures to serve a narrative designed to establish Geertz's position as the hero of the story and to provide his authority as an insider, as someone who can know and understand the natives. The political and historical counterpoint to this happy story intrudes in parentheses: "As always, kinesthetically minded and, even when fleeing for their lives (or, as happened eight years later, surrendering them), the world's most poised people, they gleefully mimicked, also over and over . . .," and so on. This could be read as the classic case of the imperial imagination. And the second section opens with a figure familiar to academic writing: The scholar looks over the literature, sees something that has been rarely noticed — the cockfight — and proceeds to show that what appears to be the case is not what is really happening at all. (For extended versions of this critique of Geertz and of ethnography, see the essays by Mary Louise Pratt and Vincent Crapanzano in *Writing Culture: The Poetics and Politics of Ethnography,* edited by James Clifford and George E. Marcus.)

We've taught this essay several times, and the argument we inevitably hear, whether among the staff or in the classroom, is over whether we've "caught" Geertz in making this critique, whether we've found the seams of his text that he is blind to. The counterargument goes something like this: Geertz's text offers its seams to a reader; the reason it is broken into pieces and written in different styles, the reason it is self-conscious and self-consciously playful, is that Geertz is showing the necessary limits and conditions of ethnography. The limits of the discourse are part of the subject of the essay. The parenthetical allusion to a different, historical narrative — shifting from a comic story to a story of political violence — is not a slip but a strategy. Part of the argument of the essay, in other words, is that the work is never pure, that understanding the Balinese means translating their lives into our terms, talking inevitably about Shakespeare, Dickens, or Aristotle.

In teaching the essay, we feel it is important for students to read generously before asking them to try to question the texts in these terms. It is too easy for students to dismiss the essay by saying that it is *just* a story of a white man asserting his dominance over the Third World. That can become a way of not reading. At the same time, it would be irresponsible to finesse these questions altogether. For us this is a matter of timing. While students are working on this essay, there comes a point at which we encourage these questions. If they don't emerge, we raise them ourselves, usually by returning to the opening section, which students say is the easiest and most fun to read. We use it as a way of talking about its familiarity, then about what the familiar story might represent.

4. The hardest of the four questions, this one invites students to imagine a specialized audience and its methods, issues, and concerns. Geertz is not just offering information on cockfights, and he is not just demonstrating, by his own performance, the ways an anthropologist goes about his business; rather, he is making a point to his colleagues in the social sciences. He is arguing that they need to think of themselves also as literary critics. Students can't master this argument — nor can we — but if they begin to sense its outlines, they can use the essay as a way of imagining not only the complex purposes of academic writing but also the different conventions and assumptions of the academic disciplines.

ASSIGNMENTS FOR WRITING (p. 340)

1. In the general discussion and in the second of the "Questions for a Second Reading," we alluded to stylistic differences in the subsections of the essay. Since the assignment is conceptually difficult, it is helpful for students to know that they themselves can organize their papers in terms of seven subsections. The eighth subsection is the one where they stand back and take stock of what they have done in the first seven. This is a difficult assignment and deserves time for revision, particularly if students have the opportunity to see at least some of the first drafts of their colleagues. They will learn much by seeing what others have noticed in Geertz's sentences, and in hearing what others have to say about what they noticed. This assignment will work best, however, if students write their first draft before the subject becomes an issue for general discussion. This is not to say that there should be *no* prior discussion. Students generally need to learn how to talk about sentences in just these ways. It might be best to have a general discussion of one of the subsections, and then to let students see what they can do with the rest, before returning again to open discussion.

2. This has been a successful assignment for us. It asks students to demonstrate their reading of Geertz's method by putting it to work on characteristic scenes from their own surroundings. Geertz's method can be represented by his phrase "saying something of something" — an event can do this. The cockfights are a story the Balinese tell themselves about themselves. Similarly, American teenagers walk around shopping malls, doing peculiar but characteristic things. College students decorate dorm rooms in peculiar but characteristic ways. To begin to carry out a Geertzian project, we might say then that in each case these are stories they are telling themselves about themselves. Such events say something about something else. The question is what. But what is being said? And about what? What are these stories? What are their key features? How, as a writer, might one interpret them? What are these people telling themselves about themselves? It is important for college students, if they write on college students, to insist on their separateness, to speak of *them*, not *us*. For the exercise, it is important that students act as though they are interpreting someone else's story and not their own.

The purpose of the assignment is to turn students to their own immediate culture and to invite them to imagine and carry out a Geertzian project. It is important that they act like anthropologists — that they work from recorded observations, not just from memory, which leads students inevitably to the commonplace and clichéd and deprives them of the very details that can make their work rich and interesting.

3. Following from the third of the "Questions for a Second Reading," this writing assignment asks students to write up a reading that runs against the grain of Geertz's essay. For a full discussion of that reading, see the entry for Question 3 above. While we present the assignment here as an independent one, we have often used it as a question to guide revisions of the first assignment. If students begin with this essay, it will be important to discuss it before students write. They will need to hear and imagine an argument against Geertz, at least in part. Students are asked to imagine a position either for or against that contrary reading.

MAKING CONNECTIONS (p. 341)

1. Because he writes about Bali, a distant and exotic place, Geertz is too unquestioningly an expert for most student readers. He is given a kind of intellectual authority ("the man's been there, he's suffered for his wisdom, he knows the real story") that, at least as we read the essay, he neither invites nor deserves. This assignment was designed to put Geertz (as someone who sees, interprets and records) into a more familiar context, one where students will feel some knowledge and authority of their own. The assignment asks for a comparison with Bordo, Tompkins, or Griffin. We are usually hesitant to make comparison-and-contrast assignments, since the acts of comparing and contrasting too easily become ends in themselves. Here, we think, the comparison provides the necessary starting point for an interesting project — a reflection on the possibilities and limitations of these authors' methods of interpretation.

    When we have used this assignment, we have been particularly interested in turning students' attention to methods. How does Geertz get his information? How does he, as a writer, work on it? These questions become easier when Geertz is seen next to (or through) Bordo, Tompkins, or Griffin, whose methods are more easily imagined by students (in a sense, they live in the same world of reference for the Bordo and Tompkins selections, and Griffin's are unusually visible). In addition, even though Geertz sets out to write about the act of interpretation, his discussion is difficult and illusive compared to those of Bordo, Tompkins, and Griffin.

    A word of warning: Our students were quick to argue that Bordo is "biased" or dogmatic, that she begins with arguments that predetermine what she will find to say about the material she studies. The deck is stacked, in other words, even though they tend to agree with her position. With Griffin, they want to give her work with the effects of childhood experiences enormous weight, so that they reduce her to a simple methodology in which she becomes a stick figure devoted to proving that childhood experiences are everything, when, in fact, she seems to purposely construct this position so that she can place other influences (history, circumstance, human will, and so on) in relation to the effects of childhoods on adult lives. By comparison, students found Geertz to be "open," "receptive," "objective," less of an ideologue. Our goal was to use the assignment — and Geertz — to question the notion of "objectivity" and the scholarly production of scientific truth. We might have begun with the third assignment in "Assignments for Writing" before turning to this comparison. As it was, we needed to make the revision assignment one that questioned the terms of (or the reading in) the first draft. Actually, we often engage in this process in revision assignments. The difficulty is that it produces a second draft that is, at least in conventional terms, no more "finished" than the first.

2. In the opening section of "The Loss of the Creature," Percy talks about the strategies one might use in order to recover the Grand Canyon from the "preformed symbolic complex," from those texts and expectations that make it something else. This assignment asks students to consider Geertz and his account of this experience in Bali, including his professional interpretation of the cockfight, as one of Percy's representative anecdotes. They are to work out a Percian reading of "Deep Play." Percy tells the story

of tourists in Paris, in Mexico, and at the Grand Canyon. What might he do with the story of Geertz in Bali? Has Geertz solved the problem that Percy charts in his essay?

As a variation on this assignment, you might ask students, once they have completed their essays, to write Geertz's response to Percy. What would Geertz have to say to Percy about his account of Geertz's work? The two essays represent a complex and difficult conversation about the relationship between method and understanding. While it would be dizzying for students to consider this debate in the abstract, it can be nicely represented in terms of a dialogue between these two characters. In a further essay students might be invited to bring their own voices into the conversation — to write a paper in which they identify the issues that matter to them in this conversation between Geertz and Percy, and in which they talk about why these issues matter to them.

SUSAN GRIFFIN
Our Secret (p. 345)

Our students were overwhelmed, knocked out, or as they said, "blown away" by this selection. Its methods are unusual, to be sure, and our students had never read anything like it, and as much as Griffin's methods took them by surprise, so did her passion and commitment to her subjects. And our students saw many subjects, all interconnected in this surprising reading: the effects of childhood upbringing on adult behaviors, the relations of violence to cultural patterns, the cultural patterns — like childhood habits — that seem related to Nazi hatreds, the effects of familial and national secrets, the Nazi manipulations of science and media, the intertwining of personal and cultural habits, and so on. This is a rich and deep selection and the more we worked with it in discussions and through writings, the more its subjects, its layers, and its connections became visible to us. One of the joys of working with this selection was our continual discoveries of the connections between the personal and the cultural with and through it.

Most of our students weren't accustomed to reading a selection as long as this, so we approached it by first asking them to read four or five pages in class. We then conducted a discussion of the reading, touching on Griffin's methods and where students saw connections between the various sections. We encouraged them to speculate about the connections, for example, between cell chemistry and rocketry, as Griffin lays them out in the opening pages, so that students could become somewhat familiar with the way Griffin asks readers to read between the sections and subjects to make connections that she does not explicitly bring forward. It's important, we think, that students be encouraged to find their own point of organization or reference when they read to make connections between the essay's fragments. Some will take secrets, fascism, Himmler, childhood, or sexuality as their point of departure. No single point is the "right" one, and the more ways students have of organizing their reading of this selection, the more it will open up to them.

After this class session on reading Griffin, we then asked students to read the selection in one sitting, to time their readings, and to come to class prepared to talk about what it was like reading the whole thing. From there, we went to class discussions with the "Questions for a Second Reading" and then to the "Assignments for Writing," although we can easily imagine students working directly with writing assignments after some discussion of their readings of the selection.

69

QUESTIONS FOR A SECOND READING (p. 392)

1. Here, again, the point is that there is no one "right" way into this selection, no one "right" way of organizing a reading of it. The more ways students organize their readings, the more and varied points of departure they explore, the fuller their understanding of its subjects and layers will be. When we encouraged this position toward the selection, we often heard students begin their discussions with something like, "Well, if I take secrets as a subject and connect it to families and child-rearing, here's what I make of them." As our discussion progressed and students became more comfortable with the selection, we encouraged them to look for connections among multiple subjects in the piece. How, we asked, for example, do you connect Griffin's writing about "secrets," "child-rearing," and Himmler's adult behaviors? How then do you figure the selections on RNA and DNA into your reading of those examples? What, in other words, does Griffin seem to be making of them, as examples, and the sections on secrets and child-rearing and Himmler? There are, of course, many more connections that can be made by students as they reread and work on this text, and we let the connections unfold in discussions and drew students back into them by layering them into multiple connections.

2. In many sections in this piece Griffin writes about the work she is doing, the way she imagines her research project, and the reasons she is so passionately involved with it. Students can locate those passages and speak from them in discussions of the project. They can also use her definitions of her project as a way to define all of its pieces. Why, for example, does she write about V-2 rockets? RNA and DNA? her childhood? And why does she put all of these various subjects or pieces together? What seems, then, to be her intention? It has also been interesting for our students to imagine the kinds of research Griffin had to do to write the various sections. She mentions traveling, interviewing people, and research, but the particulars of that work are left to our imagination. In our experience, students have little experience thinking through the kinds of research work one would need to do to write a selection like this. They have had little exposure to this kind of research; at most, they'll have a limited sense of it from writing out three-by-five cards for high school research papers.

ASSIGNMENTS FOR WRITING (p. 393)

1. This assignment is useful for teaching students to chart a trajectory through a complex piece of reading that allows them to re-present it to their readers. It also gives students an opportunity to describe text that doesn't proceed logically or chronologically but makes its connections and arguments through association and metaphorical relationships. There is no way, students might be warned, that they could represent all of Griffin's work in this essay, so they need to chart a trajectory of their reading, but they also need to acknowledge that it is *their* reading and to point to at least some of the other possible readings or some of the aspects of the selection they leave out or only briefly touch on.

    This is also a good assignment for students to revise once they have the opportunity to think through and discuss other students' first drafts. When using this assignment, we are careful to choose paragraphs and pages from students' essays that allow the class to see writers at work charting their readings, acknowledging other possible readings, indicating the way the piece is written and the kinds of work it asks of readers, and indicating what their readings leave out.

2. Although the work students must do for this essay echoes the work they are asked to do in the second-reading questions, it is more determined, more focused. Students receive an invitation here to take a given trajectory through Griffin's text, and it's a key one: to understand her claims for the ways we are all connected in a matrix or a field or a common past.

In order to do this work, students will need to reread the selection looking for those moments where Griffin directly writes about interconnectedness or the key terms that the assignment presents them. They will also need to reread the "white spaces" between her fragments for the implications, the connections, she implies. She never tells us, for example, how she thinks through RNA and DNA as metaphors that stand for growth or change, for instance, but she clearly implies that these metaphors have something to do with her thinking about these subjects and, too, about secrets. This has been the most difficult work for our students. They aren't accustomed to reading for implications or inferring between the lines, and they need to participate in discussions in class that seem to us like occasions for them to convince themselves that it's legitimate to infer or speculate about what something in the text, say Griffin's use of the DNA metaphor, might stand for or represent. These discussions seem to be essential, a part of the work of learning to read between the lines, and we encourage them whenever students appear skeptical or uncertain about their right to do such reading.

It's a difficult assignment, since it steps right past the kinds of questions students will want to begin with — What is "Our Secret" about? What is Griffin saying? — and moves immediately to questions about the project as a project — What is she doing? Why does she write this way? It may be best to assign a preliminary writing assignment or to work with some of the "Questions for a Second Reading." Or it might be useful to precede or follow this assignment with one that asks students to write *like* Griffin, where students are allowed to think about her project in terms of their own practice as writers. This assignment worked best for us when we made it clear to students that they should think about Griffin's writing in terms of the usual education offered young writers in the United States. They should begin, that is, *not* with the language of literary analysis ("image" or "metaphor") but with the language of the composition classroom ("topic sentence," "paragraph," "organization," "footnotes," and "three-by-five notecards").

3. Our students had a great time with this assignment and it produced some of the most interesting writing of the semester. They chose topics that ranged from parental influences, the relationship of machines and thinking, the struggle to be, as one young woman called it, in an unfriendly environment of violence, the replication of behaviors in men from different generations of the same family, and the various metaphors for space. The key to students' having a successful experience with this assignment seems to lie in the subjects they choose to write about and the stories they tell. We have told them to write about stories they know or would like to research because they are curious about them, because they sense connections to other stories or examples that they may or may not need to research. The students' involvement in the writing will push them to do the kinds of thinking through and connecting that imitates Griffin's work. This assignment demonstrates to them the kind of planning and care that Griffin's work required, and our students found that they could help themselves with outlines and charts or maps of the territories they wanted to cover. We allowed them class time, also, to test their plans with other students and with us. This proved to be time well spent, for it helped students see connections that others saw and it prevented anyone from being lost at sea for anything but a brief period. In this assignment also we took students through multiple drafts, and we assigned students to pairs at different points so that they could continually test their work against the readings of others.

MAKING CONNECTIONS (p. 395)

1. The subjects that students chose to work on with this assignment focused on surfaces and depths, visible and invisible, secret and apparent, hidden and exposed, control and surveillance. These are very abstract notions, especially for students who are unaccustomed to writing about abstractions and grounding them in particulars. In order

to prepare them to work on this project, we took a considerable amount of time discussing the second-reading questions for each selection, and we asked them to write one assignment on each selection before we presented them with this project. As a part of this project, students need to reread the two selections (that seems obvious), but they also benefit from class discussions where they point out the ways they could use ideas from one to critique or "investigate" the other. There is a strong pull for students to transform this project into a comparison-and-contrast assignment. We used the project after students had some experience writing critiques, where they took ideas or sets of ideas from one reading selection and used them as a frame or a lens to analyze or critique another reading or other examples. That's the basic move in this project, so it's important for students to be able to identify those subjects or ideas that they could use from one selection to read or analyze or investigate another.

This also turns out to be a project that poses challenges for students as they summarize and present it to their readers. The writing assignment that we used for each before we turned to this project asked them to re-present the selection's key examples and ideas to readers who had read the essay but didn't have it in front of them. We then discussed examples from these papers in class as ways of showing students how their colleagues handled the task. When we did this, we presented students with examples that could stand as interesting or compelling models of presentation that included both examples and the ideas they were meant to illustrate. This coupling of examples and ideas is particularly important for a project like this one, because it's so easy for students to get lost in the abstractions of the selections. Keeping sight of the examples that illustrate those abstractions gives them a way to think of the project at hand. What examples and ideas, then, we asked, could you use, for instance, from Foucault's selections to investigate the workings of secrets, for example, in Griffin's?

2. This assignment asks students to work from examples in both Anzaldúa's and Griffin's text. The examples should be directly concerned with how each author represents the relationships of identity to history or culture and society. Anzaldúa more than Griffin writes directly about this relationship. In long passages in her text she explicates her notions of her identity and how it is shaped by the culture around her and how in turn she imagines shaping a culture more sympathetic to her identity. Griffin writes spare statements regularly in her fragments about identity, and there are moments when she's explicit about the shaping of her identity in her childhood, but the other forces influencing her identity (e.g., violence, history, other people and their stories, and so on) are presented indirectly, more metaphorically than logically connected to her arguments about identity, so students face the challenge of reading between lines with Griffin on identity. The "Questions for a Second Reading" can give them the opportunity to discuss Griffin's text by articulating the connections they see; because these connections are mostly represented metaphorically in Griffin's text, it would benefit students to do a fair amount of discussion of this sort with the text before they begin this project.

And it's certainly not the case that the Anzaldúa text will be easy or self-evident to them, even though she writes more directly about identity and culture than Griffin. With a project of this sort, it seems to be generally helpful for students to work on each selection in discussions or prefatory writing assignments before beginning the project. The danger here, though, is that students will latch on to one or two or three seemingly "right" or "good" ways to present, for instance, Anzaldúa's notions of identity and its relationship to her Chicano culture, and you'll end up with a set of class papers all of which seem much alike. To counter this tendency, we usually choose students' papers for discussion which present diverse approaches to the assignments, and in discussions we encourage the voicing of alternative perspectives and purposely ask students to imagine other perspectives that can be built from particular sentences or moments in the text.

3. Although this assignment asks students to read Griffin's essay through Limerick's to decide if she is writing a kind of Liberick history or if she is doing something, something that is perhaps is some ways like Limerick and in some ways not like her, they are also asked to present both authors' essays to an audience unfamiliar with them. So this is a substantial piece of work that students are being asked to produce. They need to be familiar with both essays, and they need to find a way to present both without erasing or overgeneralizing either. To help them with this, you might want to let them work first on the presentation of Liberick's and Griffin's essay, or you might think about assigning this presentation not as an introduction in which they try to deal with both authors but as part-and-parcel of their analysis of Griffin through Limerick. They might do this by focusing on one or two sections of Griffin and one or two sections of Limerick and letting these represent their authors' work, with some references to other major sections of the texts, so that the sections both analyze Griffin through Limerick and present her work and Limerick's at the same time in an interweaving of analysis and reporting. Or you might ask some students to experiment with this approach while others take the more conventional tack with an introduction. Both examples, then, would be good materials to use in class discussions of students writings. Whatever students do, they will need to focus their analysis on one or two examples from each text to draw conclusions about whether Griffin and Limerick are writing similar history projects. If they try to generalize about the whole text of each author, they'll quickly slip into abstract writing that hovers just about the page and the texts with which they are working.

4. This assignment asks students to think about "Our Secret" in relation to other essays that use autobiography and family history to think about large questions — race, patriarchy, nation, war. The assignment identifies Adrienne Rich's "When We Dead Awaken" and James Baldwin's "Notes of a Native Son." Students could also write about Anzaldúa, Rodriguez, Walker, or Wideman.

    As always, the success of the writing to this assignment will depend on students taking time to present and to develop examples from the texts. Certainly summary and paraphrase will be required strategically to prepare the comparison. You can help students to feel the pressure, however, to turn to block quotation and to specific and extended points of comparison.

    It is important for students to take the final set of questions seriously. The temptation will be to say that these are great writers and of course everyone should be allowed a similar freedom of expression—or something like that. Students should feel the pressure (or students will benefit, we've found, from the pressure) to think seriously about what an essay like this can and can't do, the purposes and occasions it can and cannot serve.

5. As with most of the "Connections" questions, students here are asked to see one text through another. In order to do this, they must be familiar with both, so we suggest various kinds of work with Griffin's "Our Secret" once students seem comfortable enough with Hirsch's essay to use it as a lens for reading Griffin's. You might ask students to discuss the Griffin essay by working with one or two of the second reading questions for her essay, or you might begin them, as we often do, with a writing assignment first, then follow that with numerous discussions of Griffin through their writings about her text. That, then, can turn to or into a discussion of Griffin's text.

    With this question, the focus is on students reading Griffin's examples — her readings, for instance, of Himmler's childhood, or her readings of examples of her family history (history not available to her experience as examples of what Hirsch calls "postmemory." Clearly, students will need to be familiar with Hirsch's notions of postmemory, and we suggest using the second reading questions (Question 1 is particularly to the point) and one of the writing assignments (perhaps Question 2 — which invites students to engage in Hirsch's project — or 4) before they move on to this "Connections" questions.

Whatever strategy you follow to prepare students for this assignment, here they have the opportunity to imagine Griffin's work as the writing of a postmemorial artist, so they should (1) write about what in the work makes her such an artist and (2) write about how Hirsch might view Griffin's work as a postmemorial artist. What does Griffin see and write about that Hirsch might admire? What does she miss that Hirsch might see as important? And what does she write about that Hirsch misses? or thinks less central?

MARIANNE HIRSCH

Projected Memory: Holocaust Photographs in Personal and Public Fantasy (p. 400)

Hirsch's essay offers students opportunities to read a cultural space that she defines as postmemory — those memories we hold from narratives that predate our personal experiences but that, nevertheless, affect us in significant ways — and within this space, she's particularly interested in the uses of the images of children. She works from numerous examples to define postmemory, including one of her own experiences of her parents' hometown, Czernowitz (once the capital of Austrian Bukowina and annexed by the USSR in 1945), which stands in great detail in her memory from her parents' narratives about it but about which, of course, she has no direct experience. She is mostly compelled by postmemories of the Holocaust and within those, she seems to be driven by her desire to explain the uses of images of children in postmemory descriptions of the Holocaust. Her desire to understand the uses of these images extends beyond this dark period, though, and she concludes her piece with a powerful presentation of a story about an Israeli colonel, from Mitzi Goldman's *Hatred*, who uses, she argues, an appeal to the image of a child emerging from a home he just destroyed to erase his complicity in the destruction.

The headnote offers students a few moments from Hirsch's essay to begin their work on her use of the term *postmemory* and its visual space, but they shouldn't rely solely on the references found there. They are meant only to point the way, and students will only benefit from preliminary class discussions in which they explore Hirsch's multiple examples of postmemory and her explorations into the uses of images of children, perhaps by working in pairs to make such presentations to the class. Hirsch's use of other terms (e.g., *heteropathic identification, idiopathic, interiorizing, alterity, discursively,* and so on) deserve some initial attention also. Students might note those terms that seem difficult or unfamiliar to them as they read, then turn also to studies of those terms and, finally, finish with presentations to the class of their findings and understandings. This can occur before they begin work on the "Questions for a Second Reading" (or as a part of that work).

QUESTIONS FOR A SECOND READING (p. 421)

1. Although this set of questions focuses initially on inviting students to work with Hirsch's definitions of postmemory and her extrapolations of it as a visual, cultural space that affects personal experiences, and although this seems to be important preliminary work for students, we are particularly interested in the ways in which students might think about Hirsch's project — her reading of images, that is — as a writing lesson. How, we would ask, does her reading of these images, which she writes, of course, point to lessons for writing — perhaps for writing about such things as images and cultural memories which are held in visual spaces and various representa-

tions of the past? It is Hirsch's writing and her writing project that compel us. She can teach us methods for writing about images, cultural representations, and historical and literary experiences. After students deal with her uses of postmemory and the other terms on which she relies, we suggest turning them to a discussion of her work as a lesson on writing about such images and experiences.

2. Hirsch's notion of a "triangular field of looking" is difficult, but she prepares us for it by working through the three subject positions in her examples before she draws us to her definition — which is, itself, also complexly presented. As viewers, or readers of the images of the child, she argues that we identify and enter into the fantasy of such identification. We also view from the adult-looking-on position, and, perhaps the gaze that interests Hirsch the most, we see as the child witness, the witness to the scene, which, of course, we must imagine. We are particularly interested in how Hirsch reads these three gazes into her own readings and how she then writes them as a lesson in her writing project. Her conclusion about the triangular field of looking, then, is a large part of this writing lesson she offers us.

3. Here again we would turn students' attention to Hirsch's work as an example of the essay. How does she write? How is her piece different from the traditional essay with its introduction, body, and conclusion? Why does she write this way? How, that is, does her project define her form? Perhaps that's the key question. Students can respond to these questions by doing a close reading of Hirsch's writing methods. That's the purpose of this question and the work it invites students to do.

4. The two principle parts to this question invite students to first locate and explain Hirsch's use of particular sources, including how they might have suggested her work to her, and to then explain how she brings these various sources into her essay as a writing project. It's useful to suggest that students complete this work in pairs, with each pair taking a different source, so that when they report their work to the class, the class can see the different ways in which her sources inflect her thinking and the different ways she brings them into her writing (as this is, itself, a writing project).

ASSIGNMENTS FOR WRITING (p. 422)

1. Although this assignment appears to be straightforward in its invitation to write about "a past that belongs to you but that is not yours," students will need to be familiar with Hirsch's notions and examples of postmemory to engage in such a project, for the object here is to create postmemory, to write about a past that one shares with others through stories but that is not directly one's own personal experience. Hirsch writes, for instance, about her memories of the town in which her parents grew up, one she feels she knows intimately, yet she has never been there. She knows it from their stories. Her images are from postmemory, from the fantasies she creates in response to the stories, from the images portrayed in her parents' narratives and transformed in her imagination of them. This is similar to the projects students will need to identify for this assignment — a past that is theirs yet is not theirs.

The caveat in the assignment asks students to be careful of over generalizing about such a past, to be careful to not reduce it to a series of clichés, and they'll want to turn to her distinction between "idiopathic" and "heteropathic" identification before they engage in this writing project, so that they can understand the dangers of all too easy identification with a past that is beyond them rather than intimately connected to them in some way.

This assignment, then, asks students to take up Hirsch's project as their own, with their own examples of postmemory as a writing project. The first question for a second reading is a good place to begin if you're interested in turning students' attention, first, to ways of thinking of Hirsch's work as a writing project, as a project with writerly problems to solve having to do with the creation of images and stories surrounding them. It's a useful place for students to read her essay closely as a writing project marked by writerly methods for gathering information, using sources, telling personal stories, and drawing conclusions.

2. What are the images and stories that allow you to imagine, to know in some way, the Holocaust? This is the question at the heart of this assignment. The task then, after students respond to this question, is to write their stories, their accounts, of these images and narratives into Hirsch's, into her examples and her arguments for postmemory. First, though, the assignment asks students to re-present Hirsch's arguments and examples to readers unfamiliar with them, and although there are various ways to do this, most students will opt for summaries as introductions, and depending on your direction in your course, you might go with this or push against it and ask students to work towards integrating Hirsch's ideas and language into their narratives, use of sources, and conclusions. It might be easiest to do this by letting students initially write their summaries as introductions. Then you can use this as a base to work from, to ask how such introductions might be dispersed throughout the narratives, use of sources, and conclusions, as well as located in initial summaries. Examples of students' essays are good places to begin such excursions into other writerly methods for opening up Hirsch's project as their own.

3. Here again, as with the first and third second reading questions, we turn students' attention to Hirsch's essay as a writing project. What is its argument for writing projects? What is it saying about how one writes about images, postmemory, and cultural history? Students could benefit from working with these second readings questions to closely read the piece for its writerly methods, for the way it stakes out a claim to a certain kind of writing, before they begin this essay. Or you might ask them to produce a first draft; then, once they have work in hand, they can turn to a study of Hirsch's methods before they begin second drafts. Either way, a close reading of Hirsch as a writer working on a project that involves writing about memories, history, and personal stories offers students a way to pay attention to these, so that they can see the kinds of moves they might make in their own writing — to deliberately, for instance, write about a personal story and its relation to a cultural image or to another account of the story, perhaps a historical one, from another point of view. The aim of this assignment is to bring to the foreground Hirsch's work as writing, as a project that is marked by the ways she writes, by her methods and moves.

4. Perhaps, as the assignment suggests, it is most helpful for students to imagine that they are reviewing Hirsch's essay for those who have not read it, so that they can write to both re-present her arguments and examples and to comment on them. They can also write to relate personal stories or examples if this helps them establish a position in relation to the essay that would allow a reader to see how Hirsch's work is useful or interesting to them. You will want to use examples of students' writings in class to point them away from book review–like writing in which they quickly summarize Hirsch to more careful accounts of her project that refer to her examples and to her methods as a writer, so that readers can imagine both what she has to say and the ways she works. Within this kind of presentation, students can then write themselves, their commentaries, into their re-presentations, so that their commentaries and their presentations are integrated or woven into each other to be a piece rather than separate chunks of writing.

MAKING CONNECTIONS (p. 424)

1. As with most of the connections questions, students here are asked to see one text through another. In order to do this, they must be familiar with both, so we suggest various kinds of work with Griffin's "Our Secret" once students seem comfortable

enough with Hirsch's essay to use it as a lens for reading Griffin's. You might ask students to discuss the Griffin essay by working with one or two of the "Questions for a Second Reading" for her essay, or you might begin, as we often do, with a writing assignment first, then follow that with numerous discussions of Griffin through their writings about her text. That, then, can turn to or into a discussion of Griffin's text.

With this "Connections" question, the focus is on students reading Griffin's examples — her readings, for instance, of Himmler's childhood, or her readings of examples of her family history (history not available to her experience) as examples of what Hirsch calls postmemory. Clearly, students will need to be familiar with Hirsch's notions of postmemory, and we suggest using the second reading questions (Question 1 is particularly to the point) and one of the writing assignments (perhaps Question 2, which invites students to engage in Hirsch's project, or Question 4) before they move on to this question.

Whatever strategy you follow to prepare students for this assignment, here they have the opportunity to imagine Griffin's work as the writing of a postmemorial artist, so they should (1) write about what in the work makes her such an artist and (2) write about how Hirsch might view her work as a postmemorial artist. What does Griffin see and write about that Hirsch might admire? What does she miss that Hirsch might see as important? And what does she write about that Hirsch misses or thinks less central?

2. This is a big assignment. You might think about how you could best stage it for students. They need to be familiar with Coles's arguments that blur the distinctions between fact and fiction in documentary work, and they need to understand Hirsch's arguments about postmemorial writing — and, of course, Hirsch's work as a postmemorial artist's writing. Both authors work with photographic records, both read photographs of others and comment on them, and both imagine the cultural spaces those photographs occupy and inflect. Both authors take moral positions towards the images and the intentions of the images (and to the spaces they occupy in the culture and in their personal experiences of them). So the task for students, then, is to engage in their own writing projects that allow them to consider Coles's readings of images and Hirsch's in a similar space that defines two ways of "approaching the photographic record." One such avenue into this consideration, of course, is to first write about how each approaches the photographic records. After that, students might write about the points of similarities and differences in their approaches. For what kind of work does Coles's take the photographic record as an opportunity? How is this different from the opportunity that Hirsch pursues with the photographic records about which she writes?

3. As in the previous assignment, which asks students to read Coles's accounts of photographic records in contrast to Hirsch's, this assignment asks students to read Limerick's essay as an example of writing about the past in contrast to Hirsch's essay as a similar example. The focus here is on how both authors imagine and approach records of the past.

For students, the key method of their writing entails their close readings of specific examples of each author's writing about the past. They need to understand from the get-go that they won't be able to write about, or to generalize about, all of Limerick's or all of Hirsch's examples, so they'll need to pick what they consider to be key examples from each. They need to read those as examples of the author's writing about the past, and they need to imagine, then, in their writing how the methods of Limerick and Hirsch differ. What matters to Limerick in her writing projects about the past? What matters to Hirsch in hers? How might they — the students — account for these differences in both what matters *and* in how they write about the past?

Finally, the assignment invites students to stake a claim to their work by commenting on how the differences in these two writers' works — both, again, their differences in focus and in writing about what they focus on — bears on them as readers and writers, as people with some interest, or claim, to understanding the past. Here, with this moment in their essays, students might imagine the examples they wrote about from Limerick and Hirsch adjacent to their examples of the writings about the past. They might include one of those examples written out here in this essay, so that they could comment on it and read it in light of their work on Limerick and Hirsch. That would certainly be in keeping with the spirit of the assignment, which asks for close reading and writings of specific examples of each author's writings about the past.

HARRIET JACOBS

Incidents in the Life of a Slave Girl (p. 428)

While this is not a difficult piece to read, it presents some interesting problems in the classroom. Students read it and feel moved, yet the most appropriate response seems to be silence. What else is there to say? It seems almost disrespectful to begin talking about the text as a text, to turn this into material for an English class. One way to begin is with Jacobs's statement that she does not want a reader's sympathy. Why might she say this? What is wrong with sympathy?

Our approach to "Incidents," in fact, has been through the moments where Jacobs addresses her readers directly. In a sense, she anticipates the problem of silence, of a "liberal" reading, and teaches her reader how to read. We ask students to mark the sections where they feel Jacobs is speaking to them *as* readers, to talk about the readers Jacobs assumes and to identify the ways she wants to prepare them and revise their expectations. We also try to get students to imagine Jacobs's relationship to the conventions of storytelling, to the usual stories about growing up and having children, in order that they might find evidence of the difficulties of this relationship in the prose. This is why we introduce Houston Baker and Jean Fagin Yellin's accounts of the problems of slave narratives in the headnote.

One of the difficulties we've had teaching "Incidents" is that it so quickly becomes a familiar story, translating the experience of slavery into familiar terms, transforming an unwritten — and unwriteable — experience of slavery, love, and human relations into the general public discourse. This tendency to see the other in our own terms, to master that difference, places us in a structural relationship to Jacobs that mirrors her relations with the slave owners. We need to feel the difficulty of that position and we need to honor her attempts, as a writer, to make the problems of the "autobiographical act," in Baker's terms, part of her writing.

QUESTIONS FOR A SECOND READING (p. 465)

1. We added this question as a direct response to a problem we had as a staff (about twenty of us) teaching the Jacobs selection in our introductory course. The question says, "This text makes it impossible to say what we are prepared to say: that slaves were illiterate, uneducated, simple in their speech and thought." We were amazed at how many students said just this about Jacobs — that she was illiterate, uneducated, and so on. We decided there was some pedagogical gain in saying from the outset that "the text" made this probable reading "impossible." (We are happy to offer ourselves as figures in a classroom argument over whether it is possible to read "Incidents" in this way or not.)

It is not surprising that our students would say or write this. As a culture, we know so little about slavery and its conditions that we turn to stereotypes and pat phrases. It is through this fixed sense of The Slave that our students tried to find a way to characterize the author of "Incidents in the Life of a Slave Girl." As an author, she was invisible to them. Even as a character in a narrative, she was quickly reduced to stereotype.

We wanted students to acknowledge both the highly literate quality of the text and the position of its author. We found that we also had to make it difficult for students to grab onto the counterposition (that Jacobs wasn't "really" a slave, that her education and reading and her position in the house had made her something else, and that "slavery" was therefore not a useful term in a discussion of this text).

This process was both troubling and productive. At least it was productive when these misreadings could be cast as part of our cultural legacy, evidence of our readiness to misinterpret slave narratives rather than an indication of racism or racial insensitivity.

2–3. Both of these questions are designed to enable students to begin to read "Incidents" as a text, as an act of writing. As we have said, students will want to read the story as a window of human experience, to feel sympathy for this character, to feel that they now know and understand the real experience of slaves in the South. It is important for students to sense the limits as well as the benefits of this way of reading.

We want students to have a feel for Jacobs as a writer as well as a character, and to see in her writing a commentary on and a representation of her relationship to the dominant culture. We try to make a sharp distinction between the story in the selection and the story in the writing. The story of the writer and her relationship to her audience and her subject is also a story about freedom and slavery. The first question asks students to chart the places where Jacobs, the writer, interrupts the narrative to directly address the reader. If these, too, are part of the story, what is that story? How does Jacobs imagine her white reader? How does she imagine the problems of her relationship to that reader? The second question counters students' attempts to slot the narrative into familiar categories. It asks students to look at the codes governing the construction of the narrative, codes that challenge the readings students are prepared to perform. Students want to read, for example, in terms of a simple arrangement of black and white. Jacobs, on the other hand, works with a much more complex sense of color difference. She represents herself, for example, as different from other slaves, and she makes similar distinctions among the members of the white community. Is she judging individuals or is she working within a value system? How should we understand the distinction she draws between Dr. Flint and Mr. Sands, the father of her children, when both men could be said to treat her in the same way and represent her as the same type? Is this evidence of Jacobs giving her story over to a familiar narrative, one that requires a sympathetic lover? Her account of family lines in the South is offered as a corrective to the assumptions of "women in the North." How does the family in slave culture defy conventional representations?

ASSIGNMENTS FOR WRITING (p. 465)

1. Following up on the second of the "Questions for a Second Reading," this assignment asks students how the story of slavery is represented in Jacobs's work as a writer, in her relationship to her readers, her subject, and the usual stories of growing up, falling in love, and having a family. Students' success with this assignment will depend on their ability to work closely with the text, to select passages, to work them into their essays, and to take the role of teacher or commentator, showing readers how they might read and understand these passages. It is useful to help students make the distinction between Jacobs the writer and Jacobs the character. Your goal is to enable

students to see the narrative not as a fiction, but nonetheless as something *made*. Why, for example, does she offer "incidents"? How are these incidents arranged? Is there a predictable structure? Is it useful to have students look particularly at those passages where Jacobs interrupts the narrative to speak to the reader? What is she doing? To what degree might these be said to be spontaneous outpourings? To what degree might they be said to be strategic? It is tempting for students to assume that Jacobs is an untutored "natural" writer, someone who just wrote. You need to bring forward the drama of Jacobs's interaction with reader, text, and convention.

For revision: Students will devote most of their energies in the first draft to locating, reproducing, and describing what they take to be key sections of the text. In organizing revisions, we like to send students back to "Incidents," this time to notice what they left out, whether deliberately or unconsciously. We want students to return to the text to see how it might serve the project they now have under way, but also to challenge them to revise that project. And we want the revision to be the occasion for students to begin to ask questions of their material. Once they have described what they see, students feel they have exhausted the material. They can, however, begin to ask questions of their own experience as readers — how, for example, do they see themselves in relation to the reader Jacobs assumes? They can ask questions in terms of race and/or gender — how might the writing represent the problems of a minority writer writing to a white audience? "Incidents" seems to be self-consciously addressed to women — how does it distinguish between a male and a female reader? a male and a female reading?

2. This assignment asks for a written response to the third of the "Questions for a Second Reading." It asks students to read the narrative as a document from another culture, to look for the peculiar codes that govern human relations and the participants' understanding of human relations. The difficulty in reading this text, we've argued, is that it invokes familiar narratives; it wants to be read as more of the same, even as it describes a world outside of our familiar representations. Students who choose this assignment will need to pay dogged attention to a single area of slave life as represented in the narrative. They will need to understand that the details that matter most will come forward only after several readings. A student might trace the family connections between blacks and whites to see how these color differences cover a complicated set of relationships. Who were Jacobs's grandmother's parents? Who were Jacobs's? How does she define her relationship to other slaves? To what degree does she speak of them as different from her? What terms mark those differences? Or a student might chart out the relationships between men and women. The point is that students will need to understand that they are *searching* for material, for a hidden code or logic or system. They are not simply describing what they take to be obvious — nor what Jacobs seems to offer as obvious.

For revision: Students will most likely need to return to the text to complete their projects. They should look for material that doesn't fit quite so quickly or conveniently, either to complete their case or to make it richer. The difficulty lies in reading against Jacobs, in working as though she is not a source of pure understanding (a slave who can tell the truth about whites and about slavery, a position Jacobs defines as her own) but a product of competing ways of seeing, some of them belonging to slave culture and some to the white world. This is the difficult burden of Houston Baker's account of the slave narratives. If we read them to feel that we know the truth of slavery, we are ignoring their cultural context, the ways in which they participate in the very representational system that justifies and organizes slavery.

MAKING CONNECTIONS (p. 467)

1. This assignment asks students to consider how Jacobs might fit as an example in Walker's argument and to imagine why her name is missing from Walker's litany of

African American women. The answers are simple. While the text of "Incidents" was available to scholars at the time Walker was writing "In Search of Our Mothers' Gardens," it was the work of Jean Fagin Yellin and her 1987 edition of *Incidents in the Life of a Slave Girl* that brought Jacobs's text forward as an important and authentic slave narrative. Whether Walker had access to "Incidents" or not, the assignment is designed to give students a way of thinking about the range of names and examples in Walker's essay. (Our point is not to question whether or not Walker had done her homework.) Students will certainly not be familiar with all the artists Walker alludes to; they will be familiar, or can become familiar, with some. Jacobs provides a way of thinking about these names as a specific set, as something other than a comprehensive reference to all African American women. Some women are more appropriate examples than others.

The point of this assignment is to enable students to question Walker's representation of the past by asking them to imagine what she might do with "Incidents." Would she find inspiration in Jacobs's narrative — where? and why? In what ways might "Incidents" be said to invite or resist Walker's reading of the past?

2. This assignment is similar to the first of the writing assignments above, with the exception that it asks students to frame their reading in terms of Rich's argument about revision, the past, and the position of women within a patriarchal culture.

3. Mary Louise Pratt's essay, "Arts of the Contact Zone," provides a useful alternative to Houston Baker's account of the slave narrative. For Baker, the "authentic, unwritten self" is necessarily displaced — or appropriated — by the public discourse. In her representation of "autoethnography" and "transculturation," Pratt allows us to figure the author differently, so that we can imagine Jacobs engaging with the standard representation of an African American woman and her experience, and with the standard representation of a woman of virtue, but not giving up or giving in to it; where the point is, in Pratt's terms, to "intervene" with the majority understanding, where the purpose is corrective, and revisionary, and where the writer is allowed a position from which work can be done (where the writer can do more than merely repeat the master narrative).

This assignment asks students to begin with and to use Pratt's terms ("autoethnography" or "transculturation"). It is important for students to see this as something other than a dictionary assignment ("According to Webster, 'ethnography' is . . ."). The point, in other words, is not to come up with the "right" definition but to see how these words, together with the text that accompanies them and the example of Guaman Poma, can provide a way of reading "Incidents." Students need to work back and forth between the two essays, seeing how and where Jacobs might be said to demonstrate her own version of the "literate arts" of the contact zone.

PATRICIA NELSON LIMERICK

Haunted America (p. 471)

Limerick's essay offers students a way to understand the complexities of history when it's viewed and written from multiple points of view. She demonstrates that simple renderings of wars between whites and Indians erases the complexities, and complicities, of individuals and groups who by no means can be generalized as monolithic. There is no white man. No Indian. There are individuals in the stories, and groups, who can be studied for their differences and similarities and their involvements in situations that are contextually situated in shifting landscapes of motivations, accidents, misunderstandings, and cross-purposes. She is quick to debunk simple narratives, and her work here points to the writing of history as a writing problem with much to teach students.

This isn't a difficult essay, but neither is it a conventional piece. Her methods of gathering information and writing it into her essay can teach students methods of writing history, critique, and narrative. Her work offers students many opportunities to see how she handles material that has otherwise been overgeneralized and stereotyped, and as such, it can serve as a series of lesson for students to do similar work in the spirit of Limerick's.

QUESTIONS FOR A SECOND READING (p. 505)

1. This question goes to the heart of Limerick's project as an historian. Her historical research allows her a way of thinking and writing about the details of moments in history that are (and have been) easily fitted to preconceived narratives designed to render them into stereotypes and overgeneralizations. It gives her a way to complicate history by foregrounding multiple points of view on historical events and moments, and it gives her ways to critique textbook and scholarly renditions of history that ignore multiple perspectives from those involved in the moments from the past. Her research earns her the right to question romantic narratives, one-sided tellings and retellings, and to develop, then, her own retellings that complicate rather than simplify matters.

   Students can learn how she conducts her research and how to follow in her footsteps by close readings of her examples, especially in light of more conventional historical accounts of the same examples. This question offers students the opportunity to read her examples to arrive at some sense of what one gains by working the way she does. And this is a broad question. What does one gain personally as a historian? What does history gain? What do those involved (or who were involved) gain? and what do readers gain? and students who are learning to be readers and writers? In the spirit of Limerick, this question is designed to complicate the answers of what is gained, and by whom, when research like Limerick's is valued.

2. Limerick's examples of history as a writing problem come from both her work and the work of other historians. Through her writings about historical moments, students can study her writing style. And through the examples of other historians' work, some of which she critiques, students can imagine her writing as commentary on the ways other historians write history. While students engage in discussions about history as a writing problem, they will need to work from these examples, drawing their conclusions about writing from both her work and from their comparisons of her writing to those of others that she offers. If writing history requires attention to multiple perspectives, as she argues directly and through her examples, what then are the writing problems? If conventional narratives of adventure and heroism and triumph fall far short of accuracy, what then are the places of narratives in historical writing? What problems must writers overcome when they use and rely on narratives of history? And how might narratives benefit historians?

3. Limerick's essay is full of interesting surprises, since she is careful to keep her understandings of issues and events complex and multidimensional. The surprises come in some of the materials she provides, materials that challenge our learned, conventional notions of "good guys and bad guys" in the dramas of whites and Indians. Some of the surprises come from her writing, from the ways she interweaves her conclusions about these dramas with her tellings of their stories. And some of the surprises come in her responses to other historians' accounts of these dramas and moments in history. She also offers us interesting, and surprising, conclusions or principles about the patterns she observes in these clashes between white and Indians. When students work with this question, as usual, they will need to work closely from particular examples of her writing. Like the other two "Questions for a Second Reading," this one is de-

signed to immerse students in Limerick's examples, so they should be prepared to work from them either individually or in groups of two or three.

ASSIGNMENTS FOR WRITING (p. 505)

1. This is a big assignment, so we suggest that students work in stages, perhaps writing one position or point of view and then another. They can also follow this pattern in the class discussions of their writings. As they write from additional points of view, the discussions can turn to the problems, for instance, of representing those various points of view (working, of course, from examples in students' writings), so that their connections to the events are clear while their differences are also clear. One of the great qualities of Limerick's writings is in the way she presents the tangles of perspectives without losing the event or the players.

    Option "a," the library research project, offers students opportunities to research multiple perspectives on single events and to write their own histories from this research in the spirit of Limerick's work. Option "b" invites them to work from family or neighborhood records to do a similar kind of research, but in many ways this might be the more difficult project, although it may seem to be the easiest for students at first blush. To create a history in the spirit of Limerick's work for this option, they'll need to work from similar multiperspective materials, and this might be difficult to do with family or neighborhood histories. If they choose this option, you might suggest ways that they can research these multiple perspectives. The clearest way to do this is to focus on one or two events and to interview various people about them, so that the perspectives have a way to develop as a part of the research. They might also ask different people about the same photographs or family lore to see if and how multiple perspectives emerge. Whatever you offer students as help, it should be clear to them that they are not writing single point-of-view narratives for these family histories. They are working in the spirit of Limerick, so they are working against myths and singular narratives towards multiple perspectives.

2. This assignment is designed to engage students with the ways that Limerick's essay might be useful as "history" to the general public. What, in other words, might others learn about History from her work? And what might they learn about the particular history that she researches and writes about? You might find it useful to help students make this distinction — between History and the history that Limerick writes — as they prepare to write. Clearly there is much to be learned from her accounts of the Indian and white dramas that played out in our past, but it may not be as evident to students that there is also much to learn about History, about our ways of thinking about it, and about conventional accounts of historical dramas that romanticize and narrate myths rather than unfold accurate accounts.

    As students work on this assignment, they'll best serve themselves if they stay close to Limerick's essay and write from one or two key examples about what they can learn from Limerick's history and from her proposal of what constitutes History. The danger for students is to generalize away her particular accounts and to then lose sight of her arguments against such generalizations, unless they are grounded in accounts of historical events that take multiple perspectives into account.

3. This is a complex assignment that invites students to find a way to read a textbook or textbooks through Limerick's notions of what constitutes good historical research and writing, especially as it reports on conflicts between Indians and whites. The assignment is further complicated by the request to students to present Limerick's arguments to readers who are unfamiliar with her essay. This means that students will need to find a way to present both the substance of her arguments about historical reporting on conflicts and the larger issue of what she takes to be the goals and methods of historical writing.

It might be a good strategy to ask students to take a pass at a first draft of the complete assignment after they have done the research and close readings of the textbooks (something they might best do with a partner in pairs) in light of their reading of Limerick. We'd expect their first drafts to be occasions, then, for discussions in class of how they manage these various pieces of the assignment — the presentation of Limerick to an audience unfamiliar with her work, the analysis of the textbooks in light of her claims about historical writing and her "Twelve-Point Guide to War." Plenty of examples of students' work, perhaps in the form of excerpts from their essays, would give them a sense of the range of possibilities and occasions to talk and think about how well their colleagues accomplish these various tasks. Final revisions might, then, under such circumstances, take an additional week's worth of work.

MAKING CONNECTIONS (p. 507)

1. This assignment is designed to be fairly wide open to students' different ways of imagining what is being asked of them. Mitchell's text is difficult, and students' will need to have spent considerable time reading, writing about, and studying it before they can tackle this assignment. Mitchell offers students methods and language for thinking about the relationship of pictures and texts in the spirit of providing what he calls "a pedagogical primer or prompt-books for classroom experiments," and this assignment is designed to give students the opportunity to conduct such an experiment with the Brooks book, the Limerick text, and the photographs it accompanies. With the Mitchell essay as the ground for this study, students have many options for thinking about the Limerick text and the Brooks photographs. They might, for instance, write about the independence of the photographs, or the co-dependence of the photographs and the text; they might write about the "ethics of production affecting the work of the writer and photographer"; and they might imagine the book as a photographic essay and question it as Mitchell does the photographic essays that he uses for examples. These are only a few examples of the possibilities open to students with this assignment, but it should be clear that in order to engage in this work, students must be familiar with Mitchell's essay. It won't work if they try to read it quickly, as it's a challenging piece, and they'll need to understand the various arguments he makes about the possibilities of photographs and texts existing in the same space if they're to use any of these in their essays on the Brooks book.

2. Like Limerick, Tompkins discovers, through her attempts to understand Indian and white relationships in the past by reading historical accounts, that the perspective of the historian matters tremendously in the telling of the facts. This assignment is designed to put students in the position of writers who study both essays to determine how they differ — in their methods and in what they have to say about the reading and writing of history — while viewing them as a part of a single project which investigates the problems of writing history and of understanding the past. Of course students will need to be familiar with both essays, and once they are, they'll want to focus their close readings on particular examples from each to write about the methods each author uses and the particular conclusions that they draw having to do with writing and reading history. It will be interesting for students to note that Tompkins is not a historian and to consider how (or if) this matters to her work. Does she work differently than Limerick because she's not trained as Limerick is, or does she work differently for other reasons having to do, perhaps, with her motives for writing or her methods of approaching the subject and the texts she reads? And, finally, students are asked to comment on how the differences (in methods, motives, writing, and conclusions) bear on them. What's the difference, then, in reading Tompkins as opposed to Limerick? What might account for the differences? their different responses to each text?

3.   Although this assignment asks students to read Griffin's essay through Limerick's to decide if she is writing a kind of Limerick history or if she is doing something that is perhaps in some ways like Limerick and in some ways not like her, they are also asked to present both authors' essays to an audience unfamiliar with them. So, this is a substantial piece of work that students are being asked to produce. They need to be familiar with both pieces, and they need to find a way to present both without erasing or overgeneralizing either. To help them with this, you might want to let them work first on the presentation of Limerick's and Griffin's essays, or you might think about assigning this presentation not as an introduction in which they try to deal with both authors but as part-and-parcel of their analysis of Griffin through Limerick. They might do this by focusing on one or two sections of Griffin and one or two sections of Limerick and letting these stand for their authors' work, with some references to other major sections of the texts, so that they are both analyzing Griffin through Limerick and presenting her work and Limerick's at the same time in an interweaving of analysis and reporting. Or you might ask some students to experiment with this approach while others take the more conventional tack with an introduction. Both examples, then, would be good materials to use in class discussions of students' writings. Whatever students do, they will need to focus their analysis on one or two examples from each text to draw conclusions about whether Griffin and Limerick are writing similar history projects. If they try to generalize about the whole text of each author, they'll quickly slip into the kind of abstract writing that hovers just above the page and the texts with which they are working.

W. J. T. MITCHELL

The Photographic Essay: Four Case Studies (p. 510)

Mitchell's essay will challenge students. It's complex, dense, and raises issues having to do with the relationships of photographic images to language. As such, it can be the centerpiece of academic inquiry into the images that are so much a part of our daily lives and the ways in which they shape us, our desires, and our perceptions of others and of objects. As a central text for inquiries into these matters, it connects with Berger's, Coles's, Pratt's, Bordo's, and Griffin's essays. With any of these or any combination of these and Mitchell's, students can make the study of images and language a segue or a substantial piece of a semester's work or a whole semester's work.

This is an essay, however, that asks for careful attention. Mitchell begins by asking three questions about the relationship of images to language, and once he plays around with those questions and locates them in a historical context of thinking about them, he goes on to apply his thinking in these matters to four case studies of the photographic essay: *Let Us Now Praise Famous Men* by James Agee and Walker Evans, *Camera Lucida* by Roland Barthes, *The Colonial Harem* by Malek Alloula, and *After the Last Sky* by Edward Said and Jean Mohr. Although Mitchell provides substantial examples from these texts for his arguments, and although a chapter from *After the Last Sky* appears in this edtion of *Ways of Reading*, students will benefit from working with the actual texts, so you might consider rounding up copies in the library (or locating them on the Internet), and making them available to students if they are going to do sustained work with the Mitchell essay.

Students will benefit too from multiple readings of Mitchell's essay. The first of the "Questions for a Second Reading" asks them to reread noting the structure of the essay. For each "chunk" or section, we've posed questions that might help them get a sense of the ideas at play and how Mitchell evolves them into the case studies. The case studies are, of course, his significant examples, and there are many opportunities for students to work with his readings and uses of them and for them to reread his examples and his readings of them.

QUESTIONS FOR A SECOND READING (p. 547)

1. Here's a big project for students to engage with as preliminary work to writing about the essay. The question invites students to follow the structure of Mitchell's essay and to answer questions specific to each "chunk" or section of the essay. Students will want to take notes (and reread sections when they sense the need to do so). They should take this opportunity to underline or note key terms and questions, and these can be presented to the class for further discussions. They shouldn't feel that if they don't understand, then they don't get it. You might want to let them know this ahead of time. Mitchell is a specialist, so like specialists, he has technical language that he uses that readers won't be familiar with, so the noting of that language is what readers do when they work on the essay.

    Once the students get into the case studies, they can note, as the question poses, those moments where Mitchell focuses on what he calls the dialectic of exchange and resistance between photography and language. This is his central argument in the opening sections of the essay — that photographs and their accompanying language (and by implication, the language of those readers who read photographic essays) play off each other in an interchange, in a dialectic where they both elaborate on and resist each other. He's particularly interested in the ways that photographs resist the coding of language, but it's pretty apparent that if this is a dialectic, as he argues, then the exchange and resistance are mutual movements. Students might wonder out loud about this proposal of Mitchell's. What does it mean to say that photographs and their accompanying language, including their readers readings, exchange and resist each other?

2. This is a straightforward invitation to students to compile a glossary of Mitchell's technical, or specialist's, terms, so that they might be available to other readers new to Mitchell's work. Although students are invited to treat these as dictionary-type definitions, they'll benefit from constructing them in the contexts that Mitchell uses them. It might be helpful to students, then, to begin thinking of this work in those terms, so that they'll be prepared to write paragraphs in which they explain a term, Mitchell's specific use of it in context, and, perhaps, offer an example or two in two or three sentences of its use and application in the larger argument of this essay.

3. Mitchell makes much of the dialectic of exchange and resistance between photography and language, and this question invites students to examine that dialectic by locating specific moments in the four case studies where Mitchell focuses on this dialectic. Dialectic is, of course, one of Mitchell's specialized terms, and he uses it pretty much as you might expect — to signal an exchange, a give-and-take, between photographs and language. They speak to each other. They play off each other. In this speaking and playing, they exchange meanings, code and recode subject's and reader's positions, and resist each other's desires and intentions. The key to students' work with this question has to do with their working from specific examples in the case studies. They will need to locate those examples, explain the dialectic as Mitchell offers it, and speculate about why this dialectic is so important or significant to Mitchell's argument in the essay. Students can also find a place in this question for their own positions by studying their readings of the case and the accompanying photographs as other essays that are about photographic essays, so they could examine the dialectic of exchange and resistance between their readings and the photographs and the language, including Mitchell's, accompanying the photographs.

4. With this question, students are invited to conduct research on the books of photographic essays that Mitchell uses for his cases. Most libraries will have copies of these books, or they can be ordered from interlibrary loan ahead of time by the instructor and made available to groups of students if there are not multiple copies, or students can take turns using them. Students will need to read the books and come to class with

one or two examples, examples that Mitchell does not use in his essay, and build a case, as Mitchell does, either for their inclusion in the essay as further examples of his argument or as challenges to his arguments — in the sense that the photograph and accompanying language could be said to be monolithical, as opposed to dialectical, with both the image and the language working to gel or congeal rather than to exchange or resist.

ASSIGNMENTS FOR WRITING (p. 548)

1. Mitchell does not say much about the differences in the four books of photographic essays that he studies for his four cases, but a reader gets the sense that each case extends his arguments in a particular way, that each book of photographic essays contributes differently to his work. Students are invited to study the implied differences in these four books, and this invitation to study is framed in Mitchell's terms, in terms, that is, that foreground the dialectic of exchange and resistance between the photographs and their accompanying texts. How, in other words, could it be said that each book enacts this dialectic differently from the other books? What does one contribute to the overall picture of the dialectic that the others do not? Students will also need to represent the photographic essays to readers, so a part of their job in this essay is to summarize each of the four books so that readers unfamiliar with them might be able to picture them and their relation to Mitchell's argument for the dialectic. And, finally, students are invited to take a position on the range of the photo-essay as a genre, based on their work with the differences in these four texts. What, in other words, might be possible with the photo-essay? What are its possibilities? its limits?

2. Here students are asked to take up Mitchell's project by working with examples that he does not use from the four photographic essay books or with examples from other photographic essays. The work in this project is two-fold: students are invited to extend Mitchell's project with their readings of the relationships between photographs and languages in the texts they choose, and they are asked to represent this material and Mitchell's argument to readers who are familiar with Mitchell's essay but who do not have it in front of them.

3. This is a good assignment to use to ask students to think about the ways in which authors figure or prefigure readers into their essays. It's also an opportunity for students to think about the ways in which Mitchell reads as he writes about his examples. At times, as the assignment points out, Mitchell reads for us as "we," and at other times he reads for himself as "me" or "I." Why? Or, what seems to be at work here, figuring into the different positions that he takes as a reader? What, in other words, comes into play when he says "we" about readers? when he says "me" or "I"?

Students will need to sort out for themselves the ways Mitchell figures readers into his essays. They might ask themselves what assumptions he makes about readers at various moments in the text. Are, for example, his assumptions about readers changing? Are they different when he writes theory in the first two sections as opposed to when he writes his cases? Are they different in the different cases? or in moments in the cases? All of this inquiry can lead students to write about what Mitchell seems to be saying about appropriate ways to read — appropriate ways (for Mitchell, of course, and the establishment he might be said to represent) to read theory, cases, and photo-essays.

Finally, students can take a position in relation to the claims for reading that they see Mitchell making. How do they think theory should be read? cases? photo-essays? What examples of reading can they use to position themselves in relation to Mitchell? It may be obvious to you that students need to work from examples as they write about Mitchell's assumptions about reading and readers, but it's always helpful to remind them about this. And it's helpful also to remind them to work from their own examples of themselves as readers to establish their positions on ways to read these various kinds of texts.

MAKING CONNECTIONS (p. 550)

1.   This assignment invites students to use Berger to study Mitchell or to use Mitchell to study Berger. Berger writes about the differences in paintings and photographs, and he argues a particular position different from Mitchell's on the relationship of images and language. Berger seems more inclined to make images subjects of language, rather than to put images and language in a dialectic with each other, and Berger might be inclined to think of Mitchell's argument differently if he were actually engaged with it. Elsewhere in his essay, Berger argues strongly for the dialectic between paintings and contemporary readers of those paintings that ground themselves in the context of the paintings that reveals painters positions towards their subjects. This isn't, then, a clear-cut comparison, and it can be figured many ways, depending on the arguments that students build. It's interesting also to test Berger's sense of critical mystification on Mitchell's readings of the photo-essays. Would Berger claim that Mitchell mystifies the photo-essay? What evidence could be used to argue this either way?

Looking at Berger's through Mitchell's text is just as challenging as looking at Mitchell's through Berger's. Mitchell, of course, makes much about the relationship of images and language, so this offers students a way into Berger. Where does Berger write about this relationship? Students will need to locate moments where he does, and they'll need to stand Berger's claims for the relationship next to Mitchell's. Its an odd comparison because there are differences, but they seem to evaporate or change in different contexts, particularly when Berger argues for contemporary readings of paintings and when he examines reproductions that are accompanied by texts. Would it be possible to claim, students might be asked, that Berger argues for a dialectic between images and language as Mitchell does in one of his case studies? That is, are Berger's examples close to any of those used by Mitchell?

2.   Since this project invites students to study two different readings of *Let Us Now Praise Famous Men*, they would benefit from being able to study the whole text firsthand. Often libraries will have multiple editions of this book, as it is quite famous and well-known to various audiences. It was originally produced for a general reading audience, so it once had wide circulation, and since then it has been studied extensively by artists, sociologists, literary critics, and cultural theorists. To begin this project, after they have read the original text, students might locate those examples that both Coles and Mitchell use. They might then ask themselves how each author reads the examples. What are the different approaches to the photo-essay evident and implied in their different readings? Unlike Berger, Coles takes a strikingly different position on the photo-essay because, at least in part, he's using it for a different purpose than Mitchell, but also, one feels, because he's much more reverential toward it and what it represents historically.

Once students have read the common examples, they can move to the other examples from Coles and Mitchell, choosing one or two from each, and write about the different ways in which each author reads the examples. They will want to be able to write about the underlying concerns of each author as a determining factor in how each reads, so they'll need to come to some kind of general statement that points back and forth to their examples to play out their sense of the underlying concerns of each author. And, finally, students are invited to take a position. Whose readings and uses of the photo-essay might they align themselves with? Why? What, in other words, compels them to take that position? Here again students will need to work from examples —either of their readings of the different authors or of the different authors readings of the photo-essays — to say what compels them to take a particular position.

3. With this assignment, students are invited to study the political situation of the photo-essays. Mitchell writes about this in particular when he comments on *The Colonial Harem* and *After the Last Sky*, but there's still plenty of work for students to do with these and the other photo-essays. Students might begin this work by thinking about the gazes of the photo-essays. Who is looking at whom? Who is writing about whom? It might be a question of how the subjects of the photo-essay are being positioned by the photographer and the writer. It might be a question of the others, the subjects of the photo-essays, being victimized in some way by the culture that encouraged the photo-essays or by the artists who participated in that cultural project. Or it might be that the photo-essays represent subjects of different positions interacting with the culture of the photo-essays and that culture's representatives in the artists who did the work. Is it, in other words, a matter of the rich gazing at the poor? Opportunists taking up cultural opportunism to gaze at others (most often poor or marginalized in some ways)? Students can be invited to think about the political situation here and the various ways it might be represented as they read the Pratt essay. Pratt's essay offers multiple paths through the political representation of others, so it is not a question of students getting it right, but of finding a way to imagine the photo-essay as a political project that reveals its politics in the relationship of the subjects to the agents (including, of course, to the culture that promotes the relationships).

ALICE MUNRO

The Albanian Virgin (p. 554)

This compelling, double story, with two narratives running alongside each other, moves us back and forth between the story of Lottar — a kidnapped British woman, told by a woman named Charlotte, who is in many ways just as mysterious as the Lottar she tells us about — and the story of Claire, a recently divorced Canadian who runs a bookstore. The memorable characters all seem to be connected in ways that are loosely hinted at in the story, but Munro leaves the work of figuring those connections to her readers, although in an interview she hinted that the story is a romance of sorts.

The work for students here is in keeping the two stories and their characters straight and in imagining how these stories might be connected or thought of as comments on each other or as a single project. As usual, with complex, substantial selections, we suggest students read the piece through once, then a second time, with one of the "Questions for a Second Reading" in mind. We often follow up students' second readings with work in pairs, asking them to respond to the question(s) before turning to a larger class discussion.

QUESTIONS FOR A SECOND READING (p. 583)

1. We begin by assuming the Munro is carefully orchestrating the unfolding of these two stories (and all their subplots), so we designed this question to focus students' attention on the ways in which Munro organizes her story and positions the reader. As students work on the organization, they should ask themselves why it matters. What happens to them as readers because of the way the selection is organized? How would the story be different if, for example, it began with Claire's story rather than with Lottar's as narrated by Charlotte? How, in other words, does Munro control, or position, readers? And how would students define this positioning at various key moments? What (using their own language) would they name the strategies she uses?

It might also be interesting for students to chart their responses to and expectations for the story at moments they feel are key or critical. The identification of those moments is also another tack that students might take as they work on charting the organization of the selection.

2. This is a great question for students. It asks them to take the two story lines and make sense of them as one project. What might these stories have to do with each other? How could they be imagined to be connected? At what points do they seem to play into or with each other? to what ends? And what kinds of conclusions might one draw about the relation of these stories to each other?

    We think students benefit from imagining such connections in the same way that they benefit from imagining stories and poems as arguments with something to say, and, as the language puts it, with points to make. So what's the point here, then, with these two stories so closely woven together? If Munro wanted them to be separate, she could easily have written two stories, but we don't suggest falling into the trap of trying to second-guess her. Rather, we think students should imagine for themselves as readers the connections between these parallel stories. In the spirit of close reading, the question suggests that they begin by imagining what the similarities and differences are, and we should reiterate that it is important for students to work from moments in the stories, rather than from vague generalizations about the two stories, as they figure this problem.

3. Here is another close reading question for students that focuses them on Charlotte's narrative about Lottar, the Albanian Virgin. We designed this question to put students into the text, to get them to read closely for moments that they might use in imagining how the story wants us as readers to think about whether Charlotte is Lottar or whether Charlotte is, as she claims, just making up the story of Lottar for a movie. Where in the text might students find moments to turn to speak to this question? That's the task of this assignment — to read closely, to point to moments in the story that could be said to point to a way to read Charlotte's narrative.

4. Although this question directs students to report on one of the literary figures associated with Claire in the story, it can be easily imagined as an invitation to students to consider why a particular figure would be important to Claire or what we might learn about Claire by thinking of her in terms of the literary figure. This is, then, a research question. Students will have to find out something about the figure and they will need to read something written by the figure to get a sense of the work that Claire might be said to admire or that might have something to do with her sense of herself. It should be clear that students need to work closely from the moments in the story they can associate with the figures they've chosen and with moments in the texts of those figures or particular aspects of their lives if they are going to connect the figures and Claire.

ASSIGNMENTS FOR WRITING (p. 584)

1. This assignment is broadly drawn to offer students an opportunity to imagine Munro as a presence in her story who takes "The Albanian Virgin" as an occasion to think about stories. Students are invited to write about what she might be said to be saying about stories — where they come from, what they accomplish, and what they are good for. They are also invited to write about their sense of this story in the same way, responding to the same questions that they use to think about what Munro might be saying: Where do they think the story comes from? What does it accomplish? What is it good for?

    Students will need to work from particular moments in the story to do both kinds of work — to say what Munro could be said to be thinking about through this story and to say what it does for them. It seems obvious that some students will want to divide the essay into two sections, one for each part of the task, but students will benefit if they imagine it as an integrated whole, with one section in conversation with the other. Here, they might write something like "in this passage Munro seems to be saying that this story is trying to accomplish this, and as for me, I think it is doing this." We don't mean to wrap it up in one sentence, but to demonstrate how students might interweave their work on both parts of the assignment while writing closely from particular moments that they identify as key to the tasks.

2. As the assignment suggests, before students write, they might turn to the first two "Questions for a Second Reading" to guide their close reading of the story and the way it is organized to unfold two stories that are connected in ways not immediately obvious to readers. Once they have become familiar with the story, they'll need to design or imagine one of their own that proceeds, as Munro's does, with two story lines, perhaps with one of those being a story narrated by one of the characters. The challenge here is to create the two stories that readers can imagine as linked, and to do so in ways that carefully orchestrate their unfolding. We generally don't turn students to creating outlines, but in this case, such work might be useful once they have drafted their stories, so that they can then use the outline work to think how they might organize the story in the spirit of and in a fashion similar to Munro's.

     Students who have not written stories before might find this a perplexing assignment, but they should feel free to work from autobiography if they want or to imagine stories that begin in or use autobiography in some way. They might also want to reread Munro's story a number of times after they have had the opportunity to study it in order to get a sense of its movements and outline.

3. This is a terrific assignment to use that follows the spirit and concerns of Munro's stories. She writes almost exclusively about women and their circumstances, so here students are invited to think about what she might be said to be saying about women (and men, consequently). What, then, might her argument about women be? To respond to this question, students will need to identify key moments in the story that allow them to bring forward what they imagine to be Munro's argument about women. They will need to consider both story lines and the three female characters (Lottar, Charlotte, and Claire), and some will want to consider the men also as foils to, or backgrounds for, the women. The men seem to be transparently drawn — they certainly aren't given the depth of the female characters in their obsessions with themselves and their artifacts. For those students who take this tack, the question might be one having to do with why Munro figures men so superficially. Is it simply because they are background? Or is there something being said here that also relates to her arguments about women?

     The assignment also asks students to say how the argument positions them as readers. How do they think Munro, in other words, intends them to read her argument? Are they to be sympathetic readers? Critical? Cynical? Does she imagine that readers will identify with the women? disparage or ignore the male characters?

MAKING CONNECTIONS (p. 585)

1. Students are invited in this assignment to think and write about the conventions and forms of writing by studying Munro's rather unconventional story and one of the other experimental selections in *Ways of Reading*. We ask them to put aside distinctions between fiction and nonfiction and to focus instead on what they might take to be the lessons for writers in experimental writing. A part of this entails thinking about the differences in these pieces of writing from what they take to be conventional forms of writing — most likely the kinds of writing they have been doing all of their academic careers. In light of those conventions, how do they understand the work of the two experimental writers? How could their work be said to be written "against" standard

forms of writing? And how might their projects be thought of as similar? or similarly motivated?

In order to work with this assignment students will need, of course, to be familiar with both the Munro story and the other selection they decide to work with. You might imagine a way to give them some structure, perhaps by letting them work in pairs on the second selection or setting up study groups for the second selections and bringing that work into class before they begin writing this assignment. And as they work on this assignment, they'll need to turn to those moments in the selections that define for them the experimental characteristics of those selections. They'll need to present those moments to readers, and they'll also need to present readers with examples of what they take to be the "standard" forms and conventions they write about. They might take these examples from their own writings or from other selections in the book.

2. Once students are familiar with Bordo's essay (perhaps from discussions drawn from the Second Reading Questions), they'll need to imagine that Munro is making an argument in her story about women. Certainly the female characters, are foregrounded to the male characters, who seem lightly sketched compared to the women. What might they say her argument is, then, about women? How can they think about the connections among the women — Lottar, Charlotte, and Claire — in the story? How might it be said that Munro's drawing of them points to an argument she is making about women? What moments in the story might they, the students, use to argue for that argument or those arguments about women?

Bordo's work on women is foregrounded in her essay, so students will need to identify key passages that allow them to write about what she could be said to be saying about women. But the assignment asks for more than finding ways to write about the arguments being made in these two selections. Students are also asked to write to readers not familiar with these selections, so they will also need to find ways to present these selections, their outlines and substance, to their readers. Consequently, this is a substantial piece of work that students are being asked to produce, and you may want to stage it over two or three weeks of classes with considerable class time given to the presentation and study of excerpts from students' writings, so that they can see a range of work and imagine revisions from their class discussions of each other's essays. They could benefit from examples of the ways they present Munro's and Bordo's selections to their readers, of course, and from examples of how they imagine the arguments here about women. You might want to specifically focus some of this discussion on their use of sources to make these arguments and on the ways they explain the links between the sources they use and they arguments they write.

WALKER PERCY

The Loss of the Creature (p. 588)

In the assignments, we define Percy's method in "The Loss of the Creature" as an enactment of his argument: The world is disposed of by theory; to strive for a more immediate experience of the "thing," one must resist packages and packaging; the job for the writer is to resist the desire to translate examples into generalizations; the job for the reader is to attend to the varied richness of detail, not to search for the hard outline. Percy talks about the value of the indirect approach and shows how it works and how it feels once you climb inside.

Percy does his best to unsettle his readers, to keep them from turning his argument into a fixed, abstract statement. Students, to be sure, will try to sum the essay up — to tame it and make its weirdness manageable — by saying something like "Percy says that we have to work hard to be individuals" or "We must try to live every day to the fullest." When you place these sentences against Percy's own ("The layman will be seduced as long as he regards beings as consumer items to be experienced rather than prizes to be won, and as long as he waives his sovereign rights as a person and accepts his role of consumer as the highest estate to which the layman can aspire," text p. 600), or when you place them against those wonderful, almost parable-like anecdotes (the weary, sophisticated tourist who seeks out the Greyhound package tour with the folks from Terre Haute), you sense the degree to which this writing resists a reader's desire to put it into a box and tie it up with a bow.

The terms of the argument resist summary or translation into common terms. The examples seem almost to deflect, rather than to support or to illustrate, the argument. Sometimes, in fact, the argument seems playfully, or willfully, absurd: Are we really to believe that Cárdenas saw the Grand Canyon without any preconceptions? that he didn't see it as an example of God's grandeur or as property for his queen? And what about the bogus precision of assigning a fixed value (*P*) to the experience of seeing the Grand Canyon? And the examples, as they accumulate, seem to say to readers not that they are getting closer to a final, summary statement but that they are going to somehow have to find the point of all this somewhere in the spaces between the examples. They all approximate something that is ultimately beyond saying.

We find students alternately puzzled, frustrated, and entranced by this essay. Percy doesn't do what a writer is supposed to do. Yet he seems to be upbeat, and on the side of students, in favor of freedom and against dull courses. "What if we wrote like that?" We have been asked. "Give it a try," We've said. When students talk or write about the essay, we have found it important for them to focus on the examples, particularly on those that seem mysterious, that defy their efforts as readers. When students talk about the tourists at the Grand Canyon, they inevitably turn to the examples of tourists who get off the beaten track ("That's what Percy is saying — we have to take the road less traveled") and ignore the difficult talk about dialectic and the complex soul who sees through the predicaments of others. The former comes to students without effort; the latter is hard to explain (or there is no ready explanation). The complexities become invisible or unimportant to students unless a teacher brings them into the foreground.

When we teach this essay, we are interested in keeping track — for the class — of what students notice and what they fail to notice, of what they take as significant and what they allow to disappear from attention. Then we can ask why they read the essay as they do, and ask how their difficulties with the essay fit into Percy's argument about the problems of seeing the Grand Canyon or a dogfish. Students, we've found, read on the assumption that the examples are equivalent, that they all illustrate the same thing. It is harder to look for differences, or to imagine why Percy has piled example on example ("If they are all the same, then why wouldn't one or two do the trick?"). We insist that they work on a phrase like "dialectical movement," both because it is a powerful phrase — in the academy and in this essay — and because it marks a point at which Percy's essay makes an argument with more precision and rigor than the version students will offer in everyday language ("Be yourself! Don't fall into the same old rut!"). Percy talks about elaborate packages and coverings; students will want to talk about hidden meanings. The problem of translation is a central one in the essay. We want students to go back and *work* on this essay — to do more than just take pleasure in its anecdotes. We want them to see the demands the structure of the essay makes on them as readers; we want to call attention to the difference between the language of the essay and the language students will bring forward to represent and displace it.

The discussion and writing assignments begin with particulars and move outward. There is a point at which we want students to work on the largest structural problem in the essay — the relation between the first and second sections. An appropriate question would ask students, given their reading of the essay and their sense of its method and agenda, what sense it makes to compare the experience of the tourist with that of the student. The

93

essay insists on the comparison — or contrast — without coming forward and making it, without speaking directly of the relationship between parts I and II. Students will have to fill in this silence, and at the risk of making fixed and simple that which is presented as open and complex.

There is a way in which this essay is a trap. It is extraordinarily difficult to write about it without packaging it, and thereby becoming a consumer or a theorist and wearing the Percian badge of shame. Still, it is extraordinarily powerful to feel the problem of knowledge and representation in just this way. If you are concerned about leading students down this shady lane, then perhaps the most appropriate writing assignment is one that asks students to imitate Percy's project rather than write *about* it, hence the seeming indirection of the two "Assignments for Writing" on text pages 601–02.

If we can lead students to sense that there is a trap in this essay — or that Percy is playing a slippery role, having his theories and denying them at the same time — we will have some successful classes. The difficulty is getting a class to move beyond the certainty that Percy is simply telling them, if elegantly, what they already know.

QUESTIONS FOR A SECOND READING (p. 601)

1.   The first of these directs students to what we referred to earlier as Percy's method. It asks students, as they reread, to think about what it is like to read this essay or to think about the demands it makes upon them. We've found that this distinction is a surprising but often an enabling one for students. When students consider that the essay is, in a sense, teaching them how it wants to be read, they suddenly have a very different sense of what an essay is and what it means to be a reader. They are not, in other words, receiving information the way they might receive it from a textbook. The essay makes different assumptions about the nature of information and the roles of both reader and author.

2.   Students are asked to imagine that the essay is not just performance — that Percy has an argument to make, however indirect the presentation, and that the argument has bearing on the life of a student. It is, for that matter, an essay *about* the life of the student. The problem with inviting students to reread the essay with the argument in mind is that it can be an invitation to misread if students are not given advance warning that Percy is trying to undo them as readers. Without a warning, many students will read the essay as though it were no different from a piece in *Reader's Digest,* and see it as saying exactly what they have learned to say to each other: Be yourself, beware of school, count every daisy, don't lose the trees in the forest. With the warning, a rereading with these questions in mind can give students a way of beginning to talk back to Percy. Once students can make Percy's terms work for them, they can begin to imagine what it would take to stand outside that argument and speak back: Why must the "thing" be beyond words? What is the argument against this theory of education? (Rodriguez, in "The Achievement of Desire," offers one counterargument.) What about the people who can't afford trips or Sarah Lawrence — do they have an equivalent loss? What would be the consequences for a person who could step outside his or her culture and see the Grand Canyon? If such a thing is impossible, and if people nonetheless care about seeing natural phenomena, then what else might we struggle for or worry about?

3.   This question is intended to make it possible for students to imagine the essay as the demonstration of a method, and to imagine how that method might be said to be problematic. There are written accounts of first encounters with the Grand Canyon dating back at least two centuries. And, of course, there are Native American accounts of the canyon. It would be possible to conduct a scholarly analysis of what actual people have actually said. Percy's essay can be read as a deliberate rejection of the

archive, the interview, and the survey. Once students begin thinking about the essay in these terms, it is interesting to ask what is gained and what is lost. It is surprising that an essay about the limits of cultural packaging deals largely in stereotype and caricature — in the quick, representative example (his tourist, his islander, his student, and his "great man"). At the same time, one could argue that the figure of the novelist or artist, while not named directly in the essay, stands behind Percy's essay as the expert who stands outside time and culture. This is a familiar longing, and the essay can be used as a way of examining a general desire to imagine such a position.

ASSIGNMENTS FOR WRITING (p. 601)

1.   Here is a writing assignment that frees students from the burden of theorizing about an essay that condemns theorists. It asks them, rather, to do a Percian thing — to carry out a Percian project. The assignment points students in two directions. On one hand, they will have to be good storytellers; whether they should tell Percian anecdotes is another issue. On the other hand, they will have to arrange and comment on their stories using Percy's terms and methods. This is the occasion to work on the use and meaning of a word like "dialectic" (and to work on the use and meaning of the word as Percy uses it and makes it meaningful). It is not the occasion to "forget all that stuff" and turn naively to personal experience. The experience is important, but the way it is shaped and phrased by a writer who is carrying out Percy's project is equally so.

We don't want to underplay the difficulty of this, and it is a difficulty that can be represented in a cycle of drafts and revisions. Students will have access to related stories, and they will care about those stories well before they sense the attention that is required to work on them in Percy's spirit. Such Percian work may make more sense to students when they are working on a later draft, particularly if you direct comments or discussions of sample papers in class toward the relationships between the stories and the shape of the essays or the presence of a voice that speaks in general terms.

A note on the final sentence: It seems rather weak to say "Feel free to imitate Percy's style and method," as there is much teaching to be done if students are to take up the invitation. One issue, however, is whether students will ground their papers in "real" stories from their own experience or representative anecdotes crafted to serve the occasion. The latter is much harder for students to do well, but to realize this is to realize something telling about Percy in this essay. In this apparent guidebook to daily living, he never turns to the detail of his own life, and this allows him a purity and status that students won't have if they bring forward memories of family trips or favorite teachers.

2.   This assignment takes the central metaphor of the common and the complex and asks students to use it to imagine that there is more than one way of reading "The Loss of the Creature," that reading can be imagined as a matter of struggle and strategy. Students are asked to imagine a common reading and to write an essay showing what it might look like. Then they are asked to plan and to put into action a strategy to enable another form of reading, one they would be willing to label complex. Finally, they are asked to step back and comment on what they have done.

The all-at-onceness of this assignment is hard for students. This too is an assignment that benefits from stages. If students work on one reading before the other, they are more likely to develop essays on "The Loss of the Creature" that are real essays — in length and seriousness — than if they are preparing miniatures. The same could be said for the final section of the essay. If it is to serve as the occasion for reflection, that reflection can be greatly assisted by time and by group discussion of sections I and II.

MAKING CONNECTIONS (p. 603)

1. We offer this same assignment also in the "Making Connections" questions after Geertz's essay "Deep Play: Notes on the Balinese Cockfight."

In the opening section of "The Loss of the Creature" (text pp. 588–95), Percy talks about the strategies one might use in order to recover the Grand Canyon from the "preformed symbolic complex," to see it from a position outside of culture and its expectations. This assignment asks students to consider Geertz and his account of his experience in Bali, including his professional interpretation of the cockfight, as one of Percy's representative anecdotes. Geertz talks at length about his assumptions and methods — about theory — yet he seems content that he has seen something that is there. Is he simply blind to Percy's concerns and gloom?

Percy tells the story of tourists in Paris, in Mexico, and at the Grand Canyon. This assignment asks students to imagine what he might do with the story of Geertz in Bali. Has Geertz solved the problem Percy charts in his essay? Where would he place Geertz's story in the essay? How would he tell it? What would he notice and miss? Or what would he include and leave out? What would he say about it?

The goal is for students to work from within a set interpretive frame, to read one essay in terms of another. The difficulty is that Geertz keeps leaping out of the frame of what he is saying — first the narrative, then the professional account — to comment on what he has done. Students might do best if they ignored the last two sections while working on the paper. They might go back to them when they are done, particularly as a way of considering what Geertz might have to say to Percy, imagining now that Geertz has had a chance to read this Percian account of his work.

2. This assignment is a variation on the first. Here students are asked to add to the repertoire of representative anecdotes, to use their story as a response to the stories featured by Percy and Rodriguez. The key to students' success will be time spent working with the stories in "The Achievement of Desire" and "The Loss of the Creature." Rodriguez's essay, like Percy's, depends upon anecdotes — the scholarship boy, Rodriguez's parents, his life in England, and so on. Rodriguez's anecdotes, however, are drawn from recollected experience, not invented for the occasion, as are Percy's. Rodriguez is clearly creating a figure of himself in this presentation on his schooling, one that we can hold alongside Percy's great man with the grubby thumb. You will want your students to think not only about the story they will tell but also about storytelling, or about themselves as storytellers and the figures they create to stand alongside the textual Rodriguez and Percy's great man.

One decision you will face with this assignment is whether you want it to stand as a commentary on Rodriguez and Percy, whether you want your students to name Rodriguez and Percy and to allude to their work in their essays. When we have taught versions of this assignment we have made this an issue for revision, since we do not want the students to acknowledge Percy and Rodriguez as sources in their work. Without any reminders, the first draft will most likely be primarily a story. This, we think, is a fine place for students to begin — thinking about their story and about the type of story they want to tell. In revision, we remind them of the other context — the relationship of their story to Percy and Rodriguez. We ask them to make it clear to the reader, when they revise, how their account is a commentary on those prior essays.

MARY LOUISE PRATT

Arts of the Contact Zone (p. 605)

For a long time we felt that Mary Louise Pratt's work — particularly her essay, "Linguistic Utopias," and her book, *Imperial Eyes* — had much to offer those interested in writing and the teaching of writing. So much of the work on writing pedagogy was, in her terms "utopian," assuming as its end a common language commonly valued; and while we understood why teachers were prone to utopian beliefs, often expressed in the name of "community," we felt that the current version of the promised land worked against those conceptions of writing and teaching that gave priority to the social, historical, and political contexts of the classroom (and the individual act of writing). We had been greatly helped by Pratt's representation of writing and the classroom, and we had been looking for a piece of hers we could use in our undergraduate courses. We finally settled on "Scratches on the Face of the Country; or, What Mr. Barrow Saw in the Land of the Bushman" (first published in *Critical Inquiry*; there is a version of it in *Imperial Eyes*).

We taught this, we felt, with some considerable success. The essay is a wonderful demonstration of close reading (Pratt is reading excerpts from eighteenth- and nineteenth-century accounts of travel in Africa), which makes it very hard for students to write the conventional paper about exotic others (travel essays, essays about roommates, and so on). "Scratches on the Face of the Country" was on our list for inclusion in the third edition of *Ways of Reading*. However, the essay was also very difficult reading, particularly the first five pages, which are written in the style of 1980s poststructuralism (with puns on "sight" and "cite," for example).

We heard "Arts of the Contact Zone" when it was first delivered at the literacy conference in Pittsburgh and then saw it in *Profession 91*. Partly because it was written as a lecture (and partly, we believe, because Pratt had been working on this project for several years), its argument (about "contact zones" and the clash of cultures as represented in the production and reception of written texts) was similar but much more direct and would certainly put fewer roadblocks in the way of undergraduates. Parts of "Arts of the Contact Zone" serve in the introduction to *Imperial Eyes*, which we also considered, but that piece removes the references to education and the undergraduate curriculum. It was these references, we felt, that made obvious the connections we wanted to make in our classes between colonial expansion, travel writing, a letter to King Philip III of Spain, and the contemporary American classroom.

The teaching problems the essay presents are fairly straightforward. We don't get to see much of Guaman Poma's text, so the demonstrations of close reading come with the discussion of the illustrations (which are wonderful). We have supplemented this discussion with a photocopy of a page from "Scratches on the Face of the Country," in which Pratt works with the text of an early travelogue. It is important to get students to feel that they can talk about Guaman Poma (and not just Pratt's kids and baseball cards). Students will be thrown a bit by "autoethnography" and "transculturation," which is the point. Turning these into working terms requires going back to the essay (not the dictionary). It was important to some of our students to note that Guaman Poma was himself a member of the elite. We can cast him as the subaltern in his relation to King Philip, but on his home turf who knows what role he played in representing the lower castes of the Inca empire? (Positions, in other words, are situated, not pure.) The passages that provoked the most pointed discussion are those we point to in the assignments. They include those in which Pratt defines her alternative (for many students, counterintuitive) sense of community and culture, as well as those in which she lists the arts of the contact zone. The lists were extremely useful in prompting discussion, helping students to think out instances of the "rhetoric of authenticity," for example, or to imagine "unseemly comparisons" and how they might function for a student writer.

QUESTIONS FOR A SECOND READING (p. 619)

1. It is interesting for students to imagine the intellectual context in which one might turn quickly from children's talk, to the *New Chronicle*, to the undergraduate curriculum. On the one hand, there is a training or sensibility evident here that erases what seem to be obvious barriers of time and place, of personal and professional. On a second reading, we want students to try to imagine Pratt's imagination — her way of thinking about and reading the material around her as she prepares to write. On the other hand, we want students to go back to the argument of the essay and to its key terms (like "community" and "contact") to see how they hold together the pieces Pratt presents for discussion.

2. We've found that both students and teachers are sometimes frustrated by this essay. Teachers wish there was more work with the text — more on the pictures, more on Guaman Poma. That textual work appears in Pratt's book *Imperial Eyes*, although even that book, despite its extensive readings of the work of European travelers, has only a few examples of "native" texts. The reading of texts was simply not part of Pratt's original lecture which serves as the text for "Arts of the Contact Zone." Students are frustrated because they don't see the connection between the opening section (about Pratt's son) and the later discussion. Nor do they have the sense of which texts she may be alluding to when she talks about the texts of the contact zone. One way we have found for students to question the text is to imagine places within the flow of its presentation (or its delivery, if they imagine it as a public lecture) where they might have questions for the author.

3. This is, for us, a standard application question. We want to direct students' attention to the material that they can command and use to extend Pratt's project — in this case, the classroom. As a frame for rereading, the question asks students to look for passages and terms they could bring to bear in an examination of their own educations.

4. This question emerged from our experiences in class, specifically concerning the obviously difficult terms. We wanted to acknowledge that the difficulty is strategic — part of the text, not part of students' "poor" preparation — and we wanted to suggest when and where and how a dictionary can be useful. But we also wanted to point to what was for our students the hardest term to get a handle on: "culture." In particular, we wanted to focus attention on the ways in which Pratt revises the essay's usual use for her readers (making the "unnatural" definition the operative one, arguing against utopian thinking). To this end, we wanted students to think from both positions (a linguistic version of the "face and cup" pictures that appear in psychology textbooks).

ASSIGNMENTS FOR WRITING (p. 620)

1. The first assignment is an "inventory" assignment, asking students to collect documents that could stand, like the *New Chronicle*, as evidence of the literate arts of the contact zone. Pratt's essay provides a frame to organize the search. Students should imagine that they can break this frame; that is, they can take it as a challenge to find the document that would surprise Pratt, that she would overlook or never think of. Her essay thus provides the terms for a discussion of the material, or representative examples from that material that they collect.

This assignment offers two options. The first sends students to a library (or historical society) to find documents from the past. We tried to suggest the many possible moments of contact in local history (between slaves and owners, workers and management, women and men, minority and majority). This assignment was prompted by Jean Ferguson Carr's teaching at Pitt (her courses almost always include some kind of archival project) and Pat Bizzell's teaching at Holy Cross (where she has students research local accounts of European settlements written by Native Americans). We were frustrated by the degree to which students feel removed from library archives and the degree to which our teaching (and the textbook) seemed to enforce that remove. Needless to say, this option will seem to be the harder of the two and students will need some prompting or challenge or rewards to choose it. One thing to remember is that an assignment like this will take more time than usual, since it takes time to find the library and spend enough time in the stacks to make the experience profitable, more than a quick search for the one book that will get you through the assignment. We've also found that we needed to make the process of search and selection an acknowledged part of the work of the course. We ask students to collect folders of material, to present them to others (to the class, to groups) and, in their essays, to talk about how they chose the material they chose to write about.

The second option sends students out into their local culture to look for the "documents," which can be defined loosely to include music (like rap), transcripts of talk shows, films, documentaries, and so on. Students should feel that they can follow Pratt's lead and turn to their brothers and sisters (or their children) and to educational materials, including papers they are writing or have written recently. You should think carefully about whether or not you would want students to choose papers from your course. It is an interesting possibility, but it will be hard for students to write about you and your class as anything *but* a utopia, paradise on earth. You may be disappointed if you invite students to take your classroom as an example.

With either option, students are asked to present their material as part of a project Pratt has begun. We have found it important to remind students that they need to *present* "Arts of the Contact Zone," even to their fellow students who have read it. You cannot assume, we remind our students, that readers have it freshly in mind or that they will be willing to get the book off the shelf and turn to pages. And we have found it important to help students imagine the role they will play in this text. They will need, in other words, to do more than simply cite from or summarize what they have gathered in their inventories. They will need to step forward as Pratt does to teach, translate, make connection, explain, comment, discuss, think this way and that. Students, at least our students, are often too quick to let the wonderful material they gather speak for itself.

2. Whereas the other assignments in this set ask students to use Pratt's term, "contact zone," in an intellectual project, this assignment asks them to write an "autoethnography" from the contact zone, to show how they understand Pratt's argument through their practice.

   It is important, as a starting point, to ask students to imagine how this task might be different from writing an "autobiography." In a sense, autobiographies have historically been read as "autoethnographies." But as these terms define a *writer's* motive, it will be important for many students to imagine from the outset that they occupy a position likely to be ignored or unread or misread. It can be useful to think of the ways writers signal that they are "engaging with representations" others make of them ("many people would say . . . ," "I have been called. . . ," "some might refer to this as . . . ," "from a different point of view . . ."). This is also a good time to return to the lists Pratt offers of the literate arts of the contact zone ("parody," "unseemly comparisons," "bilingualism," "imaginary dialogue," and so on). These lists can serve as a writer's tool kit or, perhaps, as a way of beginning to imagine revision.

3. This assignment is the most straightforward of the three. It asks students to use Pratt's key terms in an essay in which they provide the key examples, in this case examples of "scenes" of education (Assignment 1 asked for examples of texts). We have found it useful to ask students to provide parallel accounts of a scene (the utopian and antiutopian, the pre- and post-Pratt). You could cut this if it seems too arbitrary or distracting. We added it not just as an exercise in thinking from alternative points of view but also as preparation for the final question, which asks students to think about

the consequences of this shift — the practical consequences as well as the consequences to one's sense of the order of things. As we usually do, we try to phrase assignments asking students to take a position in such a way as to remind them that their "position" is not autonomous but links them, whether they choose the connections or not, with a more generalized interest, a "group."

MAKING CONNECTIONS (p. 622)

1. This is an interesting assignment — and a bit tricky. To make the most of it, students should have some access to pages from the source material. The most obvious use of Pratt in reading Mitchell is to highlight the differences between *After the Last Sky* and *Let Us Now Praise Famous Men*. Pratt is interested in the ways those living under subject speak *back* to the institutions of power. She allows students, for example, to think about the figures in the Agee/Evans text as asserting some control over the image. They can't focus or crop; they do, however, have control over pose and gaze. It is particularly challenging to turn to the Barthes example, since he complicates the idea of "contact" beyond that which is understood by either Mitchell or Pratt. In teaching this assignment, it is important to be sure that students work closely with examples — a limited number of examples — and that they think about differences and the usefulness of one text over the other. You will want students' summaries of the texts, in other words, to serve strategically in a larger project.

2. This assignment requires something of a leap from students, since "Arts of the Contact Zone" does not provide an example of a close reading of a text. It provides the terms that can organize a close reading (and provide the grounds for evaluation), but the only extended example is the reading of the images from the *New Chronicle*. There are plenty of examples of close reading in Pratt's book, *Imperial Eyes*. It might be useful to xerox a page or two — pages where she works closely with a block quotation. (This can help students get a sense of the format and mechanics of a written close reading.) Whether you provide this supplement or not, it is interesting to ask students to begin to rework Baldwin's and Jacobs's texts by trying to organize passages under the terms Pratt uses to describe the "arts of the contact zone." Pratt's terms give them an angle on the ideology of style — thinking about "parody," or "autoethnography" or "comparisons" or the "rhetorics of authenticity." It is crucial that students spend time looking over possible examples from the texts but, when they begin to write, that they limit themselves to two or three. The goal should be to work closely with extended passages in block quotation, not simply to provide a list of passages organized under Pratt's headings.

ADRIENNE RICH

When We Dead Awaken: Writing as Re-Vision (p. 627)

While the opening sections of this essay may sound like shop talk to students, once they get beyond them, students are taken by the force of Rich's argument and a sense that the essay addresses a familiar but controversial topic. Students feel the force of Rich's argument, and they feel empowered to speak their own versions of women's or men's rights, but without careful teaching they will do so without paying attention to detail — that is, to the poems that Rich uses to ground what she has to say. As a consequence, their conversations and essays will consider the social behavior of men and women rather than, as Rich would have it, the problems women have finding a way of speaking inside the language and structures of a patriarchal culture. This is ultimately an essay about reading and writing — students tend to read it as an essay about "life." Students speak and write well when they attend to detail; they speak and write dreadfully when they speak and write about "life" (or at least when they begin with this as their motive).

The best way to teach this essay might be to show students how to pay attention to the details. Use the language and structure of the essay itself as a way of testing and extending Rich's argument. As students pull out sections that address the situation of the woman writer, it becomes interesting to turn what Rich says back on her own essay. Another approach is to spend time working on the poems Rich brings forward as evidence. Even for a professional reader, the bearing of the poems on the argument is not self-evident. We find that we have to stop and read the poems the way we read poems; we can't pass through them as quickly as we can exemplary material in other essays we read. This is one of the things we admire about this essay — Rich's willingness to put her own work in this context, and her patience in including the poems whole, rather than in fragments.

The essay provides the occasion for a teacher to talk with students about poems as they belonged to a moment in a poet's life and allowed her to work on a problem — a language problem, but one not as divorced from real life as students like to imagine. Rather than lecture students on the poems, ask students, after reading one poem out loud, to imagine just where it is in the poem that they find the illustration the essay calls for. Once sections have been identified — and we doubt there will be agreement — ask just what it is that is being illustrated. Let students work on the poems in the spirit of the essay — don't try to remove them and treat them as poems in an anthology. We are interested in hearing from students just how the poems are different, how they chart the progress of a poet. We ask them to move from the changes in the poems to what Rich says about the changes in her work as a writer.

When we think of the poems in context, the most interesting to us is the last one in the essay, the one on Caroline Herschel that concludes the sequence. The placement puts a certain burden on it, at least within the structure of the essay. Rich says of the poem, "At last the woman in the poem and the woman writing the poem become the same person" (text p. 638). This is a statement whose meaning seems constantly to elude us. We think we know what it means until we get back inside the essay again. It is one of those statements that wonderfully frame a real conversation a teacher can have with students. We're interested in what it means and in what students can say about how the poem serves the argument of the essay. Rich includes it without any direct final commentary. We want to encourage students to take the challenge and do what they can to complete their reading of the essay.

QUESTIONS FOR A SECOND READING (p. 646)

1. We've found that the central problem in this essay is imagining how a feminist argument can be applied to writers and writing. Students are familiar with arguments about housework and the social and sexual relations between men and women, but the argument about language and culture seems difficult and mysterious. One agenda for rereading is to focus on the argument as an argument about writing, one appropriating familiar terms like "revision." Simultaneously students must attend to the essay as a text that can demonstrate or deny the very argument it is making. It is important for students to think of the piece in relation to its genres — autobiography, academic discourse, political oratory. They need not only to hear familiar refrains but also to see where and how Rich resists the familiar even in the very act of mixing genres. And they need to see the consequences of assigning gender to conventions of discourse, to think about conventional phrases and structures as belonging to a patriarchal culture.

2. This variation on the first question directs students' attention not to the text but to its unusual examples, the poems. By studying the poems and the surprising things Rich notices and says about them, students can read them in context — in the context of an argument about women's writing, of a poet's discussion of their place in her own

history, of a poet's sense of what makes a poem interesting. It is possible for students to go back through the essay to learn how to better read it, and also to become better readers of poems.

3.   After teaching this essay several times, we realized that students had little sense of the names Rich mentions in passing. Since they stand as one version of the "tradition" Rich writes about, it seemed to us useful for students to be able to make use of these names as points of reference. We have a policy of not glossing names or words in the text, since glossing always presents the image of a reader who knows everything, and since we are arguing that you can work on a text without knowing everything. So instead of providing glosses, we use these names as a way of getting our students into the library. We put students in groups and make each group responsible for researching some of the names. When they come back to class they report on what they have found and how, knowing what they now know, they might read Rich's essay differently.

4.   The anthology is a useful device for setting pieces in important, striking, or suggestive contexts. With one piece per author, however, students are denied a view of the context provided by the author's continued work. This is particularly problematic with "When We Dead Awaken: Writing as Re-vision." Rich turns her attention to her own work and ends, where she must, with the poems at hand. Revision, of course, continues as part of her project as a writer. "When We Dead Awaken" was written in 1971; much important work has been written since then — in fact, Rich continues to write and publish, thirty years later. A friend and colleague, Kathryn Flannery, noted that teaching the essay alone had the effect of freezing Rich in amber. "It seems that the student is invited to respond to the essay in formalist terms — to think about revision and to put aside whatever else Rich is up to. Ironically, it is as if Rich never gets a chance to revise her stance, and students get only this relatively early version of her gender politics." Flannery in fact, suggested that we look to *Your Native Land, Your Life*. She said:

> When I taught the essay last Fall, I brought in several poems from *Your Native Land, Your Life,* not her latest collection but a collection that I think represents an important turn in her work. She has several prose poems to her father and her former husband, both of whom are dead. In a sense, she writes to them to forgive her own narrowness (to her father: "I met you again as the face of patriarchy, could name at last precisely the principle you embodied, there was an ideology at last which let me dispose of you, identify the suffering you caused, hate you righteously as part of a system the kingdom of the fathers . . . I did not see beneath it . . . ") — a narrowness that is evidence in the revision piece and that students understandably react to — a reaction that gets expressed unhelpfully as homophobia. Because the essay is not for me simply an occasion to talk about revision but is also inevitably a place for students to think about sexual orientation . . ., sometimes their first opportunity in a school setting, I want it to be the best opportunity. I don't want to dodge the issue behind some formalist reading, but I also don't want to simplify her thinking by defending a position she herself has abandoned. Her poetry has not stood still. . . .

We have provided a selection of poems from *Your Native Land, Your Life*. Ideally students will also go out (perhaps in pairs) to find her other books and to look for poems that can be placed in interesting conversation with "Orion" or "Snapshots" or "Planetarium." When we have had our students do this work, we have asked them to also think formally, to think about form and style as well as subject matter, argument, and point-of-view.

ASSIGNMENTS FOR WRITING (p. 647)

1. Rich says that language can transform by renaming the world, and this anthology is designed to showcase pieces of writing that have just that power. This can be a local phenomenon, however. There are phrases or words that grab a reader and add not just a word to a vocabulary, but a way of seeing or understanding what we would otherwise miss or take for granted. Ordinary terms suddenly have extraordinary power, and a person can use them as tools to reorganize textual material. Rich does it here when she renames writing by calling it "re-naming." This is a powerful term, and the assignment is designed to enable students to feel its power by using it as a tool for analysis. In a sense, the assignment asks students to put Rich to the test — if writing is renaming, take one of her poems and talk about it as an act of renaming. What is transformed into what? and to what end? With this term to organize their analysis, students should be able to do something with, or to, the poem that they could not have done before. The assignment asks them to use this language to speak of a poem, and then to reflect on what they have done.

2. In the course of her essay, Rich says, "I have hesitated to do what I am going to do now, which is to use myself as an illustration" (text p. 631). For illustration she uses her own story, but she also selects and presents five of her poems, each of which represents a moment in her growing understanding of her situation as a woman writing. This assignment asks students to enter into the argument of the essay and to extend it by considering, at greater length than Rich, the history that is represented by the poems. Students are asked to consider what they take to be the key differences in the poems, to construct an account of what those differences represent, and so compare that account with Rich's.

    As the final note says, the best papers will be built around carefully presented, detailed examples from the poems. A general discussion will never reach the level of language present in the poems. In speaking of the poem, "Planetarium," Rich says, "At last the woman in the poem and the woman writing the poem become the same person" (text p. 638). Students might look at the speakers in the poems to see what they say about the changes they see. Rich's statement that only in the last poem are the speaker and the poet the same is not obviously the case; there is something for students to work on here. Rich has set a problem for her readers, but it is not one she neatly solves.

    It is probably best for students to work with the poems in context — to begin with the challenge the essay raises, to see the poems as illustrations of a poet's development or of a writer solving certain language problems. We would not invite students to begin their essays by working out the kinds of readings they may have learned to perform in an introduction-to-poetry course. Students should begin with the poems themselves, and then with the task of imagining a method (a way of talking about those poems) that is in keeping with the spirit of Rich's presentation of them.

3–4. Both of these assignments were new to the second edition of *Ways of Reading*. Rich speaks powerfully about the need to turn criticism to the material of daily life, yet our original assignments kept students working with her essay solely as a textual problem. There were no assignments asking students to read their experience in Rich's terms. Some of our graduate students argued that we were avoiding the central, and difficult, questions raised by the text. While we hadn't chosen to avoid them, our students were right, and we set out to write additional assignments. We have used both of them over the last nine years with considerable success.

    Both assignments ask students to write from inside the "we" of Rich's discourse, to imagine that the essay is addressed to them. They take these as key phrases: "Until we can understand the assumptions in which we are drenched we cannot know ourselves" and "We need to know the writing of the past, and know it differently than we have ever known it; not to pass on a tradition but to break its hold over us."

Assignment 3 asks students to follow Rich's lead and to write autobiographically, not in celebration of their individuality but in order to cast themselves as representative of the way a certain group — named perhaps in terms of age, race, class, or gender — is positioned within the dominant culture. It asks them to use the occasion to try out some of Rich's key terms, like "revision" and "patriarchy." The difficulty students will have is in imagining their personal experience as representative of a collective one. You will, in other words, not get papers about the pressure of culture but about key individuals — fathers, mothers, teachers, lovers, grandparents, and coaches. In some ways this is inevitable. Both our students' age and the distinctly American versions of personal experience lead our students to write "frontier" stories, stories with no sense of the social, the political, or the historical. These are the concerns we highlight for revision: In what ways is this story more than your story? Where can we find the cultural context? In what ways are you, as a character, cast in relation to ways of speaking, habits of mind?

Assignment 4 asks students to imagine that the writing of the past is made up of more than a literary tradition, that it includes the practice of all writers, that it is handed down not only through Great Books but also through popular writing and lore, that its evidence can be found in the predictable features of students' own writing. Tradition is not just sonnet form; it is also topic sentence and book report. Students' success with this assignment will depend greatly on their ability and willingness to turn quickly to a close reading of actual examples, as Rich does with her poems. Students will need texts to work with. We have used this as a retrospective assignment, where students reflect over the work they have done over a semester, in our course and others, but we have also used it early in the term for students who have files containing old work. This assignment is an occasion for students to think about their own writing; it is also, however, an occasion for them to think about how writing has been represented to them by their culture and through their education. They hear, often for the first time, much of the emptiness of the usual talk about writing and they have a chance to reflect on whose interests are served in those representations of writing — where ideas are meant to be controlling ideas, where examples must support conclusions, where conclusions take us back to where we began.

We have found that students tend to avoid or overlook the final questions in their first draft. They devote their energy to a study of their own writing and do not step back and reflect on how or why, in their terms or Rich's, one would want to revise the writing of the past, to break its hold. This has been our primary concern when students revise the essay.

5. See "Questions for a Second Reading," 4. This is a kind of assignment that encourages (and perhaps requires) draft and revision. In order to work forward to poems beyond "When We Dead Awaken," students need to have a command of the essay, its arguments, and the ways that the arguments might be represented in "Snapshots," "Orion," and "Planetarium." The poems are presented without extended commentary. It would make sense to have students write about "When We Dead Awaken" first, and then, in a later draft, to expand as well as revise. We found it useful to give students the license to write as though they were revising "When We Dead Awaken," inviting them, that is, to talk about what Rich *might have said* if she had included two or three later poems in the body of her essay, or to talk about how she might have revised the final section, the "I had a dream" speech.

MAKING CONNECTIONS (p. 649)

1. This assignment asks students to think about "When We Dead Awaken: Writing as Revision" in relation to other essays that use autobiography and family history to think about large questions — race, patriarchy, nation, war. The assignment identifies Susan Griffin's "Our Secret" and James Baldwin's "Notes of a Native Son." Students could also write about Anzaldúa, Rodriguez, Walker, or Wideman.

   As always, the success of the writing to this assignment will depend on students taking time to present and to develop examples from the texts. Certainly summary and paraphrase will be required strategically to prepare the comparison. You can help students to feel the pressure, however, to turn to block quotation and to specific and extended points of comparison.

   It is important for students to take the final set of questions seriously. The temptation will be to say that these are great writers and of course everyone should be allowed a similar freedom of expression — or something like that. Students should feel the pressure (or students will benefit, we've found, from the pressure) to think seriously about what an essay like this can and can't do, the purposes and occasions it can and cannot serve.

2. This is a different kind of assignment altogether. Rather than asking students to read one text *through* another, it asks them to compare and contrast. The material to be held together is a selection of two or three essays by feminist writers. The assignment pressures students to look for differences, and it does so in order to allow students a more complex sense of feminism than they would be allowed if they were invited to reduce all three to a single statement. If students look for similarities, they will tend to fold all three essays into a set of overriding issues and reduce the rich and difficult work of the feminist project to its lowest common denominator. It is better, then, for students to look for variation, to make fine distinctions, to see that Rich, Anzaldúa, and Bordo could be making not only different arguments but different kinds of arguments. Finally, the assignment is the occasion for students to account for these differences, to think about the role of history, experience, and ideology in the construction of these positions. With the other "Making Connections" assignment, this one is ambitious enough that students will benefit from working through at least one draft with your help. The first draft may be the occasion for drawing the material together, the second for rethinking what to do with it.

3. Once students are familiar with Rich's essay (perhaps from discussions drawn from the second reading questions), they'll need to imagine that Munro is making an argument in her story about women. Certainly the female characters are foregrounded to the male characters who seem lightly sketched compared to the women. What might they say her argument is, then, about women? How can they think about the connections among the women — Lottar, Charlotte, Claire — in the story? How might it be said that Munro's drawing of them points to an argument she is making about women? What moments in the story might they, the students, use to argue for that argument or those arguments about women?

   Rich's work on women is foregrounded in her essay, so students will need to identify key passages that allow them to write about what she could be said to be stating about women. But the assignment asks for more than finding ways to write about the arguments being made in these two selections. Students are also asked to write to readers not familiar with these selections, so they will also need to find ways to present these selections, their outlines and substance, to their readers. Consequently, this is a substantial piece of work that is being asked of students, and you might want to stage it over two or three weeks of classes with considerable class time given to the presentation and study of excerpts from students' writings, so that they can see a range of work and imagine revisions from their class discussions of each other's essays. They could benefit from examples of the ways they present Munro's and Rich's selections to their readers, of course, and from examples of how they imagine the arguments here about women. You might want to specifically focus some of this on their uses of sources to make these arguments and the ways they explain the links between the sources they use and the arguments they write.

RICHARD RODRIGUEZ
The Achievement of Desire (p. 652)

Part of the power of the Rodriguez essay in an undergraduate class is the way it allows students to frame, even invent, a problem in their own lives as students. Throughout *Hunger of Memory* Rodriguez argues that his story is also everyone's story. It takes some work on the part of a teacher to make this connection work, however. Students will read Rodriguez with either sympathy (because he is an oppressed person) or annoyance ("What's he got to complain about — he got good grades, he went to a good school, he was offered a good job"). But it is not at all uncommon to hear students claim that their situations are different: "Well you see, I'm not on a scholarship. I'm not a scholarship boy." It takes some teaching, then, to get students to imagine "scholarship boy," or "scholarship girl," as a metaphor representing a complex relationship between a student, his or her past, and school and teachers.

Those who praise Rodriguez's book often praise it in just these terms, by saying that Rodriguez's story is "everyone's" story, that he had identified a universal in human experience. This is a problematic reading of the text, since it erases the ethnic and class distinctions that could be used to explain and describe Rodriguez's position. Those who are not sympathetic to the book say that Rodriguez not only turns his back on his parents and his Hispanic roots, he writes a general justification for this act of turning away. (Note the two reviewers in the headnote.) If Rodriguez's story is everyone's story, then there is no reason to investigate the particular determinates of ethnicity and class in America. Rodriguez's conclusion to "The Achievement of Desire" reflects this thematic displacement of class. He talks about the tradition of pastoral: "The praise of the unlettered by the highly educated is one of the primary themes of 'elitist' literature." But the relationship of high to low, of Hispanic laborers to this graduate of Berkeley, is defined finally not in terms of an elitist culture but in terms of the difference between the "passionate and spontaneous" and the "reflective" life.

We need to find a way of enabling students to read the essay, as Rodriguez says he read Hoggart's *The Uses of Literacy,* to frame their experiences — as a tool, that is, to enable a certain form of analysis and understanding, both in the terms and metaphors it offers and in the example it provides of a process of self-examination. In graduate and undergraduate classes, this essay has inspired some of the best personal essays we have ever read.

Students read the essay to frame experience and as an example of the process of self-examination — we can use this claim to describe two approaches to the essay. We have had students write a kind of "framing" exercise for ten minutes or so at the beginning of a class. We have asked them to go to a phrase or a scene, to write it out and to use it as the starting point for a kind of reverie drawing on their own memories. The same opening move can function in discussion or in more formal writing assignments. The basic assumption is this: something in this essay will grab you, and often for reasons you can't begin to describe. For us it is the phrase "middle-class pastoral," the story of the "hundred most important books of Western civilization," and the ambiguity of the final phrase "the end of

·ducation." One can begin here, in the manner of a preacher working from a text, to draw forward and shape (or "frame" — as in "frame" a house, "frame" a painting, and "I was framed") the recalled (or invented) stuff of one's own experience. This is a way of paying attention to the text — if not to its argument then to its richest moments — and of drawing a connection between it and oneself. It is also a Rodriguez-like thing to do.

We are also interested, as in the case of many of these essays, in having students turn to rich examples, like the story of the boy's reading program, and moving back and forth between their own and Rodriguez's ways of accounting for them. We want students to see Rodriguez's stories as open texts, but we also want them to feel the difference between his characteristic ways of interpreting those stories and their own.

Students as we have said, can read the essay as an example of a process of self-examination. We like to make this a minute, textual issue. One of the most characteristic features of Rodriguez's style, for example, is his use of parentheses. They are a sign of his desire to speak in two voices at once — what he might call a public and private voice — or to say contradictory things and mean both at the same time ("I wanted to be close to my parents, I wanted to push away from my parents"). If you ask about the characteristic features of Rodriguez's sentences, students will turn to the parentheses, or to the sentence fragments and the sentences that trail away to nothing. Once you gather together three or four examples, you can start a conversation about what they represent. Why are they there? What's the effect? What do they tell you about Rodriguez as a writer? about his skill? about the problems he has as a writer? We think the parentheses, in other words, are a method in miniature, a way of using language to shape experience. They provide a tool that Rodriguez uses over and over again. Our students begin relying on parentheses in the papers that follow their reading of Rodriguez.

We will give one more example of a close-up look at Rodriguez's method. Students generally have difficulty working quoted material into their own essays. On the one hand, this is a mechanical problem, and students have to learn about punctuation, ellipses, and the conventions of block quotation. But the concerns a writer faces in using someone else's words are not just mechanical ones. It is interesting to consider Rodriguez's use of Hoggart. He first quotes Hoggart on page 654, but we don't hear about Hoggart until page 655. Then, as you look at the block quotations, you find an interesting variation in the relationships between the words that are quoted and those that surround the quotations. There are occasions where the two become indistinct, as though Hoggart could speak for Rodriguez and Rodriguez for Hoggart. On other occasions, Rodriguez insists on a position beyond the quoted passages — a position from which he can claim his own authorship, that allows him to comment, to disagree, to put Hoggart into perspective. Since the essay is about the relationship between students and teachers, or about the relationship between mimicry, imitation, and identity, the small scene in which Rodriguez struggles to define his relationship to Hoggart's words represents a larger issue, in which Rodriguez struggles with his parents, his teachers, and the public world of middle-class, English-speaking America.

QUESTIONS FOR A SECOND READING (p. 670)

1. This essay is not ostensibly difficult, so students will not feel the need to reread to bring it generally under control. Our purpose for sending students back to the essay is to allow them to complicate matters. The purpose of this question is to have students read as though the story could serve as a means of framing their own experience, as though Rodriguez could stand to them as Hoggart does to Rodriguez. This is an invitation to call Rodriguez's bluff — to say, "Wait a minute" to his desire to place the burden of his sadness on all of us, to offer his story as everyone's story.

2. In the preface to *Hunger of Memory*, Rodriguez speaks about the double nature of his text: it is both essay and autobiography. He refers, in fact, to his refusal to grant his editor's wishes and make it more of a series of personal sketches (his editor has asked

for more stories about Grandma). He refused because he felt he had an important argument to make — about education in general and about bilingual education in particular. This question asks students to reread the chapter in order to pay attention to the argument it contains both in the exposition ("His story makes clear that education is a long, unglamorous, even demeaning process — *a nurturing never natural to the person one was before one entered a classroom*") and in the arrangement of anecdotes and argument.

ASSIGNMENTS FOR WRITING (p. 671)

1. These assignments represent, in written exercises, the two concerns raised in the opening discussion. The second asks students to frame their story in Rodriguez's terms and style. This one asks them to turn Rodriguez's argument about education — about the relationship between students and teachers — back on the essay by considering the relationship between Rodriguez and Hoggart as a case in point. The general question is this: Is Rodriguez still a scholarship boy? Is he still reading "in order to acquire a point of view"? The earlier general discussion explains why we send students to look at the use of quotations. There are other ways of talking about the relationship between these two writers, but our concern is to make these problems textual problems — problems that hold lessons for readers and writers.

    This can be a more complicated question than it appears, depending on how far you want to push it. Some students will argue that Rodriguez is still a blinkered pony. Some will take his argument on its own terms and argue that he rejects Hoggart in the end for being "more accurate than fair" to the scholarship boy. There is the larger question of Rodriguez's use of Hoggart's book *The Uses of Literacy*, a book about the class system which strives to speak in the general and not to sentimentalize individual stories. It is possible, if you and your students have the time, to send students to Hoggart's book in order to construct a more complicated and comprehensive account of this reading.

2. Here, students are asked to reinvest their own lives by framing their stories in Rodriguez's terms. It becomes a more powerful exercise if students try to do it in Rodriguez's style. As an opening exercise, they might write out a paragraph of his, using the shape of his sentences but filling in the names and details from their own experience. There is no reason, however, why students cannot write a personal essay that is more loosely suggested by Rodriguez's. They might lay a Rodriguez-like commentary over it, or include one with it.

    The revision process will differ in each case. If students are concerned first with telling their own stories and then in speaking of them in Rodriguez's terms, then that commentary may be the focus of revision. If the essay is more completely a stylistic revision, then we would reverse the emphasis. The first thing students want to attend to is the form that will enable the writing — sentences and paragraphs and the relationship of anecdote to commentary. Then, in revision, they can best attend to the richness and detail of their own stories. As Scholes says about autobiography, the tension is between beauty and truth. You want to shape a story but also to honor the details of memory and investigation. In the revision we would ask students to try to honor the truth of the stories they are telling.

3. Essentially, this is an assignment that asks students to locate and characterize Rodriguez's methods, his "ways of speaking and caring," his ways, that is, of presenting and valuing what he presents. He's making an argument about being a scholarship boy and, finally, about the differences between the reflective and the "passionate and spontaneous" life. Students need to consider how he presents his arguments, his materials (Hoggart, his recollections, and so on), and how he thinks through them on the page. They need, too, to name and characterize the ways he "speaks" and to figure

out what it is he cares about now, in this text, and what he cared about during the various stages of his education. What can he do now, in writing and in his thinking, that he says he couldn't do earlier, in other moments of his evolution into a "speaking and caring" guy?

MAKING CONNECTIONS (p. 672)

1. Freire spent much of his life teaching peasants. There are many reasons why Rodriguez should not be considered a peasant. But Freire also speaks generally about the relationship between students and teachers and the way that that relationship determines the nature and status of knowledge in the classroom. At first glance, Rodriguez seems to offer both a perfect example of oppression (an ape and a mimic) and, in his success, an example of the conservative counterpoint to Freire's plan for a democratized education. If students can work out a Freirian critique of Rodriguez in such black-and-white terms, we are not sure that they are violating the spirit of Freire's project. We are not convinced, however, that Rodriguez can so easily be labeled a conservative and Freire a liberal, or that Rodriguez as a child received little more than deposits from his teachers. And we would want to push against students' attempts to organize their essays in such set terms.

2. This assignment requires something of a leap from students, since "Arts of the Contact Zone" does not provide an example of a close reading of a text. It provides the terms that can organize a close reading (and provide the grounds for evaluation), but the only extended example is the reading of the images from the *New Chronicle*. There are plenty of examples of close reading in Pratt's book, *Imperial Eyes*. It might be useful to xerox a page or two — pages where she works closely with a block quotation. (This can help students get a sense of the format and mechanics of a written close reading.) Whether you provide this supplement or not, it is interesting to ask students to begin to rework Rodriguez's text by trying to organize passages under the terms Pratt uses to describe the "arts of the contact zone." Pratt's terms give them an angle on the ideology of style — thinking about "parody," or "autoethnography" or "comparisons" or the "rhetorics of authenticity." It is crucial that students spend time looking over possible examples from the text but, when they begin to write, that they limit themselves to two or three. The goal should be to work closely with extended passages in block quotation, not simply to provide a list of passages organized under Pratt's headings.

3. This assignment asks students to think about "The Achievement of Desire" in relation to other essays that use autobiography and family history to consider large questions — race, patriarchy, nation, war. The assignment identifies Adrienne Rich's "When We Dead Awken: Writing as Re-vision," Susan Griffin's "Our Secret," and James Baldwin's "Notes of a Native Son." Students could also write about Anzaldúa, Walker, or Wideman.

As always, the success of this assignment will depend on students taking time to present and to develop examples from the texts. Certainly summary and paraphrase will be required strategically to prepare the comparison. You can help students feel the pressure, however, to turn to block quotation and to specific and extended points of comparison.

It is important for students to take the final set of questions seriously. The temptation will be to say that these are great writers and of course everyone should be allowed a similar freedom of expression — or something like that. Students should feel the pressure (or students will benefit, we've found, from the pressure) to think seriously about what an essay like this can and can't do, the purposes and occasions it can and cannot serve.

EDWARD SAID

States (p. 678)

When we first read *After the Last Sky*, we were struck by its combination of beauty and power. It is, as we said, a writing with pictures, and it was the writing that made the images both beautiful and powerful. The photographs themselves do not possess the beauty common to images in travel books or books of photojournalism, and yet with the text that accompanies them (instructing you on how to look and what to notice) they become an opportunity to look through (or behind) the standard representations of Palestine and Palestinians. The license plate on the Mercedes in the opening photograph, the hands of the bride and groom, the relation of foreground to background — when you understand what you are looking at, these oddly ordinary scenes become memorable, and some, for us, unforgettable. The power of the essay's argument on behalf of the Palestinians resides in quiet attention to detail and to arrangement. The ability to read an image — for our students, the equivalent lessons were in art history classes — here is combined with political motive and a powerful argument for the importance of seeing beyond stereotype and thinking beyond formulas.

Having said all this, we should add that the chapter, "States," needed to be taught to our students. The most significant problem it presented in the classroom is the one that Said announces in the introduction to the book.

Yet the problem of writing about and representing — in all senses of the word — Palestinians in some fresh way is part of a much larger problem. For it is not as if no one speaks about or portrays the Palestinians. The difficulty is that everyone, including the Palestinians themselves, speaks a very great deal. A huge body of literature has grown up, most of it polemical, accusatory, denunciatory. At this point, no one writing about Palestine — and indeed, no one going to Palestine — starts from scratch: We have all been there before, whether by reading about it, experiencing its millennial presence and power, or actually living there for periods of time. It is a terribly crowded place, almost too crowded for what it is asked to bear by way of history or interpretation of history.

We were working with *After the Last Sky* when Said's account of his experience in Palestine was being challenged in the press as false (See Justus Reid Weiner's article "My Beautiful Old House' and Other Fabrications by Edward Said" in *Commentary*, September 1999.) This was just a few months before the publication of Said's autobiography, *Out of Place: A Memoir*. We found the attack to be ugly and biased, an example of bad reading. We were reminded by it, however, that Said himself, at least in our circles, is also a crowded place, almost too crowded for what he is asked to be by way of history or interpretation of history.

It would be foolish and wrong to teach the essay as though it had nothing to do with current events (whatever is happening in Israel, Syria, and Lebanon) or nothing to do with students' positions on or understanding of the Middle East, its history and crisis. At the same time, as Said warns us, current events and prior positions can make the essay unreadable. What we would suggest is that you use the passage above to frame and enable the discussion. What *can* one learn by pausing, by leaving the present and its polemics, and attending carefully to these photographs and texts? They, too, of course, have an argument to make. What is it? And what can be made of it?

We found it important to provide motive and context for careful attention to the text. It was also important to provide motive and context for students to learn about the history of Israel and the Palestinians and to have the chance to speak from their beliefs and concerns (particularly so as not to silence students identifying either with Israel or with the Palestinians). The background work is probably best done through group research and reporting, and the presentation of beliefs and concerns through an open discussion where you are at the front, using the blackboard and serving as recorder. Whether this should occur before or after close work with *After the Last Sky* was, on our campus, a matter of debate. We believe that the discussion will have a different and more useful focus (to establish a way of thinking from the text, perhaps in response to Said) if it comes after.

The other difficulty our students had with the essay was in simply learning to take time to read the photographs, to see them as something other than "illustrations" meant to provide nothing more than a moment's rest or to provide that one dominant impression to accompany the text (as in the standard textbook photo). We found it useful to call attention to the paragraphs following the opening three photographs, reading out loud and asking students to talk about what they see and what they heard. (And asking, "What is Said *not* noticing? What is outside his field of attention?) Then we would ask students (in groups) to prepare discussions of the relation of text to image in the subsequent pages.

QUESTIONS FOR A SECOND READING (p. 712)

1. This question was designed to address the problem identified above — the degree to which students are prepared to either ignore images in texts or to treat them as quick statement. To read this essay is to return to the photographs, to learn to see them by means of the discussions in prose. And, since one of the writing assignments asks students to prepare such a text, a combination of words and images, it is important for students to think about the *different* relationships Said establishes between text and photograph — sometimes writing from them; sometimes writing back to them; sometimes writing alongside, in adjacency. We found some exercises like this to be absolutely necessary. It allowed students to think about what it meant to *become* a reader of this text (rather than just reading it); and it produced pleasure in the text (and interest in what it was trying to do) that was crucially important when students began to write.

2. This question is a variation on the first, this time using Said's discussion of the necessity of an "alternative mode of representation" to call attention to style, method, and arrangement. It asks students to read the essay as an experiment, as a piece of writing set against the norms and conventions of, in Said's terms, journalism, political science, and popular fiction. For students, "States" can best be read against what they take to be the conventions of report and argument, usually represented by a term like "the essay." Questions about style and method are common in *Ways of Reading*, and this question is echoed in the "Questions for a Second Reading" following many of the selections: Anzaldúa, Wideman, Griffin, and Baldwin, and Hirsch, among others.

    It has been important to us to teach students to see writing as "work," including a work against, or in response to, habit and convention, and for students to think about the ideology of style. Writing is not just fitting new content into standard forms. And, again, since one of the writing assignments ask students to write *like* Said, a discussion such as this can be crucial in allowing students to make the connection between what they read and how they write.

3. It has become increasingly important for us to send students to the library. (We don't have to send them to the Internet! They go there all too quickly.) And this essay, in particular, invites research projects. We know Palestine through the image of Arafat and young men throwing rocks. We know so little, generally, about Palestinian artists, intellectuals, and politicians that it is valuable to track down some of the names offered by Said. It is our habit to insist on the library (and photocopies) as part of student presentations. As students turn to the Internet (and this is often a perfect way to begin), in this case more than most others it is important to consider sources and the interests they represent. In the case of the Middle East, many sources that present themselves as balanced or objective are serving a particular point of view.

4. The book *After the Last Sky* teaches a reader to become observant, an observer. At the end of the book, Said questions the role he has been promoting. It is a striking challenge and stands as its own invitation to a second reading:

> I would like to think, though, that such a book not only tells the reader about us, but in some way also reads the reader. I would like to think that we are not just the people seen or looked at in these photographs: We are also looking at our observers.

This question asks students to reread in order to think about how they have been positioned by the text, not only in relation to the photos (where they occupy the position established by the camera and its lens) but in relation to the text (where Said assumes certain habits and predispositions). It is a wonderful opportunity to think about reading as reading and to think about entering and leaving a text. For students who are interested in doing more work with Said, it is a perfect introduction to *Orientalism.* This question is also useful for leading towards John Berger's "Ways of Seeing."

ASSIGNMENTS FOR WRITING (p. 714)

1. We had great success with this assignment (and with similar assignments working from Agee and Evans's *Now Let Us Praise Famous Men*). Students are asked to compose a Said-like reading of a set of photos. The following assignment sentences are important and worth calling attention to in advance:

> These can be photos prepared for the occasion (by you or a colleague); they could also be photos already available. Whatever their source, they should represent people and places, a history and/or geography that you know well, that you know to be complex and contradictory, and that you know will not be easily or readily understood by others, both the group for whom you will be writing (most usefully the members of your class) and readers more generally. You must begin with a sense that the photos cannot speak for themselves; you must speak for them.

Students, that is, are not just describing photos; they are using the photos to represent people and places, history and/or geography, to an audience unprepared to understand them. The selection and arrangement of photos is important, in other words. It is part of the work of writing this text. And the text that accompanies these photos should approximate the style and method in *After the Last Sky.* The prose is not simply captions, one after another. There should be an essay, a text with its own integrity, that is written with pictures. So, it is important to have students think about audience and occasion. What is the project? To whom are they writing? What is their relationship to subject and reader? And it is important to let students know in advance that they need to take time selecting the photographs and thinking about how they might be arranged. (It is useful to have them talk about what they left out and about plans they abandoned.) And they need to think about the writing. They are not writing captions; to think about what they might write, they can return to "States" to think about what it is that Said was doing and to think about how he did it. The writing can (perhaps should) be homage or imitation, an attempt to do something similar.

2. If you give students a choice of assignments, this will be a popular one. It is also the most difficult of the three. As Said remarks,

> For it is not as if no one speaks about or portrays the Palestinians. The difficulty is that everyone, including the Palestinians themselves, speaks a very great deal. A huge body of literature has grown up, most of it polemical, accusatory, denunciatory. At this point, no one writing about Palestine — and indeed, no one going to Palestine — starts from scratch.

Students who feel prepared for this essay will be prepared with arguments for or against the state of Israel. It is certainly in keeping with the spirit of "States" that these arguments should be engaged. The writing problem will be to work with the text; the pedagogical problem will be to make that work important, necessary, to ensure that the text is part of the project and not just a stepping-off point.

It is for this reason that we have asked students to begin with a summary. Summary and paraphrase are important skills to learn; they require attention to the text and, in particular, to those part of the texts that are difficult, surprising, unexpected; and they require generosity, a willingness to enter into the text's argument. Summary and paraphrase, in our teaching, are always strategic, however; they are never an end in themselves. They allow a writer to position something they have read for work that will follow. In this assignment, we suggest that what follows might be statement, response, or extension. Students are asked, "As you are invited to think about the Palestinians, or about exile more generally, or about the texts and images that are commonly available, what do you think? What do you have to add?" You should not feel limited by the language of this section of the assignment. The work in your classroom might suggest other projects, not "statement, response, or extension" but something else — dialogue, appreciation, memorial, parody.

3. As we said above, the conclusion to the book, *After the Last Sky* is both striking and challenging:

> I would like to think, though, that such a book not only tells the reader
> about us, but in some way also reads the reader. I would like to think
> that we are not just the people seen or looked at in these photographs:
> We are also looking at our observers.

This assignment asks students to think at length about what it means not only to read but to be read by a text. It will be important for students to think differently about image and text. That is, the images alone position the reader as equivalent to the photographer (or, perhaps more appropriately, since there is little agency involved, as equivalent to the lens of the camera). The text positions them differently, both in relation to the images and as a reader. Said, in other words, makes certain assumptions about his readers, their habits, affiliations, and ways of seeing.

There are subtle distinctions to make, in other words, and students can be usefully assisted in making them. It is also important that they work from specific examples — long discussion of particular photographs and passages. We have found it important to insist upon extended discussions of a few examples (since students will most likely be drawn to brief discussions of several).

MAKING CONNECTIONS (p. 715)

1. The first of these assignments asks students to think of "States" as experimental prose, where the experiment is a political necessity driven by the inadequacy of standard forms and styles available to a particular community. In this case, students are asked to think about the two essays by Gloria Anzaldúa, "Entering into the Serpent" and "How to Tame a Wild Tongue." Other selections could be substituted here. The assignment can be assisted by the second "Questions for a Second Reading."

The assignment includes extended passages from the chapter and the introduction to *After the Last Sky*. Here Said offers an account of the writing. There are similar passages in the selection from Anzaldúa and in the headnote and apparatus. It is important for students to try to work with these passages and their terms, to summarize and paraphrase, to deploy to key terms. But it is equally important that they work with the prose itself, with the arguments enacted in the ways of writing. There should,

113

then, also be long block quotations, foregrounding representative passages, and close discussion of what the prose does (not just what it says).

2.   The point of this assignment is to enable students to write, as experts, in response to W. J. T. Mitchell's use and representation of *After the Last Sky* in "The Photographic Essay: Four Case Studies." For this reason we have staged the writing in two parts. These could easily be represented as draft and revision.

The first draft is an account of "States." The assignment for this is, in a sense, written out in the first of the "Questions for a Second Reading":

> The first three paragraphs provide a "reading" of the opening photo-graph, "Tripoli, Badawi camp, May 1983." Or, to put it another way, the writing evolves from and is in response to that photograph. As you re-read these paragraphs, pay close attention to what Said is doing, to what he notices, to what prompts or requires commentary. How would you describe and explain the writing that follows? What is he doing with the photo? What is he doing as a writer? What is he doing for a reader? (How does he position a reader?)
>
> It might be useful to begin by thinking about what he is *not* doing. It is not, for example, the presentation one might expect in a slide show on travel in Lebanon. Nor is it, the kind of presentation one might expect while seeing the slides of family or friends or slides in an art history or art appreciation class.
>
> Once you have worked through the opening three paragraphs, re-read the essay paying attention to Said's work with all the photographs. Is there a pattern? Do any of the commentaries stand out for their force, variety, innovation?

The second draft, then, would begin with a rereading of Mitchell's essay, with particu-lar attention to the discussion of *After the Last Sky*. Students would need to be able to summarize, paraphrase, and quote from Mitchell's argument, and then to add their own response. The second assignment says,

> Once you've written that draft, read Mitchell and bring his analysis into the conversation. You will want to refer to the general frame and the terms of his argument and to the specific discussion of images in *After the Last Sky*. What does Mitchell bring to the essay? How would you de-fine his expertise? What do you see that he doesn't? How might you define your position or point of view in relation to his?

The key is to insist that there be a space in the essay where students speak, too, where they speak on the same plane as Mitchell. While the assignment uses the metaphor of "conversation," and while we believe this is a useful metaphor, others are certainly possible. What we have found most persuasive, however, is insisting on space, on a paragraph or paragraphs, sections of the text, where students can be found speaking for their sense of Mitchell, Said, and the questions that are on the table.

3.   This "Making Connections" assignment is out of the ordinary, since it does not make connections with another selection from *Ways of Reading* (only an oblique connection to John Berger and "Ways of Seeing," since it refers to Berger's work with Jean Mohr). All the questions and assignments focusing attention on "States" focus on Said and his work. We wanted one assignment for students who were interested in Jean Mohr and who would like to think more about a photographer and photography and how and why it is valued by writers like Said and Berger. *A Seventh Man* is well worth the time it will take to locate and read it. Students should be encouraged to think about the differences between that project and the one represented in *After the Last Sky*.

JANE TOMPKINS

"Indians": Textualism, Morality, and the Problem of History (p. 718)

Jane Tompkins's essay, "Indians," is a wonderful opportunity for students to look behind the scenes of academic life. The essay is surprising and engaging, and it offers a powerful corrective to notions of what "research" is all about. It offers an alternative to the story told all too often in the textbooks, where research is a fairly mechanical matter of going to the library, finding books, pulling "facts" or "truths" out of those books, and then fussing over organization and footnotes.

The story Tompkins tells is one of reading and writing, of research as it involves the process of interpretation, as it questions truths that appear to be self-evident. Our students have taken great pleasure in this essay's style and its willingness to show that scholarship engages a person, that it is neither a dispassionate nor an impersonal matter. In a sense, it is the character that emerges in this essay — this "Jane Tompkins" — that students find most memorable. They are either confused or disappointed by the conclusion ("Is that all this was leading to?"), but they love to imagine that they have seen into real lives.

There is a powerful lesson for students in this essay, one whose consequences they can feel in a way they don't when they read Wideman, for example. The lesson comes in the way Tompkins represents a proper relationship to books. Students may have been told that they need to read their sources critically, but they have a hard time imagining what that means. They believe, most often, that they have to catch the author in an error or a logical fallacy. Tompkins demonstrates that reading critically is a matter of working out a book's point of view and imagining the consequences of it — what it inevitably notices and what it inevitably misses. When students write about this essay in retrospect, they return to this theme again and again — how Tompkins shows them something about books and the library (and their possible relations to books and the library) that they had never understood. They had believed that you went to the library to find the truth and that the truth lay in either the biggest or the most recent book on the shelf.

The essay presents few difficulties for students. They need, as we say in the "Questions for a Second Reading," to work out the conclusion and its importance to its audience, if only as a way of imagining such an audience. We decided it was best to finesse the reference to poststructuralism. In the fourth paragraph Tompkins says, "This essay enacts a particular instance of the challenge poststructuralism poses to the study of history." We felt a lecture on poststructuralism would put students in an impossible relationship to the text, particularly since Tompkins says the essay enacts an instance of this challenge. We decided to go at this inductively. After students had read the essay, we asked what they thought this word might mean, what this challenge might be — who would feel it as a challenge, and why. In many ways the discussion could best begin with the title — by asking why "Indians" was in quotation marks, what morality had to do with library research, and why and how history might be imagined as a problem.

QUESTIONS FOR A SECOND READING (p. 735)

1. In *Lives on the Boundary,* Mike Rose talks about how students are so often excluded from the work we present them because that work presumes a familiarity with a conversation that has been going on for some time. It is hard to jump into an academic controversy. The first of the questions asks students to imagine Tompkins's immediate audience, to piece together the rituals and assumptions that bind the members of this tribe, those who find themselves in what Tompkins refers to as the "academic situation." The questions are designed to prepare students to make sense of the con-

clusion. It would be misleading, and somewhat dangerous, if students were to see only Tompkins's growing sense of the "situatedness" of her sources, and to conclude, "Oh, I get it. It's all just a matter of personal opinion."

2. The questions here are meant to give students a way of stepping out of the narrative and asking questions of Tompkins's work. We are taken with the way the essay makes connections between lives lived inside and outside the library. Tompkins says that the essay replicates her childhood encounter with Indians. It seems to us important to ask how this also might *not* be true, particularly since all of the "naive" historians are implicated in similar "narcissistic fantasies of freedom and adventure." It is also worth asking questions about the *process* of research as represented here, where misconceptions are peeled away, one after the other, in careful order. Finally, we have found it useful to ask students to imagine alternate readings to the long passages Tompkins cites, particularly those on text pages 725–29.

ASSIGNMENTS FOR WRITING (p. 736)

1. This assignment is similar to several in *Ways of Reading*. It asks students to locate in their own work what Tompkins identifies as the problems of reading and writing. These assignments serve a dual purpose. They are an invitation for students to imagine that they are a real audience, not just naive observers. The assignments ask students to imagine themselves a part of the "we" of this essay. And an assignment like this is, in miniature, a course of instruction; it gives students a model or a scheme they can use to systematically review and assess their own work. It allows students to name what they have learned to do, to identify it as a stage or one method among several and it puts students in a position to push off in a new direction. If students write the first of the two essays, it is imperative that they have a body of work to review and quote. They will need a file of papers, either a high school term paper or work they have done or are doing in college. If they work only from memory, the essay will lose its bite; it is simply too easy to be the hero or the victim in a narrative invented of whole cloth. If students are investigating a textual problem, they will need to work from passages from books they read or from papers they wrote. They do not, of course, need to tell the same story as Tompkins — most likely such a story would be impossible. It is a rare student who has learned to reread one of his or her sources. The essay can be the occasion, however, for students to look at how they used sources, to imagine why, and to imagine how those sources might be reread.

    The second option allows students to imagine that the problem Tompkins alludes to is not literally a textual problem — that it does not necessarily involve one's work with books. It says, in effect, treat your memories — your past conversations, your ways of understanding things, the tropes and figures that dominate (or dominated) your way of thinking and speaking — as text. Imagine that they are situated and that they situate you. Ask questions about point of view, about implication and origin.

2. Students write this essay with considerable pleasure. It allows them to imagine themselves as insiders to the routines and the secrets of academic life. They can imagine that they have more to offer new students than survival knowledge, that they can help introduce them to the systems that govern work in the academy. Students feel empowered by this position and they write with energy and verve. The problem for us has been that students tend to lose sight of Tompkins and what she says about the problems of research. We find that we need to turn students back to the text, but this is perhaps best done after students have written a draft in response to their own desires.

MAKING CONNECTIONS (p. 737)

1. Like Limerick, Tompkins discovers, through her attempts to understand Indian and white relationships in the past by reading historical accounts, that the perspective of the historian matters tremendously in the telling of the facts. This assignment is designed to put students in the position of writers who study both essays to determine how they differ — in their methods and in what they have to say about the reading and writing of history — while viewing them as a part of a single project which investigates the problems of writing history and understanding the past. Of course students will need to be familiar with both essays, and once they are, they'll want to focus their close readings on particular examples from each to write about the methods each author uses and the particular conclusions that they draw having to do with writing and reading history. It will be interesting for students to note that Tompkins is not a historian and to consider how (or if) this matters to her work. Does she work differently than Limerick because she's not trained in the same manner as Limerick, or does she work differently for other reasons having to do, perhaps, with her motives for writing or her methods of approaching the subject and the texts she reads? And, finally, students are asked to comment on how the differences (in methods, motives, writing, and conclusions) bear on them. What's the difference, then, in reading Tompkins as opposed to Limerick? what might account for the differences? their different responses to each text?

2. We have used several assignments asking students to consider Wideman as an expert, to see his methods of inquiry alongside Geertz's or, in this case, Tompkins's. In retrospect, we're not completely happy with the last sentence of this assignment — it is important, we think, to name the distinction between Tompkins and Wideman, but the phrase "creative writer" is so overused and misused that it is likely to create more problems for students than it will solve. You might want to warn them that they should be working very closely with Wideman's text, particularly with what he says about writing and with what he does as a writer, in order to give quite precise definition to the kind of writer he is and how he differs from Tompkins. Both could be called "creative writers"; both could be said to be something else. Students need to feel the pressure to create a working vocabulary here. They should not assume that this tired phrase carries all of its explanations. It is important that students work closely with the text, with the problems of writing as they are represented in Wideman and Tompkins's work. If their papers deal only in commonplaces, in generalizations that are true whether one looks at Wideman and Tompkins or not, then they are likely to be a disappointment.

3. One of the pleasures of teaching these two essays is the ways they take "academic" concerns about memory, the past, the point-of-view, and situate them (urgently) in lived history, in personal terms. Both Tompkins and Hirsch demonstrate that these issues matter to them personally; the problems of knowing press on them crucially; they feel them and worry about them. It is important for students to accept each essay's invitation to see the author as character, as a character asking for identification. And, in their writing, it is important for students to locate these issues in relation to pressing concerns, to things that matter. We ask students to resist the urge to write a book report. Tompkins and Hirsch write as if the writing matters (that's the effect we want students to see as a product of the text); see if you can write similarly (and that's the point we want to make; it is not just a question of what or how students feel but of what and how they write).

ALICE WALKER

In Search of Our Mothers' Gardens (p. 739)

This essay is especially interesting for the way in which Walker develops her notion of "contrary instincts" or conflicting feelings — those feelings or intuitions that rub against socially appropriate behaviors. She points to her mother as a person who felt bound to maintain the status quo as a black woman in a white world but who, at the same time, felt compelled to express herself as a black woman with her own creative instincts. Walker also points to Phillis Wheatley, a slave in the 1700s, whose loyalties were so divided by contrary instincts that, when she struggled to write, she ended up praising her oppressors. Walker calls her situation "cruelly humorous," and the irony in Wheatley's "singing," as Walker calls it, about freedom and liberty is visible and painful.

QUESTIONS FOR A SECOND READING (p. 747)

1. To work with this problem students have to reread Walker to locate those moments in her essay where she discusses "contrary instincts." Once they've done that, they need to go on to say what contrary instincts are. When they've dealt with the definitions offered by Walker, they need to turn to her discussion of Phillis Wheatley, specifically to those passages where Walker explains why she thinks Wheatley was able to praise her oppressors while writing about such things as freedom and liberty. A key question for students has to do with the answers to the Wheatley question that the essay makes possible. Walker offers her notion of contrary instincts as a possible answer, and, if students address it, they'll need to refer to the passages that allow them to explain how contrary instincts might account for Wheatley's behavior. She offers possibilities of other answers, e.g., that the irony of the situation wasn't visible to Wheatley, that Wheatley felt genuine warmth toward her mistress, who treated her well. Students will have to be pressed to find the moments when Walker alludes to such other explanations, and then they'll need to cast their readings of her into their own language.

2. For this discussion, students will undoubtedly need to do some library research to locate works by and references to the artists, black and white, so that they can look for commonalities (and differences) among the artists to whom Walker alludes in her essay. It's difficult to say what names students will recognize, but it's almost certainly the case that they won't know much about their works or their lives and the circumstances of their creativity. You might consider taking this opportunity to introduce students to the works of these artists by asking them to read both a selection and biographical information about a number of them; alternatively, students could work in groups to conduct this research. When you ask students in discussion what they make of these artists being listed together, you'll want them to consider the subjects of their works, the conditions of their creativity and lives, and the heritages they represent. Students will also need to read the Walker essay closely to study how she uses and refers to these artists. What purpose do they serve for her? What do they represent for her?

3. To do justice to Walker's seriousness and individuality, students will need to locate passages in the essay that address or allude to her feelings about her mother, herself, and the pressures on blacks living in a predominantly white culture. Once they've found the passages they want to use, they'll need to make something of them, to say what they reveal about Alice Walker and her feelings about her mother, herself, and the pressures on blacks. They might also address the question of Walker's voice. What's her attitude, in each specific passage, toward her subject, herself, and her readers? How might you characterize her tone? Is she angry? reconciled? resentful? pleased?

. Do the passages point to contradictions or ambivalences? Are there places or moments in the essay where she talks about reconciliation, for instance, in an angry or hurt voice?

ASSIGNMENTS FOR WRITING (p. 747)

1. The parenthesis in the middle of this assignment is crucial. At least, it has been crucial in our teaching. Without the parenthesis, the assignment asks students to think about the race politics in the essay. It is important, of course, that Walker brings white, European, "high" culture into the history of women's work. It is harder, however, for students to feel the importance or the urgency of this reference. It is not likely that many will have a sense of what is represented by the allusion to Virginia Woolf. And even students who have given much thought to the history of relations between black and white Americans most likely have not thought in terms of cultural history, the changes produced by and reflected in the novel, for example. We have wanted students to feel firsthand the transgressive pleasure of rewriting someone else's words. In general, students understand this to be forbidden. They think: "You are not allowed to do that." In doing it, and in thinking about how and why rewriting can serve, they get a felt understanding of their relation (of a possible relation) to tradition and authority. Most composition classes teach summary, quotation, and paraphrase. These acts are not necessarily subservient. A writer does not have to disappear. (It is our practice, in fact, to always teach summary, quotation, and paraphrase as strategic acts—ways of getting someone else's words and ideas out on the table.) Walker, however, provides a fourth term: summary, quotation, paraphrase, and *revision*. In this sense, she enacts an argument very similar to the argument of Adrienne Rich's essay, "When We Dead Awaken: Writing as Re-vision."

2. This assignment draws students' attention to Walker's essay as a creative project. It's unusual for students to think of essays as creative projects (their schooling in genres almost always defines "creative writing" as stories and poems and then includes essays among all other writing). This assignment gives them the opportunity to study how Walker uses the texts of the past, including Wheatley's and Woolf's, within her own project. Students will need, of course, to define Walker's project and what it allows her to know or learn about herself, the spirit of African American women, and her own mother. Within the context of defining her project, they need to consider how she reconceived, or rewrote, the texts from their original sources or contexts to serve her project. They'll need to ask themselves, for instance, how the Wheatley work existed, what position it held — or what were its purposes — when Wheatley wrote it. The same kinds of questions will be helpful to students when they study Walker's use of Woolf's term, "contrary instincts"; and it would be useful for students to turn to "A Room of One's Own" to study Woolf's use of the term before drawing conclusions about how Walker uses it and makes it a part of her project. How did Woolf originally use the term? for what purposes? for what audiences? How is Walker's use different from Woolf's? for what purposes? for what audiences? Walker's use of her mother's work is also an important part of her reconceiving of other peoples' projects. You'll want to draw students' attention to this, because they're likely to see it as so integral to the piece that they may overlook it as a "rewritten" source. Again, students should consider how Walker uses her mother's creativity. What were the purposes of, and audiences for, her mother's work? How does Walker reconceive those purposes and audiences for her own project?

3. Walker's essay includes references to many examples of women who expressed creativity in the face of oppression — Bessie Smith, Roberta Flack, Phillis Wheatley, Zora Neale Hurston, Virginia Woolf, her mother, and, of course, herself. Students won't be familiar with all of these artists, and even if they recognize names, they'll need to do some research to fill in for themselves the nature of their works and lives. Once they've

done this research, they'll be in a better position to understand what these references stand for and mean to Walker. They'll then need to consider how Walker uses these references and what they allow her to imagine in her argument. What would she not be able to do if she didn't refer to these other artists, including her mother? How are these references related to the issues she raises? How does she connect or draw together this "evidence" from the past? Walker's use of these artists is an important method, especially given that she reconceives them and their works, and students will need some help understanding this. They'll also need help directing their attention to how Walker understands her audience. To whom does she seem to be writing? What methods of hers might be said to represent her consideration of audience? These issues — Walker's rewriting of the past and her consideration of audience — can usually be presented to students in discussions of their drafts, while subsequent revisions can reflect added considerations. Making these kinds of references and suggestions is a tricky business, though, because you'll want students to invent their own terms and names for what Walker does, and you'll want to be careful to let them imagine how Walker works with artists from the past rather than, say, telling them that she reconceives or rewrites them.

MAKING CONNECTIONS (p. 749)

1. If students haven't already dealt with the issue of contrary instincts in the Walker selection, you might turn to the first of the "Questions for a Second Reading" and use that as a way to get them into it. They'll need to discuss the questions or use them to guide their writing about the Walker essay and the way she portrays her mother's contrary instincts. Since the notion of contrary instincts frames this assignment, you might find it well worth your time to turn first to the "Questions for a Second Reading."

    John Edgar Wideman doesn't name as "contrary instincts" his brother's conflicting feelings about wanting to make it in the white world and yet remain uniquely himself, but it's certainly possible to see them that way. For students this is immediately a problem of reading and rereading the Wideman essay to find those places where Robby might be said to be talking (through his brother) about those conflicting feelings or contrary instincts and also to find those moments when he is acting them out or caught in them. Students will have to ask themselves what his conflicting feelings are about, since they are not the same as Walker's mother's. They'll need to ask themselves how John's understanding and portrayal of Robby's contrary instincts differ from Alice Walker's understanding of her mother's.

    Since John is talking for Robby and telling his story, students might best help themselves by seeing him in a role similar to that assumed by Walker, but they'll need to identify the passages in both essays that they'll use to make the contrast. Once they have the passages and some notes on what Robby's and Walker's mother's contrary instincts might be, they're ready to write.

    Robby's conflicting instincts pit him and his sensitivity to love and good people in the "square world" (like his friend Garth) against success in the street world where the slick guy, the gangster with flashy cars and women and cash, is admired. Students will have to locate those moments in the selection that bring forward those conflicting instincts and they might turn first to a close reading of the epigraph to the Wideman selection. John, in Robby's voice, lays out the gist of contrary instincts. Students could find moments in the essay that elaborate on these instincts and make them visible enough to use in their papers.

2. One of the pleasures of teaching these two essays is the ways they take "academic" concerns about tradition, memory, and the past, and situate them (urgently) in lived history, in personal terms. Both Walker and Hirsch demonstrate that these issues mat-

ter to them personally; the problems of knowing press on them crucially; they feel them and worry about them. It is important for students to accept each essay's invitation to see the author as character, as a character asking for identification. And, in their writing, it is important for students to locate these issues in relation to pressing concerns, to things that matter. We ask students to resist the urge to write a book report. Walker and Hirsch write as if the writing matters (that's the effect we want students to see as a product of the text); see if you can write similarly (and that's the point we want to make; it is not just a question of what or how students feel but of what and how they write).

JOHN EDGAR WIDEMAN

Our Time (p. 752)

This excerpt from *Brothers and Keepers* tells such a compelling story with such a powerful voice that students are easily drawn into it. John's younger brother Robby is in prison for his role in a robbery and murder. The excerpt picks up the story near the end, and focuses on Robby's friendship with Garth; his growing up in Homewood, a black neighborhood in Pittsburgh; and his mother and his grandfather, John French. Throughout the selection, John asks himself how this could have happened to Robby, how he could end up in prison and John a Rhodes scholar and a college professor with a national reputation as a writer. The problem of writing about Robby bothers John, especially since the book is an occasion for him to get to know his brother for the first time in his adult life, and because John questions his own motives. Am I, he asks, exploiting Robby or am I telling his story, or is it something else I am up to?

QUESTIONS FOR A SECOND READING (p. 790)

1. "Our Time" is about Robby and Homewood, about a family and a community, but it is also about the act of writing, and in this sense it is primarily John's story. This question points to moments when John interrupts the text to talk about its composition. It asks students to consider why he would call attention to the text as a text. It asks them to consider how John might be said to address the problems he faces as a writer. Students will not have any trouble identifying these sections once they reread with these questions in mind. They will, however, have trouble understanding just what Wideman's problems are, and what they have to do with writing. And they will have trouble finding a position on the question "Why?" If he does not want to tell his story, if he does not want to deflect attention from Robby, then why does he do so? And what does he do to overcome the ways in which writing inevitably makes Robby's story his own? Are the author's intrusions a solution? What about the use of fictional devices? and the sections in Robby's voice? All of these are questions that allow you to bring forward the problems of reading and writing as they are represented in the text.

2. There are major passages in this selection where John speaks in Robby's voice, offering talk that might be said to be Robby's but is, in fact, John speaking to us in the voice of his brother. Students will need to locate those moments and to use sections of them that represent Robby's point of view. How do these passages reveal Robby's view of the world? What do they tell you about how he understands and represents the way the world works?

Once students have discussed these questions, they'll need to turn to passages where John is speaking. Direct them to pay attention to the language, not so much to the subject of the talk. They'll need to look at the differences in Robby's and John's language. What aspects of the ways they use language, the ways they use their voices, can you point to as indicating differences in how they understand and represent themselves? the worlds they live in? You might ask students to think about the voices. How does the voice in the passages where Robby talks treat his subjects, his readers, and himself? Who talks like this? For what reasons? To whom? And what about John's voice? What does the voice in his passages tell you?

3. To answer the questions on the differences it would make if John started the story with different episodes, students will need to turn to the way he does start the story — with Garth's death. They'll need to reread, looking for moments in the beginning that frame the rest of the selection. You might ask them to look for passages later that use or rely on the opening to present a point of view. Students will need to discuss the point of view of the given opening. What does the passage on Garth's death do for the rest of the story? How can you demonstrate what it does by showing how other passages rely on that opening for their sense or impact?

Once students have discussed the opening, they can turn to the other sections in the selection — the house in Shadyside and Robby's birth — that might be used to begin. They'll have to imagine those episodes starting the piece, and from there try to say how those passages would change or alter the point of view. What would those moments do to other major moments in the selection if they were used to begin it? Students will want to generalize after imagining other beginnings and you should press them to relate how their readings of specific passages in the selection change when the beginning changes.

ASSIGNMENTS FOR WRITING (p. 790)

1. This is the written response to the first of the "Questions for a Second Reading." If you haven't already, you might want to see what we say about those questions and the reasons for asking students to think about the author's intrusions into the narrative.

We've taught this assignment several times and we've found it important for students to work directly from passages in the text. The first thing they need to do is to reread the selection and choose their material. The assignment asks them to choose three or four passages; this may turn out to be too many. Once they have located their material, students do not have great difficulty describing it. They do, however, have trouble turning the discussion to the issue of writing — either the writing of "Our Time" or writing as a general subject. In their first draft, students should be encouraged to turn from their material to the question of *why* Wideman interrupts the narrative. We have found that students write well and at length about *what* Wideman says, but, when the space is open for them to comment or explain, they feel they have nothing to say. Students can imagine several routes to this question, several ways of imagining their authority. They can talk as fellow writers, imagining from that perspective why a writer might want to bring forward the problem of writing. They can talk as readers, explaining the effects of these intrusions. Or they can talk as students — that is, through their knowledge of other attempts to represent an understanding of race, family, crime, drug addiction, or the black community.

For revision: Our experience with this assignment suggests that students can best use the time allotted for revision to work on the general issues raised in this paper. What might they say about Wideman's narrative intrusions? More particularly, what might this have to do with the writing they are doing — or might do — as students in the academy? What would the consequences be of producing a text that calls attention to itself as a text, as something produced?

2. This assignment turns to "Our Time" as first-person sociology, pushing to the side the question of the text as text. It asks students to use Wideman's account of Robby's family and neighborhood as a way of framing an answer to Wideman's underlying question: What is Robby's story? The question can be rephrased in a number of ways:

Who is Robby? How can you explain the differences between Robby and John? In what ways is a man or woman the product of family and environment? How did Robby end up in jail?

Ideally students will be working closely with the text. The evidence they have is here — not in whatever generalizations they can dredge up about crime or the ghetto. And students will need to do more than retell what they find in the text: They will need to assume a role similar to John's. In fact, one way students might get started on the project is to measure their sense against John's, to set themselves apart as someone who can see what he can't.

3. In order for students to step into Wideman's methods as a writer and write their own Wideman-like piece, they need to be familiar with the selection, and they need to spend some time studying and discussing Wideman's methods. We use the first two of the "Questions for a Second Reading" for class discussions that focus on the methods of this selection, and after two or three sessions our students seem ready to begin this writing project. Most students will write about their neighborhoods and family, and this works fine, we think, as long as they demonstrate an allegiance to Wideman's methods by writing in different voices, or at least in two voices, the voice of the narrator and the voice of one other person whose story is being told, at one point, and who, at other points, is telling his or her own story. Students can break their essays into sections, as Wideman does, either while they're writing or as the work of revision. They should ask themselves why they think Wideman has broken his piece as he has, and they should have reasons for breaking theirs. They can use different typefaces to signal different voices or the "essay" part of their writing. And, as Wideman does, they should allow their voices as narrators to be heard, to show their thinking about how to tell the other voices' stories, about how to do justice to the other voices. For most students this will mean "thinking aloud" in paragraphs about the problems they encounter as they try to evoke other voices with depth and credibility. This speaking aloud on the page is an important part of this project, as it allows students to do the kind of self-reflective thinking and writing that writers must do when they recreate others through their representations of their voices, as Wideman does. Students won't have great success with this reflective writing in their early drafts, and you should anticipate that this part of the project, and the telling of others' stories in their own voices, will be a large part of the work of the revision for this assignment.

    We have found it useful with this kind of assignment to turn students' attention regularly, throughout the students' work, to self-reflective questions about this kind of "mixed" writing. It's helpful for them to think about what this kind of writing can do that a more traditional essay can't. In this light, we ask them how it might serve them as students. Where, in what situations, might they want to write like Wideman? And why, do they suppose, is this kind of writing not taught in school?

MAKING CONNECTIONS (p. 791)

1. Much more challenging for students than it first appears to be, this project puts them in the position of doing a large share of the work for it on their own. To begin with, they'll have to study Wideman's selection closely for its methods. Much of this work can be done as a class with the first two of the "Questions for a Second Reading." Once they have spent two to three classes discussing Wideman's piece in terms of method, they need to select another piece from the assignment's listing to read alongside the Wideman. Students will pick different selections, and will need to find a way to examine the selections' methods. We have grouped students by two's or three's according to the selections they chose so that they could help each other. We have directed individual students and groups to the second-reading questions for their selections so that they might start with a set of method-related questions to open up their readings. And at other times we

123

have limited the selections to two or three from the list so that we can then assign students to groups and plan on some class work with each selection.

Whatever approach you take, students will need to write essays in which they explain their two chosen projects and their methods to readers who have not read the selections; this requires a fair amount of summary. They also need to comment on each selection so that these naive readers can understand their thinking about what each selection's author is able to accomplish through experimental writing. These two tasks — summarizing and commenting on the accomplishments of each piece — are not separate, and students who treat them as such will get themselves tangled in long, unwieldy essays. Students need to know from the start that the examples they choose to summarize the selections to readers unfamiliar with them should also serve them, as writers, as the examples they'll refer to when they comment on what each selection does or gains or accomplishes through its experimental work.

2. It is quite interesting to read the Jacobs and Wideman texts side-by-side. Both are black authors and both call attention to themselves as writers and to their relationship to their readers and their subjects. Both are trying to explain something that can't be explained, and in both cases what can't be explained is the position of a black man or woman in a white-dominated culture. There are many important differences, however, not the least of which is the difference between the 1860s and the 1970s.

This assignment asks students to take each of the texts as a case of the problem of writing, either as generally conceived or as it is determined by the position of a minority writer in a dominant culture. It asks students to locate and describe the differences between the two cases. It is too easy, and misleading, to assume that they are both the same — that there is no fundamental difference between the texts.

It also asks students to name and explain the differences they see. The danger here is the way this assignment becomes an invitation to generalizations students can't handle — generalizations about history or race or writing. But this is also the pleasure of the assignment. It asks students to think not in terms of individual texts and authors but in terms of broad historical and cultural forces as they converge in reading and writing, where students are the readers Jacobs and Wideman had in mind and where they need to imagine a response. This is an ambitious assignment; students will benefit from being given the chance to rework a first draft, particularly if you can help them see the terms of their emerging project in it.

3. This assignment points to the obvious connections with other selections written by African American writers (James Baldwin, Alice Walker, and Harriet Jacobs) that, in one way or another, and in relation to a particular period and audience, have tried to think through what Baldwin refers to as "the American Negro problem." The Baldwin connection is perhaps the most interesting and promising, particularly as an example of another generation of writers considering a common project, since he too places a family narrative against the larger questions of race in America. As always the success of this assignment will depend on students taking time to present and to develop examples from the texts. Certainly summary and paraphrase will be required strategically to prepare the comparison. You can help students feel the pressure, however, to turn to block quotation and to specific and extended points of comparison.

Part III: Working with the Assignment Sequences

For a complete commentary on the selections in each sequence, please be sure to read each essay's selection in this manual, particularly the opening discussion. While we will cull materials from the discussions of individual assignments, we won't reproduce the introductions. And, while the sequences provide writing assignments, you should think about the advantages (or disadvantages) of using the "Questions for a Second Reading." In every case, students should read the headnotes in the textbook, which are designed to serve the assignments and sequences.

o–o–o–o–o–o–o–o–o–o–o–o–o–o–o–o–o–o–o–o

SEQUENCE ONE

The Aims of Education (p. 799)

In the introduction to this sequence, we say that these essays confront the relationship between the individual, and structured ways of thinking represented by schooling. The goal of the sequence is to give students the feel of what it would be like to step outside of the assumptions that have governed their own sense of school, assumptions that would otherwise be invisible or seem like a "natural" part of an adolescent's landscape. The rhythm of the sequence has students moving in to look at textual problems in the essays — to look at the essays as methods, as ways of seeing and questioning education — and then moving out to apply this new frame of reference to their own familiar surroundings. The final assignment is, in the broadest sense, a revision assignment. The first seven assignments lead students to develop a single-minded view of "alternatives" to conventional education. Assignments 6 and 7 ask students to imitate them to study an unconventional academic project (Griffin's), one created by a desire to understand but written outside the usual conventions of history or the social sciences. The last assignment is a "taking stock" assignment. It says, in effect, now that you have been studying a single problem for some weeks (we would think twelve or thirteen), let's see what you have to say if you stand back from what you have done and make a final statement. Because the final assignment asks for a major revision — a radical reworking of earlier papers — any work students do revising the earlier papers along the way might best be "local" revision: working on the relationship between examples and generalizations; working on papers by going back to the essays to look for ways to extend or counter positions taken in a first draft.

. . . .

ASSIGNMENT 1

Applying Freire to Your Own Experience as a Student [Freire]

The most powerful and accessible part of Freire's essay for students is the banking metaphor. They will be able to use (or explain) this long before they can speak or write well about "problem-posing education" or about the "structure" of oppression. Structural analysis of social systems is a method they will learn. The banking metaphor gives a way of imagining teachers and students, not as individuals, but as tokens bound into a social structure. The assignment begins, then, with what students will do best. It asks them to take this metaphor and use it to frame (or invent) an episode from their own schooling. In addition, the assignment asks students to try their hand at using some of Freire's more powerful (or puzzling) terms and phrases. We want students to see how they might understand terms like "alienation," "problem-posing," or "dialectical" by putting those terms to use in commenting on their own experience. The final paragraph of the assignment is really a carrot for the best students — those who will get inside Freire's frame of mind, make his argument, and then feel that they have been denied the fun of speaking back or carving a position of their own. So, in Freire's name, it says, "Don't just do this passively. If you are going to carry on his work, you are going to be expected to make your own contribution, even at the expense of challenging this new orthodoxy."

For revision: When our students have written this essay, their first drafts, at their best, tell lively stories of an individual's experience in school or provide a tightly organized demonstration that their experience shows that Freire was "right." The goal of revision, we feel, should be to open these accounts up, to call them into question.

Perhaps because they are often young adults, and perhaps because they are (by and large) Americans, students translate Freire's account of social, political, and historical forces into a story of individuals — a mean teacher and an innocent student. One way to challenge this interpretation in its revision, then, would be to send students back to Freire's essay to see how he accounts for "agency" — "who is doing what to whom" in Freire's account of education. Once students have reread the essay with this in mind, they can go back to their own piece, making this story of individuals a story of "representative" individuals, where teacher and student play predetermined roles in the larger drama of American education, where teacher and student are figures through which the culture works through questions about independence and authority, about the production or reproduction of knowledge, about the relationship of the citizen to the society.

It is also the case, however, that the first drafts make quick work of Freire. We asked one of our students how he was able to sum up everything Freire said in three tidy pages. He replied, "It was easy. I left out everything I didn't understand and worked with what I did." This is a familiar strategy, one that is reinforced by teachers who have students read for "gist." Another strategy for revision is to have students go back to the sections of Freire's essay that they didn't understand or couldn't so easily control and to see how they might work those sections into what they have written. This is an opportunity for students to have a dialogue with Freire — not a debate, but a chance to put his words on the page and to say, in effect, "Here is what I think you are saying." This revision will pressure students to be resourceful in including quotations and representing and working on text. It makes a big difference, for example, whether a student uses Freire to conclude a point or whether a student uses Freire's language as material to work on. And, we should add, these different uses of Freire provide handy illustrations for a discussion of "problem-posing" education.

. . . .

ASSIGNMENT 2

Studying Rich as a Case in Point [Freire, Rich]

This is a more difficult assignment, partly because Rich's essay seems more accessible than Freire's. Students feel that they "know" the feminist argument (often as an argument about housework or job opportunities) even though what they know rests on relatively unexamined assumptions about the roles assigned to men and women; and most likely what they understand will have little to do with culture or writing. Rich's argument about language and culture seems difficult and mysterious. And then, to top it off, her essay turns to *poems* for its examples. Students tend to skip these, since they are not prose, and to assume that the language of the poems doesn't matter.

You will need to prepare students for the strange shifts and turns in this essay, particularly the way the poems function as examples in Rich's argument. Students will often feel that poems belong to a completely different order of discourse — that they require a different set of tools (a knowledge of prosody, a dictionary of symbols) and they don't say what they mean in the ways that "ordinary" language says what it means. We ask our students to read the poems as part of the essays. If the poems are weird or difficult (as the last couple of poems are), they should assume this is the point — that they *are* weird and difficult. Students feel that the problems these poems create belong only to them, because they are students. They need to recognize that the difficulty is one of the features of the poems they need to confront: If "Planetarium" is somehow a sign of Rich's achievement, how do you account for the fact that it is so disjointed, so hard to read?

And students must learn to read Rich's commentary carefully. They can't, that is, just assume that any combination of words on the page can be attributed to "Adrienne Rich." We have found it useful to ask students to distinguish between several speakers: (1) the character or voice in the poem; (2) the Adrienne Rich who wrote the poem; and (3) the Adrienne Rich who wrote the essay commenting on the Adrienne Rich who wrote the poem. Students will not have too much trouble imagining how and why Aunt Jennifer might not be exactly the same person as Rich, but they will have a much harder time charting the different voices in "Snapshots" and "Planetarium." You might begin by asking how they might account for the quotation marks. Who is speaking? Who is trying to draw the line between persons speaking? And why? We have also found it useful to ask students why Rich might have left the poem, "Planetarium," to stand on its own. It gets a little preliminary commentary, but the end of the poem marks a major transition in the essay.

The "Freire" questions in this assignment stand as a wild card. In a first draft students will most likely write a three-part account of the poems. You will probably want students to return to their discussion of the poems. We found that students fail to distinguish between the person in the poem and the person writing the poem. Students might return to the text to ask "Who is speaking? And to whom?" When assigning a revision, we found we also wanted to give students a way of stepping outside of the poems as they first saw them (and outside the interpretations Rich encourages in her commentary). Freire is particularly helpful here. The second draft, with the Freire questions, can be the occasion for students to ask some questions about what the progression in Rich's poems might (and might not) be said to represent about revision, transformation or criticism, about the possibilities of breaking the hold of the past.

. . . .

ASSIGNMENT 3

Tradition and the Writing of the Past [Rich]

This assignment asks students to write from inside the "we" of Rich's discourse, to imagine that the essay is addressed to them. They take these as the key phrases: "Until we can understand the assumptions in which we are drenched we cannot know ourselves" and "We need to know the writing of the past, and know it differently than we have ever known it; not to pass on a tradition but to break its hold over us."

Assignment 3 asks students to imagine that the "writing of the past" is made up of more than a "literary" tradition, that it includes the practice of all writers, that it is handed down not only through Great Books but through popular writing and popular lore, and that its evidence can be found in their own practice, in the predictable features of their own writing, including the writing they have done and are doing for school. Tradition is not just sonnet form; it is also topic sentence and book report. Students' success with this as-

127

signment will depend greatly on their ability (and willingness) to turn quickly to a close reading of actual examples (as Rich does with her poems). Students will need texts to work with.

This assignment is the occasion for students to think about their own writing; it is also, however, the occasion for them to think about how writing has been represented to them — by their culture, through their education. They hear, often for the first time, much of the emptiness of the usual talk about writing and they have a chance to reflect on whose interests are served in those representations of writing — where ideas are meant to be controlling ideas, where examples must support conclusions, where conclusions take us back to where we began.

We have found that students tend to avoid (or overlook) the final questions in their first draft — that is, they devote their energy to a study of their own writing and do not step back to reflect on how or why (in their terms or Rich's) one would want to revise the writing of the past, to break its hold. This trend has been our primary concern when working with students in revising their essays.

. . . .

ASSIGNMENT 4

The Contact Zone [Pratt]

This is a powerful assignment that gives students the opportunity to represent schooling through stories or images from their experiences. Pratt's argument for the classroom as a "contact zone," a place where oppositional discourses rub against each other, clashes with conventional notions of the classroom as a community of like-minded individuals working toward common purposes. As students begin to imagine the classroom as a "contact zone," as they settle into the identification of experiences and images, they'll want to classify them as "community" examples or "contact zone" examples, and you'll want to push them to see the possibilities between the polarities that Pratt establishes, or to imagine other ways of representing their experiences that don't set up polarities.

Once students have read Pratt, it'll be difficult for them not to classify their experiences, but this assignment relies on them to present representative examples of their experiences and images of schooling, those that come to mind almost immediately when they think of school, and they'll first need to present those. When they turn to interpreting their examples in Pratt's terms, they'll have a way to push against her by taking up the question of what they have to gain or lose if they adopt her ways of thinking.

It might be helpful for students to do the initial draft of this assignment with most, if not all, of their attention focused on rendering the representative experiences of schooling that they want to work from. They'll want to create (or re-create) the people involved in the scenes, the dialogue, and the landscape. Most students aren't accustomed to this kind of detailed scene setting; they'll need to render it carefully enough for readers not familiar with their experiences to see the people at work and the kinds of interactions going on, so that when they discuss the scene as representing (or not representing) a "contact zone," readers will be able to discern the oppositions, resistance, and alternatives being played out. The same holds true if they are representing a community.

The second draft or revision could then focus more directly on students weaving their comments into or alongside the scenes. This would be the paper, then, where they read their experiences in Pratt's terms and come to conclusions about what they stand to gain or lose by seeing their schooling in her terms.

. . . .

ASSIGNMENT 5

The Pedagogical Arts of the Contact Zone [Pratt]

For this assignment students are asked to imagine their writing class, the one that has presented them with this assignment, as a possible "contact zone." To this end, they are invited to take one of the "exercises" that Pratt presents and discuss how it might work in their class. You'll want to be sure that students think about this invitation in terms of turning their classroom into a visible "contact zone," into a place, that is, where differences are visible and taken as occasions for learning. So, for instance, if students decide to fold storytelling into their work, they need to say what kind of storytelling. What will the stories be about? What will they learn from them? How will the stories act to turn the class into a "contact zone"? The same need for definition holds true for whatever "exercise" students decide on. If they would like to critique, then they need to say what they would critique and how critiquing would act to establish a visible "contact zone." For a number of the "exercises" that Pratt suggests (e.g., "experiments in transculturation," "unseemly comparisons"), students will need to imagine what these are and how they would work in a writing classroom. There's room to move here, but they'll need to read Pratt closely to flesh out her more abstract pedagogical arts.

If students decide to imagine comments a teacher would make on one of their papers so that its revision might be one of these "exercises," they have the same problem of definition to deal with. What would the comments ask them, for instance, to tell a story about? How would the revision act to establish a visible "contact zone"? What would they learn from this kind of revision?

. . . .

ASSIGNMENT 6

Writing against the Grain [Griffin]

Our students had a great time with this assignment and it produced some of the most interesting writing of the semester. They chose topics that ranged from parental influences, the relationship of machines and thinking, the struggle to be, as one young woman called it, in an unfriendly environment of violence, replications of behavior in men from different generations of the same family, and the various metaphors for space. The key to students' success with this assignment seems to lie in the subjects they choose to write about and the stories they tell. We have told them to write about stories they know or would like to research because they are curious about them, because they sense connections to other stories or examples that they may or may not need to research. The students' involvement in the writing will push them to do the kinds of thinking through and connecting that imitates Griffin's work.

This assignment demonstrates to them the kind of planning and care that Griffin's work required, and our students found that they could help themselves with outlines and charts or maps of the territories they wanted to cover. We allowed them class time, also, to test their plans with other students and with us. This proved to be time well spent, for it helped students see connections that others saw but that they had not and it prevented anyone from being lost at sea for anything but a brief period of time. We also asked for multiple drafts of this assignment, and we assigned students to pairs at different points through their work so that they could continually test it against the readings of others.

. . . .

ASSIGNMENT 7

The Task of Attention [Griffin]

To involve themselves in this assignment, students will need to reread Griffin to locate those moments where she reveals her methods. At times she tells us exactly what she is doing (looking at an etching, studying an interview, thinking about her past, imagining her subjects in their pasts, and so on), and students should pay attention to those moments; at other times, students will need to infer (or imagine, as she imagines) the work she had to do (to learn, for instance, about the V-2 rocket development or about Himmler's childhood or recordkeeping as a Nazi). The weight of their work, though, should fall on the methods that Griffin reveals and directly writes to her readers about. How do the methods shape her study and make it hers? And students will need to consider, then, how her methods might be taught in a curriculum. What would they like to see taught? Why? What would they (and others) learn from it? Where might her work fit in a curriculum? in a particular subject area course or courses? in English classes? as a part of the writing curriculum?

. . . .

ASSIGNMENT 8

Putting Things Together [Freire, Rich, Pratt, Griffin]

This assignment is really meant to allow students to feel that the work they have done has brought them somewhere. There is no epiphany at the end of the sequence, no set of words a teacher (or textbook writer) can speak to make it all cohere, but it is possible for students to begin to fashion those words for themselves. That is the purpose of this assignment. It says, in effect, "Listen, you're not a beginner with this anymore. You've developed some expertise on this subject. Let's hear what you have to say." It is important, however, that students feel empowered to draw on their early work. This is not just a matter of saying that it is okay, but of providing the technology to make it possible (like cutting and pasting, for example). Students should begin this task by carefully rereading everything they have written and imagining what the important pieces are and how those pieces might be put together. There should be new writing, of course — students should think of this as a new project — but they shouldn't have to feel that they are starting from scratch.

O–O–O–O–O–O–O–O–O–O–O–O–O–O–O–O–O–O–O

SEQUENCE TWO

The Arts of the Contact Zone (p. 809)

The great pleasure of teaching Pratt's essay is watching students put to work the key terms of her interpretive system; "contact zone," "autoethnography," "transculturation." These terms allow students to "reread" or reconceive familiar scenes and subjects; they also provide a rationale (as well as tools) for working against the grain of the usual American valorization of "community." At first her argument seems completely counterintuitive, then it begins to make powerful and surprising sense. At least this was our experience when we taught the essay. It was difficult, in fact, to get students (at the end of their work) to stand a critical distance from Pratt's position — that is, the image of the contact zone provided a perhaps too easy answer to the problem of difference; or it led students to an

130

unexamined reproduction of "liberal" values: sympathy, respect, different strokes for different folks.

This sequence allows students to work at length with Pratt's essay, first with (and on) her terms, later in conjunction with the work of others. You can imagine the sequence working in two directions. It is, in keeping with a standard pattern in *Ways of Reading,* designed as an exercise in application. Students take the general project represented in "Arts of the Contact Zone," work those terms out through close reading and through application to an example from the students' experience, and then apply it to essays in *Ways of Reading* that could be said to represent examples of the literate arts of the contact zone — essays by Gloria Anzaldúa, Harriet Jacobs, and James Baldwin. Our goal in teaching this sequence, however, was also to invite students to begin to imagine that, through their work with Anzaldúa, Jacobs, or Baldwin, they were in a position to talk back to Pratt — adding examples, perhaps counterexamples, testing the limits of her terms, adding new terms, thinking about Pratt's discussion of Guaman Poma and her discussion of "community," its usefulness and its limits in a more extended project, drawing not only on the resources of *Ways of Reading* but also on students' readings of documents drawn from their local communities.

If you wanted to shorten the sequence, you could drop one of the readings (Anzaldúa, Jacobs, or Baldwin). There are several selections in *Ways of Reading* that could be substituted for those we have included here: Wideman's "Our Time," Geertz's "Deep Play," Griffin's "Our Secret," Rodriguez's "The Achievement of Desire," Walker's "In Search of Our Mothers' Gardens," Tompkins's "Indians." It is surprising how many of the pieces in *Ways of Reading* can be imagined as representative of the arts of the contact zone.

We chose the selections we did for this sequence because we were interested in working with material new to this edition; we also wanted to focus the term "contact" on racial, ethnic, and linguistic difference. If you add other selections (Tompkins, Griffin, or Geertz, for example), you might want to focus attention on the range of differences (age, class, nation, institutional or intellectual status) that can be highlighted under the term "contact zone."

For a complete commentary on the selections in this sequence, please be sure to read each essay's selection in this manual, particularly the opening discussion. While we will cull materials from the discussions of individual assignments, we won't reproduce the introductions. And, while the sequences provide writing assignments, you should think about the advantages (or disadvantages) of using the "Questions for a Second Reading." In every case, students should read the headnotes in the text, which are designed to serve the assignments and sequences.

. . . .

ASSIGNMENT 1

The Literate Arts of the Contact Zone [Pratt]

The first assignment is structurally a bit complicated. It offers two options, an "inventory" assignment (for which students collect examples of writing from a contact zone) and an "autoethnography" assignment (for which students imagine themselves, as writers, working in a contact zone). What complicates things is that the inventory assignment also offers two options. There are really three writing assignments listed here, grouped into two categories. You may want to make the choice of assignment for your students, depending on the goals of your course. The autoethnography assignment focuses the issues of Pratt's essays within students' own self-representations, within the context of the "personal" essay. The inventory assignment focuses attention on students as readers (and archivists) of other writers' work. Whichever direction students take, we would suggest letting them come back to revise their essays later in the semester, perhaps after assignments

2 and 3 in the sequence. If you plan to work this way, it might be useful to tell students that they will be working on a draft they can come back to later.

1. The first of the two options in assignment 1 is an "inventory" assignment, asking students to collect documents that could stand, like the *New Chronicle*, as evidence of the literate arts of the contact zone. Pratt's essay provides a frame to organize the search (a frame students should imagine that they can break — that is, they can take it as a challenge to find the document that would surprise Pratt, that she would overlook or never think of), and it also provides the terms for a discussion of the material they collect (or representative examples from that material).

The assignment suggests two ways of conducting the inventory. The first sends students to a library (or historical society) to find documents from the past. We tried to suggest the many possible moments of contact in local history (between slaves and owners, workers and management, women and men, minority and majority). This assignment was prompted by Jean Ferguson Carr's teaching at Pitt (her courses almost always include some kind of archival project) and Pat Bizzell's teaching at Holy Cross (where she has students research local accounts of European settlements written by Native Americans). We were frustrated by the degree to which students feel removed from library archives and the degree to which our teaching (and the textbook) seemed to enforce that remove. Needless to say, this option will seem to be the harder of the two and students will need some prompting or challenge or rewards to choose it. One thing to remember is that an assignment like this will take more time than usual, since it takes time to find the library and spend enough time in the stacks to make the experience profitable, more than a quick search for the one book that will get you through the assignment. We've also found that we needed to make the process of search and selection an acknowledged part of the work of the course. We ask students to collect folders of material, to present them to others (to the class, to groups) and, in their essays, to talk about how they chose the material they chose to write about.

In the second "inventory" option, students might go out into their local culture to look for "documents" (which can be defined loosely to include music, like rap, transcripts of talk shows, films, documentaries, Web pages, and so on). Students should feel that they can follow Pratt's lead and turn to their brothers and sisters (or their children) and to educational materials, including papers they are writing or have written recently. You should think about whether or not you would want students to choose papers from your course. It is an interesting possibility, but it will be hard for students to write about you and your class as anything *but* a utopia, paradise on earth. You may be disappointed if you invite students to take your classroom as an example.

Taking either direction, students are asked to present their material as part of a project Pratt has begun. We have found it important to remind students that they need to *present* "Arts of the Contact Zone," even to readers who have read it. You cannot assume, we remind our students, that readers have it freshly in mind or that they will be willing to get the book off the shelf and turn to pages. And we have found it important to help students imagine the role they will play in this text. They will need, in other words, to do more than simply cite from or summarize what they have gathered in their inventories. They will need to step forward (as Pratt does) to teach, translate, make connections, explain, comment, discuss, think this way and that. Students, at least our students, are often too quick to let the wonderful material they gather speak for itself.

2. This assignment asks students to write an "autoethnography." The inventory assignments in this set ask students to use Pratt's term, "contact zone," to read the work of others. This assignment asks students to write from the contact zone, to show how they understand Pratt's argument through their practice.

It is important, as a starting point, to ask students to imagine how this might be different from writing an "autobiography." In a sense, autobiographies have historically been read as "autoethnographies." But as these terms define a *writer's* motive, it will be important for many students to imagine from the outset that they occupy a position likely to be ignored or unread or misread. It can be useful to think of the ways writers signal that they are "engaging with representations" others make of them ("many people would say . . . ," "I have been called . . . ," "some might refer to this as . . . ," "from a different point of view . . ."). This is also a good time to return to the lists Pratt offers of the literate arts of the contact zone ("parody," "unseemly comparisons," "bilingualism," "imaginary dialogue," etc.) These lists can serve as a writer's tool kit — or perhaps, as a way of beginning to imagine revision.

. . . .

ASSIGNMENT 2

Borderlands [Pratt, Anzaldúa]

One of the pleasures of working with Pratt's essay is that it gave us a new way of reading our table of contents. There are several pieces that could stand as examples of writing from a contact zone (or that could be said equally to illustrate the "literate arts of the contact zone"). This assignment turns students' attention to the "mestiza" text, *Borderlands/La Frontera*. You could also use the selections by Rich, Rodriguez, Walker, and Wideman.

This is an application assignment — it asks for a generous reading and extension of Pratt's work. As always, students should feel free to exceed their example — to argue with Pratt, to notice things she wouldn't notice, to add to her list of the literate arts of the contact zone. And as always, it will help to give students a sense of what they will need to provide for their readers. They will need to present Pratt's essay (establish it as a context). They cannot simply assume that it is there, in full, in their readers' minds. And they will need to present their example, providing an introduction to (let's say) "Incidents" and working closely with the text, including passages in quotation. (Since Pratt does not provide examples of the close reading of passages in "Arts of the Contact Zone," it might be useful to provide supplementary examples.) We have worked with pages from "Scratches on the Face of the Country" (from Pratt, *Imperial Eyes*). You might also help students prepare by working on a set passage from Anzaldúa in class.

For us, every assignment (or almost every assignment) in a sequence, goes through at least one revision. We would, that is, spend two weeks on most assignments. If students revise this essay, we would suggest two prompts for their work. When they revise, they should begin by rereading Anzaldúa, looking for those parts of the text that have *not* been accounted for in the first draft. Students shouldn't simply be pasting in more examples but looking to see the interesting examples that were left out and asking why, on a first pass, these fell outside their range of vision/understanding/desire. And they should be looking for ways (or places) to speak from their own positions as authors/scholars. Students should, that is, be looking to see how and where they can find a place in their essays to speak from their own learning and concerns. Here is the place where students begin to talk about the limits and benefits, for them, of Pratt's work.

. . . .

ASSIGNMENT 3

Autoethnography [Pratt, Jacobs]

"Arts of the Contact Zone" provides a useful alternative to Houston Baker's account of the slave narrative. For Baker, the "authentic, unwritten self" is necessarily displaced (or appropriated) by the public discourse. In her representation of "autoethnography" and "transculturation," Pratt allows us to figure the author differently, so that we can imagine Jacobs *engaging* with the standard representation of an African American woman and her experience (and with the standard representation of a woman of virtue), but not giving up or giving in to it; here the point is, in Pratt's terms, to "intervene" with the majority understanding, where the purpose is corrective or revisionary, and where the writer is allowed a position from which work can be done (and can do more than merely repeat the master narrative).

This assignment asks students to use Pratt's terms ("autoethnography" or "transculturation"). It is important for students to see this as something other than a dictionary assignment ("According to Webster, 'ethnography' is . . ."). The point, in other words, is not to come up with the "right" definition but to see how these words (and the text that accompanies them and the example of Guaman Poma) can provide a way of reading "Incidents." Students need to work back and forth between the two essays, seeing how and where Harriet Jacobs might be said to demonstrate her own version of the "literate arts" of the contact zone.

We would spend two weeks on this assignment, asking students to treat their first draft as a draft and directing a revision in the second week. We would follow the same guidelines we outlined above in the discussion of the Anzaldúa essay.

. . . .

ASSIGNMENT 4

Writing from Within [Pratt, Baldwin]

This assignment extends the analysis from the slave narrative to Baldwin's 1955 essay, "Notes of a Native Son." The essay defines a dramatic context in which Baldwin is thinking for himself (writing for himself) about his father, his father's death and, as he says, "the Negro's real relation to the white American." It was, however, published in *Harper's Magazine* and Baldwin was beginning to think of himself (and to establish himself) as a writer who could speak to white Americans about the situation and the experience of black Americans. In this sense, it is autoethnographic and it is not inappropriate for students to think of it as addressed to a white readership. The lists Pratt provides at the end of the essay, provocative lists naming the possible arts of the contact zone, can be useful in thinking about and naming the style and method in "Notes" — "parody," "unseemly comparisons," "bilingualism," "imaginary dialogue," "the rhetoric of authenticity."

. . . .

ASSIGNMENT 5

On Culture [Pratt, Anzaldúa, Jacobs, Baldwin]

We often end our sequences with "retrospective" assignments. This one asks students to return to Pratt's essay and to the work they have been doing with it in order to represent that work to someone who is an outsider. For the first time, however, the issue has been represented through the more inclusive term, "culture." This assignment is a way for students to connect the work they have been doing with Pratt with larger questions of culture and community, reading and writing. Directing the assignment at an audience new to this material allows students to work from their strengths and to imagine the distance between what they have learned to say and where they began. To this end, it is important for this assignment that students imagine their audience to be a group of peers, people like them who have not been in this course. Without this warning, students tend to represent the "intellectual other" as a child or a simpleton. The stakes have to be high for this paper to work — students need to imagine that they have to address and hold the attention of their sharpest and most intellectually impatient colleagues.

An alternative to this assignment would be one directed not to students but to Pratt. We often end sequences with this other retrospective, in which the goal, we say, is for students to take their turn in a conversation begun by Pratt. Here the pressure on them is to achieve some critical distance from Pratt, to find a way of challenging or supplementing what Pratt says on the basis of what they (the students) have learned over the course of their work with this sequence.

As we suggested earlier, it might be useful to ask students to go back and work again on the first assignment in this sequence in a second or third draft. That way the issues as they have bearing on what students do (how they read and write) and not just on what they know (in summary statement) will be forward in their minds. From this they can begin to write to Pratt, or to students, perhaps students who would be reading the same materials in this course next semester. After a semester, you will have some of these essays on file. We have handed them out at the beginning of the term as a preview, and then brought them forward again at the end, in a discussion framing students' work with this final assignment.

o–o–o–o–o–o–o–o–o–o–o–o–o–o–o–o–o–o–o

SEQUENCE THREE

Autobiographical Explorations (p. 816)

People often speak of *Ways of Reading* as though it were an argument against "personal writing." It is certainly *not* an argument against having students write autobiographically, drawing their subjects and expertise from prior knowledge and past experience; almost every selection is followed by such assignments. Nor is it an argument against the genre of the personal essay; several selections in the anthology belong to that genre. And the course we teach always asks students to write from "life" as well as from texts.

There are arguments here, however. For the moment let us say that they have to do with (1) how students learn to imagine the sources of their autobiographical writing and (2) how they learn to imagine its revision.

In one tradition of instruction, autobiographical writing begins with a set of relaxation and self-awareness exercises. Take a deep breath. Pretend this isn't school. Look into your heart and write. If you look at the assignments in this sequence, they all argue (if indirectly) that a writer *begins* by imagining a genre (a history of autobiographical writing) and the problems of representation, problems that are easily overlooked (or suppressed) when writers write about themselves. In this sequence, students always begin with a prior text (part of a history of what we refer to as an "American" genre) and with a discussion of that text as an attempt to rework the genre, to experiment or to work on the problems of representation and problems of understanding. It is not just that Baldwin is a lovely writer or gives us a provocative glimpse into an earlier period in American race relations. He is also working on a *kind* of narrative that stands against (or outside of) the strident, action-oriented, more overtly politicized arguments more characteristic of public statements on race.

We tend not to build the revision assignments into the sequence, but this sequence (like all the others) assumes regular revision, where students work on a first draft one week and a revision the next. In the look-into-your-heart school of instruction, revision is a search for greater authenticity — finding a voice, providing more grounding detail. In our courses, it is not unusual for us to direct attention to "voice" and "detail," but the position of the writer is more combative. Rather than asking students to seek a voice or to look for details, most of our instruction is instruction in reading — in learning how to read their own texts (and their colleagues') with the same close critical attention they have used for

Baldwin (or any of the "real" authors in the course). The assigned readings serve as models of writers' work *on* writing problems, problems represented by words like "voice" or "detail." And the work we do with them as a class teaches an attention to language that a writer can use to revise. Students, then, learn to see the work of revision as a work with (and against) the language of the first draft, not "finding" a voice but finding where the language on the page is "voiceless" or "voiced" in ways that are troubling, where "voice" becomes a useful term to describe a kind of work with sentences (and not a therapeutic search for a pure center).

In a sense, then, the assignments in this sequence provide a repeated exercise in inauthenticity. Students write like someone else, someone else writing with a deep sense of the problems of identity and representation; in doing so, they learn something about "autobiographical" writing. And they get to work with materials close to home and close to the heart. We couldn't imagine teaching a writing course where students didn't feel that something was at stake — with both the first offering and the work of revision. Locating the problems of writing for students in "my voice" and "my experience" is a powerful way of producing those effects.

. . . .

ASSIGNMENT 1

Exploring Character [Baldwin]

The assignment begins with an extended passage from Richard Wright's *Native Son;* it is unlikely that first-year students will have read *Native Son;* and we wanted to give some sense of Bigger Thomas and how he is represented. The assignment says, "The speaker in 'Notes of a Native Son,' like the 'Thoreau' in *Walden*, is one of the exemplary characters of American letters." And it asks students to write an essay on the character of the speaker, or narrator, in "Notes of a Native Son." It is important to help students to distinguish between the character of the narrator (represented by a way of speaking), and the character James Baldwin, that is part of the narrative. The essay is not asking students to summarize a series of actions and events but to write about a way of thinking about and representing family, nation, and race. The assignment may not put enough emphasis on the question, "How does he think and speak?" You may need to call attention to it as you prepare students to write. And the assignment asks students to think about "a comparable twenty-first-century voice." Comparable does not have to mean similar. We are looking for students to turn to an example from contemporary texts (our students tended to write about Spike Lee movies or sitcoms). These are not likely to be similar. In fact, it might be useful to prompt students to think about differences.

. . . .

ASSIGNMENT 2

Autobiographical Explorations [Baldwin]

We have had great success with assignments like these. This one asks students to consider the style and method of "Notes of a Native Son," then to write an essay that is in direct imitation or an essay that is an act of homage. The first step, of course, is crucial. Students need to develop a sense of what Baldwin does and how he works before they can try to write from inside his example. The key here, we've found, is for students to think primarily about method rather than subject. They don't have to write about fathers, in other words. They should think about a family story that can be written against the story of nation, state, city, or community. And you should take time to think with your students about voice and style. As starting points, we would recommend some short, in-class exercises in writing Baldwin-like paragraphs. You need to have the Bible deeply in your history to write Old Testament narrative or to work within a sermonic style. It is perhaps a more useful instruction to ask students to work from within the discursive world of the central secondary character in their narrative (the figure occupying the father slot) and to move into and out of that discursive frame.

. . . .

ASSIGNMENT 3

Desire, Reading, and the Past [Rodriguez]

There is less stylistic experimentation in Rodriguez than in Baldwin (and, as a consequence, you will be asking for less in your students' essays). It makes sense, then, to begin with the preceding assignment on Baldwin so that students can imagine the work *as a* work with language and convention. When our students wrote these essays, what they took from Rodriguez was a tone (elegiac, negative, brooding) and a theme, a frame for the story of their own experiences (using the themes of family and schooling). Some of the most interesting essays followed Rodriguez's formal lead quite closely by including something the student writer had read (the student's equivalent of the Hoggart passage). Without question these were the papers that most caught students' attention when we reproduced papers for class discussion. This device prompted students to think (with Rodriguez) about how thinking *like* someone else allows you to "be" yourself, but, more important, students took pleasure in realizing that personal experience can *also* be intellectual experience. It is *not* that students don't read books or have intellectual lives, but that the usual classroom genre of the personal essay puts a premium on action and consequence. Rodriguez allowed students access to a different representation of the "personal," and this was both surprising and (for some) invigorating.

A quick note: If you are concerned with how quickly students cast themselves as Rodriguez in their first drafts, it might make sense to organize the revision around sorting out the differences.

. . . .

ASSIGNMENT 4

A Photographic Essay [Said]

It has been important to us to teach students to see writing as "work," including a work against, or in response to, habit and convention, and for students to think about the ideology of style. Writing is not just fitting new content into standard forms. A discussion like this can be crucial in allowing students to make the connection between what they read and what they write.

This assignment uses Said's discussion of the necessity of an "alternative mode of representation" to call attention to style, method, and arrangement. It asks students to first reread the essay as an experiment, as a piece of writing set against the norms and conventions of, in Said's terms, journalism, political science, and popular fiction. For students, "States" can best be read against what they take to be the conventions of report and argument, usually represented by a term like *the essay*.

After this preparation, students are asked to compose a Said-like reading of a set of photos. In the assignment, the following sentences are important and worth calling attention to in advance:

> These can be photos prepared for the occasion (by you or a colleague); they could also be photos already available. Whatever their source, they should represent people and places, a history and/or geography that you know well, that you know

to be complex and contradictory, and that you know will not be easily or readily understood by others, both the group for whom you will be writing (most usefully the members of your class) and readers more generally. You must begin with a sense that the photos cannot speak for themselves; you must speak for them.

Students, that is, are not just describing photos; they are using the photos to represent people and places, history and/or geography, to an audience unprepared to understand them. The selection and arrangement of photos is important, in other words. It is part of the work of writing this text. And the text that accompanies these photos should approximate the style and method in "States." The prose, in other words, is not simply captions, one after another. There should be an essay, a text with its own integrity, that is written with pictures. So — it is important to have students think about audience and occasion. What is the project? To whom are they writing? What is their relationship to subject and reader? And it is important to let students know in advance that they need to take time selecting the photographs and thinking about how they might be arranged. (It is useful to have them talk about what they left out and about plans they abandoned.) And they need to think about the writing; they are not writing captions. To think about what they might write, they can return to "States" to examine what it is that Said is doing and he does it. The writing can (perhaps should) be homage or imitation, an attempt to do something similar.

. . . .

ASSIGNMENT 5

Personal Experience as Intellectual Experience [Tompkins]

This assignment asks students to imagine themselves as part of the "we" of Tompkins's essay. It also asks students to locate their work in what Tompkins identifies as the "problem" of representation (of reading and writing). In asking students to imagine that Tompkins is writing for and about them, the assignment allows students to take the essay as a writing lesson and use it to imagine their own work as students of writing. Tompkins identifies a problem, gives it a name. The assignment asks students to take stock of their own work to imagine its future.

There are two options in this assignment. If students choose the first, they will need a file of papers, with a high school term paper or work they have done or are doing in college. If they work only from memory, the essay will lose its bite; it is simply too easy to be the hero or the victim in a narrative invented of whole cloth. If students are investigating a textual problem, they will need to work from passages. They do not, of course, need to tell the same story as Tompkins — most likely such a story would be impossible. It is a rare student who has learned to reread one of his or her sources critically. The work on this assignment can be the occasion, however, for students to look at how they have used sources, to imagine why sources were required or assigned, and to imagine how those sources *might* be reread.

The second option helps students to understand that the problem Tompkins alludes to is not literally a textual problem — that it does not necessarily involve one's work with books. This option says, in effect, treat your memories — your past conversations, your ways of understanding things, the tropes and figures that dominate (or dominated) your way of thinking and speaking — as text. Imagine that they are situated and that they situate you. Ask questions about point of view, about implication and origin.

. . . .

ASSIGNMENT 6

The "I" of the Personal Essay
[Baldwin, Rodriguez, Said, Tompkins]

This retrospective assignment asks students to review their work in this sequence, thinking it over in terms of its underlying argument. We've used assignments like this as a regular feature in courses we teach. While they are often a useful exercise, a way of taking stock or focusing on the "theory" in the course, they don't always produce good writing. The prose is sometimes mechanical or dutiful. For the writing to be good, students will need to be serious about working *with* their own prose. They will need to be as careful in selecting and presenting passages as they are when they work from passages in Rodriguez or Baldwin. Even though you have been their teacher and editor for several weeks, they must now imagine a reader needing an overview of their prose (or they need to be reminded that you have not committed their work to memory, nor do you keep it by your bedside). They need to think of this assignment as a *writing* assignment (and not just as an end-of-term exercise). We have identified this text as a "Preface." Since our students are also turning in a portfolio, the text becomes the lead-in to a collection of essays. The hard work is convincing students to think of us as readers and not simply as teachers who are about to give them a final grade.

o–o–o–o–o–o–o–o–o–o–o–o–o–o–o–o–o–o

SEQUENCE FOUR

Autobiographical Explorations (II) (p. 823)

These assignments can be added to those in Sequence Three or they can serve as substitutes for individual selections. For an introduction to the sequence, see the introduction to "Autobiographical Explorations" (manual, p. 135). The Rich assignment, like the Rodriguez and Tompkins assignments, asks students to think about *traces* of their past as those traces are represented in writing. And the assignment asks them to write about themselves in order to write about others, about a class of experience, others who have had similar experience. It is not simply a "personal essay." The Frith assignment provides a language and context for talking about "voice," including personal voice. The Monro and Wideman assignments are offered as examples of experimentation with the genre of the personal essay — and, at least with Wideman, of a greater concern for the liabilities, the dangers, of conventional forms and idioms.

. . . .

ASSIGNMENT 1

A Moment of Hesitation [Rich]

This assignment asks students to write from inside the "we" of Rich's discourse, to imagine that the essay is directed to them as writers (and this includes the men in the course). Rich's key phrases include "Until we can understand the assumptions in which we are drenched we cannot know ourselves" and "We need to know the writing of the past, and know it differently than we have ever known it; not to pass on a tradition but to break its hold over us."

139

This assignment asks students to follow Rich's lead and write autobiographically, no in celebration of their individuality or specialness but in order to cast themselves as repre sentative of the way a certain group — named perhaps in terms of age, race, class, or gen der — is positioned within the dominant culture. It asks students to imagine this as risky as something to be done only with hesitation. And it asks them to use the occasion to tr out some of Rich's key terms, like "revision" and "patriarchy." The difficulty students wil have is in imagining their personal experiences as representative of a collective one. You will thus not get papers about the pressure of culture but about key individuals — father mother, teacher, lover, grandparent, or coach. And you will get familiar narratives of self discovery, of hard work and nose to the grindstone, of "Believe in yourself" and "You can' tell a book by its cover." This is inevitable. Both their youth and the distinctly American versions of personal experience lead students to write "frontier" stories, stories with no sense of the social, the political, or the historical. These are the concerns Rich is addressing in her essay — she would correct this kind of thinking. And these are the concerns we highlight for revision: In what ways is this story more than *your* story? Where can we find the cultural context? In what ways are you, as a character, cast in relation to a familiar story (a fairy tale)? In what ways are you, as a speaker, as a person defined by the language or the page, cast in relation to predictable ways of speaking or habits of mind?

. . . .

ASSIGNMENT 2

Adjacency [Munro}

As the assignment suggests, before students write, they might turn to the first two "Questions for a Second Reading" to guide their close reading of the story and the way it is organized in order to unfold two stories connected in ways not immediately obvious to readers. Once they have become familiar with the story, they'll need to design or imagine one of their own that proceeds as Munro's does with two story lines, perhaps with one of those being a story narrated by one of the characters. The challenge here is to create the two stories that readers can imagine as linked, and to do so in ways that carefully orches- trate their unfolding. We generally don't ask students to create outlines, but in this case, such organization might be useful once they have drafted their stories; they can then use the outline work to think how they might organize the story in the spirit of Munro's and in a fashion similar to hers.

Students who have not written stories before might find this a perplexing assignment, but they should feel free to work from autobiography or to imagine stories that begin in or use autobiography in some way. To get a sense of its movements and outline, they might also want to reread Munro's story a number of times after they have had the opportunity to study it.

. . . .

ASSIGNMENT 3

Old Habits [Wideman]

With this assignment our intent was to focus on features of the text that could be transported to students' writing — the provisional openings ("What if I started here"), the use of italics to mark different ways of speaking, the line breaks in the text, the authorial intrusions. We wanted students to begin with formal concerns and, from those, to think about the life story or the family story. This is primarily a writing assignment, in other words, and only secondarily an exercise in "discovery" or "revelation." The goal was not to see what students could learn about their families but to see what they could learn about writing and "real" life by conducting a Wideman-like methodological experiment. This has been a particularly successful assignment for us. The use of italics seems to authorize students to bring other voices and points of view into their writing, and often with dramatic effect (where we hear two parents speaking rather than hearing about an abstraction, Parents). And students feel the power of the fragmented (as opposed to the hierarchically organized) text. It allows them to follow a train of thought through structures of elaboration usually excluded from the writing classroom. And it is wonderful to finesse the problem of the "beginning."

. . . .

ASSIGNMENT 4

Voice [Frith]

The chapter we have chosen, "The Voice," is a wonderful demonstration of critical scholarship, in our minds an ideal introduction for students to how and why popular culture can become the subject of serious work, how writing about pop music might be something an interested adult could do for a living. In the best tradition of criticism, Frith takes something that seems simple and obvious, the presence of "voice" in song, and renders it complex and problematic, not so simple at all. And the language of analysis is drawn from the traditions of rhetorical analysis — that is, the discussion of "voice" (and style and rhetoric) in popular music can serve discussions of voice, style, and rhetoric in writing. Frith begins, for example, by making a careful distinction between voice as "gesture" and voice as "utterance" — the standard distinction in a writing class where students are asked to consider not only what the language says but what it does. Later, in talking about voice as "person" and as "character," he is making another distinction fundamental to the writing class, the distinction between writer and the "I" on the page.

This assignment asks students to use Frith's terms to discuss voice as it might be said to be present in one or two of the selections they've read in this sequence. Students can organize the discussion under the four headings provided in the text — voice as instrument, as body, as person, and as character. They will need to work out equivalences for "instrument" and "body." (There is no single answer here.) And they will need to work closely with examples, most often from extended block quotations. In writing about writing (in presenting a close reading), writers have the advantage of being able to work the primary text into their texts.

. . . .

ASSIGNMENT 5

The "I" of the Personal Essay [Rich, Munro, Wideman]

This retrospective assignment asks students to review their work in this sequence, thinking it over in terms of its underlying argument. We've used assignments like this as a regular feature in courses we teach. While they are often a useful exercise, a way of taking stock or focusing on the "theory" in the course, they don't always produce good writing. The prose is sometimes mechanical or dutiful. For the writing to be good, students will need to be serious about working *with* their own prose. They will need to be as careful in selecting and presenting passages as they are when they work from passages in Rich or Munro. Even though you have been their teacher and editor for several weeks, they now must imagine a reader needing an overview of their prose (or they need to be reminded that you have not committed their work to memory, nor do you keep it by your bedside). They need to think of this assignment as a *writing* assignment (and not just as an end-of-term exercise). We have identified this text as a preface. Since our students are also turning

141

in a portfolio, the text becomes the lead-in to a collection of essays. The hard work is convincing students to think of us as readers and not simply as teachers who are about to give them a final grade.

o–o–o–o–o–o–o–o–o–o–o–o–o–o–o–o–o–o–o

SEQUENCE FIVE

Close Reading/Close Writing (p. 828)

This sequence is a set of exercises designed to encourage close attention to linguistic detail. These exercises represent a kind of work we have been doing in our classes for several years now, work that began with our frustration about the difficulties we had talking about writing at the level of the sentence. We knew we needed to have a way of talking to students about sentences, even if we did not have a shared vocabulary for the naming of parts. We began by asking our students to write sentences in parallel with interesting sentences we had drawn from the readings, sentences with a syntax students would be unlikely to produce on their own. We did this as a classroom exercise, pushing students to not only reproduce the syntax but to think of it as doing a particular kind of intellectual work. We found, in fact, that we were able to change both the kinds and lengths of sentences our students were writing, and in ways that we found encouraging. We found that the exercises gave us a way to teach punctuation. What we also learned, however, was that these exercises helped students with the readings. Thinking about sentences gave our students a familiarity with a writer's characteristic syntax, a way of negotiating and anticipating that style, and a way of thinking about difficult sentences as linguistic structures that are doing a particular kind of "work."

You could use these assignments as exercises. If you wanted to combine them with longer writing assignments, you could link them with the assignments following each selection that ask students to write Wideman, Baldwin-like, Berger-like, or Griffin-like prose. Or you could combine them with the assignments that ask students to perform close readings and to account for the work of writing as it is represented in characteristic passages from the essays.

. . . .

ASSIGNMENT 1

Language, Rhythm, Tone [Wideman]

The assignment points students' attention to sentence length (and sentence fragments) and toward the ways Wideman manipulates the rhythms and idioms of speech and writing in these passages. He has a remarkable ability to set multiple voices at work at once. The formal arrangement of "Our Time" has a reader thinking in terms of two voices: John's and Robby's. These names mark linguistic identities in relation to an urban vernacular (Robby) and the language of formal, advanced education. John Wideman the writer, of course, moves between these and manipulates them to represent the worlds of his characters and to situate his reader (perhaps uneasily) in relation to them. The references in the first passage range from Ichabod Crane to Wilt the Stilt. The final sentence has the rhythm and ring of the street and of spoken language ("You'd look at him sometimes as he was trucking down Homewood Avenue and think that nigger ain't walking, he's trying to remember how to walk"); in fact, in the absence of punctuation, a reader *must* get into the speech pattern to make the sentence work, to make the bridge from statement to quotation: You'd look at him and think, "That nigger ain't walkin, he's trying to remember how

142

to walk." And this is poised in relation to sentences notable for their manipulation of the shape and rhythm of the sentence as it alludes to traditions and conventions of writing (rather than speaking):

> Lying there in the bed with his bones poking through his skin, it made you want to cry. Garth's barely able to talk, his smooth, medium-brown skin yellow as pee. Ichabod legs and long hands and long feet, Garth could make you laugh just walking down the street. On the set you'd see him coming a far way off.

The second example points to the one long sentence, one that both accumulates speech patterns and organizes them as writing in a distinctive, bravura performance:

> French girls had that fair, light, bright, almost white redbone complexion and fine blown hair and nice big legs but all that was to be appreciated from a distance because they were nice girls and because they had this crazy daddy who wore a big brown country hat and gambled and drank wine and once ran a man out of town, ran him away without ever laying a hand on him or making a bad-mouthed threat, just cut his eyes a certain way when he said the man's name and the word went out and the man who had cheated a drunk John French with loaded dice was gone. Just like that.

Students should be encouraged to find and present representative or exemplary passages of their own selection in "Our Time."

The writing assignment asks for patterned imitation. We have sometimes simply reproduced passages with triple spacing to allow students to write between the lines. The point of the assignment is practice, to allow students the practice of writing within these forms. They can, then, serve simply as exercises. If you want to move students to longer pieces of writing, you could ask them to write extended Wideman-like memoirs or essays, as indicated in the third "Assignment for Writing" following the selection.

. . . .

ASSIGNMENT 2

Punctuation [Baldwin]

We have wanted more and more to focus students' attention on sentences. Baldwin is a remarkable writer of sentences. One of the characteristic sentence patterns is represented in the example:

> He was not a young man when we were growing up and he had already suffered many kinds of ruin; in his outrageously demanding and protective way he loved his children, who were black like him and menaced, like him; and all these things sometimes showed in his face when he tried, never to my knowledge with any success, to establish contact with any of us. When he took one of his children on his knee to play, the child always became fretful and began to cry; when he tried to help one of us with our homework the absolutely unabating tension which emanated from him caused our minds and our tongues to become paralyzed, so that he, scarcely knowing why, flew into a rage and the child, not knowing why, was punished.

For discussion, we like to ask "What do these sentences do?" We are not looking for a formal description (or a formal description alone). We want students to note the length of the sentences and the use of commas and semicolons in relation to an expressive project — as a necessary or determined way of doing something with words. Baldwin is not, for example, being dismissive even though he is being critical. This is not the rhetoric of simple statement: "He was outrageous and demanding with his children. He never established contact. He caused his children to become paralyzed with a fear of his rage." Thus, the long elaborated sentences. The semicolons insist on the link and proximity of utterances the father's experience as a child and adult; the form of his love; his failure to establish contact. And the forward movement of the sentences, their inevitability, are regularly interrupted with qualifications and secondary statements. It is not "He flew into a rage and the child was punished." It is, rather, "He, scarcely knowing why, flew into a rage and the child, not knowing why, was punished." Rather than simply resting agency in the father both the father and the child are products of moment (a family moment, a national moment) that neither can understand or control.

. . . .

ASSIGNMENT 3

Character, Point of View [Berger]

Berger, in writing about the painting *The Calling of St. Matthew*, creates a drama, a drama within the painting (the story of St. Matthew as represented by Caravaggio), but also a drama within the person viewing the painting (the character, "John Berger," represented in the prose). It might be useful first to have students reread and discuss the passage as it presents a character. (Students tend to be inclined to assume that there is no speaker and that the paragraphs are simple transcriptions of what is there in the painting.)

The passage is filled with dramatic gesture:

How many thousands of decisions to leave have resembled Christ's hand here! The hand is held out towards the one who has to decide, yet it is ungraspable because so fluid. It orders the way, yet offers no direct support. Matthew will get up and follow the thin stranger from the room, down the narrow streets, out of the district. He will write his gospel, he will travel to Ethiopia and the South Caspian and Persia. Probably he will be murdered.

And behind the drama of this moment of decision in the room at the top of the stairs, there is a window, giving onto the outside world. Traditionally in painting, windows were treated either as sources of light or as frames framing nature or framing an exemplary event outside. Not so this window. No light enters by it. The window is opaque. We see nothing. Mercifully we see nothing because what is outside is bound to be threatening. It is a window through which only the worst news can come.

You might ask, for example, why "mercifully"? Or, how should one understand the exclamation point after the opening sentence above? This is someone who clearly knows painting and the history of painting; it is also someone who reads his own story (or who reads familiar stories) into the scene of Matthew and Christ, and who invests or projects emotion into the scene.

It is appropriate to note the larger context of *And our Faces, My Heart, Brief As Photos,* from which this selection is drawn; Berger (or "Berger") is writing to a lover and so the painting (in this case) is one way for him to present himself as desirable.

As students write in imitation of this, they should begin with an understanding that there are two goals to the assignment. They need to present a painting as a dramatic action. And they need to present a character (or to write from a point of view) invested in that drama. It might be useful to help students to think of an audience for such a performance. This is not, in other words, to be "simply" a classroom exercise or an essay (for example) for an art history course. It is something they are writing to a someone who has reason to be interested in the painting because they are interested in the writer.

144

. . . .

ASSIGNMENT 4

The Paragraph, the Essay [Griffin]

Our students had a great time with this assignment and it produced some of the most interesting writing of the semester. They chose topics that ranged from parental influences, the relationship of machines and thinking, the struggle to be, as one young woman called it, in an unfriendly environment of violence, the replication of behaviors in men from different generations of the same family, and the various metaphors for space. The key to students' having a successful experience with this assignment seems to lie in the subjects they choose to write about and the stories they tell. We have told them to write about stories they know or would like to research because they are curious about them, because they sense connections to other stories or examples that they may or may not need to research. The students' involvement in the writing will push them to do the kinds of thinking through and connecting that imitates Griffin's work. This assignment demonstrates to them the kind of planning and care that Griffin's work required, and our students found that they could help themselves with outlines and charts or maps of the territories they wanted to cover. We allowed them class time, also, to test their plans with other students and with us. This proved to be time well spent, for it helped students see connections that others saw and it prevented anyone from being lost at sea for anything but a brief period. In this assignment also we took students through multiple drafts, and we assigned students to pairs at different points so that they could continually test their work against the readings of others.

. . . .

ASSIGNMENT 5

The Paragraph, the Essay [Baldwin]

Irving Howe referred to Baldwin as a writer whose essays represented an art form, "a form with possibilities for discursive reflection and concrete drama." And, he said, "The style of these essays is a remarkable instance of the way in which a grave and sustained eloquence . . . can be employed in an age deeply suspicious of rhetorical prowess."

Our age is not deeply suspicious of rhetorical prowess. It is either blind to it or drawn by it. Because our age is preoccupied with autobiography, testimonial and life stories, we do, however, have much to learn about the possibilities for "discursive reflection and concrete drama."

This assignment asks students to consider the style and method of "Notes of a Native Son" and then to write an essay that is in direct imitation or to write as an act of homage. The first step, of course, is crucial. Students need to develop a sense of what Baldwin does and how he works before they can try to write from inside his example. The key here, we've found, is for students to think primarily about method rather than subject. They don't have to write about fathers, in other words. They should think about a family story that can be written against the story of nation, state, city, or community.

And you should take time to think with your students about voice and style. As starting points, we would recommend some short, in-class exercises in writing Baldwin-like paragraphs. You need to have the Bible deeply in your history to write Old Testament narrative or to work within a sermonic style. It is perhaps a more useful instruction to ask students to work from within the discursive world of the central secondary character in their narrative (the figure occupying the father slot) and to move into and out of that discursive frame.

145

. . . .

ASSIGNMENT 6

Classroom Lesson

The final assignment is designed to bring the work of this sequence into the context of the "lessons" and "rules" prescribed in handbooks and rhetorics. We have chosen a brief example from *A Writer's Reference* by Diana Hacker (Bedford/St. Martin's, 1999). You may choose to supplement this with some examples of your own. The point of this assignment is not to dismiss handbooks — far from it. We have always required a handbook in our courses. It is, rather, to show the limits of the handbooks and to show the wonderful elasticity of language when it is in the hands of good writers.

o–o–o–o–o–o–o–o–o–o–o–o–o–o–o–o–o–o–o

SEQUENCE SIX

The Documentary Tradition (p. 836)

The six assignments in this sequence involve students in an extended study of documentary writing and photographic essays. They begin by examining Coles's arguments about images in photographic essays and the ways they are shaped by a photographer's vision or by editing (in cropping, for instance) to bring forward his claims that doing documentary work is something other than just simply collecting and presenting information. From there students move on to study Mitchell's four case studies of photographic essays to get a sense of what he means when he claims that photography and language are in a dialectic of exchange and resistance. They are then asked to use this study of Mitchell's arguments to foreground the ways in which it would be possible to say that the four cases he studies are different from each other, different enough, that is, so that they each allow him to see and say things specific to them. This difference gives Mitchell examples that allow him to build a case that's complex and multifaceted. The third assignment gives students the opportunity to study Coles and Mitchell studying the same photographic essay, *Let Us Now Praise Famous Men*, so that they can comment on the ways in which the authors' concerns shape the differences in their projects. The next assignment introduces Edward Said's essay "States," from *After the Last Sky*, to the work the students have already done, and in doing so, it asks them to consider a position on documentary work in relation to Coles's and Mitchell's. Similarly, the fifth assignment introduces Marianne Hirsch's essay "Projected Memory" and asks students to consider a position on the use of the photographic record. The final assignment gives students the opportunity to compose a photo-essay of their own, situating it in relation to the examples studied throughout the sequence.

. . . .

ASSIGNMENT 1

Images [Coles]

This writing assignment follows well from the third of the "Questions for a Second Reading" in which students are asked to study the three examples of cropped photographs that Coles uses. This assignment picks up that invitation by asking students to both represent the photographs, their history, and the points that Coles seems to be making about them for readers who are not completely familiar with the essay. Then the assignment invites students to find a way to enter into the discussion of those cropped photographs. Do they think the decisions to crop them as they are cropped were good decisions? What, then, constitutes a good decision about documentary work? How would they argue for or against those original decisions? What is at stake here when they are cropped? if they were not cropped?

The important part of this assignment is the invitation for students to enter the discussion with their thinking about the photographs and the issues that they raise having to do with the ways they were cropped and the fact that they were cropped. Students' first drafts will want to hover around the representations of the photographs and Coles's arguments about them; the work of revision will be to get students to enter the discussion, to see their thinking carrying weight in the essay along with their representations of Coles's thinking.

. . . .

ASSIGNMENT 2

Image and Text [Mitchell]

Mitchell does not say much about the differences in the four books of photographic essays that he studies for his four cases, but a reader gets the sense that each case extends his arguments in a particular way, that each book of photographic essays contributes differently to his work. Students are invited to study the implied differences in these four books, and this invitation to study is framed in Mitchell's terms, in terms, that is, that foreground the dialectic of exchange and resistance between the photographs and their accompanying texts. How, in other words, could it be said that each book enacts this dialectic differently from the other books? What does one contribute to the overall picture of the dialectic that the others do not? Students will also need to represent the photographic essays to readers, so a part of their job in this essay is to summarize each of the four books so that readers unfamiliar with them might be able to picture them and their relation to Mitchell's argument for the dialectic. And, finally, students are invited to take a position on the range of the photo essay as a genre based on their work with the differences in these four texts. What, in other words, might be possible with the photo-essay? What are its possibilities? its limits?

. . . .

ASSIGNMENT 3

Let Us Now Praise Famous Men [Coles, Mitchell]

Since this project invites students to study two different readings of *Let Us Now Praise Famous Men*, they would benefit from being able to study the whole text firsthand. More libraries will have multiple editions of this book, as it is quite famous. It was originally produced for a general reading audience, so it once had wide circulation, and since then it has been studied extensively by artists, sociologists, literary critics, and cultural theorists. To begin this project, after they have read the original text, students might locate those similar examples that Coles and Mitchell use. They might then ask themselves how each author reads the examples. What are the different approaches to the photo-essay evident and implied in their different readings? Unlike Berger, Coles takes a strikingly different position on the photo-essay because, at least in part, he's using them for a different purpose than Mitchell, but also, one feels, because he's much more reverential toward them and what they represent historically.

Once students have read the similar examples, they can move to the other examples from Coles and Mitchell, choosing one or two from each, and write about the different ways in which each author reads the examples. They will want to be able to write about the underlying concerns of each author as a determining factor in how each reads, so they'll need to come to some kind of general statement that points back and forth to their examples to play out their sense of the underlying concerns of each author. And, finally, students are invited to take a position. Whose readings and uses of the photo-essay might they align themselves with? Why? What, in other words, compels them to take that position? Here again students will need to work from examples — either of their readings of the different authors or of the different authors readings of the photo-essays — to say what compels them to take a particular position.

．　．　．　．　．　．　．　．　．　．

ASSIGNMENT 4

States [Said, Mitchell]

The point of this assignment is to enable students to write, as experts, in response to W. J. T. Mitchell's use and representation of *After the Last Sky* in "The Photographic Essay: Four Case Studies." For this reason we have staged the writing in two parts. These could easily be represented as draft and revision.

The first draft is an account of "States." The assignment for this is, in a sense, written out in the first of the "Questions for a Second Reading":

> The first three paragraphs provide a "reading" of the opening photograph, "Tripoli, Badawi camp, May 1983." Or, to put it another way, the writing evolves from and is in response to that photograph. As you reread these paragraphs, pay close attention to what Said is doing, to what he notices, to what prompts or requires commentary. How would you describe and explain the writing that follows? What is he doing with the photo? What is he doing as a writer? What is he doing for a reader? (How does he position a reader?)
>
> It might be useful to begin by thinking about what he is *not* doing. It is not, for example, the presentation one might expect in a slide show on travel in Lebanon. Nor is it the kind of presentation one might expect while seeing the slides of family or friends, or slides in an art history or art appreciation class.
>
> Once you have worked through the opening three paragraphs, reread the essay paying attention to Said's work with all the photographs. Is there a pattern? Do any of the commentaries stand out for their force, variety, innovation?

The second draft, then, would begin with a rereading of Mitchell's essay, with particular attention to the discussion of *After the Last Sky*. Students would need to be able to summarize, paraphrase and quote from Mitchell's argument and then to add their own response. The assignment says,

> Once you've written that draft, read Mitchell and bring his analysis into the conversation. You will want to refer to the general frame and the terms of his argument and to the specific discussion of images in *After the Last Sky*. What does Mitchell bring to the essay? . . . How would you define [his] expertise? What can he allow you to say or do? And, in return, what do you see that he doesn't? How might you define your position or point of view in relation to his?

The key is to insist that there be a space in the essay where students speak, too, where they speak on the same plane as Mitchell. While the assignment uses the metaphor of "conversation," and while we believe this is a useful metaphor, others are certainly possible. What we have found most persuasive, however, is insisting on space — on a paragraph or paragraphs or sections of the text — where students can be found speaking for their sense of Mitchell, Said, and the questions that are on the table.

* * * * * * * * *

ASSIGNMENT 5

Projected Memory [Hirsch, Coles]

This is a big assignment. You might think about how you could best stage it for stu-dents. They need to be familiar with Coles's arguments that blur the distinctions between fact and fiction in documentary work, and they need to understand Hirsch's arguments about postmemorial writing — and, of course, Hirsch's work as a postmemorial artist's writing. Both authors work with photographic records, both read photographs of others and comment on them, and both imagine the cultural spaces those photographs occupy and inflect. Both authors take moral positions toward the images and the intentions of the images (and to the spaces they occupy in the culture and in their personal experiences of them). So the task for students, then, is to engage in their own writing projects that allow them to consider Coles's readings of images and Hirsch's in a similar space that defines two ways of "approaching the photographic record." One such avenue into this consider-ation, of course, is to first write about how each approaches the photographic records. After that, students might write about the points of similarities and differences in their approaches. What does Coles's take the photographic record as an occasion for? How is this different from the opportunity that Hirsch takes with the photographic records about which she writes?

* * * * * * * * *

ASSIGNMENT 6

A Final View [Coles, Mitchell]

We have had great success with this assignment. Students have prepared some re-markable and memorable photo-essays. In the assignment, the following sentences are important and worth calling attention to in advance:

> The photographs can be prepared for the occasion (by you or a colleague); they could also be photos already available. Whatever their source, they should repre-sent people and places, a history and/or geography that you know well, that you know to be complex and contradictory, and that you know will not be easily or readily understood by others, both the group for whom you will be writing (most usefully the members of your class) and readers more generally. You must begin with a sense that the photos cannot speak for themselves; you must speak for them.

Students, that is, are not just describing photos; they are using the photos to represent people and places, history and/or geography, to an audience unprepared to understand them. The selection and arrangement of photos is important, in other words. It is part of the work of writing this text. And the text that accompanies these photos should approxi-mate the style and method of one of the sources: Evans and Agee, Said and Mohr, or Hirsch. The prose, in other words, is not simply captions, one after another. There should be an essay, a text with its own integrity, that is written with pictures. So — it is important to have students think about audience and occasion. What is the project? To whom are they writing? What is their relationship to subject and reader? And it is important to let stu-dents know in advance that they need to take time selecting the photographs and thinking about how they might be arranged. (It is useful to have them talk about what they left out and about plans they abandoned.) And they need to think about the writing; they are not writing captions. To think about what they might write, they can return to their sources, "States," for example, to examine what it is that Said does and how he does it. The writing can (perhaps should) be homage or imitation, an attempt to do something similar.

o–o–o–o–o–o–o–o–o–o–o–o–o–o–o–o–o–o–o–o

SEQUENCE SEVEN

Experimental Readings and Writings (p. 842)

This sequence is designed to give students opportunities to try out different kinds of experimental writing in loose imitation of the selections they read and study. The four selections (Griffin, Hirsch, Wideman, Anzaldúa) are quite different in their methods, styles, and in the subjects they address. Griffin's writing is purposely associative. She places passages of text about Heinrich Himmler's life as a Nazi, for instance, next to passages about child-rearing in Germany, next to passages about her own upbringing. She leaves to the reader the connections, which multiply limitlessly, it seems. The Hirsch assignment offers students opportunities to work within her project on postmemory by writing about a past that belongs to them but that is not theirs. It is the past they make theirs from the stories they hear, perhaps from parents, and from the culture that carries those stories and memories. The difficulty for them is to keep a balance between identification with those memories and an apppropriate distance that prevents easy overgeneralization of those memories. Hirsch refers to these distinctions as "idiopathic" and "heteropathic" identification, and students will need to feel comfortable with her concerns here, particularly with her desires to keep postmemorial writing from degenerating into cliché and sentimentality.

Wideman writes his piece on his brother Robby in many voices, including the voice of the writer who thinks aloud on paper about the problems of such writing. Wideman is particularly concerned about his voice erasing Robby or Robby's voice, and he writes on that very dilemma. For students, the challenge here is to create a piece that is partially memoir, partially reportage, and partially a writer's self-reflection on the problems or process of such writing. Wideman's essay is a powerful piece, and students will learn how to write in his spirit by closely studying the moments in which he shifts voices, and these are fairly easy to identify if one is looking for them (something they might do in pairs or as a class). Anzaldúa's bold mixture of prose, poetry, memoir, epistle, and critique moves between issues of sexual and cultural identity. Driven and passionate, her writing has a sense of immediacy that sweeps readers into it.

Once students have tried the various kinds of writings for themselves, including an assignment that invites them to use Hirsch's or Griffin's selection to read the other's, the sequence moves to a final assignment that asks students to consider the place of such writing in their development as writers and students. It affords students an opportunity to think about experimental writing as an occasion for learning to think differently from the thinking that's possible in more conventional writing, and as writing that is not taught in school but could be.

. . . .

ASSIGNMENT 1

A Mix of Personal and Academic Writing [Griffin]

Our students had a great time with this assignment and it produced some of the most interesting writing of the semester. They worked with the essay for a week before they tackled the writing assignment, and it seemed important that they had the opportunity to do so. We used the "Questions for a Second Reading" to get them into the piece and to ask questions about its methods. Although it might be possible for students to come to this assignment cold after reading the essay, we would caution against this. Generally, students need to work with the selection that they will be loosely imitating so that they can become familiar with the methods and procedures they will imitate. It sounds obvious, but students don't, for instance, automatically see the relationships among the various fragments in this selection. They want it to be linear, to present an argument and then to go on to prove it and to conclude. So they need to spend some time studying Griffin's use of fragments before they take on this assignment.

Once they were ready, our students chose topics that ranged from parental influences, the relationship of machines and thinking, the struggle to exist (as one young woman called it) in an unfriendly environment of violence, the replication of behavior in men from different generations of the same family, and the various metaphors for space. The key to students' having a successful experience with this assignment seems to lie in the subjects they choose to write about and the stories they tell. We have told them to write about stories they know or would like to research because they are curious about them and because they sense connections to other stories or examples that they may or may not need to research. The students' involvement in the writing will push them to do the kinds of thinking through and connecting that imitates Griffin's work.

This assignment demonstrates to them the kind of planning and care that Griffin's work required, and our students found that they could help themselves with outlines and charts or maps of the territories they wanted to cover. We allowed them class time, also, to test their plans with other students and with us. This proved to be time well spent, for it helped students see connections that others saw but that they had not and it prevented anyone from being lost at sea for anything but a brief period. We also asked for multiple drafts of this assignment, and we assigned students to pairs at different points through their work so that they could continually test it against the readings of others.

. . . .

ASSIGNMENT 2

Postmemory [Hirsch]

Although this assignment appears to be straightforward in its invitation to write about "a past that belongs to you but that is not yours," students will need to be familiar with Hirsch's notions and examples of postmemory to engage in such a project, for the object here is to create postmemory, to write about a past that one shares with others through stories but that is not directly one's own personal experience. Hirsch writes, for instance, about her memories of the town in which her parents grew up, one she feels she knows intimately, yet she has never been there. She knows it from their stories about it. Her images are from postmemory, from the fantasies she creates in response to the stories, from the images portrayed in her parents' narratives and transformed in her imagination of them. This is similar to the projects students will need to identify for this assignment — a past that is theirs yet is not theirs.

The caveat in the assignment asks students to be careful of overgeneralizing about such a past, to be careful to not reduce it to a series of clichés, and they'll want to turn to her distinction between "idiopathic" and "heteropathic" identification before they engage in this writing project, so that they can understand the dangers of all too easy identification with a past this beyond them rather than intimately connected to them in some way.

This assignment, then, asks students to take up Hirsch's project as their own with their own examples of postmemory as a writing project. The first "Question for a Second Reading" is a good place to begin if you're interested in turning students' attention to ways of thinking of Hirsch's work as a writing project, as a project with writerly problems to solve having to do with the creation of images and stories surrounding them. It's a useful place for students to read her essay closely as a writing project marked by writerly methods for gathering information, using sources, telling personal stories, and drawing conclusions.

. . . .

ASSIGNMENT 3

Writing the Past [Griffin, Hirsch]

Students have a choice with this assignment to work with Griffin through Hirsch or to work with Hirsch through Griffin. They might best begin by thinking about both of these essays as parts of a larger project that involves the difficulties of writing about history. The assignment points to some of these — that writing history is not just a matter of having facts or information; that a large part of the difficulty resides in the relationship of the writer to language and, through language, to the past; that there are always questions of representation, of where to begin, what stories to tell, how to tell them, and how to conclude. So the spirit of this assignment is one that asks students to think of Griffin and Hirsch as writers who are engaged in projects of history writing. From this standpoint, what do they share? How are they different? And how might one writer's project throw light on the other's? Or how might one writer think about the other's project? What would that writer notice? comment on? What might those comments look like?

Although it seems obvious to say it, students should be encouraged to work from particular moments in each selection. That is, they might identify what they take to be a key moment in Griffin that allows them to comment on another moment they consider significant in Hirsch. The idea here is to stay close to the texts and avoid generalizations about the writer's subjects and methods. By staying close to the texts, they'll be able to write about what Griffin, for example, might admire in a particular passage of Hirsch's. From our experiences, students benefit most from this kind of close textual work that teaches, then, how to avoid writing abstract, generalized prose about texts.

. . . .

ASSIGNMENT 4

Turning This Way and That [Wideman]

In order for students to step into Wideman's methods as a writer and write their own Wideman-like piece, they need to be familiar with the selection, and they need to spend some time studying and discussing Wideman's methods. We use the first two of the "Questions for a Second Reading" for class discussions that focus on the methods of this selection, and after two or three sessions our students seem ready to begin this writing project. Most students will write about their neighborhoods and family, and this works fine, we think, as long as they demonstrate an allegiance to Wideman's methods by writing in different voices, or at least in two voices, the voice of the narrator and the voice of one other person whose story is being told, at one point, and who, at other points, is telling his or her own story. Students can break their essays into sections, as Wideman does, either while they're writing or as the work of revision. They should ask themselves why they think Wideman has broken his piece as he has, and they should have reasons for breaking theirs. They can use different typefaces to signal different voices or the "essay" part of their writing. And, as Wideman does, they should allow their voices as narrators to be heard, to show their thinking about how to tell the other voices' stories, about how to do justice to the other voices. For most students this will mean "thinking aloud" in paragraphs about the problems they encounter as they try to evoke other voices with depth and credibility. This speaking aloud on the page is an important part of this project, as it allows students to do the kind of self-reflective thinking and writing that writers must do when they recreate others through their representations of their voices, as Wideman does. Students won't have great success with this reflective writing in their early drafts, and you should anticipate that this part of the project, and the telling of others' stories in their own voices, will be a large part of the work of the revision for this assignment.

We have found it useful with this kind of assignment to turn students' attention regularly, throughout the students' work, to self-reflective questions about this kind of "mixed" writing. It's helpful for them to think about what this kind of writing can do that a more traditional essay can't. In this light, we ask them how it might serve them as students. Where, in what situations, might they want to write like Wideman? And why, do they suppose, is this kind of writing not taught in school?

. . . .

ASSIGNMENT 5

A Crazy Dance [Anzaldúa]

This is a wonderful assignment that invites students to experience the creation of a mixed style from their various positions, voices, and backgrounds. A number of our students produced their most engaging writing of the semester for this assignment. Even though students have not been prepared to write this kind of text, Anzaldúa's example is strong enough to enable them to do so. The key question in the assignment asks students to consider the different positions they occupy. What does this mean? Resist the temptation to tell them. Let them come to see that they are students, sons and daughters, friends, authorities, novices, swimmers, skateboarders, lovers, bikers, enemies, ballplayers, music listeners, concertgoers, writers, inheritors of various cultures and traits. Let them realize that these various selves have voices — often contradictory — that students can bring forward in writing, as Anzaldúa does, when they set out to explain who they are, how they understand their experiences, and in particular, what their key or significant experiences are and in what form or style they might be presented.

. . . .

ASSIGNMENT 6

Writing and Schooling [Griffin, Hirsch, Wideman, Anzaldúa]

The actual assignment here is stated quite broadly, but the work students do will have to be quite specific if they are to make anything of the experimental writings they did for the sequence and the ways those writings stand against or differ from conventional school writings. The methods the assignment begs are scholarly: students need to identify and write about specific moments in their experimental writings and in examples from more conventional writings they have done for school. Once they locate these examples, they need to write about what the experimental writings (the particular moments they are using) allowed them to do that they could not have done in conventional writings. They will need to place those specific examples of conventional writings next to their other examples to avoid writing overgeneralized statements that they may try to use to represent all their past conventional writings. From the start, it's wise to direct students to specific examples from both kinds of writing; most of them will have to hunt through their college or high school writings to find the pieces they'll use to stand with the experimental writings they did for the sequence.

After doing close readings of their different kinds of writings, students need to do more than say they're different, or they're different and they allow me to use my personal experience. Students will want to draw such conclusions (not only because they are accurate, but also because they are the quickest and easiest things to say), and they'll need to be helped to think about the role these experimental writings might play in conventional courses (both writing and subject area courses). They are, in fact, being asked to imagine their own education as writers as one that includes these kinds of experimental writings. Where would such writing be useful? What can they learn from it? When? At what time could they have benefited from writing of the sort they did for the sequence?

153

SEQUENCE EIGHT

Experts and Expertise (p. 849)

We use the metaphor of apprenticeship several times in the textbook. This is the assignment sequence that features this particular use of texts. The assignments invite students to take on the key terms and angle of vision of each essay, to imagine that each author has begun a project and that the students' job, once they have been given the tools and have gotten the hang of what is going on, is to carry it on in the spirit of the master. The last assignment, in the name of Walker Percy, asks students to look back at what they have done and to question just what is at stake or what can be gained by taking on someone else's way of thinking and speaking in just this way. While we want students to have the opportunity of looking critically at this kind of imitation, we also want them to feel the power of it. It is, as we say, heady work. Students are given ways of thinking and speaking that they would not invent on their own — at least not so quickly and not in such rapid succession. And they are given a sense of Mitchell, Rich, Wideman, and Geertz that goes well beyond an encyclopedia-like recitation of the authors' key ideas.

Note: In the case of each assignment, it would be a good idea to go to the sections in the manual on each author and review what we say there as well. There are statements about the essays and about writing assignments that have bearing on the sequence but that we won't repeat here.

. . . .

ASSIGNMENT 1

Words and Images [Mitchell]

This assignment requires students to do work in the library, so it would make sense to organize their schedule in stages. We asked our students to find documentary materials over the weekend and to be prepared to present them at the beginning of the following week. This both insured that students weren't all hitting the library at the last minute and it allowed the class to see the range of possible examples and to begin to work out a language for describing them in relation to those in Mitchell's essay. It might even make sense to have a preliminary writing assignment that is nothing more than the document introducing and focusing attention on the materials they bring to the project. Students need to learn how to incorporate visual materials into their text — including the necessary rhetorical skills. While some students can scan material into a document, others simply xerox and cut and paste. All students, however, need to think about how to introduce a reader to the material and, more importantly, how to prepare their reader's attention for the images, and, finally, how to comment on the images. At the simplest level, this is a matter of calling attention to what comes before and after the placement of the image in the text. Mitchell is not necessarily a great example, since the images in his text stand more as sidebars than as parts of paragraphs or parts of the exposition. We find it is important to have students do more than Mitchell does — both for their sake and for their reader's.

It *is* important, however, to insist that students work from Mitchell's analytical frame. (If students write a first draft focusing solely on the documentary text they have chosen, this might come in revision.) Here is what the assignment says:

> Your work is to put Mitchell to the test — to extend, test and perhaps challenge or qualify his account of the genre. As with his project, the basic questions are these: "What relationship between photography and writing do [these ex-

154

amples] articulate? What tropes of differentiation govern the division of labor between photography and writer, image and text, the viewer and the reader?"

We would insist that students write sentences where they try to make use of terms like "tropes of differentiation."

. . . .

ASSIGNMENT 2

Looking Back [Rich]

Rich speaks powerfully about the need to turn criticism to the material of daily life. This assignment asks students to write from inside the "we" of Rich's discourse, to imagine that the essay is addressed to them. It takes this as its key phrase: "Until we can understand the assumptions in which we are drenched we cannot know ourselves."

Assignment 2 asks students to follow Rich's lead and to write autobiographically, not as a celebration of their individuality but to cast themselves as a representative example of the way a certain group — named perhaps in terms of age, race, class, or gender — is positioned within the dominant culture. And it asks them to use the occasion to try out some of Rich's key terms, like "revision" and "patriarchy." Students need to find a way of describing Rich's methods — both the method she calls for and the method enacted in her essay. It is easy to declare Rich a "great writer" or a "famous person." It is harder to imagine what this talk of "re-vision" might be about, and how it might have bearing on the work of a student. The goal of this assignment is to narrow the distance between Rich and the student, to enable the student to imagine that she or he can both understand and try out Rich's project.

The difficulty students will have is in imagining (or representing) their experience as representative of a collective experience. You will not, in other words, get papers about the pressure of culture but about key individuals — fathers, mothers, teachers, lovers, grandparents, and coaches. In some ways this is inevitable. Both our students' age and the distinctly American versions of "personal experience" lead our students to write stories with no sense of the social, the political, or the historical. These, then, are the concerns we highlight for revision: In what ways is this story more than your story? Where can we find the cultural context? In what ways are you, as a character, cast in relation to ways of speaking, habits of mind?

. . . .

ASSIGNMENT 3

Seeing Your World through Geertz's Eyes [Geertz]

At the heart of Geertz's method is the process of taking a characteristic cultural event and seeing it as "saying something about something else." The cockfight is a story the Balinese "tell themselves about themselves." This, in miniature, is an invitation to share in the rigorous form of cultural analysis represented by Geertz's work. This assignment asks students to apply his method to a scene from their own familiar culture. Students, we've found, take great pleasure in this assignment. They are given a method, as well as an occasion, for speculating on the meaning of events central to their own lives. It is important, however, for students to work with real observation. If not, they will be inventing television scripts or cartoon versions of their own lives. The value of Geertz's method is that it is a way of opening up an unfamiliar culture. It is difficult for students to assume that their own culture is mysterious or unfamiliar. They must begin with this assumption, however, and they must work to maintain a conceptual distance from the events they closely observe. They should, for example, be careful not to personalize or to refer to themselves, even to the extent of saying "us" when referring to a population of college students.

For revision: Students, we've found, write this essay with considerable skill and enthusiasm. We have used students' first drafts to begin to direct a critical rereading of Geertz. The seams in students' texts are larger and more immediately visible than in Geertz's. By dramatizing the way students "master" the scenes they describe (by objectifying other people, by writing an interpretation that is total and final, by dealing in stereotypes, by telling familiar stories as though they were new), we can prepare them to look for similar gestures (and motives) in Geertz's essay. And by discussing the way Geertz could be said to be working on the problems of writing in this essay (the ways his expertise includes his work as a writer), we can set the terms for students' revisions of their own essays. If, in fact, the problems we highlight are not problems that can be overcome (all writing is interested, every writer is situated), then what are the options for a writer who wants to work on his or her writing? Geertz, it could be argued, solves the problem of making the problem part of the writing. He is not, in other words, just "reporting" what he "discovered" about the Balinese. And so we would like our students to imagine that they need to think of their drafts as writing problems — not just problems of reporting what they saw.

. . . .

ASSIGNMENT 4

Wideman as a Case in Point [Wideman]

Wideman, unlike Geertz, announces that he is writing about the problems of writing. This assignment asks students to look particularly at those sections where he interrupts the narrative to call attention to his situation as a writer.

We've taught this assignment several times and we've found it important for students to work directly from passages in the text. The first thing they need to do, then, is to reread the selection and choose their material. (The assignment asks them to choose three or four passages. This may turn out to be too many.) Once they have located their material, students do not have great difficulty describing it. They do, however, have trouble turning the discussion to a critical analysis of writing — either the writing of "Our Time" or writing as a generalized subject. In their first draft, students should be encouraged to turn from their material to the question of *why* Wideman interrupts the narrative. We have found that students write well and at length about *what* Wideman says, but when the space is open for them to come forward and comment or explain, they feel they have nothing to say. Students can imagine several routes to this question — they can talk as fellow writers, imagining from that perspective why a writer might want to bring forward the problem of writing. They can talk as readers, explaining the effects of these intrusions as they experienced them. Or they can talk as students — that is, through their knowledge of other attempts to represent an understanding of race, family, crime, drug addiction, or the black community.

For revision: Our experience with this assignment suggests that students can best use the time allowed for revision to work on the general issues raised in this paper. What might they say about Wideman's narrative intrusions? And, more specifically, what might this have to do with the writing they are doing (or might do) as students in the academy? What would the benefits or consequences be of producing a text that calls attention to itself as a text, as something produced? In particular, we want them to consider how Wideman's writing might stand beside Geertz's and Rich's. His authority rests, we think, on somewhat different grounds. And we would like students to consider his language (and theirs) next to the language they find in their textbooks or other "academic" writing assigned in their courses. If, in fact, these writers might be said to be "experts," how might their expertise be valued in the academic community as students have experienced it (or as they imagine it)?

. . . .
ASSIGNMENT 5

On Experts and Expertise [Mitchell, Rich, Geertz, Wideman, Percy]

The first four assignments repeat a basic pattern. They ask students to take on the ways of speaking and thinking of other powerful thinkers — to be apprentices. They imagine (with the aid of a text) a "Mitchell," "Rich," "Geertz," and "Wideman," and then work in his or her spirit. This assignment invites students to reflect back on what they have done, this time in the name of a "Walker Percy" who says that there is nothing more dangerous for a student than to get into the hands of an expert theorist. Students, in a sense, are being invited to fold their own story into the anecdotes about students in the second section of "The Loss of the Creature." This will be a difficult assignment for students who have done no prior work on Percy. It might be useful, in fact, either to allow time for a preliminary assignment or to allow time for this essay to go through several drafts. Percy's argument lends itself so easily to cliché (partly because he refuses to come forward as a theorist and provide a useful analytical language of his own) that students will need to have a complicated sense of how his essay works if they are to do justice to this assignment. (You don't, in other words, want students to be trapped in the corner of talking about nothing more than "the need to be an individual.") It is also important that students focus in on their work in the previous assignments: they will need, that is, to have good stories of their own to tell as well as the encouragement to select and quote from their own texts.

o–o–o–o–o–o–o–o–o–o–o–o–o–o–o–o–o–o–o

SEQUENCE NINE

History and Ethnography:
Reading the Lives of Others (p. 855)

We had a great time teaching this sequence. Students took great pleasure in becoming local or family historians, in turning "anthropological" intent on the scenes and expressions of their immediate culture. One of our goals in designing this sequence was to demonstrate in precise terms the ways in which intellectual work — in this sequence, work that goes under the names "history" and "ethnography" — is the work of reading and writing. We wanted to define the academy in terms of its practice (or practices) so that it could stand as something other than a museum of ideas or a collection of geniuses; we wanted to define intellectual work as reading and writing so that students could see firsthand their connectedness to academic disciplines and how and why they might be able to develop discipline-specific expertise — to become historians or cultural anthropologists (at least of a certain school).

The opening assignments are fairly straightforward. Geertz and Limerick are offered as representatives of their disciplines. Students work with and on their projects — extending them, reading them closely. We added Wideman to the list in order to yank "reading and writing the lives of others" out of the academy and put it into the realm of "ordinary life" or, perhaps more properly, the general (as opposed to academic) culture. And the Pratt assignment provides students with a motive and a set of terms for an attempt to theorize the representation of the "other."

We also, you will notice, built a series of revisions into this sequence. The point of the revision sequence is to allow students to think of the process of revision as something more than the perfecting or "finishing" of an essay. This sequence is designed to make students first of all see that they are involved in a sequential project, in which they will go

157

back to add more to what they have begun. Secondly, while revision is defined here as "addition," this sequence tries to illustrate how addition can be addition with a difference — adding not simply more of the same, but rather material that was hidden or forbidden or lost to the project as it was conceived the first time through. Students look to the "experts" to see how they have represented the problems of reading and writing the lives of others, then they go to their own work to see what they might add to make their texts more "expert" and less "naive."

If you wanted to shorten this sequence, the best way to do it would be to drop the Pratt assignment and perhaps also the third revision of the opening essay. If you wanted to work in book-length readings, we would recommend Geertz's *Works and Lives: The Anthropologist as Author,* Pratt's *Imperial Eyes,* Simon Schama's *Dead Certainties (Unwarranted Speculations),* Renato Rosaldo's *Culture and Truth,* or Robert Coles's *The Call of Stories.*

For a complete commentary on the selections in this sequence, please be sure to read each essay's selection in this manual, particularly the opening discussion. While we will cull materials from the discussions of individual assignments, we won't reproduce the introductions. And, while the sequences provide writing assignments, you should think about the advantages (or disadvantages) of using the "Questions for a Second Reading." In every case, students should read the headnotes in the textbook, which are designed to serve the assignments and sequences.

. . . .

ASSIGNMENT 1

Ethnography [Geertz]

This has been a successful assignment for us. It asks students to demonstrate their reading of Geertz's method by putting it to work on characteristic scenes from their own surroundings. Geertz's method can be represented by his phrase "saying something of something." He insists that scenes and events can be said to do this, to speak and tell a story, even to offer a key to the interpretation of a culture. The cockfights, he says, are a story the Balinese tell themselves about themselves. Similarly, our students walk around shopping malls, form groups and subgroups, and express themselves through ritual and routine. These scenes and activities seem to stand beyond commentary — either as just naturally there or as obvious in meaning and intent. One of our students said, "I don't have a 'culture.' I go home, we watch TV, our Mom brings the dinner into the TV room, she clears it away, we watch until the news, then I do my homework and go to bed. What else is there to say?" Learning both the motive and the method to finding that "what else" is one way of representing Geertz's project.

To begin to extend Geertz's work, students must begin with the assumptions that the scenes and events they describe contain stories they are (without knowing it) telling themselves about themselves. Such events say something about something else. The question is what. What is being said? And about what? What are these stories? What are their key features? How, as a reader, might one interpret them? How, as a writer, might one present them and explain/justify/rationalize one's interpretation? It is important for college students, if they write on groups close to them, to insist on their separateness, to speak of *them,* not *us,* to work from the outside. For this exercise, it is important that students act as though they were interpreting someone else's story and not their own.

It is also important to steer students away from the grand, national generalizations Geertz makes. (This is a route to one way of critiquing Geertz — how does he get to speak for *all* Balinese people?) If they begin to write about America, they will have trouble getting beyond the national narrative of America. They will have an easier time writing about local subcultures, local scenes and characters and routines.

The purpose of the assignment is to turn students to their own immediate cultures and to invite them to imagine and carry out a Geertzian project. It is important, then, that they begin with the motive to act like anthropologists, even if that means little more than writing something *other* than the usual classroom composition. This is partly a matter of style and arrangement; but it is also a matter of preparation. Students should work from recorded observations, not just from memory. Memory will lead inevitably to the commonplace and the clichéd, to the "life story" as it is enshrined in the composition curriculum, and will thus deprive them of the very details that can make their work rich and surprising.

Students should be reminded that they will have a chance to come back to this essay later.

. . . .

ASSIGNMENT 2

History [Limerick]

There are two options in this assignment. The general goal is to have students perform a reading of Limerick by writing a history — showing, in a sense, what they have learned in what they can do, defining the presence of the writer (Limerick) through the possible ways in which she might influence other writers.

The first option sends students to the library or local historical society. This assignment was prompted by Jean Ferguson Carr's teaching at Pitt (her courses almost always include some kind of archival project) and Pat Bizzell's teaching at Holy Cross (where she has students research local accounts of European settlements written by Native Americans). We were frustrated by the degree to which students feel removed from library archives and the degree to which our teaching (and the textbook) seemed to enforce that remove. Needless to say, this option will seem to be the harder of the two and students will need some prompting or challenge or rewards to choose it. One thing to remember is that an assignment like this will take more time than usual, since it takes time to find the library and spend enough time in the stacks to make the experience profitable, more than a quick search for the one book that will get you through the assignment. We've also found that we needed to make the process of search and selection an acknowledged part of the work of the course. We ask students to collect folders of material, to present them to others (to the class, to groups) and, in their essays, to talk about how they chose the material they chose to write about. Selection is of some special importance for this assignment, since Limerick's work points to the importance of finding the otherwise hidden alternative story.

The second option cuts out the library time, although it will work best if students take the challenge of making this more than a "personal essay." In fact, when we gave students this assignment, "personal essay" became a useful negative term, a way of indicating what their work needed to transcend in revision. Here is how we made the distinction between "history," as represented by Limerick, and "personal essay." Gathering materials was important — that is, essays became "histories" when they incorporated materials (like photos, diaries, and interviews) that would not have been found if a writer had not felt responsible for more than his or her own immediate experience. And structure became important. Essays became histories when they included more than two "stories" and more than a single point of view. In fact, much of the work of revision was represented in just these terms. Students went back to write more stories (counterstories, in Limerick's style) and to write from points of view not their own (their parents', a neighbor's, a friend's, a teacher's). Students added stories, added points of view, and worked to establish paragraphs (like those in Limerick) where they stepped forward to speak as an historian about the material they had gathered. The key moments in the best essays we received came when students realized they had to break the "unity" they had been trained to value, when they added the story that didn't seem to fit or wrote from outside their own point of view.

159

. . . .

ASSIGNMENT 3

A Writer's Guide [Wideman, Geertz, Limerick]

If you have time, this assignment could actually become two assignments. It asks students first to read Wideman as an alternative to the "historian" and the "ethnographer" as they have been produced by the academy. Wideman comes to a similar project with a background as a fiction writer. For him, the problems are located more generally in the problematics of writing (and, although he is less open about this, in the problematics of the family, *its* master narratives). Students might take time to work out first an account of Wideman as a counterexample to Geertz and Limerick. The advantage of doing this first in writing is that it will allow students the time and motive to choose and work closely with representative passages from "Our Time."

The assignment also asks students to produce a "Writer's Guide." This can be formatted as a guide — that is, as a set of tips or guidelines with illustrative examples. When we taught this assignment we used a handbook as a model.

You could set this up as two separate assignments. You could let the work on "Our Time" take place in a journal, or in material prepared in groups for class discussion. It will be useful to share examples of the "Writer's Guides" or to create a composite "Guide" from the more interesting material you collect. Students should learn to read and to value these guides before they go on to the revision assignments.

. . . .

ASSIGNMENT 4

Revision [Geertz, Limerick, Wideman]

This assignment asks students to choose one of the opening two essays and to begin a major revision. We have received wonderful work from both the "history" and the "anthropological" essay. (In fact, we have had students win prizes in our campus writing contest with essays from these assignments.) It is important to allow students to finally define "history" and "ethnography" through their practice and their readings of the selections. Students will not write what might strictly speaking be called an "ethnography," for example. But the point of the assignment is not to insist upon disciplinary rigor or to force their work to fit a predetermined mold. Students are imagining, approximating disciplinary work. The ways in which they get it "wrong" will be as potentially interesting and productive as the ways in which they get it "right."

Choosing which essay to work on will be a hard decision for many students. Our standard advice is for them to choose the one they feel drawn to. We impose only one general rule: Never choose the essay that was a disaster or that you (the student) think the teacher didn't like. We want our students to think of revision as a chance to take a good piece of work on to its next step, not to compensate for a bad start.

We also make much of this distinction made in the assignment between fixing or finishing an essay and taking it on to its next step. When students set out to "finish" an essay, their goal is to preserve the text they have begun. We want to encourage students to think of revision as opening up a text, changing it fundamentally, finding a way of bringing in material that challenges or frustrates its unity or certainty, its transitions and conclusions.

When our students have worked with the guidelines suggested by Geertz, Limerick, and Wideman, they have usually written the following: a text with marked sections, a text in a variety of voices or styles, a text that moves from predictable to unpredictable examples, a text with sections representing different points of view, a text with sections in italics, a text in which they stop and talk as writers about the writing.

. . . .

Reading Others [Pratt]

We think of this assignment as a way of returning students to the practice of "reading and writing the lives of others," but this time with a bit more conscious theorizing — a little more worry about who (really) is doing what to whom. Pratt, in her work, is one of the most powerful and most generous critics of history and ethnography. She advocates the practice, that is, while pointing to the interests it has served in the past and limits that have been imposed on the genres. At the end of this assignment, we want our students to be in a position to theorize on what they have done and to consider as they prepare to revise that the very skills they have developed can also be conceived of as problematic.

This assignment is an "inventory" assignment, asking students to collect documents that could stand, like the *New Chronicle*, as evidence of the literate arts of the contact zone. Pratt's essay provides a frame to organize the search (a frame students should imagine that they can break — that is, they can take it as a challenge to find the document that would surprise Pratt, that she would overlook or never think of), and her essay provides the terms for a discussion of the material they collect (or representative examples from that material).

This assignment offers two options. The first sends students to a library (or historical society) to find documents from the past. We tried to suggest the many possible moments of contact in local history (between slaves and owners, workers and management, women and men, minority and majority). (For more information, see our discussion on how this assignment was prompted, on manual p. 98.)

The second option sends students out into their local culture to look for the "documents" (this can be defined loosely to include music, like rap, transcripts of talk shows, films, documentaries, whatever). Students should feel that they can follow Pratt's lead and turn to their brothers and sisters (or their children) and to educational materials, including papers they are writing or have written recently. You should think about whether or not you would want students to choose papers from your course. It is an interesting possibility, but it will be hard for students to write about you and your class as anything *but* a utopia, paradise on earth. You may be disappointed if you invite students to take your classroom as an example.

In this assignment, whether students choose to work with historical or contemporary documents, they are asked to present their material as part of a project Pratt has begun. We have found it important to remind students that they need to *present* "Arts of the Contact Zone," even to readers who had read it. You cannot assume, as we noted earlier, that readers have it freshly in mind or that they will be willing to get the book off the shelf and turn to pages. And we have found it important to help students imagine the role they will play in this text. They will need, in other words, to do more than simply cite from or summarize what they have gathered in their inventories. They will need to step forward (as Pratt does) to teach, translate, make connections, explain, comment, discuss, think this way and that. Students, at least our students, are often too quick to let the wonderful material they gather speak for itself.

. . . .

ASSIGNMENT 6

Revision (Again) [Geertz, Limerick, Wideman, Pratt]

This is the "final" revision. We go to great lengths to put the word "final" in quotation marks, so that it doesn't seem to indicate the end of the road or the end of thinking, so that it doesn't seem to call for some kind of ultimate, oracular conclusion, the peace that passes all understanding. We have, however, found it important to distinguish between a draft that is primarily a draft (where a student continues to work on the intellectual project) and one that must also be "finished" (almost in a carpenter's sense, with a finish applied to the surface). We want our students to worry through the problems of proofreading, format and presentation, and we want to make this process a formal part of the sequence. We do this, in fact, with every course we teach, although we don't always represent this in every assignment sequence in *Ways of Reading*. The second paragraph of the assignment, then, is an attempt to direct students to the task of producing a "finished" essay, even when we know (or hope) that they aren't finished with the issues that have been raised, or even with the projects they have begun to work on.

As we said in the discussion of the previous assignment, we want this revision to be one where students take on the burdens of history and ethnography — understanding how these textual forms have been used in the past, a sense of their participation in that tradition, a sense of the weight of convention (and not just its support). One possible way of formalizing this process is to ask students to write a separate section, modeled on the final two sections of Geertz's essay, in which the writer steps out of the project to reflect back on it, its writing, and its possible good. Students, we've found, need to be reminded of the pressure to write this final section — or else to find some other way of bringing this level of commentary into their text. Without a reminder, they will simply "finesse" this part of the assignment.

o–o–o–o–o–o–o–o–o–o–o–o–o–o–o–o–o–o–o

SEQUENCE TEN

On Difficulty (p. 862)

Difficult texts, like the ones in this sequence, present students with problems they are not accustomed to solving. They will see writers at work, thinking on paper (as Wideman does, for instance, when he questions his own writing on his brother's story), working through complex ideas (as Foucault puzzles through the relationships of surveillance, controls, power, and knowledge), and presenting unusual and challenging positions (as Hirsch does when she imagines postmemory as a familial or cultural artifact that individuals identify with). For most students, even the idea of working with texts like these will be challenging and new. Traditionally, educational enterprises "dummy down" texts for students, and that has been one of the great failures of American education. Rather than teaching students how to work with and how to write difficult texts, the educational community has moved farther and farther toward providing students with easier and easier texts as the solution to students' problems with reading. The underlying assumption of presenting students with easy texts, texts that students can "get" in one reading, is that reading is easy, that problems, then, are indications of a writer's or a reader's failures. This sequence begins with the assumption that difficult texts often present students with challenging, complex thinking, and that for students to develop into complex, critical thinkers, they need to learn the work of reading and writing difficult texts. The metaphor for this sejuence is "work." The work students will do here is textual, and the experience of that work is designed to teach them that a great deal of important reading is hard work and not at all easy or instantaneous.

The six assignments in this sequence invite students to consider the nature of five difficult texts and how the problems they pose might be said to belong simultaneously to language, to readers, and to writers. It is assumed that these texts are difficult for all readers, not just for students, and that the difficulty is necessary or strategic, not a mistake or evidence of a writer's (or a reader's) incompetence.

Since the sequence was designed to serve teachers interested in having their students study the problems of difficult texts, it might be helpful to think of using it (or some of the assignments) after students work with these selections either in class discussions (using the second-reading questions or the writing assignments as discussion questions) or in writing assignments or in some combination of both. You could also use the kinds of questions posed by these assignments for other difficult texts that students work with.

. . . .

ASSIGNMENT 1

Uneasy Confrontations [Hirsch]

Perhaps, as the assignment suggests, it is most helpful for students to imagine that they are reviewing Hirsch's essay for those who have not read it, so that they can write to both re-present her arguments and examples and to comment on them. They can also write to relate personal stories or examples if this helps them establish a position in relation to the essay that would allow a reader to see how Hirsch's work is useful or interesting to them. You will want to use examples of student writing in class to point students away from book review–like writing that quickly summarizes Hirsch and guide them toward more careful accounts of her project that refer to her examples and methods as a writer, allowing readers to imagine both what she has to say and the ways she works. Within this kind of presentation, students can then write themselves, their commentaries, into their re-presentations, so that their commentaries and presentations are interwoven as a piece rather than separate chunks of writing.

. . . .

ASSIGNMENT 2

Foucault's Fabrication [Foucault]

Students don't usually have trouble with Foucault's examples — the stories he tells about the plague, for instance, or his elucidations on examples of the Panopticon. This assignment picks up on his examples and the way Foucault uses them throughout the selection to create an argument for the relationship of surveillance, control, power, and knowledge. Students will need to focus on Foucault's examples, and they'll need to invent a way to trace the examples from the beginning of the text through to the end as they summarize Foucault's developing arguments on surveillance and power. This task will be difficult. The writing is more exploratory, more thinking on the page, than it is summative, and even the most attentive students (and instructors) will find the last section, on power and knowledge, challenging and elusive. But this is an occasion for students to work at the problem (rather than to "get" it or to get it right); they can find a way into it by studying Foucault's examples of surveillance — particularly how they might or might not be similar — and the way in which he uses them to represent control and power. The students' summaries should proceed by examples, following Foucault's text if they wish, because it

163

is through the examples that they'll be able to draw out and ground his arguments about the relationships of control and power and knowledge.

. . . .

ASSIGNMENT 3

A Story of Reading [Wideman]

This assignment asks students to take an unusual stance toward Wideman's selection — to read it as a text that wants to break readers' habits — and it asks them to take an unusual stance toward themselves as readers and writers — to write down and comment on how they read Wideman's text. Students might begin by identifying moments in the text that they want to refer to, moments where they feel Wideman is deliberately working on his readers, defying their expectations and directing their responses. They'll also need to comment on what it was like for them to read those passages, and to this end, they might help themselves with a version of a double-entry notebook, or rather a triple-entry notebook, because the assignment also asks them to comment on what Wideman is doing and why he's doing it. The first column of their notebook might note in some way the passages they've identified where Wideman seems to be deliberately working on his readers. The second column could tell the story of their reading those sections (in the context of their reading the entire selection), and the third column could indicate their thinking about what Wideman is doing, why he seems to be doing it, and how it affected them as readers. Students will need to read the selection at least twice, but they should begin their note taking for the story of how they read it the first time through so that they can record their reactions to those sections where Wideman seems to be working on his readers. Once they've got their notes fleshed out, students will then need to tell the story of their reading, with careful reference to those passages they identified and with careful accounting of their reactions to their first reading of them. They'll need to continually step aside, so to speak, in their writing — as Wideman does — to comment on the habits Wideman assumes in his readers and why he wants to break them. For students, this paper is a story of reading with references to the Wideman text, narratives on their reactions to it, and asides commenting on Wideman's demands on readers. This, then, is an assignment to read a challenging text and to create another challenging text in response to it.

. . . .

ASSIGNMENT 4

Story Lines [Munro]

This assignment is broadly drawn to offer students an opportunity to imagine Munro as a presence in her story who takes "The Albanian Virgin" as an opportunity to think about stories. Students are invited to write about what she might be saying about stories — where they come from, what they accomplish, and what they are good for. They are also invited to write about their sense of this story in the same way, responding to the same questions that they use to think about what Munro might be saying: Where do they think the story comes from? What does it accomplish? What is it good for?

Students will need to work from particular moments in the story to do both kinds of work — to say what Munro could be said to be thinking about through this story and to say what it does for them. It seems obvious that some students will want to divide the essay into two sections, one for each part of the task, but students will benefit if they imagine it as an integrated whole, with one section in conversation with the other. Here, they might write something like "In this passage Munro seems to say that this story is trying to accomplish this, and as for me, I think it is doing this." We don't mean to wrap it up in one sentence, but to demonstrate how students might interweave their work on both parts of the assignment while writing closely from particular moments that they identify as key to the tasks.

. . . .

ASSIGNMENT 5

A Sense of an Ending [Benjamin]

This assignment extends the fourth "Question for a Second Reading" into a writing project by asking students to explain the epilogue as a conclusion. Students also are invited to write for readers who have not read Benjamin and who do not have the text in hand, so they will need to re-present Benjamin's essay and his epilogue to those readers. This itself is a substantial piece of writing, one that students will have difficulties with because Benjamin's essay is complex and they'll want to reduce it to a string of generalizations about art. They'll need to be reminded in revisions that they also have to present his arguments about the superstructure, changing human perceptions, and changed notions of art (the loss of the authentic, for instance). As students work on re-presenting Benjamin to these readers, they'll need to find ways to explain to these readers the ways in which his essay prepares readers in general for the epilogue on war while, at the same time, coming to a conclusion about Benjamin's two accounts of war and his position on war, art, and aesthetics.

This is, to be sure, a demanding piece of work, and students might imagine it in stages or a week's worth of writing drafts. You might help them stage it by building it into class discussions over a week's worth of time, so that they can see examples of how their colleagues have handled the tasks. A writing workshop environment might offer everyone the flexibility to do both individual and group work over that week before they set about producing final versions.

. . . .

ASSIGNMENT 6

A Theory of Difficulty
[Hirsch, Foucault, Wideman, Munro, Benjamin]

Students are asked in this assignment to produce a guide that might be useful to other students who will be asked to work with difficult texts and assignments. It's important for students to understand their stance in this piece of writing. Although they are writing a guide that offers advice, they must write from examples of their reading and writing. The examples must come from their past work on this sequence, and they should feel free to cite and explain everything — from class discussions to note taking to revising papers. The danger with retrospective assignments like this one is that students will turn immediately to generic platitudes, that they'll say what they think is expected of them ("Be prepared to work hard," "Don't see difficult texts as your failure or the writer's failure"). To push against these kinds of moves, you'll need to ask students to work from those moments in their past work that highlighted (for them) ways of reading and writing difficult texts, ways that might help other students who haven't done the kinds of work that they have. Here again they might use double-entry notebooks, first to identify the moments in their work they want to discuss, then to explain what that work stands for or taught them about difficult texts. In their papers or in a third column, they can begin those discussions that tie together what they have to say into a theory of difficulty. Whatever they do with their note taking, they'll need it to stand as an example of good practice in reading and writing about difficult texts. And it's from those examples and illustrations that they should derive their theories of difficulty. While a theory is drawn from generalizations, these in turn are drawn from or anchored in illustrations or cases. So if students don't work from the examples they have at hand, their theory will be based on generalizations alone and will be a string of platitudes instead of an argument rooted in example.

o–o–o–o–o–o–o–o–o–o–o–o–o–o–o–o–o–o–o

SEQUENCE ELEVEN

Reading Culture (p. 868)

As we say in its introduction in the text, this sequence asks students to imagine culture as a large organizing force, one in which they are situated, implicated, one that shapes, organizes, and controls the ways we think, speak, act, and write. There is a power in this form of analysis that students can feel and share, but it comes at the expense of the usual celebrations of freedom, free will, and individuality. The usual ways of talking about experience will be displaced by this sequence. You and your students will have to work hard from the opening moments of the course to keep a watchful eye open for vestiges of the "old" ways of speaking; to stop, now and then, when you hear it at work in language, for instance, about what is "natural" or "true" or "obvious"; to bracket it; to put its key terms on the blackboard; and to imagine why it is attractive and how one might understand its limits. The pattern in this sequence is fairly straightforward. Students read the work of several critics, and they are asked to reproduce (or revise) their methods in critical writing of their own.

The sequence moves back and forth between summary and application. Students are asked to reproduce a form of critique (extending Bordo's project, for example) and then to work closely with the assumptions behind a critical project (like Berger's and Foucault's), asking fundamental questions: How do they do their work? Why? How might their projects be thought of as similar? The final assignment asks students to bring all of the work together, to select, edit and revise, and to write a longer, more finished essay on the topic of visual culture.

.   .   .   .

ASSIGNMENT 1

Looking at Pictures [Berger]

The Berger assignment is designed to familiarize the exotic (by asking students to "converse" with high art). Berger argues that criticism should turn to everyday language, to force connections between life and art. Berger turns against "academic" criticism to represent what he would like us to believe is the human reality of art and the perception of art. This is both compelling and problematic. Berger speaks in a voice students admire. It is difficult, however, to get students to read against that voice, to question the ease with which Berger assumes he knows the reality of history or the ease by which he assumes a kind of universal human experience, one that he understands because he has cut through the crap.

We've had a good deal of success with this assignment. Ideally, students should have ready access to a museum. Berger talks about the ways we have come to experience paintings in museums, and a trip to a museum to look at a painting will give students a way of adding to or reflecting on Berger's argument. But he also talks about reproductions, so we felt justified in adding the option for students to go to art books in the library. If you can reasonably expect your students to get to a museum, however, we think the trip will hold some interesting surprises for you. We usually schedule a class meeting at the museum — just to get the students in and walking around to think about which painting might be "theirs." Warn students against docents and taped tours — for your purposes these prepared readings of paintings will be a real barrier to writing.

The students who have had the most success with this assignment have been fairly literal in their sense of what it means to have a "conversation" with a painting. Their essays, that is, have not read as museum-guide-like interpretations but as more open-ended and speculative pieces, sometimes cast as a narrative with dialogue, sometimes as pure dialogue. The key is to invite students to "talk" to the painting, to ask questions, and to imagine rich and ambiguous responses. It is best to have students avoid papers that begin with an idea of what a picture is about and simply impose that reading on the material. The painting needs to be imagined to talk back, to counter or open up a student's desire to master and control.

For revision: In some cases we've found we needed to send students back to the painting and the original assignment, usually because students were more concerned to push through a single reading than to have a conversation with their material. In most cases, however, we used the revision as the occasion to send students back to the Berger essay. As they become involved with the museum assignment, students (in a sense) forgot about Berger, and so we used the revision to send them back, to see what use they can make of his way of talking about paintings or about the museum. (For example, "How could you use the example of your essay to explain what Berger might mean when he talks about 'history'?") The idea here is to engage them in a conversation with Berger, where your students can draw on their expertise to enter his argument.

. . . .

ASSIGNMENT 2

The Ideology of Hunger [Bordo]

Our students like working with this assignment. It does not, however, teach itself. Students need to take their "research" responsibilities seriously — choosing not just the first set of ads that come to hand but choosing carefully after searching. We have, for example, asked students to write a preliminary note about what they rejected — or to keep (and to let us see) a larger file of material from which they made their choices. And we found it important to insist that a "set" of advertisements had to include more than two (three at a minimum) so that students didn't fall into a simple set of binaries. It also helps to let this assignment go through two drafts. Much of students' energy and attention will go into presenting the material. It is only later that they can begin to think about their examples in relation to the specifics of Bordo's argument — specific passages and terms. Once we receive the first drafts, we would copy two or three of them (those that had done something interesting in presenting the ads (done more, for example, than "objective," newspaper style description or more than parody or mockery). We would first ask students to talk about the point of view of the writer — trying to establish the presence or absence of the student's work with the examples; then we would ask where the essay was (or might begin to be) in conversation with Bordo. Almost all of our students forgot (or were too timid) to draw conclusions about the ideology of hunger at the turn of the twentieth century in America. This, too, began a focus for revision in the second draft.

167

. . . .

ASSIGNMENT 3

Ideology and Agency [Bordo, Berger]

This assignment requires some preliminary work by students. They are asked to work with John Berger's essay, "Ways of Seeing," along with Bordo's to define a larger project, that of reading the design and intention of images, to discover whether Berger and Bordo are saying the same things in different context with different kinds of examples. The answer, of course, is "yes and no." Students don't need to chart the obvious differences — Berger writes about classics and museums; Bordo writes about ads and magazines. The interesting comparisons come to play when students consider the different ways they represent the viewer/reader (what he or she knows and doesn't know) and the source of agency (who is doing what to whom and why). The second reading questions should help to open these two essays up to this kind of discussion. Students should reread the selections with comparison in mind. (This might, in fact, be an exercise in advance of class discussion.) The work for students will come in representing both essays (providing "strategic" summaries) and then in moving to a close reading of passages that will allow students to discuss what, for them, are the most significant or interesting differences. We know from experience that students rarely put themselves into this discussion as a person with a point of view — either a theory of why and how the projects differ or an account of which they find more useful and compelling. Students don't have the knowledge to do much with the assignment's invitation to think about time and history (the dates of the essays). They can, however, theorize and/or take sides.

. . . .

ASSIGNMENT 4

On Agency [Foucault]

This is a two-part assignment. It can, in fact, be represented as two drafts of a larger work-in-progress. The first asks for a strategic summary, one that will allow students to write out a working account of Foucault's argument. We have found that it is not only useful but almost crucial for students to be invited to write sentences about what they *don't* understand. They need to be able to bracket out the ideas, sections, terms, or phrases that lie beyond them; and they need to feel that they are allowed to venture tentative translations or paraphrases. The second half of the assignment asks students to bring Foucault into the discussion they began in assignment 3. One way to stage this project would be to ask for the summary of Foucault and then to ask students to work from that paper to revise the essay that they wrote on Bordo and Berger.

. . . .

ASSIGNMENT 5

Reading Images [Mitchell]

In many ways, this is the most difficult assignment of the sequence, since it asks students to work at a level of remove from Mitchell's argument. They are asked to look at where and how he figures "the reader/viewer" in his essay. It will help to provide some modeling of this and then to ask students (either at home or in class in groups) to reread the text to find examples they can put on the table. The assignment assumes that students both know how to perform a "close reading" and how to represent a close reading in a text. Our experience suggests that both acts are foreign to them. This is certainly the occasion to each students about the use of the block quotation — not only how to punctuate it but how to make use of it as a device of presentation. You might bring in an example in order to talk about what precedes a block quotation, what follows, about highlighting and returning to key phrases and examples. (Mary Louis Pratt, in *Imperial Eyes,* or Stephen Greenblatt, in *Marvelous Possessions,* have been our favorite sources for such examples.) It makes sense for students to think through their close reading of Mitchell before turning again to Berger and Bordo. If you are extending these assignments over the semester and have time, this is another assignment that could be staged out over two drafts: the first to work out a reading of Mitchell; the second to rework Mitchell and to work in passages from Berger and Bordo.

. . . .

ASSIGNMENT 6

Visual Culture [Berger, Bordo, Foucault, Mitchell]

We have made much use of this kind of retrospective assignment. Students probably have had *little* experience writing this way and so will need help in conceiving of the task. Our goal is to have students assemble all of their work for the term and to think about how to work from those previous essays to a longer essay. They can, of course, incorporate whole sections from what they have already written. In fact, part of the challenge here is to do just that kind of editorial work. We have often asked students to assist each other as editors —that is, to read each other's work to make suggestions about where to begin, what to save, what order to work from, and so on. This is not, however, a simple exercise in cut and paste. The idea is for students to think about how to work *from* these earlier texts toward a more extended and synthetic, a smarter and more finished discussion, one (as the assignment says) where they too need to be present as a person with something to say. Some of our colleagues have asked their students to also write a brief preface, a statement about the history and evolution of the piece designed to introduce the reader to the project as a project.

o–o–o–o–o–o–o–o–o–o–o–o–o–o–o–o–o–o–o

SEQUENCE TWELVE

Reading Culture (II) (p. 875)

This sequence provides an alternate set of readings for sequence eleven, "Reading Culture (I)." It begins with the work of Walter Benjamin, a key source for John Berger and, although not cited directly in *Performing Rites,* an important figure for British cultural studies and, by extension, for Simon Firth. As you prepare your students to write (and as you prepare to read and respond to their work), it is important to remember the context of an introductory writing course. It is very unlikely that students will be famliar with Benjamin or with the traditions and preoccupations of cultural studies. Our advice would be to resist the temptation to provide background materials or lectures. The key is for students to find a way of working with and from these essays. This work is possible, it is exciting, and it is useful. (And it may send some students off to other books or other courses.) The assignments move back and forth between summary and application. Students are asked to represent Benjamin's argument and then to think forward to examples of their own, to cases from present time. The quality of the writing will depend heavily on the time students' take to present and develop the examples they bring to the text. Most of our class time is spent working with student papers. We would focus attention on the most interesting and compelling examples students had brought to the discussion. And, when asking students to revise, we were most often asking for more — not for additional examples but for time spent *with* examples.

. . . .

ASSIGNMENT 1

The Work of Art in the Age of Mechanical Reproduction [Benjamin]

One could argue that a key to Benjamin's argument about the change in art (and in the superstructure of the culture because of the change) resides in his relegation of "authenticity" and "aura" in connection to art, to a tradition that is forever changed by the possibilities of mechanical reproduction of art. Traditional notions of art as authentic, or of art as having an aura about it, no longer have bearing in a world where art can be reproduced on a large scale for the masses. There are major passages in the text where Benjamin makes these arguments, and, of course, he uses fairly extended examples involving painting and drama and photography and film.

When students work on this assignment, they'll want to be certain that they first follow Benjamin's arguments about the traditional notions of authenticity and aura through to the end of the essay, because Benjamin continues to build and modify them, especially when he writes about photography and film toward the end of his essay. The assignment also asks students to work with examples of their own that they might place alongside his to extend his argument with twenty-first century examples.

. . . .

ASSIGNMENT 2

Thinking about Cases [Benjamin]

Extending Benjamin's work, as this assignment invites students to do, involves the creation of arguments about art forms (such as film and video, or painting, music, and so on) and about the interrelation of these forms to the superstructure of the society. Students will need to begin by, in some way of their own, representing Benjamin's arguments about both the evolution of art forms and their connections to the culture's superstructure. How, they might then ask themselves, after they have represented Benjamin's work, have the forms they are writing about evolved since Benjamin's time? How has the superstructure of the culture evolved? What marks these evolutions? What visible signs, that is, would they point to, to say, "This is what Benjamin sees and this is what we see now" (while keeping Benjamin's underlying notions of the superstructure)?

Once students set the ground for their work by providing that careful account of Benjamin's arguments (for art forms and their relation to the superstructure), they can go on and extend his work by writing about a single area of art they know well enough to focus on. They might write a fairly traditional piece in which they say, "This is what Benjamin thinks and this is how my example fits into it," or they might take a more challenging tack and write in conversation with Benjamin's piece by picking up his notions, weaving in their own with examples, using footnotes as he does, and taking their examples to some conclusion about the culture, as he does with the final epilogue on war. Benjamin's piece itself can serve as an example of how one might write in conversation with others' ideas. Students could study the ways he uses his sources before they begin this so that they might have a sense of writing that speaks to other writing before they begin.

. . . .

ASSIGNMENT 3

Ways of Seeing [Berger, Benjamin]

This is a lovely assignment for students to study the influences of one author on another. Berger, as the assignment points out, acknowledges his debt to Benjamin by including a picture of Benjamin at the end of his essay, but the influence is much more particular than this gesture. He appropriates and transforms much of Benjamin's arguments, and his own terms, so there is much for students to learn and do with these two pieces.

After completing the first two assignments in the sequence, students can move on to Berger with an eye toward locating those ideas and terms that he takes from Benjamin's work. They might work in small groups to identify those ideas and terms in Benjamin that Berger appropriates before they begin writing individually. At times students help themselves if they can work together and see what others identify and the connections they make to Berger. This could easily evolve into a whole class project, with students doing all the work, so that you don't inadvertently value a particular set of connections and end up reading about them in everyone's essays. After the class work, the individual writing might begin. With this, students will need to experiment with ways to present these connections so that every essay does not read like "Benjamin says this and Berger says this." Class discussions of students' work in their first drafts could focus on the connections students make and the ways they write those connections, so that the class could see multiple examples of different ways of working and, then, imagine other methods as well.

. . . .

ASSIGNMENT 4

Ways of Listening [Frith]

This writing assignment begins with an exercise. It invites students to take the models presented in the opening pages of the chapter and to write their own descriptions of voice in performance, working with an example that is close to them, that they know well and care about. The task is to put onto the page something that is not writing. (In this sense, the problem falls into the range of W. J. T. Mitchell's concerns in "The Photographic Essay: Four Case Studies.")

We suggest that the assignment involve draft and revision. If this is possible, the first draft (or drafts) would be the production of the exercises — descriptions of voice in the manner of Sandow, Day, Gould, and Frith. The revision would be to bring these examples to a discussion of Frith's project in "The Voice." This would involve summary and paraphrase and then (or also) a move from Frith to a consideration of the student's examples and how they extend, engage, or modify his argument.

. . . .

ASSIGNMENT 5

Back to Benjamin [Frith, Benjamin]

Frith's work is shaped by the traditions of British cultural study which were shaped by the Frankfurt school. Students do not need to have the history or to know the theory in order to work on this assignment. Good work can be done trying to think through the differences between Benjamin and Frith and to think them through in detail (thinking about the differences in time and place, thinking about the differences in film and music, thinking about the different positions the two writers take on popular culture and its audiences).

Adorno is the representative Frankfurt figure for Frith. Here are some sections of a 1991 article in *Diacritics* (Winter 1991, 102–15) in which Frith thinks through his objections for the Frankfurt representation of the consumer. The first begins with a discussion reproduced in "The Voice":

> In universities, then, just as in high schools, there is still a split between what Frank Kogan describes as the discourse of the classroom (with its focus on a subject matter) and the discourse of the hallway (with its focus on one's feelings about a subject matter). In this respect (and despite first impressions) academic approaches to popular culture still derive from the mass cultural critiques of the 1930s and 1940s, particularly from the Marxist critique of contemporary popular culture in terms of the production and circulation of commodities. For the Frankfurt School, analyzing the organization of mass production on the one hand, and the psychology of mass consumption on the other, the value issue was, in a sense straightforward — if it's popular it must be bad! — and Adorno and his colleagues developed a number of concepts (such as standardization) to show why this must be so.

He says,

> In the cultural studies tradition with which I'm most familiar, British subcultural theory, this reworking [to look for the redeeming features of commodity culture in the act of consumption] took on the particular form of identifying certain social groups with what we might call "positive mass consumption" (which became — and remains — the pithiest academic definition of "popular" culture). The value of cultural goods could therefore be equated with the value of the groups consuming them — youth, the working class, women, and so forth.

And continues,

> It is hard to avoid the conclusion that the more celebratory the populist study, the more patronizing its tone, an effect, I think, of the explicit populist determination to deny (or reverse) the usual high/low cultural hierarchy. If one strand of the mass cultural critique was an indictment of low culture from the perspective of high art (as was obviously the case for Adorno, for example), then to assert the value of the popular is also, certainly, to query the superiority of high culture. Most populist writers, though, draw the wrong conclusion; what needs challenging is not the notion of the superior, but the claim that it is the exclusive property of the "high."

In the end, Frith wants to maintain the distinction between high and low but to deny that it is distributed along lines of class or defined by the traditions of high culture. Popular music, he argues, *can* contain serious pleasure; distinctions of value belong not just to the bourgeoisie but to all consumers; and the goal of academic criticism should be to improve the ways we (all of us) talk about and think about the cultural materials we value.

· · · · · · · · ·

ASSIGNMENT 6

Conclusions [Benjamin, Berger, Frith]

All three — Benjamin, Berger and Frith — conclude by imagining a vision of the future, all assuming that criticism can and must change the course of history.

In the epilogue, Benjamin offers two accounts of war. These are oddly placed in relation to the rest of the essay, but powerfully present in relation to history. Berger concludes as well by thinking about the relation of past to present. Frith's chapter, "The Voice," moves toward a conclusion but it does not articulate one. (It is a chapter, after all, and in service of the larger structure of the book.) The question provides students with a passage at the end of the book, one that can stand as a conclusion (and it might be useful to have some discussion of this passage in class). Students can then reread, thinking about where and how the discussion of voice is leading to these conclusions:

> It follows that an identity is always already an ideal, what we would like to be, not what we are. In taking pleasure from black or gay or female music I don't thus identify as black or gay or female (I don't actually experience these sounds as "black music" or "gay music" or "women's voices") but, rather, participate in imagined forms of democracy and desire, imagined forms of the social and the sexual. And what makes music special in this familiar cultural process is that musical identity is both fantastic — idealizing not just oneself but also the social world one inhabits — and real: it is enacted in activity. Music making and music listening, that is to say, are bodily matters; they involve what one might call *social movements*. In this respect, musical pleasure is not derived from fantasy — it is not mediated by daydreams — but is experienced directly: music gives us a real experience of what the ideal could be.

The question also invites students to engage with this argument. We focused on two elements: the statement that "music gives us a real experience of what the ideal could be," and a view of the ideal as imagined forms of democracy and desire (the social and the sexual).

In considering the three together, students might think about the differences in the times of these essays; they might (and rightly) consider them as part of a single project, unfolding as scholars read and work in relation to one another (with Benjamin as the crucial earlier point of reference); or they might think about the difference in materials: film, painting, and music. In an assignment like this, we like to remind students that conclusions (as in the case of the conclusions represented here) do not have to sum things up, tie things up, or bring a discussion to a close. They can be provisional ways of thinking back on a problem or a project; they can be tentative and they can be of two or three minds; they can raise questions and point to the future. In that sense, students should imagine that they too are implicated in the past and future indicated in each essay; ideally, they should write as though they have something important at stake in these arguments, at stake as consumers of these cultural forms and at stake as citizens.

o–o–o–o–o–o–o–o–o–o–o–o–o–o–o–o–o–o–o

SEQUENCE THIRTEEN

Uses of Reading (p. 880)

This sequence focuses attention on authors as readings, on the use of sources, and on the art of reading as a writer. It combines technical lessons with lessons on the rhetoric of citation. The first assignment, for example, calls attention to the block quotations in Richard Rodriguez's essay, "Hunger of Memory." On one level, Rodriguez provides students with a useful example of how (strategically as well as technically) to use a block quotation. Our concern has also been to call attention to the ways in which (as in the case of Rodriguez) a writer need not always identify with the words of others. We make much in our teaching about the space that comes before and after the block quotation. Here is where a writer has work to do — setting a reader up and providing a way of reading, including critical reading. The next two assignments look at two writers from significantly different moments in history, with significantly different relations to their sources, and to the culture represented by those sources: Walter Benjamin and Alice Walker. Both offer more striking examples of revisionary work, examples that students can imitate as well as describe. Imitation will take them outside the conventions of "academic writing," at least as that is represented by term papers.

Walker, for example, takes the past and writes herself into it, revises in order to make the words work. We have wanted students to feel first hand the transgressive pleasure of rewriting someone else's words. In general, students understand this to be forbidden. They think: "You are not allowed to do that." In doing it, and in thinking about how and why rewriting can serve, they get a felt understadning of their relation (of a possible relation) to tradition and authority. Most composition classes teach summary, quotation, and paraphrase. These acts are not necessarily subservient. A writer does not have to disappear. (It is our practice, in fact, to always teach summary, quotation, and paraphrase as strategic acts — a way of getting someone else's words and ideas out on the table.)

The last assignment turns back on the introduction to the textbook. This is a way for students to think again, to think retrospectively, about the book and the course. It would be lovely to believe that over the next few years, as students are assigned material to read, they continue to read as writers, asking not only "what does it say" but "what does it do" and "would I want to do something like that?"

· · · · · · · · · · ·

ASSIGNMENT 1

The Scholarship Boy [Rodriguez, Hoggart]

These assignments represent, in written exercises, the two concerns raised in the opening discussion. The second asks students to frame their story in Rodriguez's terms and style. This one asks them to turn Rodriguez's argument about education — about the relationship between students and teachers — back on the essay by considering the relationship between Rodriguez and Hoggart as a case in point. The general question is this: Is Rodriguez still a scholarship boy? Is he still reading "in order to acquire a point of view"? The earlier general discussion explains why we send students to look at the use of quotations. There are other ways of talking about the relationship between these two writers, but our concern is to make these problems textual problems — problems that hold lessons for readers and writers.

This can be a more complicated question than it appears, depending on how far you want to push it. Some students will argue that Rodriguez is still a blinkered pony. Some will take his argument on its own terms and argue that he rejects Hoggart in the end for being "more accurate than fair" to the scholarship boy. There is the larger question of Rodriguez's use of Hoggart's book *The Uses of Literacy*, a book about the class system which strives to speak in the general and not to sentimentalize individual stories. It is possible, if you and your students have the time, to send students to Hoggart's book in order to construct a more complicated and comprehensive account of this reading.

· · · · · · · · · · ·

ASSIGNMENT 2

Sources [Benjamin]

For this question, students might work in groups of two or three to identify one or two footnotes, and in their work together, they could connect those to the text in whatever ways they imagine. The idea is to see how the footnotes work with the text, so they might find examples in the footnotes that elaborate on the text, serve as examples to it, pose additional problems, or situate the text in some way. This is a good assignment to teach students about the objective of footnotes, and they get to work with a master footnoter

174

whose primary works, according to political theorist Hannah Arendt, were his notebooks filled with notes, clippings, and footnotes.

. . . .

ASSIGNMENT 3

Contrary Instincts [Walker]

There are really two parts to this essay. Students will first need to go to the library (and we think it is important to insist on this — they should not do *this* research via the Internet) to find out something about the authors and the books on Walker's list. This information could be gathered in groups. In class, the students can make presentations, and these presentations should include handout copies from the texts they have chosen. The discussion should move to a consideration of the difference in the types of references and allusions in "In Search of Our Mothers' Gardens." And the guiding questions should be something like these: "What does she do with authors and texts?" "How does she define the appropriate and possible uses of tradition?" "What might one learn about the library, writing, and research'?"

There is a wonderful essay addressing these very questions that we highly recommend: Matthew Fike, "Jean Toomer and Okot p'Bitek in Alice Walker's "In Search of Our Mothers' Gardens," in *Melus*, Fall/Winter 2000.

. . . .

ASSIGNMENT 4

Ways of Reading [Bartholomae and Petrosky]

Over the years we have heard from many readers about the usefulness of the introduction to *Ways of Reading*. This assignment asks students to work closely with its language and its argument and to use it retrospectively about your course and about learning to write in a college or university setting. If students do particularly well with this, we would be interested in receiving copies of essays. We can't promise to respond (we get many letters from students); we might, however, include copies in the Instructor's Manual for the next edition.

o–o–o–o–o–o–o–o–o–o–o–o–o–o–o–o–o–o–o

SEQUENCE FOURTEEN

Ways of Seeing (p. 884)

The five assignments in this sequence introduce students to the problems posed by how we look at art and what these problems have to do with history, as Berger sees it, the making of meaning, and the expectations and strategies that we use to construct both history and meaning. Mitchell's essay gives students another way to imagine the relationship between images and language, and their use of it to evaluate Berger's readings of paintings gives them the opportunity to think about the differences in language's relationship to paintings as opposed to its relationship to photographs.

Berger's essay also allows us to extend our understanding of what it means to read beyond the written text to the way one "reads" paintings or images and to the way one "reads" one's culture. He seems to purposely want to take common terms like "history" and "meaning" and make them problematic just as he wants to take familiar images and give us other ways of seeing them; yet he isn't pushy about definitions, and these terms remain open for discussion. For students, this means that they can reproduce his project beginning with a close examination of his argument, then an examination of the process whereby they interrogate a painting to get it to speak. From here, students are invited to study Berger's readings of two paintings, Rembrandt's *Woman in Bed* and Caravaggio's *The Calling of St. Matthew,* so that they can use at least one of these as an example to restate Berger's argument for what we might do with and because of paintings. In the fourth assignment, students have the opportunity to use Mitchell's arguments about the relationship of images and language to evaluate, or weigh, Berger's arguments in both "Ways of Seeing" and in readings of the Rembrandt and Caravaggio paintings. Assignment 5 offers students the opportunity to revise the essay that they wrote for the second assignment now that they have had the opportunity to study Berger's readings of the two paintings and to work closely with Mitchell's essay on the relationship of images to language.

* * * * * * * * * * *

ASSIGNMENT 1

Ways of Seeing [Berger]

This first assignment is an opportunity for students to closely study Berger's essay to resay his arguments about what gets in the way when we look at paintings and what we might do to overcome the barriers. Berger claims, in a broad sense, that culture gets in the way of our readings of paintings and history, but his examples are examples of culture as it appears in different enacted forms — in the machinery of mystification, for example and in the social positioning of experts or critics. So students will need to work closely from Berger's examples of things and people getting in the way and to use these examples as the grounds for making their claims for his argument. With this assignment, students also are asked to imagine that they are writing to an audience unfamiliar with Berger's essay.

* * * * * * * * * * *

ASSIGNMENT 2

A Painting in Writing [Berger]

We've had a good deal of success with this assignment. Ideally, students should have ready access to a museum. Berger talks about the ways we have come to experience paintings in museums, and a trip to a museum to look at a painting will give students a way of adding to or reflecting on Berger's argument. But he also talks about reproductions, so we felt justified in adding the option of using art books. If you can reasonably expect your students to get to a museum, however, we think the trip will hold some interesting surprises for you. We usually schedule a class meeting at the museum — just to get the students walking around to think about which painting might be "theirs." Warn students against docents and taped tours — for your purposes, prepared readings of paintings will be a real barrier to writing.

The students who have had the most success with this assignment have been fairly literal in their sense of what it means to have a "conversation" with a painting. Their essays do not read like museum-guide interpretations, rather like more open-ended and speculative pieces, sometimes cast as a narrative with dialogue, sometimes as pure dialogue. The key is to invite students to talk to the painting, to ask questions, and to imagine rich and ambiguous responses. You want to avoid papers in which students begin with an idea of what a picture is about and simply impose that reading on the material. The paintings need to be imagined to talk back, to counter or open up a student's desire to master and control.

For revision: In some cases we've found we needed to send students back to the painting and the original assignment, usually because they were more concerned to push through a single reading than to have a conversation with their material. In most cases, however, we used the revision as the occasion to send students back to the Berger essay. As they became involved with the museum assignment, students forgot about Berger, so we used the revision to send them back to see what use they could make of his way of talking about paintings or the museum. "How, for example, could you use the example of your essay to explain what Berger might mean when he talks about 'history'?" The idea is to engage students in a conversation with Berger, where they can draw on their expertise to enter his argument.

. . . .

ASSIGNMENT 3

Berger Writing [Berger]

Berger offers interesting and compelling readings of Rembrandt's *Woman in Bed* and Caravaggio's *The Calling of St. Matthew* as ways to talk with his lover. Students will see a slightly different Berger in these two pieces than in "Ways of Seeing," and this assignment offers them both the opportunity to use these readings to clarify and elaborate on Berger's claims that he makes in "Ways of Seeing" for what it means to read paintings and as the opportunity to see readings of paintings created in meditative space as a part of a long love letter. How, they might be asked, does this kind of reading differ from the readings in his essay? What would account for those differences? What, in other words, are these readings able to accomplish that the readings in the essay do not or cannot?

. . . .

ASSIGNMENT 4

Picture Theory [Berger, Mitchell]

Berger writes about the differences in paintings and photographs, and he argues a particular position different from Mitchell's on the relationship of images and language. Berger seems more inclined to make images subjects of language, rather than to put images and language in a dialectic with each other, and Berger might be inclined to think of Mitchell's argument differently if he were actually engaged with it. Elsewhere in his essay, Berger argues strongly for the dialectic between paintings and contemporary readings of those paintings that ground themselves in the context of the paintings that reveals painters' positions towards their subjects. This isn't, then, a clear-cut comparison, and it can be figured many ways, depending on the arguments that students build. It's interesting also to test Berger's sense of critical mystification on Mitchell's readings of the photo-essays. Would Berger claim that Mitchell mystifies the photo-essay? What evidence could be used to argue this either way?

Looking at Berger through Mitchell's text one might ask, of course, what Berger makes of the relationship of images and language, so this offers students a way into Berger from Mitchell. Where does Berger write about this relationship? And how might an argument about the relationship of paintings to language be different from or similar to Mitchell's argument about the relationship of photographs to language? Students will need to locate moments where Berger writes about this relationship, and they'll need to stand Berger's claims for the relationship next to Mitchell's. It's an odd comparison because there are differences, but they seem to evaporate or change in different contexts, particularly when Berger argues for contemporary readings of paintings and when he examines reproductions that are accompanied by texts. Would it be possible to claim, students might be asked,

177

that Berger argues for a dialectic between images and language as Mitchell does in one of his case studies? That is, are Berger's examples close to any of those used by Mitchell?

. . . .

ASSIGNMENT 5

Revision [Mitchell, Berger]

Students are invited with this assignment to revise the papers that they wrote for the second assignment in the sequence, the assignment, that is, in which they interrogated a painting for what it might say to them and reported on the kinds of questions they asked and the results of the whole process. Now they have the opportunity to bring the work they have done after this assignment to bear on the paper. They now have Berger's readings of the Rembrandt and Caravaggio paintings and Mitchell's essay to help them reimagine the kinds of questions they might ask of paintings, and they can test out those questions by going back to the paintings and seeing what happens when they approach them from these perspectives. How is it different to write about a painting as a part of a personal communication, such as in a love letter, than as an example in an essay? What might an interrogation of a painting and the language they used to present it yield up as test of Mitchell's claims for dialogic tensions of elaboration and resistance between the images and the language?

o—o—o—o—o—o—o—o—o—o—o—o—o—o—o—o—o—o—o

SEQUENCE FIFTEEN

Working with the Past (p. 889)

As the sequence introduction points out, students are asked to work with texts by Rodriguez (and Hoggart), Hirsch, Jacobs, and Walker from a perspective that focuses their attention on how authors (and texts) directly or indirectly write under the influences of others. This is an unusual position for students to take. Our students want to see the past as fixed, as certain, and they tend to treat texts the same way. For them, then, the past and past texts exist as recoverable artifacts, moments and ideas that can be accurately and objectively recovered and represented. The idea that the past changes as the lenses used to recover and represent it also change is new to our students; so is the notion that working with texts from the past involves more than simply accurately presenting them.

The beauty of this sequence lies in the way it asks students to reimagine the past and texts from the past as something other than fixed, objective artifacts, to regard them as materials, that is, that are reimagined and revised as different authors work with them for varying purposes. Work with this sequence can give students the opportunity to understand the larger cultural and historical field that bears on authors and their writing, and it can give students ways of imagining "creativity" and "originality" in the contexts of the influences of the past, rather than as the expression of "genius" free from the influences of the past and past writings.

Some of the assignments in this sequence are adapted from writing assignments in the book. You should be sure to read those assignments and the entries on them in this manual.

. . . .

ASSIGNMENT 1

The Scholarship Boy [Rodriguez, Hoggart]

Rodriguez makes extensive use of Hoggart's work in his presentation of the scholarship boy, and the extended section of Hoggart's discussion of the scholarship boy makes an interesting contrast both to Rodriguez's notion of a scholarship and to his presentation of Hoggart's ideas. Needless to say, students will need to come to an understanding of how both Rodriguez and Hoggart create and use this notion of a scholarship boy. You might consider asking students to do this kind of work from their readings of the individual pieces (Rodriguez's and Hoggart's) before they begin working directly with the sequence assignments. This first assignment is straightforward and if students follow its sequence of directions and questions they'll see that initially they need to understand how Rodriguez uses Hoggart. The important question they need to deal with has to do with what Rodriguez says Hoggart is saying about scholarship boys. The third paragraph of the assignment lays out the questions that can help students read from outside Rodriguez's point of view to establish a sense of how he could be said to be revising Hoggart while using his text and ideas. Our students, for example, have been quick to point out that Hoggart's working class scholarship boy is British and living in a culture quite different from Rodriguez's or that of most Americans. Our subsequent question back to them then asks how this distinction (being British and working class) makes Hoggart's scholarship boy different not just from the one Rodriguez imagines but also from the boy Rodriguez imagines Hoggart to be.

The fourth paragraph of the assignment turns students' attention to what they might attribute Rodriguez's strategy in using and revising Hoggart. We assume, as is evident from the assignment, that Rodriguez does reimagine and revise Hoggart, so it's a question of where, how, and why he does. The case isn't clear-cut, of course, because Rodriguez doesn't completely rewrite Hoggart, and students should have a good deal of leeway to make their cases for the where, how, and why of Rodriguez's revision of Hoggart's text. The excerpt from Hoggart is lengthy and substantive enough for students to do the kind of comparison readings this assignment calls for; and Hoggart's tone, or stance, along with his notions of the scholarship boy and how he comes into being and acts out his role, is apparent and detailed. More than anything, though, this assignment is designed to introduce students to the notion of authors working under others' influences and to the idea of the malleability of the past. Both Rodriguez and Hoggart serve as good examples of these.

. . . .

ASSIGNMENT 2

Projected Memory [Hirsch]

Perhaps, as the assignment suggests, it is most helpful for students to imagine that they are reviewing Hirsch's essay for those who have not read it, so that they can write to both re-present her arguments and examples and to comment on them. They can also write to relate personal stories or examples if this helps them establish a position in relation to the essay that would allow a reader to see how Hirsch's work is useful or interesting to them. You will want to use examples of student writing in class to point them away from book review–like writing that quickly summarizes Hirsch and guide them toward more careful accounts of her project that refer to her examples and methods as a writer, allowing readers to imagine both what she has to say and the ways she works. Within this kind of presentation, students can then write themselves, their commentaries, into their re-presentations, so that their commentaries and presentations are interwoven as a piece rather than separate chunks of writing.

. . . .

ASSIGNMENT 3

The Project of Postmemory [Hirsch]

Although this assignment appears to be straightforward in its invitation to write about "a past that belongs to you but that is not yours," students will need to be familiar with Hirsch's notions and examples of postmemory to engage in such a project, for the object here is to create postmemory, to write about a past that one shares with others through stories but that is not directly one's own personal experience. Hirsch writes, for instance, about her memories of the town in which her parents grew up, one she feels she knows intimately, yet she has never been there. She knows it from their stories about it. Her images are from postmemory, from the fantasies she creates in response to the stories, from the images portrayed in her parents' narratives and transformed in her imagination of them. This is similar to the projects students will need to identify for this assignment — a past that is theirs yet is not theirs.

The caveat in the assignment asks students to be careful of overgeneralizing about such a past, to be careful to not reduce it to a series of clichés, and they'll want to turn to her distinction between "idiopathic" and "heteropathic" identification before they engage in this writing project so that they can understand the dangers of all too easy identification with a past that is beyond them rather than intimately connected to them in some way.

This assignment, then, asks students to take up Hirsch's project as their own with their own examples of postmemory as a writing project. The first "Question for a Second Reading" is a good place to begin if you're interested in turning students' attention, first, to ways of thinking of Hirsch's work as a writing project, as a project with writerly problems to solve having to do with the creation of images and stories surrounding them. It's a useful place for students to read her essay closely as a writing project marked by writerly methods for gathering information, using sources, telling personal stories, and drawing conclusions.

. . . .

ASSIGNMENT 4

A Life Story [Jacobs]

Jacobs's methods in her narrative are fairly transparent, at least for readers with some experience in the kinds of close readings that would allow them, for example, to identify shifts within the text in the kinds of writing she's doing. She is certainly telling a story, complete with remembered dialogue and conversations, but she also, at times, creates a polemic, a passionate plea for the reader's understanding of the life of slaves, one not likely to be received with sympathy by all of her possible readers of the time. There are moments, too, when it seems as though her writing might be called epistolary, others when it is poetic. She uses sources, she quotes people and texts, and she imagines readers as certain kinds of people.

Students will need to reread Jacobs at least twice to identify those shifts in the text that signal the materials she's presenting and the methods of writing she's using. When students do this work, they will need to the take the perspective that they're reading a writer who is working with the past — both as remembered and imagined materials and as a writer influenced by conventions and traditions of writing. How, too, they'll need to ask themselves, does she imagine her readers? What can they find in the text that gives them clues or signals about the kinds of readers Jacobs imagines? How would they characterize these readers? Why might Jacobs be imagining these kinds of readers? What influences are at work on her as she creates readers in her imagination?

. . . .

ASSIGNMENT 5

Working with the Past [Walker]

Once students have been working with the notion of a writer creating from written materials from the past, they should be able to move into this assignment without much trouble. It's straightforward, without any unexpected turns, and students will find plenty of examples of texts within Walker's to work with. Our students have turned almost immediately to Walker's use of Wheatley's poetry, which she pretty clearly imagines in ways other than Wheatley might have intended; but even within these examples, there's plenty of room for students to move as they imagine how Walker uses her poetry and the story of Wheatley's life for her project. When we used this assignment in Pittsburgh, the most interesting part was the question that asks students to consider how Walker's essay, with all of its uses of texts and stories from the past, might be read as a part of the tradition of creativity that she charts in her own essay. In other words, how does Walker's project chart the creativity of an African American woman in the face of oppression? How, too, does her use of the texts and stories of the past allow her to revise that past, to imagine it as a part of her project now?

Students will need to do library research to find the discussion of "contrary instincts" in Woolf's book and address the question of how Walker revises Woolf's use of the phrase. It's certainly clear that Woolf wasn't addressing an African American audience and that she was concerned with the contrary instincts of women trying to write, trying to create intellectual lives; but students will need more than these conclusions to flesh out the differences in Woolf's use of the term and Walker's.

. . . .

ASSIGNMENT 6

Legacies [Walker, Jacobs]

Actually, this assignment is a revision of assignments 4 and 5, and students should feel free to use what they wrote for those (this is, of course, another example of working with texts from the past), but the purpose of this assignment is considerably different from these other two, and they'll need to reread Jacobs and Walker before proceeding. Essentially, this one asks students first to consider Jacobs as another example for Walker's project and then to imagine how Jacobs's example alters or changes the project. Of course, it can alter it in any number of ways — for example, by changing the focus to Jacobs's desires, or by enriching and broadening Walker's arguments through another strong example — and students should feel free, in their own "creative projects," to speculate on how Jacobs's text might serve or alter Walker's argument.

o–o–o–o–o–o–o–o–o–o–o–o–o–o–o–o–o–o

SEQUENCE SIXTEEN

Working with the Past (II) (p. 904)

As the sequence introduction on page 904 notes, you could use these five assignments to add to those of sequence fifteen or to replace some. The Baldwin assignment here (2) could, for example, easily replace the Rodriguez assignment (1), the Said assignment here

(3) could replace the Hirsch assignment in sequence fifteen (1); and final assignment here (4) could become the final assignment of sequence fifteen. Or the sequence could be used on its own as a minisequence. We are sure that there are other ways to use these assignments along with those from sequence fifteen, and we hope that you take these assignments as an invitation to invent your own sequence from these assignments and those in sequence fifteen, or to write your own assignments using other texts that revise texts from the past to reinvent this sequence.

. . . .

ASSIGNMENT 1

The Albanian Virgin [Munro]

This is a great question for students. It asks them to take the two story lines and make sense of them as one project that represents the past. What might these stories have to do with each other? How could they be imagined to be connected? At what points do they seem to play into or with each other? to what ends? What do they tell us about the past?

Students might approach this assignment in various ways. They might, for instance, take it as an occasion to draw conclusions about what Munro might be saying about the past, its relationship to the present, and the problems of writing about it. They might also take the story as an occasion to write about the ways that Munro writes about or represents the past. How does she bring the past into the story? How does she position it in relation to the two story lines? And, as the assignment asks, students might also write about how the story positions them in relation to Charlotte and Claire, in relation to the past and present.

However they proceed, they will need to work closely from moments in the story. If they identify passages that they can use in their work, they'll be able to ground their work in examples, rather than make sweeping generalizations about the presence of the past in the story.

. . . .

ASSIGNMENT 2

Notes of a Native Son [Baldwin]

This assignment was prompted by our students' frequently phrased concern for the appropriateness (or the ethic) of Baldwin's treatment of his father. It is an appropriate question, rooted more (we think) in what students are used to reading than in a different experience or sense of obligation, child to parent. The text provides the frame for this question — Baldwin invites it, that is, in the way he presents the funeral and in the extended discussion of eulogy. We direct students' attention to this section, although we don't suggest (in the wording of the assignment) that their response should be based on a reading of this section. A reading of this section, however, might be useful as a form of preparation. You could read from this section aloud in class (or invite readings). It is brilliantly readable. And then you could ask students to discuss what Baldwin is saying about eulogies in the black church. And then you could ask how he might be using this section to address a reader and to answer questions a reader might harbor.

The students' essays, though, should ideally reach beyond this section to address "Notes" more generally. The essay begins, "I had inclined to be contemptuous of my father for the conditions of his life, for the conditions of our lives." The essay does not idealize the father; it struggles against simple sentimental narratives (or simple dismissal); it is not, however, contemptuous. That is a position marked in the past tense — "I had inclined to be." In fact, *inclination* is an important word here, since it begs the question of who or what had put the speaker in a position to take this attitude.

As with the previous assignments, students will need to work closely with passages from Baldwin's essay. They'll need to identify moments that they can use to explain Baldwin's representation of his father and to relate those moments to the end of the essay and the eulogy. To work on the problem of the uses that Baldwin makes of his father and his story, they'll want to stay close again to the examples from the essay and to think about the complete essay as both a son's public account of his father and as Baldwin's writing to understand him, the past, and the present.

. . . .

ASSIGNMENT 3

States [Said]

This assignment is designed to help students think about how Mohr and Said teach us how to read and use photographs. One difficulty our students had with "States" was simply learning to take time to read the photographs, to see them as something other than "illustrations," there to provide nothing more than a moment's rest or to provide that one dominant impression to accompany the text (as in the standard textbook photo). Said's opening reading of "Tripoli, Badawi Camp, May 1983" photograph is an enormously powerful piece of writing that frames his work in this selection. He tells us, for instance, that he can't anecdotally read the photographs. He wasn't there when they were taken, but he reads this associatively and through analogies. For students, the questions of this assignment have to do with how he associates with this photograph. What does he bring forward as he comments on the details of the photograph? How does he render his analogies in response to these details? This is difficult, close reading for students, and they'll need to identify those moments in the opening where Said makes a move from details of the photograph to his comments on it and ask themselves what it is that he is doing there, in those moments where he makes that move.

This opening piece of work for students is the key to their work with the rest of the photographs in Said's essay. Once they are familiar with Said's commentary on the "Tripoli" photograph, they can identify two or three moments in his comments on other photographs, moments where he moves, that is, from the details of the photographs to his readings of them, and ask themselves, again, what it is that he's doing. We've found it useful to read out loud from the paragraphs following the opening three photographs, asking students to talk about what they see and what they hear. (Ask "What is Said *not* noticing? What is outside his field of attention?) Then we ask students (in groups) to prepare discussions of the relation of text to image in the following pages. After they've studied a number of the photographs, they can then ask themselves if there's a pattern to his work.

Now students are ready to write the assignment, which was designed to address the problem identified above — the degree to which students are prepared to either ignore images in texts or to treat them as quick statement. It is important for students to think about the *different* relationships Said establishes between text and photograph — sometimes writing from them, sometimes writing back to them, sometimes writing alongside, in adjacency. There are subtle distinctions to be made, in other words, and students can be assisted in making them. It is also important that they work from specific examples — long discussion of particular photographs and passages. We have found it important to insist upon extended discussions of a few examples (since students will most likely be drawn to brief discussions of several).

The assignment is purposely broad, so that students have considerable space to think about Said's use of the photographs and how he defines his relationship to Palestinians and their history through these photographs. Ancillary questions have to do with how this relationship of Palestinians and their history is already defined for him — defined by what he knows, what he sees in the photographs, his position, and so on. And then, finally, students have to ask how this relationship is defined for them — defined here in this project, defined in the artifacts of our cultural currency and the information that circulates broadly and might be called artifactual or anecdotal — received information — about Palestinians and their history. They'll need to interrogate this cultural currency having to do with Palestinians and their history, and they can (and should) certainly use Said's essay as a ground for that questioning of what they hold as received knowledge.

- - - - - - - - - -

ASSIGNMENT 4

The Work of Art in the Age of Mechanical Reproduction [Benjamin]

Extending Benjamin's work, as this assignment invites students to do, involves the creation of arguments about art forms (such as film and video, or painting, music, and so on) and about the interrelation of these forms to the superstructure of the society. Students will need to begin by, in some way of their own, representing Benjamin's arguments about both the evolution of art forms and their connections to the culture's superstructure. How, they might then ask themselves, after they have represented Benjamin's work, have the forms they are writing about evolved since Benjamin's time? How has the superstructure of the culture evolved? What marks these evolutions? What visible signs, that is, would they point to say "this is what Benjamin sees" and "this is what we see now" (while keeping Benjamin's underlying notions of the superstructure)?

Once students set the ground for their work by providing that careful account of Benjamin's arguments (for art forms and their relation to the superstructure), they can continue and extend his work by writing about a single area of art they know well enough to focus on. They might write a fairly traditional piece in which they say, "This is what Benjamin thinks and this is how my example fits into it," or they might take a more challenging tack and write in conversation with Benjamin's piece by picking up his notions, weaving in their own with examples, using footnotes as he does, and taking their examples to some conclusion about the culture, as he does with the final epilogue on war. Benjamin's piece itself can serve as an example of how one might write in conversation with others' ideas. Students could study the ways he uses his sources before they begin this so that they might have a sense of writing that speaks to other writing before they begin.

o–o–o–o–o–o–o–o–o–o–o–o–o–o–o–o–o–o–o

SEQUENCE SEVENTEEN

Writing History (p. 907)

This short sequence could be thought of as an introduction to the academy or, more specifically, to "history" as a disciplinary activity, a way of writing about the past valued and preserved in colleges and universities. Limerick's chapter and Tompkins's essay are presented as opportunities for students to peer behind the veil and get the "true" story of intellectual labor. Limerick's chapter tells the story of professional writing and professional preparation. Tompkins's chapter tells a more general story of intellectual life, of the ways in which knowledge is made, preserved, and transformed.

The first two assignments put students in the position of the "expert," representing (or translating) Limerick's and Tompkins's work for someone who has not read the selections. We specify the audience for two reasons. We want students (as writers) to think about presentation. The problems they will face, then, are characteristic problems in academic writing — working closely with texts, re-presenting the ideas and positions of others, presenting textual material to those who will not have the text before them, engaging readers with ideas, establishing a position in relation to the work of the others. The other reason for specifying the audience is to put students in the position of speaking as though they were academy insiders. We want students to feel their authority in just this way (as an act of will and appropriation); we want them to imagine learning as just this kind of work with the writing of others. It is important, though, that as students imagine their audience, they imagine it as composed of their sharpest and most intellectually demanding peers. Little is gained if students write to children or to simpletons. The stakes need to be high for students to feel the pressure to become engaged with these essays beyond the superficial level.

If the opening assignments ask students to play the role of the expert, the final assignment situates them as novices, outsiders, trying their hands at writing a history. We have had great success with this assignment. We do not want to argue that students can become "historians" in three or four weeks. Neither are we concerned to design a specific formula for the production of "history." We are interested, rather, in pushing students to imagine that history is, if nothing else, something other than what they would normally write, something other than what they have been prepared to do. And this is how we have worked with that assignment — by letting students formulate their own working definitions of history from their reading of Limerick and Tompkins and through their own work as writers. We don't know what a "history" is, we say, but we know what it is *not;* it's not just a personal essay or a description or a narrative or something written about the past. Something else is involved. This approach puts students in the position of imagining history as a problem rather than a given, as something achieved beyond the ordinary uses of language. That, we found, was a productive motive for students' work, to work from the given to the unknown rather than to any formula or set definition.

This short sequence can be used as it is or it might be profitably added to other sequences: "Working with the Past," or "History and Ethnography," to name two. And it is possible to imagine other readings that might be dealt into this sequence: Wideman's "Our Time," Jacobs's "Incidents," Berger's "Ways of Seeing," Foucault's "Panopticism," Geertz's "Deep Play," Griffin's "Our Secret." All of these selections can be read both as "histories" and as reflections on the problems of writing about the past. It is this mix of practice and theory that we are pointing to in this sequence.

For a complete commentary on the selections in this sequence, please be sure to read each essay's selection in this manual, particularly the opening discussion. While we will cull materials from the discussions of individual assignments, we won't reproduce the introductions. And, while the sequences provide writing assignments, you should think about the advantages (or disadvantages) of using the "Questions for a Second Reading." In every case, students should read the headnotes in the textbook, which are designed to serve the assignments and sequences.

. . . .

ASSIGNMENT 1

Haunted America [Limerick]

This assignment is fairly straightforward. It is important, we found, to ask students to pay attention to the different representations of the problems facing a historian in the chapter, as problems of myth and point of view.

Students will need to be able to produce (not only as readers but also as writers) a close reading of Limerick's text. There are several fairly important matters of technique students need to learn to carry this off. For one thing they need to learn how to set up and introduce a text for discussion. They need to learn the mechanics of block quotation and the mysteries of paraphrase. Perhaps most important, they need to learn to feel the pressure to fill the space after the block quotation or lengthy presentation of text. They need to step forward as a reader (one who writes sentences) or a teacher or a commentator. We find it important to reproduce student papers and to point to the space (usually unfilled) that students need to learn to fill.

It is worth directing attention to the final question in the assignment which opens out the context of the assignment. The issue is more than simply, "What does Limerick say about the writing of history?" The writer is asked to talk about why any of this might be important to a student at the early stages of a college or university career. The quick answer is that most students will be required to take a history course. The more interesting answer looks to Limerick's essay for what it says more generally about reading and writing and intellectual life.

. . . .

ASSIGNMENT 2

"Indians" [Tompkins]

This assignment mirrors the first assignment in the sequence; much of what we said there applies to this assignment as well. The Tompkins essay is harder to read than the Limerick chapter. It might be worth spending some class time preparing for a second reading (see the "Questions for a Second Reading"), since Tompkins works against students' commonsense understanding of "fact" and "objectivity." We found, in fact, that the most useful way to work with a rereading of the essay was to begin by asking what seem to be simple questions: What is the story Tompkins tells about her own scholarly project? What are the key moments? What happens at each one? How are they resolved? What is the final chapter?

We've said this before, but it is worth repeating. With both of these assignments, students should imagine that they are writing for their peers, perhaps for students who will be taking the same course and reading the same readings next semester or next quarter. After you have a course under your belt, you will have some of these essays on file and you can use them for class discussion. It is important for students to believe that their job is to give the most subtle and sophisticated possible reading of Tompkins rather than the reading that makes it all clear and simple. In most cases, students are prepared to think that summary (the work of representing someone else's ideas) is *ideally* reductive. You will need to counter this assumption for the assignments to work well.

You may very well find that aiming high becomes the work of revision, where students take the "simple" version of Limerick or Tompkins as a pushing-off point ("what most readers would say," "what most people believe"). If students read their drafts to bracket the obvious and the commonsensical, this will help to clear space for them to begin to write about the subtle and difficult, to take as their goal the revision of "what most people believe" into a knowledge that requires intellectual labor and special understanding.

. . . .

ASSIGNMENT 3

Writing History [Limerick, Tompkins]

There are two options in this assignment. The general goal is to have students perform a reading of Limerick and Tompkins by writing a history — showing, in a sense, what they

186

have learned about defining the presence of the writer (Limerick) through the possible ways she might influence other writers.

The first option sends students to the library or local historical society. This assignment was prompted by Jean Ferguson Carr's teaching at Pitt (her courses almost always include some kind of archival project) and Pat Bizzell's teaching at Holy Cross (where she has students research local accounts of European settlements written by Native Americans). We were frustrated by the degree to which students feel removed from library archives and the degree to which our teaching (and the textbook) seemed to enforce that remove. Needless to say, this option will seem to be the harder of the two and students will need some prompting or challenge or rewards to choose it. One thing to remember is that an assignment like this will take more time than usual, since it takes time to find the library and spend enough time in the stacks to make the experience profitable, more than a quick search for the one book that will get you through the assignment. We've also found that we needed to make the process of search and selection an acknowledged part of the work of the course. We ask students to collect folders of material, to present them to others (to the class, to groups) and, in their essays, to talk about how they chose the material they chose to write about. Selection is of some special importance for this assignment, since Limerick's work points to the importance of finding the otherwise hidden alternative story. For Tompkins, each new source marks a turning point in her conception of her project. Tompkins's narrative of discovery and revision takes place over a greater period of time than is available to students in a writing course. It is unlikely that students will work through sources following the pattern set by Tompkins. It is reasonable to expect, however, that once students have found a way of reading the material, they can (after Tompkins) also begin to call it into question, suggesting how and where and why they might responsibly begin to doubt themselves.

The second option cuts out the library time, although it will work best if students take the challenge of making this more than a "personal essay." In fact, when we have asked students to write this assignment, "personal essay" became a useful negative term, a way of indicating what their work needed to transcend in revision. Here is how we made the distinction between "history," as represented by Tompkins or Limerick, and the personal essay. Gathering materials was important — that is, essays became "histories" when they incorporated materials (like photos, diaries, and interviews) that would not have been found if a writer had not felt responsible for more than his or her own immediate experience. And structure became important. Essays became histories when they included more than two "stories" and more than a single point of view. In fact, much of the work of revision was represented in just these terms. Students went back to write more stories ("counterstories," in Limerick's style) and to write from points of view not their own (their parents', a neighbor's, a friend's, a teacher's). Students added stories, added points of view, and worked to establish paragraphs (like those in Limerick) where they stepped forward to speak as an historian about the material they had gathered. The key moments in the best essays we received came when students realized that they had to break the "unity" they had been trained to value, when they added the story that didn't seem to fit or wrote from outside their own point of view.

o—o—o—o—o—o—o—o—o—o—o—o—o—o—o—o—o—o

SEQUENCE EIGHTEEN

Writing Projects (p. 910)

This sequence is designed to bring together pieces of writing that foreground problems of representation. The assignments ask students to think from within the context and arguments of the selections, and they ask students to imagine the consequences of such writing and thinking to their own projects. John Edgar Wideman, discussing his position as a writer telling his brother Robby's story in "Our Time," puts it this way. "Temporarily at least . . . I had to root my fiction-writing self out of our exchanges. I had to teach myself to listen. Start fresh, clear the pipes, resist too facile an identification, tame the urge to take off with Robby's story and make it my own." For our purposes in this sequence, we are interested in posing the boundaries between fiction and fact as a problem for students to work on, not a problem for them to solve, but one that they can work on through writing and studying fiction and nonfiction.

Students can have a lot of fun with this sequence, but there are dangers. One of them concerns how unquestioningly people view facts as easily verifiable and objective; even though the assignments ask students to think about "fact" and its relationship to writing, at least some students will want to argue for the "real" being objective writing and fiction being simply made up. All of the selections, can confuse those perspectives, but students will need to be willing to engage the questions, to play with the idea that the borderlines pose knotty problems that can't be dismissed by assertions of the "real" as objective and verifiable. You'll help yourself and your students if you offer this sequence in the spirit of "play," as an opportunity for students to work with the plasticity of writing, to suspend their larger philosophical notions of fact and fiction so that they can engage the questions in the assignments and allow themselves to read the selections as "real" and as "fiction." It'll be important, too, to help the class keep its discussions and writings close to the texts and away from abstract declarations about the "real" — except, of course, when those kinds of statements can be tested against the texts they're working with.

· · · · · · · · ·

ASSIGNMENT 1

Words and Images [Said]

We had great success with this assignment (and with similar assignments working from Agee and Evans, *Let Us Now Praise Famous Men*). Students are asked to compose a Said-like reading of a set of photos. In the assignment, the following sentences are important and worth calling attention to in advance:

> These can be photos prepared for the occasion (by you or a colleague); they could also be photos already available. Whatever their source, they should represent people and places, a history and/or geography that you know well, that you know to be complex and contradictory, and that you know will not be easily or readily understood by others, both the group for whom you will be writing (most usefully the members of your class) and readers more generally. You must begin with a sense that the photos cannot speak for themselves — you must speak for them.

Students, that is, are not just describing photos; they are using the photos to represent people and places, history and/or geography, to an audience unprepared to understand them. The selection and arrangement of photos is important, in other words. It is part of the work of writing this text.

And the text that accompanies these photos should approximate the style and method in After the Last Sky. The prose, in other words, is not simply captions, one after another. There should be an essay, a text with its own integrity, that is written with pictures. So, it is important to have students think about audience and occasion. What is the project? To whom are they writing? What is their relationship to subject and reader? And it is important to let students know in advance that they need to take time selecting the photographs and thinking about how they might be arranged. (It is useful to have them talk about what they left out and about plans they abandoned.) And they need to think about the writing; they are not writing captions; to think about what they might write, they can return to

States" to examine what it is that Said was doing and how he did it. The writing can (perhaps should) be homage or imitation, an attempt to do something similar.

· · · · · · · · ·

ASSIGNMENT 2

Story Lines [Munro]

As the assignment suggests, before students write, they might turn to the first two "Questions for a Second Reading" to guide their close reading of the story and the way it is organized to unfold two stories that are connected in ways not immediately obvious to readers. Once they have become familiar with the story, they'll need to design or imagine one of their own that proceeds as Munro's does with two story lines, perhaps with one of those being a story narrated by one of the characters. The challenge here is to create the two stories that readers can imagine as linked, and to do so in ways that carefully orchestrate their unfolding. We generally don't turn students to creating outlines, but in this case, such work might be useful once they have drafted their stories, so that they can then use the outline to organize the story in the spirit of Munro's and in a fashion similar to hers.

Students who have not written stories before might find this a perplexing assignment, but they should feel free to work from autobiography if they want or to imagine stories that begin in or use autobiography in some way. They might also want to reread Munro's story a number of times after they have had the opportunity to study it to get a sense of its movements and outline.

· · · · · · · · ·

ASSIGNMENT 3

Writing the Present [Baldwin]

This assignment asks students to consider the style and method of "Notes of a Native Son" and then to write an essay that is in direct imitation or to write as an act of homage. The first step, of course, is crucial. Students need to develop a sense of what Baldwin does and how he works before they can try to write from inside his example. They key here, we've found, is for students to think primarily about method rather than subject. They don't have to write about fathers, in other words. They should think about a family story that can be written against the story of nation, state, city, or community.

And you should take time to think with your students about voice and style. We would recommend some short, in-class exercises in writing Baldwin-like paragraphs as starting points. You need to have the Bible deeply in your history to write Old Testament narrative or to work within a sermonic style. It is perhaps a more useful instruction to ask students to work from within the discursive world of the central secondary character in their narrative (the figure occupying the father slot) and to move into and out of that discursive frame.

· · · · · · · · ·

ASSIGNMENT 4

A Project [Rich]

This assignment asks students to follow Rich's lead and to write autobiographically, not in celebration of their individuality but in order to cast themselves as representative of the way a certain group — named perhaps in terms of age, race, class, or gender — is positioned within the dominant culture. It asks them to use the occasion to try out some of Rich's key terms, like "revision" and "patriarchy." The difficulty students will have is in imagining their personal experience as representative of a collective one. You will, in othe words, not get papers about the pressure of culture but about key individuals — fathers mothers, teachers, lovers, grandparents, and coaches. In some ways this is inevitable. Both our students' age and the distinctly American versions of personal experience lead our students to write "frontier" stories, stories with no sense of the social, the political, or the historical. These are the concerns we highlight for revision: In what ways is this story more than your story? Where can we find the cultural context? In what ways are you, as a char-acter, cast in relation to ways of speaking, habits of mind?

. . . .

ASSIGNMENTS 5

Commentary [Said, Munro, Rich]

Assignment 5 is a commentary, a retrospective assignment. It asks students to think about what they have written in the previous assignments, in relation to the reading they have been doing. If students elect to write a preface, it can provide the discursive space where they can talk about why and how they chose to work with these authors, what they chose *not* to adapt to their own writing, how they see their work in line with that of these well established figures in American letters.

Additional Assignment Sequences

Here are four additional assignment sequences. You are welcome to duplicate these materials for your students.

. . . .

Reading Walker Percy

Walker Percy
Richard Rodriguez
Clifford Geertz

This sequence is designed to provide you with a way of reading Walker Percy's essay, "The Loss of the Creature." This is not a simple essay, and it deserves more than a single reading. There are six assignments in this sequence, all of which offer a way of rereading (or revising your reading of) Percy's essay; and, in doing so, they provide one example of what it means to be an expert or a critical reader.

"The Loss of the Creature" argues that people have trouble seeing and understanding the things around them. Percy makes his point by looking at two exemplary groups: students and tourists. The opening three assignments provide a way for you to work on "The Loss of the Creature" as a single essay, as something that stands alone. You will restate its argument, tell a "Percian" story of your own, and test the essay's implications. Then Richard Rodriguez and Clifford Geertz provide alternate ways of talking about the problems of "seeing." And, in addition, they provide examples you can use to extend Percy's argument further. The last assignment is the occasion for you to step forward as an expert, a person who has something to add to the conversation Percy began and who determines whose text it is that will speak with authority.

. . . .

ASSIGNMENT 1

Who's Lost What in "The Loss of the Creature"? [Percy]

Our complex friend stands behind his fellow tourists at the Bright Angel Lodge and sees the canyon through them and their predicament, their picture taking and busy disregard. In a sense, he exploits his fellow tourists; he stands on their shoulders to see the canyon.

191

Such a man is far more advanced in the dialectic than the sightseer who is trying to get off the beaten track — getting up at dawn and approaching the canyon through the mesquite. This stratagem is, in fact, for our complex man the weariest, most beaten track of all. (p. 590)

– Walker Percy
The Loss of the Creature

Percy's essay is not difficult to read, and yet there is a way in which it is a difficult essay. He tells several stories — some of them quite good stories — but it is often hard to know just what he is getting at, just what point it is he is trying to make. If he's making an argument, it's not the sort of argument that is easy to summarize. And if the stories (or anecdotes) are meant to serve as examples, they are not the sort of examples that quickly add up to a single, general conclusion or that serve to clarify a point or support an obvious thesis. In fact, at the very moment at which you expect Percy to come forward and talk like an expert (to pull things together, sum things up, or say what he means), he offers yet another story, as though another example, rather than any general statement, would get you closer to what he is saying.

There are, at the same time, terms and phrases to suggest that this is an essay with a point to make. Percy talks, for example, about "the loss of sovereignty," "symbolic packages," "sovereign individuals," "consumers of experience," "a universe disposed by theory," "dialectic," and it seems safe to say that these terms and phrases are meant to name or comment on key scenes, situations, or characters in the examples. You could go to the dictionary to see what these words might mean, but the problem for a reader of this essay is to see what the words might mean for Percy as he is writing the essay, telling those stories, and looking for terms he can use to make the stories say more than what they appear to say (about a trip to the Grand Canyon, or a trip to Mexico, of a Falkland Islander, or a student at Sarah Lawrence College). This is an essay, in other words, that seems to break some of the rules of essay writing and to make unusual (and interesting) demands on a reader. There's more for a reader to do here than follow a discussion from its introduction to its conclusion.

As you begin working on Percy's essay (that is, as you begin rereading), you might start with the stories. They fall roughly into two groups (stories about students and those about tourists), raising the question of how students and tourists might be said to face similar problems or confront similar situations.

Choose two stories that seem to you to be particularly interesting or puzzling. Go back to the text and review them, looking for the small details that seem to be worth thinking about. (If you work with the section on the tourists at the Grand Canyon, be sure to acknowledge that this section tells the story of several different tourists — not everyone comes on a bus from Terre Haute; not everyone follows the same route.) Then, in an essay, use the stories as examples for your own discussion of Percy's essay and what it might be said to be about.

Note: You should look closely at the differences between the two examples you choose. The differences may be more telling than the similarities. If you look only at the similarities, then you are tacitly assuming that they are both examples of the same thing. If one example would suffice, presumably Percy would have stopped at one. It is useful to assume that he added more examples because one wouldn't do, because he wanted to add another angle of vision, to qualify, refine, extend, or challenge the apparent meaning of the previous examples.

. . . .

ASSIGNMENT 2

Telling a "Percian" Story of Your Own [Percy]

> The situation of the tourist at the Grand Canyon and the biology student are special cases of a predicament in which everyone finds himself in a modern technical society — a society, that is, in which there is a division between expert and layman, planner and consumer, in which experts and planners take special measures to teach and edify the consumer. (p. 599)
>
> – Walker Percy
> *The Loss of the Creature*

For this assignment you should tell a story of your own, one that is suggested by the stories Percy tells — perhaps a story about a time you went looking for something or at something, or about a time when you did or did not find a dogfish in your Shakespeare class. You should imagine that you are carrying out a project that Walker Percy has begun, a project that has you looking back at your own experience through the lens of "The Loss of the Creature." You might also experiment with some of his key terms or phrases (like "dialectic" or "consumer of experience" but you should choose the ones that seem the most interesting or puzzling — the ones you would want to work with, that is). These will help to establish a perspective from which you can look at and comment on the story you have to tell.

. . . .

ASSIGNMENT 3

Complex and Common Readings of "The Loss of the Creature" [Percy]

> I do not refer only to the special relation of layman to theorist. I refer to the general situation in which sovereignty is surrendered to a class of privileged knowers, whether these be theorists or artists. A reader may surrender sovereignty over that which has been written about, just as a consumer may surrender sovereignty over a thing which has been theorized about. The consumer is content to receive an experience just as it has been presented to him by theorists and planners. The reader may also be content to judge life by whether it has or has not been formulated by those who know and write about life. (p. 594)
>
> This dialectic of sightseeing cannot be taken into account by planners, for the object of the dialectic is nothing other than the subversion of the efforts of the planners. (p. 591)
>
> – Walker Percy
> *The Loss of the Creature*

Percy charts several routes to the Grand Canyon: you can take the packaged tour, you can get off the beaten track, you can wait for a disaster, you can follow the "dialectical movement which brings one back to the beaten track but at a level above it." This last path (or "stratagem"), he says, is for the complex traveler. "Our complex friend stands behind his fellow tourists at the Bright Angel Lodge and sees the canyon through them and their predicament, their picture taking and busy disregard. In a sense, he exploits his fellow tourists; he stands on their shoulders to see the canyon."

When Percy talks about students studying Shakespeare or biology, he says that "there is nothing the educator can do" to provide for the student's need to recover the specimen from its educational package. "Everything the educator does only succeeds in becoming, for the student, part of the educational package."

Percy, in his essay, is working on a problem, a problem that is hard to name and hard to define, but it is a problem that can be located in the experience of the student and the experience of the tourist and overcome, perhaps, only by means of certain strategies. This problem can also be imagined as a problem facing a reader: "A reader may surrender sovereignty over that which has been written about, just as a consumer may surrender sovereignty over a thing which has been theorized about."

The complex traveler sees the Grand Canyon through the example of the common tourists with "their predicament, their picture taking and busy disregard." He "stands on their shoulders" to see the canyon. What happens if you apply these terms — *complex* and *common* — to reading? What strategies might a complex reader use to recover his or her sovereignty over that which has been written (or that which has been written about)?

For this assignment, write an essay that demonstrates a common and a complex reading of "The Loss of the Creature." Your essay should have three sections (you could number them, if you choose).

The first two sections should each represent a different way of reading the essay. One should be an example of the work of a common reader, a reader who treats the text the way the common tourists treat the Grand Canyon. The other should be an example of the work of a complex reader, a reader with a different set of strategies or a reader who has found a different route to the essay. You should feel free to draw on either or both of your previous essays for this assignment, revising them as you see fit to make them represent either of these ways of reading. Or, if need be, you may start all over again.

The third section of your paper should look back and comment on the previous two sections. In particular, you might address these questions: What does the complex reader see or do? And why might a person prefer one reading over another? What is to be gained or lost?

. . . .

ASSIGNMENT 4

Rodriguez as One of Percy's Examples [Percy, Rodriguez]

Those who would take seriously the boy's success — and his failure — would be forced to realize how great is the change any academic undergoes, how far one must move from one's past. It is easiest to ignore such considerations. So little is said about the scholarship boy in pages and pages of educational literature. Nothing is said of the silence that comes to separate the boy from his parents. Instead, one hears proposals for increasing the self-esteem of students and encouraging early intellectual independence. Paragraphs glitter with a constellation of terms like *creativity* and *originality*. (Ignored altogether is the function of imitation in a student's life.) (p. 667)

– Richard Rodriguez
The Achievement of Desire

"The Achievement of Desire" is the second chapter in Rodriguez's autobiography, *Hunger of Memory: The Education of Richard Rodriguez.* The story Rodriguez tells is, in part, a story of loss and separation, of the necessary sacrifices required of all those who take their own education seriously. To use the language of Percy's essay, Rodriguez loses any authentic or sovereign contact he once had with the world around him. He has become a kind of "weary traveler," deprived of the immediate, easy access he once had to his parents, his past, or even his own thoughts and emotions. And whatever he has lost, it can only be regained now — if it can be regained at all — by a complex strategy.

If Percy were to take Rodriguez's story — or a section of it — as an example, where would he place it and what would he have to say about it?

If Percy were to add Rodriguez (perhaps the Rodriguez who read Hoggart's *The Uses of Literacy* or the Rodriguez who read through the list of the "hundred most important books of Western Civilization") to the example of the biology student or the Falkland Islander, where would he put Rodriguez and what would he say to place Rodriguez in the context of his argument?

For this assignment, write two short essays. In the first essay read Rodriguez's story through the frame of Percy's essay. From this point of view, what would Percy notice and what would he say about what he notices?

Rodriguez, however, also has an argument to make about education and loss. For the second essay, consider the following questions: What does Rodriguez offer as the significant moments in his experience? What does he have to say about them? And what might he have to say to Percy? Is Percy one who, in Rodriguez's terms, can take seriously the scholarship boy's success and failure?

Your job, then is to set Percy and Rodriguez against each other, to write about Rodriguez from Percy's point of view, but then in a separate short essay to consider as well what Rodriguez might have to say about Percy's reading of "The Achievement of Desire."

. . . .

ASSIGNMENT 5

The Anthropologist as a Person with a Way of Seeing [Geertz]

For the anthropologist, whose concern is with formulating sociological principles, not with promoting or appreciating cockfights, the question is, what does one learn about such principles from examining culture as an assemblage of texts?
(p. 330)

— Clifford Geertz
Deep Play: Notes on the Balinese Cockfight

You've gone from tourists to students and now, at the end of this set of readings, you have another travel story before you. This essay, "Deep Play: Notes on the Balinese Cockfight," was written by an anthropologist. Anthropologists, properly speaking, are not really tourists. There is a scholarly purpose to their travel, and, presumably, they have learned or developed the complex strategies necessary to get beyond the preformed "symbolic complex" that would keep them from seeing the place or the people they have traveled to study. They are experts, in other words, not just any "layman seer of sights." One question to ask of "Deep Play" is whether Geertz has solved the problem of seeing that Percy outlines.

Anthropologists are people who observe (or in Geertz's terms "read") the behavior of other people. But their work is governed by methods, by ways of seeing that are complex and sophisticated. They can do something that the ordinary tourist to Bali (or Mexico or the Grand Canyon) cannot. They have different ways of situating themselves as observers, and they have a different way of thinking (or writing) about what they have seen. What is it, then, that anthropologists do, and how do they do what they do?

If this essay were your only evidence, how might you describe the work of an anthropologist? Write an essay in which you look at "Deep Play" section by section, describing on the basis of each what it is that an anthropologist must be able to do. In each case, you have the chance to watch Geertz at work. (Your essay, then, might well have seven sections that correspond to Geertz's.) When you have worked through them all, write a final section that discusses how these various skills or arts fit together to define the expertise of someone like Geertz.

. . . .

ASSIGNMENT **6**

Taking Your Turn in the Conversation
[Percy, Rodriguez, Geertz]

> I refer to the general situation in which sovereignty is surrendered to a class of privileged knowers, whether these be theorists or artists. A reader may surrender sovereignty over that which has been written about, just as a consumer may surrender sovereignty over a thing which has been theorized about. The consumer is content to receive an experience just as it has been presented to him by theorists and planners. The reader may also be content to judge life by whether it has or has not been formulated by those who know and write about life. (p. 594)
>
> – Walker Percy
> *The Loss of the Creature*

It could be argued that all of the work you have done in these assignments has been preparing you to test the assumptions of Percy's essay, "The Loss of the Creature." You've read several accounts of the problems facing tourists and students, people who look at and try to understand what is before them. You have observed acts of seeing, reading, and writing that can extend the range of examples provided by Percy. And you have, of course, your own work before you as an example of a student working under the guidance of a variety of experts. You are in a position, in other words, to speak in response to Percy with considerable authority. This last assignment is the occasion for you to do so.

For this assignment, you might imagine that you are writing an article for the journal that first printed "The Loss of the Creature." You can assume, that is, that your readers are expert readers. They have read Percy's essay. They know what the common reading would be and they know that they want something else. This is not an occasion for summary, but for an essay that can enable those readers to take a next step in their thinking. You may challenge Percy's essay, defend and extend what it has to say, or provide an angle you feel others will not have seen. You should feel free to draw as much as you can on the writing you have already done, working sections of those papers into your final essay. Percy has said what he has to say. It is time for you to speak, now, in turn.

. . . .

A Way of Composing

Paulo Freire
John Berger
Adrienne Rich

This sequence is designed to offer a lesson in writing. The assignments will stage your work (or the process you will follow in composing a single essay) in a pattern common to most writers: drafting, revising, and editing. You will begin by identifying a topic and writing a first draft; this draft will be revised several times and prepared as final copy.

This is not the usual writing lesson, however, since you will be asked to imagine that your teachers are Paulo Freire, John Berger, and Adrienne Rich and that their essays are addressed immediately to you as a writer, as though these writers were sitting by your desk and commenting on your writing. In place of the conventional vocabulary of the writing class, you will be working from passages drawn from their essays. You may find that the terms these teachers use in a conversation about writing are unusual — they are not what you would find in most composition textbooks for example — but the language is powerful and surprising. This assignment sequence demonstrates how these writers could be imagined to be talking to you while you are writing and it argues that you can make use of a theoretical discussion of language — you can do this, that is, if you learn to look through the eyes of a writer eager to understand his or her work.

Your work in these assignments, then, will be framed by the words of Freire, Berger, and Rich. Their essays are not offered as models, however. They are offered as places where a writer can find a vocabulary to describe the experience of writing. Writers need models, to be sure. And writers need tips or techniques. But above all writers need a way of thinking about writing, a way of reading their own work from a critical perspective, a way of seeing and understanding the problems and potential in the use of written language. The primary goal of this assignment sequence is to show how this is possible.

. . . .

ASSIGNMENT 1

Posing a Problem for Writing [Freire]

Students, as they are increasingly posed with problems relating to themselves in the world and with the world, will feel increasingly challenged and obliged to respond to that challenge. Because they apprehend the challenge as interrelated to other problems within a total context, not as a theoretical question, the resulting comprehension tends to be increasingly critical and thus constantly less alienated. Their response to the challenge evokes new challenges, followed by new understandings; and gradually the students come to regard themselves as committed. (p. 266)

Paulo Freire
The "Banking" Concept of Education

One of the arguments of Freire's essay, "The 'Banking' Concept of Education," is that students must be given work that they can think of as theirs; they should not be "docile" listeners but "critical co-investigators" of their own situations "in the world and with the world." The work they do must matter, not only because it draws on their experience but also because that work makes it possible for students to better understand (and therefore change) their lives.

This is heavy talk, but it has practical implications. The work of a writer, for example, to be real work must begin with real situations that need to be "problematized." "Authentic reflection considers neither abstract man nor the world without men, but men in their relations with the world." The work of a writer, then, begins with stories and anecdotes, with examples drawn from the world you live in or from reading that could somehow be said to be yours. It does not begin with abstractions, with theses to be proven or ideas to be organized on a page. It begins with memories or observations that become, through writing, verbal representations of your situation in the world; and, as a writer, you can return to these representations to study them, to consider them first this way and then that, to see what form of understanding they represent and how that way of seeing things might be transformed. As Freire says, "In problem-posing education, men develop their power to perceive critically *the way they exist* in the world *with which* and *in which* they find themselves; they come to see the world not as a static reality, but as a reality in process, in transformation."

For this assignment, locate a moment from your own recent experience (an event or a chain of events) that seems rich or puzzling, that you feel you do not quite understand but that you would like to understand better (or that you would like to understand differently). Write the first draft of an essay in which you both describe what happened and provide a way of seeing or understanding what happened. You will need to tell a story with much careful detail, since those details will provide the material for you to work on when you begin interpreting or commenting on your story. It is possible to write a paper like this without stopping to think about what you are doing. You could write a routine essay, but that is not the point of this assignment. The purpose of this draft is to pose a problem for yourself, to represent your experience in such a way that there is work for you to do on it as a writer.

You should think of your essay as a preliminary draft, not a finished paper. You will have the opportunity to go back and work on it again later. You don't need to feel that you have to say everything that can be said, nor do you need to feel that you have to prepare a "finished" essay. You need to write a draft that will give you a place to begin.

When you have finished, go back and reread Freire's essay as a piece directed to you as a writer. Mark those sections that seem to offer something for you to act on when you revise your essay.

. . . .

ASSIGNMENT 2

Giving Advice to a Fellow Student [Berger]

Yet when an image is presented as a work of art, the way people look at it is affected by a whole series of learnt assumptions about art. Assumptions concerning:

> Beauty
> Truth
> Genius
> Civilization
> Form
> Status
> Taste, etc. (p. 108)

> — John Berger
> *Ways of Seeing*

Berger suggests that problems of seeing can also be imagined as problems of writing. He calls this problem "mystification." "Mystification is the process of explaining away what might otherwise be evident." Here is one of his examples of the kind of writing he calls mystification:

> Hals's unwavering commitment to his personal vision, which enriches our consciousness of our fellow men and heightens our awe for the ever-increasing power of the mighty impulses that enabled him to give us a close view of life's vital forces.

This way of talking might sound familiar to you. You may hear some of your teachers in it, or echoes of books you have read. Teachers also, however, will hear some of their students in that passage. Listen, for example, to a passage from a student paper:

> Walker Percy writes of man's age-old problem. How does one know the truth? How does one find beauty and wisdom combined? Percy's message is simple. We must avoid the distractions of the modern world and learn to see the beauty and wisdom around us. We must turn our eyes again to the glory of the mountains and the wisdom of Shakespeare. It is easy to be satisfied with packaged tours and *Cliffs Notes*. It is more comfortable to take the American Express guided tour than to rent a Land Rover and explore the untrodden trails of the jungle. We have all

felt the desire to turn on the TV and watch "Dallas" rather than curl up with a good book. I've done it myself. But to do so is to turn our backs on the infinite richness life has to offer.

What is going on here? What is the problem? What is the problem with the writing — or with the stance or the thinking that is represented by this writing? (The student is writing in response to Walker Percy's essay "The Loss of the Creature," one of the essays in the text. You can understand the passage, and what is going on in the passage, even if you have not read Percy's essay. Similarly, you could understand the passage about Franz Hals without ever having seen the paintings to which it refers. In fact, what it says could probably be applied to any of a hundred paintings in your local museum. Perhaps this is one of the problems with mystification.)

For this assignment, write a letter to the student who wrote that paragraph. You might include a copy of the passage, with your marginal comments, in that letter. The point of your letter is to give advice — to help that student understand what the problem is and to imagine what to do next. You can assume that he or she (you choose whether it is a man or a woman) has read both "The 'Banking' Concept of Education" and "Ways of Seeing." To prepare yourself for this letter, reread "Ways of Seeing" and mark those passages that seem to you to be interesting or relevant in light of whatever problems you see in the passage above.

$$\cdot \quad \cdot \quad \cdot \quad \cdot \quad \cdot \quad \cdot \quad \cdot \quad \cdot \quad \cdot$$

ASSIGNMENT 3

Writing a Second Draft [Freire, Berger]

> Problem-posing education, as a humanist and liberating praxis, posits as fundamental that men subjected to domination must fight for their emancipation. To that end, it enables teachers and students to become Subjects of the educational process by overcoming authoritarianism and an alienating intellectualism; it also enables men to overcome their false perception of reality. The world — no longer something to be described with deceptive words — becomes the object of that transforming action by men which results in their humanization. (pp. 269–70)
> – Paulo Freire
> *The "Banking" Concept of Education*

There is a difference between writing and revising, and the difference is more than a difference of time and place. The work is different. In the first case you are working on a subject — finding something to say and getting words down on paper (often finding something to say by getting words down on paper). In the second, you are working on a text, on something that has been written, on your subject as it is represented by the words on the page.

Revision allows you the opportunity to work more deliberately than you possibly can when you are struggling to put something on the page for the first time. It gives you the time and the occasion to reflect, question, and reconsider what you have written. The time to do this is not always available when you are caught up in the confusing rush of composing an initial draft. In fact, it is not always appropriate to challenge or question what you write while you are writing, since this can block thoughts that are eager for expression and divert attention from the task at hand.

The job for the writer in revising a paper, then, is to imagine how the text might be altered — presumably for the better. This is seldom a simple, routine, or mechanical process. You are not just copying-over-more-neatly or searching for spelling mistakes.

If you take Freire and Berger as guides, revision can be thought of as a struggle against domination. One of the difficulties of writing is that what you want to say is sometimes consumed or displaced by a language that mystifies the subject or alienates the writer. The problem with authoritarianism or alienating intellectualism or deceptive words is that it is not a simple matter to break free from them. It takes work. The ways of speaking and thinking that are immediately available to a writer (what Berger calls "learnt assumptions") can be seen as obstacles as well as aids. If a first draft is driven by habit and assisted by conventional ways of thinking and writing, a second can enable a writer to push against habit and convention.

For this assignment, read back through the draft you wrote for assignment 1, underlining words or phrases that seem to be evidence of the power of language to dominate, mystify, deceive, or alienate. And then, when you are done, prepare a second draft that struggles against such acts, that transforms the first into an essay that honors your subject or that seems more humane in the way it speaks to its readers.

. . . .

ASSIGNMENT 4

Writing as Re-Vision [Rich]

> For a poem to coalesce, for a character or an action to take shape, there has to be an imaginative transformation of reality which is no way passive. And a certain freedom of the mind is needed — freedom to press on, to enter the currents of your thought like a glider pilot, knowing that your motion can be sustained, that the buoyancy of your attention will not be suddenly snatched away. Moreover, if the imagination is to transcend and transform experience it has to question, to challenge, to conceive of alternatives, perhaps to the very life you are living at that moment. You have to be free to play around with the notion that day might be night, love might be hate; nothing can be too sacred for the imagination to turn into its opposite or to call experimentally by another name. For writing is renaming. (p. 635)
>
> – Adrienne Rich
> *When We Dead Awaken: Writing as Re-Vision*

This is powerful language, and it is interesting to imagine how a writer might put such terms to work. For this assignment, go back to the draft you wrote for assignment 3 and look for a section where the writing is strong and authoritative, where you seemed, as a writer, to be most in control of what you were doing. If, in that section, you gave shape and definition (perhaps even a name) to your experience, see what you can do to "transcend and transform" what you have written. Play around with the notion that day might be night, love might be hate; nothing should be "too sacred for [your] imagination to turn into its opposite or to call experimentally by another name."

Rewrite that section of your essay, but without discarding what you had previously written. The section you work on, in other words, should grow in size as it incorporates this "playful" experimentation with another point of view. Grant yourself the "freedom to press on," even if the currents of your thought run in alternate directions — or turn back on themselves.

. . . .

ASSIGNMENT 5

Preparing a Final Draft [Freire, Berger, Rich]

> Their response to the challenge evokes new challenges, followed by new understandings; and gradually the students come to regard themselves as committed. (p. 266)
>
> – Paulo Freire
> *The "Banking" Concept of Education*

A piece of writing is never really finished, but there comes a point in time when a writer has to send it to an editor (or give it to a teacher) and turn to work on something else. This is the last opportunity you will have to work on the essay you began in assignment 1. To this point, you have been working under the guidance of expert writers: Freire, Berger, and Rich. For the final revision, you are on your own. You have their advice and (particularly in Rich's case) their example before you. You have your drafts, with the comments you've received from your instructor (or perhaps your colleagues in class). You should complete the work, now, as best you can, honoring your commitment to the project you have begun and following it to the fullest conclusion.

Note: When you have finished working on your essay and you are ready to hand it in, you should set aside time to proofread it. This is the work of correcting mistakes, usually mistakes in spelling, punctuation, or grammar. This is the last thing a writer does, and it is not the same thing as revision. You will need to read through carefully and, while you are reading, make corrections on the manuscript you will turn in.

The hard work is locating the errors, not correcting them. Proofreading requires a slowed-down form of reading, where you pay attention to the marks on the page rather than to the sound of a voice or the train of ideas, and this form of reading is strange and unnatural. Many writers have learned, in fact, to artificially disrupt the normal rhythms of reading by reading their manuscripts backward, beginning with the last page and moving to the first; by reading with a ruler to block out the following lines; or by making a photocopy, grabbing a friend, and taking turns reading out loud.

. . . .

Ways of Seeing

John Berger

This sequence asks you to examine claims that John Berger makes about our ways of seeing art. The first assignment invites you to consider what he says about how we look at paintings, pictures, and images, and what all this has to do with "history." The second asks you to write about a painting, giving you an opportunity to demonstrate how the meaning of this piece of art from the past belongs to you. The third assignment then turns you back on your own writing so that you can examine it for the expectations and strategies that came into play when you wrote about the painting you chose. The final assignment invites you to review your first paper in the sequence so that you can enter in to conversation with Berger about what gets in the way when we look at pictures, paintings, and images, and what all this might have to do with "history."

. . . .

ASSIGNMENT 1

Berger's Example of a Way of Seeing [Berger]

We are not saying that there is nothing left to experience before original works of art except a sense of awe because they have survived. The way original works of art are usually approached — through museum catalogues, guides, hired cassettes, etc. — is not the only way they might be approached. When the art of the past ceases to be viewed nostalgically, the works will cease to be holy relics — although they will never re-become what they were before the age of reproduction. We are not saying original works of art are now useless. (pp. 124–25)

– John Berger
Ways of Seeing

Berger argues that there are problems in the way we see or don't see the things before us, problems that can be located in and overcome by strategies or approaches.

For Berger, what we lose if we fail to see properly is history: "If we 'saw' the art of the past, we would situate ourselves in history. When we are prevented from seeing it, we are being deprived of the history which belongs to us." It is not hard to figure out who, according to Berger, prevents us from seeing the art of the past. He says it is the ruling class. It *is* difficult, however, to figure out what he believes gets in our way and what all this has to do with "history."

For this assignment, write an essay explaining what, according to Berger, it is that gets in the way when we look at pictures, paintings, or images, and what this has to do with history.

. . . .

ASSIGNMENT 2

Applying Berger's Methods to a Painting [Berger]

A people or a class which is cut off from its own past is far less free to choose and to act as a people or class than one that has been able to situate itself in history. This is why — and this is the only reason why — the entire art of the past has now become political issue. (p. 127)

– John Berger
Ways of Seeing

Berger says that he real question facing those who care about art is this: "To whom does the meaning of the art of the past properly belong? To those who can apply it to their own lives, or to a cultural hierarchy of relic specialists?" As Berger's reader, you are invited to act as though the meaning of the art of the past belonged to you. Go to a museum or, if that is not possible, to a large-format book of reproductions in the library (and if that is not possible, to the reproduction of Vermeer's *Woman Pouring Milk* that is included in the essay). Select a painting you'd like to write about, one whose "meaning" you think you might like to describe to others. Write an essay that shows others how they might best understand that painting. You should offer this lesson in the spirit of John Berger. That is, how might you demonstrate that the meaning of this piece of art from the past belongs to you or can be applied in some way to your life?

Note: If possible, include with your essay a reproduction of the painting you select. (Check the postcards at the museum gift shop.) In any event, you want to make sure that you describe the painting in sufficient detail for your readers to follow what you say.

. . . .

ASSIGNMENT 3

A Way of Seeing Your Way of Seeing [Berger]

> What we make of that painted moment when it is before our eyes depends upon what we expect of art, and that in turn depends today upon how we have already experienced the meaning of paintings through reproductions. (p. 125)
> – John Berger
> *Ways of Seeing*

Return to the essay you wrote for assignment 2, and look at it as an example of a way of seeing, one of several ways a thoughtful person might approach and talk about that painting. You have not, to be sure, said everything there is to say about the painting. What you wrote should give you evidence of a person making choices, a person with a point of view, with expectations and strategies that have been learned through prior experience.

For this assignment, study what you have written and write an essay that comments on your previous essay's way of seeing (or "reading") your painting. Here are some questions that you should address in preparing your commentary:

1. What expectations about art are represented by the example of the person you see at work in your essay?

2. What is the most interesting or puzzling or significant thing that the viewer (you) was able to see in this painting? How would you characterize a viewer who would notice this and take it as central to an understanding of the painting?

3. What do you suppose the viewer must necessarily have missed or failed to see? What other approaches might have been taken? What are the disadvantages of the approach you see in the essay?

4. Is there anything you might point to as an example of "mystification" in that essay? "Mystification" is the term Berger uses to characterize writing that sounds like this: "Hals's unwavering commitment to his personal vision, which enriches our consciousness of our fellow men and heightens our awe for the ever-increasing power of the mighty impulses that enabled him to give us a close view of life's vital forces.") Is there anything in your essay you might point to as an example of mystification's opposite?

5. Berger says, "If we 'saw' the art of the past, we would situate ourselves in history." As you look back over your essay, what does any of what you wrote or saw (or failed to write or see) have to do with your position in "history"?

6. Berger says that what you write depends on how you have already experienced the meaning of paintings. What are the characteristic features in the work of a person who has learned from Berger how to "experience the meaning of paintings"? If you were to get more training in this — in the act of looking at paintings and writing about them — what would you hope to learn?

. . . .

ASSIGNMENT 4

Reviewing the Way You See [Berger]

Now that you have had the opportunity to work with Berger's examples of "seeing" and with your own examination of a painting (and your way of seeing it), this final assignment invites you to return to the first paper you wrote in this sequence, to review it with an eye to revising what you had to say about what gets in the way when we look at pictures, paintings, or images. When you first worked on this assignment, you were untangling Berger's ideas about what gets in the way. This assignment is an occasion for you to speak with him, comment on his ideas, or challenge them. You know more now, after having written about a work of art and then studied that writing for what it could be said to show about your expectations and strategies. You have firsthand experience now with the problem Berger poses, and that experience should inform your review.

Write an essay in which you revise your first essay for this argument. This time you are in a position to add your response. Your revision, in other words, will do more than tighten up or finish that first attempt. The revision is an opportunity for you to come forward as both a speaker and an authority. Berger's text becomes something you can use in an essay of your own. Or, to put it another way, in this draft you are in a position to speak with or from or against Berger. He will not be the only one represented. Your revision should be considerably longer than your first draft, and a reader should be able to see (or hear) those sections of the essay which could be said to be yours.

. . . .

Working with Foucault

Michel Foucault

This sequence is designed to give you a chance to work your way through "Panopticism" by summarizing Foucault's argument, by interrogating the summary (as it does and doesn't "capture" Foucault), and by putting Foucault to work in a Foucauldian analysis of primary materials. The first two assignments are summary assignments, in which you grapple with Foucault's argument. You will be asked to look for what you missed or left out on a first reading and to account for these absences as meaningful rather than simply accidental or "mistakes." And you will be asked to consider the consequences of a project whose goal is to "master" an author who is a critic of mastery. The second two assignments ask you to apply Foucault's terms and methods to material outside his text. The final assignment asks you to reread Foucault once again, to discuss his essay and your work with it.

. . . .

ASSIGNMENT 1

Foucault's Fabrication [Foucault]

About three-quarters of the way into the chapter, Foucault says,

> Our society is one not of spectacle, but of surveillance; under the surface of images, one invests bodies in depth; behind the great abstraction of exchange, there continues the meticulous, concrete training of useful forces; the circuits of communication are the supports of an accumulation and a centralization of knowledge; the play of signs defines the anchorages of power; it is not that the beautiful totality of the individual is amputated, repressed, altered by our social order, it is rather that the individual is carefully fabricated in it, according to a whole technique of forces and bodies. (pp. 244–45)

This prose is eloquent and insists on its importance to our moment and our society; it is also very hard to read or to paraphrase. Who is doing what to whom? How do we think about the individual being carefully fabricated in the social order?

Take this chapter as a problem to solve. What is it about? What are its key arguments? its examples and conclusions? Write an essay that summarizes "Panopticism." Imagine

204

that you are writing for readers who have read the chapter (although they won't have the pages in front of them) and who are at sea as to its arguments. You will need to take time to present and discuss examples from the text. Your job is to help your readers figure out what it says. You get the chance to take the lead and be the teacher. At the same time, you should feel free to acknowledge and write about sections you don't understand.

After you have written a draft, go back over it and Foucault's chapter. What did you leave out or miss? What did you pass over or ignore? Why? What questions might you ask to open these sections up and make them "readable"?

Write a one-page "coda" to your essay in which you account for these omissions as evidence of a "technology" (perhaps unacknowledged) for dealing with a difficult text. You are not apologizing for the omissions, but describing what might otherwise seem a natural or inevitable way of responding to a difficult text.

. . . .

ASSIGNMENT 2

The Technology of Mastery (A Revision) [Foucault]

After rereading "Panopticism" and taking note of what you left out of your summary for assignment 1 (and taking note, perhaps, of what other students in your class or group left out), go back and revise your summary. Again, you should feel free to acknowledge and write about sections you don't understand. You can make understanding tentative, provisional ("I'm not sure what Foucault means in this passage, but I think it is . . ."). Again, your goal is to provide a summary that will be useful to others who have read this chapter (although, again, they won't have the pages in front of them and hence you will have to include passages in quotation). You may want to translate difficult terms and turn to examples that are local and familiar for your audience.

When you are done, reread your revision and write another one-page "coda." This time, use the coda to talk about the technology of mastery and control. What is it that allows you to begin to control, to discipline, this unruly and resistant text? In Assignment 1 you looked back at Foucault to see what you left out. Here you will be looking at your text to see how and where you establish your authority as a reader.

. . . .

ASSIGNMENT 3

Prisons, Schools, Hospitals, and Workplaces [Foucault]

Perhaps the most surprising thing about Foucault's argument in "Panopticism" is the way it equates prisons with schools, hospitals, and workplaces, sites we are accustomed to imagining as very different from prison.

At the end of the chapter, Foucault poses two questions about the relationship between prisons and the other institutions which he leaves unanswered:

> Is it surprising that the cellular prison, with its regular chronologies, forced labor, its authorities of surveillance and registration, its experts in normality, who continue and multiply the functions of the judge, should have become the modern instrument of penality? Is it surprising that prisons resemble factories, schools, barracks, hospitals, which all resemble prisons? (pp. 252–53)

For this assignment, take the invitation of Foucault's conclusion. No, you want to respond, it is not surprising that "experts in normality, who continue and multiply the functions of the judge, should have become the modern instrument of penality." No, it is not surprising that "prisons resemble factories, schools, barracks, hospitals, which all resemble prisons." Why isn't it surprising? Or — why isn't it surprising if you are thinking along with Foucault?

Write an essay in which you speak from your work with Foucault. In that essay work out the resemblances he points to, and then assess the significance of those resemblances. Are the resemblances significant? superficial? In relation to what? And what are the important differences you note? How would you argue their significance to an audience concerned with "experts in normality" or the key sites for surveillance and control?

. . . .

ASSIGNMENT 4

Writing, Surveillance, and Control [Foucault]

At the end of this assignment you will find four essays written by twelfth graders in 1923 as part of an evaluation project. The project was designed to normalize grading practices in English departments across the country. Teachers, it was proposed, would all assign the same topic. The question for the essays included here was this: Write an essay describing how you learned a lesson. All students would write under the same conditions, for fifty minutes in class under a teacher's supervision. All the essays would be graded against a set scale, one that could be used by teachers anywhere in the United States. The following essays were chosen to establish the scale. They represent the lowest possible score (1), the middle scores (5 and 6), and the highest possible score (10).

For this assignment, treat these student essays as examples chosen by "experts in normality," by judges, perhaps, who would want them to stand as a centralization of writing evaluation, and use them as a way of talking, after Foucault, about control, normality, constraint, and surveillance.

You can assume that even though methods of evaluation may have changed since these essays were written, the order of the essays (the hierarchy of value) would be preserved by schools and agencies across the country. The order 1 through 10 represented here, in other words, would be taken for granted as natural, right, inevitable. Your job is to jolt your reader out of the "natural" view in order to see it as representing a particular agenda and set of values. This is not an easy job — to step out of the discourse of the normal, the usual way of thinking, speaking, valuing. Here are two sets of questions you might ask to interrogate this material:

1. Imagine, for a minute, that you can become an English teacher and adopt an English teacher's values. How would you explain and justify the order of these essays? What terms are available? What arguments? What assumptions about writing and schooling and intelligence and mastery? Now, ask yourself why it is so easy for you to adopt that point of view. And ask what it would take to step out, to see the "popo bush" essay as preferable to the "Grub Hollow" essay. How many alternative orders can you imagine? How would you explain or justify or rationalize them? What light do they throw on the explanations that belong to "English"? How, in fact, do they allow you to argue with or throw new light on "English" and its technologies of value and order?

2. Think about how and where you can bring passages or examples from Foucault to bear on your examples. You may need to work back through the text to do this. Remember — Foucault points to connections between prisons and schools. You are working with and not against Foucault if you make these associations. In particular, see how you can bring his discussions of control and surveillance to bear on these essays and their order. What knowledge is represented in incremental stages by the order in these essays? What

loes it have to do with "hierarchical surveillance" and "classification"? What knowledge s represented by this method of analysis — that is, what knowledge is represented by the **e**xpert judgment that chose these essays and ordered them? What might it have to do with **c**ontrol and constraint? What knowledge of writing is excluded here? what alternative **a**ccounts of mastery and expertise are excluded?

Write an essay that presents these examples and uses them to develop an argument **a**bout knowledge and constraint, about control, supervision, and classification. You can **a**ssume that your readers will have read Foucault's chapter but that they will need your **h**elp to see its application to these materials. You should assume that they do not have the **e**xamples of these essays in front of them, that you have come across them in an old book **i**n a back quarter of the library. Part of your work, and not a small part, will be to present **t**he examples so that a reader can understand and be interested in them.

How I Learned a Lesson (1923)

. . . .

SAMPLE 1

When I chewed tobacco and they found it owt they whipped me for about fifteen minnutes with popo bush. they broke ten switches out on me. but i kept on chewing. they **f**ound it out and my papa and Mamma whipped me for abowt twenty minnutes and learn **m**e a lesson.

Score: 1

. . . .

SAMPLE 2

It is said that experience is a dear teacher and *that* is one of the lessons I learned along with the real lesson.

One day I came home from school (as I have been in the habit of doing for the past **e**leven years) to find the house locked. When our house is locked up and the family go out **t**here are just two ways I know of to get in. The first and by far the easiest is to get the particular key that belongs to the lock in the front door and after inserting it in the lock, **t**urn it, push forward and the door will come open. If a key cannot be obtained there is just **o**ne way left, as I know of (and I have had years of experience) and that is to get a good heavy brick and heave it thru the window. Not that I have ever tried this method but its the **o**nly sure remidy left as I *have* tried all the others my brain could conjur up.

Score: 5

. . . .

SAMPLE 3

Two years ago I worked for a meat shop. Every day I spent a good deal of money on such things as soft drinks, ice cream, and other good things. I did this all summer. My **m**other warned me against it, but I kept indulging in these things.

By the time school commenced I began to have stomach trouble. Mother made me **q**uit eating anything I wanted, and kept me on a diet. Finally I was cured of the trouble. **S**ince then I do not "eat drink and be merry" as much as then.

Score: 6

. . . .

SAMPLE 4

When I sat down to think over the experiences of my life that have been profitable to me my memory wandered back to one of the big lessons I learned when I was yet a little child.

I was in the sixth grade in a little country school. Here I mingled with children from all stations in life and made friends with them all. There was, however, something insincere with my friendship for the poorer children. It was due, I now believe, to a feeling of superiority over them. I resented the ravenous manner in which they ate the lunches I divided with them; I detested their furtive glances when we talked; and I could not tolerate their tendency to lie. In all, they had an uncouth bearing that I could neither understand nor forgive.

That spring our teacher invited me to go with her while she took the enumeration. After visting a number of homes we came to a place called Grub Hollow where several of our school patrons lived. In one little shack we found the family huddled around a little stove, the walls and floors bare, and everything most squalid and depressing. In another, a dirty, miserable hovel, we found a blind father, an indolent, flabby mother, and three mangy children. Finally we found a family of fourteen living in one room amid unspeakable conditions.

On our way home Miss Marxson was strangely silent, and, child that I was, tears stood in my eyes. I had heard "the still sad music of humanity," and it had given me a new understanding. Never again did I feel haughtily toward those children; and all through life that experience has modified my judgment of human conduct.

Score: 10

. . . .

ASSIGNMENT 5

The Two-Step [Foucault]

This assignment has two parts. For the first, go back to your summary of Foucault's chapter in assignment 2. Once again, go back to the chapter to see what you have skipped, ignored, missed, or, from your new vantage point, misrepresented or misunderstood. Mark those passages that continue to befuddle you, that seem to defy understanding. And ask, Why? What makes them difficult? What would it take to make them available to you? Then go to those passages you now feel you understand. Again, Why? What has made them available? Write a short essay, two to three pages, in which you use the example of Foucault's chapter to talk about difficulty and mastery, about the process of coming to command a difficult text.

Once you have completed this essay, go back for the last time (at least in this sequence) to revise that summary. As before, you should try to write the kind of summary that acknowledges (rather than ignores or finesses) those parts of the text that seem to defy summary. You should focus on (rather than write over) the difficult sections, doing what you can to translate, explain, provide additional examples. You could imagine, in other words, that you have learned to write a different kind of summary in this sequence, and that its final version is represented here.

Part IV: On *Ways of Reading*

With the exception of the papers by Bill Hendricks and Dawn Skorczewski, the essays that follow were written by current and former graduate students in our department as a part of their work in a seminar on the teaching of composition. We include them here because we thought it would be helpful for you to hear from people who had taught for a year, and in some cases for the first time, from *Ways of Reading.* We hope that the discussions of their teaching and their experiences with selected readings and sequences will be helpful to you as you teach from our book. We would also like their essays to stand for the kind of work people can do in graduate seminars that make use of *Ways of Reading* for the study of the teaching of composition and literature. (Some of the essays refer to selections in previous editions of *Ways of Reading.*)

o—o—o—o—o—o—o—o—o—o—o—o—o—o—o—o—o—o

GENEROUS READING:
CREATING A GENERAL WRITING LANGUAGE
by Melissa Bender

Students often come to the General Writing (GW) classroom with certain expectations that are not met. In the classes I have taught some of these expectations surfaced at the very beginning of each semester when I asked my students to read and respond to the introduction to *Ways of Reading*. Many of them found the introduction to be empowering and affirming. They were anxious and excited at the proposed reading and writing ideas. And they could identify with the "old" way of teaching reading and writing that is outlined in the introduction with such phrases as "finding information," or "identifying main ideas." This is what they had expected GW to be like. And yes, they had done that before, and they were tired of doing it. Finally, they seemed to be saying, someone was asking for their opinion. However, in spite of all of its "ready to wear" terms, the introduction does not supply students or teachers with the vocabulary that is necessary for speaking about reading/writing in such a new and unusual way. Terms, if they are to work at all in the GW classroom, must be collectively defined and understood. And, until new terms for talking about reading/writing are defined, the only way to speak about these acts is through the "old" language, the language of expectations.

I didn't realize this immediately, however. I was as mystified by the introduction as my students were. I liked what it had to say about reading and writing but I hadn't considered exactly what it meant, or how I should use it. In my classroom I threw around terms like "framing" and "making a mark" and "reading against the grain," and in return my students stared at me.

At nearly the same time that I was struggling with this issue we discussed a paper written in response to Ralph Waldo Emerson's "American Scholar," which was included in the second edition of *Ways of Reading*. A student, David, wrote: "If I, as the reader, am to make use of these points, I will not take Emerson's word as *law*. . . ." He continued to use the word *law* throughout his paper. "Emerson stresses that books are not *laws*. Anything that is written should not be taken as *law*, but should be left to the reader to make his own interpretation." Perhaps because it was an easy metaphor, or because it reaffirmed their own previously established ideas of reading, or because of the abundance of what I call "courtroom terms" in their vocabularies, my students borrowed the word *law* from David's paper and turned it into a way of defining a reading. In spite of the fact that David seemed to be saying something quite the opposite, the class began to talk about essays as if a reader could "prove" what the author meant. Without necessarily realizing that this definition of reading was being formed right in front of me, and perhaps because I, too, was taken in by the ease of the language, I went along with the class.

Before I knew it, we were talking about how student writers might look for "evidence" in quotations, in order to "support" their "argument." After a few days of this I left the class thinking, "What happened to *ways* of reading, and forging a reading? What happened to student readers who 'can take responsibility for determining the meaning of a text' " (*Ways of Reading*, p. 6)? The language that we were using to discuss reading/writing was working against seeing these acts in a new way. And this language seemed to represent that "old" and "usual" way of talking about reading/writing that Bartholomae and Petrosky imply in the introduction when they write, "This is an *unusual* way of talking about reading, we know," (p. 1, emphasis mine). I was amazed at how easy it was for both me and my students to shy away from the challenge of this "new" and "unusual" way of writing and slip back into the "old."

In an effort to revise some of this "court talk," I directed my class back to the introduction of the book, and perhaps this is the moment when our own work as definers began. By collectively rereading parts of the introduction and making lists comparing "court words" and *Ways of Reading* words, we were able to see that, instead of aiding our entry into a new way of reading and thinking about reading, our "court talk" allowed us to do what we were most familiar with. It was time for us, as the introduction states, to begin the work of "imagining other ways of reading." In place of our "court words" we chose and defined terms, some from the introduction and some from students' papers or class comments that seemed to facilitate a way of thinking about reading that was different from reading for facts or main ideas. And, we created a term that now seems to me to symbolize the actual act of thinking about reading in new ways. Instead of the "old" reading position, which one student decided positions the writer as someone who is in a superior position to the reader, we fashioned what became known in my classroom as a *generous reading position*. The word *generous* first came from the "Reading with and against the Grain" section of the introduction:

> A reader takes charge of a text; . . . a reader gives generous attention to someone else's (a writer's) key terms and methods, commits his time to her examples, tries to think in her language, imagines that this strange work is important, compelling, at least for the moment. (p. 10)

However, as we molded it into our own term, it came to mean something more than just giving generous time to a writer's words, which to many of my students didn't seem that different from the old hierarchical configuration of writer as teacher, reader as student. The meaning of *generous reading* came from combining ideas — generous attention, strong reading, close reading, and reading against the grain. A generous reading is one that balances that "difficult mix of authority and humility" (p. 10). It allows a reader both to give attention to the writer's language, ideas, and terms and to "take responsibility for determining the meaning of the text."

Although we did not eliminate the terms *reading with the grain* or *reading against the grain* from our GW vocabularies, I found that using the term *generous reading* was in fact, more generous to both the reader and the writer. Implied in the idea of reading with the grain or reading against the grain is a choice. A student must choose whether she is going to be generous to the writer, and therefore read/write with the grain, or she chooses not to be generous to the writer so that she can read/write against the grain. While reading with or against the grain implies that the reader is really or rhetorically either agreeing with the writer or disagreeing with the writer, a generous reading allows the reader to do both in the same reading. It gives students a way of thinking about such difficult texts as Michel Foucault's "Panopticism" without getting caught up in whether or not they agree with the writer, and therefore allows them the time to create an enriched and complicated reading.

The term *generous reading* offers students a way of thinking about how they might negotiate the difficulties of balancing privilege between the reader and the writer. A reader can both give time to the writer's ideas and, in the same reading and/or paper, give time to her own ideas — which may or may not conflict with the published writer's. Therefore, from a generous reading position, reading with and against the grain are not necessarily separate acts.

In addition to becoming a tool for my students, generous reading fits well into my own evolving pedagogy. It offers me a format for thinking about the ways in which I, as teacher, negotiate terms and languages in my classroom. This became clear to me while reflecting on the class's discussion of the use of the word "Saint" in Alice Walker's essay

"In Search of Our Mothers' Gardens."

Many of my students interpreted Walker's use of the word "Saint" as a positive renaming of black women. They assumed this in their writing in spite of the fact that Walker states, "they became 'Saints.' Instead of being perceived as whole persons, their bodies became shrines" and "[They] were not Saints, but Artists" (*Ways of Reading*, p. 695). Many of my students seemed to be falling comfortably into a preconceived definition of the word *saint*, one that did not necessarily agree with Walker's definition and I felt as though I should work with them on this reading. I did so, first, because it did not seem to show a close reading of the text, and second, because I thought that it would be a good opportunity for us to again discuss the way meanings of words are constructed.

I asked them to make two lists. One list contained words they would use to describe the word *saint*. The second list was composed of words that Walker uses to describe "Saint" in her essay. When I put these up on the board it was easy for my students to see that their list, which included terms such as "holy," "chosen by God," "exalted," "looked up to," "martyr," was much different from Walker's list, which included such terms as "sexual object," "crazy," "lunatic," "wild," "loony," "suicide," "pitiable." When I had time to think about this class I saw myself as the negotiator of definitions. I moved (figuratively and literally since the lists were on the board) between the two definitions. In fact, I was demonstrating a generous reading for my students by moving back and forth between the writer's terms and the reader's terms. However, in this case, I seemed to direct the class toward working more in the realm of the writer's words, assuming that Walker's definitions were more accurate in conjunction with her work than were those of my students.

In retrospect, I believed that I was working with, as Kenneth Burke says, the "impurities and identifications lurking" around the word *saint*. However, the more I thought about it, the more I could not decide which list represented the "impurities." On one hand, my students' list of defining words (their communal definition of *saint*) had prevented them from seeing that Walker might be negating this term. On the other hand, Walker's definition of "Saint" is both dependent on another assumed definition (something close to my students' definition of that term, I suppose) as well as some negative "identifications" with that term. That is, she had to assume that her readers had some idea of what a saint is before she could write of the inappropriateness of that name. Moreover, Walker's readers needed to have some presupposed definition of the word *saint* before they could understand her work with that word.

In my mental revision of the class I would spend more time working in space where the two definitions overlapped. This, it seems, would be a more generous reading — a way of privileging both Walker's words as well as my students' — but also significantly more difficult work. It would require a strategy for linking the two lists so that it is apparent why one is dependent on the other.

One of the questions I might use in the classroom to begin this more generous reading would be, "Why is it necessary for us, as readers, to understand *your* definition of *saint* before we can make sense out of Walker's?" If students had a difficult time answering this question I would direct them to the place in the text where Walker's definition appears:

> In the selfless abstractions their bodies became to the men who used them, they became more than "sexual objects," more even than mere women: they became "Saints." Instead of being perceived as whole persons, their bodies became shrines: what was thought to be their minds became temples suitable for worship. These crazy Saints stared out at the world, wildly, like lunatics — or quietly, like suicides; and the "God" that was in their gaze was as mute as a great stone. (pp. 694–95)

While constructing her definition of "Saint," Walker draws on her reader's preconceived notion of that word. She does this by using words that have religious or "saintly" connotations in describing these women, and then she turns these words into indicators of oppression and suffering. Walker's "Saint" is pivotal only because of the existence of my students' definition.

The religious self-sacrifice suggested by "selfless abstraction," becomes the means by which these women's bodies are used as sexual objects. These numbed and abused bodies are described as "shrines." Their crazy, lunatic minds are "temples suitable for worship." They have a "God" in their gaze, but he is as unresponsive as the men who oppress them. They are "more even than mere women," they are wild, suicidal saints. *The selflessness, the shrine, the temple, the worship, the God, the elevated position* are all easily related to the list my students compiled. Likewise, they are all words that Walker uses to describe the "Saints" that black women become when their unjustifiable oppression is made acceptable in the name of spirituality. My students' saint and Walker's "Saint" are not the same, but they are both necessary to this particular reading of Walker's text.

A generous reading, then, is both a description of the ways in which I negotiate language in the classroom and in my thinking about my teaching as well as an example of one of the terms my students and I have created together as part of our common GW language. Where the students are concerned, however, it will only work if they clearly understand what it means. And, as with almost everything I have noticed about teaching GW, it takes more than one class period, more than one mention, more than one session of defining, for a term to become part of the language of the classroom. Again and again, as issues of the relation between reader and writer surfaced in our textbook and in student papers, I returned to the term *generous reading position*. I asked: "How is this student writer taking a *generous reading position* in relation to the text? What prevents her from doing so? What is her position? How could that position become more *generous*?" After a few weeks of asking these kinds of questions, in class and in my comments on papers, students started to use the term on their own.

I have also found that working with my students on creating a metaphor for a term helps to facilitate their use of it. Our metaphor for generous reading came out of the assigned reading of the Joyce Carol Oates story, "Theft":[1]

> It seemed to [Marya] at such times that she was capable of slipping out of her own consciousness and into that of the writer's . . . into the very rhythms of another's prose. Bodiless, weightless, utterly absorbed, she traversed the landscape of another's mind and found it like her own yet totally unlike — surprising and jarring her, enticing her, leading her on. (4th ed. p. 474)

The landscape, which the class decided on as mountains, became our metaphor for reading. And we agreed that the reading Oates is describing here was similar to our idea of generous reading. The character, Marya, allows herself to be both "enticed" and "absorbed." However, she does not minimize herself as a reader. Students pointed to such words as "jarring" and "totally unlike" as indications that Marya privileges her own mind as well as the writer's. Marya is able to find a way of entering a text — stepping into the "rhythms of another's prose," giving "generous attention to a writer's language" — without blindly accepting and admiring a text.

A position of blind admiration of a writer and text, one student said, would position a reader at the foot of the mountain, looking up in reverence at the peak. A position at the top of the mountain symbolized not giving any attention to the writer's "key terms" and ideas. The middle of the mountain, where the foot and the peak are both in sight, was the place where my students found that a generous reading might be possible.

Middle of the mountain then became a working metaphor for generous reading. In their midterm retrospectives more students than ever began to use the term *generous reading position*. I think this is because our "mountain landscape" made more visible to them what this term means in relation to reading and writing. I also had a few students who used the

---

[1]Oates's piece appeared in the fourth edition of *Ways of Reading*.

mountain as a term for describing their own position as readers within their individual papers.

This is not to say that our work, even with this one term of our "GW language," was entirely successful. Some students were resistant to the idea of leaving the "old" language behind for the "new." I have found that these students were most often the ones who had, in the past, successfully learned to position themselves in English or writing classes where the "old" language was part of the structure of the class. That is, they had performed well in classes where they were at the bottom of the hierarchy, where their main responsibility was to reiterate what the writer's "main idea" was or what the teacher had to say. Naturally, these students wanted to hang on to the "old" language, the language that fulfilled their expectations, because they already knew that they could "do" reading that way. They were not so sure about this "new" stuff. The very idea of a generous reading — one where they had to share the responsibility for creating meaning with the writer — caused them to question all that they had assumed about reading and writing.

Some of these students, in an attempt to please me, used the term *generous reading* and the mountain metaphor as buzz words in their papers without showing that they used this language to think about reading. One student, Trish, wrote in her midterm retrospective, "If I had to categorize myself as a reader, I would say I am somewhere in the middle of the mountain," and gave me no further indication as to why she thought that she was in that position. I believe that Trish used this classroom metaphor in the hope that she was fulfilling some requirement of mine. This hope is grounded in a truism of the "old" language. *The teacher seems to like this word. She uses it all the time so it must mean something. If I use it in my paper I'll be writing the right way.* In Trish's paper the way of reading became the teacher's way, and the "new" language, in spite of itself, reinforced the "old" language of assumptions about students, classrooms, and teachers.

Another student, Eric, who seemed quite angry with me, wrote, "If Ms. Bender would just tell me what she means by a generous reading I would do it." Eric's resistance to the "newness" of the GW language was extreme. The very fact that he addressed me as Ms. Bender (I always make it clear to my students that they may call me by my first name) showed me that, as a student, he was more comfortable in a traditional ("old") classroom where the teacher and writer are the bearers of knowledge and the students the receptacles. Eric perceived me as the keeper of the definition in spite of the fact that *generous reading* was a term that the class had defined together. Just as Eric did not want to take responsibility for determining the meaning of the texts he read, he did not want to take responsibility for defining generous reading.

These moments of resistance to the "new" language are not, however, complete failures. They are signs of crises for students who are on the threshold of beginning to question their own assumptions about reading and writing. Trish and Eric were not quite there, but they were well on their way. I responded to both of them by directing them back to themselves. To Trish I wrote, "Why? What reading practices of yours allowed you to categorize yourself as middle of the mountain? How does this show in your writing?" To Eric I wrote, "How would you define *generous reading* based on the things you have read this term, and the discussions we've had in class?" These questions allowed me to respond to my students without giving them an actual answer, which would have fulfilled their expectations in the "old" language instead of helping them work toward building a "new" one.

The work of building a language in the GW classroom is a slow and tedious, but necessary process. Without giving any attention to language we use in the classroom we (teachers and students of GW) risk true communication with each other. If we rely on our "old" ways of talking about reading/writing, like the "courtroom talk" that slipped into my class, it is unlikely that we will ever be able to think about reading/writing in a "new" way. Even the myriad of available terms that can be lifted from the introduction to *Ways of Reading* will not form a vocabulary for talking about reading/writing, unless teachers and students of General Writing work together to give those terms meanings.

o–o–o–o–o–o–o–o–o–o–o–o–o–o–o–o–o–o–o

RESISTING THE (GENDERED) SPACE OF THE ESSAY: TEACHING "A ROOM OF ONE'S OWN"
by John Champagne

> Once again I'm faced with the same situation presented in a new fashion. The situation is that of equal rights for women. The English department may say that we are discussing gender, but what is gender today — it's equal rights.
> – Chuck Hatalsky

Several times this past year I have had occasion to tell the story of my first attempts at teaching a freshman reading and writing assignment sequence that took gender as its subject. I invariably divide my semester into two halves: the first, in which I felt as if I were failing miserably, and the second, in which I achieved some amount of success. While this narrative is undoubtedly a fiction, it allows me to make sense of my experience teaching the course, to isolate what I feel were some of the pedagogical problems I encountered, and to offer to myself some suggestions as to how I might avoid such problems in the future.

The epigraph to this essay was written by one of my students during what I have come to name the "failure" half of the semester. Chuck, who was particularly resistant to what he understood the focus of the course to be, helped me to recognize that I was enacting in my teaching one of the worst-case scenarios of a composition course examining questions of gender. For, while I had hoped that I was teaching a course in which my students and I would explore how gender influences our reading and writing, Chuck's comments made me realize that I was in fact engaging my class in a series of debates on such issues as "equal rights for women" — debates that I of course won.

While I would dispute neither the power nor propriety of bringing issues of equality into the composition classroom, Chuck helped me to identify what was disturbing me about my teaching that semester. For the class had begun to feel strangely "unteachable." My students were coming to associate the discussion of gender issues with the accepting of a correct political position — my position — and one that they learned very quickly to mouth on cue. Class work consisted of identifying the pernicious effects of sexism. Issues of reading and writing fell by the wayside. Worst of all was my realization that while students seemed to recognize some of the negative effects of a sex-gendering system, they could not imagine challenging its *inevitability*. This was made clear to me when, during a class discussion, rather than questioning a way of knowing the world that insisted on someone inevitably being the oppressor and someone else inevitably being the oppressed, my students merely acknowledged that yes, men oppress women, "but why shouldn't they? Someone has to be 'on top,' why shouldn't it be the physically stronger?" As Chuck explained in one of his essays,

    I think that if all of us would take the male point of
    view for a moment this might make a little more sense.

215

```
Since the beginning of our country or even time as we
"humans" know it, the male has been the dominant figure in
our society in most cases. Then all of a sudden women want
to be equal in every manner. That thought alone sent shiv-
ers down the spines of the men in this country. Their
position on top could be gone, and if you have ever been on
top you know how it feels. You don't want to come down and
lose it so you try to find a way to keep it.
```

How had a course that had hoped to explore the ways we read and write as men and women managed to deteriorate into a discussion of who ought to be "on top"?

Not surprisingly, it was the readings in the course that helped me to make the transition from the "failure" to the "success" half of my teaching that semester. Specifically, it was the choice of one essay in particular, Virginia Woolf's "A Room of One's Own,"[1] that enabled me to shift the focus of my class away from political debates and toward questions of reading and writing.

When I first read Woolf's essay, I feared that its admittedly guarded feminist polemic might lead class discussion into yet another round of debates on "equal rights." But eventually I was able to see how I might use "A Room of One's Own" to build on the work the class had already accomplished. I decided to concentrate not on the specifics of Woolf's polemic, but on the argument enacted by her in the essay's very writing. What did the style of Woolf's essay, its rhetorical turns and formal devices, have to do with the overriding question the class was just beginning to explore: the relationship between gender and reading and writing?

In her essay "Killing Priests, Nuns, Women, Children," Jean Franco argues that cultural spaces are gendered not by the actual biological sex of those who construct and inhabit them, but by the (gendered) values that such spaces accrue.[2] Thus, in different historical moments, real women may have entered — and perhaps even flourished in — spaces gendered as masculine. The particular results of these "transgressions" of gender need to be specified in order to understand the shifting and contested history of a space's gendering. Extending Franco's analysis to the space we call an essay, a space that "constructs" us in the sense of compelling us to write (and read) according to certain culturally defined, gendered conventions, we might ask how a historical figure such as Virginia Woolf managed to find a place for herself as an essayist.

"A Room of One's Own" provides us with a compelling account of a woman in 1928–29 attempting to inhabit and transform the space of the essay, a space that has historically been gendered as masculine.[3] However, this account lies not in the essay's polemic, but in Woolf's own efforts to resist, in the writing of "A Room of One's Own," what she perceives to be the (masculine) conventions of essay writing. Through this act of resistance, Woolf

---

[1] "A Room of One's Own" appeared in the fifth editon of *Ways of Reading.*

[2] Jean Franco, "Killing Priests, Nuns, Women, Children," *On Signs,* ed. Marshall Blonsky (Johns Hopkins University Press, 1985). This piece appeared in the second edition of *Ways of Reading.*

[3] My assumption that the essay has been historically gendered as masculine is drawn from a number of feminist texts on writing as gendered. See, for example, Hélène Cixous, "The Laugh of the Medusa," *Critical Theory since 1965,* ed. Hazard Adams and Leroy Searle (Tallahassee: Florida State University Press, 1986), pp. 309–20; Jane Gallop, *Reading Lacan* (Ithaca: Cornell University Press, 1985); Luce Irigaray, "The Power of Discourse and the Subordination of the Feminine," *The Sex Which Is Not One* (Ithaca: Cornell University Press, 1985), pp. 68–85.

transforms the essay into a "space" of her own, a room where she can accomplish her work as a woman writer.

Rereading the essay, I was struck by the number of times Woolf outlines what she understands to be her "proper" task as an essay writer, only to go ahead and ignore that task. In her efforts to "defy convention," she seems to be exploring whatever avenues of resistance may have been open to a woman writing in the late 1920s. If there is such a thing as gendered writing, as certain feminists have suggested,[4] Woolf's attempts at defying convention might be gendered as feminine — since she appears not simply to inhabit the (masculine) space of the essay, but to transform that space, bringing alternative values to it. What "alternative," "feminine" values might Woolf, in the writing of "A Room of One's Own," be attaching to that masculine space of the essay? According to Susan Deysher,

> [In "A Room," Woolf] creates for herself a space where she can "offer you an opinion upon one minor point--a woman must have money and a room of her own if she is to write fiction." Therefore, she sets herself up not as an authority on "Women and Fiction," but rather as an authority on her own opinion, as she is the only one who could explain it. This is very different from the way male writing assumes authority.

One of the most commonly explored themes in feminist writing of the past twenty years is that of authority. Throughout its history, feminism has attempted to pose alternatives to a patriarchal, phallocentric conception of authority. In "A Room of One's Own," Woolf confronts, on a number of occasions, the issue of the writer's authority. Throughout her essay, she insists on "shirking her duty" as a writer, refusing to hand her audience "a nugget of pure truth to wrap up between the pages of (their) notebooks." "Lies will flow from my lips," she tells us, "but there may perhaps be some truth mixed up with them; it is for you to seek out this truth and to decide whether any part of it is worth keeping."

It might be argued that the position of authority Woolf occupies in her essay both challenges the gendering of the essay as masculine and is profoundly feminist. Woolf questions her own status as knower *while continuing to speak.* She calls into suspicion rigid distinctions between the true and the false, and suggests to her audience that they may be the ones ultimately authorized to determine the value of her work to their own lives. Her insistence on speaking through a multitude of identities — Mary Beton, Mary Seton, Mary Carmichael, her "own person," — threatens to erode the boundaries between "author" and "character," the knower and the known, the subject who "speaks" the essay, and that which the essay takes as its object. It might be argued that all of these moves work to challenge the essay's masculine gendering. Stated in Lacanian feminist terms, Woolf's attempts both to claim and call into question her own authority as a writer serve to confuse the strict epistemological boundaries of a phallocentric culture, which separates those who "possess" (truth, power, value, the authority to speak) from those who "lack."[5] Woolf presumes neither to speak from a place of mastery over language nor to occupy the silent, unauthorized place reserved by phallocentrism for the feminine. Instead, she attempts, in her writing of "A Room of One's Own," to occupy some alternative place between these poles, and thus transforms the (masculine) space of the essay.

[4]See note 2.

[5]For an excellent explanation of the Lacanian terms utilized in this essay, and a more detailed account of patriarchy as an epistemology, see Gallop, ibid.

In their own writing about Woolf's essay, students in my course sometimes made gestures similar to those made by Woolf in "A Room of One's Own." Forced to inhabit (as both readers and writers) the space of the essay, a space that they felt they were not completely authorized to enter, students moved both to claim and reject authority simultaneously. Compelled by the work of the course to speak as "experts," and yet fearing that this expertise was somehow unearned, they moved uneasily between asserting their interpretation of Woolf's essay and apologizing for their lack of understanding. At first glance, there would seem to be a tremendous difference between Woolf's deliberate attempts simultaneously to confirm and to call into question her own authority as a writer and students' less conscientious moves in similar directions. And yet both Woolf and my students faced cultural and historical circumstances that positioned them in very similar ways vis-à-vis the problem of the writer's authority. For both Woolf and my students were gendered by their culture as "feminine."

What I am arguing is that the space of "student" is, regardless of the biological sex of those who inhabit it, a space our culture genders as feminine. Our cultural understanding of "student" is "the castrated other" that desires the phallus/knowledge that the patriarch/teacher is authorized to give. The physical setup of the traditional classroom, the prohibition against speaking without being recognized by the teacher, the subordinate place student writing occupies in most classes — all attest to this gendering of "student" as feminine (and "teacher" as masculine). As "feminine" students attempt to transgress the boundaries of the "masculine" space of the essay, they face the same options faced by Woolf in the writing of "A Room of One's Own": to speak as a (culturally constructed) man (and thus to inhabit the space of the essay without attempting to resist and transform its gendering); to refuse to speak altogether (and thus occupy the place of "lack"); or to resist the gendering of the space, and attempt to forge a place in it for a "bi-sexual" voice of one's own.[6]

In response to "A Room of One's Own," I asked my students to write an essay in which they located places in her essay where Woolf appeared to be "defying convention," and to hypothesize why Woolf may have been defying convention in these particular ways. Here is a section of Jennifer Gottschalk's response to this assignment:

> One thing I noticed that Woolf does, is to pick out small details. These minute details make the essay more interesting to me. I know that I am not a critic of any sort, [emphasis mine] but I like how Woolf does that. She added details about the riverbank, the food at lunch and dinner, and also about the stray cat. These details are important because they are characteristic of a woman's writing. Men are not seen as writing this way, and usually ignore tiny details. The way Woolf uses details is a very definite feminine style.

---

[6]I borrow the term "bisexual" from Cixous, to indicate writing which contains traces of both genders. As Cixous insists, in a patriarchal, phallocentric culture, the masculine can never be fully eclipsed; a "little bit of phallus" must remain in all writing (because the feminine can be defined only in a relation of opposition to the masculine, and never in and of itself). Thus, it is probably more accurate to speak of "masculine" and "bisexual" writing, rather than "masculine" and "feminine." See Cixous, ibid.

```
This reminds me a lot of my own writing, not for
class, but on a more personal level. Most people would
ignore objects of a passing glance, as the male writing
style has taught us. I guess I admire her because her
writing is similar to my own. I know that I should not think
of it in that order, [emphasis mine] because it was her
idea in the first place, she had done it before I did. In a
way I am very protective of my own writing.
```

Although I am somewhat uncomfortable with her nonhistoricized description of "masculine" and "feminine" writing (fearing, for both of us, accusations of "essentialism"), what seems most significant to me here are Jennifer's attempts simultaneously to claim and not claim authority over both her reading of Woolf and her own writing. She has enough confidence in her reading to draw attention to what she perceives to be ways in which Woolf defies the conventions of essay writing, and to name Woolf's defiance "feminine." Yet she is quick to point out that she is "not a critic of any sort." Although she recognizes a certain similarity between Woolf's writing and her own (an "unauthorized," nonpublic writing that she feels compelled to protect from the "masculine" voice of academic criticism), she scolds herself for daring to compare herself with Woolf, and assumes a posture of humility before her.

Two additional aspects of these paragraphs are worth noting. First, Jennifer's insistence that men *are not seen* as writing this way" implies that gender is a cultural construction — that while a real man may in fact write "like a woman," we have no means culturally of recognizing this writing as feminine.[7] Secondly, her recognition that certain kinds of writing are "not for class" implies not only that the university requires one to learn some other, nonprivate kind of writing, but that this writing may be gendered in opposition to one's own "feminine," "personal" writing.

In his response to "A Room of One's Own," Jim Lakeley notices what he perceives to be a certain failure of nerve on Woolf's part. He is disappointed and confused by the move in her essay away from the richly descriptive fictive passages with which it begins, toward the more sober and directed polemic found in the essay's conclusion.

```
In the beginning of the essay she doesn't express her
feelings in direct dialogue, instead she creates a space
for the reader to enter so that readers can reflect upon
the "story" and perhaps draw their own conclusions. In the
end, she flat-out tells the audience what is on her mind.
I no longer have the pleasure of traveling through her
space and almost becoming a part of the essay. Instead, I
am lectured to about the history of women, and of "the very
low opinion in which (women) were held by Mr. Oscar Brown-
ing . . . Napoleon and Mussolini." There is nothing out-
wardly wrong with using this style of writing, but in the
```

---

[7]Cixous insists on something very similar when she claims Genet, Joyce, and Kleist as male writers who write the feminine. See Cixous, ibid.

219

```
context it is very confusing. Perhaps she has not enough

confidence that her audience has been receptive to her use

of imagery and fiction. Honestly, I do not know why [empha-

sis mine] she might go back on her earlier promise. All I

can do is guess [emphasis mine] that maybe she felt that

her use of fiction was not strong enough, and she had to

speak plainly and directly to make sure her point was made.
```

Like Jennifer, Jim notices a significant aspect of Woolf's essay, her decision to end the essay in her own person so as to anticipate two criticisms. He even offers some interesting suggestions to account for Woolf's shift in tone. But also like Jennifer, Jim litters his essay with hesitancies such as "perhaps," "maybe," "honestly, I do not know," "all I can do is guess," the effect of which is to undermine his authority as a writer. Like Jennifer, he appears to be both claiming and not claiming a place for himself within the essay. As a student (thus occupying a feminine space) Jim finds in the (feminine) beginning of Woolf's essay a place where he feels comfortable, capable of making an interpretation. But when the tone of the essay shifts to what he perceives to be a more "masculine" polemic, he feels excluded from the essay, and unauthorized to speak back to it. Interestingly, he is careful to note that there is "nothing outwardly wrong" with this "masculine" writing; he merely finds it confusing in the context of Woolf's essay, and a hindrance to his pleasure.

What is particularly interesting about this passage is the way that, in the midst of all his hesitancies, Jim has some perceptive ideas. Perhaps Woolf did experience a failure of nerve near the conclusion of her essay. Fearing the consequences of too resistant a stance, perhaps Woolf, in an effort to be taken seriously, chose "to speak plainly and directly," like a (culturally constructed) man. Perhaps in the moments of the essay's conclusion, she chose to inhabit the masculine space of the essay without resisting it. All of these ideas are suggested by Jim. One might quarrel with his easy attribution of Woolf's alleged failure of nerve to her, personally, rather than to the historical and cultural pressures brought to bear on her as a woman writer. One might also take issue with his rather monolithic reading of the essay's conclusion, a reading that ignores the fact that Woolf ends her essay with another fictional narrative. But here I want to draw particular attention to the way Jim struggles with the space of the essay, attempting both to occupy and resist a space in which he feels both authorized and unauthorized to speak. Like Jennifer, he neither fully abdicates, nor fully inhabits, the spaces of "reader" and "writer."

How are we as teachers to respond to this double movement in student essays, this gesture both toward and away from the claiming of a certain authority over one's reading and writing? Do we wipe out the traces of students' reluctance, insist that they delete their "I am not a critic of any sort," their "honestly, I do not know why"? Admittedly, my first response as a teacher would be to suggest that they take a stand, forge a reading, omit from their essays the symptoms of their unknowing. But in the act of doing so, I would be removing from their essays all trace of their (feminine) resistance to that masculine space. I would be forcing them to speak as men, to inhabit the space of the essay without transforming it. I would, in effect, be erasing the feminine from their writing. And yet, isn't it my job as a teacher to teach my students how to write with confidence, to write with authority and expertise, as if they are in command of their material? Isn't this the kind of writing the university respects and demands?

I am suggesting that, as teachers of writing, we have a conception of "good" writing. And that conception may well be gendered as masculine. When we force our students to inhabit their essays as if they can assume unquestioned authority over their reading and writing, we are, in effect, acculturating our students into a "masculine," phallocentric position, erasing their attempts to "feminize" the space of the essay. We are reproducing the epistemological distinctions on which patriarchal phallocentrism is based.

Rather than compel students to remove all (feminine) resistance to the essay, all traces of this movement both toward and away from authority, I would suggest that we move them toward their resistance, to make it, in effect, the subject of their writing. We might encourage our students to follow Woolf's example and attempt to defy the conventions of essay writing. We might ask them to explore in greater detail just what it is they are resisting in the essay and why they feel compelled to resist. What might they be able to write through this act of resistance that they felt unauthorized to write before? We might also suggest that they examine what parts of the essay they do *not* wish to resist — those "masculine" aspects which they feel are of value. In Jennifer's case, we might encourage her to explore in her work the boundaries between a "personal" and "public" writing, to attempt to discover how much heterogeneity the space of the essay can bear. To Jim we might suggest that he imagine why Woolf may have chosen to speak in both "masculine" and "feminine" voices. What did this shift from ("feminine") fiction to ("masculine") polemic allow her to say that she might not have been able to say otherwise?

While we are suggesting to our students that they examine their "feminine" resistance to the essay, we obviously need to reconsider our own masculine gendering as teachers. We need to call into question our own status as the site of knowledge and resist the cultural and institutional pressures to position ourselves as (patriarchal) authorities.

Following the Woolf assignment, my class and I were able to move in some of these directions. Our task became to imagine what might constitute a "feminine" practice of essay writing today. I asked my students to reconsider their own writing in terms of issues of gender, to name places in their work as "masculine" and "feminine."

Here is Todd Simmon's reconsideration of his first essay written that semester, in which he wrote a response to Adrienne Rich's "When We Dead Awaken."

> At times during the semester I have written in this style that I can now call masculine. My understanding of writing through your gender has often been difficult. It was in my first paper on Adrienne Rich that I can now see what I couldn't see before. What was I doing when writing this essay? Basically, what I've been doing all my life. I guess you could say I was thinking, "OK, here's my assignment, now I've got to try to convince my teacher that what I'm saying makes sense." I was very confused with what I was doing in the first place but despite that fact I still felt like I had to assume authority and write like I knew perfectly well what was going on. My second paragraph starts out, "Rich speaks of 'anger' about herself and of women. Anger from male dominance over the female and a female society that has accepted this dominance and. . . ." That is what my whole paper is about. Rich does this, Rich does that, she means this and wants to say that. I did not even say that that is what I believe but what was also indeed the correct assumptions about Adrienne Rich and her

essay. I only started to use the ever-so-controversial pronoun "I" in the last paragraph. Why even use it then? I don't know, I probably never even thought about it at the time and the fact that I can recognize it now signifies a substantial change in the things that I notice when reading essays now.

There are several things that strike me as significant in this paragraph. First of all, there is the seriousness with which Todd considers his own work. He has the ability and confidence to name his previous writing as masculine, and to argue for this gendering with a specific reference to one of his own texts. Todd recognizes that his writing has changed over the course of the semester, and is capable of articulating how it has changed. He acknowledges the limitations of his previous conception of reading, a conception that required him to presume to know "the correct assumptions about Rich and her essay." He questions his previous understanding of his own authority as a writer, one of the effects of which was a belief that he had constantly to "cover over" his inadequacy in order to have the right to speak.[8] As Todd puts it, despite the fact that he was confused, he felt compelled to write as if he "knew perfectly well what was going on." There is now a place in Todd's writing for knowing and unknowing, a space for that "ever-so-controversial pronoun 'I'" as well as for a more formal, less private voice. In his essay, Todd resists and inhabits those ways of reading and writing he "can now call masculine," so that a space might be opened up in his work for both the masculine and the feminine. As he explains, "After doing the Woolf assignment I was prepared to begin using my understanding of what feminine writing might be in my own writing."

If, as Hélène Cixous has argued, writing is the very possibility of change,[9] perhaps students' efforts at both resisting and inhabiting the (masculine) space of the essay are gestures toward a radical epistemology to come, an epistemology incorporating the bisexual. Students' willingness to acknowledge both the masculine and feminine in their own writing may in fact represent a profound act of cultural resistance. Perhaps they already sense what Cixous has argued: "In one another we will never be lacking."[10]

[8]Here, I am paraphrasing Jane Gallop, who insists that one of the effects of phallocentrism is that "one must constantly cover over one's inevitable inadequacy in order to have the right to speak" (Gallop, p. 20). Thus, Todd's reconception of this authority as a writer might be considered feminist.
[9]Cixous, p. 311.
[10]Cixous, p. 320.

o–o–o–o–o–o–o–o–o–o–o–o–o–o–o–o–o–o

WHAT THEY DON'T KNOW THEY KNOW: STUDENT WRITERS AND ADRIENNE RICH

by Christine Conklin

There is a line in Adrienne Rich's essay, "When We Dead Awaken: Writing as Re-Vision," that has haunted me since I first read it as an undergraduate. Rich writes, "But poems are like dreams: in them you put what you don't know you know." At eighteen, I was an English major and wanted to be a poet, and those lines were a direct and personal message. Ten years later, having worked with Rich's essay in my introductory composition classroom, where most of my students are neither poets nor English majors, I have come to see that those lines also work as a metaphor for reading; I substitute "readings" for the word "poems." For me and for my students, reading can be a way of coming to know more, not just about a particular subject but about the process of reading itself. And we can work out together the crucial, unarticulated connections between reading, writing, and revision.

My students are in general unaware of what "strong reading" involves and of how it is connected to "strong writing." I hope, in using Rich's essay as I do, to enact and examine reading with them in the classroom. By starting with Rich's poems and moving outward to her text, students can experience what it means to know more about poems and texts than they knew they knew — and therefore also to know more about reading and writing.

In her essay, Rich also "models" for students the way in which closely reading herself empowers and frees her. In doing so Rich presents and complicates several important issues for student readers and writers. She writes,

> Re-vision — the act of looking back, of seeing with fresh eyes, of entering an old text from a new critical direction — is for women more than a chapter in cultural history: it is an act of survival. Until we can understand the assumptions we are drenched in we cannot know ourselves.

Rich has worked best for me in the middle of the term, providing a very real crisis and turning point in a term-long discussion of reading and writing. Students who have struggled already with one or two complex essays have begun to imagine the difficulties of strong reading though they probably won't yet know what it means to perform it.

Rich's is the only essay that I discuss in class before students write on it. I require that students read and mark the essay or make some notes on it before coming to class; in some cases I've also had them write a two-page "position paper" in which they must identify specifically a "difficulty" in their reading of Rich and then suggest a solution to it. (This often surfaces and diffuses tensions about Rich's politics.) The class discussion that follows this initial reading focuses very specifically on two poems in the essay and then moves outward to connect text and poetry, general and specific, past and present. With this plan I hope to model reading, enact strategies, and make concrete some connections between reading and writing, reading *as* writing.

I didn't invent this plan alone nor do I want to present it as a simple formula. It grows out of Ann Berthoff's "double-entry notebook" method and is one way to get started that other teachers and I have used successfully. I can detail this plan here on the page, but I cannot say anything more than how and, perhaps, why it has worked for me and my students.

I ask students to draw a vertical line down the center of a piece of notebook paper. I tell them that I'm going to read the poem "Aunt Jennifer's Tigers" aloud while they read and mark whatever strikes them in the poem, and that I will give them five minutes to write notes on the right side of their paper when I have finished reading aloud. These notes won't be collected, although, I tell them, the notes may be useful when they sit down to write their papers. These notes can be anything that comes to mind after the reading: questions, images or words that strike them for some unknown reason, problems, thoughts, or phrases. Here, I think, is the beginning of a reading, an act of attention or "noticing," divorced for the moment from any purpose except paying attention.

After we've read and they've made their notes, I ask students to describe the structure of the poem. They will notice that it looks square or even "box-like" on the page, that lines rhyme and are equal in length. They may say that it is "traditional" poetry. From there I might ask them to notice what is "inside" the square or box — or who? And, "What words in the poem connect to being in a box?" I've asked. And what images are not "trapped"? Students can then take the discussion in a number of directions — to talk about what Aunt Jennifer's activity is, how she created the scene she creates, what its implications and limitations are. Basically, students take over doing what the New Critics would call "close reading," but their reading goes beyond achieving some single correct meaning, because there can and will be multiple interpretations. I require evidence from the poem for each reading, but I don't make any sort of judgment. As students begin to see the possibilities and demands of this kind of reading and supplying of evidence they become engaged with this poem and with their various readings of it. One important move for students to make next is outward: from the poem to what Rich says in the text immediately surrounding the poem and throughout the essay. I ask specifically what passages in Rich's text they can connect to the readings we have made of her poem.

Often students go to the text immediately surrounding "Aunt Jennifer's Tigers," to Rich's description of her "deliberate detachment" and to her "asbestos gloves" metaphor. We discuss these, and I ask them to locate another passage in the essay that seems to connect to whatever we have said. Because they have read the essay ahead of time, they will have underlined passages that struck them in reading, and often they will cite the lines about poems and dreams. They can suggest that Rich's project in "revision" is to look at her own writing to see what she didn't know she knew as she wrote. They may see Rich as a kind of model reader who uses "old" texts to learn something new both about her history and her present. A text can somehow be both a solid record and a malleable one, changed by a new reading/reader.

The passage on revision as an "act of looking back with fresh eyes" is useful here, and if they don't take me there, I take them. I push students to look at the whole paragraph and at Rich's ideas of "how our language has trapped as well as liberated us" and what it might mean to say that her job is "not to pass on a tradition but to break its hold over us." Whatever passages students offer can be worked with, toward the idea of making connections between the poem and the text, and between different sections of the text.

What I hope is happening here, right before students' eyes and because of their own work in discussion, is a modeling of the reading process that involves noticing, thinking, analyzing, selecting, rejecting, connecting, moving constantly back and forth, from text to thought to text. Students can begin to see that it is possible to range through the whole essay; that there are ways into this difficult essay, and there are as many ways to move within it as there are readers.

After this discussion, I tell students that I'll read "Aunt Jennifer's Tigers" aloud again and that then again they will have time to write, this time on the left side of their pages. This shows, I hope, that rereading is necessary and often surprising; it is another way to look again, to revise from a differently informed position. Students can respond in their notes to questions they wrote earlier, to points in discussion, or they can notice new images, words and connections. When they've made these new notes I ask them to look at both sides of their notes and write a paragraph about what they see as having moved or changed — or more generally what they see as having moved or changed in the hour we've spent in this class. Again, I'm hoping to model that reflexiveness, that necessary "vision and re-vision" that reading and writing require. In pointing toward the assignment (and I've used several different Rich assignments from *Ways of Reading*), I hope that students will see that their writing will grow out of these readings and subsequent ones; they will be forced to re-read and then to write again.

I do the same exercise with Rich's poem "Planetarium"; students divide a fresh notebook page, I read aloud, they make notes, and again I begin by asking about structure: "How does this poem look on the page?" They will notice that there is more "space" than there is in "Aunt Jennifer's Tigers," or that it is "more open" or "free verse." They will notice that punctuation is missing, but white space links or separates the fragments and italics and quotations. They may say this poem is about space or about a woman who isn't weighted but "levitates." They can then connect some of the passages in the text, perhaps in terms of "breaking traditions" or questioning assumptions. They can begin to say that here is some specific evidence, in two "records" of Rich, of what it looks like to revise and to rename and to transform one's writing and/or one's self.

This plan has been, for me, a powerful way to enact reading and finding a way to engage with a complex text. The papers that students write after this exercise, however, are not always (or even often) dazzling. Many students simply transfer the class discussion onto paper, or string quotations ("evidence") together; but those moves, too, can provide a way of talking about what *more* is involved in reading and writing a paper that matters. Students in the class who have tried to do more than repeat the discussion will call into question a paper that settles for that tactic. It's a way to talk about notetaking and collaboration and quotation as a starting point, rather than as a satisfactory "answer."

Students have more often taken significant steps in revising these Rich papers. Rich almost forces some movement or decision from writers, I think because she presents a direct way to observe and define the power and complexity of reading and revision. One term, I received revisions from two writers, Kelly and Monica. The two were friends and seemed, by their comments in class and their written work, to have deliberately allied themselves against the idea that a paper ought to be more than clear, logical, coherent, and correct.

Kelly and Monica were responding to assignment 2 in the "Aims of Education" sequence, which asks students to "use" one of Rich's early poems to "test and extend" Paulo Freire's argument in "The 'Banking Concept' of Education." Students are asked to consider "structures of oppression" and "transformation" and "what Rich learned to do."

Kelly's original paper, which I used in class (anonymously, as always), opens with mention of Rich's oppression and argues that her re-vision is a "transcendence" of "the male style of writing." She also quotes from Freire in this first paragraph, to show that she's "doing" the assignment. I asked students to notice, as I read the rest of the paper aloud and they marked it, how well this writer had read Rich, and how well she had used Rich. Since I ask students to put the page number in parentheses after any quotation, students noticed that Kelly quoted a lot, and that she followed almost exactly the order of Rich's essay. She also inserted some quotations from Freire. In between, she does work at interpreting "Aunt Jennifer's Tigers"; some but not all of her ideas come out of our class discussion.

Kelly gets trapped in her own strategy, however, when she gets to the end of her paper. In effect, allowing Rich to dictate her paper's order means that Kelly can't really move to her own discoveries in writing or concluding. She has to make up a generalized and happy ending in which she assumes the language of the assignment and of class discussion without the burden of evidence.

> Rich can now write in her own style; she doesn't have
> to write for her father, male writers or teachers. Women
> can now "name" by themselves without looking at men's
> examples. Rich "renames" and also "revises" herself by
> breaking out of her old self. In conclusion, Freire's
> argument about the way people can bring about change is
> thus extended through the use of Rich's examples.

Initially, this ending looks pretty good to students, because it seems to answer the assignment and even manages to bring Freire back in. When I asked students to push at it, though, it began to seem unearned. Mainly, each sentence contains an idea or assertion (smart ones, even) that hasn't been introduced or developed elsewhere. These ideas seem general, huge and too "easy" when simply stated and abandoned. Students will say they *want* to believe the writer's ideas because she has shown evidence in her preceding pages that she has read Rich closely. She has done the work to get where she does but she gets trapped into rushing to a general close. She has followed Rich so closely that when Rich stops writing so does Kelly. Rather than using her work with Rich to tease out the threads of her own reading, the writer shuts down her paper with an "in conclusion" flag. As some students said, this sentence tells, rather than shows, that the writer has "done her job." This last sentence seemed particularly easy. A writer who had read and documented as much as Kelly had could do more; perhaps she could make the work pay off in a revision structured by her own reading of Rich — one that she begins to get to in the end — rather than by Rich's order. If the writer could learn to work or control Rich, to listen to what struck her and could be connected by her, then the writer could compose her own essay, not merely echo Rich's.

Monica's original paper shares some of the "problems" of Kelly's in that quotations are strung together in predictable order, but Monica has used more of Freire, intercutting Rich and Freire in a kind of A-B-A-B pattern. Students said that this seemed promising, if in revision the writer worked more to connect the two. As in the poetry/text reading exercise, we had been working all term toward a definition of reading that included "connecting." That is, a reader notices something in an essay and elsewhere she notices something else. When the reader puts two words, sentences, passages, or ideas next to each other on a page and tries to work out for herself in writing *why* she seems compelled to notice them, she is beginning not only to construct a reading ("These two things interest me") but also to consider the process and its product — further reading, writing, rereading, connections, leading to more connections ("These two things together interest me because . . . "). In between the "things" is where the reader does the work of reading, interpreting, connecting, making meaning.

Monica had put passages from Freire and Rich together, but students saw that a *reading* was entirely missing. There wasn't, in this draft, a place where meaning or connections were made. There were opportunities, because the writer had noticed and placed passages next to one another, but at the moment these were "like strangers on a bus" — sharing the same vehicle but not interacting in any way. The writer was going to have to rethink and rewrite pretty aggressively in order to produce an essay in which connections were made. The class said that both writers seemed to "have their work cut out for them" in revision, but at least they had a place to start, with readings to work from.

Before students turned in their revisions, I asked each of them to write a note telling me what they would like me to notice about their revisions. I used both Kelly's and Monica's revisions in the next class, but before students read either revision, I also handed out copies of the notes Kelly and Monica had written to me.

I started with Monica's note, before students saw her revision, and asked what they would expect her revision to look like based on her note. Monica had written,

```
This revision is not much different from the original,
in fact it is quite similar. The more I read the original
the better I thought it was. I didn't think it was that
bad.  It had some errors and a few problems, which I tried
to clean up. I also added a few sentences and changed a few
things to try to make the paper more understandable. I
changed it mostly where there were comments written. This
paper is trying to show Rich's life as a writer; and how
she changed in her writing. There's no hidden meaning. I'm
just trying to show Rich's transformation in writing from
an oppressive style to a free thinking style of writing. I
think it's pretty straightforward. I don't know, though.
You be the judge!
```

Students could see that if, as the writer said, her revision wasn't going to be "very different" then it probably wasn't going to represent much rethinking or reworking or rereading of Rich. Moreover, the writer sees me, the teacher, saying her paper is "bad," rather than saying that it can be worked on to extend meanings or make connections. She sees the teacher's comments as condemnation rather than dialogue, and she reacts by saying she has "cleaned up" a few "errors" but otherwise doesn't see that there's anything so terribly wrong. She's changing a few things "mostly where there were comments," to please the teacher and to be "good."

Yet, the writer isn't as submissive as she says she is. She insists, perhaps as a way of warding off further prodding from me, that her mission and her ideas are simple: "I'm *just* trying to show Rich's transformation . . . it's pretty straightforward." In our ongoing definition of "strong reading," complexity was often an issue. With the classroom reading of Rich we saw together that readings can be multiple, and can change; and within readings connections can be contradictory but not necessarily exclusive. A willingness to consider and to complicate ideas can certainly lead to chaos but sometimes also to richer understanding.

I asked the class, "What is this writer resisting?" and they said, "Hidden meanings." I wrote "I hid the _____" on the board and asked students to finish the sentence. We listed their answers: money, keys, books, socks, tapes. Then I asked what these things had in common and students said, eventually, that they are all concrete items that you could put somewhere safe and then find them again exactly as they were. Someone else who knew where you hid them could also find them as you would. I asked, "So, if this writer is talking about meanings being hidden, what are her assumptions about meaning in a text?" This was a way to look back at discussions on making meaning in reading as opposed to finding "it" as a unit, ready-made. The assumptions behind "hidden meanings" are that there is one "correct" little gem of insight that an author has buried, that a clever student could unearth, so the teacher could say "right."

I asked how the phrase "hidden meaning" positions the writer and how it might be a different positioning from that of a writer who thinks that meaning is not already "there" but is made by the reader as well as the writer. I asked the class, "How does this positioning relate to this writer's assumptions about revision?" They said revision seemed to be a

227

"fix-it" notion, a mechanical or formulaic view that related to a mechanical view of the text as having discrete components of meaning, waiting to be "correctly" excavated. I asked, "How are her assumptions about revision related to her assumptions about what a teacher is?" The writer is a victim, a defendant against a "judge" and, as such, I asked, "How might such assumptions trap her?"

This allowed us to move back into Rich, thinking again about that passage on poems and dreams and the one on revision. In reading her note now, would the writer see things she didn't know she knew? Could there be advantages to that "fix-it" strategy? Could there be disadvantages?

From Monica, I had received exactly the same paper she had turned in the preceding week, with new sentences tacked onto the end of every other paragraph. In copying her paper for class, I bracketed these additions, so that her strategy would be obvious immediately. We didn't spend long on her paper. Once the class saw that their expectations of a "nonrevision" were confirmed, and that her assumptions probably had prevented her from doing the work of the assignment, it wasn't worth spending much more time on.

My intention in this discussion was not to reduce or berate Monica but to ask her — and her classmates who may share some or all of her views — to look at the trap her own language and assumptions create and to imagine ways out of that trap — as Rich does. The ways out have to do with risk and ambiguity and struggle, rather than clarity, coherence, and correctness.

I also handed out Kelly's note and asked students to imagine how the revision would look and how the writer had read Rich and herself. Kelly had written:

> I'd like you to look at the use of quotes in my essay and the way I connected my ideas through the quotes. I tried to put more of Freire in the essay, so I'd like you to look and see if there's more of a connection between Rich and Freire. I also described more of what I meant by the "space" in Rich's poem "Planetarium." Also, I didn't follow Rich's essay from beginning to end, but tried to start with "Planetarium" and work back to "Aunt Jennifer's Tigers." I still have things from our class discussion about the poems, but I felt this information was important in explaining Rich's transformation and transcendence.

Students picked up on the cheerleading tone in Kelly's note; it sounds as though she is trying to sell the paper as a "true revision." Although students said they would see for themselves in reading her revision whether this was true, they saw in the note that it might be, if she really did what she said she had. Students also saw that, like Monica, Kelly was reacting to the teacher: the teacher's comments had probably said (as did the class discussion) not to string quotations together, not to follow Rich's order too closely, not to rely too heavily on class notes. But, the class said, to be practical, this is what all students have to do — react to the teacher. Sometimes it's entrapping, like Monica's defensive resistance. Refusing to look for "hidden" meaning precluded all attempts to read strongly; Monica saw herself as having to choose between false polarities — "hidden" or "straightforward." At this point, someone said that maybe there is a difference between reacting and responding. This writer might have responded to the teacher's suggestions because they made sense to her, not because she had to. Maybe this writer could have a conversation with the teacher and learn something about how to revise. I asked for evidence.

Students said that, in this note, the writer directs the teacher to "look at," and "to see if . . ." This writer, unlike Monica, isn't asking to be "judged"; she is asking for continued dialogue about her revision. As such, I asked, "How are this student's assumptions about revision also tied to her assumptions about teachers and students?" She seems, in her tone, in her directions, and even in her defense of certain inclusions, to position herself to speak, to listen, and to respond.

I asked, "How does this relate to a willingness to consider complexity?" Monica's portrait of teacher/student is black and white, whereas Kelly seems to be able to imagine a gray area (they have, after all, read Freire) where students are teachers and teachers students, where dialogue, exchange, and response occur. Kelly can imagine and begin to compose a different relationship of student and teacher and therefore of student, teacher, text, and revision. The writer of this note, students said, could see revision as an opportunity for dialogue rather than as a punishment; this opened up possibilities to see, hear, and know more about and *through* her own text by revising it. She had hope of coming to know, in revision, more than she knew she knew.

From Kelly, I had received a paper that looked and sounded different. While she still opens with her idea of "transcendence," she also tries to connect that, in the first paragraph, to what it might mean to "rename" and "revise." She seems to begin where she had had to end in her draft; thus she is able to use her initial work as a reader to find a place to start. The ideas of transcendence, renaming, and revising allow her to work with Rich, to connect and examine what she has noticed in the essay. Rather than generalizing and concluding, she sets herself up to move from the general to the specific, with a reading of "Planetarium" and back toward "Aunt Jennifer's Tigers." In rethinking her own structure and rereading Rich, the easy "happy ending" disappears. Kelly attempts to show rather than tell her own connections in her revision. She moves from her reading of the poems to an attempt to define "renaming" as a form of transcendence that she connects to Rich's imagery of Caroline Herschel. This paper is getting somewhere in a way that Monica's cannot.

In her revision, Kelly has worked Freire and Rich hard enough to be able to use them as a filter through which she reads herself. At the end of her paper, Kelly writes,

> Rich finds new meaning for her life by examining her
> old work and ways of thinking and thus Rich creates a new
> work, her essay, in which she shows a Freire-like transfor-
> mation. She defines through her own self-examination, a
> method for anyone to find their own meaning, independent of
> meanings that others expect them to follow.
>
> Rich enters old texts and old ways of thinking and by
> questioning these she has a dialogue with herself and her
> work. Through "acts of cognition"--questioning, challeng-
> ing, thinking of alternatives--she renames her experience
> in her own terms.
>
> Rich's revision of herself from not knowing her own
> oppression to at least trying to know says to me that I

```
might do the same thing. Like Rich, I might find meanings
by looking back and redefining myself and my experience in
new terms.
```

In some ways, Kelly's move echoes Rich's authorial one and grows out of the class discussion and assignment on "structure." Kelly sees herself attempting the work that Rich defines, "enter[ing] an old text from a new critical direction." Kelly works from within what she knows to revise it into a new way of thinking and defining herself as a student/writer. While Rich works at reforming poetry and patriarchy, some of my students, through Rich, work at renaming reading as experience and process.

o–o–o–o–o–o–o–o–o–o–o–o–o–o–o–o–o–o–o

"PLEASE MAKE YOUR PAPER MORE INTERESTING": WAYS OF READING THE PAPERS IN THE MIDDLE[1]

by Ann Dean

My classroom practice in my first semester as a composition teacher was based on looking for moments of confusion, discord, and rupture in student papers. These moments are often signals that point toward the particular difficulty a student writer is having, as well as toward the better paper that revision might produce. As a class, my students and I practiced finding places where a paper was confusing or where it seemed that the writer had more to say than was on the page. Then we worked on rewriting, laying out some of the ideas that were tangled in the moment of discord.

With some students, I found this strategy of moments of discord to be effective. Students who had a great deal of difficulty writing were able to see their sentences as another reader might see them. Very able students were able to engage with the complexity of the readings and identify and write about contradictions in their own thinking. But this strategy was not helpful for a group of students whose work fell somewhere between these two extremes. This middle group wrote clear, correct sentences and neat, organized, bland essays. These essays did not have any moments of discord or confusion. As a reader, I found them uninteresting. As a teacher, I found them opaque. I had no method, no critical terms, no way of reading that could help me make sense of these papers.

Christian's sixth essay is an example of this "middle" kind of writing. The assignment asked him to consider a series of questions that the narrator asks himself about writing in John Edgar Wideman's "Our Time." His paper included this paragraph:

> Wideman describes his writing as a tool for himself to
> use as a means of escaping from the problems of the day.
> "Wasn't there something fundamental in my writing, in my
> capacity to function, that depended on flight, on escape?"
> (667). He uses his writing to get away from anything that
> may be bothering him. He does not have to fear anything
> that is going on around him. This is another trait that
> Wideman has acquired from growing up with his mother.
> Wideman's mother never allowed herself to be fearful of
> anyone or anything.

The syntax and grammar in this passage are almost error free, if not impressively elegant. Christian shows that he can integrate a quote from the reading into his own writing and

[1]This essay refers to previous editions of *Ways of Reading*.

231

that he can write grammatically correct sentences. There is nothing obviously wrong with the paragraph, and yet it is somehow not what I wanted at all. It is, as I thought to myself when I first read it, flat, boring, superficial, too controlled. I was surprised by this because it differed from Christian's contributions to class discussion, which were always much more thoughtful and complex.

As I continued to work with writing of this kind, I found that there are things to notice in it, ways to approach it, and places to intervene in it. In order to intervene, I have to concentrate not on what the writing is like but on what the essay does. What work has the student done? Are there any patterns of word use or sentence construction? How does she treat quotations? What is the argument and where did she put it? These questions provide the beginnings of a language so that I can describe the essays to myself and then to my students. And once I have described a student's essay to her I am able to suggest new kinds of work she might try, particular tasks in the revision process.

For Christian's paragraph above, this approach provides a way of reading and a language for talking about revision. Looking at the patterns of word use and sentence construction, it becomes obvious that Christian's writing is vague. Wideman escapes from "the problems of the day," "anything that may be bothering him," and "anything that is going on around him." This is a pattern in the paper. Christian writes in his concluding paragraph that Wideman "wants to be able to extend the benefit of the doubt to his brother and not allow himself to draw *certain conclusions* about him" [emphasis mine]. My first response to this sentence is to ask "what were those conclusions?" But it is more helpful to me, and would be more helpful to Christian as he revised, to recognize that this phrase is part of a pattern in the paper. Then the conversation I have with Christian would be about his writing, rather than about my question. He would rewrite in response to a sense of what his paper is about, rather than in response to an objection of mine.

It is also helpful to notice Christian's treatment of quotations. His paraphrases generalize and simplify the quotations he uses, as when he quotes Wideman asking himself this question: "And even if I did learn to listen, wouldn't there be a point at which I'd have to take over the telling?" Christian paraphrases it this way: "Wideman becomes the narrator after he listens to the facts that are given to him by his brother. Once his brother tells him what he has to, Wideman then writes down what he feels important on paper." This paraphrase turns a question into a statement and then uses that statement as a piece of advice. The same thing happens in the passage quoted above, where Wideman's questions ("Wasn't there something fundamental in my writing . . . that depended on flight?") become answers, descriptions of the right way to do things, for Christian.

Christian uses quotations, in other words, as moral maxims or summaries. This, too, is a pattern in the paper. He quotes Wideman's description of his mother's attitude, which can be read as a maxim: "You gave people the benefit of the doubt. You attempted to remove your ego, acknowledge the limitations of your individual view of things" (660). But he does not use a quote when he is attempting to characterize Wideman's writing. He claims that "this is what Wideman brings to his writing. He tries to hear what his brother has to say before he writes or says anything that is his own opinion." Then, rather than using quotations to give the reader an idea of what writing is like when a writer brings these ideas to it, Christian changes the subject and goes on to discuss a different essay.

Unfortunately, these aspects of Christian's work were not apparent to me when I first read the essay. This is because I responded to it and other "middle" writing in aesthetic terms, rather than in terms of its content and argument. I only knew that the writing did not have the kind of feel that I enjoy in good academic writing and try to achieve in my own. Rather than expecting the writing to do certain things, such as read quotations critically or question its own assumptions, I expected it to have a certain character: complex sentences, lumpy bits of detail, flashes of personality. This kind of character, of course, is difficult to achieve without the kind of careful thinking, close reading, and difficult questioning I was trying to teach my students to do. But by focusing my own reading on the character of the prose, rather than on the activities that form that character, I made it diffi-

:ult to describe to myself or to my students what this writing did and what I wanted it to
do differently.

One of my problems in reading this kind of writing was that nothing stuck out. So
when I tried to help the writer to revise or to think about strategies for her next paper, I
:ouldn't find a handle, a place to start. One solution to this problem is to look at the paper
as a whole, and ask what work it does. How does the student connect ideas? What provides structure for the paper? This approach provides a way to describe a paper such as
Rena's second assignment. In this paper, Rena refers to Stanley Fish's essay "How to Recognize a Poem When You See One," which appeared in the third edition of *Ways of Reading*.
Rena concluded with these two paragraphs:

> Fish discusses two basic ideas in his essay "How to
> Recognize a Poem When You See One." The first idea deals
> with the lists of words he used in his classroom experi-
> ment. His students used their *"poetry-seeing eyes"* to make a
> poem from the words. Fish remarks on this by writing *"It is
> not that the presence of poetic qualities compels a certain
> kind of attention results in the emergence of poetic quali-
> ties"* (143). We have been influenced by society to look
> beyond the face value to grasp a concept; just as Fish's
> students looked past the list of words as names of lin-
> guists and saw a religious poem. Mary Louise Pratt writes
> about a similar topic in her essay *"Arts of the Contact
> Zone"* when she explains how her son Sam looked past the
> face value of the baseball cards and learned many different
> things about people and society.
>
> Each individual must learn how to take what they learn
> or are exposed to and apply it to their own life. This, in
> turn, will make them into *"strong readers."*

Like the paragraph from Christian's paper, this passage seems firmly "in the middle."
It has no major errors, beyond the odd use of italics. It does many of the things the assignment asked for ("write an essay in which you work with Fish's idea of 'shared ways of
seeing' in order to explore the issue of reading as Bartholomae and Petrosky and Pratt
describe it"). It relates the three pieces of writing. It concludes. It quotes. But there is nothing particularly noticeable or striking about it. What can be said about it?

The first question to ask is what kind of work the writer has done. "Fish discusses two
basic ideas in his essay . . ." tells us what is *in* Fish's essay. It is a report on the reading.
Further on, Rena tells us that "Mary Louise Pratt writes about a similar topic in her essay."
Again, Rena reports on the topic. Rena uses the quotation to support these summaries,
introducing it with the phrase "Fish remarks on this [his 'basic idea'] by writing . . ." The
quotation serves to tell us what is in the essay. This is probably a more important thing to
notice about the quotation than the fact that Rena has left out several words of it. (The full
quotation should read "It is not that the presence of poetic qualities compels a certain kind
of attention but that the paying of a certain kind of attention results in the emergence of

poetic qualities.") Restoring those words would not involve doing a different kind of work or (necessarily) reconsidering the quotation or the act of quoting it.

Rena's word use also contributes to an understanding of the work she has done. The word "similar" is very important to this conclusion. It means that the cognitive task that this writing has done is a comparison. She has noticed something similar. This, along with the reporting on topics, is the source of the sense of simplicity I had when I first read the passage. Rena has made the assignment into an exercise in comparison and contrast. Looking through the rest of the paper, I can see that this is a pattern. The first sentence explains that

> the intent of this paper is to explain both the differences
> and similarities between Stanley Fish's "How to Recognize a
> Poem When You See One" and Mary Louise Pratt's "Arts of the
> Contact Zone." In order to fully understand these similari-
> ties, one must be familiar with the views that each author
> has, as well as with the concept of "strong reading."

Thus Rena introduces her project as a comparison that will be supported by reports on the content of various essays.

The paper is actually more interesting than Rena's description makes it sound — it contains a strange anecdote about her high school English class as well as a discussion of a question that came up in class: "Does Fish think that we are all robots?" But Rena structures the paper by linking one section to the next through words for similarity and difference. She introduces new ideas or topics with phrases like "I can relate to the example used by Fish due to an incident that occurred in my English class last year"; "This, in turn, brings about an example used in Mary Louise Pratt's essay . . ."; "This brings about a question that was addressed during class one day." The repeated use of "brings about" is unsatisfying because it does not say what the relationship is between the things being brought about. And Rena does not go beyond thinking that that relationship is some sort of similarity or difference. The work she has done, then, is comparing and contrasting.

When I first read Rena's essays, I did not know how to respond. I looked for polite variations on "Spend more time on your writing" and "Do you really think so?" Now that I have a way of describing them, however, I also have a way of responding. An understanding of this essay's structure and important terms allows me to talk with Rena about strategies for revision and about future papers.

In order to help Rena imagine doing other kinds of work, I would talk to her about the way she uses the term "face value" in this paragraph. She uses it to establish a similarity; both Fish and Pratt talk about reading as a question of whether or not you take things at face value. Rena uses this term, in other words, as a tool for making sense of the two essays, bringing them together and coming to a conclusion. She learned the term, as she explains in the paper, from her high school English class. The next assignment asked Rena to do a similar kind of work, but using a new term, "shared ways of seeing," instead of an old one. Talking about this new task in terms of the work she has already done would give Rena a place to start and something to try as she revises.

Unlike Rena and Christian, Matthew entered my class equipped with language for making arguments and using quotations. A transfer student with forensics experience, Matthew could explain claims, make distinctions, and fill pages comfortably. Like Rena and Christian, however, he wrote papers in which nothing seemed to be happening. This disjunction made me, as a reader, feel disoriented and lost and actually distracted me from the positive possibilities and suggestive moments in Matthew's writing.

For his second essay, Matthew was asked to reconsider his first essay in light of Walker Percy's "The Loss of the Creature." He begins with these two paragraphs:

> Reading Walker Percy's essay, "The Loss of the Crea-
> ture," has caused me to think of my experience with college
> roommates in a slightly different manner. I believe that he
> would have much to say about my experience. Viewing my
> experience in Percy's eyes has revealed quite an abundant
> amount of information and insight.
>
> Percy would probably have a field day with my first
> paper entitled, "Discovering Roommates." In that paper, I
> discussed what living with friends from high school was
> like in college and the changes that I noticed in these
> friends. Percy would take statements such as "My roommates
> began acting differently than they had previously" and
> psychoanalyze my roommates and me. I believe that Percy
> would readily incorporate my paper into his next essay and
> use it as one of his many examples.

Matthew leans heavily on adverbs and other modifiers. They make his sentences sound more complicated than those of many freshman writers: "Percy would readily incorporate my paper into his next essay." They also give the impression that careful distinctions are being made: "caused me to think . . . in a slightly different manner," "quite an abundant amount of information." Pointing this out, however, might not be the most helpful response for Matthew. The problem with this paragraph is not the modifiers, but the argument. We are told that Percy "would have much to say," but not what that would be. There would be "quite an abundant amount of information and insight," but we are not given any of that information or insight. Percy could use Matthew's paper as an example, but we are not told what it would be an example of. The only claim Matthew makes is that claims are possible.

Although I might not immediately point it out to Matthew, identifying his pattern of adverb use helps me, as a reader, to locate one aspect of my discomfort with the style and tone of Matthew's prose: the sense that he is trying to snow me, fake me out. Having done so, I can move my attention away from questions of style and toward more specific tasks I could give to Matthew as he revises and as he continues to write.

As it was, my general sense of disorientation when reading this prose prevented me from seeing places in the essay that did real work with Percy. Rereading now, I notice an interesting paragraph on page 3:

> After thinking of Percy's point of view, I now think
> that I had greatly preconceived notions of what living with
> friends would be like. This is something that I had not
> thought of previously. I also feel that I have gained much

> knowledge. I see my experience with my first roommates as a
>
> "discovery," and my college experience now as a "recovery."

This paragraph could be the introduction to an essay in which Matthew looked at his previous writing through the new framework suggested by Percy. That would be exactly the kind of work the assignment asked for. Matthew carries this idea of discovery and recovery through to the end of the paper. A useful comment would have pointed this out to him and suggested doing this kind of work from the beginning of his next paper.

Looking at Matthew's essay helps me to define another aspect of this kind of writing which made it unpleasant as well as mystifying to me. Each of these students assumes, to some degree, an air of confident mastery. As a teacher and reader, I am more attracted to a tone of naive doggedness. I think it is important to see this confident tone as a way of taking on the voice of the academic writer, a way of finding a place to stand in a scary and unfamiliar endeavor. But understanding the combinations and resonances of style in student essays is not as important as having aspects other than style to look for. If I can focus on what kinds of work students do in particular pieces of writing, and where and in what words, my own prejudices and identifications with respect to style will have less importance in my responses. I will be able to challenge my students with particular obstacles and particular tasks. And I will be able to show them that, rather than an infinite sea of undifferentiated possibilities, the realm outside of controlled, safe writing includes usable tools and recognizable landmarks.

The work that Matthew did in his next paper demonstrates one way that students can make use of the kinds of comments I am recommending. The assignment asked students to imagine Jane Tompkins using Walker Percy's essay for an academic project. We used Matthew's first draft as a sample paper for class discussion. It began with this paragraph:

> Jane Tompkins, in her essay "'Indians': Textualism,
>
> Morality, and the Problem of History," seems to have a
>
> natural attraction to relations and relationships. In this
>
> essay, she writes:

> > My story stands for the relationship most non-
> >
> > Indians have to the people who first populated this
> >
> > continent, a relationship characterized by narcis-
> >
> > sistic fantasies of freedom and adventure, of a life
> >
> > lived closer to nature and to spirit than the life
> >
> > we lead now. (619)

> This quote clearly displays her affinity for relationships
>
> and her interest in finding the origin or root cause of
>
> them. However, let us not assume that just any relation-
>
> ships fascinate her. The relations focused on in her essay
>
> center on people. Researching the relationship between the
>
> ocean and paper clips is something better left to Walker
>
> Percy. I have therefore decided to assign Tompkins the

```
project of researching the relationship between writers and

readers.
```

Matthew goes on to say that Tompkins will use Percy's essay to help her with this project.

What work has Matthew done in this passage and what words does he use to describe it? The paragraph is structured around several general words — "relationships," "people," "readers and writers" — which are linked together like a chain. The quote from Tompkins includes the word "relationship." The relationship is between people. People read and write, and so we will look at reading and writing. This strategy allows Matthew to create a structure, to make something out of nothing. The problem with the strategy is that it takes Matthew away from the specificity of Tompkins's essay. After all, there are many other good reasons for Tompkins to consider the relationship of readers and writers besides the fact that she is interested in people. Rather than considering these reasons or other specific issues raised by reading Tompkins, Matthew structures his paragraph around the "natural attractions" between certain words.

In discussing this draft with the class, I used one of the questions I ask myself about student papers. I asked them to look at how Matthew had used the quotation. What was it for? What purpose did it serve in the paragraph? Before they could answer we spent a good deal of time trying to figure out what the sentence he quotes from Tompkins actually says. The sentence's structure is quite complicated and the students had difficulty understanding which group had the "narcissistic fantasies of freedom and adventure." It also took some time to make sense of how a relationship can be characterized by fantasies.

Then I pointed out that the rest of Matthew's paragraph had not suffered from the fact that none of his readers could understand his quotation. Matthew's writing neither explains the quotation nor depends upon the reader's ability to explain it. In fact, like his argument in the paragraph as a whole, the quotation is linked to the rest of the paragraph by one word, "relationship." This is a pattern in the draft — Matthew's strategy is consistently to choose quotations because they contain a single word that he has been using. I suggested that he and his classmates think about reading the quotes as part of the activity of the paper, rather than something the reader is supposed to do on her own. Then the essay would pay attention to the quotes, rather than just attaching them to a structure that would be the same without them.

I also spoke to Matthew alone and suggested that he leave out the question of readers and writers and focus on Tompkins's original project. Again, I was attempting to propose an alternative structure for the work of the paper. Rather than the chain of linked words, the paper could be structured around a single problem and various possible solutions or approaches. In retrospect, I wish I had talked more with Matthew about different structures, rather than telling him what to do, because it would have provided him with a way of thinking about the arguments of future papers as well as this one.

When Matthew revised, he made two kinds of changes. He omitted some things — the references to readers and writers, some of the quotations that he had not paid attention to in the previous drafts. But he also wrote some new material in which he began to do a different kind of work. In the first paragraph, he left what he had written intact but added an explanation of the quote. He followed the explanation with the claim that

```
I feel that Tompkins wants to look to the past to better

explain the relationships of today. I have therefore de-

cided to assign Tompkins the project of using the writing

of Walker Percy to better explain relations between Europe-

ans and Indians described in her essay.
```

In the previous draft the argument was built out of a series of associative links and stood apart from Tompkins. Here, the argument comes out of the quote and out of Matthew's sense of what work Tompkins's project is and why she took it on. In other words, the work Matthew is doing here is the kind of work the assignment asks for: thinking about what Tompkins is like as a reader and a thinker and why she might do one thing rather than another.

Revising his idea of the work that the essay could do also helped Matthew with the rest of the essay. For his first draft, Matthew had written a promising paragraph in which he claimed,

> I believe Tompkins would readily find a link between
> Percy's idea of the "loss of sovereignty" and her own idea
> of "perspectivism." This link is that when people are
> locked into their own time period and suffer from the
> points of view of their era, they tend to lose full control
> over their own thought process. Therefore, they lose their
> sovereignty and suffer from perspectivism at the same time.

Having made this link, Matthew could have done a variety of different kinds of work with it. In the first draft, the conclusion becomes a statement of truth. He applies it to his generalized "readers and writers":

> The effect on relations between readers and writers here is
> that the influence goes only one way . . . the reader is
> powerless to influence the writer, yet the writer can
> influence readers in much later periods.

Because Matthew does not write about any particular readers or writers (Percy or Tompkins, for example) this move further separates him from his readings and from any work that he might do with them. Through this strategy, in other words, he finds answers but no further work to do.

In the next draft Matthew continued to work with the two terms and to worry about what it would mean to make the link he had made. Instead of writing about unnamed readers and writers, he speculated that

> this [perspectivism and the loss of sovereignty] would help
> to explain European-Indian relations by helping to under-
> stand exactly why the people in the colonial period had the
> points of view or perspectives that they did. This is
> almost like making an excuse for the Europeans of the
> colonial era. Of course, others would argue that the Euro-
> peans never had sovereignty and therefore could not lose
> it. In any case, that would be something for Tompkins to
> decide, and I believe that she would argue back and forth
> and probably not come to a decent conclusion about it.

As in his previous paper, Matthew deals with difficulty by claiming that an argument could be made rather than by making it. But this passage has gone a step beyond the place in his essay on Percy where he claimed that "Percy would have much to say." This time he is undecided about a particular question. And before falling back on saying "she would argue back and forth," he argues back and forth himself for a few sentences. He considers the issues raised by Tompkins's essay and uses her essay to raise problems for Percy's. When he says, "Of course, some people might say that . . . ," he is bringing up problems, running into difficulties, making it interesting.

This new draft is not the perfect essay. But the important thing is that this time Matthew's writing suggests further revisions. This passage is a moment when things become difficult, a place where disagreement is possible. It is now an essay that invites response.

The worst moments for me as a beginning composition teacher all involved papers that left me speechless, papers to which I had no response at all. Developing a list of things to pay attention to in such writing has helped me to make sense of it for myself and to talk about it with my students. I have learned to respond to papers that do not invite response. Rather than giving the desperate order, "Please make your paper more interesting," I can have conversations about this writing that can lead to revision and further writing.

"LA CONCIENCIA DE LA MESTIZA": [1]
CULTURAL IDENTITY AND THE POLITICS
OF PERSONAL WRITING [2]

by Bianca Falbo

When I decided to put the excerpts from Anzaldúa's *Borderlands* on the syllabus for my General Writing Women's Studies class, I was worried about two things. One was the difficulty of having students work with the essay itself — not only the shifting languages (since I was fairly sure students could understand how this is inherent to the point Anzaldúa is making about the politics of negotiating cultural identity), but in addition I was uncomfortable with the implications of my asking students to imagine themselves as something other than unified subjects. To the extent that such an idea could be empowering, I knew it could also seem threatening. Consequently, I was worried about how I'd know whether I was challenging students' assumptions or simply alienating them.

The second thing that worried me came from my own resistance to assignments that ask for "personal" writing. In my experience as a teacher, I've come to realize that the "personal" is not readily available to students, that their "own experience" is not simply there for them to write about, that, in fact, it's difficult for students to write interestingly and purposefully about their own lives. This is not to say that their lives are uninteresting, but that the dominant paradigms for writing about a life — the ones students tend to come to college knowing how to produce or, at least, imagine they need to reproduce — do not generate the kind of "academic" writing I imagine as part of the project of General Writing, the kind of writing that they will be expected to do in the university courses they go on to take, writing that engages with, appropriates, and extends someone else's critical project.

This is an essay about how the experience of working with my students on Anzaldúa's text challenged my ideas both about what I imagined my students' experiences to be and about the place of and possibilities for personal writing in an academic classroom. I'll look first at the writing my students produced in response to the assignment, and then at their comments later on in the course about what it was like to work with Anzaldúa's text. For my part, I hope readers will find the glimpse into someone else's classroom practices (as well as anxieties, mistakes, and oversights) useful.

. . . .

Let me begin, though, by giving you some background about the work that preceded our work with Anzaldúa. In the spring of 1994, I had put together a sequence of *Ways of Reading* essays that included the selections from Jacobs's "Incidents in the Life of a Slave

---

[1] My title is taken from a *Borderlands* chapter ("*La conciencia de la mestiza*/Towards a New Consciousness") that appeared in the third edition of *Ways of Reading*. In this chapter, Anzaldúa imagines the development of a new kind of consciousness — one that permits, among other things, a tolerance for ambiguity, the juggling of cultures, the breaking down of paradigms.

[2] A version of this article was presented as part of a panel on the uses of personal writing in the classroom at the Tri-State Teaching Women's Studies Conference, Indiana University of Pennsylvania, March 11, 1995.

Girl," the chapters from Limerick's *Legacy of Conquest*,[3] the Anzaldúa chapters, and Rich's "When We Dead Awaken." The point of the reading and writing assignments was to think about the problems of writing from a position outside the dominant culture or some traditional paradigm (i.e., Jacobs writing as a slave, Limerick as a revisionist historian, Anzaldúa writing out of or toward a *"mestiza"* consciousness, Rich as a woman poet writing into a tradition defined by men). The Anzaldúa essay assignment (the first of the "Assignments for Writing") was third in the sequence, and we hit it about midway through the term — just after midterm grades — so many of my students were feeling anxious and worrying about improving their grades in the second half of the course. And then I was feeling anxious myself not only because of my ambivalence toward personal writing, but also because this would be the first time I'd worked with Anzaldúa's text.

In preparation for this assignment — and, to be honest, because I was concerned that students would lose patience with the text because it looked difficult — I asked them to come to class prepared to talk about the third of the "Questions for a Second Reading":

> Although Anzaldúa's text is not a conventional one, it makes an argument and proposes terms and examples for its readers to negotiate. How might you summarize Anzaldúa's argument in these three chapters? How do the individual chapters mark stages or parts of her argument? How might you explain the connections between the chapters? As you reread this selection, mark those passages where Anzaldúa seems to you to be creating a case or argument. What are its key terms? its key examples? What are its conclusions? (p. 46)

I split the class into groups to discuss the responses they had prepared and asked them to decide, as a group, on two or three exemplary passages from the text where, as the assignment proposes, Anzaldúa seems to be "creating a case or argument." It was my hope that this kind of close, specific work on the text would help students think about how to construct their own "mixed" narratives.

From the discussion that followed once the individual groups reconvened as a class, it seemed as though students weren't necessarily having any more difficulty articulating a first response to Anzaldúa than they had with any of the other essays we'd read up to that point in the term. In fact, students seemed to be looking forward to writing about themselves and when, during the last ten minutes of class, we turned to discuss the essay assignment, they had a lot of questions about what they were being asked to do and on what terms. (This is a situation I always take as a sign that students are thinking seriously about their work.) I directed their attention to the last paragraph of the assignment since it offered them a way to begin thinking about the project:

> To prepare for this essay, think about the different positions you could be said to occupy, the different voices that are part of your background or present, the competing ways of thinking that make up your points of view. (p. 46)

In response to my reading this passage aloud, one student raised her hand and said she didn't understand the part about occupying different positions. What did that mean? Another student — Jenna, a junior taking the class for her women's studies certificate, whose familiarity with the discourse of feminist theory often intimidated other students in the class — preempted my response and said emphatically, gesturing with her arms, "FIRST of all, you're a woman! A WOMAN! Don't you see?" The first student, Cheryl, looked puzzled and remained silent.

It was a particularly uncomfortable moment — exactly the situation I wanted to avoid. If, on one hand, students needed to consider the different positions they saw themselves occupying, on the other hand, I didn't want them to feel pressured, by me or their classmates, to see themselves through one lens more so than another. If a student didn't see herself positioned in terms of her gender, I didn't want her to feel her success in the course depended on doing so. The point of the assignment was for students to use their writing to

---

[3]These chapters appeared in previous editions of *Ways of Reading*.

explore and examine the complicated nature of their cultural identity — not fit themselves into prescribed slots and preordained oppressions.

Because Jenna's perceived "expertise" often gave her comments in class discussion a certain authority, I realized it was important for me to step in here, and so I did what I knew how to do — I turned the question back out to the class. "What would it mean to say that being a woman is occupying a particular cultural position?" I asked. In spite of the fact that we had just talked about Anzaldúa's essay in similar terms, students had little to say about this when pushed to examine their own lives.

"I'm not sure if this is what you're looking for, but are you saying you want us to write about what it means to be a woman?" someone asked.

I tried to explain that the richness of Anzaldúa's writing came from her examination of the ways in which the *different* positions she occupied inflected and contradicted one another. But then I've been teaching long enough to know that talking at students — summarizing, condensing, clarifying — is infinitely less successful than having students struggle with the text (assignment, question, problem) themselves. I also know that no matter how much an assignment is discussed ahead of time, the moment of truth comes when students sit down and put pen to paper (or more likely fingers to keyboard), but I was feeling pressed for time since our class was nearly over and so I tried to fashion some nugget they could take away with them. Using my own experience as an example, I explained how I could imagine writing an essay about the conflicts among my identities as a woman and as an academic, as well as someone who is the product of a middle-class, Italian American, Roman Catholic family.

Not surprisingly, class ended on a disappointing note: students were frustrated because they didn't have a handle on what I *wanted* (through my attempts to pare down the assignment, I'd come to be identified with its expectations) and I went home fairly sure that yet another personal essay assignment was doomed to failure.

．．．．．．．．．．

As it turned out for most students, though, the writing they produced in response to Anzaldúa proved to be the most interesting and complicated work they did all semester. The set of first drafts I received was both surprising and troubling — surprising for the variety of ways they'd found to make Anzaldúa's project meaningful to them, but troubling for what was revealed about my students' experiences of prejudice and alienation. And so I had to think carefully about how I wanted to respond.

Here are two first drafts with my comments. In my opinion, they are good working papers because of the ways the writing appropriates and extends the kinds of gestures Anzaldúa makes. In addition, they're typical of the ways my students were working to figure out what it would mean to construct a nonlinear, nonstraightforward narrative. As you read through them, you'll notice that my comments focus primarily on these aspects of the writing. In addition, I try to call attention to the moves they're making as writers trying to read their own experience.

Jakrita S. Sherman
March 18, 1994

"I'll Fly Away"

Thus saith the Lord, the heaven is my

✓ throne (thrown) and the Earth is my footstool:

Where is the house that ye build unto me?

And where is my place of rest?

– Isaiah

Black: 1. adj. without light, or not able to reflect it ||
colorless or so dark as to appear colorless || the opposite
of white || lowering, black clouds || not hopeful, *the
prospects look black* || (rhet.) sad, *a black day for our
team* || angry, sullen or disapproving, *a black look* || very
dirty || (rhet.) wicked, *black villainy* || evil, *black magic*
|| dark skinned, belonging to a race with dark pigmentation
|| reflecting discredit, *a black mark* || illegal, *black
market* || inveterate, a black Republican, a black liar ||
(Br.) not to be handled or worked in by trade unionist
while other trade unionists are on strike || (of the mem-
bers of a religious order) wearing a black habit || of or
concerning black or blacks 2. n. a black pigment, fabric
etc. || dirt, soot || (board game) the dark-colored men or
pieces or the player having these || a person whose natural
skin color is black 3. v.t. to make black || to polish
with blacking || v.i. to become black, blacken to black out
to darken, cause to give out or receive light || (esp. of
pilots of planes pulling out of a dive or very sharp turn)
to lose consciousness or memory usually temporarily
(*BLACKOUT)

White: 1. adj. of the color sensation stimulates by a
combination of all the wavelengths of visible light, or
resulting from combinations of certain pairs of wave-
lengths, being the color of e.g. milk || (of hair) gray or
silver || (of hair) very blond || (of wines) very pale
yellow || free from sin, pure || pale, white with terror ||
of or relating to the Caucasian division of mankind ||
covered with snow || blank, not printed upon, leave the
rest of the page white || (of silver and other metals)
unburnished || (of the members of a religious order) wear-
ing white to bleed (someone) white to get money from (someone) until there is no more to be had 2. n. a white
pigment, fabric etc. || a member of the Caucasian division

of mankind || the white part of the eye surrounding the
cornea || any of various breeds or species of white hog,
white horse, white butterfly etc. || (printing) a blank
space between words or lines || (archery) the outermost
ring of a target || (archery) that shot that hits this ring
|| (board games) the light-colored man or pieces, or the
player having these || (pl., pop.) leakoiihea

An effective   – New Webster's Dictionary and Thesaurus
beginning   of the English Language, copyright <u>1992</u>

Ode to a Genius

    The history of man begins at a place of uncertainty.
✓ No one really knows how ~~[it,]~~ life/ was ~~[all]~~ started or where
it all began. We are born by the fertilization of an egg
and we die because of a physical shutdown of the systems of
the body, but when did this cycle first originate and when
will it end? <u>Some</u> people believe that an all-powerful,
all-knowing entity created man and the universe by the
motion of a thought. Others believe that a scientific
phenomenon marked our creation. I agree with <u>Some</u>.

    Man and his home came from the mind of the ultimate
genius. *God* created the idea of man and produced a proto-
type in which he housed a program of regeneration of the
being in different forms. He set these forms on a platform
called Earth and surrounded it with other creatures and
other worlds. I have believed in <u>*God*</u> for most of my life,
doubting him only on occasions of emotional distress. I
was born to believe in him.

<u>History can only be written by the survivors.</u>

    God has been a comfort to <u>black</u> Americans for hundreds of
years. As a people we were severed from our original
beliefs, culture, speech, heritage, and homes. When some
<u>blacks</u> accepted *God* in the terms dictated to them by

Europeans they discovered a means of survival. They took

✓ the reality of _God_ and made it their own by seeing ~~their-~~ *themselves*

~~selves~~ as not the property of their white captors but as

children of _God_. However, there were black people who after

conforming to Euro-American thought became even more self-

hating because they started to believe that _God_ hated them

or even, in some cases, that the *devil* made them while

✓ whites were made by _God_. As time passes ~~both feelings~~ both   *Why*
not —
✓ feelings continue to flourish, but the ~~later~~ *latter* is well dis-   *what are*
you
guised. Now it is not easy for everyone to recognize the   *getting*
at?
self-hate within blacks as being an attribute to the past.

In my American history class in high school I was told

about white people and their heroes, conquerors; their

fight for freedom from British rule, their inventions,

their innovations, philosophers, scientists, doctors,

builders, fighters, etc. I also heard about a few popular

black people, Martin Luther King, Nat Turner, Harriet

Tubman, and Thurgood Marshall. I would estimate that such

issues as Slavery and The Civil Rights Movement were covered

in only three of the thirty-six weeks spent in school. I

learned about Malcolm X and Marcus Garvey through a black

history program I was in that consisted of about ten other

black students. My high school was thirty percent black.

but? (Is this misquoted?)
The eyes see not thyself ~~for~~ in reflection.

There have been studies done on the mentality of black

children and how they view themselves. Many black girls

when given a choice to play with either white or black

what do
you base dolls would choose the white dolls. When my mother was a
this?
child there were no black dolls made available to her, so

she, like most poor black girls, would make dolls out of

tall weeds, grass, and string.

There is a product that many black American women use

on their hair, to make it straight, called *Relaxer.* As a

245

young lady, if you are fortunate, you can get your hair straightened by *relaxer* so that your hair can be manageable. I got my first *relaxer* or *permanent* in the third or fourth grade. I remember fondly how my hair was before this incident. It was dark and thick and it hung down my back. There was a boy that liked me and he used to pull my hair. My sister would fix my hair in pony tails or braids with colorful beads. After my *perm* clumps of my hair fell out because the beautician left the "white cream" on my hair for too long. It took a while for my hair to grow back and of course it will never be the same again. I get a *touch up* (the perms that you receive after your first one) almost every month now. My hair is addicted to the chemicals in the *relaxer*. If I do not get a *touch up* my hair will break off and become too unmanageable. I wonder how my black female ancestors dealt with their untamed hair. The only way that I can return my hair back to its natural state is to shave it all off and start over. I do not yet have the inner courage it would take to do that. We, black girls, are taught that in order to be considered somewhat beauti-

✓ ful your hair has to be nice and straight. ¶Sometimes it is hard to see myself as beautiful. My dark skin, big lips,

✓ protruding mouth, large feet, and other "black features" have not been pronounced to me as "naturally beautiful." I *have been*
~~was~~ taught [through example¹, history², tradition³, and
⁴
unspoken criticism] that my looks are inferior to that of
[1, 2, 3, 4]
white women. It takes a conscious effort on my part to ignore this deceit that has been embedded in my psyche since birth.

By whom, what context? In what ways/forms has this been presented to you as the norm?

In what ways does that effort manifest itself?

A child cannot be dangerous.

In my home *God* was a given and it was an automatic rule that we were to believe in him. It was inconceivable or intolerable for anyone not to. However, I did not grow up attending church. I do not know whether it was because my mother did not have time to take me, for she worked two jobs and had an illness that kept her preoccupied, or because she did not have faith in the "institution of churches." My mother stressed education through schools and the strengthening of the mind so that one day you can

What precedes this? be very successful. <u>Success</u>, <u>by her definition</u>, means having an excellent career that affords you the privilege of obtaining certain luxuries, once unattainable by <u>blacks</u>.

This definition is a reasonable one and it is definitely a welcome substitution for the all-too-common scenario of <u>blacks</u> doing the hard and dirty work while receiving no benefits. It is also better than the gang-bangin, <u>black</u>-on-<u>black</u>, self-destructive behavior that many of our <u>black</u> youth are participating in these days. In my opinion, though, success as my mother defines it is not the

Is your proposal related to A.'s proposal for a "mestiza" consciousness? Look back at what she is — can u use her here? Does she give you a way of extending our argument about education here? solution. We as <u>black</u> people <u>need to find our way back</u> to our natural state. We need to start over from the beginning <u>through our children</u> by instituting in them the things that were denied to us by history. Those things are: <u>self-respect, dignity, self-worth, self-love, pride, peace, inner happiness, unity, truth, knowledge, power, freedom,</u> etc. We need to give our children the vision to see themselves clearly through their own perceptions and not those of others, <u>white</u> or <u>black</u>. The more fortunate children, white children, need to be <u>taught</u> as well, but we cannot *Taught what?* wait for the <u>"individuals in power"</u> to change. To do that is to say that they are in control of our futures and only God occupies this position.

<u>I'm going to heaven and I'll take my bear with me!</u>

When I was eight or nine years old I went Christmas shopping with my mother at Macy's Department store. We were in the toy department when I saw this shelf full of stuffed animals. I went to reach for one when I looked up and saw <u>Herbert</u>, a medium-sized brown teddy bear with big <u>black</u> eyes, who at the time looked huge. I pulled him down and started hugging him. I begged my mother to buy him, but she said that she did not have enough money. Herbert cost nearly a hundred dollars.

✓   At this time my family and I were living in a place called La~~s~~ke Lucerne, which sounds like a nice place to live, but it was just the opposite. Lake Lucerne is a deteriorating housing complex in <u>Miami</u> with only <u>one way in and the</u> *Effective* <u>same way out, which was convenient for the local police</u> *put* <u>because it made it easier to catch the drug dealers or</u> <u>other such unsavory characters that lived there.</u> There were many nights when my family and I would be woken up by the sound of gunfire. My mother would always make us sit in her closet in her bedroom. She had a huge walk-in closet that made a perfect hiding place.

After my sisters and I finished opening our presents that Christmas morning, my mother told me to go into her room and get something out of her closet. I walked into my mother's room with my head down low and my eyes drooping because I was sad that I had not gotten <u>Herbert</u> for Christmas, but I walked out of the room screaming with my eyes bulging out of my head squeezing <u>Herbert</u> tight in my arms. I named my bear <u>Herbert</u> after Herbie Hancock, who was one of my older sister's favorite musicians at the time. <u>Herbert</u> has been with me ever since. He has been the one constant in my life that I never had a genuine fear of losing. I could take him everywhere with me if I wanted. He will never die, like my grandmother, or he will never get so sick that I am afraid that he is going to die, like my mother, and he will never abandon me, like my father. Till this day, that moment when I saw <u>Herbert</u> sitting on my mother's closet floor was one of the happiest moments of my life.

The day will come when my happiness will know me and I will know it.

Use quotation marks to clarify "The day will come when my happiness will know me and I will know it" is a phrase that I wrote some time ago when I was feeling optimistic about my status in this world that we exist in. I have a tendency to vacillate between stability and instability as far as the level of tolerance of the intolerable I have. I remember one time in the tenth or eleventh grade a boy in my French class (who was, by the way, extremely attractive) came up to me and said, in a rather serious tone of voice, "You are too serious for your own good." There are lots of times that I wish that my

These seem very different but your sentence structure denies that.

mind was filled with shallow and immature thoughts, or at least with a profound dedication towards accuracy, good grades, and success, instead of the worries and emotional burdens of everything. Life is a bad dream that one person is having. I wish that person would wake up -- I wrote that saying in high school during one of my down spells. However, despite my history, the parts that came before and after my birth, and my present, which is filled with fear and hope ("Where there is fear there is hope"), I know that I am going to be okay, that everything is going to be okay in the end.

This seems a less interesting ending gesture than your argument about education two sections earlier.

To the man with no future,

To the man with no future I bid you peace for I have somewhere to go and people are waiting for me there.

—me

21 March

Jakrita —

This is thoughtful and interesting writing — nice going. I've made more specific comments in the margins and you should come talk to me if you have questions/comments.

If you choose to work further on this, consider developing in particular your argument about education (see comments in the last section).

Thanks for your work.

Bianca

Christine Schrodi

Assignment #3

3/18/94

SELF-UNDERSTANDING

Solo figure on crowded ground
Her stubborn chin held high,
Asking nothing, receiving nothing
Defiance in her eye.[1]

I guess one could say that I grew up in the average middle-class neighborhood. It was tucked away in a nice suburban area surrounded by beautiful farm land -- fifteen minutes from the city yet a world away. It appeared that I had all the advantages with a supportive and loving family and an education from a good school. From the outside everything looked comfortable and safe . . . simple. But, even with all the advantages, there were and still are hurdles I have to overcome, situations that need to be understood, and experiences that need to be lived. I can't seem to go through these things unscathed. I always find some internal conflict.

Delicate child who's seen too much
Who's learned to hurt too soon,
Letting loose, a wild dance

250

Here beneath the moon.

She swings her head, her body moves

frustration drains away;

She can't forget the angry words

The things that people say.

I am an American citizen. Because of the fact that I
am Asian, I never really feel accounted for and accepted.

Once, while I was at work, a woman asked me if I
celebrated Easter in my country. Isn't America my country?
I am a citizen.

Her pounding feet refuse to stop;

A tear slides down her face;

She clings to her compassion as

Hatred tries to steal the place.

The more people alienate me from this country, my
home, the more I want to be accepted. The more I want to
be accepted, the more I hate myself. Why would I ever want
to be part of a country where I feel as though I am an
outsider to the dominant culture, the white culture? Some
even have the idea that I can't speak English. English is
my first and primary language. So I am Asian.

Whipping round, her back is arched

Her hands attack the sky;

She gives so much to others

No return, she wonders why.

There is a saying in Korea that it is not enough to be
born in Korea, but one has to be socialized as a Korean. I
was socialized as an American. So I am an American.

America says I am Asian. Gloria Anzaldúa says that "to be close to another Chicana is like looking into the mirror. We are afraid of what we'll see there. Pena. Shame" (43). I also feel shame when I encounter other Asian people. At first, this was because I was ashamed of being Asian. Now, it is because I am not. I may look Asian, but I grew up in an Irish/German/Polish/white family. This is what was presented to me, and this is how I was raised.

G.A. is talking specifica[...] about feminist[...] no? Does that change your use [...] her here?

Learning about being Asian has been a learning process for me, it is not something that comes natural on a subconscious level of understanding. But just as African Americans feel pride in their culture and heritage, so do I as an Asian American.

Can you elaborate? How are you defining "white culture?" or "Irish/ German/ Polish"?

Can you say some[...] thing abo[...] the ways [...] which this [...] manifest[...] itself?

> Beating heart pumping blood;
> One thousand eyes, they stare
> as silently her body leaps to slice the heavy air.

White culture has always dominated my life. It is my parents, a large percentage of my classmates, and most of my teachers. I still have not had an Asian teacher. Because of this situation, I feel as though I have assimilated into the white culture. But this is the same culture which excludes me. This is the culture which tells me I am Asian yet sometimes punishes me for it.

This is a nice laying out of the issue.

What wou[...] you expec[...] to learn from her?

> Landing light, she cannot breathe;
> She longed for just one chance,
> The moon retreats behind a cloud
> Let lonely dancer dance.

Am I proud to be Asian? Yes, because that is who I am. I finally realized that being Asian doesn't make me

n G.A.'s less American, it only adds one more dimension to my per-
ise of a son. It is to my advantage because I have more than one
"estiza" viewpoint. In a country like America, we have to realize
"scious-
ness? that not all white people are the devil, that black is

beautiful, and that not all Asians carry cameras. I'm just

You glad that my experiences have allowed me to do just that.
haven't
y shown Note
s — why
"ntion it 1. All poetry excerpts from "Lonely Dancer" by Jen
the end
here? Niemeyer.

Christine —   23 March

*This is interesting and thoughtful work — I really enjoyed reading it. I had thought
about xeroxing it for class but hesitated in the end because I figured your classmates
would know it was yours, and I wasn't sure how you'd feel about that since this is a
more "personal" essay than we have so far written.*

*I've made more specific comments in the margins and you should come talk to me
if you have any questions/comments. In general, I think your paper gets at the key
issues raised by Anzaldúa's text. If you would like to take this further, you should think
about working in sections — you have several powerful anecdotes/stories to offer here
and they might be more productively developed into individual sections. In addition —
while I like the way you weave Niemeyer's poem into your text — you might consider
other kinds of texts (cultural myths, e.g., or legends, traditions, or customs) on which
you could draw to represent your "mixed sensibility."*

Thanks for your work,

Bianca

Both Christine and Jakrita reproduce Anzaldúa's project in terms of issues of racial
identity. Although this is a somewhat reductive reading of Anzaldúa's project (she is concerned more broadly with cultural identity), it's clear from the ways in which the writers
are working to produce "mixed" texts that, like Anzaldúa, they are trying to imagine that
identity in terms of conflicting pressures. Jakrita's text is, perhaps, more self-consciously
mixed in its use of multiple cultural texts — the biblical epigraph, dictionary definitions,
stories of school experiences, bits from her diary. And then all of this is emphasized by her
use of bold and italic type and separately titled sections (both of which echo gestures
Anzaldúa makes).

Christine's story is intertwined with only one other text, but I think her use of that text
is striking for the way in which it can be read as a commentary on or frame for her own
story. See, for example, the way the lines "She can't forget the angry words / The things
that people say" introduce

Once, while I was at work, a woman asked me if I

celebrated Easter in my country. Isn't America my country?

[manual p. 254]

253

In addition, the repetition of "So I'm Asian" / "So I'm American" emphasizes the fact that she is simultaneously part of and alienated from two cultures.

To my mind, these are already strong papers even though they're only first drafts, because it's clear to me that they depend on the writers' careful observation of Anzaldúa's characteristic ways of working. In trying to figure out how I wanted to comment on these pieces, I decided that my responsibility would be to try to bring out the kinds of gestures —some more direct than others — students were already making toward putting their project into some kind of relationship to Anzaldúa's. This is usually a priority I have when commenting on student papers. For the Anzaldúa papers, it proved particularly useful because, in calling attention to the kinds of formal gestures students were making as readers and writers and in focusing on their writing as a rereading of Anzaldúa's text, I didn't put myself in the position of commenting on the (often) intensely personal material they were exploring in their writing

Because I wanted to focus my comments in this way, another thing I noticed about these two papers was the way they entertain the possibility of the kind of educational project Anzaldúa proposes in her section *"La conciencia de la mestiza* / Towards a New Consciousness" [which appeared in the third edition of *Ways of Reading*]. Anzaldúa puts it in these terms:

> Through our literature, art, *corridos*, and folktales we must share our history with [middle-class whites] so when they set up committees to help Big Mountain Navajos or the Chicano farmworkers or *los Nicaragüenses* they won't turn people away because of their racial fears and ignorances. They will come to see that they are not helping us but following our lead.

Jakrita proposes something like this in her essay:

```
We need to give our children the vision to see them-
selves clearly through their own perceptions and not those
of others, white or black.  The more fortunate children,
white children, need to be taught as well. . . . [manual
p. 250]
```

And Christine makes a similar kind of move in the last paragraph of her paper: "In a country like America, we have to realize that not all white people are the devil, that black is beautiful, and that not all Asians carry cameras" [manual p. 256]. On one hand, I couldn't be sure whether these imitative gestures were intentional — Christine's paper, in particular, only gives the whole idea a sentence or two. But on the other hand, I thought these places would bear further exploration, and so in my marginal comments I pushed each writer to define her project more specifically in relation to Anzaldúa's.

In my General Writing course, students can revise a paper as many times as they want. Although Christine and Jakrita both wrote two more drafts of their papers, most of the changes were local ones and very little was altered in terms of the original structure. In spite of my final comments to Christine, she chose neither to work in separate sections nor to incorporate different kinds of cultural texts. And neither Christine nor Jakrita did significant work toward thinking through the idea of the national education project alluded to in their first drafts.

In fact, like many of my students, Christine and Jakrita were not only invested in their Anzaldúa papers, they were adamant about their intentions. This isn't so unusual in writing courses when it comes to the issue of revision — although I try to represent it as an occasion (an invitation, even) to imagine their papers as works in progress, students tend to see the work of revision as more burden than opportunity. With the Anzaldúa papers, however, it was clear to me that something more was at stake. Although most students could imitate Anzaldúa's methods, there were some, like Christine and Jakrita, whose investment in composing their "own experience" in a way that seemed to break the rules for conventional narrative also prevented them from undertaking a substantive revision. This is the opposite response from that of the student who refuses to revise a personal essay because "that's the way it happened." Rather it seemed that because students already felt they were operating outside "the system," they had more license to resist my suggestions for revision.

Now I'd like to turn to Staci's essay, one where revisions turned out to be more substantial, because I think that paying attention to the ways in which it was revised — what was changed, struggled over, added, left out altogether — says something more about students' attempts to work with Anzaldúa than is perhaps visible in the previous papers. Staci's first draft is written entirely in the first person: although she acknowledges her conflicted identity, she doesn't use her writing to exploit that. The intentions behind my comments to Staci are the same as in the preceding essays by Christine and Jakrita, but I'm also more overtly concerned with questioning and disrupting the seamlessness of the writing.

Staci Wenitsky

Assignment #3

3/18/94

My Positions in Society and in Life

✓ What exactly is my role in society? A woman, a Jew, a
✓ student() they all apply, but what do they mean? While
having no control of how or ~~under~~ *under* the circumstances ~~in~~
which I was born, I have to use my individual characteristics to not only adapt to society but also to overcome its
hurdles.

✓ *positions?*
My position in society is one that can be stretched to   *Not sure*
how you
whatever situation may arise at that particular time. By   *mean this.*
being a woman I have had to work to extreme limits in order
for me to attain my goals. Problems such as racism and
prejudice have arisen which only occurred for the mere
reason that I am Jewish and I am a woman. Being a woman in
the United States has become easier throughout the years,
what?
but (it) should not be underestimated, and being a Jewish
what?
woman can in some instances make (it) that much harder.

✓ With the upsurge of the woma(ns) movement throughout the
seventies, women today in the United States are finally
working side by side with their male counterparts as
equals. Who would have ever thought twenty years ago that

✓ my mother would be a neurologist(.) Sometimes when people ask me what my parents do, they give me a funny look after I tell them that my mom is a neurologist and my dad is a teacher. It seems kind of funny that their gender roles have been switched according to our society. Twenty years ago a woman was certainly not expected to be a doctor -- her role was probably a teacher or else raising her children at home while her husband worked nine to five.

Do you ha a specific incident i mind? Wh would it mean to retell it a personal anecdote that you then ana- lyze in terms of how it has shaped/ informed your notio of cultural identity?

Being a woman in today's society has had both its advantages and disadvantages. Of course some attractive women may get a little farther in life, but it also can backfire. Throughout high school I have seen people I know being called stupid, ignorant terms such as jap and prin- cess. For what reason? For being a woman? For being a Jewish woman? I have had people look at me because I have worn a star upon my neck for the sole reason of being proud to be a strong Jewish woman.

Again does G.A. give you a way to relate a more specific e.g.? What would it mean to expand this ¶ into its own section?

My identity in society will change as time goes on, but my beliefs and intuitions as a woman I will have for a lifetime. I believe that as a woman I think and observe the world different than my male counterpart. *why may?* Some may call my ideals slanted or strange, but as a woman in Ameri- can society my convictions are important not only to my views of the world, but how I live them. My views as a woman are strong yet I am sometimes timid when sharing them with others.

What produces this belief? How can you tell? What moments in your life would you point to? Are there other kinds of texts that sup- port your claim here?

When I was thirteen years old I got to express my pride and knowledge of the Jewish faith at my Bat Mitzvah. It was on this day that I told to a large congregation of family and friends just how important being a Jewish woman was.

If this is important, why only a two- sentence ¶?

I recall just a few years ago a conversation that I had with my parents about marriage. I was told that marry-

ing within the Jewish heritage was very important to them.
My aunt had married a man who was not Jewish and it ended
in divorce. My mom told me that I must raise my children
Jewish or she would have nothing to do with them. My views
on Judaism are strong, but certainly not as strict. [I
think, because my parents were raised in times where segre-
, *prejudice, and racism were*
gation ~~was~~ still quite evident and people believed that
^
Jewish people had horns growing out of their heads, that
along
their views have not changed with the times. But if we are
^
discriminated against as Jews, and they know how it feels,
then why must they discriminate against other minority
groups? This is where I differ greatly with the views of
my family. My uncle married a Filipino woman and faced a
large amount of hostility from my grandparents and his
brothers and sisters. But why? Being Filipino is a minority group just as much as being a Jew is.]

t do you
mean?

[All in all, your race, ethnic background, gender, ~~and~~
little positions such as being a brother, sister, daughter,
father, etc., help to mold you into your own individual.
Each person perceives their role in society and even in
life in a different perspective than others may perceive
them. Everybody is equally as special and important in
their own way whether they are within the minority or the
majority.]

So, are
there other
positions
you've
chosen not
to consider
here?

21 March

Staci —

This is thoughtful and interesting work. You've begun to suggest in powerful ways how being a woman and being Jewish are neither easily reconciled nor wholly opposed. You have also gathered together a number of very interesting personal anecdotes. Now I'd like to see you turn your narrative into the kind of "mixed" text that Anzaldúa writes. What would it mean to reconceive what you have here into separate sections that, as hers do, mark stages or parts of a larger argument about cultural identity? What would it mean to construct your paper not as a straightforward narrative but rather as a "mosaic" or "montage"? What other kinds of texts (poems, e.g., cultural myths or stereotypes) could you draw on? What other languages and/or ways of seeing do you have at your disposal as a result of the different positions you see yourself occupying?

If you have comments/questions about anything I've said here or in the margins, I'll be happy to talk further with you.

Bianca

Like many of my students, Staci had a number of interesting stories to tell. Additionally, her essay is ambitious for the set of cultural histories it tries to link together with her own story: the rise of the women's movement, her parents' experience growing up Jewish in the mid-twentieth century. Consequently, I tried to use my comments to help her work with the interesting material she had already compiled — pushing her to use Anzaldúa as a model for reimagining the overall shape of her essay.

Here is her second draft:

Staci Wenitsky

Assignment #3

3/24/94

My Positions in Society and in Life

My parents decided when I was four years old and my sister was six years old to move our family to a suburb called Richboro.

"It is in our best interest to move," my mom told me.

"But why, Mommy? I'm going to miss all of my friends," I replied.

That didn't seem to matter. Our family picked up to relocate to a very large house as opposed to the so-called lower-class neighborhood that I had grown up in thus far in my life. There was a huge field behind my house leading to absolutely nothing. The block was empty instead of clustered as I was used to. I knew nobody. My sister and I played together, not knowing any of the other children in the neighborhood.

later?

Race and Religion. I ~~latter~~ was old enough ~~to be able~~ to understand the reason for the move. My parents wanted a good education for me and my sister. Both of my parents had never had the opportunity to go on to a higher schooling such as college and they wanted better for their children. The school system that I would have been raised in was the Philadelphia School District. When people think of Philadelphia they may think of the city of "Brotherly Love," but my parents believe Philly was more ~~of~~ *or* less ~~as~~ a city of crime. There were a lot of black people moving into my old neighborhood.

Prejudice: Negative or hostile attitudes toward, and beliefs about a group of people.

I never thought of my parents as racist, but rather they described their views as being cautious and looking out for "our best interest."

and how do you understand this?

While having no control of how or the circumstances under which I was born, I have to use my individual charac- teristics to not only adapt to society but also overcome its hurdles. I am a white Jewish woman. That is the obvious. I can't hide behind this, nor would I want to. I am proud to be what I am. Although I was born into these conditions I feel it is important to learn about what I am ethnically and to take pride in it.

beliefs?

Not sure what you mean.

Problems such as racism and prejudice have arisen in which only occurred for the mere reason that I am Jewish and I am a woman. With the upsurge of the women's movement throughout the seventies, women today in the United States are finally working side by side with their male counter- parts as equals. Twenty years ago most people would be surprised at the fact that my mother is a neurologist.

✓

Do you mean to underline this?

[Grade school.] Boys hated girls and vice versa. Chil- dren were selfish and spoiled. It was my first day being a "big shot" third grader. We had to get to know our class- mates and I was paired with a boy. The question he asked me was what my parents did. When I replied that my mom was

a neurologist he laughed at me and made fun of me. I know
that it seems kind of funny that their gender roles have
been switched according to our society, and I guess that is
why the boy laughed at me. Twenty years ago a woman was
certainly not expected to be a doctor -- her role was
probably a teacher or else raising her children at home
while her husband worked nine to five.

<u>Anti-Semitism:</u> prejudice and discrimination against

Watch pronoun agreement Jews. This is something that I believe (every) Jew has faced at some point in (their) life. I was lucky to be raised in an area populated heavily with Jewish people.

"Oh, you live in Little Israel," my friend Meredith
replied to me as I gave her directions to my house.

for

This was the term ~~that~~ the development in which I live, *Nice juxtaposition* ~~in is labeled as.~~ Other words such as calling me and my friends JAPs (Jewish American Princesses) were hostilely used to put me down throughout high school. I have had people look at me because I have worn a star upon my neck for the sole reason of being proud to be a strong Jew.

Reading from the <u>Torah:</u> the whole body of Jewish
religious literature at my Bat Mitzvah allowed me to express to a congregation of friends and family my pride in
my religion. I had been studying Hebrew and learning about
the history of the Jews for about four years now. The
✓ pride in my relati(ves) eyes on this day made all of my hard
work worthwhile. Relatives of mine were killed in the
Holocaust and I felt a sense of necessity to be Bat
Mitzvahed as my way of showing the world that I was proud
to be a Jew.

This sound like an important experience for you — there more you can do with it? Other ways to draw on it?

Marriage is a sacred thing. It has been strongly

expressed to me by my parents that I should marry a Jewish

man. My mom refuses to have contact with her grandchildren

unless they are raised Jewish. My views towards my

is is very ethnicity are strong, but certainly not as strict. I think
nicely
developed that because my parents were raised in times when segrega-
— you give
thought- tion, prejudice, and racism were still quite evident, their
ful account
of your views have not changed along with the times. But if we are
conflict.
discriminated against as Jews, and they know how it feels,

then why must they discriminate against other minority

groups? This is where I differ greatly with the views of

my family. My uncle married a Filipino woman and faced a

large amount of hostility from my grandparents and his

brothers and sisters. But why? Being Filipino is a minor-

ity group just as much as being a Jew is.

My identity in society will change as time goes on, *Not sure*
  how you
but my beliefs and intuitions as a white Jewish woman I *mean this.*

Not sure will have for a lifetime. All in all, your race, ethnic
why you
want to background, and gender help to mold you into your own
end with
this. individual. Each person perceives their role in society

that — at and even in life in a different perspective than others may
this point
— is your perceive them. Everybody is equally as special and impor-
sense of
our larger tant in their own way whether they are within the minority
project?
or the majority.

Staci,
  This is a nice revision. You've really reimagined the shape of your paper,
and I can see how you're working hard to develop/explore ideas introduced in
your first draft. I've made more specific comments in the margins, and you
should come talk to me if you have any questions.
  Thanks for your work,
  Bianca

Although her sentences seem awkward and tangled at times (due, I think, to attempts
to overcorrect them), and although the writing still lapses into uninteresting generalities,
Staci is working hard in her second draft to construct a "mixed" narrative. The way she
juxtaposes the sections of her essay, as well as smaller sections within the bigger ones
(although at times it's hard to distinguish separations) is very effective. For example, her

parents' concern that "there were a lot of black people moving into my old neighborhood" is directly followed by a dictionary definition of "prejudice" [manual p. 262]; similarly, her comment "I was lucky to be raised in an area populated heavily with Jewish people" is immediately undermined by her friend's remark about "Little Israel" [manual p. 263]. I was also intrigued by the way Staci uses stories in the second draft to selectively amplify particular moments from the first draft: for example, she begins the second draft with a story that inflects the questions she raises in the first draft and then carries over in the second about her parents' prejudices; also, the paragraph in the first draft on the women's movement is divided into two separate sections in the second draft, one of which is an anecdote about explaining her mother's unusual occupation to a classmate.

Obviously there is still much more that Staci could do here, but in my opinion the fact that the changes she's made have opened up more possibilities is precisely what makes this a productive revision. In addition, because the moves she makes in the second draft — the way she juxtaposes modes of telling (stories, definitions, dialogue) — echo the kinds of moves that can be observed in the *Borderlands* essays, Staci's revisions also reflect her revised understanding of Anzaldúa's project.

. . . .

Whether or not students managed successful Anzaldúa revisions, when, at the end of the semester, they had to write a retrospective essay about their work as writers in the course, nearly everyone had something positive to say about how this assignment freed them up from conventional essay writing. Tamarrah explained it this way:

> In all of my years of English composition, I was always told to write a five-paragraph essay. This included an introduction, three supporting ideas, and a conclusion. With my Anzaldúa assignments, I was asked to write a mixed text, which could include poems, quotes, stories, a combination of languages, or sporadic sentences here and there. This helped me a great deal, for when I sat down to write my essay, I felt more in control of my paper. I could pick and choose from many different creative options. . . .

Another student, Cheryl, wrote, "This assignment, unlike the others, gave me the freedom I felt I had previously been denied" (3–4). And Christine, the author of "Self-Understanding," explained, "We had to take everything that we had learned, technically, about writing and leave it in the gutter" (3–4).

At the same time that Anzaldúa's essay represented a kind of freedom, though, students — often within the space of the same essay — also reverted to very familiar metaphors for talking about personal writing as opposed to "academic" writing and as a direct representation rather than re-presenting of their experiences and feelings. "I am very proud of my efforts with [the Anzaldúa] paper," one student admitted, "It is raw and straight from my gut" (Bulawa 4–5). And another student who had written about her family's experience immigrating to America explained, "The freedom that I felt when writing this paper was unlike anything else. The fact that creativity was encouraged instead of suppressed made it possible for me to truly and freely express what was on my mind" (Nemirovsky 4).

Notwithstanding my students' enthusiasm, I was intrigued by the way these discussions obscured not only the point I think Anzaldúa is trying to make about the limitations of any single language or sign system to represent her identity, but more interestingly the successes my students had experimenting with multiply voiced narratives. When I think about why this might be the case, my sense is that it has less to do with students' sophistication, or insight into their own writing practices than it does with the kinds of assumptions students have about personal writing in the first place, before they ever walk into General Writing. Ideas about the importance of self-expression, about the autonomous, free-thinking individual in society, are deeply embedded in American culture. So, to the extent that Anzaldúa's writing forces us to question these kinds of assumptions about the possibility of a unified identity, it's not surprising that students would still struggle with how to talk about the consequences of asking such questions.

But, I need to say that if students didn't have the theoretical language to articulate what was different about the writing they produced in response to Anzaldúa, the experience did, nonetheless, refocus their attention on issues that were central to the course. In the comments I quoted above, for instance, there is the sense that, writing into or out of a tradition, a writer necessarily makes choices about how to proceed. Additionally, in our class discussions and in the comments I wrote on their papers, thinking about Anzaldúa's writing in terms of different kinds of "strategies" gave us a way to talk about her writing, and consequently their writing, as negotiable, as a way of working out/through complicated ideas, as imagining (facilitating, complicating, undermining) the role of the reader.

These are all reasons I would teach Anzaldúa again, if the opportunity arose. They are also reasons that I've been forced to reconsider my own assumptions about the value of personal writing. And finally it's on these terms that I can begin to account for my students' success with Anzaldúa — and I do think their efforts were successful. In asking students to think and write about the traditions/ideologies Anzaldúa was responding to, what proved to be valuable was the way it brought to the surface the class's assumptions — mine included — about the limitations and possibilities for writing about personal experience.

WORKS CITED

Bartholomae, David, and Anthony Petrosky. *Ways of Reading: An Anthology for Writers*. 4th ed. Boston: Bedford/St. Martin's, 1995.

Bulawa, Jenny. "The Final Analysis of a Never-Ending Process." Unpublished, University of Pittsburgh: 1994.

Nemirovsky, Vita. "Growth and Development." Unpublished, University of Pittsburgh: 1994.

Schrodi, Christine. "Retrospective." Unpublished, University of Pittsburgh: 1994.

———. "Self-Understanding." Unpublished, University of Pittsburgh: 1994.

Sherman, Jakrita. " 'I'll Fly Away.' " Unpublished, University of Pittsburgh: 1994.

Thomas, Tamarrah. "Reseeing My Own Writing." Unpublished, University of Pittsburgh: 1994.

Wenitsky, Staci. "My Positions in Society and in Life." Unpublished, University of Pittsburgh: 1994.

All student papers are used with the permission of their authors, to whom I am grateful.

I would also like to acknowledge the help of Pitt English Department colleagues David Bartholomae, Angie Farkas, and Kurt Simonds, who kindly offered valuable advice as I worked on this paper.

o–o–o–o–o–o–o–o–o–o–o–o–o–o–o–o–o–o–o

RIDING THE SEESAW: GENERATIVE TENSION BETWEEN TEACHING MODELS

by Gwen Gorzelsky

In the end we're all freshman writers. This is a notion I've absorbed through many conversations with fellow University of Pittsburgh writing teachers, though it suggests different implications to its different hearers and users.

Let me begin to explain my sense of the implications through a short digression. Recently, I've watched my husband work on a pencil portrait based on an old black-and-white photo of his mother holding his infant sister. Because the photo itself is an unflattering representation — its lighting draws harsh lines and pales the woman's and child's faces — my husband subtly alters some of its aspects in his penciled version. The piece evolves through his process of working back and forth between the ideal of exact imitation and the ideal of artistic embellishment aimed at producing a more aesthetically pleasing effect. Like writing, drawing entails a combination of manual and intellectual activities that generates a material product. Like drawing, writing entails a set of back-and-forth moves between particular intellectual practices.

I like the portrait metaphor because it embodies the relationship between, on one hand, the back-and-forth moves between intellectual practices (here, the use of various artistic ideals as guides to ways of seeing and ways of drawing) and, on the other hand, the generation of a material aesthetic product. But there are other, more concrete comparisons that can serve as a shorthand to express the notion of a back-and-forthness between intellectual practices. A friend who swing dances has explained to me how the dancers simultaneously pull away from and hold onto one another to produce the couple's pirouettes. She says that this combination of seemingly conflicting motions generates a "creative tension" that enables the dance itself. Similarly, kids on a seesaw work simultaneously against and with each other's balance and weight to generate the material experience of the seesaw's sustained motion. This generative tension of the swing dance and the seesaw is a combination of moves that seems crucial to me in both the activity of writing and in the use of models in theorizing writing and its teaching.

Because this generative tension, in the form of back-and-forth moves between intellectual practices, is as much a part of "freshman writing" as it is of "advance composition" or of professional and scholarly writing, I see the term "freshman writing" as sort of a misnomer. That is, so many of the issues with which freshman writers grapple are issues that beleaguer experienced writers as well. An easy example is the tendency of writers to get balled up in sentences expressing complex thoughts and, as a result, to produce confused grammatical structures. (And my writing should certainly stand as an instance.) But there are issues —like finding and explaining the "right" piece of evidence, pitching a piece to your audience, developing the complexities of an argument, and hammering out that felicitous turn of phrase — that dog experienced as well as freshman writers. For me, the term "freshman writing" doesn't stand for a set of preliminary skills but for a set of com-

264

plex issues that are problems, in different ways, for *all* writers. In a sense, I hear the phrase as an argument against a developmental model of freshman writing.

Others, though, hear the term as compatible with the developmental model. And conversations with some of these folks have pushed me to think about how different models might be useful.

And for the moment, what seems most useful to me is a set of back-and-forth moves between models, the generative tension of the seesaw and the swing dance. This kind of back-and-forthness is one of the things I like about Dave Bartholomae's essay "The Tidy House: Basic Writing in the American Curriculum." I see it as similar to the back-and-forth between producing narratives and producing critiques, which is one of the moves I read in "The Tidy House," or the back-and-forth between generous readings and against-the-grain readings.

My back-and-forth in models of freshman writing is this: on one hand, I believe in complex reading and writing assignments and in class discussions that address this complexity; on the other hand, I use commenting practices that draw on a developmental model. One way to explain this is to acknowledge that my comments have gotten more directive over the past year. As I'm a relatively new teacher, this might just be part of a developmental trajectory. On the other hand, I taught basic writing, a course sometimes seen as "prior" to the usual freshman writing course, for the first time this year. I often found myself writing, in response to a general, unsubstantiated claim about a text, versions of this comment: "*First*, you need to show readers evidence by quoting a place in the text. *Then*, you need to show us your interpretation of that quote and how that interpretation enables you to make your claim." This kind of comment certainly suggests a developmental model to me, and I must admit that I find it not just useful but indispensable.

The danger of such prefab comments, though, is when they become automatic, when they're the only response I can make, or bother to make, to a paper. The back-and-forth I'm striving for demands that I look for ways to intersperse these prefab comments with other kinds of comments that respond with real questions to an intellectual issue, problem, argument, or question raised in the paper.

To talk about why it's so important to me to hang onto complex reading and writing assignments and to engage actively in intellectual discussion with student texts, I want to read through sections of a paper by a student of mine, John B ———. The assignment that prompted the student's writing is below:

Wideman Paper Assignment

Step One in class M 2/6, W 2/8, F 2/10

Step Two due M 2/13

Step Three due M 2/20

Step Four due W 2/22

Step Five due F 2/24

Step One

Choose a passage that seems significant to you, one in which Wideman shows his problems with representations, with reconstructing events and people's lives through writing. Quote this passage using the correct format. (Use your handbook or check with me if you need to.) Then, do an interpretation of the passage. (Your interpretation should be at least two or three substantial paragraphs.)

Step Two

Go back to your interpretation and reread it. Then, choose two or three places from *Brothers and Keepers*. These should be places where you see Wideman trying to cope with the difficulties of writing described in your interpretation. What kinds of writerly techniques does he use to do this coping? You can discuss broadly things Wideman does throughout the book (e.g., things like using both ghetto dialect and academic English), but be sure to interpret in detail two or three passages from the book.

Step Three

Reread your own identities paper (the paper was modeled on Wideman's book). Explain your paper's problems with representation, with reconstructing events and people's lives through writing. Then, choose two or three places from your paper where you, as a writer, are trying to cope with these problems. What kinds of writerly techniques do you use to do this coping? You can discuss broadly things that you do throughout the paper, but be sure to interpret in detail two or three passages from your paper.

Step Four

Reread your interpretations of *Brothers and Keepers* and of your own paper. For each text, discuss the effectiveness of the writer's attempts to cope with her or his particular problems with representing the world through writing. Use the passages that you've interpreted from each text. Build on your interpretations to explain how and why the writer's attempts to cope with her/his problems are and/or aren't effective.

Step Five

Reread all of your work from the previous steps of this assignment. Based on your work, what do you think are effective ways for both writers and readers to deal with the problems of representing the world through writing? Be careful to use the work you've done up to this point to build your argument and support your conclusions.

The combination of the above assignment and the assignment for the identities paper, which this assignment's Step Three requires students to reread, asks them to seesaw, to move back-and-forth, between different practices of reading and writing. John B ——'s response to Steps Three and Four of the assignment follow:

III

In the biography <u>Brothers and Keepers</u> we saw that there was a problem with reconstructing people's events and lives in a totally unbiased way. This runs true throughout most biographies including the biography of John B —— and Lauren D ——. In order to compensate for these problems I try to cope with bias to make it the best interpretation as far as dealing with unbiased goes.

The general problem with this biography, and most other biographies in general, is the selective memory of the author. Surely there are many events that I choose not to remember or that I modify in my brain. When I retell the events that shaped our lives, this will make the recreation highly unreliable. What needs to be considered as well is that there could be events that shaped my life that were more important than the ones listed, but this just needs to be understood by the reader and he or she needs to keep this in mind when reading any biography, including my own.

The language of the paper is going to be written in a manner of a freshman engineering student since that is my identity. The part that deals with the dialog from Lauren's childhood will definitely suffer from this. I try to compensate for the difference by working with Lauren for using phrases that her and her mother were likely to use back then. Lauren's interpretation is better than mine alone, but it also has the same selective-memory problem.

The other method of coping is in my part of the biography. I still go fishing with my dad, so many of the events and feelings of the first day have become ritualized. I can therefore cope by using my present-day recollections from the event of fishing. I therefore am not detached from the whole ceremony and this makes it a more accurate retelling of events.

I also tried to cope by mentioning a number of times that it was not the fishing ritual so much that was important as was the decision to follow my dad. This also runs true in Lauren's biography when at the end of the painting scene I dropped in the idea that the event could have been anything, just as long as Lauren was with her mom. This releases the stress of the importance of the exact details and points to the decision that was made during these two activities in our lives.

IV

Gwen, my feelings towards the usefulness of coping are expressed below. I did not answer the question in the way that it was asked, but I spent a good portion of the paper dealing with why coping is self-defeating. I do at the end talk about coping in my John Wideman papers but did not expand. I just wanted to test the waters and see if you think that my reasoning is good enough to make valid not including big explanations on effectiveness in coping. Please give me your input on this approach. If you think it is still necessary let me know if I should expand the coping effectiveness at the end!

It is my opinion that the human is formed from a complex series of experiences. Each experience either reinforces or contradicts a previous one. In the early stages of our lives we learn the most important things we will ever learn. I believe that it is an effect of childhood experiences in why we like some things and shun others. I also believe that no two people are even closely alike. There are many things that go unsaid, perhaps more things than are said. In light of the complexity and variety of every human there is no way to form a biography that everyone can relate to or understand. It is therefore my thought that a writer should not attempt to deal or cope with bias from his paper.

The reason that I feel so strongly about this is that when an author copes he is altering in some way the emotions conveyed by the paper to suit a certain audience. It is impossible to please everyone so when writing a biography I feel that when you cope you are again making a bias towards the story.

The author is shaped by certain events. If he or she is free to express them as he or she remembers them then they are more accurate than if he makes an attempt to recreate them exactly. This may sound a bit ascewed but let me reason it out.

A person experiences thousands of events in their lives. Each event offers some aspect on life and a way of acting towards it. When I live through an event I inter- pret it and store it how I feel it can assist me in making myself a better person. When I recall stories that shaped my personality I need not cope with my bias, because it is with this bias I live. If I were to cope, this bias would not be part of the image I drew of myself and therefore would be false. Since the point of a biography is to create events that shaped my life I need to include the events in the way I interpreted them and remembered them not the way they factually happened.

The methods of coping used by both John Wideman and myself were done in such a manner that they drastically changed the event as it was interpreted not as it histori- cally happened. Wideman is trying to write a biography of his brother. This is the reason that the book was pub- lished, but I assert that the real reason is to figure out why he is not in the big house. His family was never really that close and he wanted to see if there were dif- ferences in himself and Robby. Wideman oftentimes finds himself not listening to Robby. He does not say that he changed his final draft and if he asked Robby to repeat this missed stuff. I am assuming that it never was and it is better of not because Wideman, at first was looking to find himself and his relationship to his brother. Since this is the case the stories that Robby tells are not as important as what Wideman writes since it is Wideman's head that we need to get into. There is no point when Wideman

269

> begins to write in order that others may experience what he
> and his brother have, the keepers and the prison system.
> Before this point though there is no need for coping be-
> cause Wideman is dealing with a personal issue so any bias
> adds to what is in his head.
>
> There is need for coping in the way Wideman tries to
> express Robby's hate at the end of the book, though, and he
> does this by including Robby's poems. This is a direct
> path into Robby and is an effect manner of coping because
> it gives us a firsthand look into Robby's head.
>
> In my biography the coping occurs in the events re-
> told. This coping does not affect the point, since the
> point is that Lauren and I decided to be like our parents
> not the actual event that happened on those two respective
> days. The coping is indifferent to the point of recollec-
> tions.

In these paragraphs, John B ———'s paper is working against the grain of class discussions that emphasized objectivity as Wideman's problem and "objective" depiction of Robby as the standard by which to measure the effectiveness of Wideman's solutions. John B ———'s paper determinedly insists on *not* "addressing the assignment" and instead on redefining the problem.

A straight developmental model of freshman writing would, I think, argue that I should never have asked my students to read a complicated, controversial text like Wideman's, much less given them such a complex assignment. John B ———'s paragraphs display difficulty with sentence structure and boundaries, with constructing logic in ways a reader can follow. Surely a developmental model would hold that their writer is far from ready to call the terms of his assignment into question. But it's precisely that thoughtful, provocative line of questioning I'd like to encourage for freshman writers, for all writers.

I'm not making any claims for John B ———'s status as an example of the kind of resistant, excluded student described in "The Tidy House." In traditional terms, he's probably the "best socialized" student I've ever had: unasked, he presented me before the fact with absence excuses signed by his commanding officer and submitted typed homework and copies of in-class writing assignments. During discussions, he spoke enthusiastically, thoughtfully, confidently, politely. He never deviated in the slightest from class rules without first seeking permission. I wouldn't mark him as a resistant student.

Nonetheless, these paragraphs mark him as a freshman writer in institutional terms. But these freshman writing paragraphs also make the move of using an idea that John B ——— insists is important to him as a way of questioning class discussion and the terms of the assignment. "It is . . . my opinion that the human is formed from a complex series of experiences." He *acknowledges* that this is his belief, not a premise he's proven, and then *uses* that belief as a frame to develop his critique and an argument about the text, an argument shaped by a belief and an approach in which he has significant stake.

This move seems crucial to me. I believe in the project of prompting our students and ourselves to question foundational assumptions. But I think that the kind of negotiation between students and the academy called for in "The Tidy House" demands that students find ways to bring their foundational assumptions *into* their academic writing projects. I can't imagine producing a paper that was more than a mechanical exercise in conventionality without working in and through my foundational assumptions. The generative tension between bringing foundational assumptions *into* academic writing, on one hand, and questioning those foundational assumptions, on the other, is a crucial instance of the back-and-forth intellectual moves that make successful pieces of writing pirouette so that they push readers' ways of thinking and seeing.

So whether John B ——— is a "disfranchised" student or not, whether he's a fresh-man writer, an advanced composition student, or a professional or scholarly writer, his is the kind of move I want to encourage. While students' production of critiques of texts in response to assignments, class discussions, and/or teacher comments can be a valuable learning experience, that move isn't the same one John's text performs. The teacher-prompted critiques are moves that, in one sense, are obedient responses to authority. John B ———'s paper is thoughtful, engaged questioning of the framework provided by authority. A notable move. And, I think, a way of interacting with texts, with teachers, with authority's frameworks that I don't know how to solicit but would certainly like to promote. It is a way of writing that intersects with ways of seeing and of being in the world.

Now, I continue to struggle with how to mediate between models, between kinds of comments, class work, and assignments. I'm striving to work out a balance between teaching calculated to help students enable students "to negotiate the full range of expectations in the university" ("Tidy House," 20) and teaching calculated to help enable students to pursue, develop, and push on their texts' ideas and moves. This struggle for balance — for the seesaw's and the swing dance's generative tension — might, I hope, be useful to students in defining new ways of relating to authority and its frameworks. I'm working with two models: one of development and one of writing as a means of social transformation. Both enable particular kinds of work. Both produce problems. As I mentioned above, the developmental model can become automatic and thus prevent teacher engagement with the intellectual work happening in student texts. The social transformation model can prompt a focus on student papers' potentials and successes and allow teachers to lose sight of the real and extensive pressures students face to learn and use academic conventions.

So I'm suggesting a model of how to use models, a model of back-and-forthness, of sustained efforts to move into and out of models, using, critiquing, and perhaps improving, them. In the end, we all struggle with problems of articulating complexities and of negotiating between our own agendas and academic conventions. We're all freshman writers.

WORKS CITED

Bartholomae, David. "The Tidy House: Basic Writing in the American Curriculum." *Journal of Basic Writing* 12. 1 (1993): 4–21.

o–o–o–o–o–o–o–o–o–o–o–o–o–o

ON TEACHING *WAYS OF READING*

by Bill Hendricks
Temple University

Imagine the beginning: the class has met three or four times. The teacher has introduced the course to her students, talked about her expectations, about what will be required of the students, about classroom procedures. The students have read the introduction to *Ways of Reading*, and the teacher has assigned a first reading, say the Walker Percy essay. The students have read "The Loss of the Creature" and used the "Questions for a Second Reading" in their rereading; they've talked about those readings in class. Today the students handed in a paper for one of the "Loss of the Creature" writing assignments. The teacher sits down in front of this first stack of student papers and thinks about how the course has gone so far.

She was pleased with the class conversation about the introduction. She had been apprehensive that the students would be puzzled by, maybe even hostile to, an essay on reading that deemphasizes information-gathering, summarizing, and reading for main ideas in favor of "strong reading," an aggressive and challenging way of reading that few students are likely to have thought much about. But, happily, the students seemed intrigued, and a little flattered, to imagine reading as enabling them to pursue academic projects that they are responsible not only for maintaining and shaping but, in some ways, initiating. "I like the idea of being able to begin with what I notice," one student said, "of not just having to throw in a couple of sentences at the end of a paper about whether I agree or disagree with what I've read." True, some students objected to Bartholomae and Petrosky's claim that reading is a social interaction, but other students insisted that to deny that claim is really to affirm it. "How can anybody object to this essay's saying that reading is a social interaction," one student said, "without doing exactly what the essay talks about — making a mark on it and talking back to its writers?"

At the next class meeting, when the class discussed readings of "The Loss of the Creature," several students wanted to talk more about the course introduction, saying that the Percy essay reminded them of it. "I'm not sure I know just who a 'consumer' is," said one student, "but he probably isn't a 'strong reader.' The consumers Percy talks about seem pretty passive." The teacher noted this student's use of one text as a frame for understanding another, and she felt generally hopeful about the class's readiness to see acts of reading as involving construction and struggle.

Thinking about these class conversations, the teacher anticipates a satisfying semester, and she begins to read the student papers in front of her with high expectations. Many of these papers, she suspects, will offer rich readings of the problem Walker Percy investigates in "The Loss of the Creature." "The society of today is mechanical," begins the first paper, "and so are the people of this society. They do what they are told, when they are told, and how they are told to do it." The teacher pauses, taken aback by a reading of "The Loss of the Creature" that reduces the dilemmas Percy works with to terms of universal authoritarianism and regimentation — and marveling at how easily this writer has managed to free himself from such pervasive constraints. The teacher begins a second paper, less portentous than the first, which talks about the writer's success in eluding the preformed symbolic complexes that have threatened him: "the solution is to keep an open mind." But the writer seems to think that this formula needs no explanation. The slogan, maddeningly, stands alone. The teacher turns to a third paper, one which begins with what seems like a commitment to look closely at Percy's essay: "In 'The Loss of the Creature,' Walker Percy tries to understand some very important problems," the paper begins. "Such as," it continues, "how to see the Grand Canyon. This is important because if everyone saw the Grand Canyon in the same way the world would become a very boring place to live."

The teacher reads on. A few of the papers seem more promising, better ways to begin the difficult work on reading and writing she has in mind for the semester, but she finds none of the papers very satisfying. She is surprised most by how little most of the readings notice. Few readings notice Percy's distinction between "experts" and "planners"; no one wants to do anything with "dialectic." Many papers make no attempt to bring forth Percy's key terms and examples through direct quotation, relying instead on paraphrases that do not so much translate Percy's language into the writer's as translate it out of existence: "According to Percy, until people actually make an experience their own, or express their own ideas in their own words, the problem of missing the gift will not be solved, and people will be left merely to admire all the pretty packages." Here, quite neatly, the writer avoids the puzzle of what to do with Percy's "preformed symbolic complexes" by implying that "loss of sovereignty" is a dilemma only for the morally lazy: be true to yourself, and the creature is recovered. There are too many papers willing to portray the problems of the social construction of perception as cartoon conflicts: the expert or planner or "society" is plotting to cheat "individuals" of their rightful claims to authentic experience, and we all need to resist these encroachments through keeping an open mind and appreciating how special and unique we and our surroundings are. But few papers want to extend this fervor for resistance to doing a little resisting of Percy. The teacher finds only two or three papers that question Percy's conclusions about what Cárdenas or Terre Haute tourists see in the Grand Canyon; she finds no papers at all that question the liberating potential of apprenticeship to "great men" or majestic educators.

And she wonders: given the promise of the first few classes, how is it that this first batch of papers is so disappointing, so thin? And what is she going to do next?

Reading and Writing

In every course I have ever taught, there has been a moment like this. Always my students' first papers have been not what I hoped for, less than I wanted. Stubbornly, I continue to be a little surprised by such moments ("This semester," I have told myself, "things will be different"). But at least I have gradually developed, I think, ways of understanding the disparity between my expectations for my students and their initial performance — and strategies to narrow the gap by the end of the semester.

Even if *Ways of Reading* is being used for a first course in college reading and writing, students come to the book with considerable experience as readers and writers. But most students will not have been prepared by that experience for a course in which reading and writing are so tightly bound together — in which, for example, students' readings of an essay are validated largely through what they can do with that essay in writing essays of their own, and in which, further, the writing thus produced is ordinarily responded to with a request that the students validate *it* through going back to do more work on reading, and so forth. This back-and-forth movement between reading and writing creates, I think, special challenges and opportunities for both students and teachers of *Ways of Read-*

ing. In this essay, I am not suggesting that there is a "right" way to teach the book and that I know what it is. I offer just one teacher's reading of the book, of the questions I imagine *Ways of Reading* posing for teachers and students, and the ways my teaching experience suggests to me to work with those questions.

Like the rest of us, students are practiced at getting along. As you together discuss their readings of the Introduction to *Ways of Reading*, your students may well cheerfully assent to Bartholomae and Petrosky's ideas about new ways of looking at reading — partly because of the excitement of thinking about reading as a powerful tool for intellectual achievement, partly because of the great respect for students evinced by Bartholomae and Petrosky, and partly because *Ways of Reading* is your students' textbook and you're their teacher. The temptation is very strong: "Yes, now I see. Here's how I can be a better reader and writer and get more out of reading and writing." But as they write their first papers, your students will be relying on what they already know how to do, and what they know how to do probably does not include a way of treating reading as a constructive activity extending over time, as a process.

Reading and writing are not inevitable, not "natural." What people learn when they "learn to read" depends on their culture's (or cultures') ways of teaching and valuing reading. Much in your students' education has probably suggested to them that reading is a highly unusual form of interpretation: while one's parents or friends may inspire baffling mixtures of comfort and irritation, a well-written book is perfectly clear; while two workers may have good reasons for their conflicting evaluations of the same job, if two readers disagree, one of them is probably a better reader; while people may make very different judgments, over time, of their children, their neighborhood, their country, the meaning of a text is properly fixed, unalterable; life is a process, reading happens all at once.

For students to pursue the questioning and aggressive reading process suggested by *Ways of Reading* is difficult, moreover, because their education has often seemed to imply that intellectual pursuits, especially in school, are bounded by fairly rigid categories. It is not just reading and writing that have been presented as separate activities. Disciplines and texts and courses of study have also often been seen as self-contained, discrete, each in its predetermined place: tenth-grade biology, eleventh-grade chemistry, twelfth-grade physics; *The Scarlet Letter* "belongs to" American Literature, but not to History of Psychology; students are expected on a final exam in their Systems of Government course to "know the material," but are probably not asked how they could apply what they have learned to improving the governments around them. The student who identifies "how to see the Grand Canyon" as a significant problem presented by Walker Percy's essay, significant because "if everyone saw the Grand Canyon in the same way the world would become a very boring place to live," is probably not in the habit, as a reader, of seeing one thing in terms of something else. A metaphor is something that poets use.

As the students in your course work at being more self-conscious about and critical of their reading and writing, you can expect that they will become increasingly articulate about their reading and writing processes. The student quoted earlier who talked about Percy, the gift and its trappings, wrote midway through the semester:

> Generally I play one of two roles as a reader. For an essay based on an assigned reading, I take what I call the everything-fits-in-a-neat-little-package-and-you-can-tie-it-all-up-in-a-bow approach; for an essay based on personal experience, I use what I refer to as the sounds-like-I-know-what-I'm-talking-about-but-I'm-lying approach. The names are long but quite easily understood.

The systematic everything-fits-in-a-neat-little-package-and-you-can-tie-it-all-up-in-a-bow approach is best applied in essays which analyze the assigned text of any author. My favorite example: "According to Percy, until people actually make an experience their own, or express their own ideas in their own words, the problem of missing the gift will not be solved, and people will be left merely to admire all the pretty packages." In a way, it is somewhat incredible if you stop to consider what I did. In one slightly longer than average sentence, I wrote what it took Walker Percy ten-and-a-half pages to say! I summed up an entire essay, all its examples, problems and complications, in one sentence. How? I omitted anything he said that confused me and pretended that the complications didn't exist. That way I sounded as though I had Percy all figured out lock, stock, and barrel, case closed, the end. Granted, it is good to have a strong idea and to go somewhere with it, but in the process, I killed Percy. Not really; but I do sound as though I learned everything there was that Percy had to offer, used him up, and am finished with him. That is awful because I am probably sacrificing a lot of interesting ideas in my attempt to appear so conclusive. Perhaps if I dared to explore what confused me, I could have generated some new ideas even if they were not all neatly resolved in the end.

But your students' capacity to be reflective about and modify their ways of reading won't emerge quickly. To work at reading by writing takes opportunity and practice, repeated attempts, time.

It isn't that your students initially can't conceive of the interrelatedness of reading and writing, abstractly considered. They can, but different students will arrive differently (and take varying lengths of time) at ways of putting this interrelatedness to work for them. You can expedite this in part through the language in which you conduct your class, referring, for example, to class conversations and student papers as "readings" of the subject or assignment at hand, but the process of learning to see reading and writing as aspects of a single activity probably won't proceed far until students see the advantages, in the contexts of particular acts of reading and writing, of honoring the interconnectedness. For example, the student who writes, "People do what they are told, when they are told, and how they are told to do it" can be questioned about how he has conceived the relation between reading and writing. This student can write, and he can read, but he is trapped by acting as if there were only the slenderest of connections between reading and writing. He has read the Walker Percy essay, noticed that it could be said to have something to do with conformity, mentally scanned the commonplaces he has stored under "Conformity," and written a perfectly lucid sentence that makes nonsense of Percy and his own experience. He could use his sentence to prove that he has read the essay, or to prove that he can write correctly, but he couldn't use it to show why anybody, himself especially, should take his reading seriously. If, now, this student is asked to account for the reading his sentence represents, he will need to write better sentences, but he can't do that unless he simultaneously makes a better reading and goes to work on his and Percy's texts.

Reading here, writing over there: *Ways of Reading* is designed to help students work against such fragmentation. This is obviously true of the "Making Connections" assignments and the extended assignment sequences, which ask students to write about how two or more essays or stories might illuminate both each other and academic projects that they can be made to further. But it is also true of the "Questions for a Second Reading" and the initial "Writing Assignments," where students are asked, for example, to apply Paulo Freire's term "problem-posing" to their own educational experiences. There are a number of ways that you can reinforce your students' efforts to practice this sort of constructive, amalgamative reading and writing. For example, in introducing a writing assignment on, say, John Berger's *Ways of Seeing*, you might bring forward a student comment from your class discussion of Berger, that wondered whether Emerson's original audience for the "American Scholar" oration[1] might be seen as having been in a position analogous to the audiences for art before mass reproduction. And both in class discussions and in your marking of student papers, you can attend to and encourage comments in the form of "X reminds me of Y" — the sort of comment that may have been dismissed as irrelevant in your students' previous school experience with reading.

Rewriting, Rereading

But while for most readers to notice that one part of their experiences can be connected to another part, that one text recalls another, that "X reminds one of Y," is by no means irrelevant, it is of only rudimentary usefulness.

In order to read or write a text, any reader, any writer, makes many linguistic connections. Students who in high school have read long books and made A's on tests on those books, and who have written correct and coherent papers in a number of courses, have a legitimate claim to a certain expertise as readers and writers. And even if (maybe especially if) students coming to a course in college reading and writing have been very successful in high school, they won't necessarily be discouraged by a comment on their work that says, in effect, "That's wrong." (They have, after all, a lot of experience in setting things "right," and college is supposed to be harder than high school.) But they may well be baffled and angered by a response to their work that says, in effect, "So what?" "How do you account for this reading? What passages or moments in the text might you use to bring it forward? What is it good for? What does noticing that X reminds you of Y allow you to do that you haven't done already? What's the next step?" Suddenly for such students "to reread" must mean something other than reading an essay twice, and "to rewrite" must mean something other than fixing errors or being clearer — but just what these "others" might be will not be immediately apparent. What lies beyond one more academic hurdle successfully negotiated, one more teacher's approval duly registered?

In trying to assist students to sort out for themselves what might be "in it for them" to pursue writing and reading as ongoing, open-ended, and mutually supporting activities, I have found that I need to combine a number of considerations. Any group of student papers addressed to some question or questions about an assigned text will encompass a great variety of readings. Teachers of college reading and writing encounter, every day, the problem of trying to see these readings on their own terms, different as those terms may be

[1]Emerson's essay appeared in the fifth edition of *Ways of Reading*.

from what the teachers themselves might have chosen to do in addressing the assignment. And this problem is likely to be more acute than usual in a course based on *Ways of Reading*, partly because these essays and stories resist easy pigeonholing or categorization (and thus the variety of student readings may be unusually broad) and partly because in almost every writing assignment students are asked to try to see one thing in terms of some other thing or things — a Percian reading of Clifford Geertz's travels in Bali, a progression in the creative development of Adrienne Rich's poetry seen through the language of John Berger. Thus, a teacher is faced with a multiplicity of readings of complex cases. Both in commenting on student papers and in class discussions, I struggle (not always successfully) to suspend the strong readings I myself have made of these cases sufficiently to see what my students' readings have attended to. In class discussions, I often find it enormously tempting to propose my own reading of an assignment question or problem my students are working with. But when I have succumbed to the temptation, I have almost always regretted it. ("Well," too many students think — or at least act as if they do — "that settles it. He's paid to know what he's talking about.")

Usually I can resist the lure, but the more interesting pedagogical problem is how to tie the various readings that emerge in a classroom discussion to further acts of reading and writing. One of the most fruitful class discussions I've been involved in recently had to do with how students read the phrase "the end of education" in Richard Rodriguez's "The Achievement of Desire." Some students argued that the "end" of education means a formal stopping point, Rodriguez's way of acknowledging the completion of his academic training. Other students insisted that "end" here means "goal" or "object," that Rodriguez is identifying the aim of education as an ability to reconcile present and past. Still other students proposed that the phrase suggests a renunciation, Rodriguez's recognition that to desire the past would entail his no longer being able to participate in what he had been calling "education." The class discussion had begun in response to one of the "Questions for a Second Reading" that you'll find after the Rodriguez essay in *Ways of Reading*, but it seemed to me, as I listened to students forcefully articulate these completing responses to a troubling moment in "The Achievement of Desire," that here was an occasion to do more than acknowledge the variety and richness of readers' reactions to a powerful text. It seemed to me that the right move now was to draw on the excitement and energy of this discussion by turning the reading question into a writing problem, by sending students back to the essay to see how they might work out, through writing about yet another reading, their interpretations. The resulting set of student papers was one of the strongest I have received lately. Whatever interpretations they were able to articulate in their writing, all students, as they went back to read Rodriguez's essay again, had somehow to take into account — acknowledge, react against, incorporate, consciously ignore — the other voices they had heard in our discussion.

In a course that provides opportunities for students to read and respond to their classmates' writing students will get further experience in seeing not only the anthology pieces but their own papers as subject to multiple interpretations. However, as I have suggested, it is probably naive to think that students will hear a teacher's comments as only one more voice in the dialogue. Teachers are readers, but they are also their students' teachers; they are responding from a privileged position, even if they wish that this were not so. But I think that it is possible for teachers to take advantage of the power relations implicit in institutional writing to become their students' allies in resisting the silence to which it is all too easy for readers and writers to acquiesce. Later in this essay, I show my marking of a sample student paper on Rodriguez, a paper that I thought was — though coherent and sometimes arresting — distressingly silent just when it most needed to speak up. For now, let me offer a few general remarks on how I approach helping students to become more articulate about what their readings have revealed to them.

Often I get papers in which an odd paragraph stands out, something that is hard for me to integrate with the rest of the paper; not what I'd call a "silent" paragraph exactly, but a paragraph that is speaking poorly — perhaps verbose, or seemingly extraneous or misplaced. Some years ago, when I would routinely comment on such a paragraph — with something like "Is this paragraph necessary?" I'd get back revisions with the offending paragraph (that's how students heard my questions) obediently cut. But it seems to me now that though teachers can always shut students up, they ought to be more than a little nervous about deciding to do so. And now I am generally concerned to encourage students to say more, not less. They aren't writing an essay about Percy or Geertz just to prove that they can do it and end there. I try in my comments to help students advance the work on projects which they have begun or might begin, asking them to make connections, in their revisions, with other essays and stories, or with other papers they have written, or between various parts (especially odd paragraphs) of the paper I am commenting on. And I am more likely than I used to be, faced with a puzzling paragraph, to ask questions about it that direct the student back into the essay of which it is a reading.

After one or more revisions of a paper, students may indeed decide that some sentence or paragraph or section of the paper is extraneous, that it doesn't advance the project they are working on. But rather than knowing what they are going to say or how they are going to say it before they begin to write, students will work out what they have to say as they write, and rewrite. In order to write about a text, students have to listen to what an author says and then, in their turn, talk back to the voice they hear. And then a teacher speaks to the voices in the students' papers, commenting both about ways of reading and ways of writing. And though, as I have implied, I think that it is possible for a teacher to say too much too soon about a paper's rhetorical effectiveness, some of my ways of asking students to be more articulate are very much in keeping with traditional rhetorical concerns. On the most basic level, if I read a sentence or paragraph that seems to me so tangled that I can only respond, "I don't understand," I tell the student that I don't understand. I consider this to be providing the student with humble but useful information. And certainly I often request that a writer extend some remark by supplying elaboration or qualification or specific illustration. My problem, always, is to balance my desire, as a reader, for a stronger argument, against my perception, as a teacher, that there are other lines of argument that might also be profitably pursued — or lines of argument that, though hesitantly or confusedly, the writer might in fact *be* pursuing. "The text provides the opportunity for you to see through someone else's language, to imagine your own familiar settings through the images, metaphors, and ideas of others," students of *Ways of Reading* read. Ideally, this model of reading applies not just to students reading assigned texts.

Teachers respond in their comments not only to a particular paper addressed to a particular assignment, but also to what they know about the student's reading and writing development. I have found that my acknowledging a new direction, a new achievement — something that a student has not been able to do before — can have considerable effect in motivating that student to sustain and increase his or her articulateness. This may entail my praising something that, were I to notice it in the writing of a colleague or a professional writer, I would not ordinarily remark on. It isn't plausible that students will in the course of a semester become as expert as professional writers. But expertise is not really the issue. The essays and stories in *Ways of Reading* "leave some work for a reader to do. They require readers willing to accept the challenge and the responsibility, not experts; perhaps the most difficult problem for students is to believe that this is true." For students to improve as strong readers and writers requires that they take some risks; a teacher can honor their risk taking.

Before I turn to a discussion of some representative student papers and my marking of one of them, I want to say that I think teachers commenting on student papers have to develop some way to mediate between all that they *might* say about a paper and what they *do* say about it. Perhaps you have had the experience, as I have, of responding to a student paper with more words than the student wrote: comments snake about everywhere, densely interlining the text, crawling down every margin, turning corners to the back of the page; end comments expand into small essays. I now think that for students, unless they are already unusually good readers, trying to interpret so much commentary may mean that they can't interpret anything; staring at so many words may mean, strangely, that they can't *see* any of them. And, for the teacher, who doesn't have just one student but twenty or forty or sixty), such mammoth expenditure of time and energy can quickly sink a labor of love into a dispiriting and debilitating trap. I think that the improvements students make in a college reading and writing class will occur gradually, over time — and continue, at the best, long after they have finished with the class. Certain kinds of instrumental writing may be totally successful at once: a grocery list gets the goods, a memo may be recognized by all concerned as having accomplished some purpose. But I think that most acts of strong reading and writing entail dissatisfactions of compromise. Understanding in reading is never complete; the performed understanding represented by a piece of writing may occasion, for its writer, just as much anxiety over what it has failed to accomplish as satisfaction in what it achieves. Paradoxically, this dissatisfaction probably increases along with skillfulness. The stakes keep going up. Writers' consciousness that some goal has been achieved, their *knowing* that they know, is often accompanied by a sense of further goals fleeing before them. As a teacher, I ask myself what I can reasonably expect my students to achieve in one semester and try to pitch my comments accordingly. And I try not to ask students to achieve everything at once. One thing I do to restrain the urge to speak volumes on a single paper is to keep a record (very brief) for each student of the accomplishments and problems I note on their growing portfolios of papers. This way I have a firmer sense of what each student has done so far as I sit down to read and comment on a fresh batch of student papers. And I'm more likely to be able to assist them in moving from the writing they have done so far to the writing they might do next.

Ways of Reading and Revising: Some Sample Student Papers

Reading begins with predispositions. When students read "The Achievement of Desire," they do so having already read a headnote that says something about Rodriguez's background and educational concerns, and something about the reception of Rodriguez's book *Hunger of Memory*. In addition, they begin to read with certain assumptions (different for different readers) about the purposes of education, about Chicanos and working-class families, about autobiographies. Further, students come to "The Achievement of Desire" with characteristic ways of reading, strategies that have worked for them in the past in making sense of texts in academic settings. Readers never notice everything that might be noticed; what they notice when they come to a text for the first time largely depends, then, on what they are predisposed to notice. Moreover, in rereading, as students try to articulate what they have noticed about a text through writing a text of their own, they can't write about all they have noticed. Even given the focusing instrument of an assignment question or problem, their rereading, their writing, will have to attend to some things that they might say about the question or problem and ignore others. This narrowing of the field of vision need not be seen as merely confining; it can also be seen as empowering. The selective and structuring acts of attention required by writing can transform what students have noticed into texts they must account for, the beginning of a performed understanding.

In commenting on a student's reading of an assigned text with an eye to having the student revise, I am commenting both on the understanding of what the paper represents, asking that it be strengthened and extended, and on the way of reading that the paper brings forward, asking about what it allows the writer to do and about how alternative ways of reading might enable the student to construct further, possibly more satisfying or complete, readings.

Let me illustrate by looking at some student papers written in response to an assignment that asks students to talk about Richard Rodriguez as a reader by examining the ways Rodriguez makes use of Richard Hoggart's *The Uses of Literacy* in writing "The Achievement of Desire." The assignment is closely similar to the first "Assignment for Writing" on Rodriguez in *Ways of Reading*. Here is the first paper.

Rodriguez used Hoggart's "scholarship boy" as a role model to a certain extent. Rodriguez modeled his education around what Hoggart made the "scholarship boy" out to be. After he read Hoggart, Rodriguez thought he might become all the more educated and know so much more if he followed the ideals of the "scholarship boy."

In the beginning, Richard's education and learning became his first priority. He often resorted to hitting the books because his family life was folded around him. The isolation which he felt became the obsession for his hard work and constant classroom participation. The time spent on schoolwork made the division between his social and secluded life apparent. The lack of understanding and support he felt that was not coming from his parents made him draw further away as his family life fell to pieces. The only way for him to escape the confinement which he believed was around him was to view his teachers in astonishment. His admiration stemmed from their praise of his work and dedication. His work and efforts were directed toward some mystical goal, the goal to be like the "scholarship boy."

In conclusion, I understand and admire Rodriguez's perseverance and dedication to learn. I once wrote in a speech, "Anything of any worth or value has to be worked for. Oftentimes it is a struggle, but when you persevere and you reach your goal, there is a sense of accomplishment. And I do feel that sense of accomplishment." And so does Rodriguez.

Ways of Reading assumes that the essays and stories it asks students to read are worth the active questioning and recasting they require of their readers; and *Ways of Reading* also assumes that student papers written in response to these texts are worth similar effort. As I read and respond to papers my students have written, I am trying to see what their readings have noticed and trying to suggest ways in which, when they revise, they might do more with what they have attended to. When I begin to read a set of student papers, the question that guides my first reading is usually: "Which of these papers represent readings that grow out of acts of attention?" Or, as the question could also be put, "Which of these papers do some work with a text, and which don't?" That is, I believe that some papers are not worth revising, and this paper on Rodriguez is one of them.

Consider this sentence: "[Rodriguez's] work and efforts were directed toward some mystical goal, the goal to be like the 'scholarship boy.' " I was puzzled by the sentence, initially, because I couldn't understand how this writer is imagining the young Rodriguez to be pursuing a goal he had never heard of. It occurred to me, of course, that the sentence might represent this writer's way of saying that, retrospectively, the mature Richard Rodriguez was renaming his past through Richard Hoggart's language. (And the same thing could be said, hypothetically, about the sentence "Rodriguez modeled his education around what Hoggart made the 'scholarship boy' out to be.") But I had no way of reconciling these conjectures with the sentence "After he read Hoggart, Rodriguez thought he might become all the more educated and know so much more if he followed the ideals of the 'scholarship boy'" followed by a paragraph describing the young Rodriguez trying to become more educated. Bizarrely, the paper suggests that Rodriguez used *The Uses of Literacy* not as a way of retrospectively framing his experience but as a sort of twentieth-century conduct book guiding, *while* it was occurring, his education.

What way of reading does this paper represent? I believe that this writer has read "The Achievement of Desire" at breakneck speed, probably only once, and attended to very little, grasping at just enough to dash off a paper to hand in — never mind the assignment or trying to become engaged by the text. He has a paper, but he hasn't given himself a chance to make sense out of a puzzling text or a challenging problem. He begins with an assignment asking him to discuss Rodriguez as a reader of Hoggart; he scans the text for the first reference to Rodriguez reading Hoggart and finds this: "Then one day, leafing through Richard Hoggart's *The Uses of Literacy*, I found, in his description of the scholarship boy, myself. For the first time I realized that there were other students like me . . ."); and he goes on to grab enough from the essay to prove that, yes, Rodriguez found himself in the "scholarship boy." The student will not be swayed by assignment language that asks him to "look closely at Rodriguez's references to Hoggart's book," to "compare Rodriguez's version of the 'scholarship boy' with Hoggart's," or to examine "the way Rodriguez handles quotations, where he works Hoggart's words into paragraphs of his own"; he has no time to elaborate on his intriguing claims that "[Rodriguez] often resorted to hitting the books because his family life was folding around him" or "the lack of understanding and support he felt that was not coming from his parents made him draw further away as his family life fell to pieces"; and he especially gives himself no opportunity to wonder about what use Richard Rodriguez is making of Richard Hoggart's *The Uses of Literacy*.

In commenting on this paper, I said to the student, in greatly abbreviated form, what I have just said here, and asked him to go back and write a paper on the assignment. I did not ask him to "revise" his first paper because, for one thing, I believed that to do so would trivialize my idea of revision, a re-seeing of some act of attention. Also, I believed that to ask this student for a rewriting of his first paper would be to patronize him. I think that I would have been saying, in effect, "Sorry, you're just not bright enough to read Rodriguez or do this assignment, but maybe you can polish your prose a bit."

"The Achievement of Desire" is especially suitable to a study of the practices of academic reading and writing because of the many ways in which it could be said to suggest that intellectual achievement, as recognized by (contemporary American) academic communities, involves a continuing mediation between invention and imitation, between freedom and constraint. Students engaged in most academic projects are expected to articulate well-considered personal positions within limits not of their own choosing — limits that, unfortunately, probably cannot even be seen *as* limits in the absence of particular acts of reading and writing. That is, teachers cannot resolve their students' reading and writing dilemmas in advance. And students cannot resolve them until they experience them, until they begin, for example, to work at reading an essay through articulating in an essay of their own what their reading has paid attention to. "What strong readers know is that they have to begin regardless of doubts or hesitations."

I think that, in contrast to the first writer, the writer of the following paper has begun a project that she might usefully revise.

> Richard Rodriguez finds himself in Richard Hoggart's
> <u>The Uses of Literacy</u>. I thought I identified parts of
> myself in my psychology texts, but I was not so feverish
> about finding them. The anxiety in Rodriguez's life makes
> his reading of Hoggart more dynamic.
>
> His unease can be seen in the way he jumps from
> thought to thought throughout "The Achievement of Desire."
> On almost every page, there is an example of Rodriguez
> questioning himself. The power that is bound to his anxi-
> ety is shown by the emphasis that he puts into his confes-
> sion.
>
> What I am about to say to you has taken me more
> than twenty years to admit: <u>A primary reason for my</u>
> <u>success in the classroom was that I couldn't forget</u>
> <u>that schooling was changing me and separating me from</u>
> <u>the life I enjoyed before becoming a student</u>. That
> simple realization!
>
> He sets the confession apart to give it more emphasis
> and throws in the italics and exclamation for good measure.
> It is this angst that characterized Rodriguez before he
> reads Hoggart.
>
> When the author finally finds Hoggart, it is a relief
> for him. He gets much satisfaction from being identified.
> The description of a "scholarship boy" is held up as a
> theme to his life. "Then one day . . . I found, in his
> description of the scholarship boy, myself." For most of
> "The Achievement of Desire," there is a pattern to
> Rodriguez's use of Hoggart. He gives an excerpt of
> Hoggart's description and then tells of his early experi-
> ences. The way Hoggart is employed almost convinces me
> that Rodriguez based his life on the writing of Hoggart.

I must point out that the writer is able to distinguish himself from the generality. In my psychology courses, I would read about the different personality traits and think that I was an example of all of them. Under close inspection, though, I was able to see that I was more complex than any one category could portray. Rodriguez shows reservations about committing himself, too. He adds qualifications to Hoggart's view of the "scholarship boy." One instance of setting himself apart comes when he says that Hoggart only "initially" shows "deep understanding." Throughout the essay, we go from Hoggart's concept of a "scholarship boy" to the more specific reality of the author's life. Rodriguez sees the differences between the two, but he is content to call himself "a certain kind of scholarship boy."

Why is it so important for him to call himself a "scholarship boy"? He is not content to trust his own words to describe himself. The revelation was made by himself, but he felt a driving need to find "mention of students like me." This insecurity parallels his problems as a youth. I have to wonder if he has really come very far from the imitator he was. In an autobiography, we expect to hear an account in a personal, original, and direct manner. Here we get Rodriguez's life framed in the work of Hoggart. I do not want to say that using Hoggart is not effective for our understanding of a powerful part of his life. There are so many ways of presenting the subject, however, and his choice strikes me as being odd. He is very willing to give up his authority to an "expert."

He felt that he must find himself in the reading. A great deal of energy was bound to his feelings of loss. He had to pacify his anxiety. Hoggart gave a description that was close enough for identification and Rodriguez jumped at it. The reason that he gives us for reading Hoggart is

```
that it gave him a measure of his change, but I see it as

proof that he has changed very little.
```

When I got this paper, which was submitted for the same assignment in the same class as the paper I looked at earlier, I saw it as a worthwhile opening move in the construction of a strong reading. The tack that this writer takes in this reading, her insistent emphasis on Rodriguez's "anxiety," was not a direction that most of her classmates chose to pursue, nor one that I would have chosen myself, but it seemed to me that this paper, as I interpreted it, did grow out of an act of attention, one that I felt it worth my time and hers to ask her to question and extend.

Our class had already worked with reading and writing assignments based on Walker Percy's essay "The Loss of the Creature," and I noted this writer's allusion to Percy at the end of the fifth paragraph. I also noticed that the allusion was *only* that, not a genuine recasting of experience through new language. It was what we had been calling a "gesture." Certainly, I thought, her re-seeing her paper in conjunction with Percy's treatment of authority might give this writer more to say about Rodriguez-as-anxious-reader. At the same time, I did not want to overemphasize what for this reader might be seen as only tangential, an issue which, if she pursued it strenuously, might serve to turn her paper into my paper.

We had also, in our class, talked about readers' "roles," and it seemed to me that at times this paper (notably in the last sentence of the fourth paragraph) might profitably be questioned on the basis of the limiting roles it was asking me to assume as a reader — particularly since, in the fourth paragraph, the writer herself speaks of having declined to be limited by a certain kind of reading.

One of my strongest reactions to the paper was, as you might imagine, unease at the paucity of demonstration, illustration, and qualification of the claims being made — even though I was quite taken by a number of the claims. Here the task ahead will sound familiar: to deploy my own variants of the writing teacher's old refrain, "Show me." (Our class's term for unexplored assertion was "labeling.") This is how I responded to the paper.

```
     Richard Rodriguez finds himself in Richard Hoggart's

The Uses of Literacy.  I thought I identified parts of

myself in my psychology texts, but I was not so feverish

about finding them.  The anxiety in Rodriguez's life makes

his reading of Hoggart more dynamic.

     His unease can be seen in the way he jumps from

thought to thought throughout "The Achievement of Desire."

On almost every page, there is an example of Rodriguez

questioning himself.  The power that is bound to his anxi-

ety is shown by the emphasis that he puts into his confes-

sion.
```

*Signifi-
cant? W‌
have you‌
chosen ‌
to demo‌
strate t‌
in your
paper?*

```
     What I am about to say to you has taken me more

than twenty years to admit:  A primary reason for my

success in the classroom was that I couldn't forget

that schooling was changing me and separating me
```

from the life I enjoyed before becoming a student.
That simple realization!

He sets the confession apart to give it more emphasis
and throws in the italics and exclamation for good measure.
It is this angst that characterized Rodriguez before he
reads Hoggart.

O.K., a reader can grant that you recognize his confession as worth noticing. So how do you account for its significance? Why not give us the interpretation? Is "angst" not self-explanatory.)

When the author finally finds Hoggart, it is a relief
for him. He gets much satisfaction from being identified.
The description of a "scholarship boy" is held up as a
theme to his life. "Then one day . . . I found, in his
description of the scholarship boy, myself." For most of
"The Achievement of Desire," there is a pattern to
Rodriguez's use of Hoggart. He gives an excerpt of
Hoggart's description and then tells of his early experiences. The way Hoggart is employed almost convinces me
that Rodriguez based his life on the writing of Hoggart.

True? Important? Where's your reading?

*This is the one para-
graph in
your read-
ing that
parallels
the "dyna-
mic" read-
ing you say
Rodriguez
makes of
Hoggart.
Here your
Rodriguez
can dis-
criminate;
elsewhere
he is over-
whelmed.*

I must point out that the writer is able to distinguish himself from the generality. In my psychology
courses, I would read about the different personality
traits and think that I was an example of all of them.
Under close inspection, though, I was able to see that I
was more complex than any one category could portray.
Rodriguez shows reservations about committing himself, too.
He adds qualifications to Hoggart's view of the "scholarship boy." One instance of setting himself apart comes
when he says that Hoggart only "initially" shows "deep
understanding." Throughout the essay, we go from Hoggart's
concept of a "scholarship boy" to the more specific reality
of the author's life. Rodriguez sees the differences between the two, but he is content to call himself "a certain
kind of scholarship boy."

What can you make of this split?

And then?

*What role
are you ask-
ing a reader
to play when
you imply
that the
quoted
phrase
contradicts
Rodriguez's
ability to
see differ-
ences?*

Well? Why is it so important for him to call himself a
"scholarship boy"? He is not content to trust his own

words to describe himself. The revelation was made by himself, but he felt a driving need to find "mention of *Only* students like me." This insecurity parallels his problems *labels* as a youth. I have to wonder if he has really come very far from the imitator he was. In an autobiography, we expect to hear an account in a personal, original, and direct manner. Here we get Rodriguez's life framed in the *How is it* work of Hoggart. I do not want to say that using Hoggart *effective?* is not effective for our understanding of a powerful part of his life. There are so many ways of presenting the subject, however, and his choice strikes me as being odd. *Do you have* He is very willing to give up his authority to an "expert." *something in mind by the allusion to Percy?* He felt that he must find himself in the reading. A *Can you* great deal of energy was bound to his feelings of loss. He *You need make this* had to pacify his anxiety. Hoggart gave a description that *say more more of a* was close enough for identification and Rodriguez jumped at *gesture?* it. The reason that he gives us for reading Hoggart is that it gave him a measure of his change, but I see it as proof that he has changed very little.

I admire your willingness to see Rodriguez's achievement at an advanced stage of his education, his way of reading Hoggart, as having roots in long-standing feelings and habits. But I don't think your essay yet demonstrates the reading it wants to claim. Your word "category" struck me. What categories besides "anxiety" could you incorporate in your reading of Rodriguez's relation to Hoggart?

And here is the revision that the student handed in the following week.

In Richard Rodriguez's essay "The Achievement of Desire," we get a sort of record of how Rodriguez responded to reading a book by Richard Hoggart called The Uses of Literacy. But what I can't understand is how to separate how Rodriguez reacted to The Uses of Literacy when he first read it in the British Museum from how he is reading it when he's a professional writer writing an essay he wants to publish.

In the British Museum, Rodriguez says, he found in Hoggart's

> description of the scholarship boy, myself. For the
> first time I realized that there were other students
> like me, and so I was able to frame the meaning of
> my academic success, its consequent price--the loss.

At various points in "The Achievement of Desire," we see Rodriguez working out how what he read about the scholarship boy helps him understand why he feels so bad about his academic success. "Good schooling requires that any student alter early childhood habits," Rodriguez paraphrases Hoggart, and then Rodriguez remembers how "after dinner, I would rush to a bedroom with papers and books. As often as possible, I resisted parental pleas to 'save lights' by coming to the kitchen to work." Rodriguez wasn't as upset as his parents were about his need to be alone to study. When he first entered school, he remembers, "what bothered me . . . was the isolation reading required." But gradually, as he was tutored by one of the nuns, he began to feel the "possibility of fellowship between a reader and a writer," not "intimate," but "personal." And he also started to want a power he sensed in reading: "Books were going to make me 'educated.'" So that eventually, Rodriguez often enjoyed being alone with his books--but the enjoyment made him feel guilty and anxious: "Nervous. I rarely looked away from my book--or back on my memories." His parents, he knew, were not "educated."

Hoggart helps Rodriguez interpret his past, but as he writes "The Achievement of Desire," Rodriguez is not always grateful for Hoggart's descriptions of the scholarship boy. Rodriguez quotes a passage from The Uses of Literacy in which Hoggart says that the scholarship boy "begins to see life as a ladder, as a permanent examination with some praise and further exhortation at each stage. He becomes an expert imbiber and doler-out." Here, says Rodriguez, Hoggart's "criticism" is "more accurate than fair." When I first read "The Achievement of Desire," I wasn't sure what Rodriguez meant by calling Hoggart's description here "criticism." After he quotes Hoggart's remarks, Rodriguez restates them in a way that makes me think he sees them as a good description--but he's worried about how "fair" they are. In reading the essay again, I noticed Rodriguez's saying that the scholarship boy "realizes more often and more acutely than most other students--than Hoggart him-self--that education requires radical self-reformation." How does Rodriguez know how much Hoggart realizes? I haven't read <u>The Uses of Literacy</u>, and maybe if I did I would find out that Hoggart was not himself a scholarship boy, and this might be related to how much Rodriguez says Hoggart "realizes." Or maybe there are parts of <u>The Uses of Literacy</u> that show Hoggart not understanding what Rodriguez sees--but I don't see that Rodriguez quotes them.

I said earlier that I couldn't figure out how to separate Rodriguez's first reading of Hoggart from all the rereadings of Hoggart he must have done before he wrote and published "The Achievement of Desire." I still think, as I wrote in a previous paper, that Rodriguez "felt that he <u>must</u> find himself" in reading Hoggart, but I also think now that Rodriguez also became anxious <u>not</u> to find himself in Hoggart's book. Maybe I started to feel this way after Sylvia pointed out in class something that I hadn't noticed before: Hoggart says that the scholarship boy is unusual, not a typical working-class student, not even a typically <u>successful</u> working-class student. Most successful working-class scholarship students "manage a fairly graceful tran-sition," Rodriguez paraphrases Hoggart. It is only the exceptional working-class scholarship student--perhaps "intellectually mediocre" (Rodriguez's paraphrase of

Hoggart) and maybe "haunted by the knowledge that one chooses to become a student" (Rodriguez's interpretation of Hoggart--I think)--who becomes a "scholarship boy." I think that Rodriguez found in Hoggart's idea of the scholarship boy something he thought he could use to help him understand his own anxieties about his success. But I also think that Rodriguez must have understood at some point (when I'm not sure) that Hoggart's description of the scholarship boy didn't completely correspond to his own situation. (Does Hoggart talk about race as well as class? Does Rodriguez really believe that he was himself of only average intelligence?) When Rodriguez reacts against Hoggart's description, then, you could say that it is Rodriguez, not Hoggart, who is not being "fair." But I prefer to say that Rodriguez, as he writes "The Achievement of Desire," is being what in our class we've called a "strong reader."

When Rodriguez says,

> A primary reason for my success in the classroom was
> that I couldn't forget that schooling was changing
> me and separating me from the life I enjoyed before
> becoming a student,

I read him to mean that his being unable to forget that his education was making him lose something he valued in his relationship with his family kept him continually anxious to be a big success as a student. If he were only a little successful, he would have "lost" his family without gaining anything in return. I'm not saying that as a boy Rodriguez was conscious of this (he says the "realization" took him twenty years), but I do think this is how he sees it as he writes "The Achievement of Desire." Partly, Rodriguez wanted to separate himself from his parents; he wanted to become "educated." What he found in books became what guided his feelings about who he was. But I don't think that it's exactly right to say that Rodriguez wanted, in Walker Percy's words from "The Loss of the Creature," to "surrender" his "sovereignty" to "experts," his teachers and the authors of the books he read. At some point, Rodriguez had to see that his way of pursuing education only made sense if <u>he</u> became the expert. In a way, I know that when I read my psychology texts and find myself there, I am only playing at psychology. Even when I realize that I am more complex than any one psychological "category" can portray, I also know that I don't yet know enough psychology to feel very sure about just where I do or don't fit into the language being used. And I could understand someone's saying that I am still caught up in believing, in Walker Percy's words, that "the thing is <u>disposed</u> of by theory." But I also suspect that if I want to become a psychologist (and I do), I can't just ignore psychological theory. I can't just go <u>around</u> the words and categories of "psychology"; somehow I have to go <u>through</u> them. And I think that Rodriguez was doing something like this when he reread Hoggart. In the British Museum, he wanted an "expert," somebody his education had taught him to respect, to give him a handle on his life. But he was also anxious, as he wrote "The Achievement of Desire," to go <u>beyond</u> Hoggart, to show that his expertise was greater than Hoggart's. He needed to show that he was better able to explain his own life than his teacher was. I think that if Richard Hoggart were to read "The Achievement of Desire," he might feel both complimented and astonished.

When I compared this revision to the original paper, one of the things that struck me was the change in the writer's manner of using quotations. In the original, the material quoted is all drawn from a cluster of three pages in "The Achievement of Desire"; in the revision, the writer has ranged through much of Rodriguez's essay for her citations. In reading the original, I felt a disjunction between phrases like "on almost every page," "for most of 'The Achievement of Desire,' " "throughout the essay," and the nonarticulation of readings those phrases only gesture at. In the revision, it seemed to me, the writer has needed to lean less on summarizing assertions because she has demonstrated her readings through a much closer working relationship with Rodriguez's text.

But I would not want to say that I think the revised paper "supports" its "points" better than the original (though I can certainly imagine a teacher's saying something like that). Ways of reading that emphasize repeated readings and writings, that posit back-and-forth movements between reading and writing, are probably not well served by talking about "support" (supporting "thesis" statements, for example, by "adding detail"). Students can learn fairly quickly how to generate and support theses; but to present that activity as a goal of writing about readings can mean that that's all students will learn. To write a paper is to perform a reading. Strong reading is dependent on attentiveness, on curiosity; if students see their job as primarily to support a thesis, attention declines, curiosity withers.

I do not think that the writer of the original paper has seen her reading as simply supporting a thesis. She's done more than that. A strong reading of "The Achievement of Desire," one that allows itself to be curious, is likely to end up with a proposition different from the one it begins with. And to some extent this is what happens in the original version of the paper. Like the writer of the first Rodriguez paper I looked at, this writer, in her original paper, begins with Rodriguez's claim to have found himself in Hoggart's description of the "scholarship boy." But she hasn't approached Rodriguez's declaration blankly; she hasn't, that is, adopted the role of a reader who is content to take Rodriguez at his word, a reader who has been entrusted with the key to the essay and need now only locate and assemble all those instances in the text that show that the key works. In fact, almost immediately, the writer decides that her reading of "The Achievement of Desire" will tease out not *that* or *how* Rodriguez finds himself in Hoggart, but *why* he chooses to do so. And this project is further modified by the writer's incorporating a comparison between a reading of her own experiences and Rodriguez-as-reader-of-Hoggart, which leads to her becoming (if only temporarily) cautious about and critical of what she is doing: "I must point out that the writer is able to distinguish himself from the generality. . . ." Throughout the essay, we go from Hoggart's concept of a "scholarship boy" to the more specific reality of the author's life.

But, I think, the writer does not sustain her strong reading. Perhaps daunted by the work she senses it would take to follow up on the differences between Hoggart's "concept" and Rodriguez's "specific reality," or perhaps feeling impelled to conclude her reading unwaveringly, she ties up loose ends with her final sentence: "The reason that he gives us for reading Hoggart is that it gave him a measure of his change, but I see it as proof that he has changed very little." I like the sentence. I find it gutsy and intelligent. But I also think that the sentence is a kind of giving up. It indicates, to me, a writer who does not yet have a way of reading that allows her to be more than sometimes curious about what she is saying.

In the revised paper, the writer takes the risk of beginning with a puzzle that she is not going to be able to solve — no more than any reader could. My guess is that the risk is calculated: that though she knows there is no way to separate with certainty Rodriguez's early and late readings of Hoggart, she recognizes that the problem she poses is one that leaves room for multiple strong interpretations. And it's the sort of problem that she can tie to more ways and acts of reading than Rodriguez's reading of Hoggart in the British Museum. While making a strong reading of Rodriguez, she is also beginning readings of the relations between reading and writing, between reading and rereading, between individual and collective participations in language. Interestingly, these connections emerge (and, yes, they are mostly implicit — there are more papers to be articulated here), I think, *because* she has decided to work curiously and attentively with reading and rereading Rodriguez. In strong reading, the commonplace, "You can't see the forest for the trees," makes little sense. For strong readers, the forest is not a given but a field of possibilities, and whatever possibilities are realized require detailed attention to lots of trees.

Talking about Reading and Writing

As they work through the reading and writing assignments of *Ways of Reading*, students will have many opportunities, in a variety of contexts, to attend to the construction of meaning. Occasionally they will be asked to paraphrase or reconstruct a difficult passage. More often, they will be asked to interpret what they have read, with some specific purpose in mind: framing something in their own experience with the key terms and methods of another writer, in order to learn more about both that writer's methods and their own experience; or turning an essay back on itself by testing out its claims or reconsidering its examples; or seeing how they might use one text to interpret another. Frequently, students will be asked for revisions of their papers, revisions in which they can continue projects suggested by the assignments and their responses to the assignments. Always students are asked, implicitly or explicitly, to reread what they have written, to rewrite what they have read.

Much of this work will go on in the classroom. Students' dormitory rooms or library carrels or kitchen tables are not their only arenas for making meaning; the assignments and anthology pieces, the papers students write and the comments a teacher makes on those papers, are not a class's only forums for engaging in the conversations of reading and writing. What happens in the classroom can reinforce or redirect those other exchanges — and serve to make them more fruitful.

I find that class conversation is facilitated when a class begins to develop early its medium of exchange — a language about language that can be shared. Whatever ways students have, individually, for talking about reading and writing, they probably bring with them to a course in college reading and writing a sort of lingua franca from their various high school English courses: "coherence," "organization," etc. Certainly college teachers and their students may choose to draw on these terms to talk about the work of reading and writing, but I have often been surprised at how slippery this seemingly stable language can be. A couple of years ago, for example, when I returned a set of student papers on which I'd commented to some writers that they were "summarizing," two students approached me after class. The first said that he had just reread the assignment carefully and didn't see it asking him anywhere to "summarize," and that that was certainly not what he had done in his paper, though he could have if he'd been asked. The second student thanked me for the comment but wondered if I'd found anything "wrong" with his paper. Both students, that is, revealed to me that my class had not so far provided a context for these readers to do anything with the word "summarizing." In the absence of our class's having worked out a distinction between "summarizing" and, say, "interpreting," these students could only conclude that "summarizing" meant exactly what they knew it meant: a routine performed by students in English classes — ordinarily when asked but sometimes, miraculously, unbidden.

What I like to try to do is have my reading and writing classes construct — gradually, accretively — a language for language that has had to be interpreted, a language for which we have had to make sense. Many terms in my marking of the student paper discussed earlier — "labels," "gesture," readers' "roles," "demonstrate," writing about a text as "reading" it — are terms that that class had been slowly accumulating since the beginning of the semester. Generally these terms first surfaced in class discussions. Sometimes they were first proposed by me, sometimes by students, as linguistic tools for our class to use to make sense of some text before us. Sometimes the terms first appeared in an assignment. Obviously not all classes will fashion the same tools, and one semester's key terms, metaphors, are not likely to be identical to what gets used the next semester. In redeploying these terms to comment on student papers, a teacher models a version of what students are engaged in as they read and respond to the pieces in *Ways of Reading* — seeing their own projects through the frame of language they have had to come to terms with, redefining preexistent language and routines for their own purposes.

I think that there are certain benefits in devoting much of a class's time together to discussions of student papers. Students whose papers are being discussed get multiple responses to what they have written, and possibly insights into how they might revise. The whole class gets a chance to look at other writers struggling with dilemmas similar to those that they themselves have been wrestling with in their own papers.

Classroom discussion of their papers gives students opportunities to explore the possibilities and problems involved in moving from writing to rewriting, from a reading that has noticed something significant to a reading that can better articulate and account for the significance of what has been noticed. The revised paper on Rodriguez I looked at earlier grew not only out of what the writer was able to do with my comments on her first version but also, as it happened, out of a class discussion of the original paper. Students generally liked and were impressed by the paper, but they were puzzled at times by the reading. One student wondered what the writer meant by saying that Rodriguez "jumps from thought to thought" in "The Achievement of Desire." A second student said that, whatever the writer meant, she should have shown how this "jumping" works. Someone else said that she wasn't sure why Rodriguez's jumping from thought to thought, if he does, might be important in the first place, but a fourth student said that obviously it could indicate, as the writer says, Rodriguez's "unease," an "anxiety," just as Rodriguez's "questioning himself" could — provided the writer demonstrated that. "But self-questioning doesn't always mean anxiety," said a fifth student. "I don't think I'm very anxious, and I question myself all the time. Self-questioning could mean that a person doesn't know enough." "Right," said another student, "or that he knows too much." The conversation continued. This sort of discussion provides not so much a chance for writers to hear that they haven't said what they meant (though it may do that), as an occasion for writers to become more curious about just what they *do* mean. The writer of this paper, as she learned from the discussion, couldn't do a rewriting of her paper, not in any important sense, without doing some more reading, getting back into Rodriguez's text and hers.

And class discussions of the papers students write can offer substantiations of the assumption that there are multiple ways, and many good ways, to read. I talked earlier about a class discussion in which students argued about the interpretation of the phrase "the end of education" that concludes Rodriguez's essay. When I read the set of papers that came in for the writing assignment I made, I picked out and duplicated three of them for class discussion. The first writer argued that his interpretation of "the end of education" as the completion of Rodriguez's academic training derived from noticing that "The Achievement of Desire" is constructed as a series of commentaries on important moments in an academic's schooling; that Rodriguez speaks early on of trying to figure out — "in the British Museum (too distracted to finish my dissertation)" — what that schooling amounts to; and that by the last words of the essay, "the end of education," Rodriguez has come to a resolution — though, this writer conceded, he could also see that Rodriguez retained some unfulfilled "desires." The second writer insisted, also quite convincingly, that, according to her reading, "the end of education" must be the accomplishment the essay's title foregrounds — "The Achievement of Desire"; that the significant incidents in Rodriguez's education can be read (she gave readings) as his holding the past at arm's length; and that Rodriguez is able to stop this repression only when he becomes secure enough in his "educated" identity that it can't be undermined by regret for what he has sacrificed; so that, finally, he can turn "unafraid to desire the past." The third reader, in her paper, while saying that she understood the "end" of Rodriguez's education to be in one sense its completion, thought it most important to notice that Rodriguez calls his schooling, early and late, "miseducation," and that, whatever Rodriguez learns in school, he can't understand himself until he gets outside the boundaries of schooling ("too distracted to finish my dissertation"); so that, as this writer reads the essay, "education" is opposed to both "desire" and understanding. I don't do these readings justice with this outline, but I thought that one of the most interesting outcomes of our class discussion of them was several students' remarking that, since they found all three papers persuasive, they judged that not only do different readers read differently, but a single reader might read a text in various ways. Discussions of student papers, texts articulating readings of other texts, parallel the practice of looking at one thing through something else, which most of the course's assignments ask students to perform. For a class to examine student papers with the same attention and care brought to discussions of the anthology selections by themselves augments students' belief in the value of the strong reading they are being asked to pursue.

A teacher's decisions about how to use student papers in class — which papers to use, how much student text can be profitably addressed in a single class period, what questions to use in guiding the discussion, just how a discussion of some particular paper or papers serves broader discussions of reading and writing — all depend on a teacher's experience, agenda for a course in college reading and writing, and way of imagining how *Ways of Reading* fits into that agenda. I'll end here with just a few more notes from my own experience. I have found that student papers duplicated for distribution and class discussion can focus on the acts of reading and writing represented by the papers rather than on uneasy exchanges governed by diffidence about or defense of the emotional investments that the papers also represent. Generally speaking, students adapt to the convention of authorial anonymity quickly and easily. As much as possible, I try to choose papers for discussion that will give the class opportunities to notice, wonder about, and question efforts at performed understanding — rather than papers that I think exhibit little effort, nonperformance. Ideally, I want my students to see a discussion of papers as an occasion not for sniping at lousy work but for talking about how good work might be extended. For example, I can imagine my using the first Rodriguez paper I looked at earlier only in an early semester class discussion — using it as a way of talking about nonreading, perhaps pairing it with a much stronger paper. But after the first few weeks of a semester, I would think that that paper no longer has a place (and, indeed, its writer did not seek a place) in our class conversations.

If you are teaching *Ways of Reading* along with other teachers at your college, and if some of you have made similar selections from among the scores of assignments available in the book, you might want to share some student papers along with the other things you are sharing about teaching the course, thus giving each of you a bigger pool from which to draw the kinds of papers you want for class discussion.

o—o—o—o—o—o—o—o—o—o—o—o—o—o—o—o—o—o—o

RESTLESS AND HOPEFUL: TEACHING TOWARD DIFFICULTY IN FREIRE'S "THE 'BANKING' CONCEPT OF EDUCATION"
by Jennifer Lee

Each semester, I step into the General Writing classroom with a strange mixture of romantic idealism and anxiety. Part of me imagines the twenty-two mostly first-year students and myself embarking together on what Paulo Freire calls the "restless, impatient, continuing, hopeful inquiry" that makes us human. The other part of me remembers that General Writing is a required course — few students manage to "test out" — and for many incoming freshmen, the prospect of a semester spent reading and writing rarely elicits excitement. Some students hope General Writing will provide them with useful skills, but few envision finding the course particularly stimulating. If I forget, momentarily, this divergence between my expectations for the course and students', I am reminded when I read the first batch of essays. How, I ask myself again, will I get students to "open up" the way the read and write? How will I get students who carry eighteen credit hours, maybe work at night, invested in the process of reading and writing their way into difficult and complex terrains? How will I enable them to see the limitations of writing only about what they understand, or make it possible to see writing as something that rather than capturing its subject moves toward it?

On the first day of class, I ask students to respond to an excerpt from the introduction to *Ways of Reading,* one in which the editors talk about reading as "social interaction" — "You make your mark on a book and it makes its mark on you" — and set this approach against "finding information or locating an author's purpose" (*Ways of Reading* 1). As we look at samples of their responses during the next class, I ask students what it would mean, or for that matter what it would look like, for a writer to actually make her mark on a text. In one form or another, we will circle around this notion all semester. But one of the most important ways I suggest making a mark might be possible is by reading toward difficult moments in a text. A significant part of students' work will be to write "difficulty papers," informal responses to the assigned readings where students think through a moment they find particularly confusing, hard to understand or decipher, or a passage that surprises or angers them. These "difficulty papers" then serve as the center of class discussions, students reading selections during class and using them to lead us in and out of the text at hand.

At the same time, I ask questions in the margins of their essays and attempt to trouble their assumptions by playing devil's advocate, trying to get them to tease out their ideas. Combined, these strategies usually initiate dialogue about writing that continues all semester, a conversation with difficulty and uncertainty at its heart. As students become familiar with the routine and we establish a rhythm of work, their essays get progressively messier. By midsemester, the five-paragraph essay has all but disappeared. Paragraphs lengthen, sometimes taking up a full page. Comma splices begin to appear in the writing of students who, at the beginning of the semester, were fine-sentence boundary managers. Things begin to feel a little out of control. When I read essays at this point in the term, there is a discernable momentum to the way students think through their ideas on the page, and

295

with it, a kind of chaos. No longer attempting to present what they know in neat little packages, there are redundancies, digressions, moments of ambivalence and uncertainty.

At least, that was the story until this past spring when my tried and true methods just didn't work. It was only by way of working with Paulo Freire's essay, "The 'Banking' Concept of Education," that I was forced to slow the process of reading down, both for my students and for myself, forced to make visible the way a reader forges her path through a difficult text. What I found was that, in a sense, Freire's text demands a certain attention and humility. It is nearly impossible for a reader to wave her hand and say simply, "I get it." In light of the essay's complex, abstract language, any attempt to "sum up" the essay's main idea feels conspicuously incomplete. Each reading elicits textual nuances and meanings that surface only after a second, third, or fourth reading, and while this may be true for any text, Freire's essay makes the notion of layered meanings impossible to ignore. Students cannot help but notice the partial nature of their work, something they do not readily see when reading "easier" — meaning more narrative, more "straight forward" — texts. As they attempt to control Freire's essay by summing it up, they know they are leaving so much out. The idea of shaping an explicitly partial reading begins to make more sense. Besides, students readily admit, attempts to account for the whole leave them with little to say. What Freire's essay made possible for my students and I, just as the class seemed to be grinding to a painful halt, was actually *seeing* what writing and reading toward difficulty could accomplish. Working on Freire's text over the course of three weeks, we began again, this time taking small, creaking steps toward making a mark.

It was midsemester by the time we made it to "The 'Banking' Concept of Education," and as I read through the students' essays, I encountered one attempt after another to read for Freire's "main point." I could almost hear the sentences putting one foot in front of the other, playing themselves out along a script. *Do this, then this, now go here and there.* Many of the essays were quite short. In their introductions, writers often reiterated the assignment prompt: "The banking concept of education describes how in the classroom, students are transformed into 'containers' and are 'filled' with information by their teachers." They provided an example from their own educational experiences, as they were asked to do, and shaped their stories to illustrate the "banking" concept of education. Everything fit. The textures of the students' experiences, their ambiguities and conflicts, the complicated ways they did, and did not, play out Freire's theories, were lost. Students made sweeping proclamations: "This is wrong," or "Freire makes very powerful statements." It seemed these quick appraisals of Freire's argument were self-evident and should, without further embellishment and with little fanfare, make perfect sense to the average reader. Their analyses skipped across the surface of Freire's ideas like stones across water. I panicked. Now, looking back at the essays they had written up to this point in the semester, I could see ways the class had moved forward, but compared to other General Writing classes I'd taught, we hadn't made it very far into the land of gritty intellectual work. The silence in the room, both literal and figurative, was palpable. The essays seemed almost numb. It wasn't just that students persisted in writing along familiar, perhaps more comfortable, models, but that they seemed unengaged in the work, bored. The Freire essays were not so much a step backward as a moment in which I saw just how far we hadn't come.

Something else that caught my attention was the way many students actually quoted the same paragraph-long passage, in spite of the fact we had not yet discussed Freire's essay in class. This move was something I associated with responses written after class discussion of a text. I went back to Freire and back to the assignment prompt and found, not surprisingly, that students had chosen to represent Freire's argument by including the passage from which the assignment's language is drawn. Jillian's essay, excerpted below, represents the way many students approached the assignment, including the passage many of them quoted:

> This common way of teaching is stripping the informa-
>
> tion being taught of its significance and meaning. Paulo

Freire, a radical educator of our time, believes the methods of teaching must be changed. The student never truly
understands what they are learning, and in doing so, the
information is stripped of any life, substance, meaning.
Often a student sits in a classroom taking notes on the
facts the teacher lectures about, carefully involved in
making certain nothing is missed. But in effect, something
is missed. The teacher lectures and tells the student what
he/she must memorize in order to be "successful" and ultimately enlightened and intelligent. Freire stated:

> Narration (with the teacher as narrator) leads the
> students to memorize mechanically the narrated
> content. Worse yet, it turns them into "contain-
> ers," into "receptacles" to be "filled" by the
> teacher. The more completely she fills the recep-
> tacles, the better a teacher she is. The more
> meekly the receptacles permit themselves to be
> filled, the better students they are. (260)

This is true in classrooms in every society. The
student takes on the role of memorizer, focusing not on
what the meaning behind events are, but mainly on the
precise facts. They don't ask why, they just listen and
memorize. The better the teacher gets the students to
memorize the information, the better their grades are on
the tests, and the more successful the student and the
teacher feels. He is considered to be an excellent teacher
if students memorize enough of the information to pass. The
students that memorize what the teacher tells them to
memorize receive good grades and therefore are considered
good students.

I can easily recall sitting in the front seat of my
tenth grade American history class. My teacher, Mr. G——
walks in at the sound of the bell. . . "Get your notebooks
out" he states, and everyone responds simultaneously to his

direction. The routine has been reinforced by its daily
occurrence. "Today we will finish up our lesson on the
roaring twenties and then follow up with a review for the
test that will be taking place tomorrow in class." The
students look around at each other and begin to smile, for
we all know that the underlying meaning of "reviewing for
the test" is finding out what is exactly going to be on it.
After forty minutes of taking notes on the facts that Mr.
G—— states robotically, we switch notes and turn to the
review. "Now if I were you, I would pay very close attention to the words I say," Mr. G—— says with a wink. . . .

Each student received a good grade on the test making
Mr. G—— look like a "fabulous teacher who could get even
the worst students to pass." In reality none of us actually
learned anything or showed a desire to learn more. We just
memorized and repeated what the teacher told us to. It was
actually quite easy . . . a little time spent . . . what
could be better?

Later in the semester, Jillian would tell me she'd worked hard on this essay, and I certainly
noticed her attention to developing an example, the way she moves carefully through her
general reading of Freire. In fact, I chose Jillian's essay to duplicate and distribute for class
discussion because her essay was not only representative but, I thought, a comparatively
good effort. Like her classmates, Jillian shapes her reading of Freire around the notion of
memorization, not just as a symptom of the "banking" concept, but as its very definition.
Everything explicitly drawn from Freire's text comes from the first page and a half of his
essay — the language included in the assignment prompt, memorization as a key term.

News writers rely on a story structure called the inverted pyramid, in which the most
crucial information, the who, what, when, how and why, is crammed into the first and
perhaps second paragraphs. This way, so the reasoning goes, a reader can get what's most
important and, if time or attention are short, quit midway through the story without missing anything important. When I read the essays on Freire, I wondered if students had
similarly quit before making it to the end of the essay, or if they figured the essay's essential points could be found right up front, the remainder of the text just reiteration, unneces-
sary elaborations. But in each essay, I also saw hints of other ways of reading, threads that
echoed moments in Freire's text not talked about explicitly. Jillian, for example, focuses on
narration in her work with Freire, but her example is as much about the complicity between student and teacher as it is about narration and memorization. She has, it seems to
me, both a more particular reading of Freire to assert, and an argument against his text.
What she will name, in her second version of this essay, the "easy work bond" between
teacher and student, their mutual sense of satisfaction, she only hints at here. Mr. G——
may be lecturing "robotically," but it's clear from the smiles and winks that the students
and teacher like one another and that both parties enjoy their unspoken pact.

If Jillian's paper represents the majority of student responses to Freire, then Nick's paper, which I also handed out to the class for discussion, represents something like the kind of work I'd expected, or hoped, students would do:

> It was pounded into my head that America was the greatest place on earth and was hardly ever wrong and I believed every word of it. I did not think to question my teachers and they did not question me as to what I thought of America. Even if they had I would have only responded with a rehashing of what they had taught me because that is all I knew. Freire states, "The capability of banking education to minimize or annul the students' creative power and to stimulate their credulity serves the interests of the oppressors, who care neither to have the world revealed nor to see it transformed. The oppressors use their 'humanitarianism' to preserve a profitable situation" (Freire 350). By this pounding of patriotism into our heads at a young age the United States government is playing the role of the oppressor trying "to preserve a profitable situation" by using the banking concept of education. . . .

> > As I got older I began to see contradictions in what was taught to me by my elementary school teachers. My reality had always been that America was always right, but now I was finding things outside of school that transformed this reality. I saw people on television arguing over whether we should have dropped the atom bomb on Japan or whether we should have fought in Vietnam. . . . When I saw these contradictions I began to question my teachers I began to shape my own reality. That is when I began to engage in the act of, as Freire would call it, my own "humanization."

Though I would say Nick misreads Freire in a sense, assigning full responsibility for the "banking" concept to government, it might also be said that he is forging a strong reading, actually extending and reshaping Freire's argument. He agrees with Freire — he reads generously — yet his conspiracy theory approach also risks leaving the assignment prompt behind. He utilizes Freire's notion of education as a *system*, which he conflates with "the government," then grabs hold of contradiction as a way out. Nick, more than most of his

299

classmates, tackles difficult and not so obvious moments in Freire. He reads beyond the main point as it is set forth in the assignment prompt, and toward the link Freire makes between education and humanization.

I also included, in the essays I reproduced for class discussion, a piece in which the writer, Rae, disturbed by what she sees as Freire's assertion that she has been duped by "banking" education, asserts, "*I* think that *I* have a firm grasp on reality." Rae continues:

> Perhaps Freire's "banking concept" does exist during the foundation part of education, but it certainly does not continue for very long. If it did, the essay "The 'Banking' Concept of Education" that I have just read would have acted as my teacher, making "deposits which [, I,] the students [should] patiently receive, memorize, and repeat" (260). However, if I were merely this "receptacle" for information or also someone else's opinion, how would I ever be capable of writing anything that remotely argues against the teacher?

What struck me about Rae's essay was the way it questioned Freire — she was the only writer to do this — as well as the way Rae asserts herself in the piece — italicizing the "I" and inserting herself right into Freire's language. Her difficulty with Freire's text is made explicit and placed at the center of her response. What I found myself unable to discern finally was why, poised at midterm and having familiarized ourselves with the notion of using difficulty to read and to write, I hadn't received more essays like Rae's and Nick's. My decision to place these three essays on the table for discussion was not intended to play the good essay/bad essay game. As a matter of fact, I considered all three pieces to be quite "good" in certain ways. I felt as if I'd lost perspective and I needed a litmus test. I wanted to gauge the students' relationship to the work of General Writing, and because so many essays looked like Jillian's, I fully expected the class to see hers as the strongest. I was no longer sure what the class would say about Nick's and Rae's.

In preparation for the discussion of Jillian's, Nick's, and Rae's papers, I asked students to mark in each essay moments where they saw the writer most actively engaging with Freire's ideas. Once they had read all three essays, they were to write about a moment in one of the essays that was particularly "illuminating or surprising" in its reading of Freire. My language, drawn directly from difficulty paper assignments and class discussions, was by this time familiar to students. Much to my surprise, the class reacted to Jillian's essay with little enthusiasm. While some students liked her description of Mr. G———'s class, most wrote about moments in Rae's essay as most interesting. Her argument, many of them said, was right on target. On the other hand, students reacted negatively to Nick's essay. While they liked the writer's work with contradiction — like Rae's argument, it articulated the difficulty many of them were having with the lack of agency assigned to students — they didn't buy Nick's assertion that the government influences education. Ultimately, their discomfort with Nick's essay had less to do with seeing it as misreading Freire — only one student wondered aloud if Freire really meant the government was responsible for "banking" education — as it did with the fact that the essay seemed lopsided, that it "harped" on the notion of oppression.

With ten minutes left before the end of class, I interrupted what had become a lively discussion and asked students why their objections to Freire's ideas were so conspicuously absent from their own essays. One student responded by saying, "Well, maybe we just fit our experiences into Freire's ideas, even if they didn't really go all the way. I guess that's what we thought we were supposed to do." A few students laughed, some looked sheepish. On the way home that day, I thought about how this insightful comment wasn't, as I first presumed, merely the admission of a "good student." The class had not been simply "following orders" as they wrote their essays on Freire. Rather, I came to read this moment as evidence of the fact that I had not yet *taught* students to read their way into difficulty. The Freire essays were not anomalous at all, but indicative of the fact that students didn't know how to work their way through a text, except by summing it up. While I had made gestures toward teaching them to make a mark, I had duped myself into believing these overtures were enough. Only my students' "failure" in the face of "The 'Banking' Concept of Education," their trouble digging into its overt complexities, finally foregrounded my own short-sightedness.

For the next class I asked students to reread Freire, this time stopping at moments or phrases they had "missed," or even purposely glossed over in their first reading. I asked them to notice unfamiliar words or difficult phrases and suggested that while a dictionary would certainly help, they would also need to work contextually. I suggested they work toward a passage's meaning by reading around it and then by moving to other places in the essay where Freire seemed to be chewing on the same idea. In this way, I was asking students to be conscious of themselves as readers, to notice where they "tuned out" or avoided part of the text, and to give this occurrence a tangible weight. Then, I wanted to get them tracing that moment through Freire's essay, following a particular thread of argument rather than trying to account for the essay as a whole.

When students read from their journal entries in class, many of them isolated particular words, *dichotomy* for instance, which led one student to notice Freire's assertion that the banking concept creates a fissure between the student and the world. Someone else singled out *conscientizacao* and tried to figure out its relationship to both *banking* and problem-posing education. One student returned to the notion of oppression after the workshop, and talked about the idea that the "banking" concept oppresses by instilling student "credulity." Often, students had little trouble tracing the thread itself through Freire's essay, but when they turned to talking about what the passage *meant* exactly, they tended to resort to generalizations, like the student who noted a series of moments where Freire talked about "reality," then wrote that " 'Reality' is not one thing, at least it is something different for each person who is aware of it." None of the journal entries were revelatory; students did not suddenly "understand" the nuances of Freire's complex argument. There were entries that seemed to lead to greater confusion: "Conscientizacao refers to taking action against contradictions, like against the banking concept . . . The banking concept is conscientizacao because its the more natural way of doing things and therefore more responsible for social, political, economic contradictions." But for the first time that semester, students were moving into the text at hand. It was as if the difficult terms themselves had finally hooked students into understanding the value, and sometimes the necessity, of close reading.

Important to note here is the fact that this day's conversation was facilitated by a group of three students. While they had already prepared a set of discussion questions for Freire's essay, I asked them if they would be willing to utilize this most recent set of journal entries as part of the conversation. More than I had during other classes led by students, I worked hard this time to recede from the conversation. Given the reluctance of students to make their own ways through Freire's essay, it seemed vitally important that I avoid providing any sanctioned reading. One student led us to "praxis" by providing first a series of dictionary definitions, then taking us into the text itself to work around the passage. This in turn initiated a conversation about Freire's phrase, "Education as the practice of freedom," and led students to move around the essay as they tried to discern what exactly the "practice of freedom" meant. Dissatisfied with Freire's lack of concrete examples, students turned to a hypothetical discussion of what problem-posing education might actually look like.

When I asked students to write at the end of class about a moment they had found particularly productive during the course of discussion, many noted the way focusing in on praxis had helped them define, or "draw a line," between the "banking" concept and problem-posing education, or they talked about how defining praxis led to provocative arguments about education as dehumanizing. What happened, in other words, was that students moved in and out of attending closely to Freire's text and thinking about their own stake in his arguments. Because "The 'Banking' Concept of Education" is such a challenging text, I think students were able to see how, by slowing down and biting into difficult moments, they actually reaped tangible rewards. The more students worked with Freire's difficult terms, the more they teased out the specifics of his argument, the more

301

invested they became in the conversation. There was a sense that day that students had "opened" the text; not that we had finally arrived at the *real* meaning, but that we had truly worked our way past numbing summary and into something more substantial.

Not that any of this was really new. I had, after all, tried to *tell* students about "taking charge" of a text. But as is often the case, I found myself confusing the act of telling with the act of teaching. Until this part of the semester, I hadn't been forced to slow the process down enough to make it fully visible to my students. Of course, the revisions students produced soon after were not miraculous transformations. Many writers continued to focus on memorization, keeping, in fact, the language of the assignment intact in their essays. I wish I could say the work they did in their reading journals made it directly into their revisions, but for the most part it didn't. What did happen was that their essays, finally, began to fall apart. Their arguments digressed, weaving in and out of Freire's essay as students zoomed in on particularities. Jillian, for instance, focuses on the pact between student and teacher, and though she follows the notion of passivity though Freire's text and her own example, she never does much with the sense of satisfaction she'd noticed in her first draft. She responds to my question in the margin by saying only "at the time I liked the idea of simply memorizing information to receive a good grade, now I understand all the important information that I missed." But later in the essay, Jillian does extend her example to talk about how, while she was taught about flappers, she was never taught about the dangerous conditions in 1920s era sweatshops, which, she asserts, might have caused students to draw connections to "the sweatshops owned by Nike sneaker companies today."

Another student, Adam, revised his essay around the phrase "consciousness as consciousness of consciousness," which, in fact, he had written about in his journal. In this second version of his essay, he talks directly to his reader, making the *process* of thinking through difficult ideas on the page visible. His argument may be repetitive, even circular at moments, but he is working it out:

> Freire, as well as myself, believes that a person's reality, like their identity, is a learned and developed perception. A person develops their own identity, just as students should develop their own way of perceiving the world. Freire states, "They [students] may perceive through their relations with reality that reality is really a *process*, undergoing constant transformation" (Freire 351). In this sentence, Freire shows that each and every student develops their own reality, their own perception of the world around them and how they fit into it. Yet, by using the banking concept, by directing what students learn, a teacher ultimately shapes his pupils' reality. Another way to explain this would be, if all you know is what I have shown you, then you are a product of that, you are only able to see the world through my, the teacher's, eyes. This holds true in my biology class, I am shown only what my professor deems necessary or proper to learn. My reality has had boundaries made for me since I was little. The trick lies here, because if all I am able to learn is what people deem necessary for me to learn, then how can I see beyond those boundaries? A quick, maybe not so good analogy for this would be, I, the student, am like a horse with blinders on, except that I do not know that I am wearing blinders. Therefore, all I see is what I am shown. Freire believes that "a teacher's most crucial skill is his or her ability to assist students' struggle to gain control of their lives, and this means helping them not only to know, but 'to know that they know'" (Bartholomae and Petrosky 348). I believe that it is knowing that they know, such as understanding that you or I exist in a reality created by the society that governs us, that teachers should ultimately strive to teach and show to their students.

Many of the revisions looked like this: long paragraphs (sometimes lengthening out beyond a single page), comma splices linking a series of successive ideas together. Rather than seeing this as carelessness, what I saw was evidence of minds at work, writers grabbing hold of ideas and chewing on them. Elsewhere in the essay Adam turns to the reader and asks questions, anticipates objections: "What in the world you say? I said the same thing at first." He takes on the role of both teacher and student, approaching the notion of consciousness from first one angle and then another: "Another way to explain this. . ." or "A quick, maybe not so good analogy would be. . ." Like his classmates, Adam has not yet organized his ideas because they are still in transit, the writing still working toward its subject.

A teacher of mine once asserted that all good writing can be condensed to a single sentence. I remember the way my heart leapt into my throat, the way I felt queasy and thought, *If this is what it means to read and write, I want none of it.* Though the teacher was most likely talking about finding focus, I also knew that that this kind of reduction — of ideas, people, experiences — to a "main point," this erasing of textual difficulty and contradiction and question, was exactly what I worked against *as a writer*. When I opened the end-of-term evaluations for this General Writing course, I discovered — and this time I was not surprised — that students had consistently cited Freire's essay as the text they found most useful. One student wrote, "it was difficult because he really 'beat around the bush' a lot. . .that was confusing if you weren't giving the essay *all* of your attention." Because I value, and want to teach students to work their way through, the messiness of texts that "beat around the bush," I am inclined to begin next semester with "The 'Banking' Concept of Education." I know that Freire's text will once again force us to slow down and grapple with difficulty from the start. Then, I imagine, we might move on to "easier" texts, better able to dig in and push the kind of "beach reading" so many students are inclined to do. But considering how uncomfortable and confusing I found teaching last semester, I can't help but think I don't much enjoy mucking around in difficulty either (except, of course, when what is difficult for students is comparatively easy for me). And I wonder if falling apart in the middle of the semester isn't itself inevitable, in one form or another, or at least part of the praxis of teaching writing. As one student put it, "Even though I got frustrated with the repetition of staying with it for so long, it was kind of a 'gateway' piece for me."

WORK CITED

Bartholomae, David, and Anthony Petrosky. *Ways of Reading*, 5th ed. Boston: Bedford/St. Martin's, 1999.

"EXILED ON PLANET GARNISH": READING, REFERENTIALITY, AND THE PERSONAL IN STEEDMAN'S "EXILES"[1]

by Juli Parrish

I'm not sure exactly what my General Writing student James had in mind when he came up with "Exiled on Planet Garnish" as the title for a paper on Carolyn Steedman's "Exiles." I do know that at the time I was taken with its cleverness amidst papers entitled simply "Fiction" or "Exiles." I know that James intended the "garnish" in the title to refer to the watercress sold by a little girl in a Henry Mayhew text to which Steedman makes reference. And I know what I would like to think about James's title. I'd like to think that he was speaking on behalf of all the GW students in our class who felt when they were reading Steedman as if they were watching a science fiction movie, as if they were being asked to comprehend a strange world in which personal stories are filled with references to alien texts, as if they had been banished to this world without a decoder ring.

Whether or not James intended anything like this in his title, it's an apt description of the way I saw my students responding to Steedman's text. In an in-class writing exercise for which I asked them to address some aspect of their difficulty with Steedman, some two-thirds of them discussed the references Steedman uses in her writing — their number, their variety, their inscrutability. One student, for example, wrote that Steedman "tells a little about how she grew up but because she refers to a lot of other people who I've never heard of (authors) I can't really follow her line of thinking." Another wrote that "the author talks about her mother and then she brings up authors with quotes. I didn't understand the author and quote part. Why is she putting in quotes?" And a third wrote that "the biggest problem aside from the vocabulary, [he] had with the book was the quotes which sum up how [Steedman relates to] another author's writings and then jumps to a personal experience." These and other responses suggest a real uncertainty on the part of these first-year students about the function of references to other texts in Steedman's work and about their own role in reading those references.

For many first-year students, reading for the first time the kinds of complicated texts offered by *Ways of Reading*, grappling with references in academic writing is difficult enough. But what I discovered in teaching Steedman is that for some students, grappling with references in *personal* writing is even more difficult because, as excerpts from my students' papers suggest, students don't expect to see references to other books in personal writing. All three student writers quoted above implicitly contrast personal and academic writing in their statements of difficulty. The use of the word "but" in the first student's comment draws an opposition between personal writing, "tell[ing] a little about how she grew up," and academic writing, "refer[ing] to a lot of other people who I've never heard of (authors)." The suggestion is that this student *would* be able to follow Steedman's line of thinking if it involved just talking about how she grew up, *but* the references prevent this understanding. The second student makes a similar move in separating the personal from the academic with the word "then." She writes that "the author talks about her mother and

---

[1]Steedman's essay appeared in the fifth edition of *Ways of Reading*.

then she brings up authors with quotes." The acknowledgment of difficulty which follows has to do with Steedman's quotes, not with Steedman's mother; this student, too, sees her access to the personal narrative, which she implies is understood easily enough, as limited by the references to other authors. The third student approaches the matter somewhat differently, framing his difficulty as involving not just the references but the unclear relationship between the references and the personal writing, but here, as well, these elements are conceived of as disparate: Steedman discusses "another author's writings and then *jumps* to a personal experience."

Reading these responses pointed out to me the need to work with my students both on making sense of textual references and on developing and expanding their notion of "personal writing." I needed to help my students to begin to answer questions like, "what is Steedman doing when she refers to a nineteenth-century English study of the London poor in the context of a reflection on her father in 'A Thin Man'?" Subsequent class discussions about what Steedman's text gained by quoting from and referring to other texts in an autobiographical narrative confirmed this. Students insisted that "good" personal writing is simple, straightforward, and authentic, and that Steedman, in her rejection of these stylistic properties, is only interested in showing off her intelligence and education. She sacrifices a good story, they argued, in order to pander to an academic audience; she sells out to academia. My students were quite unwilling at this point to reconcile personal narratives with deliberate acts of referentiality, unable to see personal writing as dependent on the same kinds of constructions as academic writing.

To a point, though, their argument made sense. The idea that Steedman is showing off really depends on the idea that acts of referencing and quotation function in texts as proofs of authority, and this is a view sanctioned by many handbooks and style books, which construct referencing and quotation as valuable only for the information or the automatic authorization they provide. They advise students only to quote when they absolutely can't rephrase or when they need to bolster their argument. The introduction to *Ways of Reading* specifically works against this construction in pointing out that the authors "are not presenting our book as a miniature library (a place to find information) and . . . do not think of you, the reader, as a term-paper writer (a person looking for information to write down on three-by-five cards" (2). As the introduction rightly points out, reference and quotation are much more complex than this. Yes, it is the convention — and even the nature — of academic writing to refer to, to quote from, to build on other texts. But within that convention, there are countless ways for an author to situate a reference, to work with a reference, to use a reference in a text.

In teaching Steedman, I found that I needed ways to help students learn to engage with references — quotations, citations, epigraphs, allusions. And the ways of teaching I have continued to develop are based on my own ways of reading, on the constructions or theories or assumptions that shape my understanding of "Exiles." My ways of reading Steedman involve several connected moves — related aspects of an approach to the text which sees references and referentiality as crucial, and ultimately as accessible to students. Considering an act of reading itself both as a construction and as a metaphor can help students to understand the ways in which references function as traces of and as keys to Steedman's own positioning of reading in "Exiles." I have found that these are schooled ways of reading, that they must be taught, explicitly, to students. What I want to do here, then, is to introduce these ways of reading and to discuss their role in my teaching of Steedman.

I work, in part, from the idea that the reading of a text is an act of construction; this is a commonplace of literary studies. The reader of a text does not merely receive the text but actively participates in making it mean. The text to which a reader refers when writing is not just the words on the page but that reader's particular vision of those words; this is a text that the reader has helped to author, to construct. The introduction to *Ways of Reading* invites students to come to see just this kind of reading:

> When you stop to talk or write about what you've read, the author is silent; you take over — it is your turn to write, to begin to respond to what the author said. At that point the author and his or her text become something you construct out of what you remember or what you notice as you go back through the text a second time. (2)

As important as this notion was and is to my own work and my teaching, and as accessible as it seems to be in the introduction, I found it very difficult to teach. Class discussions about reading as construction often sent us speeding down the highway of relativity, and as I have discovered in more than one class, this highway has no exits. My students tended to reason about construction in two ways. With regard to their own *writing*, they said that if reading is an act of construction, then all constructions are equally valid, whether or not they have any grounding in the original text. With regard to their *reading* — and this is a fascinating contradiction — they argued that the author who constructs is to be blamed for her construction. I see a version of this second argument operating in the following excerpt, which includes the concluding paragraphs of a student paper on "Exiles":

> I believe Steedman has read too many books by this point. . . . I can say her imagination has gone a little over the edge. The book she read has caused her to think that [a dream about her parents cutting each other with knives] is what "grown ups" do. This is obviously false, in most cases. Steedman read this book at the age of seven, and I can see this has caused a huge impact on her reality. How a girl at the age of seven could stand to read something like that is beyond me. The fact that she has brought the book to create a situation of reality is also beyond my understandings of childrens' imagination.
>
> Steedman's use of a fictional story to create another fictional story is incredible. At this point I am not sure if she is referring to the real past or to the fictional past. My point of view is this, I know Steedman created the "picture" of her parents in that situation, but I am not sure if one may be able to call it a "history." I understand it happened in the past, but it is completely fictional.
>
> All I am able to say is, Steedman read an interesting amount of literature. I believe the works of literature that Steedman has read somehow became incorporated into her memories of her childhood. I believe since she has read such a variety of books, she unintentionally related them

```
to her life. Since this has happened she cannot distinguish

the two. She cannot remember if her past is, her past. She

is incapable of [distinguishing] her history from her

readings.
```

When I received this paper, I was somewhat disturbed by the writer's quick censure of Steedman's work, by her characterization of the narrative as "a little over the edge" and "obviously false." In this text, Steedman becomes an easily influenced hyper-reader whose misreadings of texts have damaging consequences for her own perception of her life and for her narrative. Nevertheless, I see this student text as a valuable teaching text for working with the idea of reading as construction.

In a class discussion of this text, I would direct students' attention to the second paragraph, in which the writer talks about using stories to create stories. I would ask students to talk about the way in which this writer distinguishes the "real" past from the "fictional" past, the "picture" Steedman has created of her parents from the "history" the student writer seems to want. I would ask them to think about the kind of construction to which the writer refers. What I see being constructed is not a book — not a reader's construction of "The Snow Queen" — but a past. Steedman is taking a cue from "The Snow Queen" as a way of constructing a memory of her childhood. With this in mind, I would ask students to reflect on this writer's conclusion that this construction is "unintentional," that it suggests a flaw in Steedman's work, and I would ask them to think about what it would mean if this construction were in fact quite intentional, if it suggested an accomplishment, a strategy, for Steedman. In addition to wanting them to think about this construction of the past as a strategy of *writing*, however, I would also want to push my students to think of it as a way of *reading*. What I see Steedman doing, that is, is giving the reader a sense of her own relationship to a kind of reading which is flexible and constant and active.

As the final paragraph of the student paper on "The Snow Queen" suggests, however, this kind of reading may not be entirely visible or accessible to students, even when they demonstrate an implicit understanding of the idea of reading as a construction. This student paper resists, finally, the connection between "history" and "fiction" to which her earlier paragraphs would seem to lead. She concludes by arguing that Steedman cannot distinguish "her history from her readings." This final paragraph suggests to me that this writer is not entirely aware of the valuable metaphor at work in her paper. This is a metaphor which refers to the writing of personal narrative as a "reading" of experience.

In fact, I have found myself relying on this metaphor in my own reading of Steedman each time I have returned to it. As a graduate student in English studies, it comes naturally to me to think about "reading" as a process in which I engage not just when my eyes pass over the pages of a written text but when I watch a movie or consider an advertisement or think about a dream. In discussions with other graduate students about responding to students' own narratives, we similarly talked of identifying social codes and "reading" them for the ways they give us insight into students' discussions of their experience. We take this metaphor of reading for granted. But, as I have learned through teaching Steedman, the idea that experience is a kind of text, and that writing about that experience is a way of reading that text, does not come at all naturally or automatically to my students. I realized that although it was central to my own reading and teaching of Steedman, to my students it wasn't really visible; it required a kind of reflection to which they were not accustomed. The metaphor, in other words, needed to be made explicit. After all, if "reading" printed texts and "reading" past experiences can be understood to be similar moves, then Steedman isn't really "jumping" from personal experience to another author's text at all, as one of the three student comments with which I began suggested. She is, rather, moving from one kind of text to another.

Not only is reading a constructive act, then, but it is a constructive act that does not limit itself to the printed page. Just as Steedman constructs the books she reads, so does she construct the dreams and the conversations she remembers having. This is precisely the issue raised by the author of the student paper on "The Snow Queen"; she points out the similarity in Steedman's relationship to books she has read and experiences she has had. An understanding of the metaphor of reading experience, I am suggesting, would give this student writer a way to engage rather than disparage this similarity.

As is often the case, the text in question — "Exiles" — itself offers any number of possibilities for teaching this. The ways in which Steedman embeds reading in her own reflective narrative is suggestive of this metaphor and could help to facilitate it more directly for students. That Steedman continually moves from discussions of her own memories and dreams to discussions of other texts and back indicates the extent to which reading — both literal and metaphoric — shapes her narrative. The markers of reading, in her text, are the subject of writing. For example, at one point she describes her mother's habit of refusing to allow her to answer the doorbell if it rang during a meal. "Years later I read about this reluctance to reveal the poverty of food on the table in several working-class autobiographies and thought; yes, that must have been it. . . . But the practice represented more than that" (67). An act of reading a *text* prompts Steedman to reread a childhood *experience*, and the acknowledgment that the reading alone isn't sufficient to explain prompts her to explore further the motives behind this practice. This kind of reading moment is everywhere in "Exiles," modeling the kind of reading which can help to shape narrative writing. Steedman repeatedly describes interactions with texts which prompted her to form or revise ideas about her experience, whether that experience involves having a dream, talking with her mother, or reading a book.

This goes both ways. On the one hand, experiences get "read" just as books do. On the other hand, reading (and writing) are experiences, as are dreams, conversations, memories. With this in mind, I could protest to my student who wrote about "The Snow Queen" that something Steedman remembers from a book is no less true than something that she remembers from her family life. Both are experiences. (In this sense, quotation marks or other markers of referentiality would serve only to indicate the *kind* of experience in question.) I suspect that this could be a productive way to challenge my students' separation of personal experience from reading. After all, for a student writer, this might mean that the very process by which students embed other sources and discourses in their own writing — the process by which they make their writing academic — is personal, as well.

At the same time, I want to discourage students from regarding Steedman's discussions of other texts as transparent, as simple, because the work of reading and writing which they indicate has been subsumed under the rubric of "personal experience." Their assumption already is that "experience" is more accessible, and "reading" is less so; I want to challenge this assumption. Even as I want to advocate the idea that reading and remembering and valuing books are a part of Steedman's experience (and, potentially, of students' experiences, as well), I want to work with the idea that remembering one's experience is always a form of reading, metaphorically speaking.

While the ideas both of reading as an act of construction and reading as a metaphor can be productive and thought-provoking in their own right, I would use them in the service of work with the textual features of referentiality. This, after all, is the issue with which my students have had the most trouble. If reading and "reading" are constructions, then references play a special role as the most visible manifestations of those constructions. References function as traces of an author's constructed reading. This means that in referencing or quoting another text, a writer, such as Steedman, chooses to connect her own words with the words of another author, to connect her ideas with those of a previous text; this connection in part shapes her new text, the one she is writing. And the references themselves —quotations, paraphrases, allusions to or titles of books — signal that this connection has occurred.

A reference serves not only as a representation of a previous reading experience, but as a representation of a choice made to bring that previous reading experience into the current text. Another way to say this is that an explicit reference (a quotation, a title) literally positions an act of reading within the written text. When Steedman writes that "the long lesson in hatred for my father had begun, and the early stages were in the traditional mode, to be found in the opening chapters of *Sons and Lovers* and Lawrence's description of the inculcated dislike of Mr. Morrell, of female loathing of coarse male habits" (35), for instance, we see that the language she uses to write about her father has been shaped by her reading of that novel.

Now, my students had no trouble understanding the first aspect of this; that is, they easily understood references to be the product of previous reading experiences. (A writer like Steedman can show off precisely *because* she has read so many texts.) But to students in my class, the signifiers of those previous reading experiences — the references — remained separate, disconnected. They seemed to only happen to appear in the text the students are reading. So, one student of mine read the *Sons and Lovers* passage and saw not a text being introduced to show us the way in which Steedman moves from life to text, not a reference highlighting Steedman's identity *as a reader*, rather a reflection on personal feelings abruptly interrupted by a reference to an unfamiliar novel. Seeing this, he wanted Steedman to show him how these texts *should be* connected, but he didn't see that the texts *have already been* connected. I hadn't taught this student, who insisted that Steedman needed to do the work of providing a connection between her own writing and *Sons and Lovers*, that Steedman has in fact provided a set of clues which suggest those connections.

Regarded in this light, this and other students' confusion about the function and source of references makes sense. If a reference represents a text which remains disconnected from the text in which it appears, then it makes sense for a student to want to understand that text on its own terms, to be familiar with an English ballad or "The Snow Queen" or *Sons and Lovers*. What I have tried to teach my students in response is that it is the reference itself, more than the text it represents — the process of reading — which matters. In other words, the moment in the text at which the reference occurs, by signifying the connection between the referenced text and the referencing text, tells the reader everything she needs to know about that text. As an exercise using the case of *Sons and Lovers*, for example, I would spend some time in class asking my students to tell me everything they could figure out about *Sons and Lovers* by reading the paragraph in which Steedman mentions the text. We would make a list on the board which would be likely to include most of these suggestions: (1) it is some kind of book, as opposed to story or essay or poem or article (because it includes chapters), (2) it has a character named Mr. Morrell, who has coarse habits, (3) at least one woman in the book loathes these male habits; and (4) this loathing is, according to Steedman, traditional. With only that much to go on, I would tell my class, they would have enough to discuss the reference, to work through the ways in which Steedman seems to read this text through her experience, and her experience through this text.

Of course, while this kind of exercise helps to get students working to make sense of the reference, it doesn't necessarily challenge the idea that Steedman is "showing off." If we were to stop with discussing Steedman's choice in referring to a text, or to stop with breaking down the reference on the board, we would leave class with the idea that Steedman's use of references is basically a writing strategy — a good strategy, perhaps, but still just a strategy, a stylistic choice that she makes. I can imagine students protesting: How is strategizing different from showing off?

In fact, several of my students, writing about Steedman's work with a particular text, implied just this kind of view of her use of references. Consider, for example, this opening paragraph from one student's paper, which attempts to draw connections between the Disney version of "The Little Mermaid" and Steedman's narrative:

"Up where they laugh, up where they run, up where they play all day in the sun, wish I could be part of your world." This key line from the theme song of Walt Disney's motion picture version of *The Little Mermaid* conjures up romantic images of Ariel becoming human and living happily ever after [with] Prince Eric. How is it possible that this same fairy tale can be related to Carolyn Kay Steedman's bluntly realistic *Landscape for a Good Woman?* Quite honestly, the story of the Little Mermaid is a wonderful tool used by Steedman to bridge the gap between fiction and her own personal history.

For this student, Steedman applies a strategy (referring to a text) to her narrative and comes up with a "bridge" between literature and life. The text to which she refers is a "wonderful tool." That is, the reference has no natural connection with Steedman's experience; it remains separate, something imported after the fact to perform a specific textual function. So completely does this writer subordinate the text in question to the strategy that she doesn't seem to realize that, in fact, Disney's "The Little Mermaid" and the fairy tale to which Steedman refers have very little in common. Steedman's version of the fairy tale focuses on the cut-out tongue, the pain of walking on knives, the blood of the prince, the death of the mermaid; this is quite different from the student's version, which features a catchy tune, romantic images, a happy-ever-after ending. Her whole paragraph is overwhelmed by Disney connotations; even the word "wonderful" in the last sentence bears the marks of the cartoon. For a revision, I would direct this student's attention to the fact that the Disney version of the fairy tale to which she refers does not actually help her to say anything about Steedman's text except that it is a "wonderful" tool. And saying that it is a wonderful tool tells us nothing about how Steedman is reading.

Now compare this paragraph from the opening of another paper on the same topic:

One fairy tale which Steedman uses called "The Little Mermaid" helps tell a story about her parents' relationship. Steedman does something very unique which is to either revise or compare and contrast the fairy tale in a fashion which would show what life was like and what she wanted for her mother to do. "The Little Mermaid" is about a mermaid's love for a prince and how she wishes to become a human and have legs. Her bargain with the Sea Witch causes her to go through pain, and when the prince meets her, he rejects her. In the end, although she was offered a chance to become a mermaid again by killing the prince and using his blood to transform her feet to a tail again, she refuses, sacrifices herself, and dies. Steedman takes this fairy tale and revises it. Instead she wishes for the death of her father. She understands that her mother was the one who sacrificed for her and not her father.

In some ways this paragraph might seem to be not as polished as the one in the first example. The student spends more time summarizing, and this almost takes over the paragraph. And this paragraph is similar to the first in that it still relies on a rhetoric of strategy: Steedman "uses" a fairy tale to do something with her text. But this writer's sentence order and word choice suggest a more complicated reading. First, she writes more specifically about the strategy itself. She writes not of a "tool" but of revising or comparing and contrasting. The first writer's use of the noun "tool" implies a vision of the strategy as static, as an object, whereas the second writer's use of the verbs "revise," "compare," and "contrast" suggest an idea of the strategy as a process. The strategy itself, then, is more active for this writer. Second, this idea of strategizing comes at the beginning, and not the end, of the paragraph. For the first writer, it serves as the conclusion; for the second, it is an introduction, and in fact she develops this idea. Working with the version of the fairy tale provided by Steedman allows her to consider the specific aspects of text — death and sacrifice — which seem to be most important to Steedman. And it allows her to see that text and experience are not established in a one-way relationship: it is the fairy tale, and not her life, that Steedman revises in this paragraph. For this student, then, Steedman's work with the fairy tale is not so much a strategy as a clue to a way of reading which involves both her textual and her non-textual experience.

This student, most importantly, is beginning (granted, she's not quite there yet) to see Steedman as a reader — not just a reader of texts but a reader of experiences, someone whose experience with textuality has altered her interactions with people, her consciousness as a writer, her own ways of reading. This, finally, is what is valuable in working to understand Steedman as a reader; this is what students can take away from her text. I don't want to underestimate the importance of this; one of the things I understand myself to be doing as a teacher of writing is helping my students to reinvent their own relationships to textuality through writing and reading.

This student's reading and writing on "Exiles" is work I would want to foster in my classroom by not only introducing my students to the ideas of reading as a metaphor and reading as a construction, but by giving them practice in working with the textual features that will enable them to see these kinds of reading in action. I would want consistently to draw students' attention to what I might call the "referential structures" in Steedman's text. These would be the aspects of the text which actively work to situate another text — implicitly or explicitly — in the text. In the case of quotations, referential structures might include signal phrases, brackets, ellipses, sentences and paragraphs which come before and after a quotation, citations of page numbers and names. In the case of less explicit allusions, epigraphs, mentions of texts, these structures might include some of the same elements but also titles, notes in the back of the book, and the more general context of the paragraph: the ways in which Steedman seems to be making use of the other text. This is a practice that, although we came upon it rather late in the semester, seemed really to help students to understand Steedman's function as a reader in "Exiles." When my students began to use these referential structures to make sense of how Steedman was using other texts, they were more able to engage with Steedman's readings, more able to write about those readings without seeking help outside the text. That is, they were able to use these structures to work through some of their initial difficulty not only with the references themselves, but with their understanding of Steedman's ways of reading. Most importantly, this is work in reading for them, as well, work in developing new ways of engaging with textuality.

In starting this work with my students, I introduced them to the general idea of "referential structures" but stopped short of providing them with the list above. Instead, I asked them to come up with their own lists by working in groups on a particular reference from "Exiles." One of the most productive kinds of reference for this kind of work was epigraphs, for which all but the most obvious referential structures (usually a citation) are invisible. In the case of epigraphs, students have to work harder to find referential structures, because Steedman's work in situating an epigraph in relation to the rest of the chapter is, and isn't, there. For this exercise, I asked students to choose one epigraph (there are three in "Exiles") and "read for it" in the appropriate section of the text, to see if and how the text alluded back to it. I asked them to consider whether and how the epigraph fit into the rest of the section; whether its language, its tone, its images, its themes were echoed later in the chapter; whether other references seemed to be working similarly. More often than not, students were able to find the epigraph in the text, to consider, for example, Steedman's reflections on and dreams about clothing in light of the song lyric epigraph which begins "The Weaver's Daughter." Arguably, however, the more successful cases were those groups which couldn't as easily locate the epigraph in the rest of the chapter, because these groups had to make meaning where there seemed to be none, to construct, actively, their own referential structures, and hence, their own reading of the epigraph.

In teaching "Exiles" again, I would want to try the exercises I have mentioned again, and to continue to develop new vehicles for bringing my ways of reading Steedman's text into the classroom more explicitly. I would want to work with other groups of students on making sense of Steedman's often complex use of references in "Exiles." And I would want to encourage other writing teachers to do the same. Work with ideas of reading as construction, with metaphors of writing narrative as reading experience, with "referential structures" may not bring first-year writers out of exile completely, but it can, I think, make Planet Garnish a slightly less alienating place to live.

WORKS CITED

Bartholomae, David, and Anthony Petrosky. "Introduction: Ways of Reading." *Ways of Reading: An Anthology for Writers.* 4th ed. Boston: Bedford/St. Martin's, 1996.

Steedman, Carolyn Kay. "Exiles." *Landscape for a Good Woman: A Story of Two Lives.* New Brunswick: Rutgers UP, 1986. 25–62.

I am indebted to the students in my General Writing classes in the fall of 1996 and the spring of 1997; their reading and writing on "Exiles" made much of my work possible.

SUSAN BORDO AND MICHEL FOUCAULT: TEACHING CLOSE READING A MOMENT AT A TIME
by Dawn Skorczewski

When the teaching assistants I supervise select essays from *Ways of Reading* for their first-semester syllabus, they rarely choose Foucault. Many of them have struggled to read Foucault in a theory class the previous semester, and have been amazed at the discrepancy between what they understand of the text and what their brilliant instructor presents as her reading of it. They are not confident in their reading of Foucault's text, and they tend to be even less confident in the ability of the first-year student to reach any understanding of his work at all. Bordo's "Hunger as Ideology," on the other hand, tends to be one of their first picks. They rightly believe that students will have a lot to say about the topic of eating and the body, that students will be eager to find examples from popular culture to counter or confirm Bordo's argument.

These teachers' opinions of what might or might not work in a classroom rest on the assumption that we teach best what we know best — that if we are confused, our students will be similarly confused. They also presume a level of mastery of a text to teach it successfully. And for teachers who struggle to retain confidence in their own authority, this makes sense to me. But it also makes me a bit apprehensive about the dangers of staying within our comfort zones. What is excluded from the conversation when we do this? What are we prevented from learning with, about, or from our students when we feel that we have mastered or understood a text that they cannot? For these reasons, I suggest that new teachers attempt to teach a text they feel comfortable with alongside one that they do not. I urge them to use this Bordo/Foucault sequence as an opportunity to consider what might be learned from teaching reading and writing as processes of risk and discovery for both students and teachers.

I first designed this assignment, which asks students to read Foucault and then trace his influence on Susan Bordo's "Hunger as Ideology," to help me answer a genuine question I had in mind, a question which I did not know the answer to: how much has Bordo been influenced by Foucault? To my delight, semester after semester, students teach me new ways in which she has or has not adopted his ideas. As we work with these texts a moment at a time, I attempt to teach students the value of very detailed close work with a text that can yield answers to our questions and provoke new ones as well.

. . . .

Writing Assignment

Theories of Power
Susan Bordo and Michel Foucault

[The Panopticon] is an important mechanism, for it automatizes and disindividualizes power. Power has its principle not so much in a person as in a certain concerted distribution of bodies, surfaces, lights, gazes; in an arrangement whose internal mechanisms produce the relation in which individuals are caught up. The ceremonies, the rituals, the marks by which the sovereign's surplus power was manifested are useless. There is a machinery that assures dissymmetry, disequilibrium, difference. Consequently, it does not matter who exercises power. Any individual, taken almost at random, can operate the machine: in the absence of the director, his family, his friends, his visitors, even his servants. . . . Similarly, it does not matter what motive animates him: the curiosity of the indiscreet, the malice of a child, the thirst for knowledge of a philosopher who wishes to visit this museum of human nature, or the perversity of those who take pleasure in spying and punishing. The more numerous those anonymous and temporary observers are, the greater the risk for the inmate of being surprised and the greater his anxious awareness of being observed. The Panopticon is a marvelous machine which, whatever use one may wish to put it to, produces homogeneous effects of power.

–Michel Foucault,
"Panopticism," 232–33

In "Panopticism," French philosopher Michel Foucault summarizes his theory of how power works through surveillance in the modern world. Foucault's theory has influenced innumerable thinkers, including feminist philosopher Susan Bordo. In this first assignment, you will trace the extent of Foucault's influence on Bordo. In short, you will closely read her essay "Hunger as Ideology" in relation to his theory of power articulated above in order to develop a thesis about how Bordo mimics, rejects, or expands upon Foucault's theory of "panopticism" in her essay. You will formulate your own thesis based upon a careful analysis of Foucault's and Bordo's key terms, and, in Bordo's case, textual and visual examples.

Writing Skills:

- Provide a *close reading* of Bordo's use or expansion of Foucault's key terms and concepts. "Close reading," as we will discuss in class, includes both detailed analysis of the text and the argument you make about the text, based on that analysis.

- At the beginning of your essay, *summarize* Foucault's theory of surveillance for the reader who is not familiar with "Panopticism." Begin your summary by identifying the author and the source, and state the main idea. Then present key supporting points. Don't evaluate; merely report. Use your own words and an occasional quoted phrase. Your summary should be less than a page.

- *Orient* the reader. You should address your essays to readers who have read the essay, but not recently and not in-depth. You will need to orient them with appropriate reminders (explanations of the context of quotations), always making sure these explanations serve a purpose in your essay as a whole (not just summary for its own sake). Your reader should always know where you are in the text, through the material you provide to jog their memories. As you close-read, never assume (1) that readers know what to look for, (2) that they'll read a passage in the same way that you do, and (3) that they'll draw the same conclusions. Your *analysis* of the *evidence* should persuade your readers of the validity of your claims.

- *Style:* limit your use of the verb "to be." To increase your awareness of "to be" verbs, underline every one you use in your draft and try to substitute active verbs when you revise. "To be" verbs include **is, are, was, were, be, to be, been,** and **being.** You should have no more than one per page; before you turn in an essay, be sure to circle the uses that remain.

．　．　．　．　．　．　．　．　．

DAY 1

"Panopticism": Is this written in English?

We begin with Foucault on a day when the students have just handed in an essay and have not read a word of "Panopticism." I ask them to open to his essay, and find a sentence anywhere in it that makes sense to them — a sentence that sounds, I tell them, like it might be written in English. "Pretend for now that it is written in another language, that you are trying to find words that are familiar to you." Each student finds a sentence and presents it to the class. Together we map their sentences on the board, charting their paraphrase of Foucault's words. We write these paraphrases in order of their appearance in Foucault's essay. Once we have finished, we already have a general sense of the notion of the panopticon, and of Foucault's understanding of policing mechanisms that continually produce and reconstruct individuals' identities in relation to powerful experts.

Once we have a broad sense of what Foucault is going to be teaching us as we read him, we begin to sketch out the sections of his essay in the same way. This time students work in groups to present a paragraph of the first section of the piece. Again they present their readings, and again we chart them on the board. We discuss how to keep track of our readings of this difficult text in the margins or on yellow Post-its, and I suggest that I will be looking for their "maps" of Foucault's text when they arrive next time. They then go home to read the essay.

In this initial exercise I try not to impose my reading of Foucault on the students. When they suggest what seems to me to be a blatant misreading, for example, I simply ask them to show where in the text it says that. Sometimes I let it go, and wait for someone to contradict the misreading. Misreadings like those that often appear during a first class on Foucault very often give way to stronger and more textually based readings in the classes that follow, and I am more committed to my belief in the students' abilities to read a very difficult text on their own than I am concerned that they "get it right." "Getting it right," moreover, seems to me exactly the opposite of what we want to emphasize in a course in college writing.

．　．　．　．　．　．　．　．　．

DAY 2

Building readings of Foucault: the useable text

Exercise 1.1 due: *Identify, define, and discuss at least five of the key terms Foucault uses as he describes the nature and function of "panopticism."*

In our second class on Foucault, students have read the text and are generally more confused than they were in the last. We discuss how deepening our reading of a text, or our writing of our own texts, can result in an initial sense of loss. The easy understandings we had arrived at together in the previous class have been replaced by complications and nuances that we cannot reconcile with the meanings we generated in class. I argue that persisting in our examination of particular moments in the text and connecting these moments to each other will eventually yield another understanding of it, one that goes beyond what we initially formulated and one that connects more directly to our individual experiences as readings of the text.

Students work again in this class at mapping Foucault's text, section by section. Groups of students "teach" a section of the text to their classmates, writing on the board their most important points. They then compare notes. How does each section build on the last? What does it add to the conversation about how individuals are policed and produced by the panoptic mechanisms in contemporary culture? We also draw from their exercises to generate a vocabulary list of important terms in Foucault's discussion.

Finally, each group finds examples of what foucault is talking about from their own lives, and presents them to the class. Some groups discuss the experts who sit in the center of the panopticon in our culture: doctors, lawyers, teachers, judges, parents, personal trainers at the health club, etc. This discussion prepares us to work with Susan Bordo's text in the next class.

．　．　．　．　．　．　．　．　．

DAY 3

Susan Bordo: echoing, then speaking back

Exercise 1.2 due: *Choose one quotation from each of the sections of Bordo's argument that discusses the ways in which advertisements work to shape our ideas about bodies, selves, food, and so on. Discuss what bordo argues in the quotation, and whether you believe she is correct. Choose an ad from a magazine to support your case if you wish.*

Students have many visceral reactions to Bordo's text, many of which oppose her readings of advertisements that students are familiar with. Many resist Bordo's readings because they identify ways in which unknowing consumers learn what it means to be embodied in our culture. They do not necessarily believe that they have been influenced in the ways Bordo describes. When we discuss Bordo, we usually begin here, with a listing and venting of reactions to her. I credit students for being active and critical readers at this point in the course, but I also caution that I am not certain that we are entirely doing justice to Bordo's arguments.

Once we have vented, it is time to "echo back" Bordo's arguments, to really listen to what she is saying rather than merely reacting to it. We discuss the article section by section, and students offer examples from their exercises to help us reconstruct and respond to Bordo's argument. I also ask students to bring in advertisements for this session, and we lay them out on the floor in the middle of our circle. As we discuss each section of Bordo's piece, we look on the floor for an ad that supports, refutes, or complicates what Bordo is saying. Students match quotes from Bordo with particular aspects of the ad they are studying. Often, other students use evidence from their sections of the piece to add to the conversation.

After this exercise, students are generally more fluent readers of Bordo's arguments, and they are often more generous readers of her as well.

. . . .

DAY 4

Making connections: an in-class Ping-Pong game

Exercise 1.3 due: (1) *What evidence of Foucault's concept of surveillance appears in Bordo's essay? Choose 2–3 quotations from Bordo's essay and explain how they provide an example of Foucault's concept.*

(2) *What evidence does Bordo use to suggest a different or expanded concept of how surveillance works and its limitations from the concept Foucault describes? Choose 2–3 quotations to support your argument.*

In this session, we begin to make connections between Bordo's and Foucault's texts. We are trying to figure out how, exactly, Bordo's text is in conversation with Foucault's. What has she learned or borrowed from him that informs her readings of contemporary culture? We play the "echo game" to help us decide. Students start with a quotation from Bordo, then they look for one in Foucault that somehow relates to Bordo's. (We begin with those they found when they did their exercises.) Once we have found one quotation from each text, we discuss in detail their relationships to each other. This gives us a chance to practice the close reading skills that will inform their work with evidence in the essay.

At the end of class, I ask students to write a test-run of the thesis paragraph of their essay. Here is what I ask them to do: "On the basis of your assessment of Bordo's debt to Foucault, write a paragraph in which you elaborate your own thesis about the implications of this debt. For example, does Bordo use Foucault's theory as her main lens, or way of seeing attitudes toward food and the body in contemporary culture? Do her examples make us see things that Foucault's theory does not account for or anticipate?"

Armed with evidence and a "dummy" first paragraph, the students are ready to compose their drafts.

. . . .

DAY 5

First drafts: a writing workshop (pink and yellow highlighters required for each student)

Assignment: see Writing Assignment above

. . . .

ESSAY #1

Cover Letter (due with first version of your essay)

Write a letter, addressed to your readers, in which you answer the following questions and present any other concerns that you have. As with all letters you write in this course, this one should be typed and should be about a page long.

- What argument are you making about Bordo's relationship to Foucault? Please quote the thesis statement of your essay as you explain.

- What are the biggest problems you're having at this point in the writing process?

- What is your favorite part of your essay?

- What is the number one question about your essay that you would like your reader(s) to answer for you?

- What is your plan for revision?

For this class, two students arrive with enough copies to workshop with the entire class. The remaining students bring three copies each: one for me and one for each of their two readers, who write Readers' Letters for them to be delivered in the next class session.

In our workshop, each student highlights the following: quotations from Bordo (in yellow), quotations from Foucault (in pink). They then underline the sentences in which the writers discuss the relationships between the quotations. We discuss how the writer builds an argument based on analysis of the evidence as we workshop each piece.

If there is time, the writers highlight the copies of the two essays they will write readers' letters for (see below). It generally becomes clear during this workshop that the writers need more evidence to build their arguments and that they need to discuss that evidence in more detail if they are to persuade their readers of their interpretations of Bordo's debt to Foucault.

. . . .

ESSAY #1

Readers' Letter (bring a copy for the instructor and the writer)

Revision literally means "seeing again." When experienced writers revise, they often radically alter their idea and reorganize the entire essay. By contrast, when inexperienced writers revise, they change a few words here or there but leave the essay essentially unaltered. Help your partners become experienced writers! They have several days to revise, so you can make comments that demand — and direct — a true revision. Try to make comments that you think will help the writer revise. (That said, please be respectful.)

Directions: As you carefully read and reread each essay, *draw a squiggly line* under the awkwardly expressed sentences and phrases whose meanings are unclear. Write *marginal notes* to the writer on anything that puzzles or interests you. After rereading, write a letter to the writers in which you answer these questions:

- In your own words, what is this paper about? (What's its *idea*?) Don't assume that the writer knows what his/her story is about. Mistrust the stated thesis (if there is one).

- Accept the writer's idea and try to extend the argument by providing additional examples, suggesting questions that provoke further thought, discussing parallels, and so on.

- Provide counter-argument for the writer. If you did not accept this argument, what objections might you raise? Are there other interpretations possible? Provide one and discuss it briefly.

- In the cover letter, the writer has asked one or more questions. What answer do you have to offer?

What is your favorite moment in this writer's essay?

. . . .

DAY **6**

Final Drafts

. . . .

ESSAY **#1**

Self-Evaluation Letter (due with final version of Essay 1)

This is the cover letter, addressed to me, that you should staple to the front of your revision. Each time you hand in a revision, you should attach such a self-evaluation letter. This time around, please answer the following questions and address any other concerns you have:

- What argument does this essay make?

- What do you like best about the essay overall? What specific parts work well?

- What were the two biggest problems for you in writing this essay? How did you address these problems?

- Discuss your use of evidence in your essay.

On a scale from 1 to 5, with 5 being high and 1 being low, how would you rate your final product? What's your reasoning for giving it this rating?

When students hand in the final copies of their essay, they submit the exercises, the draft (with cover letter attached), the readers' letters that they received, and the final essay, with a self-evaluation letter attached. After I respond to it, this collection becomes a piece in their final portfolios.

o–o–o–o–o–o–o–o–o–o–o–o–o–o–o–o–o–o–o

RELATIVISM: A WALL WITH MANY WINDOWS
by Ellen Smith

A little past midterm of a semester last year, in a cross-listed Women's Studies general writing course using *Ways of Reading* as its main textbook, Mary, a student who was usually cool and confident with her assignments, came to my office hours shaking a photocopy of Susan Willis's "Work(ing) Out"[1] and announced that she was "climbing the walls." Willis had so problematized the idea of women and fitness that Mary, an ardent exerciser and feminist, was angry at the critical infinity the essay had opened up. "You could just go on forever reading into popular culture," Mary noted. And she was right. She showed me a draft of her essay in response to Willis's article. The first page was devoted to venting her frustration at the way Willis's analysis glided from one paradigm to the next without closing in and making a prescriptive statement on the feminist stance toward the fitness craze of the 1980s.

I was confused, too, and started climbing the walls with her. It was, after all, my fourth try at teaching this course; and by then I'd pretty much adopted the Jean Kerr variation on the famous Kipling quote: "If you can keep your head when all about you are losing theirs [and blaming it on you], it's just possible you haven't grasped the situation." Mary took her frustrated draft back to her apartment, picked up where the frustration tapered, and in a day or two turned in an essay in which she furnished the conclusion the Willis text nobly refused to furnish. In a loud textual voice, Mary yelled back and forth with Willis and finally decided that exercise wasn't the enemy of women, but that the way exercise was marketed was a partriarchal mediation that women needed to separate from the commonsense good of physical fitness and strength.

I was very happy to see this essay. Mary had waded through the relativism that the critical reading/writing class must encounter if it is to be truly "critical." Her work made me begin to see that critical work follows a kind of ebb and flow, a passage from the sturdy banks of certainty to the Sargasso of relativism and inevitably back to some ground on which to stand, though the ground will never seem as erosion-free as it once did — not as long as there is dialogue.

Through revisions from one semester to the next, I always carry over in my course descriptions a few key concepts that I value in the teaching of composition. One of them is that of "dialogue." This concept is developed in the the introduction to *Ways of Reading* and has been helpful to me in articulating with my students the link between reading and writing. It has become a part of my classroom's critical lexicon and readerly etiquette. I emphasize dialogue because I feel that we all come to writing with strong adversarial models in place (courtroom TV, debate rhetoric). In dialogue, one needn't swing to a markedly pro or con position in relation to a text or set of ideas. The aim is not to vindicate or dismiss a text wholesale; rather, it is to engage it so that both text and reader come away modified by the exchange.

With my students, I set a scenario of a stimulating conversation among friends. It's unthinkable that constant agreement or disagreement would make such conversations

---

[1]Willis's essay appeared in the third edition of *Ways of Reading*.

worth returning to. I discuss the importance of tension and the give and take that make us return to some conversational milieus and not to others. But anyone who has ever stayed up into the wee hours engaged in an energetic dialogue knows that they never really conclude, at least not decisively. Someone points to the clock or rubs her eyes; maybe someone else offers a provisional conclusion or mentions areas of discussion that still need to be covered in a future meeting; or another throws up her hands in despair the way Mary did. The point is that in closing, we assume that someday we'll return to the discussion. The closing signals a potential beginning.

I hope that this analogy relieves student writers of the burden of having the definitive final word in response to a text. In my critical comments, I often activate the analogy to point out places where the assigned text is being shut out of the discussion and where the student is sitting back and letting it do all the talking just to fill a nervous pause. In large group readings of a student text, a key question is: "What kind of conversation does this student essay represent?"

In a reading sequence that opened with Adrienne Rich's "When We Dead Awaken: Writing as Re-Vision," two analogous reading practices emerged in the first student assignments of the semester. Assignments related to Rich's essay asked students to read certain concepts introduced by Rich through the examples of her poetry that she includes in the essay. Any text will yield these types of practices in the beginning of a freshman writing course, although the Rich piece, whose combination of poetry and expository prose the *Ways of Reading* assignments avoids separating, accentuates the causes for the two types of responses (with some overlap):

(1) The way to be in dialogue with an expository essay is to locate or invent a thesis, to abstract the thesis into issues around the text, and then to proceed to either oppose or augment this thesis.

(2) The way to be in dialogue with poetry, since it is "subjective" and only the author knows its "true meaning," is to defer as much as possible to the author's cues on how to read it; if the author's directives are absent or incomplete, one can go "out on a limb," but only if one states the disclaimer that one reader's interpretation is as good as another's.

With both types of response there are problems in terms of dialogue. I have found it useful to try to use one of each type of response in the initial group readings of student texts. I therefore try to bring in a paper ostensibly dealing with the issue of women's rights and involving very little textual work, along with a paper that refers (or de-fers) to the text with very little intervention on the part of the writer's opinions or experience. Since the notion of "dialogue" is my classroom mantra, what we read for in a large group are relationships between the writer/reader and the text.

An issue-oriented, polemical student essay entitled "Defense of a Republican Redneck" presented itself as almost a caricatural version of the first type of response. It seized not so much on the Rich text but rather on the political values the student inferred from it. It was as if they had asked Rich to "step outside" the text and duke it out over the issues. One student blamed his fighting posture on Rich's "tone":

> My point is that I can understand different ideolo-
>
> gies, but by no means can I ever approach the subject with
>
> a cool and open mind when my own values have been violated
>
> in an aggressive style, much as Ms. Rich has done. . . .
>
> Ms. Rich manages in one essay to offend all that is holy to
>
> a conservative, young, white heterosexual, old-school male.

I opened classroom discussion with this question: "With what parts of the Rich essay is this writer in dialogue?" The first student to speak looked sheepishly at me, asking if I wanted his honest opinion. His honest opinion was that he "wished he had written it." Like the student writer under discussion, this student held that the "aggressive" tone of Rich's text deserved a response in kind. If you ever teach the Rich essay, be sure to take time to develop a collective working definition of "tone"! Sooner or later, it has to be taken into a close look at Rich's use of language and how such a tone is inferred by many male (and female) writers. Anyway, the "fire with fire" principle was raised by the second student, even though we hadn't yet located the cause of the fire within the Rich essay. A woman student took the defensive, arguing that to write an essay like this, "Rich had to be 'aggressive,' to not let up."

The discussion had become impressionistic, and we needed to get into the text itself, to try to grapple with the "incendiary" material. John helped this happen by commenting that the student essay was not dealing with the assignment question, or for that matter, with "*what* Rich was saying" (as opposed to how). So we began to scout for passages in which the student made any reference at all to any aspect of the assigned text. The first gold we struck was not Rich's text, but the editors' text introducing the essay in the anthology. That was good enough for the moment; I was desperate for any intertextuality we could work with:

> It would be one thing if Ms. Rich was simply an advocate, but she goes a step beyond. She insists that she trash and deface accepted norms along her way of proving her point; for example in her <u>Of Woman Born: Motherhood as Experience</u> the editor even agrees that despite a fine job she still "calls for the destruction of motherhood as an institution."

Obviously, since the writer is drawing his material from the editors' introduction, he is already predisposed away from dialogue with the text that ensues. Finding this gave us the opportunity to discuss the influence of paratextual discourse (be it present or removed) on our readings of a given text. From there, we followed John's lead by looking for other "hookups" with the assignment or Rich texts, locating this oasis about midway through the paper:

> She [Rich] suggests that major works of literary art be re-examined to find sleeping messages that may prove new points to an "awakened" audience. . . . Not only do major works of male authors [need to be scrutinized], but more important lost and "buried" works from female authors need to be "unearthed" in order to gain the complete picture. <u>I disagree</u> with Ms. Rich on the point of "unearthing" all females' work simply because until the 1920s most women were not accepted. . . .

Here, this textual moment breaks down as the writer repairs to the political issues he infers from the text (and it is exactly this process of inference that would need to be externalized in a revision, as in "Here all we get is Z, but we, your readers, are clueless. Please walk us through the process of getting from A to Z."). From this point, the writer never returns to the text, as we noted in class, but rather culminates his detour with a chilling anecdote that serves as a conclusion:

> I'll never forget the homosexual killed in my town
>
> when I was in ninth grade, he was dragged behind a pickup
>
> truck on a rope for a mile at high speed by some seniors.
>
> They went to jail but did so freely, feeling that they were
>
> protecting a way of life, much as Ms. Rich feels she's
>
> protecting hers.

(I said it was an extreme example of an adversarial, pro and con approach.) It wasn't difficult (as it is in much more subtle versions of this approach) to move into a discussion of the incongruity not only of the frightening analogy drawn up by this text, but of the dialogical relationship between this text and the Rich essay. Also, in keeping with the question, "What aspect of Rich's text is this essay in dialogue with?" this final passage connected clearly in students' minds to the information proferred in the editors' introduction: that Rich was committed to gay and lesbian rights. This piece of information had furnished paratextual noise in many students' own readings of Rich, and so they quite readily pointed to it.

From this extreme (and clearly antisocial) example of the adversarial model over the dialogical one, which is always only ideal, we moved to a less vituperative student essay which does quite the opposite. It defers to and privileges the Rich text and keeps the student writer's voice at bay. Here is the writer's conclusion:

> She [Rich] began her career writing like men, for men,
>
> but changed. She was able to see changes in her writing and
>
> make other changes. After following tradition she actually
>
> went against it. Rich overcame conformity of men and found
>
> a way to write like a woman. She often used renaming in her
>
> poetry to get this point across.

Because the editors' assignment question had asked students to apply Rich's assertion that "writing is renaming" to a reading of her poetry, this student is careful to include the importance of renaming in this capsule summary of the Rich text. But throughout the essay, the concept itself is never worked out through reading and writing of both the prose and poetry that form "When We Dead Awaken." There is, however, a paragraph in the center of the essay that brings the idea in proximity to a reading of Rich's poem "The Loser"; and we made this our center for critical discussion in class:

> The renaming used in this poem, as I see it, is not
>
> something in the poem being renamed but the narrator being
>
> renamed. The point of view should be of the author who is
>
> female, but because females were criticized by men, Rich
>
> wrote "The Loser" from the point of view [of] a man. . . .
>
> Tradition is not renamed but only followed in "The Loser."

This is the productive center of the student's essay, where the text is engaged in understanding a concept introduced expositorily through its assumed manifestation in the poetic artifact. My mimeographed copy of this essay has marginal notes gleaned from discussion — "go back to the place where Rich discusses renaming" — this, with an arrow indicating the first sentence of the cited passage (the place where the reader makes a decision either to go back and dialogue with Rich on this idea or to move forward, following the "evolutionary" line of Rich's sequence of poems). In other words, she prematurely gave the "floor" back to Rich (or at least, back to her generalized outline of Rich's thesis and narrative).

In picking up the superficial line of Rich's expository/narrative text, the student safeguards herself against taking a plunge into "back-and-forth" reading and writing — and thus running the risk of kicking up more questions than answers. Right beyond that point is the shrug of despair that I associate with relativism. Who wouldn't want to put that off, especially in her first weeks at the university, when she doesn't know what's expected of her? And so this second student, when she notices her own insight emerging, steps aside and lets stand what the author tells her "The Loser" represents in her "evolution." Only it's doubtful the author would have needed to include the poems if that's all she wanted the reader to gather.

As the student essay stands, "renaming" is present in name only, and to follow the paper's analysis of the poem, we must refer back to Rich's text, of which the student text is only an index. But it can be more, and the work of the critical reading/writing course is to locate such places not as faults but as "windows of opportunity." As a group, we located every moment in this student's essay where the word "renaming" appeared. Each of these places was seen as an opening back to the text, where "going back" is not a penalty but a real instance of "reading against the grain." At each opening this student had a chance to do more than indicate the concept. But I think the presence of poetry in the Rich essay made her cautious — and rightly so — about stopping the progress "with the grain" of the text. It doesn't help that the phrase "writing is renaming" has a tautological aspect to it. In short, the reputedly "endless" possibilities for interpreting poetry, the spectre of relativity, were preempted by this student's referring back to the general line of Rich's essay, for which the concept of "renaming" could be seen as a transcendent rubric.

Regardless of which *Ways of Reading* essay you use to open your course, I recommend selecting two such student essays and juxtaposing them in class. In this way, you set the stage for a movement away from both the extratextual debate approach and the deferential, or indexing, approach, in both of which, the dialogue is markedly lopsided. I should point out that these essays should not be painted as failures. For instance, a student's deferring to the grain of a given text — as well as the opposite approach — is an effort to contain an abundance of ideas, reactions, and a convergence of many texts both written and unwritten. You can help to stem this overwhelm through your written comments and through in-class discussions that try to narrow the focus or find, as we did in the previously cited essay, a "productive center." For this latter student, the following Rich assignment presented a reasonable point of entry back to the poems and to the concept of "renaming": The assignment asked students to explore, again through Rich's poetry, another idea Rich offers, that "revision is an act of survival." Here, the student has two "re" words to work with. How are they related? And how might we see "The Loser" as a revision of "Aunt Jennifer's Tigers"?

Helping students to narrow the focus is one way to reduce the fear we all have (and no one more than the instructor) of opening cans of worms that can't ever be closed. It's the uneasiness we feel when a dialogue gets further and further away from the prospect of a conclusion. But this is the nature of critical reading and writing, isn't it? The first student cited, the "belligerent" one, attempted to be, in his words, "more diplomatic" with the Rich text in his revision. But the text remained for him an object to deflect in the name of larger issues external (or tangential) to it. Not one citation appeared in this second essay, although quotation marks do not necessarily guarantee dialogue, as anyone who's ever "strip-mined" a reference book for a research paper will admit. In retrospect, I think that this student might have been better served by the very model I wished he would abandon.

What might have happened had he tried (as the tradition of debate sanctions) to take on the alien perspective, that is, to debate on behalf of the Rich text? Would he, under these circumstances, have been able to keep the text at a distance, as an object? It's only recently that this "hair of the dog" intervention occurred to me. I'll take it up again shortly, in relation to John Berger's "Ways of Seeing."

By discouraging monolithic pro and con positions, I hope to discourage entrenchment and to encourage critical reading. To do this, we must question the nature of conclusions, and by implication, the construction of knowledge and discourse. A resounding, definitive conclusion may be like sealing the final car payment in an envelope, making the text one's own; but I work against this proprietary impulse and replace it with the sense that a text can never be owned outright.

By stressing that no one reader can "own" a text entirely, I find that the next wall we often encounter as a group, beyond the adversarial model, is that of relativism. Certainly, it's a wall you want to encounter. But to return to the analogy of dialogue, acknowledging the varying perspectives of the speakers is usually not an end in itself.

I would like now to work through examples of moments when students are wading in relativism, or what Jane Tompkins calls her "epistemological quandary." When a reader feels s/he can only end in relativism, I propose that, as Jane Tompkins illustrates in "'Indians': Textualism, Morality, and the Problem of History," the only way over the "wall" is a shift in the discourse, or what Tompkins calls "a change of venue." This shift can involve taking stock, backtracking, and it is usually self-reflexive and metadiscursive.

Tompkins's essay can be seen as a model of the process composition students and instructors work through in the course of a term. Like Tompkins, a group of readers and writers set out with a project. Whereas Tompkins sets out to research the relationship between Native Americans and colonists in seventeenth-century New England, the composition group has a more mixed agenda, but certainly it has something to do with getting somewhere, hitting on knowledge, and making progress.

Not long into the course, you notice the ground shifting, the compass points of progress jerking erratically in every direction. Tompkins discovers that history, even that conveyed by "primary" sources, offers varying perspectival facts about the Anglo-Native encounters in New England. This leads her back to the only "sources" left — her own subjectivity, her postmodern formation, her reading practices — all of which have contributed to her arrival at a quandary. "It may well seem to you at this point that, given the tremendous variation among the historical accounts, I had no choice but to end in relativism" (*Ways of Reading*, p. 630).

It's desirable that students, too, reach a point where they feel they have no choice but to *end* in relativism. But it's easy to mistake the beginning for the end. In Sheri's paper, a response to John Berger's "Ways of Seeing," the ending on a relativistic note becomes a way back into dialogue with the text:

> As I approach the end of my paper I ask myself what I have found. I guess really all I've found is that <u>I'm still at the place I was before I began:</u> not quite sure of what mystification is, or why it exists. However, on the positive side, I realize that the way I see something stems from who I am, where I've been, what I've done, everything that has come from my existence. I am a unique individual who is entitled to have unique thoughts. What I see is what I know, and neither can really be wrong.

To make this assertion is important to a student; it draws a connecting line between the reader and the text, recognizing that the reader does make a mark on the text; it positions the reader as active and subjective; and it recognizes that writing needn't end in mastery to be successful.

On the other hand, I read the final assertion on two levels: first, as an application of Berger's claims — that nonexperts can "read" art and the world without intervention by powerful and interested experts; and second, as a plea to me, the instructor, for indulgence about her not nailing down the concept of "mystification." To be part of the university, to admit oneself into the confederacy of subjectivities, a student does need to disown the fear of being wrong. Yet, as the editors of *Ways of Reading* point out in the anthology's introduction: "Think of yourself . . . as a writer intent on opening a subject up rather than closing one down." Declaring all opinions, perspectives, and readings as equally viable is a generous move (and a nice break from the adversarial model), but as Tompkins notes in "'Indians,'" "The notion that all facts are only facts within a perspective has the effect of emptying statements of their content" (*Ways of Reading*, p. 632). Just as the definitive conclusion closes down the dialogue between reader and text, so, too, does a disclaimer in the name of relativism. Where the former anchors down the text, the latter sends it floating like smoke with no significance apart from a reader's subjectivity.

To try to get Sheri to substantiate the text and her reading of it, I asked her to think about her own metadiscourse, the final disclaimer about everyone's being entitled to an opinion: "Why do you feel the need to assert this? Who might judge your individual way of seeing as 'wrong'?" I followed these questions up with another, having to do with the concept she was struggling with. "How might this move you make help you to understand how mystification can work against an individual's way of seeing?" Invoking relativism might be a more sophisticated way of expressing an insecurity in relation to the text or the instructor. "This is only my opinion" becomes, "Since even published writers are not totally objective, I stake out the right to go out on a limb, too." In both cases, instead of calling for these assertions to be cut, I try to use them as windows back into the reading/writing project.

If Sheri's defensiveness comes from her sense that she does not have a hold on Berger's concept of "mystification," the defensiveness itself becomes an occasion for returning to that concept. What is daunting about Berger's discussion of mystification? Which words block her (and she is not alone) from seizing what the text is trying to say? Earlier in her essay, as she tries to make meaning of the concept, she writes:

> Berger focuses mainly on mystification and its role in art. He <u>never really gives a straightforward definition of mystification within his essay</u>, but he does say that "mystification is the process of explaining away what might otherwise be evident." I took this to mean that something simple and undistorted can become obscured by searching for a hidden meaning. Being of the analytical type, I have a habit of doing this. [emphasis added]

This is a key paragraph to return to for revision, because here the writer is hitting on the problem of mystification in her very attempt to define it. By searching for a "straightforward definition," she is missing Berger's development of concepts functioning through examples. She is searching for a concise hidden meaning as if it were a bedrock in the maze of text that is actually Berger's process of showing what mystification *does* rather than what it *is*.

In an assignment requiring students to describe a work of art on their own terms and "in the spirit" of John Berger, it is necessary to understand what that "spirit" is. His discussion of mystification is at the core of it. So students' initial impulse to break off dialogue with Berger's text and go into a monologue about their chosen work of art is a short-lived but probably necessary step. A self-reflexive assignment for revision, "Ways of Seeing Your Ways of Seeing," sets the table for a return to the text, through which a student can then look at his or her description on a metadiscursive level. Here, too, is a chance to expand on the notion of mystification, to add to Berger's delineation of its function among art historians. Is it something only art historians do, by trying to put forth single, valorized (and often esoteric) meanings for works of art? How might saying, "Everyone who looks at a painting will form his or her own meaning" also be a sort of mystification?

Here, the "hair of the dog" might be helpful. I might try, for instance, to put a spin on the *Ways of Reading* assignment for "Ways of Seeing," which asks students to evaluate a work of art of their own choosing in "the spirit of John Berger." My spin — and I can't say whether it would be successful — would be to require students to pair off, each pair choosing the same work of art, but with the stipulation that the partners could not discuss their readings until after their essays were written and turned in. In-class discussion would then juxtapose these individual readings of the same work of art (with a reproduction of it available for the group to see). I am curious whether there would be a tendency to valorize one reading over another, or if, in group discussion, students would take refuge in the clause "Everyone has his or her own opinion," which so many of the Berger-related essays I've read seem to seize upon. I would hope that the classroom jury might turn to the Berger text for help in reading and commenting on the student essays. . . . If the jury didn't do this on its own, I'd ask some questions to facilitate this return to the text.

The point is not to force students to take firm positions, but rather to be aware that these positions shift during the course of a dialogue. It is important to establish through large group work with student papers that relativism, too, is a certain position assumed and gesture made by the writer to both the reader and the text discussed. It is also to call a writer's attention to her own discursive shifts. Metadiscussion is not the sole property of advanced writers. "This is only my opinion," that seeming nervous writing tic, underlies and precedes more developed instances of self-reflexivity. But if we point it out in class as a superfluous truism or as a flag in textual confidence, we lose the chance to build around it a larger discussion and a conscious way back into the close reading project.

Returning to the essay by Jane Tompkins, I'd like to discuss how my students' readings of that text show how much of a wall the point of relativism can be. The initial assignment asked students to relate their own stories of either an academic research project or a personal discovery in which, like Tompkins, they found conflicting facts and ended up reflecting on how knowledge is constructed. As with the Berger essay, this assignment gave students the chance to read their own experience, a frame of reference that easily pulls writers toward monologue over dialogue. The writer of the following essay does not succumb to this temptation. She reads her experience through Tompkins's experience; but while Tompkins gets around the wall of her quandary by changing the venue, Rhee parts company with the "'Indians'" parallel at the point of relativism:

> In my experience of being a Korean-American, no one
> can truly understand what I experience unless they them-
> selves experience it with me. I am able to tell about
> cultural shock, but **telling and experiencing are different:**
> no one can get the full effect. That is what Tompkins is
> saying; we have to be there to fully understand because

> everyone's perception of what occurred is different. [em-
>
> phasis added]

Rhee relates the dilemma of historical otherness to her own dilemma of making her experience understandable to contemporary others. Like most students I've worked with on the Tompkins text, she sustains a dialogue with the text up to the point where the quandary of perspectivism is discussed. What is more difficult for students to work with in a parallel writing assignment is Tompkins's metadiscussion on what to do about the quandary, which occupies the closing section, or "zone," of the essay. In the same paper, Rhee summarizes Tompkins's project in this way:

> Basically what Tompkins said initially is that you,
>
> the observer, had to be there to know and understand what
>
> happened, since everyone's point of view differs from
>
> others. Then, she began to research the Puritans and Indi-
>
> ans by consulting "expert" sources to see what they claimed
>
> as factual information about what had occurred between the
>
> two groups. After she had completed her research she tried
>
> to tie together what she researched, but was unable to do
>
> so. All the "experts" she consulted had slight variations
>
> in their point of view. At the end of the essay it was as
>
> if she had given up trying to formulate an opinion from the
>
> factual information she researched about their [the Puri-
>
> tans' and the Native Americans'] relationship.

Rhee concludes her synopsis with a partial quote from Tompkins. "She finally states that, 'someone else's facts are not facts because they are only the product of a perspective.'" This partial quote is interesting primarily because it has been cut to suit the needs of the summary's line of thinking and to "end in relativism." But when the clause is put back into context, the meaning is quite different. The full sentence from which it is taken is in Tompkins's metadiscussion of her quandary and how the assumptions she held about history and perspective were getting in the way of her making a moral judgment on an historical event. In effect, this discussion helps her to work her way out of her postmodern corner:

> . . . the argument that a set of facts derives from some particular worldview is no longer an argument against that set of facts. If all facts share this characteristic, to say that any one fact is perspectival doesn't change its factual nature in the slightest. It merely reiterates it.
>
> This doesn't mean that you have to accept just anybody's facts. You can show that what someone else asserts to be a fact is false. But it does mean that you can't argue that someone else's facts are not facts *because they are only the product of a perspective,* since this will be true of the facts that you perceive as well (*Ways of Reading,* p. 633).

Here is the close of Rhee's essay:

```
Even though Tompkins was unable to state a research-
opinionated statement about the relationship between the
Indians and the Puritans, she made a very important point:
You have to be there or experience the situation to under-
stand what was or is happening.
```

What interests me in this passage is the way in which Rhee is careful to distinguish between "what is" and "what was" happening, just as she made the distinction in a passage cited earlier between "telling" and "experiencing." In discussion, it was clear that her focus was, if taken to its logical conclusion, emptying history of its content, since we cannot be in history. Taking her own distinctions, together with part of the essay's title "the *problem* of history," we have something to work with beyond perspectivism. If history is history and now is now, how do we read history? How do we read "now"?

I have found it helpful to assign a second reading of "'Indians'" that examines it in terms of "zones" and gestures. Early in the essay, Tompkins announces that the essay is an enactment of "a particular instance of the challenge poststructuralism poses to the study of history" (*Ways of Reading*, p. 619). The presence of space-breaks throughout the essay assumes more than a typographical significance, and asks students to summarize each of the five zones of text — with emphasis on the final one (which we could call the "twilight zone" because it's difficult to summarize and easily eclipsed by the preceding discussion of perspectivism). In rough terms, it breaks down in this way:

I. Anecdotal introduction — preconceived impressions about Indians from childhood. Introduction of research problem. Metadiscourse about purpose of the essay.

II. Initial source — Perry Miller's *Errand into the Wilderness* (1956). Observations about the author's subjective oversights.

III. Examination of other sources from the 1960s and 1970s. Discussion of contradictions in certain revisionist accounts.

IV. Examination of captivity narratives. Expression of frustration ("It may well seem to you at this point that I had no choice but to end in relativism").

V. Self-reflexive discourse. Change of venue and reformulation of the question.

Calling attention to Tompkins's use of the phrase "change of venue" in this final, often overlooked, zone of the text raises the issue of other legal language employed in this section. Caught between the need to judge "the case" and a reading practice that makes her reluctant to accept the "evidence" of history, Tompkins appears to be using "change of venue" as a way of mediating between the adversarial model and the legacy of poststructuralism. "The change of venue, however, is itself an action taken" (p. 633).

Even though Rhee's final conclusions from the Tompkins's essay essentially beg the question and do not take Zone V into account, this idea of the perspectival nature of historical fact became one of her themes, even as the course moved into a reading of "Our Time," the excerpt from John Edgar Wideman's *Brothers and Keepers*. Comparing Wideman's text to Harriet Jacobs's "Incidents in the Life of a Slave Girl," Rhee stands by her conviction that Wideman is the more "authentic" of the two: "When I say that Wideman is objective, I mean that he tells what happens; he does use emotion but not . . . to show his bias." Rhee is on to something here, which has to do with the differences in the kinds of rhetorical/historical constraints each writer was under. Rhee continues:

```
You have to be there to know and understand what
really happened to say it is a true FACT. . . .  Wideman
```

> does [not?] tell the facts as to what happened to Robby,
> but he tells what <u>he saw</u>. Tompkins may say that what he saw
> is not a "true fact" because it was all from his point of
> view. A "true fact" to Tompkins is something like Garth
> died from a serious illness. To me, it seems like Wideman
> is telling what happened as it happened, but Tompkins feels
> otherwise, because everyone's point of view and perspective
> differs from others. She is always skeptical of what is
> written down. In other words, take what is written with a
> very small grain of salt. What Wideman wrote may be nothing
> more than one big deception on his part in Tompkins's eyes.
> Everything depends on what the observer or reader perceives
> in their eyes <u>ONLY</u>.

As you can see, Rhee still takes from Tompkins only the notion of relativism, but perhaps, too, she has taken something else: an interest in reseeing what constitutes fact and objectivity. The highly antijournalist style Wideman introduces in his nonfiction account of his relationship with his brother could be expected to put a reader on guard against seeing the text as "objective," since objectivity is more often an effect of style than it is of content. Yet Rhee admits this text into the realm of the "historical." And more important, even though she doesn't get past the relativistic disclaimer, it's on her mind enough to carry over as a theme from one assignment to the next.

Nicole first wrote an essay about a personal experience that came to the conclusion that knowledge depends on perspective, stopping at just about the same point as Rhee did. In her second essay, Nicole decided to focus on a research project; this made her parallel with Tompkins's project more feasible, although it raised its own set of questions. She discussed researching Franklin Roosevelt's presidency and encountering conflicting views. Disposed as she was to favor the Democratic president, she acknowledged how her preexisting values mediated in her sorting through the opposing facts. By the end of the essay, Nicole has moved into a self-reflexive discourse, if not a total change of venue (since, unlike Tompkins, she solves her problem, instead of reformulating another):

> I can reach a happy medium on my approach to history
> and perspective/fact by drawing <u>from my own method:</u> Gather
> the perspectives, weigh the information carefully, and
> decide what, <u>in your mind</u>, should be considered a fact.

My comments on Nicole's paper took on a different focus than they had in response to Rhee's work. Rhee's relativism did not allow for any fact in history. Nicole's method links fact to perspective, à la Tompkins, but does not anticipate conflict between the two when they are brought together to solve a problem. Which will out in the tough cases? Perspective? The weighing of evidence? Here, a further stepping away from the individual method she proposes might be helpful. If everyone approaches history in this way, how do we account for differences and similarities in conclusions? What are the consequences of such an approach? What does this say about history and our relationship to it? And to knowledge?

The stepping back needn't lapse into generalization. Even if it does, it serves to place the relativistic relationships in a larger context. In Rhee's essay, the inexperienced other is prohibited from judging an alien experience. In Nicole's, the method of judgment is contained, atomized, and at once subjective and objective. Further, the stepping back is a necessary component of any self-reflexivity; we cannot examine ourselves without examining our place within a culture and cultures.

Relativism is a wall that usually has its windows right there in the student texts and in the texts they are in dialogue with. Those windows are usually questions, questions that multiply within student essays, instructor's comments, and group discussions. Getting there is an accomplishment. Getting "beyond" it may not happen for you or for all of your students in the space of one semester. But "climbing the walls" can't go on forever, and for many reasons it's a lot more constructive than being in the trenches. I know one thing. No student who's read Susan Willis's "Work(ing) Out" will ever again go to aerobics class in the same frame of mind. Nor does that essay go unmarked. Willis may never know, for instance, how a male student tuned himself into a text by appearing in class with a skirt on, catching me so off guard that all I could think to say as he handed in the paper was, "Uh, that's a nice skirt, Dave." Later, I read the essay he had written in response to "Work(ing) Out":

> If gender discrimination is entirely the fault of men, then why do some men suffer at the hands of this discrimination? How would a man be judged if he wore a skirt? Are not hulking male body builders seen as more manly and favorable than just a healthy physique?

Now say this aloud, three times: "If you can keep your head when all about you . . . "

○–○–○–○–○–○–○–○–○–○–○–○–○–○–○–○–○–○

WAYS OF READING STUDENTS' WAYS OF WRITING: IMITATIONS OF SUSAN GRIFFIN'S COLLAGE, "OUR SECRET"
by Patricia Suzanne Sullivan

After we had spent quite a bit of class time reading, mapping, and discussing Susan Griffin's collage, "Our Secret," I asked the students in my first-year writing class to try their hand at the form, or as the assignment suggested, "to imitate it, to take it as a model . . . write a Griffin-like essay, one similar in its methods of organization and argument" (Bartholomae and Petrosky, 453). We had read parts of Griffin's collage together and slowly, talking about how we saw connections between pieces. Students worked with the first question for a second reading (Bartholomae and Petrosky, 451-452) on their own, and then in groups in class. We covered two chalkboards with the result of all our efforts: lists of themes, elaborations on themes, the various sources Griffin uses, perspectives she offers, metaphors she employs, and visual representations of some of the connections we had made as readers (with lots of lines and arrows). Then they worked in small groups discussing their plans and materials (some more prospective than actually physically present in front of them). I circulated, fielding questions, asking questions.

Yet, at the end of the class, before they were to go home and write the first drafts of their collages, one student said, amidst the chatter of other students getting ready to leave, "So, then, anything goes, right?" I looked around at the chalkboards, densely packed with notes from our class discussions, and began to worry. Another student responded to the first student, "No, not anything goes, you can't just write a regular essay, you have to mess it all up, you have to confuse the reader, make it like a puzzle." "No, it's harder than that, you have to have different points of view and everything." "Well, it's not like you can do everything Griffin does, right? We only have a couple of pages and she had fifty something pages. So, Patricia, can we just pick one or two aspects of Griffin's essay and do it like that?" There is nothing like hearing students who have been participating in a thoughtful discussion about the complexities of Griffin's text, faced with the prospect of producing their own collages, suddenly reduce all that reading and writing work into one very pragmatic and seemingly doable suggestion: "You just write a regular essay and then break it up."

The assignments in *Ways of Reading* challenge many of the assumptions students make about reading and writing. As the introduction suggests, the writing and reading assignments are carefully worded to discourage students from doing exactly what my students were doing at the end of class, that is, oversimplifying the work before them:

> When we write assignments, our goal is to point students
>
> toward a project, to provide a frame for their reading, a
>
> motive for writing, a way of asking certain kinds of ques-
>
> tions. In that sense, the assignments should not be read as
>
> a set of directions to be followed literally. In fact, they

are written to resist that reading, to forestall a writer's

desire to simplify, to be efficient, to settle for the

first clear line toward the finish. We want to provide a

context to suggest how readers and writers might take time,

be thoughtful. And we want the projects students work on to

become their own. (Bartholomae and Petrosky, "Introduc-

tion," 16)

Though several of my students were most likely trying to find "the first clear line toward the finish," it is also possible to see their comments otherwise, to see them as trying to use ways of writing they knew and with which they felt comfortable (e.g., the "essay") as the basis for leaping into completely new ways of writing (e.g., the "collage"): "You write an essay and then just break it up." An earlier assignment I had given to the same writing class had specifically and rather explicitly (at least in my teacherly eyes) cautioned students to be careful in their writing:

Write an essay that focuses on a rich and illustrative

incident from your own educational experience and read it

(that is, interpret it) as Freire would. You will need to

provide careful detail: things that were said and done,

perhaps the exact wording of an assignment, a textbook, or

a teacher's comments. And you will need to turn to the

language of Freire's argument, to take key phrases and

passages and see how they might be used to investigate your

case.

To do this you will need to read your account as not

simply the story of you and your teacher, since Freire is

not writing about individual personalities (an innocent

student and a mean teacher, a rude teacher, or a thought-

less teacher) but about the roles we are cast in, whether

we choose to be or not, by our culture and its institu-

tions. . . . Use your example, in other words, as a way of

testing and examining what Freire says, <u>particularly those</u>

<u>passages that you find difficult or obscure.</u> (Bartholomae

and Petrosky, 360)

Many, if not all, of my students had neglected some or the other key bit of advice embedded in the assignment's language: either they simply told the story of a teacher (sometimes evil, sometimes good) and a student (almost always good); or they managed to tell a complicated story from their educational past but tended to ignore Freire's text, avoiding, perhaps, the often more messy work they might produce in trying to figure out of his difficult language and ideas. I mention this Freire assignment because it seems to me that if students get a sense that the assignment is asking them to do something different, it is also true that they don't know yet how to make those new and different moves. Instead, they find ways of making the complex assignments into things they know how to do, for example, compare and contrast their experience with Freire's ideas without really letting each affect the other, use their own experience to illustrate Freire, or attempt to hide their confusion or uncertainty by oversimplifying Freire. For many of my students, writing is still about showing what you know not using writing to work out a response to a text.

I had tried to help students all semester (Griffin was the last assignment) as they revised their ways of reading and writing—took chances, faltered, resisted, forged ahead, fell back on old habits, tried out new approaches. The Griffin assignment which asked them to write a collage, however, seemed to send them a very clear message: one has got to do something very different, old ways of writing will not help (or at least that is how it might appear). What hadn't yet occurred to me at the time was that while my students would need to figure out new ways of writing, I as their teacher, might need to be figure out new ways of reading. Of course, as a graduate student in English Studies, I had more experience and practice than my students with new and unconventional forms. But would this experience, along with Griffin as a model, be enough for me in reading students' texts? Would it be merely a matter of evaluating how well they had imitated Griffin's text, or would responsibly engaging with their writing require that like my students I too would have to develop my own project?

The first thing that became apparent to me when I received my stack of student collages was the difficulty students had in resisting the inexorable pull of familiar writing conventions. The Griffin assignment had by its very form taken what were originally writing goals to work toward and turned them into traps to be avoided. Even with all our preparation, I came to realize that those traps couldn't always be avoided, those familiar writing conventions were not always so easily dismissed. As I read some of the most "coherent" essays I had read all semester, my students' interpretations of the writing assignment echoed in my ears. One student wrote about her break up with her boyfriend in the form of a linear narrative disrupted by descriptions of a roller coaster ride, clearly meant to be a metaphor for relationships. I imagined that all she had heard in the class discussion was the idea that you could write about what you wanted and then break it up a little. Another student's collage was so chaotic that I worked and worked to make connections and had finally given up. Had she decided that "anything goes," or that the whole idea had been to confuse the reader, to make the writing like a puzzle? And then there were some collages which had tried to find a balance, not too coherent, but not too confusing, moving toward the potential of a collage form, yet with traces of essay conventions in them. These were the kinds of collages I focused on in class discussions and the ones that I read here in order to highlight not only the ways in which students were and were not able to take on Griffin's project, but also the ways in which I struggled to learn how to read their attempts.

One of the first collages I read began with definitions of the word *racist* and *racism*, and went on to discuss how difficult it is for people to talk about. As the collage never leaves the topic of racism, the opening clearly functions as an introduction. Another student collage by Cecilia Rodriguez which focuses on the effect on the lives of Chileans under Pinochet, begins this way:

> `Chilean Air Force Hawker Hunters fires 18 rockets straight`
>
> `into the 300-year-old presidential palace. By 2:45 p.m.`
>
> `there was total calm. President Allende was found dead at`
>
> `his desk, surrounded by the lifeless bodies of his 14`
>
> `personal assistants.`

> General Augusto Pinochet was at the head of this
> military coup. The General, assisted by the conservative
> right wing and the North American CIA, that considered
> Allende's left tendencies a threat to democracy, was able
> to organize the military and overthrow Allende's govern-
> ment. Despite scattered resistance, the left was crushed.
> Pinochet became president and the disappearances, tortures
> and assassinations began. Within 19 days of the coup 320
> people were executed by the military, 13,500 were arrested
> and many were rounded up and tortured at Santiago's Na-
> tional Stadium. (Rodriguez 1)

Both students employ two familiar strategies of introductions: offering definitions as a way to introduce a topic ("racism") and providing necessary exposition (about Pinochet's military coup). As a class, we had discussed how Griffin's collage differed from more conventional essays, specifically in that it did not have what we usually thought of as an introduction, middle, and conclusion. Yes, we decided, it had an opening and an ending, and yes, there was movement (though not always linear) in the middle, but this was not the usual essay format. We had also discussed how the collage, as evidenced by Griffin's "Our Secret," had asked if not demanded that readers do more and different kinds of work than they were used to doing. Yet, here were some very clear "introductions" in my students' texts. Were they were wary of asking their readers to do very much work or nervous about losing their readers? An important question about writing emerged: what might be the difference between an introduction and a beginning? Though we went on as a class to discuss opening moves for these student collages, when I think back now, I wonder not just about conventional introductions in terms of their effects on readers, but the role that conventions play in enabling (or disabling) the writing process: how does one start writing without an introduction? Could it be that the convention of an introduction actually helps writing begin, and if that is the case, then how does one decide where to begin when the requirements of the assignment seem to take away that enabling device? Or does one write an introduction in order to get started and then take it away later, or move it, replacing it with something more appropriate to the collage form — a story, an image, a text that works metaphorically? Here is an example of an opening from Bernadette Loftus's first draft that resists the conventional introduction (or puts it in the second slot?):

> As the corpse of the monstrous entity Chton sinks back into
> the lava whence it rose, you grip the Rune of Earth Magic
> tightly.
>
> Now that you have conquered the Dimension of the
> Doomed, Realm of Earth Magic, you are ready to complete
> your task. A Rune of magic power lies at the head of each
> haunted land of Quake. Go forth, seek the totality of the
> four Runes!

```
I don't remember acknowledging or even caring much
when I heard about the killings in Colorado. Violence in
the news does not upset me much. Violence just kind of
melds into other television programming. "What a shame," I
remember saying. It was a shame. No one should have to die
like that, especially kids. Monsters, I thought, tortured
every day of their lives. They just couldn't take it any-
more. (Loftus 1)
```

When we discussed this opening in class, some students thought the collage was going to be about computer or video games, and though they reported feeling a little disoriented, they said they had been curious to read on and see if they were right. When we discussed the next part—where Bernie relates her response to the news of the Columbine High School shootings in Colorado—students began debating. One the one hand, the thrill was gone for some students once they realized that the collage was most likely going to focus on the relationship between violent games and youth violence (a topic that had been much in the news at the time). On the other hand, some students argued that the predictability of the connection was mitigated by their surprise at reading about the writer's apparently indifferent attitude: "I don't remember acknowledging or even caring much . . ." Either way, my students recognized that Bernie had found a way to open her collage that was different from yet similar to Griffin's opening. Whereas Griffin had opened with a definition of a "nucleus," Bernie had chosen the discourse of a video game, *Quake*, to pull her reader in before going on to imitate Griffin's next move—the use of a personal narrative (for Griffin, an interview; for Bernie, a personal narrative showing her own reaction).

Through class discussion of the ways in which Bernie's and Griffin's openings had worked, students reconsidered how they had opened their own collages, seeing that for this new form an introduction might be undesirable. Yet, in looking back at Cecilia's "introduction" to her collage on Chile, I wonder now if advising Cecilia to take away her introduction and replace it with something else is a piece of advice more easily given than taken. One of the reasons that Bernie's opening seemed to succeed so well, according to my students, was because they recognized the passage as a video game (even if they were not familiar with *Quake*). Could Cecilia rely on her reader's knowing who Pinochet was or what happened in Chile in the same way that Griffin might be able to rely on her readers' familiarity with the Holocaust or in the same way that Bernie might be able to rely on her fellow students' ability to recognize a video game? I wonder now about how helpful some of my generic advice actually was to students when the subject of their collage might pose particular problems for them not answerable by suggesting that they review their notes on "Our Secret," or work harder to imitate Griffin's collage.

The attempts to not only imitate Griffin's moves but adapt them to the specificity of their own work is evident in all three of the collages I include here. For example, though Cecilia begins her collage with exposition, her next move employs Griffin's use of definition for a different effect:

```
Within 19 days of the coup 320 people were executed by the
military, 13,500 were arrested and many were rounded up and
tortured at Santiago's National Stadium.

Fear: emotion caused by threat of some form of harm, some-
times manifested in bravado or symptoms of anxiety, and
```

<u>prompting a decision to fight the threat or escape from it.</u>

<u>(Microsoft Encyclopedia '97).</u> (Rodriguez 1)

Later, after presenting an excerpt from a personal testimony of a man who watched his wife die as the result of a car bombing, Cecilia returns to the general idea of fear, this time invoking its physiological manifestation:

> It is a strange thing, living in permanent fear.
>
> Adrenaline is constantly pumping through your bloodstream.
>
> It makes your heart race, strengthen your muscle, raises
>
> your blood sugar, and boosts your sugar metabolism. This
>
> reaction is often called the "fight or flight" response; it
>
> prepares the body for strenuous activity. (Rodriguez 2)

If my class had decided that the scientific definitions and information (particularly of the cell) in Griffin's text could be read metaphorically, Cecilia's definitions instead seem to offer something different: a way for the reader—who ostensibly has felt fear or a fight or flight response at some point in his or her life—to connect to the specific cultural fear of people staying in Chile under Pinochet's rule.

Similarly, when I first read Tony Portis's collage on racism, I noticed how his collage as a whole imitated Griffin's "Our Secret" in that it provided multiple texts, sources, and perspectives: quotations from Malcolm X, job applications, movie reviews, Web sites, excerpts from newspapers and television news, examples drawn from his own experience, and so on. However, one way that Tony apparently makes Griffin's project his own is by inserting statements that look like inter-titles into his collage, which either name topics for parts of the collage—"Application and Workplace," "The Media," "Let's Go the Movies," "Web Sites," "My Experience"—or comments on something just discussed or presented, "He Needed a Chance," Don't Judge Me Before You Know Me," "Why Do We Continue to Kill Over Color?" "Give Me a Break" (Portis, 2–8). Are these titles an instance of revising Griffin's work, or another instance of the conventions of the essay emerging to prevent the different work of the collage as a form? The inter-titles seem to have at least two effects: first, as transitions, they work against imitating the kind of abrupt shifts evidenced in Griffin's text; second, the titles seem to be another example of my students' reluctance to risk losing their reader, or their reluctance to risk being misunderstood. Moreover, I began to see these titles and their accompanying texts as creating mini-essays: a mini-essay on racism in the news media, a mini-essay on racism in the movies, a mini-essay on racism in sports, and so on. In a section titled, "*Trading Places*, Eddie Murphy," Tony describes how difficult it was for football player Jason Shorn to play cornerback for the New York Giants since all the cornerbacks in the NFL were black at the time. Tony concludes this section with the inter-title: "He Needed a Chance," titles the next piece of his collage, "Shoe on the Other Foot," and describes playing basketball with his friends in the park:

> When we play basketball in the summer at Mellon Park and
>
> there are a couple of white guys wanting to play, we pick
>
> them up to show them we just want to play basketball. I
>
> have a few friends that might say it's us four and "white
>
> boy." I say to them, "Hey, he has a name; all you have to
>
> do is ask him." Just think, if the shoe was on the other

```
foot -- if it were four whites and the "nigger" you would

be ready to fight. (Portis 4)
```

Similarly, in a section titled *"Let's go to the movies!"* Tony describes the controversy about the ways in which the character Jar Jar Binks in *Star Wars* is considered a racial stereotype. Immediately following this, in the next section titled, "The Good," Tony offers an example of a movie, *Rosewood*, that shows "how racism is defeated by people of color coming together as one" (Portis, 5). Though there is certainly a kind of collage created by all these mini-essays, and if Tony had adopted Griffin's ways of working with juxtapositions, Tony's collage lacks the kinds of associative connections present in Griffin's collage. If it doesn't seem to challenge a reader to read and think across parts (since related parts were so often adjacent to one another), could it be that Tony's collage achieves some other effect?

In fact, most of my students had clearly found this work of making associative connections, or asking a reader to think analogically across pieces, the most difficult work. Their collages were often very focused on a specific issue, or a set of clearly related issues. Surely, this was a missed opportunity and something I encouraged them to explore as part of their revision work, but was this absence of associative connections to be considered a failure? Or could it be that their collages were doing other things, going for other effects in an attempt to make Griffin's project their own?

To return to Tony's collage on racism, it had many of the markers of a conventional argumentative essay: an introduction which defined its terms, set forth the problem—"there's something about racism that puts people in denial, and they just don't want to deal with it" (Portis, 1)—and a conclusion which acknowledged that racism "is one problem that just won't go away. People of today have to realize it is here and we have to deal with it" (Portis, 8). In the end, Tony offers a list of suggestions about how to deal with it, including not prejudging and being respectful of others. One way my students had read Griffin—one path they had taken through her text—was to see her text as making an argument about the necessity of realizing we are all connected. With this in mind, many students thought that the collage form had allowed her to explore and represent the complex and often subtle nature of those interconnections. By providing a varied and critical mass of instances, perspectives, sources, and texts, Tony's collage realizes its argument by disallowing his reader's attempt to deny racism. There is a very real sense of immersion when reading his text, an immersion which challenges the reader to "deal with it," to look directly at instances of racism, rather than think about it as an abstract problem.

Similarly, when my class was discussing Bernie's collage on youth violence, one of my students asked whether or not Bernie's collage was making an argument or had an organizing theme or themes. The collage includes references to a video game, reactions to Columbine from the Internet, statistics, descriptions of the formation of two different planets (Earth and Venus), as well as Bernie's commentaries and personal narratives. All of the perspectives presented are those of teenagers and young adults, describing how ostracized, frustrated, and angry they felt during high school. If discussions in the media had seemed ask how kids could suddenly murder other kids, Bernie's commentary has a way of putting her reader at ground zero, reminding us that while it might seem that kids just lose it (out of nowhere), in actuality, their actions are often the result of a long struggle:

```
For many people school was a breeding ground for pain.

Day in and day out, being tortured by peers while other

students and administrators turned their back. How much can

one person stand before crumbling, before wanting the world

to end? It seems you have two choices: you can leave or

they can.
```

```
      But what makes people choose the lives they choose?

Hundreds of kids, millions, grow up in America tortured.

Why do some of them go on rampages . . .


Luke Woodham, 16, Pear, Mississippi, 10-1-97

2 students killed, 7 wounded, Mother stabbed to death


and how do those who don't prevent themselves acting out

their anger and pain? (Loftus 2)
```

It seems that the statistic here literally interrupts Bernie's thoughts because it interrupts her syntax, or that the statistic is offered as evidence to support the preceding phrase "go on rampages." Yet, it can also seem that Bernie's question surrounds the statistic, asking us to think not just about the kids who become statistics but about the many other kids who don't resort to murder, who are able to "prevent themselves [from] acting out their anger and pain."

If Bernie's text tries to defend troubled adolescents (or at least generate some compassion), there are also attacks on the adults whose attempts to help or handle troubled teenagers prove inadequate. For example, Bernie includes a long internet testimony from "Dan in Boise, Idaho," in which he relates how his school advisor suggested students write about their feelings about what happened in Colorado. However, when Dan wrote an article for the school newspaper, arguing that it was wrong to blame "screwed up kids or the Net," and that perhaps it was the system that was to blame and that he felt sympathy for the boys who had done the shooting, his article was "killed" and he was sent home with a letter to his parents:

```
So this is how they are trying to figure out what happened

in Colorado, I guess. By blaming a sub-culture and not

thinking about their own roles, about how fucked-up school

is. Now, I think the whole thing was a set-up, cause a

couple of other kids are being questioned too, about what

they wrote. They pretend to want to have a "dialogue," but

kids should be warned that what they really want to know is

who's dangerous to them. (Loftus 4)
```

Bernie follows this with another statistic and with two pieces: in the first one (since this paragraph is in italics, it's not clear whether it is a quote or Bernie's writing), she wonders if Columbine had an effect on the "microculture of our own household;" in the second one, she recounts a recent conversation with her father about Columbine:

```
But how many of us actually did anything differently? Spent

more time with our children, or someone else's? Came home a

little earlier? Skipped a meeting? Turned off the TV?

Called other parents, called a teacher, volunteered to help

with some after school activity -- Girl Scouts, theater,
```

```
baseball -- that will happen only if enough grown ups
show up?


I sent my father three articles from the other side. He
called me up to tell me he refuses to read them; he has
made up his mind about the situation. I told him I under-
stand these kids. I play Quake. I was tortured by others for
being different. "Did you ever want to hurt them?" he
asked. "Sure," I said, "all the time. But I knew better."
"Oh, Bernie . . ." he said, his voice heavy with the tone
of devastating disappointment. I could almost see him walk
away from me like some leprous being. Has he forgotten?
Have fifty-four years washed away the pain of adolescence?
```

(Loftus 4-5)

The story Bernie tells here emphasizes the generation gap and the difficulty that adults and adolescents have talking with one another—the misunderstandings, the fear, the mutual suspicion, the "refusal" to read or listen, the mutual disappointments. But it is the language she uses to open this section which is perhaps most telling and which led my class into a discussion about what perspectives were present and not present in her collage. She writes, "I sent my father three articles *from the other side*" (emphasis mine). What we have here, she seems to be saying, is a matter of sides, one against the other, with a lot of space or static in between. Because at the time of the class discussion, I was still caught up in trying to respond to my students' texts in terms of how well they had imitated Griffin's project, I asked them (rather leadingly, I have to admit) if Bernie's collage needed more and different perspectives, for example, texts which quoted what the media was actually saying about the connections between video games and violence, or more texts which let the adults—teachers, administrators, parents—speak. My students were adamant: absolutely not. They argued that those perspectives were already implied by the texts Bernie had chosen as responses and that adding more texts would detract from the forcefulness of the material she had already chosen. I kept pushing, asking them to consider to what good uses multiple perspectives had been put in Griffin's "Our Secret," but to no avail. Apparently there was something more at stake here than students' reluctance to do the work of revision.

In my comments on her collage and in conversation with her, I encouraged Bernie to at least experiment with including other perspectives. It would make for a tidy story if I could report here that she acted on my advice, but she didn't. My motives for pushing her seem now rather tangled. I still value the work of revision, particularly exploratory revision. In retrospect though, I wonder if I hadn't been clinging too much to Griffin's text as a model. To some degree, I felt that Bernie's collage had failed by not imitating more of Griffin's moves. I also felt that I had failed her as a teacher by not convincing her to try to do this work. Yet, both she and the class had made strong arguments for excluding those other texts and for respecting the project of the collage form as Bernie had realized it. Perhaps the mistake I had made was in holding on too tightly to the importance of students' taking on Griffin's project. And perhaps this looks like a slight mistake, a mere matter of emphasis. Yet, I am beginning to think that shifting one's emphasis might make the difference when trying to get students to take chances and write in new and different ways. Faced with a similar situation in the future, I would want to try to give more precedence to the student's writing, to be able to say, "Let me show how I see your text as different from Griffin's, and let's talk about how you might use some of her moves, adapt her moves, or create new moves in order to develop *your own project*."

If when my students tried their hand at this new kind of writing, they sometimes fell back on old ways of writing. I, too, sometimes fell back on typical ways of reading which prevented me from seeing the nature of the difficulties they were having, or even the nature of their successes. The key for me is to make my ways of reading part of the classroom discussion. I don't mean to suggest that I make my problems their problems, but that as readers and writers trying to figure out a new form, it is important to acknowledge our shared obstacles and our shared achievements. If I wanted my students to "forestall a writer's desire to simplify, to be efficient, to settle for the first clear line towards the finish" (Bartholomae and Petrosky, "Introduction," 16), then I, too, had to move beyond the kinds of readings of student work which merely compared them to Griffin and evaluated the ways in which their texts measured up or failed to measure up. I had to resist my impulse to write quick remarks on their papers like "replace that introduction with a more collage-like fragment," "cut your transitions," "provide more perspectives." In the context of my own project as a teacher, those kinds of comments represent the easier work. The harder work for me is to take the time to be thoughtful, to be able to recognize when students need help revising their ideas about reading and writing, and when they are not necessarily failing but coming into their projects.

Works Cited

Bartholomae, David, and Anthony Petrosky. *Ways of Reading*, 5th edition. Boston: Bedford/ St. Martin's, 1999.

Loftus, Bernadette. "Jocks Are from Earth, Oddballs Are from Venus." Unpublished, University of Pittsburgh, 1999.

Portis, Anthony. "Racism." Unpublished, University of Pittsburgh, 1999.

Rodriguez, Cecilia. "Truth and Reconciliation." Unpublished, University of Pittsburgh, 1999.

All students papers are used with permission of their authors, to whom I am very grateful.

I would also like to thank Keely Bowers, Juli Parrish, and Mari Pena-Jordan, who talked with me about my students' papers, or read drafts of my writing, or sometimes did both.

o–o–o–o–o–o–o–o–o–o–o–o–o–o–o–o–o–o–o

THE RETROSPECTIVE ESSAY:
"MAKING PROGRESS" IN A WRITING CLASS[1]
by Steve Sutherland

> A Klee painting named "Angelus Novus" shows an angel looking as though he is about to move away from something he is fixedly contemplating. His eyes are staring, his mouth is open, his wings are spread. This is how one pictures the angel of history. His face is turned toward the past.
>
> – Walter Benjamin
> "Theses on the Philosophy of History, IX"

Halfway through the reading and writing course I teach at the University of Pittsburgh, and again at the end of it, I ask students to write a retrospective paper in which they look back upon the work that they've done in my class in order to "look for key moments and points of transition, for things that have changed and things that have remained the same" in their writing. These two assignments could be said to stand as markers of "progress" or "development" in the class, as moments when students are afforded the opportunity to think about how their writing has changed and about how they have changed as student readers and writers. In other words, the opportunity for an act of retrospection aims at enabling my General Writing class to "see" change by constructing narratives about what has happened in the course.

In a memo to graduate students teaching at Pitt, Jean Ferguson Carr offers the following rationale for this act of retrospection: "The final retrospective assignment should direct your students back to some significant rethinking of their practices and positions as readers and writers, as they have been influenced by this course, by your comments and classroom work, by their classmates, and by the texts they have read and the papers they have written. . . . This is a difficult assignment for your students, coming at a difficult time. It can be, however, a very important experience for them and a very telling assignment for you to evaluate." At first glance, the retrospective assignments might seem to offer tidy, historical evaluations of the course, mini-chronicles of what happened and failed to happen. Yet the histories that students write are "very telling" in other ways, since they are indeed functions of what Carr calls a "difficult time." This essay is about how teachers and students work within and against the constraints of that "difficult time." It's about the difficulty of writing in/about time.

Very often, the pedagogical gesture of asking students to write a midterm and final retrospective essay reinforces their sense of the course as an unfolding history of progress, a story about a time of growth. For example, many of their retrospective narratives are structured by notion of causality ("This occurred, and it then caused that to happen") that allow students to see a chain of influence running through their successive papers. The retrospective essays are almost always chronologically structured, so that successive moments of insight serve to reinforce a linear progression toward a conclusion in which the student frequently claims to have reached a kind of educational utopia. There is, I think, a sense in which the rhetorical demand of asking students to write these essays can often

[1]This essay refers to previous editions of *Ways of Reading*.

reinforce rather than challenge unproblematic accounts of history and of what it means to *become* educated. This is because the retrospective papers that my students write frequently participate in broader cultural narratives about change and progress.

For a moment, I'd like to problematize the popular notion of "course as narrative of progress" by entertaining a somewhat absurd notion of "course as Zeno's stadium." Zeno of Elea proposed the well-known "stadium paradox." Here is his scenario: If someone were to walk from one end of a stadium to another, it would be impossible to arrive at the other end. This is because the person would have to pass through an infinite number of points:" halfway, quarter-way, and so forth, *ad infinitum*. Since it is impossible to pass through an infinite number of points in a finite period of time, it would be impossible to reach the end of the stadium or even to get to a halfway point. So much for end of term and mid-term.

Since Zeno's account precludes any kind of change or movement, it seems necessary to refute his argument, not only because he is violating "common sense" in general but, more important, because his position calls into question some "common sense" notions about teaching. Plato finds a way out by positing two worlds: one of unchanging, ideal forms, and another of change and illusion. This is a familiar Platonic position, which insists that the world of change (of "becoming") is only a reflection of a more substantial, unchanging world of "being." The argument allows Plato to account for change while still preserving an essentialist notion of an unchanging reality. According to his model, change is merely something that appears to be the case, an illusion. This illusory world is, for Plato, precisely what education should not be asking students to look at. In the *Republic* he writes, "Education then is the art of . . . this turning around, the knowledge of how the soul can most easily and effectively be turned around" in order to apprehend permanence in the world of forms (171). When Plato's students are asked to "look back," they look away from change and toward permanence — that is, in the opposite direction to my students. In fact, the whole of the *Republic* might be understood as an attempt to "look at" a utopian model "laid up in heaven" (238). Plato's moment of turning and looking (his retrospective act) fails to see change. And, I'd like to argue, this particular way of looking has pedagogical and political consequences, since it is a predictable prerequisite for establishing the kind of republic Plato desires: one that is free of change and conflict.

Although it's clear that Plato's notion of change is substantially different from that of Zeno, both arguments manage to turn change into an illusion. This way of accounting for change is of considerable importance because it allows the narrative to construct utopian spaces (like Plato's *Republic*) that are free of contradiction. Utopian fiction, for example, frequently offers mystical or unreliable accounts of the historical changes that brought utopia into existence. A kind of forgetfulness often frames utopian narratives. Since utopias are almost always narrated retrospectively (e.g., More's *Utopia* or Bellamy's *Looking Backward)*, one might say that an unwillingness to engage with history can all too easily produce utopia.

I want to argue that a similar construction of change is often at work in my reading/ writing class, both in discussions and in student papers, and that this construction of change frequently allows students to imagine an educational model that is free of complication, unproblematic, and utopian. I'll focus first on class discussions and then on student essays. During the course of the semester, students (most are in their first year of study) read five selected texts from Bartholomae and Petrosky's *Ways of Reading,* an anthology of essays for student writers. Each week, they write a paper (about five pages in length) in response to an assigned question on a particular text. These weekly assignments are sequenced and interrelated, asking students to consider among other things, the ways in which they are enacting a particular "reading/rereading" of each text. Our class discussions center on sample student papers, which I select and distribute ahead of time. I do not choose the "best" or the "weakest" essays, neither models for imitation nor pitfalls to avoid. Instead, the samples are papers that I believe will lead the class into a productive discussion, perhaps papers that enact or raise issues that seem to crop up in many essays. I some-

343

times choose papers that might seem provocative, problematic, even absurdly Zenoesque. We then talk about these essays as a way of investigating student writing, and also as a way of thinking about how students are reading the assigned texts in the anthology. Two of these assigned pieces, Adrienne Rich's "When We Dead Awaken: Writing as Re-Vision" and Harriet Jacobs's "Incidents in the Life of a Slave Girl," regularly provoke conversations that can lead to important insight into the ways in which students discuss change.

Jacobs's text, an excerpted slave narrative written in order to further the abolitionist cause, is accompanied by a second-reading question which asks students, "What is Jacobs doing in this text? What might her work as a writer have to do with her position (as a female slave) in relation to the world of her readers?" (p. 411). The first writing assignment asks students to "consider the ways she [Jacobs] works on her reader . . . and also the ways she works on her material," emphasizing that students "will need to reread the text as something constructed" (p. 412). In our class discussions, students usually see Jacobs's narrative not as a constructed account but rather as a kind of window into her life, one that allows her to "show" her story "just as it is." Students often use optical words (like "reveals") to describe Jacobs's work; they seldom use words like "selects," or "organizes." In this way, Jacobs's story is frequently seen as an accurate display of the truth, and as an autobiography that is *inevitable* in the sense that it is dictated solely by Jacobs's real life rather than by her choices as a writer. What students frequently do not see is precisely what the question asks them to see, namely, that Jacobs is a writer at work, constructing a text, making decisions, making changes to her material. What seldom gets discussed is the fact that Jacobs's narrative is not identical to her life; neither is it propelled by her life in an automatic or deterministic manner.

Getting students to think about Jacobs's work as a writer might be done in various ways, but I think an effective method would probably entail managing a discussion about how Jacobs looks back on her life in a retrospective gesture that allows her to work with her material by selecting, emphasizing, ordering, or otherwise changing it. If we imagine Jacobs looking back, our account of her work can move beyond seeing only inevitability, and toward a recognition of how her narrative gets changed in the very act of writing it. Such a move can help students to acknowledge the critical choices that Jacobs makes. It's a move toward a nondeterministic/nonautomatic account of the text's production, toward seeing Jacobs as a writer who is both self-aware and aware of her choices. In this way, the absent moment, Jacobs's retrospective gesture in which changes are made, can be made present.

A similar discussion is often prompted by the two assignments on Adrienne Rich's essay, a piece about the changes she sees as she looks at a brief history of her poetry. This time, the first writing assignment asks students to choose a poem by Rich and to consider "the poem as an act of 'renaming'" by asking, "What is transformed into what? and to what end?" (p. 563). The second assignment (drawn from a previous edition) extends the first, asking students to "take three of the poems Rich offers as examples of change in her writing . . . and use them as a way of talking about revision." Both of these questions explicitly ask students to talk about "change" or "transformation." Nevertheless, the notion of change frequently disappears from our class discussions. Students are able to offer intelligent insight into the "meaning" of Rich's poetry, or passionate opinions on her homosexuality. However, they seldom talk about change. When they do, they describe an almost self-evident development in Rich's poetry. A common way of accounting for the changes they see is to imagine change that takes place *between* the poems, in a chronology that exists prior to Rich's actual writing of the essay. While this account is undoubtedly somewhat accurate, it fails to account for the revision that gets enacted by Rich's essay itself.

In order to problematize this particular construction of "change," I ask students to construct a narrative of what they think Rich actually does as a writer. They respond by saying that she writes a poem, notices that it is somehow insufficient, then writes another poem that tries to solve the problems of the earlier poem. Subsequently, Rich sees the second poem as insufficient, and she goes on to make up for its inadequacies in the third poem, and so forth. This narrative, although addressing the issue of change, locates change outside (prior to) Rich's act of writing her essay. It thus offers only one, chronologically based understanding of what our class might mean by "re-vision."

Adrienne Rich's piece reminds us that "re-vision" is an act of "looking back." I want to argue that this act, this retrospective moment, which so often disappears in our discussions of Jacobs, partially disappears in our discussions about Rich. Students frequently do not examine the absent moment in which Rich looks back on her work with a gaze that selects, connects, exaggerates, or otherwise changes her material in the very act of writing about change. My role in the discussions about Jacobs and Rich is to recuperate the moment of change, to try turning students' attention toward the retrospective gestures that could otherwise manage to disappear. In this way, I hope to provoke a conversation about how Rich and Jacobs *use* chronology, about how they construct histories, and to move beyond a discussion that views chronology only as a self-evident determinant of the texts we read.

The same might be said of the texts we write. Of course, many of the texts we read are essays written by students in the class. Our discussion of these essays is intended to get students to think about how their writing both enacts and produces a particular reading. To a large extent, then, our class is about how acts of reading and writing are connected.

When students sit down to write their retrospective assignments, they occupy what I have called the moment of constructing change, of looking backward, the same moment they learned to identify as readers. The two retrospectives ask students to "review the work you've done . . . and describe what you see. . . . You might look . . . at what stands as evidence of your efforts and achievements as a writer." As students respond to these questions, they confront rhetorical tasks similar to those undertaken by Rich and Jacobs. Students, too, have to look back on the past and construct a text that accounts for changes. They, too, are writing history; and they are rereading the readings they produced in their essays. This affords them the opportunity to enact some of what they have learned in our class discussions.

However, what frequently happens at these moments is that students again ignore what they did not initially see in our discussions of Rich and Jacobs, namely, that writers of history do not merely report, but also construct their narratives. When we talk about the retrospective papers, then, I try to get student writers to push against conventional accounts of change driven by narratives of inevitability. I remind them of the work we performed as readers of Jacobs and Rich. In short, I try to get my students to produce writing that enacts a critically self-conscious retrospection rather than utopian narratives that either banish change completely or effectively neutralize the possibility of writing a critical account of change.

Sometimes students write utopian accounts — papers that, in looking backward, turn away from change and toward closure, permanence, the end of history. At the end of my first semester teaching at Pitt, I received final retrospectives that constructed change in this way. The conclusion of Amy's paper is an appropriate example of what I've called utopian closure. She writes, "Now at the end of the term, I feel confident that I have completed the wishes of Bartholomae and Petrosky and have proved myself as an open-minded and honest writer. I see myself as a well-rounded reader with the intelligence of knowing that there are many other ways of reading, seeing, thinking, and writing." In Amy's account, the work of the course is completely over, the agenda fulfilled, the goals achieved. It's almost as if Amy's paper functions as a kind of testimony that bears witness; "I have proved myself."

This is how she describes her essay in her opening paragraph: "While I was gathering ideas for a retrospective paper I had a feeling that this paper could be considered as a confession. What I have done on the following pages was to confess to my professor what I feel I have accomplished in his class." The purpose of Amy's confession is, in part at least, to claim that she has "satisfied the desires of Bartholomae and Petrosky" in what she calls "an effort to achieve the praise of B[artholomae] + P[etrosky] and to have the satisfaction for myself." I want to point out that her paper is an astute reading of the pedagogical scene in which she finds herself. Having been asked to write about how her work has changed in the course, she reads the assignment as a request for testimony, a chance to prove to the teacher that she has performed all of the requirements. In this act of writing, though, the retrospective gesture glosses over contradictions and complexities. She does not, for example, "read against" what she sees as the "desires of Bartholomae and Petrosky," even though she describes herself as a student who is becoming a "strong and critical reader."

Rather than a precise demonstration of the changes she identifies, Amy's paper offers only a claim: "I have changed." Her essay draws on broader cultural narratives about education as an almost total transformation of the student. As such, it constructs a conversion narrative — not necessarily because Amy feels that she has converted to the course's agenda, but because she feels that this is what she is required to say.

Felicia and Damian also employ narratives of change that are relatively predictable and unproblematic. Their papers offer accounts of developmental progress that are as inevitable as organic growth. Felicia's retrospective is called "Stages," and it employs the following model as a way of talking about the changes she sees in her writing: "Just as humans go through these different stages, I strongly believe as a writer that I have encountered these stages but in a different manner. First, there is the baby stage. . . ." Felicia then goes on to talk about the "teenage stage" and the "young adult stage," comparing teenage rebelliousness with a kind of rebellion in her writing. She reinforces this developmental metaphor, but also adds a more sophisticated reading of it in her conclusion:

> One semester can't transform my way of thinking. This can be compared to being raised; once your parents have told you to behave in a certain manner, if all of a sudden others tell you differently, it will take you a while to adjust to what they tell you. I believe that I have adjusted dramatically from the beginning of the semester, but I believe it will not stay.

While I admire both Felicia's fairly elaborate deployment of the "growing up" metaphor and her resistance to the utopian closure that operates in Amy's paper, I cannot help thinking that her account of change limits her ability to reflect critically on the work she has done in my class. Her narrative presents change as a matter of growing up, but she fails to problematize her metaphor by seeing its limitations or by acknowledging that the "stages" she relies upon are also socially constructed, culturally specific stages rather than phases that are chronologically inevitable. I think her metaphor disallows a critically useful construction of change because it locates change within the familiar, predictable, sequential framework of "growing up." For example, her metaphor prevents her from recognizing that she is at work in her retrospective, seeing developments or noting significant moments while she is engaged in the very act of looking backward.

Damian's paper also accounts for change, but he uses a similarly limiting metaphor, that of swimming. Looking back on his work, Damian writes, "I see this [his early work] as being shallow, but I had to start somewhere. After all, when one goes swimming at the beach, one starts off in the shallow water. It is not possible to start in the middle of everything." Perhaps Damian's swimming metaphor is suggested by the adjective "shallow," which he uses initially in a figurative sense and then employs literally in his description of wading into the water. I had hoped Damian's paper would enact an awareness of this particular move he makes as a writer, that it would trouble this metaphor of education as wading into water. It would be interesting, for example, to see a revision of Damian's paper in which he replaces the more progressive action of wading into the ocean with a less sequential metaphor like getting thrown in the deep end, or diving into water. It might certainly be argued that students begin their work in my class *in medias res:* the first text we read is Adrienne Rich's essay, which is not shallow by any means. How, then, might Damian account for change within less sequential narratives? This is the kind of question he does not pose.

My reading of retrospective essays like Damian's, Felicia's, and Amy's led me to conclude that the work of recuperating the retrospective moment — making it more explicit — does not necessarily result in students' ability to construct powerful or critical accounts of change when they write. Strong student readers who learn to identify the kind of work undertaken by Rich and Jacobs do not automatically become more aware of the work they are performing when they write retrospectives themselves. I had hoped to see students move away from narratives of utopian closure or from unproblematic accounts of educational "progress" and change toward constructions of change as problematic, constructions that might allow them to think about their work of and their education in ways that are more critical, more self-aware.

In my second semester, I taught the same sequence of writing/reading assignments. This time I wanted to forestall utopian retrospectives by prompting my class to think about change and education from the beginning of the semester. My course description centered on a student's retrospective essay from the previous semester, which I asked the new students to read closely as a way of examining how a former student had accounted for my class and for the changes he and his work had undergone. I wanted them to see that change could be described in various ways, as something to be welcomed and also as something to be resisted.

At the end of that semester, I read the new set of retrospective essays with keen attention. All of them resisted utopian closure; all of them refused to engage in conversion narratives. Does this represent a success? I'm not sure if this change is because students now feel that they simply ought not to write such narratives, or because they are indeed able to see that such accounts do not allow for a complex assessment of what they've learned. Many of these papers still employ models of change as inevitable progress or growth. Laurie, for example, describes herself as "fifteen weeks old" at the end of a semester in my class. Her account echoes Felicia's paper; moreover, it assumes that a student entering my class is *tabula rasa,* or a newborn baby. I am troubled by this attitude, which strikes me as overly and uncritically forgetful.

As I come to the end of this my own retrospective paper, I feel perhaps the same as my students do: in need of utopian closure. How can I end with a story that might account for the ways in which my work works?

The most successful retrospective paper I received in the second semester was Steve's. What I admire most about his essay is that it troubles its own sense of accomplishment and questions the narrative of progress that it presents. It also problematizes and calls in question some of the pedagogical work I have described in this paper.

Steve begins his search for change in the following way: "I wondered how my writing might have improved . . . so a comparison between papers written before midterm and later essays seemed to be a good way to see if anything had changed. I wasn't sure what to look for." Using the midterm point as a marker, he constructs a careful discussion, which leads him to the conclusion that his earlier papers simply took for granted the kinds of implications that his words have. He explains: "In earlier essays I noticed I was using words . . . without any hint that they have many different contexts. I used them as easily as if I were talking to myself." He sees his later work as being more aware of the implications involved in using certain words. But then his retrospective takes an unusual turn, which I would like to quote at length:

So there it is . . . I can now write about "writing." I once was lost but now I'm found . . . Halleluia, I've seen the light. All is fine with the world, right? Well, I'm not sure I'd go that far. I could just savor the important things I learned about writing, but I find myself with a sense of uncertainty about what happens next.

I looked back at my writing, and as I said, my later essays said a lot more about the ways in which the texts were written. I felt my Wideman essays [the last in the sequence] were the best ones, but why then did I feel as I had once again missed something? Was I simply operating in the "General Writing frame of reference"?

I looked again at my [John Edgar] Wideman papers . . . the author's use of language, frame of reference, and other aspects that we discussed throughout the term are important for understanding him, but just how much consideration do they deserve in the scope of the overall work and its moral implications in the "real" world? I made statements like "in Wideman, we have no such simple judgment," and "we have to face disturbing questions." Earlier in the semester I would have made a judgment or dealt with those questions, not just pointed out that Wideman presents them to us with some technique. I guess that in the "General Writing frame" this is progress, but I'm not sure about the "responsibility frame." Maybe the earlier papers were the better ones. So, you see my dilemma? Here I am with a collection of texts [by Rich, Jacobs, Berger, Tompkins, and Wideman] about oppression, slavery, morality, and racial injustice, and I'm spending more time discussing the language of the author than I am the issues that he or she has made it a point to write about. An increasing amount of my time has been spent writing about "writing." I'm just not sure this is progress. I don't know what the proper balance between ethics and semantics should be. Maybe that's what I missed.

In Steve's account, a definition of "progress" is itself context-bound, not to be taken for granted. He locates his definition first in the "General Writing frame" and then in what he calls the "responsibility frame." For him, the former represents a gain, and the latter involves a very troubling loss — troubling because it questions the "proper balance between ethics and semantics." I find this formulation of change provocative and insightful, and its attendant critique of the educational process in my class presents an important challenge to much of what I have argued in this paper. Perhaps the course, in insisting on its own frame (what Steve calls "writing about writing" rather than writing about the "real" world), ends up "talking to itself"? I'm not sure. I know that I could respond to Steve's paper by asking him to challenge his division between "ethics and semantics" by examining, for example, how these two categories are intertwined. This might also produce a different reading of his distinction between the "General Writing frame" and the "responsibility frame." After all, knowing how words are put together — how they mean — is precisely what enables us to make the kind of moral judgment that Steve wishes to make.

Because retrospectives like Steve's are produced at the end of term, at that "difficult time" in which students are asked to reconstruct the fifteen-week time period of the course, they have a tendency to escape the kind of thoughtful revision that is so central to my reading/writing class. When I began my second year of teaching at Pitt, facing a new set of students, Steve, Amy, and the others were not there to respond to my comments and questions about their papers. We were unable to "go back" and rework what had been done. I think students know this, and I think their knowing it reinforces their desire to write "end of history" essays. My concern is to seek and imagine ways of turning this desire into a self-reflexive and critical account of history that brings a retrospective understanding back into the work of the course — making it present rather than invisible.

When I present my syllabus to the next reading/writing class I teach, I hope to direct the new group back to the "very telling" retrospectives of my former students. I would like these narratives to help situate our work on a continuum of constant and repeated retrospection, to build an awareness of a course history that is already well under way. What might begin to emerge is a more self-conscious understanding of the ways in which we (students and teachers) work within and against very powerful notions of what it means to make educational progress.

I may well use Steve's piece in my next course description. In this way, his project will continue, not as the utopian end of history or the fullness of time, but as an involvement in ongoing critical, educational work. As in the story of Walter Benjamin's "angel of history," there is no utopian space that is exempt from criticism and change, or from the often thwarted desire not only to look backward, but also to use retrospection in order to think critically about how "progress" gets made.

> "The angel would like to stay, awaken the dead, and make whole what has been smashed. But a storm is blowing from Paradise. . . . This storm irresistibly propels him into the future to which his back is turned, while the pile of debris before him grows skyward. This storm is what we call progress."

WORKS CITED

Bartholomae, David, and Anthony Petrosky. *Ways of Reading,* 4th ed. Boston: Bedford/St. Martin's, 1996.

Benjamin, Walter. "Theses on the Philosophy of History, IX" in *Illuminations.* Ed. Hannah Arendt. Trans. Harry Zohn. New York: Schocken Books, 1969: 257–58.

Bloom, Damian. Retrospective Essay. Unpublished, University of Pittsburgh: 1990.

Carr, Jean Ferguson. Memo on Final Retrospective Assignment 11/23/1990, University of Pittsburgh.

Gray, Felicia. "Stages." Unpublished, University of Pittsburgh: 1990.

Nicotra, Amy. "Confessions." Unpublished, University of Pittsburgh: 1990.

Plato. *Republic.* Trans. G. M. A. Grube. Indianapolis: Hackett, 1974.

Rich, Adrienne. "When We Dead Awaken: Writing as Re-Vision" in *Ways of Reading*, 549–62.

Sheaffer, Steven. "Looking Backward, Seeing Ahead." Unpublished, University of Pittsburgh: 1991.

All student papers are used with permission of their authors, to whom I am grateful.

I would like to thank Jean Ferguson Carr and Barbara McCarthy, who provided the retrospective assignment that I have cited in this essay.

I am also grateful to Phil Smith, Joe Harris, Paul Kameen, Mariolina Salvatori, and Dave Bartholomae, who gave me valuable suggestions as I worked on this paper.

o–o–o–o–o–o–o–o–o–o–o–o–o–o–o–o–o–o

OPENING A CONVERSATION WITH THE TEXT, OR "WHAT PART OF THE ASSIGNMENT SHOULD I WRITE ABOUT?"

by Kathleen A. Welsch

The question in my title was posed by one of my students after we had spent a class period closely reading and discussing one of the writing assignments in *Ways of Reading*. Although this student had been quite attentive and had dutifully taken notes during class, her frustration and exasperation at not having been told precisely what or how to write was reflected in her face and in the way she slammed her notebook closed at the end of class. She had come to class looking for answers and what she got instead was a discussion about rereading and working with the text in preparation for writing. This didn't correspond to her previous writing experiences. For her, reading and writing were two distinctly separate activities. She'd read the text already; she knew the story; the reading was done. What she wanted now was a precise definition of what she should write about: What were the important points in the text? What did I (the teacher) see as its value for students? What kind of essay did I expect her to produce? As students filed out of the classroom, she approached me in a final effort to ask, "What part of the assignment should I write about?" Because she had come to class expecting to hear an answer, she had neither seen how class work related to what she might do on her own nor heard that what she might write depended on how *she* read, what *she* noticed, why *she* was interested in this passage or image and not that one. Her final question asked for a connection to the ways of knowing and doing papers that she had come to rely on and that had worked for her in the past. In this case, however, these old ways blocked her from understanding class work and discussions, making use of the information she'd taken down in her notebook, and, ultimately, from engaging in the challenge of the assignment at hand.

This student's question, though simply stated, reveals a set of assumptions about reading and writing that many students and teachers bring to assignments like those in *Ways of Reading*. To begin with, my student wanted a clearly stated topic to *write* about, for that's what she had come to expect of a writing assignment. How reading fit into that she couldn't imagine. Her question asked me to clear a path through all the reading and to identify the topic so that she could get to work on writing her essay. Prior experience had led her to assume that an assignment defined her choices as a writer, that it possessed an authority to which she had to submit rather than being the starting point for her own work. Her readiness to tell back what an assignment asked for clashed with this new assignment that challenged her to write about her reading of a text. She didn't grasp how she could use the assignment for her own purposes: to return to the text, to open it, question it, respond to it, and then write about *that* interaction. It didn't occur to her that writing about her reading might entail looking at what she'd noticed and why, what she'd skimmed over because it seemed difficult, and what she had found outright confusing or intriguing. It didn't occur to her, because she assumed that this was the work of the assignment, not the writer. The assumptions about the roles of teachers, students, assignments, and texts embedded in her question worked to undermine her authority as a reader/writer. First, she imagined that the text presented a specific knowledge she needed to find; second, she expected the assignment to tell her what was important to find and write about; third, she assumed that I knew what it was she should focus on rather than her establishing that for herself. This last assumption frequently took the shape of the question, "What do you want?" as if I could tell a student what she would notice, connect with, find confusing, or feel compelled to write about.

Assignments in *Ways of Reading* imagine that writing is more than reporting what the text says, and that reading is more than finding a main point or getting the story. Students are challenged to write about their own acts of attention and making of meaning. This is no easy task, when one considers the level of complexity in each of the essays, or the possibility that one might notice something new or have a deeper understanding with each rereading. The complexity of the essays is reflected in the complexity of the assignments in this book, and attempting to simplify either assumes that an essay's complexities can be reduced to a single most important point or lesson — something to be "gotten" quickly. Students and teachers who assume assignments should provide a path to a pre-established meaning (or who have grown comfortable with such an arrangement) may be confused by the nature of assignments in this book. For this reason, learning to read the assignments (making meaning of them as one would make meaning of an essay) is just as important as reading the essays before one can write a response. As I've talked with students and teachers about the essays and assignments in this book, I've encouraged them to recognize and question their assumptions about what it means to read or write an essay, and to imagine alternatives to these old ways of knowing. My plan for the rest of this essay is to discuss some alternatives in relation to three assignments that challenge both students and teachers to imagine possibilities in essays rather than the right answer; to open a subject to the range of directions it might take rather than close it down with conclusions, the main point, or the lesson; to notice not only the complexity of each project but how one might read, write, and make meaning in one project in a way that leads to rereading, rewriting, and rethinking meaning in relation to another project. The assignments I've selected address the work of Harriet Jacobs and Alice Walker. They are based on Assignments for Writing and Making Connections in the book, but I have revised several questions for my course.

Assignments like the first Jacobs assignment for writing are particularly perplexing because they seem to say a lot about Jacobs's narrative and much less about what one should write. This particular Jacobs assignment opens with quotes by Jean Fagin Yellin, Susan Willis,[1] and Houston Baker, is followed by a statement about "gendered subjects" and a brief discussion of the public discourse of slavery, moves on to distinguishing between a life and a narrative, and shifts to observing how Jacobs's text reflects the circumstances of her life. All this before any writing objective is suggested, and this, too, is complicated by parenthetical remarks. In response to this mass of information, inexperienced students (and teachers) tend to grasp the one part of the assignment they understand best as their focus and generally disregard the rest. This isn't surprising, since most students have plenty of experience establishing a clearly stated topic and presenting an organized explanation of it. What they have less experience in is pursuing the numerous possibilities a text might offer. They tend to note what they understand, organize it, and keep it under control rather than consider how the one part of the assignment they *do* understand relates to the parts they don't seem to have a handle on. They are less practiced in the art of questioning what confuses them in order to make meaning; more commonly, students assume they didn't read thoroughly enough or that the material is simply beyond their comprehension.

My students and I have addressed this particular Jacobs assignment by beginning at the end — identifying the type of rereading the writing project suggests — and then turning to the rest of the assignment as a way to address that rereading. The final paragraph in the assignment states:

---

[1]Willis's essay "Work(ing) Out" appeared in the third edition of *Ways of Reading*.

Write an essay in which you examine Jacobs's work as a writer. Consider the ways she works on her reader (a figure she both imagines and constructs) and also the ways she works on her material (a set of experiences, a language, and the conventional ways of telling the story of one's life). Where is Jacobs in this text? What is her work? How do you know when you've found her? When you find her, have you found an "authentic voice"? A "gendered subject"?

In this assignment students are invited to write an essay in which they "examine Jacobs's work as a writer" by investigating how her text (chapters from *Incidents in the Life of a Slave Girl*) can be read "as something constructed." Since students have read Jacobs's text, they generally assume they know the material (the details of her narrative), and they generally assume that the narrative represents the "truth"; that is, that Jacobs doesn't deviate from or alter her experience as she writes it. To consider Jacobs's text as constructed, however, requires a different kind of reading, one in which the truth of a life is read through the truths of nineteenth-century social and literary conditions. An understanding of Jacobs's text and audience as constructed is crucial for a reader/writer who plans to reread Jacobs's narrative for the work she does as a writer. The reader needs to attend to *how* the story is told/constructed rather than being caught up in and carried along by the emotion and details Jacobs provides. The reader needs to ask: What does her text reveal about the decisions she makes as a writer with a purpose?

One way that my students and I begin talking about the kind of work one would have to do to reconsider Jacobs's story as something "constructed" is by reexamining the Houston Baker quote at the beginning of the reading from a variety of angles, since it provides a key to understanding Jacobs's text as something constructed. Baker writes:

> The voice of the unwritten self, once it is subjected to the linguistic codes, literary conventions, and audience expectations of a literate population, is perhaps never again the authentic voice of black American slavery. It is, rather, the voice of a self transformed by an autobiographical act into a sharer in the general public discourse about slavery.

The problem for many students lies in the fact that although they've read this quote, it remains an abstraction because they can't imagine how it might connect to Jacobs. So we discuss phrases that appear mystifying — "linguistic codes, literary conventions, and audience," "general public discourse" — and define them in terms of their own experience and understanding. We explore the meaning of the "unwritten self" by replacing the phrase with Harriet Jacobs's name and considering the differences between the unwritten and written Harriet Jacobs. When students have difficulty making this distinction, we shift to more personal terms by replacing the "unwritten self" with the word "student" so that they can consider what it means to them to be a written or unwritten self. For example, what linguistic codes, literary conventions, and audience expectations do they find themselves subjected to or restricted by when they go to write? We can take this question a step further by replacing the words "linguistic" and "literary" with academic codes and conventions and "audience" with teacher expectations. Such a discussion positions students to be more thoughtful about what it means to construct a text or about how what they write might be called a construction rather than a truth. We use the second paragraph following the opening quotes to establish an understanding of a "general public discourse" by exploring students' storehouses of general public discourse. The assignment explains that in Baker's formulation:

> [Jacobs's] voice shares in the general public discourse about slavery and also in the general public discourse representing family, growing up, love, marriage, childbirth, the discourse representing "normal" life — that is, life outside of slavery. For a slave the self and its relations to others has a different public construction.

Students begin to investigate what it means to participate in a public discourse by considering how they, too, are sharers in it. What do they know about slavery, life outside slavery, literary expectations for a writer like Jacobs who wants to be published? If necessary, we shift to the more personal again as students consider the public discourse that describes the life of students in the university and the academic expectations they must meet to be successful. A discussion such as this allows them to see and understand their own participation in public discourses. It also allows them to begin imagining how Harriet Jacobs participated in the general public discourses of the nineteenth century as a writer, while at the same time being positioned outside those discourses for the person she was — an African American, a slave, and a woman. We pursue this "inside but outside" conflict in Jacobs's narrative by mapping out on the blackboard the dichotomies identified in the third paragraph of the assignment.

> The passages from Baker, Willis, and Yellin allow us to highlight the gap between a life and a narrative, between a person (Harriet Jacobs) and a person rendered on the page (Linda Brent), between the experience of slavery and the conventional ways of telling the story of a life, between experience and the ways experience is shaped by a writer, readers, and a culture.

As a group students compose four parallel lists on the board that identify the differences they see between a life and a narrative, Harriet Jacobs and Linda Brent, the experience of slavery and how one is expected to tell one's life story, a lived experience and the ways in which experience becomes shaped by forces outside one's life. By the time students have completed this work, they have created a context that they can complicate and explore further by considering how the Willis and Yellin quotes relate to what Baker writes.

Students have accomplished a great deal of work by this point, but that work has not yet included writing the assignment essay. Instead, they have focused on using the assignment to work closely with Jacobs's text, rereading and rethinking it from a number of critical perspectives. Students begin to see that her text is no longer only the story of a life; it is also the story of a writer's work. For readers to arrive at this distinction, they need to be willing to see the text as something constructed rather than only the flow of the writer's memory. And that requires working with Jacobs's text more than once. When I describe the variety of ways my students and I discuss a text like Jacobs's (as I did in the previous paragraphs), I want to make clear that we aren't just talking off the top of our heads from what we remember. Our books are open; we search the text for specific passages; we go home and read it again and come back to class the next day to continue our discussion by turning to what we notice today that we didn't notice yesterday. It is only after we have worked with the text in this way that we go back to the final paragraph of the assignment where the writing project is outlined. At this point I ask students to notice the verbs in the assignment; we talk about ways they have already begun to "examine," "consider," and "reread" Jacobs's text and her notion of audience as something constructed and how they might continue this work on their own. As students construct readings of Jacobs during class discussion, they model the type of work they'll need to do to construct individual readings as they write their essays. Through class work they also identify an array of possibilities for reading the text; this task, in turn, gives them the writer's responsibility of focusing, selecting, and developing what interests them most about Jacobs's work as a writer.

Reading Harriet Jacobs's work as a writer — exploring what it means for a writer to "construct" a text — positions students to move on to investigating the work of other writers who not only have different projects but who write in different contexts. Students are thus challenged to reconsider and complicate their understanding of a text as something constructed from still other critical directions. A sequence in which students move from Jacobs to Alice Walker invites a revision and complication of how they understand the choices a writer makes as she constructs a text. In the first writing assignment following Walker's essay "In Search of Our Mothers' Gardens," students are invited to write an essay in which they "discuss Walker's project as a creative endeavor, one in which she reconceives, or rewrites, texts from the past." Unlike the Jacobs assignment, there are even fewer directions here about what students should write in their essays. The question posed to them is simply: "What would you say . . . that Walker creates as she writes her essay?" Writing an essay that answers such a broad question entails some very specific reading; the second paragraph of the assignment offers a number of questions to begin investigating her project:

> How would you say that Walker puts that term, "contrary instincts," to use within her project? What does Walker's use of that term allow her to understand about the creative spirit of African American women, including Phillis Wheatley and her own mother? And if you consider Walker's position as an African American artist of today, what would you say the process of looking back at ancestral artists helped her to understand about herself?

Where students frequently encounter difficulties with such broadly stated assignments is when they focus on what to write rather than on constructing a reading through writing. Instead of using assignment questions to open a conversation with the text, some students shut down possibilities by writing essays that read like a checklist of the assignment's questions; that is, they devote one paragraph to answering each of the questions about Walker's project. Answering the questions, however, doesn't address the larger issue of what it is that Walker creates as she writes. Before students write about Walker's project, they first need to read her text closely (as they did with Jacobs) for what the project is, what influenced its construction, and how it works.

When we talk about Walker in class, we begin by examining her revision of Virginia Woolf's passage in which she defines her key phrase, "contrary instincts." We use a strategy from our work with Jacobs as we draw up parallel lists on the board to illustrate the dichotomy between these two constructions of contrary instincts and to highlight how it is that Walker is revising a text from the past. Students test their understanding of Walker's revision by drawing up another list (in class or for homework) of all the women Walker names in her essay in order to identify each woman's creative gift and how it was or might have been subjected to contrary instincts. These discussions do not move students through the set of questions in the assignment; they do, however, provide students with ways to begin formulating answers and discovering how the questions lead to an understanding of the project. And by examining the array of women that Walker brings together and how each contributes to her revision of contrary instincts, students begin to see a process of creation. As they construct their understanding of this process through their own close reading, students don't need to rely on the assignment's questions to structure their essays. Instead, they can turn to their own authority as readers as they write about how they understand Walker's creation of a project.

Both the Jacobs and the Walker assignments challenge students to develop as strong readers — readers who notice what they pay attention to as they read — who respond to and interact with a text rather than repeating it. As they read and reread these texts, students develop a method of analysis and a set of key terms for looking at and talking about a writer's project — whether it's the work of Jacobs, Walker, or the student herself. Another type of writing assignment in *Ways of Reading* invites students to participate in a writer's project by extending it, either by connecting it to personal experience or by rereading one text through the frame of another. The first "Making Connections" assignment after the Jacobs piece calls for students to reread Jacobs through Walker's frame of contrary instincts and the creative spirit of African American women. To do this work, students need to extend what they already understand about these two texts. Instead of seeing them as separate projects, students need to reimagine each of them as contributing to a larger project: in general, how writers construct a text and, more specifically, how these two African American women construct texts within and against established discourses and traditions.

This assignment suggests that students "extend Walker's project by considering where and how Jacobs's work as a writer and artist would complement Walker's argument for the 'creative spirit' of African American women in the face of oppressive conditions." To do this, students will need to return to Jacobs's text for another rereading, this time in light of Walker's frame. And likewise, they'll need to return to Walker's text, rereading for places where Jacobs's work as a writer and artist would complement Walker's argument. The work students have done with these two pieces in prior assignments provides them with a level of familiarity with content; it can also be used as a starting point for reentering the texts, for beginning a new conversation with them.

This last point is important. It would be very easy to reenter the texts and repeat what one has already seen and said about them before. For example, the second paragraph of the assignment suggests that students note the choices Jacobs makes as a writer. They are to attend to

> her use of language, her selection of incidents and details, her method of addressing an audience, the ways in which she negotiates a white literary tradition. Where for instance do you see her writing purposely negotiating a literary tradition that isn't hers? Who does she imagine as her audience? How does she use language differently for different purposes? Why?

Students have answered questions similar to these in their first essay on Jacobs. This set of questions, however, does not serve to reacquaint students with Jacobs's work but proposes that similar questions can be answered differently in relation to Walker's argument. In their first essay on Jacobs, students focused on her work on her terms; they read her text for how she constructs herself and her story in relation to traditions and public discourses that excluded her. The third paragraph in this new assignment asks them to extend this original reading by considering a new set of questions that incorporate Walker's terms:

> How would you say that the writerly choices Jacobs makes and enacts allow her to express a creativity that otherwise would have been stifled? What type of legacy does she create in her narrative to pass on to her descendants? And, as Walker writes in honor of her mother and Wheatley, what might Walker or you write in honor of Jacobs?

Answering these questions entails still more reading. This time, however, students reread Jacobs with an eye toward noticing what makes a particular writerly choice creative and how that creativity creates a legacy that Jacobs passes on to future generations. As they reread Walker, they need to attend to those places where her argument about creativity in the face of oppressive conditions relates to Jacobs's experience as a writer. The challenge of this assignment, then, lies in reseeing and rethinking both Jacobs's and Walker's work from new perspectives and in writing an essay that presents this revision.

One way that my students and I address this challenge is by identifying what we understand as the key terms or phrases in Walker's argument, for example, "contrary instincts," "creative spirit," "artist," "legacy," and "notion of song." We talk about why we chose them and how they help us understand Walker's project. We also use these terms to reread the quotes included in the first paragraph of the assignment.

> Of her mother, Walker writes: "Her face, as she prepares the Art that is her gift, is a legacy of respect she leaves to me, for all that illuminates and cherishes life. She has handed down respect for the possibilities — and the will to grasp them." And to the poet Phillis Wheatley she writes: "It is not so much what you sang, as that you kept alive, in so many of our ancestors, the *notion of song.*"

Students consider how they understand the legacies created by Wheatley and Walker's mother — two women separated by time, living conditions, and legal status. From here students are prepared to shift to a discussion of how Jacobs, too, shares in and helps create this legacy out of a context and experience quite different from that of Wheatley and Walker's mother. It is when students have looked at all three of those women as possessing "creative spirits" and "contrary instincts," and as artists who have kept alive the "notion of song" and created a "legacy" that I invite students to consider what type of statement they would write in honor of Jacobs, as Walker has written in honor of Wheatley and her mother.

I want students to try on Walker's way of thinking and working, to test her language in relation to Jacobs's creativity, to know where it works (or doesn't) and why, to consider how they would revise her project and why. In the end, I want my students to be responsible for constructing a reading in the essays they write rather than reporting what an author says.

My students and I devote a good deal of time to developing reading strategies for writing essays that present their understanding of a text. We read assignments closely for ways to enter the texts from different directions, work through confusions, understand complicated ideas, discover what they know, and make personal connections. One can't expect to just *do* these assignments — to go off and write a paper. It's important for both students and teachers to realize that one first needs to learn to read the assignments; they provide a guide or model of how one might go about rereading, interacting with, and responding to the essays in this book. They offer keys to opening conversations with texts, and it is these conversations that the reader writes about in response to the assignments.

Part V

o–o–o–o–o–o–o–o–o–o–o–o–o–o–o–o–o–o–o

Entering the Archive:
An Interview with Jean Ferguson Carr
on Students' Library Projects

This is an interview with Jean Ferguson Carr about the freshman composition course that was taught at the University of Pittsburgh in 1993–94. Jean was part of a team directing multiple, graduate student-taught sections of freshman composition using the History and Ethnography sequence in *Ways of Reading*. Two of the assignments in the sequence have research options: Assignment 2, History; and Assignment 5, Reading Others. In the interview, Jean talks about the logistics of preparing both freshmen and local librarians for the archival projects these assignments suggest.

DAVID BARTHOLOMAE: Jean, you and the people you work with made a decision to do the History and Ethnography sequence in Ways of Reading. Can you talk to us a little bit about why you chose that sequence and what sorts of changes you made?

JEAN FERGUSON CARR: We wanted to have students doing some kind of work that took them outside the classroom, gathering materials and attempting to represent other lives, places, or times. So we were drawn to the double set of assignments in the sequence on history and ethnography. Students are in one case sent to the library to do archival work; in the other they gather materials from family, friends, or "contemporary documents from the print that is around" them. We liked the idea of doing two versions of this kind of project, one in connection with reading the essay by Limerick and one in connection with reading Pratt. For the first assignment, we specified that students work with historical materials; for the second assignment, we gave them the choice of library work or community work, of materials from the past or from the contemporary scene. In both projects, we wanted students to have a stake in what they gathered and to see that forming their topic and constructing the material that would make the topic possible was part of the work of writing the paper.

That seemed imperative in this project, because they couldn't write the paper without having done some kind of gathering. It was very difficult for them to make up material, or to write without any preparation or reading.

Indeed, the students who were irritated by these assignments were ones who habitually delayed, who therefore hadn't worked at gathering materials, and then found they couldn't write the paper.

DB: Right. And as students were making a choice about where they would go to gather information for the material that they would work on, were there patterns? That is, were there obvious places that students went?

JFC: Many of them wanted to write about what they saw as their ethnic or regional history. They wanted to write about various immigrant groups, for example, or about their town or school. They would go into the archives assuming that their town would be represented under a listing that said "my town." They were taken aback by finding themselves at a distance from what they saw as the "local," i.e., in a larger urban setting where perhaps they couldn't find their hometown newspaper or family records. Many of them did find ways to research something that had been important to their family. In some cases, that meant getting materials from home. One student, for example, wrote about a set of letters that his grandfather had written to his grandmother when he was off in World War II. Another student began with a picture of the Johnstown flood that had hung on her wall at home. Another worked from a family journal that described her grandparents' muck farm.

But they also came with a strong — in some cases, disabling — notion of what counted as "history." For many of them it had to mean a fairly big event — the Holocaust, race relations, wars, assassination attempts, the Depression. They had difficulties imagining one could write about ordinary people, and looked for documents about groups that seemed clearly marked as important historically — slaves, soldiers, politicians. Yet it was an interesting feature of doing this project in Western Pennsylvania that many of them assumed the importance of striking factory workers and of immigrants. Their sense of history was also shaped by their reading of Limerick, and so they followed her cue of representing undervalued histories of different kinds of people. One of the nice things about this assignment was that it provoked topics we would not have predicted for students. It showed interests and attitudes outside of widely shared claims about "today's student." Our sense of who the students were and what they found interesting was greatly expanded, and in many cases challenged, by this assignment.

When the students returned to archival work near the end of the course, in the context of the essay by Pratt and after reading Wideman's account of growing up in Homewood, many of them had a changed sense of what was appropriate to write about as "history." Their sense of being able to write about more ordinary people developed, which had something to do, I suspect, with moving away from Limerick (and naming their work as "history") and toward using Pratt's category of materials from "the contact zone" (and so naming their work as "culture").

DD: So the first assignment was the Limerick assignment and the second was the Pratt assignment? Isn't there a point where they are asked to think back to Limerick as a historian? Did they? or did they in useful ways? You talked about the students having a sense of history — of what it was, where you found it, and how you wrote it. Did Limerick play into that evolving sense of what they were doing?

JFC: It's hard to pinpoint how the students understood to use Limerick in their own work. Many of them referred back to Pratt's work with the letter of Guaman Poma (we had read Pratt at the beginning of the course, to introduce issues of representation and the politics of idealizing the past and others vs. acknowledging the "arts of the contact zone"). Limerick seemed to challenge, in fairly serious ways, their prior sense of what a historian was and did. You can see this in the one-page memos students wrote at the end of their Limerick assignments, memos in which they were to tell Limerick something about the "experience of a novice historian that she might find useful or interesting." These memos were both wonderful and distressing in what they revealed about how the students understood the work of history. They were, however, always a fascinating text to read. Some students took the directive of offering Limerick something "useful," and wrote to inform her what she needed to learn to write history. One student, writing to "Patricia," encouraged Limerick to "keep up the good work as a professional historian!" Another explained politely about "some of the tactics . . . that you may find helpful." This student recognized the problem of writing as a novice to a professional, writing: "If you are trying to achieve what I have just state [sic], then please disregard it as a helpful suggestion and take it as a mere observation."

The assignment was forcing them to experience the difficulty of making absolute narratives, of negotiating different perspectives; you can see this in comments in the memos about specific problems they encountered. One mentioned the difficulty of retelling "what has already been said." Another wrote that "it's hard to write a history when you have so many different opinions and secondhand views." One student discovered that "you can't just write History you have to read into it first," or, as another student wrote, "it is excessively important to try to become a part of what you are researching." Their experience with the construction of history stayed in conflict with their previous sense of what it meant to be called a historian. Several students used the memo as an occasion to challenge the construction of history Limerick represented to them, a construction they were in many cases trying out themselves in their papers. One student wrote, "I failed to understand your work as a history. Maybe it is because I have a set definition of 'history' and do not believe your work was one." As this student suggested, Limerick upset their notion of what history entails. In class discussion, they attributed this to her willingness to reflect on her own authority, to resist the notion that a single history will suffice. Limerick's efforts to see historical narratives as always problematic, as always contested, made her somehow not a real historian, and so they offered her advice about how to do better at this thing they called history.

Despite this conflict, many of them were intrigued by isolated moments in Limerick where they could see her doing historical work. If they didn't initially engage with Limerick as someone who *owns* history, they did take from her a sense of concern about how to work with quotations or with objects left behind. Many of them, for example, mentioned the illustration of cans left behind by the miners as something needing to be noticed. They started to take on ways of imitating moments in the history, while at the same time remaining fairly troubled by the argument Limerick is making about history as constructed, as contested.

DB: **Can you give an example?**

JFC: The epigraph for the assignment on Limerick asks students to imagine "it is as if one were a lawyer at a trial designed on the principle of the Mad Hatter's tea party." The students honed in on the first part of this — the lawyer at the trial — and therefore saw their job as one of arguing a case, presenting the facts, representing pro and con positions. They were then adamant that there had to be two opposing points of view. This assumption became a major barrier in their search for appropriate documents. They would dismiss perfectly interesting documents because they weren't explicitly opposite or antagonistic, but simply represented slightly different positions or articulations of an event.

DB: **Right, because they weren't pro and con.**

JFC: They were unsettled by the second part of the epigraph, which refers to a trial "on the principle of the Mad Hatter's tea party." They didn't like the idea that things might change depending upon where you sat. They were looking for authoritative history. This became a problem in how they could talk with the librarians and of how they could recognize when they had found a useful document. For many of them it remained a problem through the whole assignment — they couldn't find their material because nothing looked like what they expected to find, what they assumed they were being instructed to find.

Let me give you a specific example. This assignment was exceedingly frustrating to a student who had decided he wanted to write on the assassination attempt on the industrialist, Henry Clay Frick. As he wrote in his memo, he expected to find "personal diaries or any material of personal significance (not meant to be read by others by publishing or other means) toward the subject." When he couldn't find precisely these materials, he was surprised because, as he knew, "the Homestead strike was a controversial event." He looked for "autobiographies on Henry Clay Frick . . . so that I could get his story," and was disappointed when he "had to rely on a biography and some newspaper stories." He also used the accused assassin's prison autobiography, which he found "remarkable" in that it "leaves out a lot of information on the assassination attempt compared to other sources." This student expected to find a "private" (and never-before-published or used) account of an assassination, but expected the accused assassin to record a full version of the event, with as much information as he could read in professional histories. He couldn't negotiate the problem of writing before the fact or retrospectively, nor the various constraints (legal, journalistic) under which people wrote. He imagined his only option was to tell the true story of what happened, rather than to derive an argument about attitudes or issues that could be said to lead to such an event. If he couldn't find the documents he expected, he felt he had nothing. This student never could complete the assignment. He hovered at the entry to the archive, with his preconceptions preventing him from looking at what he could have found (indeed, in many cases, what he did find but rejected as "wrong"). He ended up using an authoritative history of the attempt, citing its quotations as his "document."

Students had difficulty negotiating the difference between their expectations — of an already constructed narrative clearly delineating pro and con positions — and what they found. They were unnerved at having to write a history from a document that didn't already have a clear narration organizing its details.

DB: **What kind of documents did students end up using?**

JFC: Students used books of interviews and letters, published memoirs, and diaries. They worked from documents in the university archives, with newspaper accounts, family letters and journals, and, in one case, from architectural plans. Two students wrote on the Depression, using books of memoirs people had written looking back to the old days.

DB: **You mean interviews by Studs Terkel? That sort of oral history?**

JFC: In one case, clearly oral history interviews. Another student used a book of letters workers wrote during the Depression about their jobs, letters that were clearly instigated by journalists or social workers to "document" problems. They were working from relatively short accounts, mostly retrospective or written under specific prompts at the time. The gap in time became a central issue in our class discussion and to both of these students; one of them actually went back to look for more materials written from the time. Both students were concerned about writing from such limited sources. They felt responsible for a general, and authoritative, history of the Depression. When we discussed these two papers, the class was agitated about the students' "presumption" to write from small evidence and without knowing "what really happened." The student writers and their colleagues shared the notion that "what really happened" exists somewhere out there in textual form. These particular writers, I think, both turned this assignment around to see that they had a responsibility to account for even the few documents they had, and that this was a complicated job in itself. One had documents from two different people and saw that they remembered comparable events differently, to make different "stories." The other student used materials written at different moments (and out of different circumstances) in the Depression, and saw that such circumstantial differences altered what the writer saw as "his story." These were among the most successful archival projects. Neither of these students was a particularly expert writer, but both worked very hard, returning to reread these materials over and over, rewriting, and reorganizing. They both produced long, elaborate, and careful revisions of this assignment, which they — and their classmates — liked and cited in their final papers.

DB: **I want to go back for just a second to the assignment. In the process that you are describing, students learned (at least for the occasion of this course) that working as a historian means learning how to work on some materials they have gathered. Then that's unsettling because they think that history is a body of knowledge about a point in time, from which they would make an argument. That is, they would know what they need to know about the Depression, and from that they would argue to some material that was in front of them, rather than working from some material that was in front of them to some sense of what it would mean to speak for "The Great Depression."**

JFC: I think they are imagining the historian's work to be to find a fairly streamlined, relatively neutral narrative that manages to incorporate everyone's experience. Two comments kept coming up that show this conception: one was the notion of wanting to know "what really happened" and the other was of wanting to know "what happened in a nutshell." Both of these concerns show an anxiety about dealing with unruly detail, with multiple strands of an event or with multiple perspectives. Both propose, implicitly, a method of cutting away what is read as unimportant, distracting, off the target. In both cases, students push toward whittling out what they see as biased or individual perspectives to find what "really" happened — which somehow exists without agents, outside time or place. These represent strongly held beliefs about fact, objectivity, truth, beliefs that the Limerick assignment pressured tremendously. By suggesting that students might locate oppositional documents, which might, in turn, produce divergent accounts, the assignment challenged this need to "discover" what has already been authorized as the event.

DB: **That's right.**

JFC: These students had clearly learned a procedure for dealing with different opinions or accounts, but difference had to be clearly presented as pro and con. They were most comfortable when a situation had a very clear villain and victim, or a clear set of preconstituted oppositions: black/white, male/female, German/Jew. They were less comfortable when they were dealing with figures who seemed somewhat aligned, but yet reported events differently. Such situations forced them not to pare the accounts down to the "nutshell," to a consensus or neutral event, but to work closely with specific versions, trying to see how different interests or conditions might influence the construction of "the event."

DB: **If you were going to do this sequence once again, or if you were going to give us some advice for the book, would you set it up differently? Would you set it up the same way?**

JFC: Some of these difficulties are what you have to work through. It is important to recognize that you have to work through students' strong and pressured sense of what it means to write as a historian. That is simply part of what this assignment demands. This sense about writing history is connected with students' strong investment in issues of objectivity and fact, in concern about bias, prejudice, subjective perspectives. I would say, however, that the assignment's hint about opposing views as a trial is misleading, since students tend to disregard Limerick's qualifications about this as a peculiar — "mad hatter" — trial. You want to suggest multiplicity without necessarily suggesting the model of the trial.

DB: **Exactly.**

JFC: Once they had settled on the model of a trial, they didn't pay attention to the rest of the assignment (references to "problems of myth, point of view, fixed ideas," for example). The trial was a solution for many of them, and they grabbed on to it desperately. I would say the other problem is the degree to which they don't know what to do with the document. They imagine that they should summarize it, or that it is self-evident. They imagine they should boil it down to a simple position. The assignment asks them to treat a document as full of details, as potentially complex, as something you don't simply retell but study, question, wonder about. This is, of course, the problem posed in all the assignments in *Ways of Reading*. This assignment brings to the surface the problem of representing another's words or account in a particularly visible and pressing way — which is useful.

We tried to deal with this textual problem by having students bring in the documents they had found before they wrote their papers. We had them work in class from these documents, treating them as "texts" for study. I think it is probably useful in this kind of assignment to break it into parts or stages. Students have a lot of trouble finding something, and so that activity probably needs to be done as a separate part, where they discuss their ideas for a project, and their strategies for finding material, then discuss the documents they have found, and then work on how to use these documents to write "a history."

I asked students to bring in their materials, with a preliminary account in which they described their document, discussed briefly the detail they found most intriguing, and indicated what they thought would need to be annotated to use this for "history." This accomplished a couple of things. It pressured them to find a document, and it also allowed them to share their work with their peers while they still had time to work on their materials. The brief written assignment helped them see that there were levels of description, that there was a difference, for example, between describing the document itself (e.g., what kind of document, how long, written by whom to whom, of what level of literacy or sophistication, etc.) and skipping over the document to describe "the event." The suggestion that they attend to specific details — and that details could be important because they provoked questions or were difficult to understand — usefully encouraged them to work within their documents, not to reduce them to a generic outline. And the request to begin imagining the document as needing annotation allowed us to discuss the problems of information, knowledge, and accessibility. Students began to negotiate the differences between what they didn't know because of the remove in time or situation and what most readers wouldn't know because of its private or local nature. This encouraged students to take some responsibility for the "larger" history available to them through reference guides and secondary histories without simply renouncing their own roles as readers of the past.

I copied out for class discussion many of these preliminary reports. In these preliminary discussions, it was wonderful to watch students teaching each other about their newly found expertise in library research. One of the nicest moments in my class was when a student explained to the rest of the class how to use the library's online catalog. He had not found what he wanted in the rare book collection, and so had taught himself how to use a "keyword" search to find a volume of Civil War letters. The other students were delighted at the idea of finding materials they could take home with them, and most seemed stunned at the idea that one could access the library's materials through such mechanisms. Similarly, students were greatly impressed at one writer's lengthy quotation from his document. Many had not located a full primary document but were instead working with dispersed quotations from a history or biography. The descriptions of documents helped such students considerably. The terms "document" and "first-person account" don't mean much to most students.

One of the major difficulties of this assignment is how their concept of the project limits their process of searching for documents. Students generally had difficulty knowing what to ask librarians, knowing how to describe what they needed or wanted, and knowing how to describe their idea for the paper in strategic terms (i.e., I want to write on Subject X, and therefore it would be useful to find these kinds of documents). I think it is probably important to work closely with the documents within the essays by Pratt or Limerick — to define discussion as coming from documentary work in specific ways. It is useful to work backwards from the essays to try to recuperate what archival work must have been done, to recover what the "evidence" might have looked like initially.

DB: **One of the things, just frankly, that I remember as a problem when I taught both Limerick and Pratt is that they don't present material very fully; they allude to material. Pratt does quite a lot with the Guaman Poma letter. In Pratt's book Imperial Eyes, you get these extended, really quite lovely close readings of block quotations that in many ways figure what you would want students to do. But they don't see enough of this in Limerick.**

JFC: Well, I think there are places in Limerick, although I agree with your sense of needing more explicit uses of documents. I have worked closely on Pratt's treatment of Guaman Poma and on Limerick's account of Narcissa Whitman. One place we discussed at length was where Limerick quotes from the journal of a woman pioneer, beginning with the instruction: "Consider Mrs. Amelia Stewart Knight." That section allowed us to talk usefully about what Mrs. Knight did "record" and what she reported but did not discuss (the work of tending to seven children). Students were intrigued by Limerick's suggestion that "one simply has to imagine what some of her terse entries meant in practice," and that became the hinge for a discussion on what constrained a historian's "imagination" and on the value of trying to connect "entries" with "practice." The passage contains at least one marker to help account for Limerick's "work" ("The older children *evidently* helped out" [my emphasis]), and it shows how one can construct a pattern out of clustered details ("The youngest child, Chatfield, *seemed* [my emphasis] most ill-fated: 'Chat has been sick. . . . Here Chat fell out. . . . Here Chat had a very narrow escape"). One of the problems, though, might be described as graphic or visual. Because Limerick quotes in dispersed fashion, breaking up passages with her own commentary, students had difficulty "seeing" where she was using documents. We spent quite a bit of class time *literally* finding quotations, which proved a very hard search. We did a similar job in working on Pratt's section on Guaman Poma.

In the Pratt essay, students could see perhaps more readily that Pratt had gathered diverse "materials" to make her account: the Guaman Poma letters, her son's classroom materials, the Stanford course debates. It's useful in that case to think of each section as having its own materials. In class we looked carefully at what are the material bases for each argument, at what kind of "document" is used, and at how some of the "evidence" is based on nontextual materials such as conversation, which is then quoted and treated as a "document" (i.e., cited, retold, interpreted). But one of the problems is the ease with which Pratt moves from section to section, the eclectic nature of this particular piece. She, like the students, assumes at times that the texts speak for themselves; she doesn't belabor her interpretation of materials. This has to do, of course, with the occasion for this particular lecture, but it poses a problem for students trying to model historical work.

I think a teacher and a class have to work fairly closely on how to use these essays as models for archival work. One of the issues that suggested students' confusion was that they couldn't decide whether they were in Pratt and Limerick's roles or in the roles represented by Guaman Poma and the western pioneers. Students tended to see themselves more in relation to the historical figures, identifying, I suspect, with the difficulty of speaking and being heard, with the position of being an unknown and unarticulated subject. Part of what the assignment calls for is having students imagine themselves as also in Pratt and Limerick's positions of authority, however much those positions are qualified or challenged by Pratt and Limerick as cultural critics.

DB: **This is the time that I should ask you to talk a bit about what remains for me one of the really remarkable achievements of this project of yours, which was that it wasn't just your twenty-two students doing this, but about twelve hundred Pitt undergraduates over two semesters. I'm imagining how they needed to make use of the region's resources to do documentary work.**

I guess there are several questions to ask here. One of them is to ask a very specific logistical question: how did you pull it off? The other question is, what led you to think that this was something you would want to do?

JFC: It was very useful for me to do this with a more dispersed group than my own class. I do considerable historical work myself and in my stand-alone courses, and I know the resources in this region fairly well. But it's very useful to figure out how to do such work with a set of teachers who are new to the area and, by and large, new to historical work.

DB: **And new to teaching.**

JFC: Yes. I was thinking about it partially as a way of showing me what is particularly difficult about this kind of work, what needs to be explained or facilitated. But I also wanted to try it out for the book, which presumably asks people to launch such historical projects without necessarily being historians, without being terribly familiar with the resources, and without time or particular interest in devoting a lot of energy to such a search.

And the book can't, of course, predict what will be available — or particularly interesting — in any particular region of the country, to any particular teacher or set of students. That is a problem, but it also seems to me a considerable advantage. It is a situation that makes apparent the kind of work teachers and students need to do to make the book useful, to make it locally appropriate. This assignment is very useful in how it challenges the model of teacher authority and knowledge. The assignment proposes that the teacher is no longer the sole resource person, the one who knows all the material best, but that students are going to have to learn how to use their own resources, to use library collections, to learn how to get help from other university experts — librarians, for example.

I think that's a useful thing. It is initially a very scary thing.

DB: **By teachers, in this case, do you mean teaching assistants? teaching fellows?**

JFC: In this case, the staff was mostly first-year teaching assistants and fellows. There were several faculty, advanced graduate students and part-time faculty who volunteered to teach the sequence and make their classes available for observation. It was unnerving for teachers to undertake this assignment without knowing from their own experience what the library had. I think most experienced teachers' inclination was to go find out what the library had and bring back a list, or at least to try out the procedure of searching for themselves. Others set up special sessions with the library's instructional staff to teach students how to access books and periodicals. I think it's important to resist providing the students with too explicit a menu, with a list of targeted materials for them to go "find." This would certainly solve some of the logistical problems, but it doesn't necessarily teach students how to do a certain kind of work. And it limits the topics they can find to what the teacher or resource person imagines are their interests.

Some of what made this assignment difficult has to do with the social history of students' library use. Most of the students in my class had never used more than the reserve collection in the library and its study rooms. The library functioned for them as a large study hall with prescribed readings and marginal levels of quiet. They had never used a card catalog, nor had much use for one since their books and articles had all been preselected for them. They didn't know that books can be taken out but manuscripts cannot. They didn't know that a researcher might have to make appointments for use of some collections or work within more limited hours. They didn't know that they might not be allowed to make a copy of a document or that they might need permission to quote from private papers. There was, in other words, a whole set of social conceptual problems that this assignment inherits. Simply getting students to the library and into rather rarified collections was a challenge. Then on the other side, the assignment done on this scale posed quite a challenge to the librarians, most of whom (for archival and rare book collections) are used to dealing with scholars and professional visitors, not with freshmen.

DB: **And not with large numbers of them.**

JFC: And large numbers of them. Yes. Well, because the librarians are used to dealing with professionals, they're used to conducting a fairly elaborate question-answer interview with a prospective user. This kind of user knows what he or she wants to do and knows a lot about how to get at it or what it might look like; what this user doesn't know is the offerings of a particular collection. Librarians were initially imagining they needed to do a full hour interview with each student, which, needless to say, overwhelmed them. These interviews stretched in some cases to two or three hours when librarians confronted the students' lack of experience with documentary collections, and their lack of understanding about historical procedure. Librarians were faced with students who didn't know what they wanted (and in many cases, couldn't explain why they wanted it). Or they were faced with students who wanted only one very specific thing and were indignant when the librarians couldn't produce it. The librarians described them as wanting the history of the world or a specific history never written. They had little sense of how to negotiate the topic, of how to find something approximate or comparable, of how to make use of a document to elaborate an interest. The librarians were concerned about students trying to do the work of professionals in amateur time (often fifteen minutes before the close of the archives) with amateur credentials.

DB: **What did you learn about working first with the librarians that was important to you? How did you prepare them?**

JFC: I learned as much about the librarians as I did about students in this project. I must say, our librarians were extraordinarily helpful, concerned, and knowledgeable, willing to put in far more time than they could spare to this project. It's very important for any teacher doing this project to meet with librarians ahead of time, to warn them that this is happening. Give them the sense of the scale and get some advice from them about how their system operates. I asked permission from each specialist librarian to include their particular collection on a memo and sent every participating librarian a copy of the assignments with the expected dates for student work. If I were doing this again, I would meet with the librarians ahead of time to discuss the aims and scope of the assignment, to show some sample papers, and to talk over what they should offer students and what they should encourage students to negotiate more independently. I wrote a memo to the students about the different libraries and what kinds of items were in each collection, about library hours, how to make an appointment, about using pencil when taking notes about a rare book. It's important to support the librarians' procedures.

DB: **How many different sites were involved? How many places were students potentially going to?**

JFC: There were about nine archive and book collections, as well as the general resources of the university and city library.

DB: **Can you name some of them?**

JFC: There's a rare book special collection, the university archives (a collection of materials about the founding of the university, about the construction of campus buildings, about university departments and organizations), the library science collection (which had an archive of children's materials, including periodicals and television programs), the local historical society (which had letters and documents), and the Labor Archives. Many students chose the university archives. They wanted to stick close to home and write about something they could visit or observe. Many of them used some kind of newspaper, periodical, or facsimile versions of local history papers. Few of them wanted to go beyond the university bounds to the historical society or city library, although they're very close to campus. Some of their choices had to do with ease of availability, with hours and location. That wasn't so much the case in the second project. They were more adventuresome after they'd done it once and were willing to go to more than one collection to find what they wanted. Once they adjusted to the idea, they respected the librarians' requests to make appointments; indeed they seemed reassured by the structure of scheduling official appointments, of going to a specific site, of physically gathering materials. The first time, the issue of scheduling was a disaster. Many students assumed they could go, en masse, to a special collection fifteen minutes before closing on a Friday and retrieve specialized materials from a collection. Many of them assumed they would enter an archive, be handed their own particular material, and take it home with them.

Several students were very angry at the librarians when they found this wouldn't work: they blamed the librarians for preventing them from carrying out their task. This greatly unnerved the librarians. They're used to arranging for scholars to get what they need. They're not used to disappointing people or having people refuse to come back later.

DB: **I just want to get you to talk for a few more minutes about the librarians' side of it. How did you establish, not only for yourself but for all of these other teachers and students, a set of working relationships with the librarians?**

JFC: I'd say that it goes two ways. One, you need to talk to the librarians to find out their procedures, their interests, and their materials. You need to prepare your students in some way ahead of time to negotiate these procedures. That was the aim of the handout I prepared. But the other thing that is important is to talk with the librarians about what you hope to get out of the assignment. It is easy to fall into a mentality of imagining the problems of such work and to avoid discussing the aims, the expectations, the possibilities. I gave the librarians copies of the assignments and copies of what the students had been reading. I talked to them about where these projects fell in the semester (the first one came at three weeks into the term; the second at eleven weeks), and I talked about how the first assignment might lead to a different level of work in the second. I talked with them some about the kinds of reading and writing students know how to do at this level but also about what they are learning but can't fully accomplish yet. In other words, you don't imagine that students become expert at such work with one try; you try to seed the ground for the second project, even for subsequent work in the curriculum. And you don't need to expect the project to fail because students stumble along the way. I talked with them not only about what students might know specifically about using libraries, but also about what they might know about formulating questions, articulating a topic, defining a document. This was an important part of the discussion.

Many of the initial difficulties we had arose from the librarians' assumptions of a certain kind of knowledge and experience and the students' assumptions of what librarians could (should?) offer or provide. Many of the students assumed that librarians could simply hand them what they needed, that they could read students' minds and concoct an appropriate source to satisfy the students' topics. Some students expected to be able to describe their interests very generally and then have the librarians fill in all the rest: out would come two opposing documents already annotated, legible, translated, etc. The librarians for the most part assumed students would know how to talk about a project, and they assumed that students knew what documents were available. Things improved considerably when I urged librarians not to take on the job of teaching students how to write their paper and not to write the paper for them. In the first go-round, I think many of the librarians were spending more time than they should with individual students and with large — and often inattentive — groups of students. They were trying to make up for lost time, to do remediation in library research, history, professional writing, etc. They tried to teach them how to read the document and produce a history the librarians knew was available. It was important to discuss how a course based on revision might differ from one with a single term paper at the end. Students in a revision-based course might be expected to reread their document, to go back later to see what else they could do with the material, to rethink their construction of history. Their first attempt didn't need to be imagined as all they could do.

It was important, then, to suggest that the students' difficulties were not just their unfamiliarity with library procedure. We could, in other words, teach them to use the card catalog, and we would still have many comparable problems to face. It was important to suggest how the problems students had negotiating the library were connected to problems in reading, in negotiating the academy more generally, in imagining themselves trying out what it means to work as a researcher. I urged the librarians to send really ill-prepared students back to their teachers, to stick to their sense of what procedure was important. I encouraged them not to feel they ought to be handing out documents at random to the twenty students who arrive at quarter to five, but that it was important to maintain their own procedures. It was useful for students to see how part of being a historian is an ability to imagine that a set of documents ought to be somewhere specific, not in some neutral reference shelf prepared for generic use. It was also useful for students to work at describing the kinds of documents they wanted to see. An experienced historian will enter an archive with a kind of confidence based on having visited other collections. She'll assume that there's likely to be something like this and it's likely to be in this kind of collection because she's found comparable documents elsewhere using similar search procedures. She'll be able to describe the kind of material she wants, even though the specific features are bound to be different in every collection she enters. She'll know that the catalogs for accessing special collections are full of information that might be hard to read initially, and she'll know how to ask for help in prying that information out of the particular format or tradition. We wanted, in part, to teach students some of that confidence, the confidence of being able to ask about what they don't know fully or absolutely. We wanted them to envision a library as a place to go to find out about what you only know parts of, or only know imperfectly.

DB: If we were to interview some of these librarians right now, would they say they had a good year? How would they remember this experience?

JFC: The initial onslaught of five-hundred-plus students in the fall term was a horror. I was surprised at how agitated the librarians were, and we were all deeply surprised at how much work this project entailed for them. I went in for an emergency meeting — twelve research librarians and me. I felt very much that I was being called on the carpet. At the same time, they were very willing to pursue the issue, to work to make it better. They did not simply want to complain or make the problem go away (although those sentiments did dominate the beginning of that first meeting). They were by and large sympathetic to the aim of getting students into the library.

As we talked, we considered a number of ways of easing the burdens, and we recognized how much we shared similar aims at the university. A lot of the initial problem was logistical: when they treated each student as a visiting scholar, the numbers soon overwhelmed them. We discussed the suggestion that we produce a model set of documents to put on reserve for all students to use; this seemed to promise to contain the chaos and to reestablish "our" oversight of the project (we could help students better because we would regain control of the materials, both physically and intellectually). The group divided on this issue, with the librarians of book collections expressing more reluctance about having inexperienced students in large numbers using their collections than did the librarians of archive collections. This is certainly understandable; the ethos of rare book collections makes one very aware of how fragile such materials are, of how each use, however careful, damages or potentially destroys irreplaceable materials. The university archivist argued, however, that we didn't want to solve the problem of library use by shutting inexperienced students out of "the library," i.e., by reproducing a set of materials to read in a reserve room. The transformation of "the library" into a study hall was an issue about which the librarians were very concerned. The debate revolved around getting students into the central collections of the library or warding them off with a prepared packet that would be used in the library or purchased for use in class. I offered to try this out. I can certainly imagine the use of a set of documents to use in preliminary discussions. But the university archivist held out, arguing, as I had, that a prepared packet doesn't get students into a part of the library (or of the academy) where they have both the intellectual and social experience of constructing a project for themselves.

The group of librarians came to agree that this was a desirable goal, and this discussion was an important one for us to have. They were willing to try the experiment a second time in the semester, as well as two more times the following semester. And we discussed how to build on this intensive project in subsequent courses across the curriculum. They saw the importance of getting students into the library in a substantive way early in their college careers, despite the difficulties and the logistical problems. There was very little turmoil in the second semester. I got joking reminders from librarians that they were undergoing extra work thanks to me. But they were pleased (and surprised) by the kinds of papers students produced out of the experience. They were pleased to imagine students might build on this experience to use the library in future work.

DB: Do you think they will?

JFC: I don't know. I think that for most students it was initially a very demanding, somewhat daunting experience; yet most students were proud of their accomplishments and recognized the substantive difficulty of the project. Many of them said it made them feel like scholars. They felt they were doing serious work, and it raised their sense of self-esteem that their university had such resources. They enjoyed questioning their families and looking for documents from their parents' or grandparents' past. They liked the sort of professionalism that the project encouraged.

Many of them spoke about the pleasure of finding their own material, of defining their own topic. We forget how much we control their work, even when we invite them to experiment, to speak their own opinion, even when we choose as texts what we imagine are "their" kinds of materials. Although this was in many ways a highly structured, disciplined project, in other ways the material was more fully theirs than are class texts. Students talked about being in "charge" of their materials, of bringing it to our attention, of bringing it into the public or the present. I think this project challenges in important ways issues of authority in the classroom. Teachers are necessarily less in charge of the material when they haven't chosen it and haven't in most cases read it. Students had more responsibility for describing, reporting, accounting for their materials. This was particularly useful for the beginning teaching assistants, although the project also caused moments of anxiety for many of them with its lack of a uniform text to order the class discussion. TAs found out how much more students could say or write when the text was not already the "property" of the teacher or of the class. In such a situation, teachers are not the ones who must persuade a resistant audience to find the material interesting or persuasive; they ask their students to explain what makes something worth reading, worth interpreting. In this case, it is a real question. This is often not the case, even when we've offered what count as "student" texts as a basis for our conversation.

DB: Can you talk about a set of rules or principles for getting students ready to work in the library?

JFC: I'd say one of the things that is important to do is not to send all students at the same time to work in a rare book or primary paper collection. Much of this work can be done in book collections or in microforms, using almost any college or city library. There are many books that reprint documents or narratives, government papers, letters, and diaries. Students who used books had the advantage of taking the book home with them, of being able to go back easily, of being able to read around their document, of reading more widely when they had the interest. I think for many students that kind of book work was very productive. Some students wanted to brave the challenges of the rare book collection or the archives, and I think for them this assignment was particularly exciting. It's useful to set up the project so students can sort themselves out, so that the most interested students can have access to look at manuscripts, to translate letters from Polish immigrants, or to read eighteenth-century handwriting. In some cases, students figured out their interests using books, and then turned to more specialized collections with their newly discovered expertise. Book sources aren't particularly easier than special collections for most students, but students are going to do less damage or be more dispersed in the general collection than when they are concentrated in special collections.

It is useful to offer some sort of general library orientation for students before the project begins, but most introductory library tours will not solve the problems this assignment recognizes. Most initiations in libraries are aimed at teaching students how to access material they can name already. This is a very different kind of project, introducing more sophisticated use of library resources. One could develop, with a librarian, a very useful one-hour session that would help students find material for this project. Such a session would have to address not simply research tools but a logic for searching and asking questions. This session might discuss using catalog searching to help develop a potential topic; it might teach students how to browse productively, how to examine a book as a possible source without reading it fully.

DB: So that would mean working with somebody who understood the project?

JFC: I would say to work closely with somebody familiar with archival projects and interested in the particular problems of inexperienced users.

DB: **So, in most textbooks, all this work is represented through the mechanics of note-taking . . .**

JFC: Term papers, collecting bibliography cards . . .

DB: **Exactly. To what degree were your students in need of or coming to you for help with things like notetaking?**

JFC: One of the things that happened that interested me in this project was that they taught each other what they needed to know. This turned into a fairly collaborative project, even though students had individual topics and materials. They ran into each other in the library and offered their different expertise. Some of them were willing to try out the interactive computer catalog and taught themselves how to access their materials through a subject index.

There is in general very little familiarity with using the library. Students had little experience with making distinctions between materials in a special collection and printed books, between facsimile letters and original manuscript documents. It is useful to work back from an essay like Limerick's or Pratt's to discuss what the documentary source must have looked like and to discuss the relationship of what is being quoted to the whole document. I can imagine it would be useful to add a packet of different kinds of primary materials as an appendix to the textbook. You could put in a facsimile letter, for example, or a section of a diary. One of the problems — and one of the pleasures — of working with original materials is dealing with handwriting, as well as working with items in multiple languages. Some students chose documents written in Lithuanian, Czech, or Slovenian. Because of the makeup of this region, some students had multiple language abilities, but they often had more difficulty with the handwriting than with the language itself. Another difficulty was reading texts without annotations. A letter would refer to something they didn't understand and that would make them feel they couldn't continue. It is useful to teach students how to piece information together by reading the context, to continue reading even when something isn't perfectly clear. It's also useful to suggest how to begin annotating such materials.

DB: **Let me move ahead to the second assignment you did. Limerick was the first archival assignment and Pratt came later. How did Pratt and the second assignment work for you? What were you and your students able to do with it?**

JFC: The Pratt assignment pressured them to think more about how the document they picked represented a group's experience, and how that experience could be seen as contested.

DB: **You're referring to Pratt's discussion of the "contact zone"?**

JFC: Yes. Students worked with documents from groups trying to explain their positions to mainstream culture. That moved the issue of pro and con to considering the questions of audience, of multiple audiences, and to issues of persuasion and representation. They worked with the documents not as simply telling facts but also as a way of trying to marshal the material to speak to a difficult audience.

DB: **And to represent a position.**

JFC: Yes. Our sequence stressed issues of representation. How could a document represent a larger group? How does an individual speak for the experience of a diverse group? The issue of bias, which kept coming up in the first assignment — triggered in part by their reading of Limerick's radical position about institutional historical bias — became an issue students negotiated better through reading Pratt. For many students, any document written by an individual is biased simply because an individual wrote it.

DB: **Do they make the same assumptions about the authors in the textbook?**

JFC: They want to believe that texts written by an authority or historian attain neutrality and somehow suppress "personal" bias. Limerick upset this opposition by asking them to think about institutional or disciplinary bias or conventions. It was then useful to reconsider the issue in Pratt's terms about the contact zone.

DB: **Would you talk a bit with some examples about the kinds of materials students found to write about? Talk about the ones that seemed to you to be particularly a mark of success and the ones that seemed to represent the sort of problems you have when you do this kind of teaching.**

JFC: I've mentioned the problems of the student writing about the Frick assassination attempt and the productive efforts of the students working with Depression-era documents. I'd say the projects that were most successful were the ones where students found an array of materials from which they selected specific parts. The Pratt assignment asks students to "conduct" a "local inventory of writing from the contact zone." The task of conducting the inventory is very useful to spend some time on. I encouraged students to consider the relationship between the array of materials they looked at more quickly and the text they selected to focus on. In the first assignment, many of the more successful pieces involved such a broader survey to set a context for the closer attention to a single document. They read more than one document to make a substantive choice for focus and so had some basis for comparison. One student wrote about letters written home by a Civil War soldier; he selected this particular soldier after looking over a volume of comparable letters. Another student wrote about letters written by inmates of [Nazi] Germany's death camps, letters written, as it were, "to the world." My sense is these students were clearly more at ease with the work because they had some knowledge or previous interest in the general topic. Sometimes, of course, their previous understandings were challenged or contradicted, which was also interesting to them and to me.

The project challenged not just the inexperienced student researcher but also the ambitious student who embarked on the project with self-directed interest. One student, for example, wrote about H. P. Lovecraft, a science fiction writer he had long admired. This student began with five volumes of Lovecraft's letters and couldn't figure out how to leave anything out. He was very devoted to Lovecraft and felt anything he could write would falsify the totality he envisioned. He kept saying, "I don't know enough. How could I represent him out of these two letters? I'd have to read all of it." He worried about the necessity of having "an opposing view": he couldn't imagine how to "oppose" what Lovecraft himself said or how to credit as opposition the letters of any of his correspondents. He ultimately recognized that the letters don't simply speak for themselves, that there was considerable work he could do as a reader — even as a devoted reader — to read Lovecraft's self-descriptions against his more mundane accounts of daily life and to do that in a concentrated way focusing on a few letters rather than the whole collection. His became one of the most successful and satisfying projects, but it took a lot of work and rethinking.

DB: **Did students tend to choose to do the historical option here? My memory of the Pratt assignment is that it gives you a choice between turning to the past or to your immediate environment.**

JFC: Yes, that's true. For the Limerick assignment, students had the choice between library materials or materials from their family "archives." Most students chose the library work because of the logistics of getting materials from home. Many students returned to this history work for the Pratt assignment, but others understood the political issues Pratt raises as more evident in current materials.

Students had comparable problems with both options, except for the specific issues of gaining access to the library materials. Those who chose to read from current culture often had more problems than those who used the library. One student, for example, wanted to write about the founding of the university's Black Action Society but had considerable difficulty imagining what a primary document would be. She was concerned because everything she considered seemed to her to be secondhand knowledge (and she was right!). She was talking to people about their sense of what must have happened. She had difficulty perceiving that this was a different strategy (i.e., it let her investigate current *attitudes* about the past) from interviewing some of the people who were involved (which might have let her investigate different *accounts* of the past). She finally worked her way back to reading the student newspaper from the past (rather than the Anniversary issue she had initially chosen, which basically preempted her work as investigator). This choice led her back — via a different interest and route — to the library. She announced one day that her problem was that she didn't have any place in the story, that there was nothing for her to do. She was right, and we had to work on what it would mean for her to construct a place for herself as a writer, as an observer, a place from which to write her own story rather than simply retell someone else's version.

DB: **Were there students who chose a contemporary piece, say a piece produced by the Black Action Society in the month of September? or a piece from the student newspaper?**

JFC: Most of my students who chose the current culture option focused on topics having to do with sports (Steelers Superbowls, for example). It was their sense of having partaken in history.

DB: I see.

JFC: These tended to be fairly unsatisfactory projects — not because of the topic per se, but because students were convinced they already knew the history of the event and wrote from memory rather than from sources.

Perhaps the opposite problem is exemplified by the student who wrote about the tearing down of Forbes Field, the baseball park, an event that he felt powerless to discuss because, as he said, "I wasn't there." He worked from a contemporary "retrospective" from a local newspaper, an account in which the reporter had in a sense already done his assignment, had gathered documents, quoted from interviews, sifted through memoirs. The student could not understand what role he could now play as a writer. He could not see that using the reporter's passages and narrative was plagiarism. He was trapped by his faith that the past had *happened* and therefore there could only be one set of "evidence" available and only one assignment carried out. He couldn't see that he might presumably tell a different story if he focused on different primary sources, or if he asked different questions of them. We went round and round on this. I don't think it was a case of unwillingness to do the assignment, or laziness about the work, but of deep incomprehension about what it means to produce "history." He would say that he could go back and read original accounts, but he wouldn't thereby change the "history" that was already there. The events, the quotes, the opinions, all already had a place in the narrative he imagined as fixed, permanent, unauthored.

DB: **What role did Pratt play in this work? Was it just an occasion for students to revise earlier work, or did she function strategically in particular ways?**

JFC: For some students, neither Pratt nor Limerick was sufficient — partially because they had difficulty reading their material in the fairly politically charged contexts of those two pieces. For several students, the key text in the sequence was Geertz's essay. Students went back to Geertz to work out how to account for something that happened, how to take it through different analytic models. For others the key text was Wideman, who allowed them to see what stake individuals might have in negotiating the representations of the past.

Many students returned to these history papers several times, using every opportunity for revision or reuse of the materials. One student wrote five revisions of his historical project, moving from a one-page paper to a fifteen-page paper in the end. He wrote on *Black Elk Speaks,* a memoir about the days of Crazy Horse (this was one of the complications: was his work about Crazy Horse or about Black Elk, or about the mediator to whom Black Elk spoke?). He had a lot of difficulty untangling what in such a book counted as a "document." But that was crucial to his success with the project: the project began to work for him when he saw that parts of the book were derived from something someone saw, parts were legend, parts were official accounts, and parts were Black Elk producing a kind of counterhistory, indirectly challenging the other histories available. Pratt was a very useful text for him; indeed, his interest in the project began in our early class discussions of Pratt. Limerick helped him see how Black Elk had to negotiate a white narrative of history, how he had to struggle to be able to "speak" a different version of the past. Geertz helped him see he could approach his project in several different ways, making it different without simply contradicting his earlier work. Pratt helped him pay close attention to how Black Elk told Crazy Horse's story, to consider specific language and narrative moves that implied a contest over meaning. He came to see Black Elk as trying to negotiate the representation of Indian culture. He came to treat Black Elk as an author rather than as a found object. He spent maybe seven weeks on this work. But it was important work for him to do intellectually.

DB: **As people say here — it was hard because it was hard.**

JFC: Many of the difficulties I have described show students grappling with what are extremely important issues in writing and reading. One difficulty is perhaps a literary issue, of seeing how to read a text closely, of how to use a text to locate a writer's positions and hesitancies. The other is perhaps more a cultural issue, that is, imagining that somebody you have understood as an object can have something to speak that may alter "history" as it has been previously narrated. Some students were struggling with the recognition that there are competing notions of what is culturally important, of what counts, of what "really happened." I count these as serious difficulties, but also as serious work to investigate.

DB: **Jean, we've been talking about the Limerick and Pratt assignments largely because I was interested in what you see as the problems and successes in sending students out to work with documentary and archival material. But I want to take a moment to ask you generally about the shape of the sequence you worked with. That is, I know that there are other readings or other kinds of writing students do, and I know that you and the group made some changes to the sequence so that it worked for you. Would you talk about the sequence and those changes?**

JFC: We worked with the history and ethnography sequence (sequence four in *Ways of Reading*). We read the introduction to *Ways of Reading,* Pratt, Geertz, Limerick, Wideman, and then Pratt again. We used Pratt at the beginning to raise some of the problems of representation, to set these up as issues that are contested in the academy, that are difficult to negotiate — even for "professionals." Pratt usefully suggests how this problem crosses many lines, not resting in only one disciplinary site. For the first assignment of the semester, we added an assignment to the sequence. We had students write from the Pratt essay on the issue of community. (This is the third Assignment for Writing following the Pratt essay.) They were asked to write about an observed community in terms of Benedict Anderson's discussion about "imagined communities" and then in terms of Pratt's "contact zone." Many of them wrote about high school groups, community groups from their past. Another change we made was that we inserted more time before each archival assignment so students had time to discuss their searches and their documents before writing the minihistories. We built in time for students to go out to gather material and sometimes to do a small assignment to work from in class. This differed somewhat in various sections. My students had to produce a short position paper when they first described their documents.

The second assignment, reading Geertz, asked them to observe a group —

DB: **It says a group or subgroup, some part of the culture you know well.**

JFC: Yes — to do an ethnography, a reading of the activities of a group or subgroup and to consider what constitutes a group and its representations. Students tended to choose local organizations, university groups, or work situations. We emphasized in this case the importance of going out now to observe, rather than relying — as many of them had for the first assignment — on memory of a group. Then we did the Limerick assignment. Then we did a revision, inviting students to choose any of their first three papers to revise (Pratt, Geertz, or Limerick). We worked with the introduction to *Ways of Reading* as they were preparing to revise and having midterm conferences.

Then we read Wideman. Instead of doing a writer's guide using Wideman, we composed an assignment more explicitly on the problems of representation in Wideman, considering how to put those into conversation with Pratt, Geertz, or Limerick. Wideman usefully complicates their sense of who has problems of representation. They've been willing to imagine it as a historian's problem, or as a problem Geertz, for some reason, takes on himself by going to Bali. When they hit Wideman, they begin to see it as a problem anyone has with the past, with others — even with others as close as family. They see how what they have understood as personal can be read as historical. Wideman quite usefully revisits the work of ethnography begun with Geertz, and brings home the work of history, as well as Pratt's concern with the arts of the contact zone. Wideman localizes and makes visible what for the students was more abstract in Pratt, even in Limerick — the sense of having different positions from which to speak, of having different authority as a speaker, of needing to negotiate dominant narratives or perspectives. So, although it's a slightly different piece than the others in the sequence, it was crucial to how the sequence worked. It was also useful for students to go back from Wideman to rethink how the other essays are shaped by the disciplines they inhabit and critique, by history and anthropology, by being offered as a lecture at a conference on literacy. After Wideman, we returned to Pratt and worked with materials representing "the arts of the contact zone." Some students revisited earlier materials, while others launched a new project at this point.

DB: **So, did some people who had started working on the Depression continue that?**

JFC: Some continued their archival projects through the Pratt assignment and into the final project as well. I'd say maybe a third of the class revised the archival work a couple of times, extending it, rethinking it.

DB: **Would you generalize from this that it would be a good idea for students to work with fundamentally the same body of materials from beginning to end?**

JFC: I think that the difficulty of finding things in the first place is so great that it is useful to continue with them when possible. On the other hand, you don't want to limit students by what they can find in the third week of class. This places too much pressure on what is already their sense that they have to find the right stuff to succeed. Some students did find wonderful materials early on, and they mined these to great effect for the rest of the semester. Others learned from their first experiment how to find something of more interest to them for the second foray. They were pleased at their growing confidence in searching, with their ability to formulate more clearly what they might want to work on. Some students used the historical assignment as a trial run for finding cultural materials. They saw then the usefulness of having a document and not just relying on a generalized sense of culture or on memory alone. They saw that one could document attitudes, that one could quote material to work on intensively. So I think that the historical project was useful both for students who caught the bug of archival work and for those who preferred to turn to more contemporary issues. I left it up to the students. I didn't want to force them to keep going with the history work unless they were so moved. But many of them were. Many of them saw it as their strongest writing, which may, of course, have had to do with my obvious interest in it. We ended the course with work on a class book. Each student contributed a revision of one of the assignments; we had these copied and bound as a book;

and the students bought them to use as our text for the last two weeks of class. In some sections of the course students all revised one particular assignment, but in others students chose to revise material from the entire course. Many of these revisions were of papers we had discussed earlier in the semester, so students saw how their classmates' early work had changed. Students really seemed to enjoy having the book, reading the essays as stories or part of a book rather than as papers to edit.

DB: **So at the end of the course everybody had a book?**

JFC: Yes. Everybody had a book, and we used it to talk about issues of representation, about how they might represent their work as student writers or represent the project of the course.

DB: **May I have the title of this book?**

JFC: Mine was called simply "Classbook," but it had a nice table of contents.

Afterword

Joe Harris, Margaret Marshall, Jim Seitz, and I were the faculty responsible for planning the first-year course and the accompanying program for beginning graduate students. Rashmi Bhatnagar, Bianca Falbo, Jean Grace, and Steve Sutherland worked with me to oversee the course and the staff meetings. I also want to acknowledge the following teachers who used this sequence and allowed beginning graduate students to observe their classes: Rita Capezzi, Nick Coles, Joe Harris, Margaret Marshall, and Paul Kameen.

I want to thank the wonderful staff of archivists and special collection librarians at the University of Pittsburgh, and especially Charles Aston, Director of Special Collections at the University of Pittsburgh, who has long helped me carry out my pedagogical extravaganzas with library projects. He was instrumental in coordinating problems and solutions, in channeling complaints my way, and in working out plans for improvement.

I want to thank the students in my section of General Writing, Fall 1993, for permission to quote from their papers.

— JFC